THE CRITICAL REPUTATION OF
F. SCOTT FITZGERALD
Supplement One
through 1981

THE CRITICAL REPUTATION

OF

F. SCOTT FITZGERALD

A BIBLIOGRAPHICAL STUDY

Supplement One through 1981

by

Jackson R. Bryer
University of Maryland

ARCHON BOOKS

1984

The paper in this book meets the guidelines
for permanence and durability of the
Committee on Production Guidelines for Book Longevity
of the Council on Library Resources.

Library of Congress Cataloging in Publication Data

Bryer, Jackson R.
    The critical reputation of F. Scott Fitzgerald.
    Includes index.
    1. Fitzgerald, F. Scott (Francis Scott), 1896–1940
—Bibliography.   I. Title.
Z8301.2.B74   1967 Suppl.   016.813'52   82–25536
[PS3511.I9]
ISBN 0–208–01489–6 (v.1)

"Affectation of candour is common enough;—one meets it everywhere. But to be candid without ostentation or design—to take the good of every body's character and make it still better, and say nothing of the bad—belongs to you alone."

Jane Austen, *Pride and Prejudice*

CONTENTS

PREFACE

This first supplement documents the great amount of scholarly and popular attention the Fitzgeralds have received since publication of *The Critical Reputation of F. Scott Fitzgerald* in 1967. It includes pre-1967 items which were inadvertently omitted, such as newly uncovered reviews of Fitzgerald's books or periodical articles from 1964 to 1966 not listed in bibliographies until after the earlier book had gone to press. But many of the added entries represent deliberate efforts to widen the scope of critical coverage; and the direction of that widening has been suggested, for the most part, by events within the past sixteen years.

As in the earlier book, the basic arrangement here is chronological. In the first two sections, Reviews of Books (G) and Articles (H), items from the pre–1967 period are listed first; in the Books (I) and Graduate Research (J) sections, material omitted from *The Critical Reputation of F. Scott Fitzgerald* is interspersed alphabetically with post–1967 items. In order to avoid confusion with the numbering system used in the earlier volume, the sections in this book are designated by the letters G, H, I, J, K, which immediately follow in the alphabet the letters used to denote the sections of *The Critical Reputation of F. Scott Fitzgerald*. Thus, cross-references to sections A, B, C, D, E, and F are to the latter. Unlike in the earlier book, in Section I, reviews of books about Fitzgerald are here numbered individually, using the section letter (I), the number of the book reviewed, and a lower-case Roman numeral (i, ii, iii, iv, etc.). These reviews are also individually listed in the Index. Similarly, in Section I, when a single book includes several relevant pieces, reprinted or original, these are also numbered individually, using the section letter (I), the number of the book in which they appear, and a Roman numeral in small capitals (ɪ, ɪɪ, ɪɪɪ, ɪᴠ, etc.). These are also individually listed in the Index. Arabic numbers have been substituted for Roman numerals for volume numbers in periodical citations. Because Linda C. Stanley's *The Foreign Critical Reputation of F. Scott*

Fitzgerald provides such complete, up-to-date, and annotated listings of foreign-language materials, what had been Section D in the 1967 book is not supplemented here.

Because of the great interest which has emerged since 1967 in the life and writings of Zelda Fitzgerald, caused principally by the success of Nancy Milford's biography, a section of reviews of various editions of *Save Me the Waltz* (Section K) has been added in the body of this book and a checklist of her writings has been added to the Appendix.

No attempt has been made to evaluate the items. Annotations are either summaries or descriptions, with summaries of scholarly articles and book chapters being more numerous here than in the earlier book. Essays and book sections which are the work of two or more authors are listed under the name of the first and cross-indexed to the main entry under the name of the author. The same procedure has often been adopted in listing several Letters to the Editor which appeared in the same issue of a periodical and referred to the same matter. Pieces in which only a few of many pages refer to Fitzgerald are included with the pages of the full item listed first and then, in brackets, those pages pertaining to Fitzgerald. In general, coverage in this volume should be considered as complete as could be achieved through 1981, with several 1982 and a very few 1983 entries included as found. The listing of Masters Essays in Section J, because it was derived principally from a survey conducted in 1980, is current only through that year; although, again, some later theses are included.

The use of abbreviations is similar to that in *The Critical Reputation of F. Scott Fitzgerald*. F. Scott Fitzgerald's name has been shortened to F in annotations, but not in quotations or titles (except, as in the case of the *Fitzgerald Newsletter*, where the shortened form actually appears in the title). Abbreviations have also been used—again, only in annotations—for many of Fitzgerald's books and for Zelda Fitzgerald's *Save Me the Waltz*. A list of these can be found following the Introduction.

***

The task of acknowledging assistance in a project which has taken fifteen years taxes both one's memory and the limitations of space. My first expression of gratitude must be to James Thorpe III and Patricia Bernblum and their colleagues at Archon Books, who waited patiently and, I think, confidently, through my various crises and procrastinations. I only hope that this end product somewhat justifies their restraint.

I am also deeply grateful for the series of research assistants provided to me by the successive heads of the University of Maryland Department of English—Morris Freedman, Shirley S. Kenny, John Howard, and Annabel Patterson—and by the Provosts of the Division of Arts and Humanities under whom they served—Robert A. Corrigan and Shirley S. Kenny. To the research assistants themselves—Roberta Robbins, Joanne Giza, Nancy Prothro, Jane DeMouy, and Ruth M. Alvarez—I can only say that there literally would not have been a book without them. Ruth M. Alvarez, in particular, who presided over the last five years of the project, has been invaluable. She is entirely responsible for the detailed and comprehensive Index to this volume. Roberta Robbins was here when I began; I only wish she were here now to see me finish.

As always, my fellow Fitzgerald scholars have been generous with their time and knowledge. Alan Margolies not only sent me word of important sources of material, he actually did some of my work for me. Matthew J. Bruccoli answered my many queries promptly and fully; and he also let me see his files and scrapbooks, in themselves a treasure trove of Fitzgerald materials. I have been helped as well by the advice and wisdom of Scott Donaldson, James L. W. West III, John Kuehl, John Callahan, Robert Sklar, Sadao Nagaoka (who provided me with photocopies of many obscure English-language articles in Japanese periodicals), Tony Buttitta (who gave me access to his file of reviews of his book on Fitzgerald), and Calvin Tomkins (who did the same with respect to his book on the Murphys).

For completeness and accuracy, a project of this sort truly depends upon the kindness and cooperation of hundreds of librarians throughout the world who have found and verified references, supplied page numbers, and provided me with photocopies. To list even most of their names here is impossible; but to them all I owe a collective debt of gratitude. My principal thanks go to Betty Baehr, Mindy Goodwin, and Louann Wall Stylianopoulos of the Interlibrary Loan Department at the University of Maryland's McKeldin Library; and to the staff of the Manuscripts and Rare Book Department at Princeton University's Firestone Library, principally Alexander Clark, Wanda Randall, Richard M. Ludwig, Jean Preston, Charles E. Greene, Mardel Pacheco, Anne Van Arsdale, and Stephen Ferguson. My numerous requests for information to the British Library were invariably handled swiftly and efficiently by John Westmancoat of the Newspaper Library; and the staff of the Newspapers and Current Periodicals Room of the Library of Congress likewise were always helpful.

My lists of reviews of books by and about the Fitzgeralds would not be nearly as complete without the assistance of the Publicity Departments of publishers here and in England: The Bodley Head, Hodder and Stoughton, Weidenfeld and Nicholson, Random House, Charles Scribner's Sons, Grosset & Dunlap, Secker & Warburg, Delacorte Press, Harcourt Brace Jovanovich, Southern Illinois University Press, and Jonathan Cape.

Finally, various segments of this project were completed during time off from teaching provided by the General Research Board and the Division of Arts and Humanities of the University of Maryland, to whom I am most grateful.

J. R. B.
College Park, Md.
October 20, 1982

INTRODUCTION

In the sixteen years since the publication of *The Critical Reputation of F. Scott Fitzgerald—A Bibliographical Study*, there have been fifteen "new" books by Fitzgerald, that is, volumes which include substantial amounts of his work never before issued in book form. These include three collections of letters, the last of which, *Correspondence of F. Scott Fitzgerald* (1980), claims to publish all known previously unpublished Fitzgerald letters. Similarly, the appearance of *Bits of Paradise—21 Uncollected Stories by F. Scott and Zelda Fitzgerald* (1973) and *The Price Was High—The Last Uncollected Stories of F. Scott Fitzgerald* (1979) brought into book form for the first time sixty-one stories by Scott, nine by Zelda, and one written by them jointly, leaving only eight of Scott's published stories uncollected. Alan Margolies' edition of *F. Scott Fitzgerald's St. Paul Plays 1911–1914* (1978) and Matthew J. Bruccoli's of *F. Scott Fitzgerald's Screenplay for "Three Comrades" by Erich Maria Remarque* (1978) made available important new specimens of Fitzgerald's writing for the stage and screen; and the 1981 publication of his *Poems 1911–1940* filled out the record of his work in verse. Editions of his *Ledger* (1973) and *Notebooks* (1978) and a facsimile of the holograph manuscript of *The Great Gatsby* (1973) provided important glimpses behind the scenes of Fitzgerald's already well-publicized writing career. If we add to this the reissue of Zelda's novel *Save Me the Waltz* (1967), the first publication of her play *Scandalabra* (1980), and the significant album of excerpts from their scrapbooks, *The Romantic Egoists* (1974), it is apparent that the past decade and a half produced more books by the Fitzgeralds than they saw into print during their lifetimes. And because these books included much material never before available in book form, most reviewers were seeing this material for the first time. Their comments, as recorded in the Reviews section (G) of this volume, thus have expanded considerably the range of Fitzgerald criticism.

That these new works by the Fitzgeralds generated critical and scholarly activity as well as reviews is testified to eloquently by the fact that, since 1967, there have been approximately forty-five new full-length books about—or primarily about—F. Scott and Zelda Fitzgerald. These include scholarly biographies, bibliographies, textual and composition studies, personal reminiscences, a concordance, collections of reprinted essays and reviews, a collection of new essays, and critical studies. The most significant of these are Matthew J. Bruccoli's biography of Scott, *Some Sort of Epic Grandeur—The Life of F. Scott Fitzgerald* (1981) and Nancy Milford's *Zelda—A Biography* (1970); Bruccoli's *F. Scott Fitzgerald—A Descriptive Bibliography* (1972) and *Supplement* (1980), and Linda C. Stanley's *The Foreign Critical Reputation of F. Scott Fitzgerald—An Analysis and Annotated Bibliography* (1980); Bruccoli's *"The Last of the Novelists"—F. Scott Fitzgerald and "The Last Tycoon"* (1977) and James L. W. West III's *The Making of F. Scott Fitzgerald's "This Side of Paradise"* (1977); Sheilah Graham's *College of One* (1967) and *The Real F. Scott Fitzgerald* (1976) and Tony Buttitta's *After the Good Gay Times* (1974); Bruccoli and Bryer's *F. Scott Fitzgerald In His Own Time* (1971), Bryer's *F. Scott Fitzgerald—The Critical Reception* (1978) and *The Short Stories of F. Scott Fitzgerald—New Approaches in Criticism* (1982), Marvin J. LaHood's *"Tender Is the Night"—Essays in Criticism* (1969), and Ernest H. Lockridge's *Twentieth Century Interpretations of "The Great Gatsby"—A Collection of Critical Essays* (1968); and John A. Higgins' *F. Scott Fitzgerald: A Study of the Stories* (1971), Robert Emmet Long's *The Achieving of "The Great Gatsby"* (1979), Robert Sklar's *F. Scott Fitzgerald—The Last Laocoön* (1967), Milton R. Stern's *The Golden Moment—The Novels of F. Scott Fitzgerald* (1970), and Brian Way's *F. Scott Fitzgerald and the Art of Social Fiction* (1980).

These books, along with the others about the Fitzgeralds, generated numerous reviews and review-essays. This was particularly so in the cases of the several which were published by trade publishers rather than by university presses. These books and the reviews they received are listed in the Books section (I) of this volume, along with the numerous chapters and sections of books devoted to Fitzgerald since 1967. Scholarly periodical articles on Fitzgerald between 1967 and 1982 averaged about fifty per year. This total was greatly aided by the establishment, in 1969, of the *Fitzgerald/Hemingway Annual*, a handsomely printed hardcover volume which by 1971 had become a book of some 380 pages, a size that it maintained steadily until its suspension in 1979. The *Annual*, successor to the more frail and ephemeral *Fitzgerald Newsletter* (1958–1968), regularly contained a dozen or so full-length critical or bibliographical articles on Fitzgerald, several briefer notes, reviews of books by and about him, and a checklist of Fitzgerald studies. Material from the *Annual* and the other scholarly and critical articles on Fitzgerald since 1967 are listed in the Articles section (H) of this volume.

Between 1967 and 1982, the Fitzgeralds received as much attention in popular media as they did in the scholarly community. Overlapping between these two areas occurred when Nancy Milford's biography of Zelda, Calvin Tomkins' profile of the Murphys, and A. Scott Berg's biography of Maxwell Perkins appeared on the best-seller lists. But popular attention began in earnest in 1974, when a third film version of *The Great Gatsby* opened after a great deal of prerelease publicity. *Newsweek* (February 4) and *Time* (March 18) did major cover stories, and a television special, "F. Scott Fitzgerald and 'The Last of the Belles,'" was aired in January 1974 to take full advantage of the *Gatsby* ballyhoo. Similarly, when a movie version of *The Last Tycoon* opened in 1976, it was preceded by another television special, "F. Scott Fitzgerald in Hollywood."

Other events which kept the Fitzgerald name in the public eye during the 1970s and early 1980s included the designation in 1972 of Fitzgerald's St. Paul birthplace as a National Historical Landmark; the 1975 reburial of the Fitzgeralds in the Catholic cemetery in Rockville, Maryland, to which they had been denied admission at their deaths; the inclusion of an adaptation of "Bernice Bobs Her Hair" in the 1977 PBS television series on "The American Short Story"; National Public Radio's 1979 series, "The World of F. Scott Fitzgerald," which presented adaptations of eight stories; and Tennessee Williams' 1980 play, "Clothes for a Summer Hotel," which was unmistakably, albeit loosely, based on the lives of the Fitzgeralds. While much of the printed commentary generated by these events concerns the Fitzgeralds only tangentially and does so in a largely uncritical and certainly unscholarly fashion, it does reflect the fact that F. Scott and Zelda Fitzgerald have become figures of American popular culture as surely as they are important in American literary history. Hence, the news items, reviews, interviews, and editorials which reflect this popular attention are an important part of the record; and they are included in the Articles section (H) of this volume side by side with articles in scholarly journals.

New movie, radio, and television versions of Fitzgerald's writings have indicated that it would be useful to include a selection of reviews of and articles about earlier adaptations. This volume thus includes material on the three silent movies made from Fitzgerald short stories, the silent film versions of *The Beautiful and Damned* (1922) and *The Great Gatsby* (1926), stage adaptations of *The Great Gatsby* (1926), and *This Side of Paradise* (1962), the sound films of *The Great Gatsby* (1949), *Tender Is the Night* (1962), and "Babylon Revisited" (1954); and the television versions of *The Last Tycoon* (1957) and "Winter Dreams" (1957). It also lists news stories about adaptations which were planned but never materialized. Articles and reviews about adaptations have been included only when they comment significantly on Fitzgerald's original work, on the quality of the adaptation, or are the work of a major critic or literary figure of the day such as George Jean Nathan or Robert E. Sherwood.

Added to this volume also are reviews of revivals of "The Vegetable," as well as newly discovered reviews of the 1923 production. The latter include two new reviews of the Atlantic City opening, as well as two reviews of a subsequent engagement which the production had in Wilmington, Delaware. These last are particularly significant because all previous accounts have indicated that "The Vegetable" was presented for one performance on November 19, 1923, and closed the same night. This now is obviously not the case; in fact, records at the New York Public Library's Lincoln Center Library for the Performing Arts suggest that the original production of "The Vegetable" played not only in Wilmington but in Boston and Stamford, Connecticut, as well. Unfortunately, attempts to locate reviews of these other two engagements have been unsuccessful. Reviews have, however, been found and included for the 1925 Baltimore revival, the 1929 first New York production, and the 1975 English production. The user of this volume will now be able to compare the receptions of several different productions of Fitzgerald's only professionally produced play, just as he or she will be able to compare reviews of the three *Gatsby* films. In this way, popular responses to Fitzgerald's writings and to their adaptations suggest changes in attitudes towards his fiction, as well as fluctuations in his popular and critical appeal between 1920 and 1982.

This new volume, then, not only updates *The Critical Reputation of F. Scott Fitzgerald* by presenting annotated listings of the considerable scholarly and popular attention which Fitzgerald's work and life have attracted in the past fifteen years; it also widens the coverage of the earlier book by including types of material excluded from it, material which further documents the quantity of words in print generated by F. Scott Fitzgerald's writings and, by extension, the remarkable popular as well as academic attention he has received.

ABBREVIATIONS

AofA	*Afternoon of an Author*
ATSYM	*All the Sad Young Men*
AF	*The Apprentice Fiction of F. Scott Fitzgerald, 1909–1917*
B&J	*The Basil and Josephine Stories*
B&D	*The Beautiful and Damned*
Bits	*Bits of Paradise*
Correspondence	*Correspondence of F. Scott Fitzgerald*
"C-U"	"The Crack-Up"
C-U	*The Crack-Up*
Ledger	*F. Scott Fitzgerald's Ledger—A Facsimile*
"Three Comrades"	*F. Scott Fitzgerald's Screenplay for "Three Comrades" by Erich Maria Remarque*
F&P	*Flappers and Philosophers*
GG	*The Great Gatsby*
LT	*The Last Tycoon*
Letters	*The Letters of F. Scott Fitzgerald*
Notebooks	*The Notebooks of F. Scott Fitzgerald*
SMTW	*Save Me the Waltz*
6TJA	*Six Tales of the Jazz Age and Other Stories*
TJA	*Tales of the Jazz Age*
TAR	*Taps at Reveille*
TITN	*Tender Is the Night*
TSOP	*This Side of Paradise*

G

Reviews of Books by
F. Scott Fitzgerald

This section includes reviews of Fitzgerald's works published or performed before 1967 and omitted from Section A of *The Critical Reputation of F. Scott Fitzgerald—A Bibliographical Study*, as well as reviews of material by Fitzgerald which has been published or presented since 1967. Works by Fitzgerald are listed chronologically in order of their first publication in English, based on the listings in Matthew J. Bruccoli's *F. Scott Fitzgerald—A Descriptive Bibliography* (1972) and *Supplement* (1980). The one deviation from Bruccoli is the inclusion of *The Romantic Egoists* (1974) as a work by Fitzgerald. This has been done because of its subtitle, *A Pictorial Autobiography From the Scrapbooks and Albums of Scott and Zelda Fitzgerald*, which in turn reflects its editors' expressed policy to "include nothing in the text which is not directly autobiographical" and to present the Fitzgeralds' "*own* story of their lives, rather than someone else's interpretation of them."

The lists of reviews of works by Fitzgerald since 1967 are, in most cases, derived from publishers' or editors' files; while this method insures that they are more complete than they would be if only available reference works were relied upon, undoubtedly some reviews are missing. No attempt has been made to locate all appearances of syndicated reviews; one such appearance is annotated, with an indication in the annotation of representative other appearances, when these are known.

Reviews which have served as vehicles for extended re-evaluations of Fitzgerald's career are marked with an asterisk; and, in a few instances, these "Review-Articles" are also listed in the Articles section (Section H) of this volume.

When a review deals with several Fitzgerald works, it is listed under each work reviewed but numbered only once, at its first appearance chronologically. Each listing of the review gives the pages of the full review and then, in brackets, the pages which concern the book by Fitzgerald which is the subject of that particular group of reviews. For reviews which cover several books, among them one by Fitzgerald, page numbers for the full review are listed and, in brackets following, the pages dealing with Fitzgerald.

Several reviews of Fitzgerald's books published during his lifetime and found as unlocated clippings in his scrapbooks at Princeton University were published in *F. Scott Fitzgerald—The Critical Reception* (1978) and are listed in Section I under that title (I73).

Reviews of Zelda Fitzgerald's novel *Save Me the Waltz* are listed in Section K.

THIS SIDE OF PARADISE
American Edition
(1920)

G1.   Phelps, William Lyon. "Books Worth Reading, Buying, and Keeping," *Yale Alumni Weekly*, 29 (May 7, 1920), 756–757 [757].

Novel is "one of the best stories of college life in America I have ever read. This book is nothing less than extraordinary, coming from youth so extreme. It naturally bears some marks of immaturity, carries at times the knowing wink of adolescence, but is full of observation, of deep reflection, and has true graces of style. The author will go far and I shall read everything he publishes in book form."

FLAPPERS AND PHILOSOPHERS
American Edition
(1920)

G2.   Anonymous. "Fitzgerald Again," Minneapolis *Journal*, October 21, 1920, p. 3.

The collection "has all the uncanny wisdom and the exuberant vitality" of TSOP.

Reprinted: Bryer, ed. (I73)

G3.   Boyd, Thomas Alexander. "Mostly Flappers," St. Paul *Daily News*, December 26, 1920, Sec. 4, p. 6.

Of the eight stories in the volume, "some...are good. Others are merely brightly colored flub-dub about surpassingly beautiful 19-year-

old debutantes...whose erudition is only equaled by their boredom and capacity for kissing."
Reprinted: Bryer, ed. (I73)

G4.   Brown, Heywood. "Books," NY *Tribune*, November 1, 1920, p. 10.
"The Ice Palace" is "a skillful study of character in environment" and it is "extremely successful in making the reader see places and persons, even though those persons are types." "The Cut-Glass Bowl" is "disquieting."
Reprinted: Bryer, ed. (I73)

THE BEAUTIFUL AND DAMNED
American Edition
(1922)

G5.   Anonymous. "Epigrammatic," *Rocky Mountain News* (Denver), April 2, 1922, Sec. 2, p. 6.
"There is no searching of ultimate values here, no shrewd penetration—only the tracing of an unimportant degradation thru scenes which (whatever the author's purpose) succeed not even in being shocking or arresting, only tiresome and rather disgusting."

G6.   ———. Review of *The Beautiful and Damned*, *Nassau Literary Magazine*, 77 (April 1922), 343.
"We have read 'The Beautiful and Damned,' and we are sorry we did. Only curiosity, not interest, made us get through with it at all."

G7.   Minot, John Clair. "Bookish Chat and Comment—Mr. Fitzgerald," Boston *Herald*, March 11, 1922, p. 5.
Although the novel "is so uneven that you are alternately exasperated and filled with enthusiasm while reading a single page," it is "an impressive and stimulating work."
Reprinted: Bryer, ed. (I73)

G8.   S[wan], M[ary] B[elle]. "Author of *This Side of Paradise* Writes Biting Satire on Modern Life," Buffalo *Sunday Courier*, April 30, 1922, Magazine, p. 22.
F's "dialogues, his characters and his gift for dramatic portrayal make him a compelling writer, and always throughout his work gleams a silver thread of spiritual projection that makes his story ring true, and makes it go with the public."
Reprinted: Bryer, ed. (I73)

TALES OF THE JAZZ AGE
American Edition
(1922)

G9.   Mencken, H. L.   Review of *Tales of the Jazz Age*, *Smart Set*, 71 (July 1923), 141.

Brief notice: It "is a book that would have been far better if it had been more rigorously edited."

Reprinted: West (H837); Bryer, ed. (I73).

G10.   S[wan], M[ary] B[elle].   *"Tales of the Jazz Age* Caviar For Jaded Taste," Buffalo *Sunday Courier*, November 5, 1922, Magazine, p. 14.

Stories "reveal uncommon imagination, richness of creative power and a technique that enables the author to put forth in his own individual way, the phases of life that have attracted his notice, since jazz was elected sovereign of an historical age."

Reprinted: Bryer, ed. (I73)

G11.   Thompson, Anita B.   Review of *Tales of the Jazz Age*, *The Messenger*, 5 (May 1923), 706, 719.

"Mr. Fitzgerald has produced another splendid book, appreciable both from 'muse and amuse' points of view."

THE VEGETABLE
(1923)

G12.   Anonymous.   "Bootlegger, President, and Postman," Boston *Evening Transcript*, May 19, 1923, Part 4, p. 2.

Brief review precedes reprinted excerpt from the text of the play. "The characteristic tricks of verbal juggling and mental acrobatics which have made many of Mr. Fitzgerald's previous pages readable to the younger generation, he has often saved in the present instance for his stage-directions, leaving to his dialogue, a super abundance of outworn 'gags' thrice-familiar on vaudeville or burlesque stages."

G13.   ———.   "Fitzgerald's Play—A Brilliant Farce Comedy With a Sociological Moral," Philadephia *Evening Public Ledger*, May 22, 1923, p. 23.

Play has "a deliciously humorous second act," there is "a bit of sound philosophy at the bottom of it," and "it is lively farce in form."

G14.   ———.   "Somnolent Rail Clerk Is Psychoanalyzed," Richmond (Va.) *Times-Dispatch*, May 27, 1923, Part 2, p. 5.

"Mr. Fitzgerald has written a clever farce, with his characters drawn skillfully. There are many humorous lines. It may be called an excellent satire."

G15.   D'Or, René [Maxwell Bodenheim]. "Books," *Chicago Literary Times*, 1 (June 1, 1923), 1, 6 [6].

"This drivel is supposed to be a satire on the vanities and incapacities of public officials, but it affords nothing save the spectacle of a breezy charlatan—the author—engaged in stuffing his mental hollows with a shallow brand of humor."

G16.   F., R. "The Day's Best Book," Richmond (Va.) *News Leader*, May 19, 1923, p. 10.

F's "satire and irony are much more effective when delivered through his youthful characters than when voiced by Jerry, or the bootlegger."

Reprinted: Bryer, ed. (I73)

1972 Edition

G17.   Anonymous. Review of *The Vegetable*, *Choice*, 9 (October 1972), 968.

New edition is of "little interest to any but the most dedicated of Fitzgerald scholars."

1976 Edition

G18.   Anonymous. "Fitzgerald, the Playwright," Baltimore *Sun*, May 30, 1976, p. D5.

Very brief descriptive review.

G19.   ———. Review of *The Vegetable*, *Choice*, 13 (September 1976), 820.

"About two thirds of *The Vegetable* is very funny stuff, and though the stage directions written for its book audience are a bit too clever-coy, the wacky actions of its principals are well worth attending to and remind one of the gang that comes to Gatsby's parties two years later."

G20.   ———. Review of *The Vegetable*, *Kirkus*, 44 (May 1, 1976), 585.

Very brief descriptive review.

G21.   ———. Review of *The Vegetable*, *Publishers' Weekly*, 209 (May 10, 1976), 82.

"Although Fitzgerald's bite wasn't deep and the play adds nothing to his stature, it's a happy read nonetheless, and good to have available again."

G22.   Brown, Dennis. "Fitzgerald's Prophetic Flop," St. Louis *Post-Dispatch*, August 1, 1976, p. 4F.
"'The Vegetable' remains an amiable curiosity."

G23.   Carey, Gary. Review of *The Vegetable*, *Library Journal*, 101 (July 1976), 1550.
"Though it contains patches of snappy dialogue and some clever scenes, the play is structurally schizoid—starting and ending as folksy realistic comedy, it swings into political burlesque for its second and best act."

G24.   Cockshutt, Rod. "New Paperbacks: Hot Times to 'Ragtime' to Race Time," Raleigh *News and Observer*, July 4, 1976, p. 6-IV.
Very brief mention: "A quick reading of the play...suggests why Fitzgerald did not pursue writing for the stage. But as a literary curiosity, the play may be of interest to Fitzgerald buffs."

G25.   Cowie, Denise. "Fitzgerald Bomb Being Revived," Hartford *Times*, June 13, 1976, p. 36.
"Even if it is never again produced here, the play is worth reading for its beautiful take-offs of political absurdities."

G26.   Dickerson, James. "Book Review—Satire Is Subtle, Penetrating," Greenville (Miss.) *Delta Democrat-Times*, June 6, 1976, p. 38.
"*The Vegetable* should not have been the failure it was in 1923, and it is likely it will now receive a more favorable reaction from a public more attuned to the nuances of political corruption."

G27.   Hall, Randy. "Fitzgerald's Play 'Vegetable' Oddity," Anniston (Ala.) *Star*, June 27, 1976, Sec. C, p. 10.
F "mistook mocking his characters' social class for satirizing their ambitions; there is an uncomfortably patronizing tone to much of the dialogue." Even so, "much of it is well written, although there is some uncertainty of treatment in the second act, and the third act is disconcertingly sentimental."

G28.   Houston, Levin. "Playing Around With Success," Fredericksburg (Va.) *Free Lance-Star*, July 3, 1976, "Town & Country" Magazine, p. 13.
"Despite the high regard" F had for the play, "it remains, if not a failure, certainly a far from successful play" because F's satire seems "unchannelled—shooting off in all directions at once. But it is good to have the chance to read this long unavailable work by one of our country's most beloved and glamorous figures."

G29.   McCormick, Ashley. "F. Scott Fitzgerald Pens a Side-Splitting Comedy," Nashville *Banner*, August 7, 1976, p. 5.
"Like most of F. Scott Fitzgerald's writing, you can't put it down until you've finished reading it. I recommend this book to whoever wants a good laugh. Now would be a good time for a theater to produce the play as this is an election year."

G30.   Sparrow, Prep. "Readers' Journal," Fayetteville (N.C.) *Observer & Times*, August 29, 1976, p. 3D.
"Although the play was a failure, it remains a classic piece of political satire and it served the author well by giving him valuable experience in literary craftsmanship."

G31.   Stewart, Susan. "Show Biz, Arts, Etc.," *Mademoiselle*, 82 (August 1976), 140, 144–145 [144].
Brief descriptive review: "The novelist Fitzgerald shows through in his characterizations."

"The Vegetable," opened November 19, 1923
Apollo Theatre, Atlantic City

G32.   Anonymous. Review of "The Vegetable," *Variety*, 73 (November 22, 1923), 16.
The play "in no way did justice to the talent of Mr. Fitzgerald, its author, the discrimination of Sam H. Harris, its producer, or the ability of Ernest Truex, who struggled bravely on as its hero."

G33.   Smith, E. F. "Ernest Truex Works Hard in New Comedy," Atlantic City *Press*, November 20, 1923, p. 2.
"The title does not belie the production, for the play may be likened to a frost-bitten rutabaga that is fairly sound at both ends and wholly gone in the middle."

"The Vegetable," opened November 26, 1923
Playhouse Theatre, Wilmington, Delaware

G34.   Anonymous. "Fine Comedy in 'Vegetable,'" Wilmington (Del.) *Evening Journal*, November 27, 1923, p. 15.
"Just the same sort of promise of things better to come seeps through the audience that sees F. Scott Fitzgerald's 'The Vegetable' as did with the reader of the young writer's first novel, 'This Side of Paradise.'...There is satire, burlesque, farce and pure comedy galore."

G35.   M., F. M. "'Vegetable' Kept Alive By Truex," Wilmington (Del.) *News*, November 27, 1923, p. 11.
"The fault [of the play] lies in too many goals. Light comedy, farce, satire even burlesque are all garbled in one play."

Revival, opened March 2, 1925
Vagabond Players Theatre, Baltimore, Maryland

G36.   Anonymous.   "Vagabonds Give 'The Vegetable' This Month," Baltimore *American*, March 3, 1925, p. 7.

F "has written a play that is real in its utter silliness, that is aimless and dull and acrid as life is, and that allows not evermuch for the efficacy of dreams."

G37.   ————.   "'The Vegetable' Given By Vagabond Players," Baltimore *Sun*, March 3, 1925, p. 13.

Basically descriptive review.

G38.   ————.   "'The Vegetable' Vagabond Offering," Baltimore *News*, March 3, 1925, p. 11.

Calls play "a somewhat dreary fantastic comedy."

G39.   F., R. B.   "Vagabonds Present 'The Vegetable,'" Baltimore *Post*, March 3, 1925, p. 7.

"To tell the truth, Fitzgerald's play fails to 'jell' and its failure on Broadway is easily explicable....The first act is slow, the second act...terribly hard to 'put over' and only in the third does the play gain speed and power. By that time it is nearly too late."

G40.   M., A. F.   "'The Vegetable,' a Comedy, on Vagabonds' March Bill," Baltimore *Evening Sun*, March 3, 1925, p. 22.

"The play itself still remains the *reductio ad absurdum* of the school of Smart-Aleckry among adolescent writers."

Revival, opened April 10, 1929
Cherry Lane Theatre, NY City

G41.   Anderson, John.   "'The Vegetable' Opens With Amateur Cast—Play in Cherry Lane Not Freshest on Market," NY *Evening Journal*, April 12, 1929, p. 29.

Play "seems to have been written on some bitter afternoon after the success of 'This Side of Paradise' and 'The Beautiful and the [*sic*] Damned.' It represents one of those 'get away from it all' moments with which such resounding acclaim frequently victimizes its recipients and leaves them in a condition of morbid jeering."

G42.   Atkinson, J. Brooks.   "The Play—Cherry Lane Vegetable," NY *Times*, April 11, 1929, p. 32.

"When it was written,...stylized satiric fantasy with a tendency toward expressionism was one of man's noblest works—very gallant in its esthetic protest against the stupidities of the nation....But, now that the state of the nation is so advanced, both the theme and the manner sound sophomoric."

G43.   B., S.   "The Theatre—Garden Variety," *Wall Street Journal*, April 15, 1929, p. 4.

"The idea came and came again, and would not down,...that here was something that belonged rightly to a room full of school children to whom a tolerant teacher had permitted an hour of spoofing, with costumes borrowed from old trunks in the garret at home, the only restriction being that the spoofing must have a semblance of dramatic form."

G44.   Bolton, Whitney.   "Deserting Village—A Last Look at 'Vegetable,'" NY *Morning Telegraph*, April 12, 1929, p. 3.

"I could see nothing fine or satirical in it...."

G45.   Gabriel, Gilbert W.   "'The Vegetable,' as Reviewed by Gabriel—Scott Fitzgerald Comedy Offered With Odd Results," NY *American*, April 11, 1929, p. S–7.

"Neither Mr. Fitzgerald nor I, nor the times in general, for that matter, can have changed so completely as to explain why 'The Vegetable' seemed such a horrific bore last night. I'm inclined to take a chance and blame it all on the production."

G46.   Garland, Robert.   "Cherry Lane Offers Satire on Habits of These United States—F. Scott Fitzgerald Comedy Has Its Manhattan Premiere," NY *Telegram*, April 11, 1929, p. 12.

"The Vegetable" is "a coherent and satisfying theatrical invention, casual, playful, as native as a nice long spit."

G47.   Hammond, Percy.   "The Theaters—Scott Fitzgerald's 'The Vegetable' at the Cherry Lane Theater," NY *Herald Tribune*, April 11, 1929, p. 22.

"After overlooking as much of last night's exhibition as was possible to a morning journalist, I suspected that Mr. Harris and Mr. Hopkins were justified in their fear that 'The Vegetable' is better upon a book shelf than upon a stage."

G48.   Littell, Robert.   "The Play—The Lenox Hill Players Drearily Revive F. Scott Fitzgerald's Dreary Satire, 'The Vegetable,' at the Cherry Lane," NY *Evening Post*, April 11, 1929, p. 20.

"Mr. Fitzgerald is one of the American novelists who can make flat dialogue sound sharp, but in this play the caricatured banalities of the morons are just one flabby pancake after another. It all seems tired and grouchy."

G49.   Lockridge, Richard.   "'The Vegetable'—F. Scott Fitzgerald's Satire Is Offered at the Cherry Lane Theater," NY *Sun*, April 11, 1929, p. 24.

"It is one act of domestic bickering, one act of only tolerably amusing satire, one act of rather too pretty sentiment. Now and then it is amusing, but at its best it is a little labored, a little uncertain, a little faint. At its best it lacks fervor and the furious mockery which satire should have—and should, of course, control. Never does it come within leagues of living up to its conception."

G50.   Mantle, Burns. "Speaking of Co-operative Theatre— 'The Sea Gull' Is Effective, But 'The Vegetables' [sic] Awful," NY Daily News, April 12, 1929, p. 51.

"Nothing more imbecilic in text and inept in performance has been offered in the local theatre within this playgoer's memory and the experience of sitting through even two acts of it was depressing and discouraging in the extreme."

G51.   McIntyre, O. O. "Theatre," Life, 93 (May 3, 1929), 24.

"Mr. Fitzgerald possibly has the nucleus of an idea in his artless travesty on American gawkery....'The Vegetable' may be transplanted to better kept gardens north of Herald Square, but even then I fear it will turn out a quince."

G52.   Nathan, George Jean. "Judging the Shows," Judge, 96 (May 4, 1929), 16, 28.

Less a review than Nathan's denial that he ever called F's play "something of a masterpiece" (as he is quoted as having said, in publicity for the production).

G53.   Osborn, E. W. "The New Plays—'The Vegetable,'" NY Evening World, April 11, 1929, p. 20.

Very brief descriptive review. Play was received "with grave doubts and a few titters."

G54.   Pollock, Arthur. "The Theater—The Lenox Hill Players Present 'The Vegetable,' by F. Scott Fitzgerald, at the Cherry Lane Theater," Brooklyn Eagle, April 11, 1929, p. A 12.

"'The Vegetable' would be better dead."

G55.   S[mith], A[lison]. "Another Play—Not Beautiful But Damned," NY World, April 11, 1929, p. 13.

"Altogether the revival seems a cruel error whose only value lies in a warning to brilliant young novelists imploring them to tear up their earlier efforts before they have a chance to reach the merciless glare of the footlights."

Revival, opened January 29, 1975
Oxford Playhouse, Oxford, England

G56.   Anonymous.   "What Makes Jerry Run," *Times Literary Supplement* (London), February 7, 1975, p. 138.

Play "sharpens our sense of the topography of early Fitzgerald, even if its merits prove to be the novelist's rather than the playwright's."

G57.   Billington, Michael.   "*The Vegetable* at the Oxford Playhouse," Manchester *Guardian*, January 31, 1975, p. 10.

Play is bad, but "with its references to Freudian analysis and demonstration of bootlegging techniques, the play nevertheless has a sociological fascination."

G58.   D[ibb], F[rank] W.   "Oxford 'The Vegetable,'" *Stage & Television Today*, February 6, 1975, p. 20.

"Some of this is not without sharply witty impact but the fires of Fitzgerald's satirical writing and his understandably undeveloped abilities in dramatic construction tend to burn rather low."

G59.   Hobson, Harold.   "Stars in Glory," London *Sunday Times*, February 2, 1975, p. 35.

In the play's "sudden switch from the audible and visible surfaces of life to the exteriorisation of the internal disturbances of an overwrought brain, Fitzgerald was anticipating in a most remarkable way much of the development of modern theatre." In "its conception," "The Vegetable" is "a more original creation than either 'The Great Gatsby' or 'Tender is the Night.'"

G60.   Nightingale, Benedict.   "Iron in the Soul," *New Statesman*, n.s. 89 (February 7, 1975), 184.

F's play emerges as "an American lower-middle-class mania for illiterate malapropisms."

THE GREAT GATSBY
American Edition
(1925)

G61.   Paterson, Isabel.   "Rags to Riches in the New Novels," *McNaught's Monthly,* 3 (June 1925), 190–191.

F "deserves much credit for *The Great Gatsby....*it is a clever, quietly satirical, extremely skilful comedy of manners—mostly bad manners—depicting a social phenomenon common to all wealthy nations and periods."
Reprinted: Bryer, ed. (I73)

ALL THE SAD YOUNG MEN
(1926)

G62.   Cowley, Malcolm. "Now the Age of Cuckoo Humor," *Charm*, 5 (May 1926), 46, 80–81 [80–81].

Most of the stories are "serious; often they are touched with a melancholy which is new in Fitzgerald's work. Incidentally, there are one or two which rank among the finest stories he has written." Reprinted: Bryer, ed. (I73)

G63.   Partridge, Bellamy. "Some Good Short Stories," *Brentano's Book Chat*, 5 (May-June 1926), 49.

"The Rich Boy" is "the best story in the collection," which, as a whole, is "well up to the author's batting average which, as short stories go, is rather high." But F's stories "never seem to have quite the quality of his novels." Reprinted: Bryer, ed. (I73)

G64.   Paterson, Isabel. "Other Books Worth Reading," *McNaught's Monthly*, 5 (May 1926), 155.

Very brief mention: "Most of these young men seem to be utterly miserable because they have nothing but money, youth and health."

TAPS AT REVEILLE
American Edition
(1935)

G65.   M., J. O. "F. Scott Fitzgerald Comes of Age in His New Story Collection," St. Paul *Daily News*, April 22, 1935, p. 6.

Collection offers "excellent and varied diversion. Its negligent, half-amused, half-humorous style, the tone of which is occasionally deepened by irony, does not disguise the author's keen sense of character and quiet tragedy."

THE CRACK-UP
(1945)

G66.   C., S. C. "A Memorial Miscellany," *Christian Science Monitor*, August 4, 1945, Magazine, p. 12.

"The historian of the gawdy nineteen-twenties has, in this collection, an abundance of evidence as to the state of mind and morals of a small, self-conscious section of the American people."

THE STORIES OF F. SCOTT FITZGERALD
(1951)

G67.   Gannett, Lewis.   "Books and Things," NY *Herald Tribune*, March 7, 1951, p. 25.

Rereading the stories, "one is astonished at their brilliance, their romantic sheen and their monotonous juvenility. They make it painfully obvious that, even in his forties, Fitzgerald was still a wistful, slightly spoiled bright boy."

AFTERNOON OF AN AUTHOR
American Editions
(1957, 1958)

G68.   Poore, Charles.   "Books of The Times," NY *Times*, April 29, 1958, p. 27.

Volume is "a remarkably appealing book of uncollected stories and sketches by Fitzgerald that Arthur Mizener has festooned with formidable critical commentaries."

THE PAT HOBBY STORIES
American Edition
(1962)

G69.   Anonymous.   "Brief Look at What's New On the Bookshelf," New Orleans *Times-Picayune*, September 9, 1962, Sec. 2, p. 19.

"The fictional character Hobby is fascinating, but fans of Fitzgerald will find the stories more interesting as a final peek into the life of the late author."

G70.   ————.   "Collections," Boston *Sunday Globe*, July 15, 1962, p. 72-A.

"This sequence bridges the last major gap in the collected writings of Fitzgerald."

G71.   ————.   "Pat Hobby Stories," Philadelphia *Inquirer*, July 22, 1962, Sec. D, p. 8.

"There's more life and poignancy in the Fitzgerald-Gingrich correspondence that makes up the introduction than in the whole Pat Hobby saga."

G72.   ———. "Pat Stories Fill Fitzgerald Gap," *Syracuse Herald*, August 19, 1962, "Stars" Section, p. 4.

Volume is "thin stuff indeed, and the troubles of Pat Hobby in the movie milieu of the late 1930s [are] downright tiresome. The fact that 21 years have passed before anyone thought it necessary or desirable to collect them is the tipoff."

G73.   ———. Review of *The Pat Hobby Stories*, *The Booklist*, 59 (September 1, 1962), 29.

"Since they are from a magazine sequence there is some repetition in each story, much of the dialog is dated, and many readers may not consider them hilarious, as the editor claims, but they fill the last major gap in Fitzgerald's collected writings."

G74.   ———. Review of *The Pat Hobby Stories*, *The Critic*, 21 (August-September 1962), 64–65.

"The stories are an uproarious commentary on the Hollywood atmosphere—satire nearly at its best—and it is astonishing that they could go unnoticed for so many years."

G75.   Beau-Seigneur, Jay. "Mr. Hyde," Palo Alto (Calif.) *Times*, July 14, 1962, "Peninsula Living" Section, p. 19.

These stories "should do little to detract or to enhance Fitzgerald's reputation as a writer," although they do present "an accurate, penetrating portrait of what Hollywood must have been like at its zenith." This is because, while the stories are "as factual as a news account," they are "curiously devoid of feeling."

G76.   Gould, Ray. "'The Pat Hobby Stories,'" Montgomery *Advertiser*, September 2, 1962, p. 4E.

"It is a slight book but to the multitudes of Fitzgerald fans it will be welcomed as the final efforts of a brilliant but frustrated career."

G77.   L., F. "Fitzgerald Reborn In Pat Hobby," Buffalo *Courier-Express,* August 26, 1962, Sec. D, p. 26.

"Here is fine, clean prose in a comic picture of Hollywood as seen through one man's bleary eyes, conveying a sense of accuracy and, in a way, vitality."

G78.   Mariano, Louis. "'The Pat Hobby Stories'—Fitzgerald's Hollywood," Chicago *Daily News*, July 18, 1962, p. 38.

"Despite the many negatives"—they are "cliché ridden" and "repetitive"—the stories "make for interesting reading" because they "reflect Fitzgerald's scorn for the Hollywood of his day and highlight in a fashion the turmoil of his life."

G79. P[rather], G[ibson]. "Fitzgerald's Last Effort," Fayetteville (N.C.) *Observer*, July 29, 1962, Sec. D, p. 3.

"The writing is superb, better than most men could achieve in their prime, because Fitzgerald, even after the flame went out, was still a master of the language."

LETTERS TO HIS DAUGHTER
(1965)

G80. Anonymous. "Fitzgerald and His Daughter—When a Father Worried," *National Observer*, October 18, 1965, p. 24.

In this volume, "there shines an innocence of character and a kind of nobility of ideals."

G81. ———. Review of *Letters to His Daughter*, *The Booklist*, 62 (January 15, 1966), 479.

Descriptive brief review.

G82. ———. Review of *Letters to His Daughter*, *Kirkus*, 33 (July 15, 1965), 736.

Descriptive favorable review: "In *loco parentis*," F is "at his best."

G83. Havighurst, Walter. "Advice the Author Ignored," *Chicago Tribune Books Today*, October 10, 1965, p. 6.

This "slender, tasteful book...makes a surprisingly complete self-portrait of the author in the years when life had closed in on him."

G84. O'Leary, Theodore M. "Whatever the Life, Love Was Constant," Kansas City *Star*, October 17, 1965, p. 5E.

"A more pertinent example of one side of the dialogue that goes on perpetually between the generations would be hard to find."

G85. P., F. Review of *Letters to His Daughter*, St. Louis *Sunday Post-Dispatch*, September 26, 1965, p. 4C.

Less a review than praise for F's daughter's Introduction.

F. SCOTT FITZGERALD IN HIS OWN TIME:
A MISCELLANY
(1971)

G86. Anonymous. Review of *F. Scott Fitzgerald in His Own Time*, *American Literature*, 43 (January 1972), 681.

Brief descriptive mention.

G87.   ———. Review of *F. Scott Fitzgerald in His Own Time*, *Choice*, 8 (January 1972), 1450.
"This miscellany...is a worthwhile addition to any library." It "will be useful to the Fitzgerald scholar, who will find relatively arcane material rendered easily accessible here; but it will prove interesting to even the most casual undergraduate reader as well."

G88.   ———. Review of *F. Scott Fitzgerald in His Own Time*, *Christian Century*, 88 (September 1, 1971), 1029.
Brief mention: "Helpful for putting Fitzgerald in proper perspective."

G89.   ———. Review of *F. Scott Fitzgerald in His Own Time*, *Journal of Modern Literature*, 3 (February 1974), 600.
Brief mention: "a major addition to the Fitzgerald canon."

G90.   ———. Review of *F. Scott Fitzgerald in His Own Time*, *NY Times Book Review*, October 24, 1971, p. 61.
Brief mention: "A feast for fans."

G91.   *Adams, Robert M. "Attis Adonis Osiris Fitzgerald & Co.," *NY Review of Books*, 17–18 (January 27, 1972), 26–29 [27–28].
"The formative stages" of F's "talent would be better served in a concise article than by reprints of his blurbs and the leftovers of his juvenilia."

G92.   Allen, Wallace. "'New' Writings By Fitzgerald," Minneapolis *Tribune*, September 26, 1971, p. 10D.
"The Fitzgerald fan club should give three cheers for some fascinating reading and scholars should be happy that so much digging has been done in their behalf."

G93.   Barra, Allen. "Early Fitzgerald," Birmingham (Ala.) *News*, December 29, 1974, p. E–7.
This is "a charming, sometimes illuminating collection: one wishes there were similar collections of writers far more worthy of study than Fitzgerald."

G94.   Brown, Adger. "Fitzgerald Era Subject of Book By Two Professors," *The State* (Columbia, S.C.), August 15, 1971, p. 4-E.
Descriptive review.

G95.   Buchen, Irving H. "A Valuable New Research Tool," Baltimore *Sunday Sun*, September 12, 1971, Sec. D, p. 4.
"What Bruccoli and Bryer... have provided specialists with is an invaluable research tool. They have done all the hard leg work, all the dating, all the confirming, all the securing of permissions, to enable

critics and literary historians to study further the evolution of a vaude-villian into a tragic comedian."

G96.   Callahan, John F.   Review of *F. Scott Fitzgerald in His Own Time*, *Saturday Review*, 54 (December 11, 1971), 57–58.

"Although throughout their foreword the editors point out that various Fitzgerald writings have been neglected, nowhere do they say that what has been neglected is of any lasting quality."

G97.   Christ, Ronald.   Review of *F. Scott Fitzgerald in His Own Time*, *Books Abroad*, 47 (January 1973), 148–149.

Book is "a performance of diligence and pack-ratting rather than one of intelligence and discernment."

G98.   Clark, Alexander P.   Review of *F. Scott Fitzgerald in His Own Time*, *Fitzgerald/Hemingway Annual*, 4 (1972), 391–393.

"This volume can be considered a 'companion' to Scott Fitzgerald, a reference work which will give the rest of the quotation, or which lets us see why the humorous lyrics were adjudged 'tops,' or why Fitzgerald's book reviews get quoted."

G99.   Drewry, John E.   "New Book News—F. Scott Fitzgerald Subject of New Books," Athens (Ga.) *Banner-Herald*, July 6, 1972, p. 4.

Descriptive review.

G100.   Harrison, Cynthia.   Review of *F. Scott Fitzgerald in His Own Time*, *Library Journal*, 96 (November 15, 1971), 3759.

"This miscellany may be of some interest to the general reader in view of the current attention being given to the Fitzgeralds, but it is basically an academic work."

G101.   *Keetch, Brent.   Review of *F. Scott Fitzgerald in His Own Time*, *Western Humanities Review*, 26 (Spring 1972), 183–185.

"The first section of the miscellany will serve as an excellent source for scholars, but the collection as a whole has an additional value; it evokes a sense of a lavish era in American history, and as many pieces in the second section of the book attest, Fitzgerald the man came to be representative, to exemplify somehow in his writings and even in his personality what it was that the nation thought it had produced in a youthful generation after the war."

G102.   L[abor], E[arle].   "News For Fitzgerald-Hemingway Buffs," *CEA Forum*, 2 (December 1971), 9–10.

Volume is "modestly named and—considering its wealth of contents—modestly priced."

G103.   M[alkin], M[ary] A[nn]. Review of *F. Scott Fitzgerald in His Own Time*, *AB Bookman's Weekly*, 48 (September 6–13, 1971), 512.
"This book fills a real gap in the spate of books about the man and his works."

G104.   Meacham, Harry M. "Miscellany: Scholars Collect Material on Fitzgerald," Richmond (Va.) *News Leader*, September 22, 1971, p. 11.
Book is "a work of enormous scholarship which students of contemporary American literature will find indispensable."

G105.   Weeks, Robert P. Review of *F. Scott Fitzgerald in His Own Time*, *Modern Fiction Studies*, 17 (Winter 1971–72), 638–639.
The *Princeton Tiger* and *Nassau Lit* material is "unlikely to lure scholars away from the best known fiction"; the other material by F "is mildly interesting because it's by Fitzgerald, but apart from that it possessed for me little intrinsic merit."

G106.   White, William. "A Fitzgerald Miscellany," *American Book Collector*, 22 (January 1972), 2.
Descriptive favorable review.

G107.   Whitman, Charles. "...and More Freight for the Fitzgerald Flyer," Chicago *Daily News*, October 23–24, 1971, "Panorama" Section, p. 16.
"If you like Fitzgerald even a bit, this book is one to read."

DEAR SCOTT/DEAR MAX—THE FITZGERALD-PERKINS
CORRESPONDENCE
American Edition
(1971)

G108.   Anonymous. "F. Scott Fitzgerald," Omaha *Sunday World-Herald*, January 16, 1972, "Entertainment" Magazine, p. 26.
Very brief squib; book is recommended.

G109.   ———. Review of *Dear Scott/Dear Max*, *American Literature*, 44 (November 1972), 529.
Brief descriptive review.

G110.   ———. Review of *Dear Scott/Dear Max*, *Amherst* (Amherst College), 24 (Winter 1972), 22.
Brief descriptive review.

G111. ———. Review of *Dear Scott/Dear Max, The Booklist*, 68 (February 15, 1972), 483.
Collection is "an essentially auxiliary volume for readers interested in Fitzgerald's career and publishing history."

G112. ———. Review of *Dear Scott/Dear Max, Choice*, 9 (April 1972), 212.
"This unnecessary book…seems an attempt to ride the current Fitzgerald wave without providing any real service either to scholars or to laymen."

G113. ———. Review of *Dear Scott/Dear Max, Kirkus*, 39 (August 1, 1971), 854.
"The editors have presented the material (annotated throughout) with a care and concern the great Max Perkins would have appreciated."

G114. ———. Review of *Dear Scott/Dear Max, MD—Medical Newsmagazine*, 16 (September 1972), 279.
"This book is illuminating with regard to biographical material about the two men, and, in addition, it is a record of a very important period of American writings."

G115. ———. Review of *Dear Scott/Dear Max, New Republic*, 166 (January 22, 1972), 28–29.
Basically descriptive favorable review.

G116. ———. Review of *Dear Scott/Dear Max, NY Times Book Review*, April 23, 1972, p. 10.
Very brief descriptive favorable review.

G117. ———. Review of *Dear Scott/Dear Max*, Portland *Sunday Oregonian*, December 26, 1971, p. 4 F.
Brief descriptive favorable review.

G118. ———. Review of *Dear Scott/Dear Max*, Savannah *Morning News and Evening Press*, February 13, 1972, Magazine, p. 8.
Brief descriptive review.

＊Adams, Robert M. "Attis Adonis Osiris Fitzgerald & Co.," *NY Review of Books*, 17–18 (January 27, 1972), 26–29 [26].
Brief descriptive mention. See G91.

G119. ＊Atkinson, Jennifer McCabe. Review of *Dear Scott/ Dear Max, Fitzgerald/Hemingway Annual*, 4 (1972), 377–381.
"Although the volume has many things to commend it, it should have been called *Selected Letters from the Correspondence of F. Scott Fitzgerald and Maxwell Perkins*. We do not yet have the thorough and informative volume containing Fitzgerald's correspondence with his

editor which is needed. Professor Kuehl's and Professor Bryer's work will have to be done again some day."

G120.   Barrett, Mary Ellin. "Cosmo Reads the New Books," *Cosmopolitan*, 172 (January 1972), 12.
Descriptive brief mention.

G121.   Beardsley, Charles. "Literary Memories: O'Casey, Fitzgerald," Redwood City (Calif.) *Tribune*, April 1, 1972, "Peninsula Living" Section, pp. 21, 22.
"This collection defines an era with stunning immediacy, and illuminates it."

G122.   Blied, Diane. "Fitzgerald-Perkins Letters an Unbiased View," Los Angeles *Herald-Examiner*, January 2, 1972, p. E–7.
The book is "interesting to the casual reader as well as to the growing number who dote on every word written on the chronicler of the Jazz Age, which he named."

G123.   Boardman, Kathryn G. Review of *Dear Scott/Dear Max*, St. Paul *Sunday Pioneer Press*, December 12, 1971, "Lively Arts" Section, p. 34.
"The letters leave the reader with the impression that Perkins suffered as deeply as Fitzgerald over the writer's personal and professional problems."

G124.   Bode, Carl. "Letters to and From a Brilliant Sinner," Washington (D.C.) *Sunday Star*, December 12, 1971, p. D–5.
"Though all the letters have been printed before, the editors' art makes this a fresh volume and an interesting one. It shows us not only Fitzgerald but the Jazz Age."

G125.   Brady, Charles A. "A New Fitzgerald Portrait Emerges," Buffalo *Evening News*, December 11, 1971, p. B–8.
Collection is "a wonderful dual portrait of two men, at once radically different and yet strangely alike: George Apley, as it were, acting as custodial trustee for a latter day Shelley."

G126.   Brown, Dennis. "Fitzgerald and Friends," St. Louis *Sunday Post-Dispatch*, June 4, 1972, p. 4D.
Book is "particularly valuable for its chronicling of the working relationship between an author and editor" and "should be of immense value to the serious student of Fitzgerald."

G127.   Bruccoli, Matthew J. "Max, the Man Who Took Care of Scott," Chicago *Daily News*, December 25–26, 1971, "Panorama" Section, p. 7.
Volume amounts to "an epistolary novel" as well as "the latest biography of Fitzgerald as a novelist."

G128.   Buchen, Irving H.   "Is Only Convenience a Justification?" Baltimore *Sunday Sun*, December 5, 1971, p. D5.

"The way this volume is grooved, with certain letters and certain parts of letters omitted, and with the field of vision artificially narrowed to two men and their letters, the entire volume is already tipped in the direction of only confirming what the editors have said."

G129.   Bunke, Joan.   "Scott and Max—A Literary History Told in Letters," Des Moines *Sunday Register*, January 23, 1972, p. 9-C.

Descriptive favorable review.

G130.   Burns, Randall.   "Collection of Letters Illuminating," Fort Smith (Ark.) *Southwest Times Record*, November 28, 1971, p. 7A.

Descriptive favorable review.

G131.   Burton, Hal.   "Books in Brief," *Newsday* (Garden City, NY), December 18, 1971, p. 16 W.

Book is "interesting to anyone who would like to fathom Fitzgerald's character and the torment he underwent."

Callahan, John F.   Review of *Dear Scott/Dear Max*, *Saturday Review*, 54 (December 11, 1971), 57–58.

"If the editors of *Dear Scott/Dear Max* had read the Fitzgerald-Perkins correspondence with more discernment, I doubt that they would have indulged the fancy that these letters constitute a compelling narrative." See G96.

G132.   Clark, George P.   "Fitzgerald-Perkins Letters," Louisville *Courier-Journal & Times*, February 13, 1972, p. F 5.

"The editors have achieved their objective to give a continuous and readable text....The man who named the 'Jazz Age' and was its principal chronicler in fiction lives once again in these pages, joined in spirit with the friend who did so much to further his career."

G133.   Cockshutt, Rod.   "Scott, Max and 'Ecclesiastes,'" Raleigh *News and Observer*, December 19, 1971, Sec. IV, p. 6.

"If you're at all interested in how a writer's mind works, or in how some of the great literature of our century was born, ask Santa for this one."

G134.   Condon, Charles R.   "Author-Editor Letters Better Than Novel," Jamestown (NY) *Post-Journal*, April 22, 1972, p. 6M.

"If you are a person who likes to read other people's letters or are interested in writing, publishing and good books, this is the book for you. I have enjoyed this book more than any recent novel I have read and can highly recommend it if you are in the group of readers aforementioned."

G135.   Dawe, Alan. "More Fascination on Fitzgerald," Vancouver *Sun*, December 17, 1971, Leisure Section, p. 33A.

"Lesser novelists have, after long effort, written worse epistolary novels than Max and Fitz have produced by accident."

G136.   Denison, James. "F. Scott Fitzgerald and His Publisher—Comments on the American Scene," *Peninsula Herald* (Monterey, Calif.), January 1, 1972, p. 21.

"Both correspondents offer penetrating comments on the passing American scene....Skillful editing has smoothed much of the jerkiness inherent in this type of book and given it the sweep of a narrative."

G137.   Donnelly, Tom. "Book Marks—Yet Another Side of Scott Fitzgerald," Washington (D.C.) *Daily News*, December 10, 1971, pp. 31, 32.

Descriptive favorable review.

G138.   Douglas, Mary Stahlman. "Friendship of Author and Editor Recorded," Nashville *Banner*, February 11, 1972, p. 47.

"'Dear Scott/Dear Max' is the record of a near-perfect relationship between author and editor that from beginning to end exhibited deep understanding, loyalty and mutual respect. All concerned with the making of books will want to read it."

G139.   Ehmann, F. A. Review of *Dear Scott/Dear Max*, El Paso *Herald-Post*, January 22, 1972, Sec. A, p. 4.

Book is "a contribution to the literate public, even if earlier publication of the letters dims its lustre as an original contribution to scholarship."

G140.   Elliott, Carl. "Scott Fitzgerald Had a Friend," Jasper (Ala.) *Daily Mountain Eagle*, February 12, 1974, Sec. A, p. 7.

Descriptive favorable review.

G141.   Fetherling, Doug. "Wet Nurse and Writer: Two Sides of Genius in Dialogue," Toronto *Globe and Mail*, January 8, 1972, p. 28.

"The effect is narrative rather than documentary, as the editors claim in their preface. And because it shows both sides of the personal and professional relationship of these two men, the book gives a better view than most of Fitzgerald's personality and private life."

G142.   Frazer, Jan. "Book Review," Naples (Fla.) *Star*, January 20, 1972, Sec. A, p. 4.

Book is "a fine contribution to the growing number of books concerned with the Jazz Age writer."

G143.   Gregson, Lillian. "Books 'n Stuff," DeKalb (Ga.) *New Era*, September 7, 1972, p. 5.

"The letters are fascinating. They portray aspects of Fitzgerald's character which do not appear in his sundry biographies."

G144.   Griffin, L. W. Review of *Dear Scott/Dear Max*, *Library Journal*, 96 (August 1971), 2509.

Collection "illumines a seminal era of American literature, gives details on the intimate relationship between an author and his editor, and reveals with a new clarity one of the giants of the jazz age as well as one of the most legendary of editors."

G145.   Hagemann, E. R. "Dear Scott-Dear Max," Riverside (Calif.) *Press-Enterprise*, February 20, 1972, Sec. D, p. 6.

"No, the myth will not enlarge with 'Dear Scott/Dear Max'; but the book should be read and re-read."

G146.   H[all], C[ody]. "'Scott-Max' a Record," Anniston (Ala.) *Star*, December 12, 1971, Sec. D, p. 2.

"'Dear Scott-Dear Max' is a warm, entertaining record of a friendship between two men and a valuable addition to the modern literary history shelf."

G147.   H[arrison], R[obert] L. "Book Adds to Literary History," Galesburg (Ill.) *Register-Mail*, December 15, 1971, p. 15.

"This book belongs in any collection of modern literary history."

G148.   Hart, Jeffrey. "Fitzgerald and Perkins," *National Review*, 24 (March 3, 1972), 228–229.

Although these letters "do not possess that order of independent interest, they are both fascinating and moving nevertheless, and fully dramatize one of the central relationships of Fitzgerald's moral and artistic life."

G149.   Hickok, Ralph. "Perkins-Fitzgerald Letters Absorbing," New Bedford (Mass.) *Standard-Times*, December 19, 1971, p. 66.

"The collection is a pleasure to read, but the editors might have made it even more pleasurable by presenting brief summaries of missing letters in the text, instead of burying the information in notes at the back of the book."

G150.   Hofmann, Virginia C. "Scott-and-Max Letters Mirror Lively Decades," Dayton *Daily News*, April 16, 1972, "Dayton Leisure" Section, p. 22.

Descriptive brief review.

G151.   Hogan, William.   "World of Books—Even More to the Fitzgerald Story," San Francisco *Chronicle*, December 2, 1971, p. 53.
"This is a bright new tile in the Fitzgerald mosaic."

G152.   Horgan, Paul.   Review of *Dear Scott/Dear Max*, *Book-of-the-Month Club News*, January 1972, p. 8.
"It is good to have this excellently edited record of a working relationship between two first-raters in their respective fields."

G153.   Houston, Levin.   "Book Review—American Literature Owes Max Perkins," Fredericksburg (Va.) *Free Lance-Star*, December 8, 1971, p. 4.
"This book, getting progressively more interesting as it proceeds, shows that being a gentleman is not an empty phrase. Both of these men were."

G154.   Irving, Maggie.   "Delightful Counterpoint," Worcester *Sunday Telegram*, December 19, 1971, Sec. E, p. 8.
"The contrast between the two men...the boyish exuberance, and innocent snobbery (and generous loyalty) of the one, and the tweedy, measured calm of the other, patting and gentling his author, like a man faced with a mettlesome horse, forms a delightful counterpoint."

G155.   Johnston, Albert.   Review of *Dear Scott/Dear Max*, *Publishers' Weekly*, 200 (August 30, 1971), 269.
"It would be difficult to equal this account of the working relationship between editor and writer."

G156.   Karst, Judith.   "*Dear Scott/Dear Max*—Exchange of Letters By Men of Letters," South Bend (Ind.) *Tribune*, January 16, 1972, "Michiana" Supplement, p. 10.
"This volume may not be as exciting as the popular book by Nancy Milford, 'Zelda,' but for those who are true Fitzgerald fans, it is excellent."

G157.   Kirsch, Robert.   "The Book Report—Fitzgerald, Editor Become Friends," Los Angeles *Times*, January 5, 1972, Part IV, p. 4.
"The book informs on many levels: the working relationship of author and editor, the glimpses of the literary life through two decades of American writing, even politics and gossip."

G158.   Knickmeyer, W. L.   "Even Writer, Editor Can Be Friends," Ada (Okla.) *News*, February 27, 1972, Sec. 2, p. 10.
"The letters themselves may not be gems of literary art, but if you have a taste for literary gossip they sure are fun to read."

G159.   LaHood, Marvin J.   Review of *Dear Scott/Dear Max*, *Books Abroad*, 46 (Summer 1972), 497.

"These letters must lay to rest, once and for all, the idea that Fitzgerald had a great deal of native ability but neither the dedication to the craft of fiction nor the common sense he needed to become really great. His letters reveal that he had both."

G160.   Latham, Aaron.   "Scott's Editor, Zelda's Friend," *Book World* (Washington [D.C.] *Post*, Chicago *Tribune*), December 19, 1971, p. 4.

"Most of the people who read this correspondence...will probably do so because of Fitzgerald, but it is really Perkins's book.... Unfortunately, Maxwell Perkins has not been as well-served by his editors as Wolfe-Hemingway-Fitzgerald were by theirs. They have made what seem serious errors of omission, having tried to carve from the correspondence a 'narrative.' "

G161.   Legate, David M.   "To and From," Montreal *Star*, December 31, 1971, p. B–3.

Descriptive favorable review.

G162.   McMahan, Allan.   "Books and Authors—Image Maker Stood By F. Scott Fitzgerald," Fort Wayne *Journal-Gazette*, December 19, 1971, Sec. E, p. 5.

"Letters between friends can be rather dull reading, at best, but those of DEAR SCOTT/DEAR MAX are fascinating. They disclose not only the acute mechanical problems of writing and publishing a book but the unlimited patience it takes to mold temperament and talent into an acceptable product. Fitzgerald and Perkins were master craftsmen at this task."

G163.   Manning, Margaret.   "Book of the Day—Letters Show a Bit of F. Scott Fitzgerald," Boston *Globe*, December 13, 1971, p. 18.

"In spite of the prosaic quality of much of the book, the characters of two remarkable men burst into life in these pages."

G164.   Margolies, Alan.   Review of *Dear Scott/Dear Max*, *Journal of Modern Literature*, 3 (February 1974), 601–602.

Descriptive favorable review: "The book makes for fascinating reading."

G165.   Meacham, Harry M.   "Letters: Fitzgerald-Perkins Correspondence Edited," Richmond (Va.) *News Leader*, December 15, 1971, p. 15.

"This is one of those necessary books, beautifully edited and put together by two distinguished scholars."

G166.   *Meats, Stephen E. "The Responsibilities of an Editor of Correspondence," *Costerus*, n.s. 3 (1975), 149–169 [163–167].

"Although many of the letters are new, the collection is far from being definitive....The editorial principles governing this edition are extremely questionable."

G167.   Moody, Minnie Hite. "A Sympathetic Editor and a Tragic Genius," Columbus (Ohio) *Sunday Dispatch*, January 16, 1972, "Tab" Section, p. 17.

"'Dear Scott-Dear Max' has the advantage of selectivity and of continuity. Careful planning has contributed greatly to the charm of this book, which does indeed add dimensions to Fitzgerald when we had about reached the point of belief that there were no more dimensions to be added."

G168.   Murray, G. E. "More on Fitzgerald—Writing Under a Wise Editor's Eye," Chicago *Sunday Sun-Times*, December 12, 1971, Sec. 5, p. 13.

"A powerful book of letters is sometimes a good book of imaginings. 'Dear Scott/Dear Max' is such a book. Its fine scholarship will please some: Its energy should move into the imaginations of young writers with a striking impact."

G169.   Murray, James G. "The Art of Reading," *Long Island Catholic*, November 25, 1971, p. 14.

Brief descriptive favorable review.

G170.   Newquist, Roy. "Books of the Week—Fitzgerald and Perkins," Chicago Heights *Star*, January 16, 1972, Sec. A, p. 14.

"Until now, because of Perkins' desire for anonymity, he has been obscured by the trio he saw through hell and high water. But in this book he emerges in his own splendid array of bold and subtle colors, and as a consequence 'Dear Scott-Dear Max' is one of the literary events of this new year."

G171.   O'Brien, John H. "A Boost to the F. Scott Fitzgerald Boom," Detroit *News*, December 6, 1971, p. 6-B.

"It all seems so long ago, yet Fitzgerald is a figure of intense public interest today and this book will delight those anxious to understand him."

G172.   O'Leary, Theodore M. "How Close the Writer and Editor," Kansas City *Star*, December 12, 1971, p. 3E.

While the book is "a kind of narrative," it also "offers an unrivaled view of that delicate and precarious relationship between editor and writer which Perkins was always able to keep in balance."

G173.   Perley, Maie E. "The Book Scene—Letters Reveal the True F. Scott Fitzgerald," Louisville *Times*, December 13, 1971, p. A 11.

"There will doubtless be some readers who will cringe at the naked revelations of Fitzgerald's soul, but letters are such that they probe far below the surface of one's personality. The unvarnished truth of a man's life and his times are brought graphically alive in a lifetime of correspondence between F. Scott Fitzgerald and Maxwell E. Perkins."

G174.   Piper, Henry Dan. "Scott Fitzgerald and Max Perkins," *CEA Critic*, 36 (January 1974), 28.

Book presents "an object lesson in the crucial role a sympathetic editor can play in encouraging as well as educating a major literary talent."

G175.   Powers, Robert L. "What To Do If It's Raining," Athens (Ohio) *Messenger*, November 28, 1971, p. 6.

"If you are acquainted with Fitzgerald, 'Dear Scott-Dear Max' is a must addition to your library. If you're not, shame on you."

G176.   Rice, Cy. "Stage Whispers—Publishing Cover Raised," Milwaukee *Sentinel*, May 17, 1972, Part 1, p. 11.

Descriptive favorable review.

G177.   Rogers, W. G. "The Literary Scene," NY *Post*, November 29, 1971, p. 22.

"There was romance in Fitzgerald's work and life, but none at all in this sobering record of a career—of two careers. This is bedrock. No other book reveals more clearly what is all important about both the editor and the writer."

G178.   Russ, Margaret C. "Scott and Max—21 Years of Letters," Buffalo *Courier-Express*, March 12, 1972, "Focus" Section, p. 14.

"The editors can be thanked for assembling this exceptional correspondence."

G179.   Satterfield, Archie. "An Important Literary Relationship," Seattle *Times*, January 16, 1972, p. D 3.

"Fortunately, neither knew how to write a dull letter, and each is a revelation to the casual reader and the serious student of literature."

G180.   Saunders, Tom. "Books—Editor and Author," Winnipeg *Free Press*, January 8, 1972, p. 20.

"It would be easy to dismiss this book on the grounds that it tells us nothing essentially new. That, however, would be a mistake. We may re-travel much old ground in these pages and the editors may claim for their work more than it actually contains, but there are still things here that are worthy of record."

G181.   Schwartz, Joseph.   Review of *Dear Scott/Dear Max*, *America*, 126 (January 22, 1972), 72.

"The letters will be of value to those concerned with Fitzgerald or with the literary period between the two great wars. There is nothing intrinsic to the letters themselves which would make them of special interest to the general reader."

G182.   Shapiro, Morton.   "Dear Scott-Dear Max," Charlotte *Observer*, December 19, 1971, p. 5-I.

Book is "a valuable addition to the two already existing volumes of Fitzgerald's and Perkins' correspondence."

G183.   Spearman, Walter.   "The Literary Lantern—Scott Fitzgerald to Max Perkins," Chapel Hill (N.C.) *Weekly*, December 23, 1971, p. 4.

"The letters are, of course, well worth reading for their illumination of the author-editor relationship and for the occasional insight they give to the characters of both men; but they seem remarkably impersonal in their approach and seldom provide the kind of warmth and insight into the problems of their individual lives that one might expect."

G184.   Sudler, Barbara.   "'Scott' Adds Dimension to the Fitzgerald Lexicon," Denver *Sunday Post*, December 26, 1971, "Roundup" Section, p. 34.

Descriptive favorable review.

G185.   Thompson, M. B.   "Gifted Writer's Letters Foreshadowed Tragedy," Ottawa *Citizen*, March 18, 1972, p. 39.

"This volume is indispensable for the reader who loves and marvels at the best works of F. Scott Fitzgerald."

G186.   Wardlow, Jean.   "Max Perkins and His 'Sons,'" Miami (Fla.) *Herald*, January 9, 1972, p. 7-K.

This is "a valuable and well-compiled book. And there's no doubt of its interest."

G187.   Wasson, Ben.   "The Time Has Come," Greenville (Miss.) *Delta Democrat-Times*, January 2, 1972, p. 11.

Book is "consistently readable" and is "specially recommended to F. Scott Fitzgerald readers and admirers."

G188.   Weeks, Edward.   Review of *Dear Scott/Dear Max*, *The Atlantic*, 229 (January 1972), 95.

Descriptive favorable review.

G189.   Weinstein, Bernard.   Review of *Dear Scott/Dear Max*, *Best Sellers*, 31 (February 15, 1972), 504–505.
"This is a book that belongs on every library shelf. It raises the consciousness of any one who has ever resisted reading a book of letters. Indeed, if there is an epistolary heaven, 'Dear Scott/Dear Max' is already there."

English Edition
(1973)

G190.   Anonymous.   "Bookshelf," *The Author* (London), 84 (Summer 1973), 87.
Descriptive favorable review.

G191.   ———.   "To the Editor," *Times Literary Supplement* (London), May 18, 1973, p. 546.
Correspondence is "a notable tribute to a perceptive and generous and dedicated editor; it is marginally revealing of Fitzgerald's professional dedication (if proof were needed); it is also a fine record of one aspect of the publishing industry in the 1920s and 1930s; but, for the rest, it makes a somewhat laboured and specialized footnote to the corpus of a great writer."

G192.   Calder-Marshall, Arthur.   "They Found Time to Write Letters Too," London *Evening Standard*, April 3, 1973, p. 26.
Descriptive favorable review.

G193.   Connolly, Cyril.   "Drafts and Over Drafts," London *Sunday Times*, March 25, 1973, p. 30.
"In the Scott-Max exchange there is enough of the artist to make them worth reading."

G194.   Dick, Kay.   "Monday Books—Gabbling On About Scott," London *Times*, December 10, 1973, p. 14.
"Is this present work really necessary?"

G195.   E., P. D.   "Letters From Scott Fitzgerald," Christchurch (New Zealand) *Press*, November 17, 1973, p. 10.
Collection "rather unexpectedly does more for the Fitzgerald reputation than do some of the longer studies of the writer already written, revealing facts instead of projecting them through the prism of critical speculation."

G196.   Forrest, Alan.   "Punctuation Marks," *Books and Bookmen*, 18 (May 1973), 11.
Descriptive review.

G197.   Freedman, Richard. "Scott Fitzgerald and His Editor," *The Observer* (London), March 25, 1973, p. 37.

"If these letters lack the lyric grace and tragic intensity of the ones Fitzgerald wrote his daughter Scottie, they are no more concerned with money—and are a lot livelier—than the letters of James Joyce."

G198.   Grigson, Geoffrey. "From the Jazz Age," *Country Life*, 153 (April 12, 1973), 1025.

Review is mostly concerned with demonstrating that F is a minor writer.

G199.   Hooker, John. "View From an Editor's Office—A Pain in the Arse First Novelist...," *Nation Review*, 3 (August 3–9, 1973), 1322.

Descriptive review.

G200.   Lambert, Gavin. "Scott Fitzgerald and His Editor," *Books and Bookmen*, 18 (May 1973), 30–31.

"I know of no other book that illustrates a writer-editor relationship so dramatically, but then there has probably never been a writer-editor relationship so close and revealing."

G201.   Nathan, Jeff. "Recycling Scott," Los Angeles *Free Press*, April 5, 1974, pp. 24–25 [24].

"No doubt the relationship between Fitzgerald and Perkins was important, but nothing in this collection illuminates their association beyond the dull business details of publishing." This review also appeared in *West Coast Review of Books,* 1 (October-November 1974), 49–55 [54].

G202.   Nye, Robert. "The Failure of Scott Fitzgerald," *The Scotsman* (Edinburgh), March 24, 1973, "Weekend Scotsman" Section, p. 3.

Although F's letters to Perkins "do not add substantially to what we already know about Fitzgerald," it is "revealing to see them put together with Perkins' replies."

G203.   Porter, Hal. "Prospect From an Author's Study—...and an Unbelievably Patient Editor," *Nation Review*, 3 (August 3–9, 1973), 1323.

"Most fascinating is the portrayal, through their letters, of the characters, intelligences, sensitivities, politics, and so on of the two men. It makes a 'gripping' book even if one had never heard of F. Scott Fitzgerald."

G204.   Powell, Anthony.   "A Publisher and His 'Sons,'" London *Daily Telegraph*, March 29, 1973, p. 8.

This is a "remarkably interesting book" whose "interest arises partly from the fact that Fitzgerald is here shown simply as a professional writer,...and partly from the way that the letters illustrate the general author/publisher relationship."

G205.   Pritchett, V. S.   "Gentlemen's Agreement," *New Statesman*, n.s. 85 (March 23, 1973), 417.

"The interest of this volume chiefly lies in its presentation of a friendship—lasting all Fitzgerald's life—that seemed unlikely on the surface." The collection is, "by its nature, too restricted to catch very much beyond Fitzgerald's professionalism, in which, it must be said, he showed a power of will, and decency amid his self-induced disasters."

G206.   Sainsbury, Ian.   "A Friend in Deed," Sheffield *Morning Telegraph*, March 22, 1973, p. 8.

Descriptive review.

G207.   Sewell, Gordon.   "The Writer and His Editor," *Dorset Evening Echo* (Weymouth), May 2, 1973, "Midweek" Magazine, p. III.

"The interaction between writer and editor represents the most vital aspect of this correspondence, since it goes beyond the autobiographical and demonstrates how a creative editor can affect serious writing."

G208.   West, Rebecca.   "When Critics Were Critics," London *Sunday Telegraph*, April 15, 1973, p. 14.

"The letters are predominantly business letters written by two hurried men, neither of whom had an attractive shirt-sleeve style, and they contain little of interest."

G209.   White, Terence de Vere.   "More For a Legend," *Irish Times* (Dublin), March 31, 1973, p. 10.

"The book offers many pleasures as well as the picture it presents of a man with more talent than intellect, more heart than character."

G210.   Williams, Herbert.   "The Dying Flame," *Western Mail* (Cardiff, Wales), March 24, 1973, p. 10.

Correspondence "makes absorbing reading" and "reveals a close and perhaps rare relationship between editor and author."

AS EVER, SCOTT FITZ—: LETTERS BETWEEN
F. SCOTT FITZGERALD AND HIS LITERARY
AGENT, HAROLD OBER: 1919–1940
American Edition
(1972)

G211.   Anonymous. "Books Explore Lives of Famous Authors,"
Portland *Sunday Oregonian*, July 16, 1972, Family, Features, Fashion,
Entertainment Section, p. 17.
Brief favorable review. "There is much new material here."

G212.   ———. "Nothing New on F. Scott," Tucson *Star*, June
18, 1972, Sec. F, p. 3.
Brief review. "Fitzgerald himself would probably be quite shocked
that his letters to Ober were considered worthy of publication."

G213.   ———. Review of *As Ever, Scott Fitz—*, *The Booklist*,
69 (September 15, 1972), 63–64.
Brief review. Collection "forms a minor auxiliary volume to major
Fitzgerald materials."

G214.   ———. Review of *As Ever, Scott Fitz—*, Burlington
(Vt.) *Free Press*, June 15, 1972, p. 20.
Volume "marks a literary event—the first study of the relationship
between a famous writer and his agent."

G215.   ———. Review of *As Ever, Scott Fitz—*, *Choice*, 9
(November 1972), 1128.
"Because Ober handled Fitzgerald's short stories rather than his novels, and because the correspondence deals primarily with financial concerns, the volume presents much dull and insignificant material."

G216.   ———. Review of *As Ever, Scott Fitz—*, *Kirkus*, 40
(February 15, 1972), 227.
"The letters, per se, are by no means as interesting as most of those
which appeared in the Turnbull complete collection (1963) or the
shorter *Letters to His Daughter* (1965)."

G217.   ———. Review of *As Ever, Scott Fitz—*, *Publishers'
Weekly*, 201 (February 28, 1972), 68.
This is a book "that adds a full cubit to the stature of a much-
misunderstood and sometimes underrated man."

G218.   ———. Review of *As Ever, Scott Fitz—*, *Virginia
Quarterly Review*, 48 (Autumn 1972), cxxxvii, cxl.
Brief review. "At last one senses the painstaking effort Fitzgerald
put into so much of his work, his sense of literary marketability, and his

remarkable endurance of his own life and troubled times with his agent."

G219.   Aulis, Jack.   "More Letters of Scott Fitzgerald," Raleigh *News and Observer*, July 16, 1972, Sec. IV, p. 6.

Collection is an "outstanding reference source book that only true Fitzgerald-philes—and maybe would-be writers—will want to read in any depth."

G220.   Blicksilver, Edith.   "Letters Reveal Author's Failure," Atlanta *Journal and Constitution*, June 25, 1972, p. 6-C.

"One questions the value of publishing for posterity every Fitzgerald bank statement or cost of living account, except that the writer's never ending financial desperation dominates every aspect of his existence."

G221.   B[rady], C[harles] A.   "Fitzgerald and Agent," Buffalo *Evening News*, August 5, 1972, p. B–18.

"Though it is good to have the harrowing record complete, these letters make dreary reading...."

Brown, Dennis.   "Fitzgerald and Friends," St. Louis *Sunday Post-Dispatch*, June 4, 1972, p. 4D.

Descriptive favorable review. See G126.

G222.   B[runsdale], M[itzi] M.   "Fitzgerald Letters: A Real Rip-Off," Houston *Post*, July 30, 1972, "Spotlight" Magazine, p. 17.

"Though it may be debated whether the details of an author's life ought to be used in the judgement of his work, surely a microscopic examination of his financial entanglements cannot replace textual analysis of manuscripts, if developmental criticism is in question."

G223.   Bryer, Jackson R.   "Fitz/Ober Letters," *Connecticut Review*, 6 (October 1972), 100–103.

"More than any previous book about Fitzgerald...this one emphasizes the rewards, the frustrations, and the uncertainties which were his lot as a professional writer, that is, a man who made his entire living from his writing."

G224.   Digilio, Alice.   "Books and Things—Scott Fitzgerald? He Wrote For Loans," Alexandria (Va.) *Journal*, September 14, 1972, p. A4.

"Bruccoli has given us an excellent collection, most of which makes entertaining reading, and all of which will be of value to anyone working in the field of American literature."

G225.   Dimick, Steve.   "'Fitz' Book Worth Wait," *Oklahoma Journal* (Oklahoma City), July 30, 1972, "Fun Guide" Section, p. 10.

"The choice of the letters and the fine editing of them bring out...subtle aspects of both men's characters. We couldn't get to know either of them completely through the letters, but there is more meat here than one would think. And as a companion to other Fitzgerald studies, it is excellent."

G226.   Duke, Maurice. "Fitzgerald's Letters to, From His Agent Give Keen Insight Into Literary World," Richmond (Va.) *Times-Dispatch*, August 13, 1972, p. F–5.

"There is more...than the professional career and personal life of F. Scott Fitzgerald contained in these letters. Particularly important, the book is a document about the general profession of authorship in the United States during much of the first half of this century."

G227.   Gingrich, Arnold. Review of *As Ever, Scott Fitz—*, *Fitzgerald/Hemingway Annual*, 4 (1972), 373–376.

It is ironic that "three at least of the best things in this book have as their common denominator the fact that Scott Fitzgerald himself never saw them. They are Scottie's Forword [*sic*], the letter that Harold Ober, essaying the role of turning worm, wrote Scott in 1939 but never sent, and the letter from Zelda to Ober right after Scott's death."

G228.   Goldstein, Laurence. "'A Business Plot—The Kind I Can't Handle,'" Providence *Sunday Journal*, June 11, 1972, p. H 21.

"The bulk of the volume is a thoroughly monotonous exchange of financial information, a ledger of publication credits."

G229.   Goranson, Brinkley. "Still More on Scott Fitz," Norfolk *Virginian-Pilot*, July 23, 1972, p. C6.

Volume is "one of the rare documentations of its kind to be found anywhere."

G230.   Harris, Paul. Review of *As Ever, Scott Fitz—*, *TV Radio Mirror*, 10 (September 1972), 9.

Brief review. Volume is "an absolute must for those interested in the life of one of the major figures in modern American literature."

G231.   Hughes, Riley. Review of *As Ever, Scott Fitz—*, *Columbia*, 52 (October 1972), 39–40.

Volume is "a sad yet enthralling story of a great artist."

G232.   Irving, Maggie. Review of *As Ever, Scott Fitz—*, Worcester *Sunday Telegram*, August 6, 1972, p. 8E.

"In general, the collection can be of but small interest to the lay reader, although it may provide the scholar with abundant detail as to the middleman's function in peddling writers."

G233.   Karst, Judith L.   "Scott Fitzgerald," South Bend (Ind.)
Tribune, July 23, 1972, "Michiana" Supplement, p. 11.

"There is nothing new or revealing in this volume and it seems almost sadistic to merely drag Fitzgerald's weakness—money—past the
bandstand again."

G234.   Kirsch, Robert.   "The Book Report—More Bits of the
Fitzgerald Mosaic," Los Angeles *Times*, May 18, 1972, Part IV, p. 19.

The letters form "another part of the mosaic," give "still another
evidence of the Fitzgerald magic, that deep appeal, almost child-like,
which could elicit from a tough-minded, square, straight literary
agent...real and deep friendship...."

G235.   Leighton, Betty.   "Letters Record Waste of Talent,"
Winston-Salem *Journal and Sentinel*, September 3, 1972, Sec. D, p. 4.

"It is a poignant, touching part of this volume that their personal as
well as business lives were so intertwined—that Fitzgerald's need was
so great and Ober's response so openhearted."

G236.   Lenson, David.   "With the Writer—Old Times, Good
Times," *San Francisco Book Review*, No. 26 (December 1972), 8–11
[8].

"To read page after page of correspondence about the placing of stories and the price Scott got for them is a joy only for the most materialistic of necrophiliacs.   Mind you, the book is a good job.   It is done,
and there it sits."

G237.   Lord, Barbara.   "'Flaming Youth,'" Austin (Tex.)
American-Statesman, July 23, 1972, "The Show World" Section, p.
32.

It is "unfortunate" that so much of the collection deals with money;
"more interesting are the passages referring to various stories and his attempts at rewriting them to make them saleable."

G238.   Lucid, Robert F.   "A Not-So-Great Gatsby in the
Business World," Los Angeles *Times*, June 25, 1972, "Book Review"
Section, pp. 1, 9.

"Reading the book really is a lot like discovering the letters in some
hidden place, and one prowls the volume at last as if it were a closet,
holding in its darkness the secret to a past world which we need to
recapture." This review also appeared in the Chicago *Daily News*, June
17, 1972, "Panorama" Section, p. 9; Baltimore *Sunday Sun*, May 28,
1972, p. D5.

G239.   McNaughton, Carol.   "New Titles," *Arizona Republic*
(Phoenix), July 23, 1972, p. 8-N.

Brief review: "a thoughtfully edited collection."

G240.   M[alkin], M[ary] A[nn].   Review of *As Ever, Scott Fitz—*, *A.B. Bookman's Yearbook*, 1972, Part 2, p. 32.

"For a picture of what the agent does for a good client, there isn't a better book around."

G241.   Margolies, Alan.   Review of *As Ever, Scott Fitz—*, *Resources for American Literary Study*, 3 (Spring 1973), 133–135.

"To the Fitzgerald scholar, to those interested in the relationship between author and agent, these letters are invaluable. Others, however, may not find them too significant. For the correspondence suggests that, to a large extent, the relationship between the two men was concerned mainly with the novelist's financial situation and the sales of his short stories."

G242.   Meacham, Harry M.   "Letters: Fitzgerald-Ober Notes Mostly Concerned Cash," Richmond (Va.) *News Leader*, July 26, 1972, p. 15.

Descriptive review.

*Meats, Stephen E.   "The Responsibilities of an Editor of Correspondence," *Costerus*, n.s. 3 (1975), 149–169 [167–168].

Volume "is notable...because it maintains its integrity as a scholarly work, even though it was published by a commercial publisher and was apparently intended for a popular as well as a scholarly audience." See G166.

G243.   Moody, Minnie Hite.   "Writer's Tragic Life Reflected In Letters," Columbus (Ohio) *Sunday Dispatch*, September 17, 1972, "Tab" Section, p. 18.

Descriptive favorable review.

G244.   Muggeridge, Malcolm.   Review of *As Ever, Scott Fitz—*, *Esquire*, 78 (September 1972), 190–191.

Collection "brings out even more poignantly than heretofore the appalling obsession with money which hung over all the other tragedies" of F's life.

G245.   Newton, Eileen.   "Scott Fitz Popularity on Rise," Wilmington (Del.) *Morning News*, June 23, 1972, p. 43.

"Bruccoli could have excluded a full third of the material and still given us a penetrating chronicle."

G246.   Norton, Hubert.   "Fitzgerald's Money Woes Revealed in Agent's Letters," Miami (Fla.) *News*, June 29, 1972, Sec. C, p. 7.

Book is "a history of Fitzgerald's shorter fiction."

G247.   Powell, Larry.   "Scott on the Rocks—Letters Chart Author's Decline," Savannah *Morning News and Evening Press*, July 9, 1972, Magazine, p. 5.

"More revealing than last year's collection of letters to Perkins, this book gives glimpses of Fitzgerald as a working writer and of the unusual relationship between agent and author, but the story it tells is sad."

G248.   R[eid], M[argaret] W.   "Money Trouble," Wichita Falls (Tex.) *Times*, August 13, 1972, Magazine, p. 4.

"The collection may be important to scholars and specialists in American literature of the 20s, but the pages and pages of laconic telegrams and letters offer little to the general reader...."

G249.   Reigstad, Thomas S.   "Fitzgerald's Letters to Ober," Buffalo *Courier-Express*, September 10, 1972, "Focus" Section, p. 16.

Although the letters contain "several informative facts," the book is "over-sized."

G250.   Sanford, Mrs. Leslie J.   "Scott Fitzgerald's Letters Document His Decline, Death," Jamestown (NY) *Post-Journal*, October 21, 1972, p. 14M.

Book is "an excellent supplement to all the previous books about Fitzgerald whose life captured more attention than his writings."

G251.   Satterfield, Archie.   "Fitzgerald's Correspondence," Seattle *Times*, October 8, 1972, p. F 4.

"These letters, telegrams and memos are a record of unhappiness, irresponsibility and petulance on the part of Fitzgerald and old-fashioned good manners, sound advice and generosity by his agent, Harold Ober."

G252.   Sessions, Lynette.   "Letters Show Fitzgerald's Appeal," Macon *Telegraph and News*, July 30, 1972, p. 10B.

Letters "reveal the Jazz Age author's immense personal appeal, his constant financial difficulties, and the nagging sorrows of his life. They reveal, also, the patient, warm loyalty of Ober."

G253.   Shavin, Norman.   Review of *As Ever, Scott Fitz—*, *Atlanta*, 12 (July 1972), 58.

"Letters not written for publication often provide the most revealing relationships....One result: views of an artist in torment."

G254.   Shroyer, Dr. Frederick.   "Titles For Scholars," Los Angeles *Herald-Examiner*, July 2, 1972, p. D–6.
Descriptive brief review.

G255.   Spearman, Walter. "Fitzgerald's Letters," Chapel Hill (N.C.) *Weekly*, July 16, 1972, Sec. 2, p. 4.
Descriptive review.

G256.   Stein, Hel[e]n. Review of *As Ever, Scott Fitz—*, Mt. Pleasant (Iowa) *News*, November 25, 1972, p. 14.
"Fans and students of Fitzgerald will find in his correspondence an interesting new dimension to the man, and some fresh insights into his feelings about Zelda, his daughter, and his work as a literary craftsman."

G257.   Stoddard, Donald R. Review of *As Ever, Scott Fitz—*, *Cithara* (St. Bonaventure University), 13 (November 1973), 90–93.
"The essential value of this collection of letters...lies in their explicit literary discussion and in their revelations of interests and attitudes reflected in Fitzgerald's fiction."

G258.   Sudler, Barbara. "Fitzgerald 'Vogue' Continues With 'As Ever,'" Denver *Sunday Post*, September 3, 1972, "Roundup" Section, p. 35.
"It is difficult to see this volume as of overbearing interest to any except those still absorbed in Fitzgeraldiana or perhaps this could be an introduction to those as yet uncaught by the story."

G259.   Weeks, Edward. Review of *As Ever, Scott Fitz—*, *The Atlantic*, 229 (May 1972), 110–111.
Letters are "for business and without literary flavor" and are "a monument to Ober's patience and integrity."

G260.   Weinstein, Bernard. Review of *As Ever, Scott Fitz—*, *Best Sellers*, 32 (September 15, 1972), 266–267.
This is "an admirable edition that illuminates heretofore unrevealed aspects of Fitzgerald's career and provides much needed biographical data, especially about Fitzgerald's career as a screenwriter in Hollywood."

G261.   White, William. "'Arrange an Advance So I Can Eat...'—The Letters of Despair By F. Scott Fitzgerald," Detroit *Sunday News*, June 11, 1972, p. 5-E.
"Not only is it a fascinating, sad, and painful account of a relationship between two capable men—each in his own often peculiar way—but we have here a portrait, half of it a self-portrait, of Fitzgerald which differs from the other portrait we thought we had before."

G262.   ———. Review of *As Ever, Scott Fitz—*, *Library Journal*, 97 (August 1972), 2604.
"Told wholly through correspondence, this is a pathetic and human tale involving a major American writer."

G263. Whitman, Alden. Review of *As Ever, Scott Fitz—*, *Saturday Review*, 55 (July 8, 1972), 60, 64.
This is a book for "devoted Fitzgeraldites"; others should skim it.

English Edition
(1973)

G264. Anonymous. "This Side of Paradise," *Times Literary Supplement* (London), January 4, 1974, p. 13.
Although the letters establish that F "was a hard-working, professional writer," the correspondence "is a dull one."

G265. Axelrod, George. "The Dutiful and the Crammed," *The Spectator*, 231 (December 8, 1973), 745–746.
"One of the problems with the book...is that it tells us not only very little that we did not already know about Fitzgerald, but in addition, I fear, presents us with a somewhat distorted picture: 'A Portrait of the Artist As A Man Totally Obsessed By Money.'"

G266. Corrin, Stephen. "Agent of Despair," London *Daily Telegraph*, January 31, 1974, p. 12.
"Has the hagiographic approach to literary agents ever before been carried to such lengths, even in the United States (where, I fancy, the breed was invented)?"

Dick, Kay. "Monday Books—Gabbling On About Scott," London *Times*, December 10, 1973, p. 14.
"Typographically this book is a mess: packed with ridiculous detail such as postmarks....the best letters from Scott are included in Mr. Turnbull's 1963 volume." See G194.

G267. Kermode, Frank. "Scottie on the Make," Manchester *Guardian*, December 22, 1973, p. 25.
The letters are "tedious, but they illustrate the struggle for money as the agent of freedom and beauty."

G268. Lambert, Gavin. "Author and Agent," *Books and Bookmen*, 19 (February 1974), 57.
"This latest raid on the Fitzgerald files leaves the barrel empty and its bottom visibly scraped." This material "certainly deserves a footnote in Fitzgerald's life, but not a footnote of four hundred and forty pages."

G269. Masters, Anthony. "The Myth of Scott and Zelda," Birmingham (England) *Post*, December 8, 1973, Saturday Magazine, p. 2.
Descriptive review.

G270.   Moynihan, John. "Scott on the Rocks," London *Sunday Telegraph*, January 13, 1974, p. 14.

Letters "are often on the dull side until Scott sinks more and more into the red and the kindly, conventional 'angel' suddenly refuses any more advances."

Nathan, Jeff. "Recycling Scott," Los Angeles *Free Press*, April 5, 1974, pp. 24–25.

"We learn nothing new in this tedious volume, and there isn't a page on which money goes unmentioned." This review also appeared in *West Coast Review of Books*, 1 (October-November 1974), 49–55 [54–55]. See G201.

G271.   Nye, Robert. "Money and Scott Fitzgerald," *The Scotsman* (Edinburgh), December 1, 1973, "Weekend Scotsman" Section, p. 2.

Letters are "noteworthy" in that they dispel the legend which "represents Fitzgerald as mean and hard, luxuriating in praise and sucking up to the rich."

G272.   Snow, C. P. "Scott and Mrs. Scott," *Financial Times* (London), December 6, 1973, p. 18.

Book is "far more fascinating than chocolate-box short stories."

G273.   Toynbee, Philip. "Fitzgerald Industry," *The Observer* (London), December 2, 1973, p. 36.

Only "a quarter" of the collection "adds a little to our understanding of this sad and impossible man."

G274.   Woods, Eddie. "Bustling Life of East End," London *Morning Star*, December 20, 1973, p. 4.

Brief review. Book tells us "little more, but at greater length, of what has already been recorded" about F.

THE BASIL AND JOSEPHINE STORIES
(1973)

G275.   Anonymous. "Fitzgerald Frenzy Is Merited," St. Paul *Sunday Pioneer Press*, October 7, 1973, "Focus" Section, p. 8.

Brief favorable review. Stories are "excellent."

G276.   ———. "Fitzgerald Remembered," Big Spring (Tex.) *Herald*, November 4, 1973, p. 3-D.

Descriptive review.

G277. ———. "For Fitzgerald Fans," Bridgeport (Conn.) *Post*, September 16, 1973, p. E4.
Brief review: "entertainment of a high order."

G278. ———. "F. Scott Fitzgerald Stories Lead November List," *Rocky Mountain News* (Denver), November 4, 1973, "Startime" Section, p. 18.
Descriptive favorable review. Collection shows that F "was also a gifted short story writer."

G279. ———. Review of *The Basil and Josephine Stories*, *The Booklist*, 70 (December 1, 1973), 368.
Brief descriptive review.

G280. ———. Review of *The Basil and Josephine Stories*, *Choice*, 10 (September 1973), 974.
"This collection, pleasant enough entertainment for the casual reader, is for the scholar another example of the proliferation of peripherally useful material by and about Fitzgerald in recent years."

G281. ———. Review of *The Basil and Josephine Stories*, *Journal of Modern Literature*, 4 (November 1974), 322.
Brief descriptive review.

G282. ———. Review of *The Basil and Josephine Stories*, *Kirkus*, 41 (July 1, 1973), 702.
F was "snobbish, childish, and hopelessly naive, and in the minor stories, like these, this comes through clearer than ever; but his hopes and failures were those of an America whose myth had not yet soured...."

G283. ———. Review of *The Basil and Josephine Stories*, *New Times*, 1 (October 19, 1973), 32.
Brief review. "Was life ever as secure as these frothy bon-bons suggest?"

G284. ———. Review of *The Basil and Josephine Stories*, Portland *Sunday Oregonian*, January 6, 1974, "Oregonian SunDAY" Section, p. 19.
Brief descriptive review.

G285. Baker, Jackson. "And Yet Another Round of Scott Fitzgerald," Memphis *Commercial Appeal*, October 28, 1973, Sec. 6, p. 6.
"Whatever this book's flaws, one's second impression comes to be a grudging assent to this publication" because it "will be a convenience to

the legion of Fitzgerald scholars" and because "there is an intensity to the volume that belies the artlessness of its several parts."

G286.   Balakian, Nona.   "Books of The Times—Beautiful and Undamned," NY *Times*, October 2, 1973, p. 41.
"Here, as always, Fitzgerald sees in the interaction between character and society poetic truths that transcend sociology. Slight as they are they delight us, as fragments of a Mozart or Chopin do because we know the work as a whole."

G287.   [Bannon, Barbara A.] Review of *The Basil and Josephine Stories*, *Publishers' Weekly*, 204 (July 16, 1973), 110.
"The stories are interesting as they reveal the aspirations and values of Fitzgerald's youth, but they have the curious overtones of period pieces in both style and content."

G288.   Bell, Mae Woods.   "Bell on Books," Nashville (N.C.) *Graphic*, November 8, 1973, p. 7.
Descriptive favorable review.

G289.   Bell, Michael Davitt.   "Fitzgerald's Josephine," *Princeton Alumni Weekly*, 74 (May 28, 1974), unpaged.
"Few of these tales rank with Fitzgerald's best work. But their combination of nostalgia and precise observation of social detail, especially in the highly autobiographical Basil stories, always makes for at least pleasant reading. And they tell us a great deal, as well, about the themes and preoccupations of their author's better-known stories and novels."

G290.   Blumberg, Leslie.   "Two Who Never Met," *New Leader*, 57 (February 4, 1974), 25, 26.
"Taken individually, the pieces by and large are shoddily executed and far inferior to Fitzgerald's best work; looked at as a whole, the volume has genuine value, for it provides an insight into Fitzgerald's often complicated and perhaps circular notions about money and the psychology of class....it gives us an idea of how Fitzgerald understood the formation of those character types that obsessed him throughout his career."

G291.   Brady, Charles A.   "Fitzgerald Memories of Buffalo Boyhood," Buffalo *Evening News*, September 29, 1973, p. C–12.
In the Basil sequence F "surpasses Tarkington for poetry of place, and its power of evoking the nascent sexuality of boyhood and girlhood can be paralleled nowhere else except—surprisingly—in the first pages of Dante's 'Vita Nuova.'"

G292.   Brown, Michael.   "Fitzgerald Revival," San Francisco *Chronicle*, January 27, 1974, "This World" Section, p. 25.
There is "much enjoyment" in this collection.

G293.   Cady, Richard.   "'Basil, Josephine Stories' Light Tales By Fitzgerald," Indianapolis *Star*, January 6, 1974, Sec. 8, p. 5.

"It would be a mistake to make more of these stories than what they are: bright, light and entertaining tales of adolescence, brought together to give the effect of a novel but really no more a novel than, say, 'Dubliners' is."

G294.   Casper, Leonard.   Review of *The Basil and Josephine Stories*, *Thought*, 49 (September 1974), 330–331.

"Is it not...possible that these stories, far from being a holiday from the psychological traumas in *Tender Is the Night*, show an awareness of the inter-penetration of past and present (as causality; as moral nexus) most grotesquely perverted in the novel's father-daughter incest scenes?"

G295.   Denison, Paul.   "Fitzgerald Prose Still Glows White," Monterey (Calif.) *Sunday Peninsula-Herald*, October 28, 1973, p. 8C.

"Writing with economy and control, Fitzgerald sharply evokes the decade before the first world war, and even more poignantly the time-less time called youth."

G296.   Dias, Earl J.   "A Plus For Fitzgerald Buffs," New Bedford (Mass.) *Sunday Standard-Times*, October 14, 1973, "Panorama of Southeastern Massachusetts" Section, p. 14.

"Although not all of the tales are of sterling caliber, at least four are excellent and should prove of great interest to Fitzgerald buffs."

G297.   Eble, Kenneth.   Review of *The Basil and Josephine Stories*, *Fitzgerald/Hemingway Annual*, 6 (1974), 261–263.

Basil stories "are as excellent in craftsmanship as any stories Fitzgerald ever wrote"; Josephine stories, while not as good, "are full of satisfying touches of precise characterization, wry observation, and Fitzgerald stylistic flourishes."

G298.   Finocchiaro, Ray.   "For Fitzgerald Addicts," Wilmington (Del.) *Morning News*, October 25, 1973, p. 59.

"Fitzgerald fans should enjoy reading or re-reading the stories from the author's admittedly flawed early work."

G299.   Flora, Joseph M.   Review of *The Basil and Josephine Stories*, *Studies in Short Fiction*, 11 (Spring 1974), 210–212.

Brief comparison of this volume with *Winesburg, Ohio*: "Because Fitzgerald's stories here deal so exclusively with youth in an almost mythic sense, only hero and heroine matter very much. Surrounding characters do not capture the imagination as they do in *Winesburg, Ohio* or in Hemingway's Nick Adams stories. Nevertheless, it is good to have the Basil and Josephine stories brought together in their present form, to be able to counterpoint so precisely George and Nick against Basil Lee."

G300.   Glotzer, David.   "A Fitzgerald Delight," *Valley Advocate* (Amherst, Mass.), November 14, 1973, p. 16.

"The quality of the writing is consistent throughout and it's got all of the Fitzgerald charm—his humor, observation, sense of drama, the ability to evoke not only the characters, but the whole world around them."

G301.   [Harris, Robert R.] Review of *The Basil and Josephine Stories*, *Library Journal*, 98 (July 1973), 2071.
Descriptive review.

G302.   Hartley, Lodwick.   "Scott Fitzgerald's 'Basil and Josephine' Tales," Raleigh *News and Observer*, October 28, 1973, p. 6-IV.

"Whatever superior value Fitzgerald's characters may have as social documentation, they are not equal to Tarkington's in their comment on the comedy of adolescence."

G303.   Jones, Cal.   "Devilish Duo's Exploits Relived," Oklahoma City *Sunday Oklahoman*, April 21, 1974, "Showcase" Section, p. 8.
Descriptive review.

G304.   Kastelz, Bill.   "Early Fitzgerald," Jacksonville *Times-Union and Journal*, October 21, 1973, Magazine, p. 9.
Descriptive favorable review.

G305.   [Keegan, Timothy].   Review of *The Basil and Josephine Stories*, *Jeffersonian Review*, 2 (Spring 1974), 65–66.

"All of these stories are very well done, for the most part humorous, but never slapstick or exceedingly sad.   They are very touching and Fitzgerald never leaves you bored.   The Basil stories are overall much better constructed and told than the Josephine stories where Fitzgerald gets bogged down trying to describe female emotions of which he reveals he knows little about."

G306.   Keister, Don A.   "Some Lesser Fitzgerald," Cleveland *Plain Dealer*, March 3, 1974, p. 8-F.

Although F was right that these stories are not his best, he "missed none of the life-giving detail of the middle- and upper-middle-class environment he grew up in, and his skillful writing makes even the trivial glow."

G307.   Kerr, Laura.   "Anti-Lib Scott," *WGA News* (Writers Guild), November 1973, pp. 12–13.

Basil stories are "light and amusing in the Penrod manner, full of nostalgia, but with an underlying thoughtfulness"; but the Josephine stories "are such a direct reflection of the author's revenge for an injured ego that Josephine emerges, not as a female counterpart to Basil, but as a vicious spoiler of people's lives."

G308. K[issel], H[oward]. "Book Making—Christmas Books," *Women's Wear Daily*, December 19, 1973, p. 18.
Brief review. Stories are "wonderful both for their social observations and their gorgeous prose."

G309. Latham, Aaron. "Stories in the Juvenile Tradition," Washington (D.C.) *Post*, September 24, 1973, p. B 4.
None of the stories "rank with Fitzgerald's best stories"; but, taken together, they are "almost a novel that is almost as good as 'This Side of Paradise.'"

G310. Long, Fern. "Taking a 'Pentimento' Journey," Cleveland *Press*, October 19, 1973, "Showtime" Section, p. 18.
Descriptive brief review.

G311. M[oody], M[innie] H[ite]. Review of *The Basil and Josephine Stories*, Columbus (Ohio) *Sunday Dispatch*, February 3, 1974, p. 7D.
To read these stories now "mixes sensations of admiration for Scott Fitzgerald's genius and nostalgia of the good old days so appealingly resurrected."

G312. Morton, Kathryn. "About Books—Fitzgerald: Our Perpetual Boy Wonder," Norfolk *Virginian-Pilot*, September 23, 1973, p. C6.
"They are stories well suited to collection. When read together they build on one another and develop an overall story of growing up."

Nathan, Jeff. "Recycling Scott," Los Angeles *Free Press*, April 5, 1974, pp. 24–25 [24].
Descriptive review. This review also appeared in *West Coast Review of Books*, 1 (October-November 1974), 49–55 [51–53]. See G201.

G313. Norris, Hoke. "Out of a Dead Past, Fitzgerald's Glittering Boy-Girl Stories," Chicago *Daily News*, October 13–14, 1973, "Panorama" Section, p. 9.
"These stories are all of very high quality. They have survived. They are antique without being old-fashioned, like fairy stories and the works of Fielding and Hardy."

G314. Salzman, Jack. "Waiting For Gatsby," *The Nation*, 218 (June 1, 1974), 700.
"When all the critical shadow-boxing is over there are still the sto-

ries. And they simply are not very good. They may tell us something about Fitzgerald's thought process, about his maturity and new insights, but as stories, as literature, most of them have almost no interest at all."

G315.   Schedl, Mary. "Fitzgerald Collection: Timeless, Nostalgic," Palo Alto (Calif.) *Times*, October 20, 1973, "Peninsula Living" Section, p. 27.

"This collection of Fitzgerald stories will delight not only old Fitzgerald fans with their nostalgic re-creation of an era which is gone, but should prove timeless in their portrayal of what it is like to be young at any time."

G316.   Scott, L. Wayne. "Fitzgerald Nostalgia Booms Big," San Antonio *Sunday Express and News*, March 3, 1974, p. 72.

"The mere fact that the stories of the lost stars of Basil and the unclear chase of Josephine can be appreciated today is sufficient reason to read an author, safely dead by 40 plus years. Anything learned can be dealt with as nostalgia, not relevant reality well captured."

G317.   Seward, William W., Jr. "Fitzgerald's Short Stories," Richmond (Va.) *Times-Dispatch*, February 10, 1974, p. F–3.

Stories "capture the two strains in their author's talent: the Irish inverted romanticism and moody sentimentalism, and the Midwestern awe at wealth and urbanity."

G318.   Sudler, Barbara. "'Basil and Josephine' Series Put Together," Denver *Sunday Post*, November 25, 1973, "Roundup" Section, p. 6.

"These stories belong primarily, as far as style goes, to the 'This Side of Paradise' period. They are not yet the rococo of 'Tender Is The Night' and they miss the greater simplicity of 'The Great Gatsby' which was written a few years before the stories."

G319.   Thomas, Phil. "The Short Stories of Scott Fitzgerald," Cincinnati *Enquirer*, April 11, 1974, p. 38.

Descriptive review. This syndicated AP review also appeared in Dubuque *Telegraph*, February 15, 1974; New Britain (Conn.) *Herald*, November 2, 1973; *The State* (Columbia, S.C.), November 4, 1973, p. 4-E.

G320.   Wellejus, Ed. "Bookshelf," Erie (Pa.) *Times*, December 23, 1973, "Foto-Feature" Section, p. 8-J.

Brief descriptive review: "a rare treat for Fitzgerald fans."

G321.   White, William. "Scott Before Princeton," *American Book Collector*, 25 (January-February 1975), 4.

"Even for those who are not on a nostalgia binge, these stories capture both what's bad and what's good about Fitzgerald and his times."

G322. Williams, Erma. "A Fitzgerald Collection—Stories Reproduce His Years as Youth," Buffalo *Courier-Express*, October 7, 1973, "Focus" Section, p. 16.
"Fitzgerald fans and others should enjoy these stories of an era and a youth presaging that of today."

F. SCOTT FITZGERALD'S LEDGER—A FACSIMILE
(1973)

G323. Anonymous. Review of *F. Scott Fitzgerald's Ledger*, *Choice*, 10 (January 1974), 1716, 1718.
"Understandably limited in readership audience to the advanced Fitzgerald scholar, it is recommended for graduate libraries where it will prove useful for research on the doctoral level and beyond." While the first four sections "provide bibliographical and biographical data, the last offers a fascinating series of insights into Fitzgerald's use of his life as a source of material for his fiction."

G324. ———. Review of *F. Scott Fitzgerald's Ledger*, *Journal of Modern Literature*, 4 (November 1974), 322–323.
Brief descriptive favorable review: "a fascinating document" and "a primary source of undisputed importance."

G325. Bene, Nota [William McPherson?]. "Briefly Noted," Washington (D.C.) *Post*, September 16, 1973, "Book World" Section, p. 15.
Brief review. "It may provide some thesis fodder besides being an unusual ornament for coffee tables."

G326. Boswell, Jackson C. "Books—Fitzgerald In His Own Hand," Washington (D.C.) *Star-News*, December 13, 1973, p. D–4.
"A few scholars and the Fitzgerald fanatics...will doubtlessly find something of value" in the book; but, after Bruccoli's "eloquent and exhaustive two-page introduction..., there is little left to ponder but Fitzgerald's handwriting."

G327. Mangum, Bryant. Review of *F. Scott Fitzgerald's Ledger*, *Fitzgerald/Hemingway Annual*, 6 (1974), 253–256.
This "will be an indispensible resource tool for those interested in exploring the integral relationship between the professional author/literary artist sides of Fitzgerald's career."

G328.   White, William. "For Fitzgerald Collectors," *American Book Collector*, 24 (January-February 1974), 4–5.

"If you're a Scott Fitzgerald collector, you don't need me to tell you that this facsimile...is something you absolutely must get.... But if you're not a Fitzgerald collector, you ought to consider the book anyway."

"THE GREAT GATSBY": A FACSIMILE
OF THE MANUSCRIPT
(1973)

G329.   Anonymous. "Gatsby In Longhand," *Times Literary Supplement* (London), March 29, 1974, p. 344.

This is "one of those scholarly monuments whose value to other scholars is not altogether clear. Certainly, there is some disproportion between the resources devoted to its production and its importance as a contribution to knowledge."

G330.   Brown, Dennis. "Uncut Fitzgerald," St. Louis *Post-Dispatch*, September 7, 1975, p. 4F.

"From first sentence to last—both of which later were re-written—this work-in-progress breathes new life into Jay Gatsby, Nick Carraway, and Daisy and Tom Buchanan."

G331.   Raymond, Landon T. "The 'Gatsby' Facsimile," *Princeton Alumni Weekly*, 74 (May 21, 1974), 13.

"Any English teacher who uses *Gatsby* in teaching American literature will find this material of unusual value in understanding the making of a novel."

G332.   Schulberg, Budd. Review of *"The Great Gatsby": A Facsimile of the Manuscript*, *Fitzgerald/Hemingway Annual*, 6 (1974), 247–252.

This is a "rare opportunity to meet Scott Fitzgerald, the tireless literary craftsman whose artistic conscience will outlive the myths, the romances, and the rip-offs."

G333.   West, James L. W., III. "The SCADE *Gatsby*: A Review Article," *Proof*, 5 (1975), 237–256.

Most of review deals with SCADE GG (I38) but there is some brief criticism of Bruccoli's Introduction to GG *Facsimile*.

BITS OF PARADISE
English Edition
(1973)

Anonymous. "This Side of Paradise," *Times Literary Supplement* (London), January 4, 1974, p. 13.
"Jacob's Ladder" is the best story in the book; and "The Swimmers" is also very good; but it is "nevertheless on balance a disappointing book." See G264.

Corrin, Stephen. "Agent of Despair," London *Daily Telegraph*, January 31, 1974, p. 12.
Except for "The Continental Angle," Zelda's contributions are "of mammoth triviality"; but Scott's talent "keeps shining through." See G266.

Dick, Kay. "Monday Books—Gabbling On About Scott," London *Times*, December 10, 1973, p. 14.
Brief review. Book is "a sad burnt offering." See G194.

Kermode, Frank. "Scottie on the Make," Manchester *Guardian*, December 22, 1973, p. 25.
F's stories are "'constructed' and delicately flecked with poetic prose about sexless feminine fragility, evenings in Paris, snow outside the shops and apartments of Fifth Avenue; but perhaps because these devices are here used rather to exploit than to confront his obsessive themes, the stories are at best merely dispiriting successes." See G267.

Masters, Anthony. "The Myth of Scott and Zelda," Birmingham *Post*, December 8, 1973, Saturday Magazine, p. 2.
Although F's stories "do not entirely transcend the limitations of his desperate desire to make money out of them, they are fascinating for two reasons: there are sharp, almost unconscious barbs in them that are of genuine Fitzgerald quality and some of them acted as catalysts to his novels." See G269.

Moynihan, John. "Scott on the Rocks," London *Sunday Telegraph*, January 13, 1974, p. 14.
Zelda's contributions "run close enough in quality to Scott's to suggest that her talent was almost equal to his...." See G270.

Nathan, Jeff. "Recycling Scott," Los Angeles *Free Press*, April 5, 1974, pp. 24–25 [24].
"Even the best of these stories appear to be a mechanical device for Fitzgerald's attraction to the rich and beautiful." This review also appeared in *West Coast Review of Books*, 1 (October-November 1974), 49–55 [53–54]. See G201.

Nye, Robert. "Money and Scott Fitzgerald," *The Scotsman* (Edinburgh), December 1, 1973, "Weekend Scotsman" Section, p. 2.

"A Couple of Nuts" is the best of Zelda's stories; "Jacob's Ladder" is "worth attention" for the way F used it in rewriting TITN. The rest are "best forgotten." See G271.

Snow, C. P. "Scott and Mrs. Scott," *Financial Times* (London), December 6, 1973, p. 18.

"By any literary standard," Zelda's writings "have no place alongside any writing" of Scott's. F's stories here, though "carefully fabricated," contain a "falsity [which] is usually—not always—rippling through and breaking up the art." See G272.

Toynbee, Philip. "Fitzgerald Industry," *The Observer* (London), December 2, 1973, p. 36.

Scott's stories "are a bit more skilful than Zelda's: there are flashes in both sets of stories which poignantly remind us of her genuine wit and talent, of his brilliance and melancholy wisdom." See G273.

American Edition
(1974)

G334.   Anonymous. Review of *Bits of Paradise*, Burlington (Vt.) *Free Press*, October 8, 1974, p. 30.

Brief descriptive review.

G335.   ———. Review of *Bits of Paradise*, *Kirkus*, 42 (September 15, 1974), 1019.

"Zelda's stories...are mostly pretty trivializations about pretty girls—save for the elderly 'Miss Ella' and 'A Couple of Nuts' which are a little more formed. Several of Scott's stories also lack narrative definition—excepting 'The Popular Girl' and 'The Dance'" and "A New Leaf," "The Last Kiss," and "The Swimmers."

G336.   ———. "Two Meteors: Scott and Zelda," Savannah *News-Press*, October 27, 1974, Sunday Magazine, p. 5F.

Brief review: "Not great literature, but precise, perceptive writing." This syndicated review also appeared in Key West *Citizen*, October 16, 1974; San Mateo (Calif.) *Times*, October 5, 1974; Killeen (Tex.) *Herald*, October 6, 1974; Bennington (Vt.) *Banner*, October 5, 1974; Trenton *Trentonian*, October 7, 1974; *Beavercreek News* (Dayton, Ohio), October 1, 1974; Cheyenne *Tribune Eagle*, November 3, 1974; Fullerton (Calif.) *News Tribune*, October 7, 1974; *The Scrantonian* (Scranton, Pa.), October 6, 1974.

G337.   Brown, Dennis. "Two Bright Meteors," St. Louis *Post-Dispatch*, November 3, 1974, p. 4C.
"Almost all these stories share a winning combination of imagination, unpredictability and craftsmanship."

G338.   Corriveau, Verna Cutter. "By Their Life Together," Worcester *Sunday Telegram*, October 13, 1974, p. 6E.
Collection "may not add a great deal to anyone's Fitzgerald library, but it does add to one's conception of the Fitzgerald mystique."

G339.   Eble, Kenneth. Review of *Bits of Paradise*, *Fitzgerald/Hemingway Annual*, 6 (1974), 263–264.
"The Swimmers," "A New Leaf," and "What a Handsome Pair!" are "major Fitzgerald stories, deserving to be rescued from oblivion"; and, taken as a group, the F stories "save readers the trouble of thumbing through old copies of *The Post* to find the realities of Scott Fitzgerald as a popular magazine writer."

G340.   Fink, Ira. "Theater—Paradise in Bits and Pieces," *Harvard Crimson*, November 12, 1974, p. 2.
Volume "represents the trappings of Fitzgerald's writing—his style, characters and themes—without the substance: the elements of paradise are very fragmentary."

G341.   Friend, Beverly. "Bits of Paradise—And Bits of Hell," Chicago *Daily News*, November 16–17, 1974, "Panorama" Section, p. 7.
Descriptive review.

G342.   Gregg, Louise. "The Flapper Years," Wichita Falls (Tex.) *Times*, December 15, 1974, Magazine, p. 4.
Stories are "refreshing, sentimental and nostalgic."

G343.   Hagemann, E. R. "Zelda in Writing Glory, and Scott in Her Shadow," Louisville *Courier-Journal & Times*, October 20, 1974, p. E 5.
Zelda's stories are "gems of the first water"; Scott's are "bad" and don't "match up" to hers.

G344.   H[all], R[ichard] R[andall]. "The Fitzgeralds as Collaborators," Anniston (Ala.) *Star*, September 29, 1974, Sec. D, p. 2.
"Unfortunately, none of the stories in this book by either of the authors are particularly good, but the ones attributed to Zelda are valuable for the light they shed upon this unhappy woman."

G345.   H[obbs], J[ohn].   "Scott's, Zelda's Stories Form 'Bits of Paradise,'" Galesburg (Ill.) *Register-Mail*, October 7, 1974, p. 9.
Descriptive review.

G346   Hogan, William.   "World of Books—Fitzgeralds Are Still With Us," San Francisco *Chronicle*, October 23, 1974, p. 47.
Stories are "a footnote to a career."

G347.   Kouidis, Virginia M.   Review of *Bits of Paradise*, *Southern Humanities Review*, 11 (Summer 1977), 70–71.
Stories by Scott "have more well-constructed and varied plots than most of Zelda's"; and, "at his best, Scott's characters reflect the soul of America and thus are more than just types of the jazz age."

G348.   Meacham, Harry M.   "Uncollected Writings: Book Marks End of Fitzgerald Canon," Richmond (Va.) *News Leader*, October 30, 1974, p. 13.
Descriptive review.

G349.   M[oody], M[innie] H[ite].   Review of *Bits of Paradise*, Columbus (Ohio) *Sunday Dispatch*, October 27, 1974, p. I–7.
Descriptive review.

G350.   Oberbeck, S. K.   "'Writer at Work,'" Washington (D.C.) *Post*, November 21, 1974, p. C 12.
"By their very superficiality the stories are still satisfying reminders of the glittering surface and sweet entropy of the Jazz Age high-jinks and hangovers of which the Fitzgeralds were so much a part."

G351.   Scott, Ellen.   "Books in Review—You Can Make Book On It: People Love Printed Word," Albany (NY) *Times-Union*, December 8, 1974, p. G–8.
Brief review. "These are definitely not Scott's most polished works but are interesting for the hints of characters and plots that later became familiar in his successful novels."

G352.   Shackelford, Arn.   "Some Choice 'Warmed-Over Fare,'" Grand Rapids *Press*, October 13, 1974, p. 2-H.
Volume "may serve to end talk of Scott and Zelda cribbing each other's material, since it makes their differences so very evident. One a professional, the other a gifted amateur, they wrote naturally from shared experiences."

G353.   Smith, James M.   "'Bits' Probably the Last of Fitzgerald Canon," Nashville *Tennessean*, October 20, 1974, p. 10-F.
"Jacob's Ladder," "What a Handsome Pair!," "The Last Kiss," and "The Swimmers" belong with F's best stories; the rest "are interesting

G354. Tolson, Michael. "Book Revives Fitzgerald Works," *Daily Texan* (University of Texas, Austin), October 17, 1974, p. 19.
"While these stories reveal nothing new about Fitzgerald's talent as a writer, they do serve to underscore the fact that he tried to maintain a high standard, even in work which interested him little."

G355. Walsh, Anne C. Review of *Bits of Paradise*, Phoenix *Gazette*, November 2, 1974, p. 22.
Descriptive review.

THE ROMANTIC EGOISTS:
A PICTORIAL AUTOBIOGRAPHY
FROM THE SCRAPBOOKS AND ALBUMS
OF SCOTT AND ZELDA FITZGERALD
(1974)

G356. Anonymous. "Christmas Books—A Continuing Joy," St. Louis *Globe-Democrat*, December 7–8, 1974, p. 6C.
Brief descriptive review.

G357. ———. Review of *The Romantic Egoists*, *Journal of Modern Literature*, 4 (Supplement 1975), 1039.
Descriptive review.

G358. ———. Review of *The Romantic Egoists*, Portland *Sunday Oregonian*, December 8, 1974, p. B22.
Brief descriptive review.

G359. ———. Review of *The Romantic Egoists*, *Time*, 104 (December 16, 1974), 96.
Brief descriptive review.

G360. ———. Review of *The Romantic Egoists*, *Wilson Library Bulletin*, 49 (May 1975), 618.
Brief mention: "It is a very personal look at two 'short and dramatic lives,' and truly one to linger over."

G361. ———. "'The Romantic Egoists,'" Minneapolis *Tribune*, January 12, 1975, p. 10D.
Descriptive review.

G362. ———. "Scott and Zelda In Their Own Pictures," Detroit *Free Press*, December 15, 1974, p. 5-C.
Brief review. "For Fitzgeraldophiles, this volume is a Christmas feast."

G363.   ———. "Unique Autobiography," *The State* (Columbia, S.C.), October 20, 1974, p. 4-E.
Brief descriptive review.

G364.   Baker, William. Review of *The Romantic Egoists*, *Antioch Review*, 33 (Spring 1975), 113–114.
"Somehow scrapbooks and albums leave a more enduring autobiographical impression than a person's own memoirs."

G365.   Barkham, John. "Scottie on Fitzgerald," Norfolk *Virginian-Pilot*, December 22, 1974, p. C6.
"Scottie Fitzgerald has never written a substantial work about her parents. This is a splendid substitute, full of riches and remembrances." This syndicated review also appeared in Youngstown *Vindicator*, December 22, 1974; Victoria (Tex.) *Advocate*, December 15, 1974.

G366.   Beirne, Roger F. *"The Romantic Egoists*—A Pictorial Look At the World of Scott and Zelda Fitzgerald," *The Record* (Bergen County, N.J.), December 5, 1974, pp. B–1, B–8.
Less a review than an extended interview with Scottie Smith and Matthew J. Bruccoli.

G367.   Bevington, Helen. "The Great and Near-Great," *NY Times Book Review*, December 1, 1974, p. 82.
"The book is irresistible, a narrative with a strange eloquence...."

G368.   Bingham, Barry, Sr. "Scott and Zelda, As They Told It," Louisville *Courier-Journal & Times*, December 29, 1974, p. E 5.
Descriptive favorable review.

G369.   Brock, Charles. "Memories of F. Scott and Zelda," *Florida Times-Union* and Jacksonville *Journal*, December 22, 1974, Magazine, p. 5.
"Scott and Zelda were the stuff of legends, and the record of their lives together is remarkably preserved here."

G370.   Brown, Dennis. "Fabulous Fitzgeralds Revived," St. Louis *Post-Dispatch*, December 3, 1974, pp. 1D, 2D.
Less a review than an interview with Matthew J. Bruccoli, who talks of the origins of the book and about its significance.

G371.   C[ady], E[rnest]. Review of *The Romantic Egoists*, Columbus (Ohio) *Sunday Dispatch*, January 12, 1975, p. J–7.
Volume is "a fitting climax to the Fitzgerald revival which shows no signs of abating."

G372.   Clarey, Kathey. "Albums, Scrapbooks of the Fitzgeralds," Fresno *Bee*, November 24, 1974, Sec. K, p. 5.
Brief favorable review: "a must for Fitzgerald fans."

G373.   Clemons, Walter.   Review of *The Romantic Egoists*,
Newsweek, 84 (December 16, 1974), 94B.
Brief review. "These snapshots, letters, telegrams and clip-
pings...have an immediacy none of the biographies gives us."

G374.   Davis, Paxton.   " 'The Romantic Egoists,' " Roanoke
Times, December 15, 1974, p. F–4.
"This is an outsized fan magazine."

G375.   Diehl, Digby. "Book Talk—Cream of the Coffee-Table
Crop," Los Angeles *Times*, December 8, 1974, "Calendar" Section,
p. 90.
Brief descriptive review.

G376.   Dooley, Donald H.   "So You're Interested in People?
Here Are Some Worth Meeting," Milwaukee *Journal*, December 22,
1974, Part 5, p. 3.
Brief descriptive review.

G377.   Duke, Maurice.   "Scrapbooks, Photo Albums Add to
Fitzgerald Saga," Richmond (Va.) *Times-Dispatch*, December 1, 1974,
p. F–5.
"If we look at the scrapbooks and photo albums of Fitzgerald with a
keen eye for discovering something about the nature of genius, we find
a great deal to hold our attention."

G378.   Eble, Kenneth E.   Review of *The Romantic Egoists*,
Western Humanities Review, 29 (Autumn 1975), 372–375.
Book's "visual attractiveness can hardly help but lead back to the
written word, and the written word shaped by Fitzgerald's hand is after
all what has created and kept alive the Fitzgerald presence."

G379.   Field, Carol H.   "Mass of Memories," San Francisco
Sunday Examiner & Chronicle, December 15, 1974, "This World"
Section, p. 35.
"It's a coffee table book, an oversized unhandsome volume, a
curious amalgam of memorabilia that only whets the appetite."

G380.   Gillbanks, Elizabeth. "Scottie Smith and The Romantic
Egoists," *The Georgetowner* (Washington, D.C.), 21 (March 5-March
18, 1975), 1.
Interview with Scottie Smith and favorable descriptive review.

G381.   Gregg, Louise. "The Flapper Years," Wichita Falls
(Tex.) *Times*, December 15, 1974, Magazine, p. 4.
Descriptive favorable review.

G382.   Hunter, Stephen. "The Books of Yule," Baltimore *Sunday Sun*, December 8, 1974, pp. D5, D6 [D6].
This is "easily the ugliest book of the year. It's also one of the best; it's sad and funny, boisterous and drunken, a little embarrassing and finally pitiful."

G383.   Lague, Louise. "Scott and Zelda AGAIN? This Time, Bio By Scrapbook," Washington (D.C.) *Star-News*, January 11, 1975, p. C–3.
"It is a charming, engrossing book, and with very little text to glue it together, it still manages to paint an objective and unromanticized picture of the two, through clues to their character."

G384.   M., E. Review of *The Romantic Egoists*, Chattanooga *Times*, December 15, 1974, p. G 8.
Brief descriptive review.

G385.   McKenzie, Alice. "Scott Fitzgerald Daughter's Story Sad, Sentimental," Clearwater (Fla.) *Sun*, January 5, 1975, p. 2-F.
"This is a lovely book. Sad and sentimental, of course, but lovely, too."

G386.   Manning, Margaret. "The Terrible Poignancy of the Fitzgerald Year," Boston *Globe*, November 26, 1974, "Calendar" Section, p. [15].
"For Fitzgerald admirers, 'The Romantic Egoists' is probably not an essential book, but fascinating it certainly is."

G387.   Martine, James J. Review of *The Romantic Egoists*, *Library Journal*, 100 (January 15, 1975), 118.
"This exceptional collection...is oddly more powerful than any book on the Fitzgeralds. A most interesting and fascinating book."

G388.   Meacham, Harry M. "F. Scott Fitzgerald: Autobiography Marks Return to 'Royalty,'" Richmond (Va.) *News Leader*, December 25, 1974, p. 11.
Descriptive favorable review.

G389.   Moloney, Kathleen. "The Life and (Good) Times of the Photogenic Fitzgeralds," Chicago *Tribune*, December 1, 1974, "Book World" Section, p. 1.
This is a book for "Fitzgerald fans" or "for the literary groupie, the person whose spirits soar at the sight of a first edition, who speaks about the Algonquin and the Left Bank in hushed tones."

G390. Neely, Mildred Solà. "Scribners' 'The Romantic Egoists': Scott and Zelda Fitzgerald in Pictures," *Publishers' Weekly*, 205 (June 3, 1974), 128.
Descriptive review: "the most fascinating Fitzgerald chronicle to appear...this year..."

G391. Norris, Hoke. "A Garden of Fitzgeralds," Chicago *Daily News*, December 7–8, 1974, "Panorama" Section, p. 6.
Book is "large, beautiful and sad."

G392. O'Rourke, Matthew R. Review of *The Romantic Egoists*, *Best Sellers*, 34 (January 1, 1975), 448–449.
Descriptive favorable review.

G393. Raymond, John. "Gift Choices—If a Book Will Do, Here Are a Few," Atlanta *Journal and Constitution*, December 8, 1974, p. 22-D.
Brief descriptive review.

G394. Rumley, Larry. "Fitzgerald Folio," Seattle *Times*, December 22, 1974, Magazine, p. 15.
"It's a feast for Fitzgerald fanciers."

G395. Sanford, Mrs. Leslie J. "Scott Fitzgerald Era Celebrated," Jamestown (NY) *Post-Journal*, December 14, 1974, p. 3M.
Descriptive review.

G396. Shroyer, Frederick. "Following the Scott Fitzgeralds Through Their Rise and Fall," Los Angeles *Herald-Examiner*, December 8, 1974, p. G–7.
Brief descriptive review.

G397. Thompson, Haynes. "'The Romantic Egoists'—A Daughter's Story of Scott and Zelda," Montgomery *Independent*, April 17, 1975, pp. 1, 7.
A résumé of F's life and an interview with Scottie Smith; volume is a "rare treat."

G398. Tolson, Michael. "Literary Darlings," Austin (Tex.) *American-Statesman*, December 29, 1974, p. 35.
"In a way this may be the most revealing book that has been published concerning the Fitzgeralds."

G399. Trueheart, Charles. "Foreword—Off the Coffee Table!" Greensboro (N.C.) *Daily News*, December 1, 1974, pp. D2, D3 [D3].
Brief descriptive review.

G400.   Whitman, Alden.   Review of *The Romantic Egoists*, *Fitzgerald/Hemingway Annual*, 7 (1975), 333–334.

"The delineation of Fitzgerald's life is all here—marvelously so—but the interior life, well, that requires a biography's sensitive interpretative skills. Even so, this book remains a splendid experience."

G401.   Yardley, Jonathan.   "Gift Books—A Look at This Year's Coffee Table Behemoths," Miami (Fla.) *Herald*, December 1, 1974, p. 6-E.

Brief review.   "The book is an invaluable companion to the existing Fitzgerald biographies, a solid biography in its own right, and an endlessly fascinating book."

THE CRUISE OF THE ROLLING JUNK
(1976)

G402.   Lucid, Robert F.   Review of *The Cruise of the Rolling Junk*, *Fitzgerald/Hemingway Annual*, 8 (1976), 280–282.

This is "the best piece of nonfictional narrative that Fitzgerald ever wrote." The "key" to its success is "Fitzgerald's narrative identity. Not unlike Nick Carraway, he is a man on the other side of the narrative divide, intimately including the reader in residence there, where together they nourish themselves on spectacles of the disintegratingly unreliable vehicles of our technology, the folly of the young, and the wildness of the unexplored American night."

F. SCOTT FITZGERALD'S SCREENPLAY FOR
"THREE COMRADES"
BY ERICH MARIA REMARQUE
(1978)

G403.   Anonymous.   Review of *F. Scott Fitzgerald's Screenplay for "Three Comrades," American Literature*, 50 (November 1978), 532.

Brief review.   "Whether this belongs in the Fitzgerald or the Remarque canon and whether such things ought to be reprinted are doubtless questions for the future."

G404.   ———.   Review of *F. Scott Fitzgerald's Screenplay for "Three Comrades," The Booklist*, 75 (October 15, 1978), 346.

"For movie buffs who will appreciate the archaic set directions and script writing; also for truly avid Fitzgerald fans who wish to see what happened to his writing in Hollywood."

G405. ————. Review of *F. Scott Fitzgerald's Screenplay for "Three Comrades," Choice*, 15 (December 1978), 1367.

"The script is, predictably, simplistic in comparison to the novel; yet even within the limitations of the genre, it is often trite and sentimental, its weaknesses leavened only rarely by glimpses of Fitzgerald's imagination."

G406. Brown, Dennis. "Uncut Fitzgerald," St. Louis *Post-Dispatch*, July 9, 1978, p. 4D.

"Fitzgerald's dialogue turns out to be amply appropriate for a screenplay—especially one in its early draft. His movie sentences are short and crisp. The overall script is too long and moves somewhat slowly (the final version was 40 pages shorter), but rewriting and cutting are two different matters."

G407. *Combs, Richard. Review of *F. Scott Fitzgerald's Screenplay for "Three Comrades," Sight and Sound*, 48 (Summer 1979), 198.

F was "evidently after...a fineness of feeling and a doomed romanticism in the story's central love affair...which was undoubtedly compromised by structural changes and rewriting.... On the other hand, Fitzgerald's writing does have an attenuated laborious quality"; and his "discomfort with images might be deduced from his whimsical notion of showing a switchboard operated in turn by an angel and a satyr during the couple's first, tentative telephone conversation."

G408. Deutelbaum, Marshall. Review of *F. Scott Fitzgerald's Screenplay for "Three Comrades," Library Journal*, 103 (September 1, 1978), 1657.

"Though it is easy to lament the loss of Fitzgerald's control over his project, the fact—not mentioned here—that the changes are fully in keeping with the melodramatic style of its director put these revisions into clearer perspective."

G409. Fuller, Richard. "...and Checks and Balances of Scott," Philadelphia *Inquirer*, March 4, 1979, p. 12-H.

Brief descriptive mention.

G410. G[etz], R[icki] R. Review of *F. Scott Fitzgerald's Screenplay for "Three Comrades," Kliatt Young Adult Paperback Book Guide*, 12 (Fall 1978), 23.

"Fitzgerald fans will be delighted with this new find and students will profit from and enjoy a comparison between the novel and the screenplay in a study of the process of adaptation."

G411.   Mahoney, John C. "5th Annual Movie Book Roundup," *West Coast Review of Books*, 5 (May 1979), 7–20, 47–52 [51].
Brief descriptive mention.

G412.   Margolies, Alan. Review of *F. Scott Fitzgerald's Screenplay for "Three Comrades," Fitzgerald/Hemingway Annual*, 10 (1978), 419–421.
"Some of the visual touches that Fitzgerald wrote in are effective"; "on the other hand, we do have a few obvious clichés"; but "it is worthwhile having this script in print."

G413.   Ray, David. "F. Scott Fitzgerald and Films," Kansas City *Star*, May 28, 1978, p. 14D.
"The script is fascinating largely for its insight into Fitzgerald's projections of his own concerns, for its fragmentary images from his novels, embedded in the hackwork like shrapnel in cheesecake."

G414.   *Vidal, Gore. "Scott's Case," *NY Review of Books*, 27 (May 1, 1980), 12–20 [15–19].
Detailed examination of F's script and of the revisions in it made by Mankiewicz.
Reprinted: Vidal (I355).

G415.   Young, Walter. Review of *F. Scott Fitzgerald's Screenplay for "Three Comrades," West Coast Review of Books*, 4 (September 1978), 64–65.
Screenplay is a "unique effort, somehow preserved, and of interest to film buffs and the Fitzgerald fans who must collect everything he wrote."

THE NOTEBOOKS OF F. SCOTT FITZGERALD
American Edition
(1978)

G416.   Anonymous. Review of *The Notebooks of F. Scott Fitzgerald, American Literature*, 51 (March 1979), 135.
Brief descriptive review.

G417.   ———. Review of *The Notebooks of F. Scott Fitzgerald, The Booklist*, 75 (November 1, 1978), 448.
"Despite the extravagant claims of editor and publisher, these jottings and sweepings remain of interest only to scholars and serious students of Fitzgerald's work...."

G418. ————. Review of *The Notebooks of F. Scott Fitzgerald*, *Kirkus*, 46 (August 15, 1978), 920.

"What these notebooks finally do is put to rest the lazy idea of Fitzgerald as golden-boy profligate, for whom everything came easy, too easy. Each entry here is a little knot of struggle to stay ahead of his craft and his life."

G419. ————. Review of *The Notebooks of F. Scott Fitzgerald*, San Francisco *Sunday Examiner & Chronicle*, November 19, 1978, "This World" Section, p. 67.

Brief descriptive review.

G420. ————. Review of *The Notebooks of F. Scott Fitzgerald*, *Southern Living*, 14 (January 1979), 69.

Brief review. "Any serious writer can learn much from Fitzgerald's thoughtful and persistent notekeeping."

G421. ————. Review of *The Notebooks of F. Scott Fitzgerald*, *Virginia Quarterly Review*, 55 (Spring 1979), 68.

"It is all pure Fitzgerald, there's no doubt about that. If you are not one of the dogged admirers, don't bother to begin the long wade through it."

G422. Baker, Mary M. "A Little Too Much Scott Fitzgerald," Wilmington (Del.) *News Journal*, November 19, 1978, p. F16.

"Ingesting more than 2,000 unrelated fragments, even Fitzgerald fragments, imposes too much of a burden on the casual reader."

G423. Bonham, Roger. "Bruccoli-Edited Works Add to Writers' Canon," Columbus (Ohio) *Sunday Dispatch*, April 1, 1979, p. K–8.

Volume "will bewitch any Fitzgerald aficionado and every writer or would-be writer."

G424. Davis, Robert Murray. Review of *The Notebooks of F. Scott Fitzgerald*, *World Literature Today*, 53 (Autumn 1979), 689.

Book underscores "the fact that Fitzgerald was essentially a lyric writer who tried, by cultivating a sense of history, to become epic or dramatic and sometimes succeeded in being elegaic. He seemed to believe that the right verbal formula could transmute anything. This is not a belief which makes a major writer, but it is far from the worst illusion a writer can have."

G425. Edmonds, B. F. "Book Review—The Notebooks of F. Scott Fitzgerald," *The Press and Banner* and Abbeville (S.C.) *Medium*, December 6, 1978, Sec. B, p. 3.

"This book will give the reader an inspiring view of the genius of F. Scott Fitzgerald."

G426. Ellis, James. Review of *The Notebooks of F. Scott Fitzgerald*, *Southern Humanities Review*, 15 (Spring 1981), 172–173.

"This is material that is of interest not only to the specialist in Fitzgerald but also to those who are more generally concerned with the processes that go into the making of a fictional work, and it is, moreover, material that for most of us would otherwise be unavailable."

G427. Fugate, Francis L. "'The Notebooks of F. Scott Fitzgerald,'" *El Paso Times*, December 10, 1978, "Sundial" Section, p. 23.
Descriptive review.

G428. Fuller, Richard. "...and Checks and Balances of Scott," Philadelphia *Inquirer*, March 4, 1979, p. 12-H.
Descriptive review.

G429. Gregory, Bob. "Old Fitzgerald," *Tulsa Magazine*, 55 (November 1978), 44.

"Toward understanding Fitzgerald's torment and his brilliance with language, his overpowering gifts, this book is invaluable and of course a continuous joy to read."

G430. H., M. P. Review of *The Notebooks of F. Scott Fitzgerald*, *Kliatt Young Adult Paperback Book Guide*, 14 (April 1980), 19.

"As well as being a storehouse for writers, *The Notebooks*...open up opportunities for the literature student who wishes to follow the development of an idea in a Fitzgerald story from first draft to published story to the aspect of the idea Fitzgerald thought worthy of further development or use."

G431. Hagemann, E. R. "For Better or Worse, Fitzgerald," Louisville *Courier-Journal*, December 31, 1978, p. D 5.

"Despite their haphazardness,...they make for fascinating reading at times; at other times, shocked reading, so mundane is his mind."

G432. Hall, Joan Joffe. "More Christmas Books for Giving and Receiving," Houston *Post*, December 10, 1978, "Spotlight on Travel/The Arts" Section, p. 10CC.
Brief review. "Although the volume is intended primarily for scholars, random reading turns up secret pleasures."

G433. Harris, Roger. "The Book Shelf—'Notebooks' Offer New Look at Fitzgerald," Newark (N.J.) *Sunday Star-Ledger*, October 22, 1978, Sec. 4, p. 24.

"This is a book to browse, not to read right through from cover to cover. But for those who love good writing, there is nothing quite like it around."

G434. Hartman, Zella. "Fitzgerald Notes Offer Intimate Glimpse of Genius," Oklahoma City *Sunday Oklahoman*, January 28, 1979, "The Oklahomans" Magazine, p. 37.

"Readers who already are familiar with Fitzgerald's works will find new delight in this intimate glimpse of genius at work and others may be inspired to read further by the 'tastes' spread forth like smorgasbord."

G435. Houston, Levin. "Fitzgerald's Complete Notebooks Are Sparkling," Fredericksburg (Va.) *Free Lance-Star*, October 13, 1979, "Town & Country" Magazine, p. 11.

"I can think of few books with the sparkle, the zany humor which it contains."

G436. Jaynes, Roger. "Genius Jottings By Fitzgerald," Milwaukee *Journal*, October 29, 1978, Part 5, p. 3.

"Fitzgerald wrote of Jay Gatsby that he possessed 'a heightened sensitivity to the promises of life.' His notebooks show he might well have been speaking of himself."

G437. Johnson, Mark. "Why Fitzgerald's Writing Has Lasted," San Jose (Calif.) *Sunday Mercury News*, December 3, 1978, p. 8B.

"This is not a book for sustained reading, and certainly anyone who has not read Fitzgerald's completed work, particularly 'The Great Gatsby,' should not bother with it. But those who enjoy Fitzgerald will find gems on every page of the notebooks."

G438. Kapsidelis, Tom. "Fitzgerald Notebooks—Disturbing Insight," *The State* (Columbia, S.C.), November 12, 1978, p. 4-E.

"For Fitzgerald enthusiasts, the book depressingly serves to remind how the author, in his own mind, probably did not achieve happiness."

G439. Keister, Don A. "F. Scott Fitzgerald—He Knew All Along What He Had Wasted," Cleveland *Plain Dealer*, January 21, 1979, Sec. 4, p. 24.

It is "good" to have the full *Notebooks* in print.

G440. Kennedy, William. "American Hero of the Word," Washington (D.C.) *Post*, November 19, 1978, "Book World" Section, p. E3.

Volume is "a superb rummage sale, an organized romp through the imagination of an American hero of the word." This review also appeared in *Rocky Mountain News* (Denver), December 17, 1978, "Now" Section, p. 49.

G441.   Kirsch, Robert.   "Insights and Introspection From Woolf and Fitzgerald," Los Angeles *Times*, November 19, 1978, "Book Review" Section, pp. 1, 29 [29].
"For Fitzgerald collectors and enthusiasts, this volume is useful, though by no means the evidence of literary intelligence...the editor claims for it."

G442.   Kosek, Steven.   "Fitzgerald Revisited: Fragments Before and After 'The Crack-Up,'" Chicago *Tribune*, October 15, 1978, "Book World" Section, p. 1.
"On the whole, the 'Notebooks' seem much less useful in understanding the author, or the times in which he wrote, than do the novels or the Jazz Age articles that initially made his fame.   Nonetheless, it is important to have access to the complete canon of our best authors...."

G443.   Leighton, Betty.   "In the '30s, 'Everything He Touched Crumbled'—Fitzgerald's Letters Were Partly a Confessional," Winston-Salem *Journal*, April 6, 1980, p. C4.
"The *Notebooks* indicate self-knowledge and an incredible sensitivity and will do much to change the stereotyped image held by some that he was an ignorant genius 'who did not understand his gift.'"

G444.   McMurtry, Larry.   "A Revealing Portrait in Fitzgerald's Notebooks," Washington (D.C.) *Star*, October 9, 1978, p. B–2.
Notebooks "can be read with interest from beginning to end and, except for the section of 'Jingles and Songs,' seem remarkably consistent."

G445.   Mason, Franklin.   "Scott Fitzgerald Took Notes on His Own Decline," Baltimore *Sunday Sun*, December 17, 1978, p. D5.
Comparing this full edition to Edmund Wilson's selection from the notebooks in C-U, "we can learn from either of them.   Working the two together, we can learn even more, see the change that has come about in a literary reputation over the years."

G446.   Milazzo, Lee.   "Hemingway, Fitzgerald Get Renewed Attention," Dallas *Morning News*, October 22, 1978, p. 7G.
"A careful investigation of the *Notebooks* should further increase our already considerable respect for Fitzgerald the artist."

G447.   Mysak, Joe.   "Notebooks of F. Scott Fitzgerald," *Columbia Spectator* (Columbia University), January 23, 1979, p. 16.
"There is lyricism, and there are ideas, but most of all there is good

crafty writing in *The Notebooks of F. Scott Fitzgerald.*"

G448.   Powell, Larry.   Review of *The Notebooks of F. Scott Fitzgerald*, Savannah *News-Press*, February 11, 1979, p. 5G.

"Much of the material sheds light on Fitzgerald's private life.   Some of the aphorisms, wisecracks and word play are funny and entertaining."

G449.   Romine, Dannye.   "'Notebooks' a Must For F. Scott's Fans," Charlotte *Observer*, October 22, 1978, p. 6F.

Notebooks are "invaluable on several counts": "for pure reading pleasure"; "they serve as a model for all other notebook keepers"; "they illustrate a type of observation, a type of sensitivity, and one to emulate"; and they "provide a further glimpse into the mind and soul of a literary genius."

G450.   Schulberg, Budd.   "Fitzgerald: Master of the Art of the Notebook," *Newsday* (Garden City, NY), November 12, 1978, "Ideas" Section, pp. 16, 13.

Only slightly revised reprinting of review from *Fitzgerald/Hemingway Annual* (G451).

G451.   ———.   Review of *The Notebooks of F. Scott Fitzgerald*, *Fitzgerald/Hemingway Annual*, 10 (1978), 429–432.

"It will be a myopic reader who does not find this irresistible.   Of all the Notebook masters, beyond Butler, Bennett, even Jules Renaud, Fitzgerald emerges—in our judgment—as not only the most thorough and professional but the most entertaining and evocative."

Reprinted (revised): Schulberg (G450).

G452.   Stacy, Paul H.   "Somewhat of a Mess," Hartford *Courant*, December 10, 1978, p. 11F.

"This volume, the least interesting, the least usable document in years, is a roaring example of having too much from an author."

G453.   Tavernier-Courbin, Jacqueline.   Review of *The Notebooks of F. Scott Fitzgerald*, *Library Journal*, 103 (November 1, 1978), 2241.

Book "makes fascinating reading for the Fitzgerald lover."

*Vidal, Gore.   "Scott's Case," *NY Review of Books*, 27 (May 1, 1980), 12–20 [12–13].

Notebooks "serve only to remind us that even in his best work, Fitzgerald had little wit and less humor." See G414.

Reprinted: Vidal (I355).

G454.   Wanner, Irene.   "Fitzgerald's Remembrances of Things Past," Seattle *Post-Intelligencer*, March 2, 1980, p. G7.
Descriptive favorable review.

G455.   Williams, Shirley A.   "F. Scott Fitzgerald—Novels Built With Fragile Bricks," San Diego *Union*, December 3, 1978, "Currents in Books" Section, p. 3.
"The star here is Fitzgerald, and Bruccoli's editorial work adds to that luster."

G456.   Zochert, Donald.   "Fitzgerald's Storehouse," Chicago *Sunday Sun-Times*, October 15, 1978, Sec. 3, p. 10.
Notebooks "remain rich with the evidence of a good writer at work."

Canadian Edition
(1979)

G457.   Anonymous.   Review of *The Notebooks of F. Scott Fitzgerald*, *Queen's Quarterly*, 86 (Winter 1979/80), 739.
Descriptive brief mention.

G458.   Duffy, Dennis.   "At Last the Truth About F. Scott Fitzgerald: Neither a Fallen Angel nor a Gloppy Keats in Vaseline," Toronto *Globe and Mail*, February 17, 1979, p. 43.
"This book may possibly temper the Fitzgerald enthusiasts. It will delight the admirers of a sensibility that never quit picking up the pieces of life, love and friendship it happened upon—and sometimes wrecked."

G459.   Powers, Gordon.   Review of *The Notebooks of F. Scott Fitzgerald*, Ottawa *Revue*, February 22–28, 1979, p. 24.
"The measure of this book lies as much in the how of writing as it does in the light it throws on Fitzgerald's art. Although bundled together, each thought remains separate from the rest, a small bright spark encased in print for handy reference."

F. SCOTT FITZGERALD'S ST. PAUL PLAYS: 1911–1914
(1978)

G460.   Anonymous.   Review of *F. Scott Fitzgerald's St. Paul Plays*, *American Literature*, 51 (March 1979), 135.
Brief descriptive mention.

G461.   *Kuehl, John.   Review of *F. Scott Fitzgerald's St. Paul Plays*, *Fitzgerald/Hemingway Annual*, 11 (1979), 439–442.

"Less skillful than the early stories, these early stage pieces nonetheless have a special significance when seen as part of Fitzgerald's lifelong fascination for the theater, a fascination often reflected in his nondramatic writings."

THE PRICE WAS HIGH—THE LAST
UNCOLLECTED STORIES OF
F. SCOTT FITZGERALD
American Edition
(1979)

G462.   Anonymous.   Review of *The Price Was High*, *Kirkus*, 46 (November 15, 1978), 1263.

"With the exception of only one story, a football one—'The Bowl'—this is Fitzgerald trading upon what was closest at hand: the softest parts of his style and the most myopic contemporaneities; churned out under obligation, not a single one of these stories takes the time to stand back and really achieve the pause, gravity, and sweetness of Fitzgerald's best work."

G463.   Anderson, David.   "Short Stories With a Touch of Class—Fitzgerald's Prose Is Still Fresh," San Jose (Calif.) *Mercury News*, February 25, 1979, p. 8B.

"This collection has Fitzgerald at his zenith and as well as at his ebb ....The price was high and so was the cost of this book, but, like Fitzgerald's life and work, it is well worth it."

G464.   Bannon, Barbara A.   Review of *The Price Was High*, *Publishers' Weekly*, 214 (November 20, 1978), 51.

Stories are "essential to a balanced assessment of Fitzgerald's work" and "still flash intermittently with that familiar Fitzgerald magic."

G465.   B[arkham], J[ohn].   "No Masterpieces In Fitzgerald's 49 Magazine Stories," Youngstown *Vindicator*, February 4, 1979, p. B–4.

"Though there's a certain dated air about these stories...narrative skill, acute observation and striking descriptions make them well worth reading."

G466.   Benson, Joseph.   "Fitzgerald's Fine Forty-Nine," Greensboro (N.C.) *Daily News*, May 27, 1979, p. G5.

"Fitzgerald still moves us since his short fiction remains a singular monument to his well used talent. We are not likely to encounter such a talented writer very soon, as *The Price Was High* attests." Singled out for specific discussion are "Myra Meets His Family," "The Unspeakable Egg," and "Dice, Brassknuckles, & Guitar."

G467.   Boardman, Kathryn. "49 Fitzgerald Short Stories In Collection," Macon *Telegraph and News*, February 18, 1979, Sec. F, p. 3.
Descriptive favorable review. This review also appeared in St. Paul *Pioneer Press-Dispatch*, January 20, 1979, p. 7B.

Bonham, Roger. "Bruccoli-Edited Works Add to Writers' Canon," Columbus (Ohio) *Sunday Dispatch*, April 1, 1979, p. K–8.
Descriptive review. See G423.

G468.   Brown, Dennis. "Fitzgerald By the Yard," St. Louis *Post-Dispatch*, February 18, 1979, p. 4C.
Volume "provides a mixed blessing. Even if it doesn't reveal Fitzgerald at his peak, it still allows us to be consistently entertained by a masterful craftsman."

G469.   Buchanan, Bill. "Last Scott Fitzgerald Collection Is a Bust," Nashville *Tennessean*, February 18, 1979, p. 10-F.
Although "there are places in these stories where the glimmer of emotion survives the commercial formula," "at best the 49 stories collected here do nothing to enhance F. Scott Fitzgerald's now secure literary reputation."

G470.   B[utscher], E[dward]. Review of *The Price Was High*, *The Booklist*, 75 (February 15, 1979), 913–914.
"This collection has to remain of more interest to scholars than discerning general readers."

G471.   Cook, Malcolm. "No Dumb Dolls," *Village Voice*, February 5, 1979, pp. 73, 82 [73].
While the stories "don't rank with Fitzgerald's best work, they are disciplined and generally well-wrought. More importantly, they provide glimpses into themes he would later develop in his novels."

G472.   Cowley, Malcolm. "A Book of Last Things," *NY Times Book Review*, March 4, 1979, p. 7.
Although "three-fourths of the stories in 'The Price Was High' are below his usual level of achievement" because they "depend too much on coincidence, melodramatic turns of plot and information withheld from the reader until the last moment so as to end the story with an O. Henry twist" and because "they reveal an innocent snobbery, a resentful tribute paid to inherited wealth and position," "almost all of them contain something to surprise us" and "such moments...are a sound reason for preserving even the weaker stories in this final collection."

G473.   Dretzka, Gary. "The Last Word(s) on Fitzgerald," Los
Angeles *Herald-Examiner*, February 4, 1979, p. F–12.

"Fitzgerald fanatics and scholars will want this book if for no other
reason than it closes a chapter on the man's literary life. The uniniti-
ated probably would do better by starting with earlier collections. For
fence-sitters in between, like me, 'The Price Was High' should be kept
conveniently near and read slowly, piece by piece, like a magazine."

G474.   Dugas, Joseph H.   Review of *The Price Was High*, Grand
Rapids *Press*, March 25, 1979, p. 7-G.

"Going through all 50 of the selections leaves the reader sad and dis-
appointed. There are too many rich boy-rich girl tales, too many tiresome magazine fiction-type endings."

G475.   Fanzone, Joseph, Jr.   "Fitzgerald and Adolescence
Mingle in the Memory," Baltimore *Sunday Sun*, March 11, 1979,
p. D5.

Volume is "a compendium not really suited for intensive reading by
amateur or reviewer. That it is as readable as it is bears witness to
Bruccoli's deft introductions and Fitzgerald's irrepressible skills."

G476.   Feeney, Joseph J., S.J.   Review of *The Price Was High*,
Best Sellers, 39 (May 1979), 42.

"The human and artistic price [exacted by F's magazine fiction] was
very high, and the occasional good story or brilliant moment only
serves to underscore the genius mixed with the journeyman, the suffer-
er with the child."

G477.   Fox, Thomas.   "Written to Pay the Bills," Memphis
Commercial Appeal, February 11, 1979, Sec. G, p. 6.

"In each, even the worst of the lot, there are those fine Fitzgerald
touches: the dazzling run of description, the opening sentence that sets
the pace of what is to come, a glowing dash of philosophy."

Fuller, Richard.   "...and Checks and Balances of Scott,"
Philadelphia *Inquirer*, March 4, 1979, p. 12-H.

Despite the "small gems" one discovers, "most of the stories" are "a
depressing contrast to Fitzgerald's masterwork, 'The Great Gatsby.'"
See G428.

G478.   Gervais, Ronald J.   "Fitzgerald's Lesser Works Re-
Examined," San Diego *Union*, February 18, 1979, "Currents in Books"
Section, pp. 1, 4.

"The colors and rhythms of the Fitzgerald style shine through the
faults and make the stories as much a pleasure as a disappointment.

And since these are the last stories we will have from him, we have to feel more gratitude than regret."

G479.   Hagemann, E. R.   "Fitzgerald Potboilers Unearthed," Louisville *Courier-Journal*, April 15, 1979, p. D 5.

"The magic of Fitzgerald, who was supposedly touched with it, is only very occasionally evident in 'The Price Was High' and almost always in the first paragraph or so of a story until about 1930; after that, even first-paragraph magic is missing...."

G480.   Harris, Roger.   "The Book Shelf—Scholar Spins a Fascinating Mystery Web," Newark (N.J.) *Sunday Star-Ledger*, February 4, 1979, Sec. 4, p. 24.

"All those who love Fitzgerald's work will want to read this book....This may be a case where the whole greatly exceeds the sum of its parts."

G481.   *Hart, Jeffrey.   "Swell Letters—Tough Professional," *National Review*, 31 (June 8, 1979), 750–751.

Collection should help "a great deal" in changing our conception of F as a writer who "crashed with the Market, spent the Thirties drunk, and revived only briefly to lament his fate and begin *The Last Tycoon*." In fact, "he prevailed over adversity, produced first-rate work throughout the Thirties, and made a fortune in Hollywood."

G482.   Hibbert, Dorothy.   "A Desperate Search For Pleasure— Memorable Fitzgerald Stories Mirror the '20s and '30s," Atlanta *Journal and Constitution*, February 25, 1979, p. 5E.

Stories evoke the 1920s and 1930s and "also bring a sigh of longing for the quality of magazine fiction common then."

G483.   Hunter, William B., Jr.   "Fitzgerald: A Career's Interesting Leftovers," Houston *Chronicle*, January 28, 1979, "Zest" Section, p. 15.

"Although it contains no fiction of exceptional merit, this collection remains readable and scarcely dated.   Admirers of the novels will certainly enjoy it...and it tellingly evokes the popular culture of the '20s and '30s in their most typical writer."

G484.   Jaynes, Roger.   "More Good Fitzgerald," Milwaukee *Journal*, March 4, 1979, Lively Arts Section, p. 5.

"There is enough good Fitzgerald to make the collection entertaining, and a few of the stories...are diamonds with only minor flaws."

G485.   Just, Ward. "Leftovers From the Files of Scott Fitzgerald," Chicago *Tribune*, December 24, 1978, "Book World" Section, p. 2.

"Only the most dedicated Fitzgerald fanatic or scholar will have the slightest interest in these proceedings."

G486.   Kirsch, Robert. "Fitzgerald's Short Stories: A Master at Work For the Masses," Los Angeles *Times*, March 18, 1979, "Book Review" Section, pp. 1, 8.

"If these were the only stories Fitzgerald ever left, they would justify calling him one of the best short story writers of his time. Maybe the best."

G487.   Kloer, Phil. " 'Price Was High' Has Beauty, Tragedy," Jacksonville *Times-Union and Journal*, March 18, 1979, p. G–7.

"Even when read 50 years after they were written, many of the stories are as good as most short fiction being written today."

G488.   Latham, Aaron. "Slick Fiction From F. Scott Fitzgerald," Washington (D.C.) *Post*, February 11, 1979, "Book World" Section, pp. 1, 4.

"These stories have a lot in common with a bootlegger's brew: They are not very subtle, but they can still show you a good time." This review also appeared in *Rocky Mountain News* (Denver), February 25, 1979, "Now" Section, p. 31.

G489.   L[atour], M[artine]. Review of *The Price Was High*, *Mademoiselle*, 85 (January 1979), 44.

Quotes Features Senior Editor Mary Cantwell as observing, " 'Fitzgerald was truly a repository of grace and fluency even when he didn't have a subject. Often the stories are forgettable, but there's always a phrase, or a statement....' "

G490.   Lavine, Harold. "Fitzgerald Payed [*sic*] High Price For Fortunes," *Arizona Republic* (Phoenix), March 18, 1979, p. ET–8.

"They are pot-boilers. And yet, they are worth reading. For, even when he was wracked by alcoholism—and despair—Fitzgerald could not write badly."

G491.   *Mangum, Bryant. Review of *The Price Was High*, *Fitzgerald/Hemingway Annual*, 10 (1978), 389–395.

Collection has several values: "No authentic study of the relationship between Fitzgerald's commercial fiction and the novels could be done" without it; it points "to the importance of the workshop theory in Fitzgerald's career as a writer: he used the popular magazines to experiment with subjects, themes, and characters that he planned to use later."

G492.   Manning, Margaret.   "No Rest for Fitzgerald," Boston Globe, February 1, 1979, p. 20.
"Publishing these stories does nothing for Fitzgerald's reputation. They haven't been collected before because in spite of the Fitzgerald publishing bonanza of the '50s, '60s and '70s they aren't very good."

G493.   Marder, Dan.   Review of The Price Was High, Tulsa World, May 13, 1979, Sec. F, p. 3.
"The women in these stories struggle to make something of themselves in a man's world, unlike the women in his novels who tend to destroy Fitzgerald's romantically idealistic men."

G494.   Middleton, Harry.   "The Last of All Scott Fitzgerald Had to Say," Figaro (New Orleans), June 25, 1979, p. 35.
"More of these stories are memorable than not, and all of them are still a pleasure to read...."

G495.   Milazzo, Lee.   "F. Scott Fitzgerald: He Truly Wrote to Live," Dallas Morning News, February 25, 1979, p. 4G.
Descriptive review: "Readers browsing through the nearly 800 pages will find both genuine nuggets and fool's gold."

G496.   Milicia, Joe.   Review of The Price Was High, Studies in Short Fiction, 17 (Winter 1980), 87–88.
"Early or late, the great majority of the stories in this volume share with the most popular Fitzgerald short fiction his gift of style and his inventive ways of expressing self-pity—with the whimsy, lyrical mournfulness, not-quite-dry detachment, or other strategies so distinctive of this writer."

G497.   Mintz, Phil.   "Fitzgerald's Potboilers," Newsday (Garden City, NY), March 18, 1979, "Ideas" Section, p. 18.
"Even the worst have their redeeming moments, and they are all infused with Fitzgerald's unmistakable style."

G498.   Mysak, Joe.   "American Writers of the 20's and 30's— Yet Another Fitzgerald Book," Columbia Spectator (Columbia University), February 13, 1979, p. 5.
"These stories may not be 100-proof old Fitzgerald, but they are much better than much of the goods being sold today. In short, if you have an interest in fiction writing, it would do well for you to read some of these stories."

G499. Noland, Thomas. "Fitzgerald's Short Stories—Writer Paid the Price," Anniston (Ala.) *Star*, February 18, 1979, Sec. L, p. 2.

"Clearly, ordinary standards of literary merit should not be applied to this volume. These laboratory pieces hold one's interest not because they are much in themselves, but because their inventor combined, refined and molded them into one great discovery."

G500. Olsen, Carol. Review of *The Price Was High*, *Arizona Republic* (Phoenix), January 21, 1979, p. N–8.

Brief descriptive review.

G501. Peabody, Richard. Review of *The Price Was High*, *Washington Book Review* (Washington, D.C.), 1 (May 1979), 16.

"Every glimmer of talent in these stories is a reminder of how good Fitzgerald was."

G502. Pintarich, Paul. "Writing Good For Study—Stories By Fitzgerald Prove Disappointing," Portland *Sunday Oregonian*, February 18, 1979, p. D4.

"While these stories—with exceptions—are not to be read at one sitting, since they tend to be repetitious and boring in too strong a dose, they should be studied for insights into Fitzgerald's style."

G503. Powell, Larry. "Scott Fitzgerald: The Other Stories," Savannah *News-Press*, June 3, 1979, p. 5G.

"They are worth reading because, while they vary in their attraction, they show what Fitzgerald was doing when they were written and sold, because they show glimpses of Fitzgerald at his best, and because, like all of Fitzgerald's work, they illuminate the author's times and his concerns."

G504. Rollings, Alane. "Fitzgerald Wrote Them For Money," Chicago *Sunday Sun-Times*, January 21, 1979, "Show" Section, p. 8.

"What is in these stories is what he called 'the extra I had,' and if they are not always Fitzgerald at his white-hot best, that's the price we have to pay, but for us it's not too high."

G505. Seib, Philip. "Fitzgerald: Fine Even at His Worst," Dallas *Times-Herald*, January 28, 1979, p. 4-G.

"Although most of the stories in this new collection cannot be considered good enough to include in a volume of Fitzgerald's best work, running throughout them is the brilliant phrasing and understated humanism that distinguishes Fitzgerald's writing."

G506. Sermon, Charles. "Last of Fitzgerald Is Notable But Not Best," *The State* (Columbia, S.C.), January 28, 1979, p. 4-E.

F's "craft, his intelligence, his sensitivity and his descriptive powers shine through even the trite stories in this collection."

G507.   Staley, Thomas F.   Review of *The Price Was High, Tulsa Home & Garden*, 3 (May 1979), 72–73.

When "judged against the contemporary competition," these stories "probably would hold up well, because you see in them the occasional turn of phrase, momentary insight, clarity of character, and imaginative depth that Fitzgerald's more important work always reveals."

G508.   Stiles, Lehman.   "Fitzgerald Stories a Curious Mix," *The Gamecock* (University of South Carolina, Columbia), March 2, 1979, p. 14.

"This volume of Fitzgerald's uncollected magazine stories is interesting in two respects: the evidences of the true nature of the creative process conveyed by Fitzgerald's own notes and the stories themselves."

G509.   Tavernier-Courbin, Jacqueline.   Review of *The Price Was High*, *Library Journal*, 104 (January 15, 1979), 210.

"A valuable addition to the Fitzgerald canon for the scholar; the casual reader will also enjoy them for they are well written and entertaining."

G510.   Thomas, Phil.   "F. Scott Fitzgerald Wrote For Money," Omaha *Sunday World-Herald*, March 25, 1979, Magazine, p. 38.

"If not the best Fitzgerald was capable of, many of the stories here are far better than the best efforts of lesser authors. Fitzgerald was a fine writer, and even though these stories were written to bring in some money they still show flashes of the author's genius." This AP syndicated review also appeared in Asheville (N.C.) *Citizen-Times*, March 25, 1979, p. 5L; Wichita Falls (Tex.) *Times*, July 29, 1979, Magazine, p. 22; Charlottesville (Va.) *Daily Progress*, March 25, 1979, p. E–4.

G511.   Vogel, Jim.   "Bad Collection of Fitzgerald Not Too Bad," Memphis *Press-Scimitar*, March 17, 1979, p. 8.

"None of these has a tremendous impact that enlightens and improves the mind, but most are at least entertaining. About half are worth reading."

G512.   Williams, Paul.   " 'The Price Was High'—Will Appeal to Scholars and Fitzgerald Lovers," *The Patriot Ledger* (Quincy, Mass.), February 23, 1979, "Limelight" Section, p. 19.

"The moods, the settings, the characters, the elan and the style are Fitzgerald's trademark. Therein lies the appeal of this book for scholars, freaks and lovers. There should be enough of them to make this book pay."

G513.   Wilson, Leon.   "Wildly Uneven Fitzgerald Tales," San Francisco *Sunday Examiner & Chronicle*, February 11, 1979, "This World" Section, p. 53.

"Even the 'lousy' stories...are worth reading, even aloud, because they have his instantly recognizable style."

G514.   Wukas, Mark.   "Scott's Shorts—Leftovers Need Salt, Pepper," *The Daily Illini* (University of Illinois, Champaign-Urbana), March 31, 1979, "Spectrum" Section, p. 9.

"The 50 stories in this collection might have been more accurately titled *The Worst of F. Scott Fitzgerald*. But even at his worst, *The Price Was High* proves that Fitzgerald is still among America's most talented writers."

G515.   Yardley, Jonathan.   "'New' Fitzgerald: Shining Moments at a High Cost," Washington (D.C.) *Sunday Star*, February 4, 1979, pp. E–1, E–8.

"Whatever his opinion of their merits, Fitzgerald wrote these stories for publication; they are part of the record, and they have to be dealt with by anyone seriously interested in Fitzgerald's work. It is vastly more convenient to have them in a single volume than to chase after them in library microfilms; that is reason enough to be grateful for this book." This review also appeared in Miami (Fla.) *Herald*, February 4, 1979, p. 7-E.

English Edition
(1979)

G516.   Anonymous.   Review of *The Price Was High*, *Harpers and Queen*, October 1979, p. 276.

Brief review: "A steep price, but an unexpectedly fat book."

————.   Review of *The Price Was High*, *Queen's Quarterly*, 86 (Winter 1979/80), 739.

"The stories in *The Price Was High* are not the author's best work, but it is good to have them in book form." See G457.

G517.   Blythe, Ronald.   "Fitzgerald's Dream-Men," *The Listener*, 102 (November 15, 1979), 685–686.

"Reading him in bulk, reading the dozen fine things, and the masses of plot and dialogue that he could never have wanted to write, his professional slog and inspired hours are, in this context, equally intriguing from our point of view."

G518.   Burgess, Anthony.   "Dollars and Dolours," *The Observer* (London), December 2, 1979, p. 36.
"It is the good writing here that is likely to infuriate the reader more than the slick pert plots. Fitzgerald should have been getting on with his novels, not wasting his talent on sub-literary prostitution." This review also appeared in *The Critic*, 38 (April 1980), 2–4.

G519.   Hill, Barry.   "Domestic Chronicles and Crass Regurgitations," *National Times* (Sydney, Australia), July 13, 1980, p. 47.
There are "no masterpieces here"; of "greater interest are the stories which relate to the novels."

G520.   Keates, Jonathan.   "Fitzgerald's Leftovers," *Literary Review*, No. 3 (November 2–15, 1979), 8–9.
Whatever the stories "may not confirm or reinforce in our judgments on the case of F. Scott Fitzgerald, their implied criticism of the mechanics of a vanished American fiction market is an effective poison to nostalgia. We may as well use our rejects, near-misses and distinguished failures for lighting the stove in the garret."

G521.   Lothian, Andrew.   Review of *The Price Was High*, *Blackwood's Magazine*, 327 (May 1980), 399–400.
"By and large, these are extremely enjoyable stories in which, with considerable lightness of touch, Fitzgerald wrings the changes on some of his favourite themes."

G522.   McNeil, Helen.   "Dream Factory," *New Statesman*, n.s. 98 (October 5, 1979), 520.
"Even in these dregs Fitzgerald could not write an ugly sentence. Indeed, the worse the story the more striking its distinctively modern disjunction between a self-sustaining authentic language and a plot that cries out to be disbelieved."

G523.   Pye, Michael.   "Short Stories—Autopsy on Fitzgerald," *Now!*, 2 (September 21, 1979), 105.
"Fitzgerald wanted to lose these stories....His skills and gloss and colour cannot mask the fact that he was absolutely right."

G524.   Reynolds, Stanley.   "Cracked Up, Still Tops," *New Society*, 50 (October 4, 1979), 32.
Volume is "a valuable book, marred by little errors in editing."

G525.   ———.   "Good Times, Bad Times," *Manchester Guardian*, November 21, 1979, p. 16.
Stories, "for all their clockwork movements of plot, are still Fitzgerald's stories, and if only a few of them are first rate, then most of them are marvellously, fantastically, superbly, second-rate." This re-

view also appeared in *Manchester Guardian Weekly*, December 9, 1979, p. 20.

CORRESPONDENCE OF F. SCOTT FITZGERALD
(1980)

G526.   Anonymous.   Review of *Correspondence of F. Scott Fitzgerald, Choice*, 18 (October 1980), 244.

"This large, engrossing volume fills a definite need in Fitzgerald scholarship and will prove interesting to Fitzgerald buffs and useful to scholars."

G527.   ———.   Review of *Correspondence of F. Scott Fitzgerald, Kirkus*, 48 (February 1, 1980), 179.

"As is frequently the case with a mop-up collection of previously unpublished letters, this one is heavy on the money matters, light on 'significant' aesthetic documents....No matter: the letters between Scott and Zelda are what is extraordinary here."

G528.   ———.   Review of *Correspondence of F. Scott Fitzgerald, Oregon Journal* (Portland), June 21, 1980, p. 13.

There is "nothing" in this collection "that will enhance Fitzgerald's reputation. His letters are not very riveting, his spelling atrocious, and his whining about his finances and health is interminable."

G529.   ———.   Review of *Correspondence of F. Scott Fitzgerald, Sewanee Review*, 89 (January-March 1981), xxxi.

Very brief review. Volume is "large and carefully edited."

G530.   Adams, Jack.   "Letters Reveal More Intimacies of Fitzgerald," *Indianapolis News*, April 26, 1980, "Free Time" Section, p. 22.

"The book is an important contribution to literary history. It should be of great interest to general readers of personal memoirs as well as to students, teachers and critics."

G531.   Baker, Mary M.   "Another Year, Another Book on Fitzgerald," *Wilmington* (Del.) *Sunday News Journal*, June 1, 1980, Sec. H, p. 6.

"Bruccoli proves magnificently that when you're dealing with a prolific letter writer like Fitzgerald, all you have to do is set his letters down in chronological order and they'll tell his life story better than most biographies could."

G532.   B[arkham], J[ohn]. "F. Scott Fitzgerald—The Man and His Legend," Youngstown *Vindicator*, June 1, 1980, p. B–8.
"These letters are the nearest we will ever come to a Fitzgerald autobiography." They are "a major addition to Fitzgerald scholarship."

G533.   Barrow, Craig. Review of *Correspondence of F. Scott Fitzgerald*, Chattanooga *Times*, August 16, 1980, p. B4.
"The portrait of the relationship of Scott and Zelda Fitzgerald that the letters provide is fascinating."

G534.   Boozer, William. "One of America's Most Gifted Writers—Letters Chronicle Fitzgerald's Rise, Fall," Nashville *Banner*, July 5, 1980, p. 5.
Descriptive favorable review.

G535.   Boulton, Richard. "F. Scott Fitzgerald's Letters," Hartford *Courant*, June 29, 1980, p. 6G.
"Except for a handful that have but recently come to light the letters in this volume were not overlooked but undervalued by previous editors....Only several from Zelda...give much rationale to the entire endeavor."

G536.   Brans, Jo. "Notes From the Jazz Age," *Lone Star Book Review* (Dallas), 2 (August 1980), 3, 20.
"For the most part, Fitzgerald's letters are undistinguished." The "best letters" in the volume "are not his at all but hers....as a letter writer, she sings and soars above his arrogant head."

G537.   Brown, Dennis. "Dear Scott, Dear Zelda," St. Louis *Post-Dispatch*, July 20, 1980, p. 4F.
"All told, the volume is yet another significant contribution to the Fitzgerald library. Some of the correspondence is just fun and light banter....But much of it is absorbing and illuminating."

G538.   Bryar [Bryer], Jackson R. "Fitzgerald Letters: Triumph of Form," Richmond (Va.) *Times-Dispatch*, November 23, 1980, p. G–5.
Most of the letters are more valuable "for what they say than for how they say it"; the "major and significant exception" are those exchanged between Scott and Zelda, especially Zelda's letters.

G539.   Cory, James M. "Ecstasy First, Then Agony Ever After," Fort Worth *Star-Telegram*, June 1, 1980, p. 6E.
"The most striking thing about this correspondence is that midway through the volume, the world turns upside down and never ever gets right again."

G540.   *Cowley, Malcolm.   Review of *Correspondence of F. Scott Fitzgerald*, *New Republic*, 182 (April 19, 1980), 30–31.

"The aspect [of the F story] most sharply revealed in this new volume is by no means an undiscovered one, but it has often been underemphasized. Briefly it is the extent to which the Fitzgerald story—whether lived or turned by him into fiction—was a collaboration between Scott and Zelda."

G541.   Davis, Paxton.   Review of *Correspondence of F. Scott Fitzgerald*, Roanoke *Times & World News*, June 15, 1980, p. F–4.

"The stuff on Zelda and her insanity is especially revealing, and adds a new dimension to what one would have thought a tale told once too often."

G542.   Dexter, Bruce.   "New Insights Into Fitzgerald—The Man," San Diego *Union*, June 1, 1980, "Books" Section, pp. 1, 5.

"In the end, more fairly than most of the writing concerned with Fitzgerald, this book gives the man's deepest character, as well as shows the exceptional talent and feelings of Zelda."

G543.   Donnelly, Jerome.   Review of *Correspondence of F. Scott Fitzgerald*, *America*, 143 (September 13, 1980), 122–123.

Although these letters "will probably do little to settle any arguments about who was to blame in the Scott-Zelda disaster or provide the final word on the Hemingway-Fitzgerald relationship," they "do add dramatically to the fullness of our understanding of Fitzgerald's life and the generation he came to symbolize."

G544.   Dorenkamp, John H.   "F. Scott Fitzgerald: A Man Whose Talent and Decline Were the Norm," Worcester *Sunday Telegram*, May 25, 1980, p. 10E.

"The letters are fascinating, and if it has been some time since you have read Fitzgerald (or if you have never read him), you may well find yourself searching out his fictional world to complement the world of fact contained in his correspondence."

G545.   Dwyer, Bill.   "Bill Dwyer's World," Trenton *Trentonian*, April 27, 1980, Editorial and Opinion Section, p. 20.

Descriptive favorable review.

G546.   Garrison, David.   "Letters," *Minnesota Daily* (University of Minnesota, Minneapolis), July 7, 1980, p. 7.

"Reading the letters *by* Fitzgerald is generally a boring, unpleasant task; he seldom writes well and is almost always in a pose. But what saves the book is the inclusion of many letters *to* Fitzgerald, especially those from his wife, Zelda...."

G547.   Gilboy, J. Thomas.   Review of *Correspondence of F. Scott Fitzgerald, Best Sellers*, 40 (October 1980), 258.

"The achievement of this volume of letters is that the editors have selectively included letters *to* Fitzgerald which give an understanding of the characters and concerns of those to whom he wrote." What are "perhaps the most worthwhile letters" are "those to, from and about the literary giants of his generation, either in criticism or praise of his work or theirs."

G548.   Goolrick, Chester.   "'Leftovers' Provide Insight to Fitzgerald," Atlanta *Journal and Constitution*, May 18, 1980, p. 4-E.

"For those who continue to admire Fitzgerald's restless talent, these letters will be a welcome addition to what has become a great body of published correspondence."

G549.   *Hall, Donald.   "Literary Reruns," *Saturday Review*, n.s. 7 (May 1980), 69–71.

The "best writing" in the collection is Zelda's—"and it is good enough to make the volume worth reading for its literary value, and not only its rehearsal of the myth.   If we learn nothing new about F. Scott Fitzgerald or his art, we find in this book some letters of Zelda's that by themselves save this collection from triviality."

G550.   Harris, Roger.   "The Book Shelf—The Final Word on Sad Letters of Scott, Zelda," Newark (N.J.) *Sunday Star-Ledger*, May 4, 1980, Sec. 4, p. 16.

"The addition of the correspondence to Fitzgerald makes this volume doubly important.   The book is magnificent."

G551.   Hillman, Serrell.   Review of *Correspondence of F. Scott Fitzgerald*, Riverside (Calif.) *Press-Enterprise*, June 8, 1980, p. C–4.

"Lots of these letters are plain boring.   The letters *to* Fitzgerald tend to be more boring than those from him, because he wrote better than most people, but even his, generally, aren't much more fun than the letters we write to, or get from, our friends."

G552.   Howland, Bette.   "Beyond Fitzgerald's Legend," Chicago *Tribune*, May 11, 1980, "Book World" Section, pp. 2, 4.

"It is only the personal letters that disappoint—the ones that tell the story everyone knows.   When Fitzgerald talks about his craft he is never disappointing; never hazy; he is always true and clear."

G553.   Hughes, Riley.   Review of *Correspondence of F. Scott Fitzgerald, Columbia*, 60 (December 1980), 30.

Volume contains "words as memorable as any Fitzgerald ever wrote."

G554.   Jaynes, Roger.   "Fitz Footnotes," Milwaukee *Journal*, June 8, 1980, "Lively Arts" Section, p. 5.
"Whether the big volume is worth $25 to anybody but a Fitzgerald collector is debatable."

G555.   Keister, Don A.   "Fitzgerald's Letters Keep Legend Alive," Cleveland *Plain Dealer*, June 22, 1980, p. 31-C.
Descriptive favorable review.

G556.   Kennedy, Joseph Patrick.   "Self-Portrait: Fitzgerald's Letters," Houston *Chronicle*, June 22, 1980, "Zest" Section, p. 36.
"This volume is essential for students of Fitzgerald. It may be perused *ad libidum* or studied completely. Whatever the method, the novel relationship between Scott and Zelda seems proportional to the evidence at hand. The greater the information the greater the incredulity."

G557.   Leon, Philip W.   "Volume Presents Two Faces of Fitzgerald," *The State* (Columbia, S.C.), May 11, 1980, Magazine, p. 10.
"Bruccoli and Duggan have supplied us with a valuable, lively insight into the life of a significant writer who contributed much to the lore of American letters."

G558.   Leonard, John.   "Books of The Times," NY *Times*, April 18, 1980, p. C27.
Volume is "full of punctilio." While the letters "are leaves raked up for the first time," most of them "are dead. The life is in the response from others, from Zelda and John Peale Bishop and Sara Murphy, plus a few reminders of Scott at his best and most vagrant...." This review also appeared in Minneapolis *Tribune*, May 4, 1980, p. 10G; Charlotte *Observer*, June 8, 1980, p. 4F.

G559.   *Makowsky, Veronica A.   "The Lees of Happiness: More Fitzgerald From Bruccoli," *Review*, 3 (1981), 247–263.
Discusses both the content and the editorial policy of the volume, suggesting that the editors left "much chaff with the wheat of Fitzgerald's correspondence...[but] are more judicious in their choice of letters to Fitzgerald." Praises selection of letters from and about Zelda and also briefly discusses other editions of F letters.

G560.   Manning, Margaret.   "Fascinating Fitzgerald Remnants," Boston *Sunday Globe*, April 20, 1980, p. 92.
Collection is "intermittently fascinating, sad, amusing"; but you "have to know a great deal about Fitzgerald to tackle the book and to

appreciate it." The "most moving" part is "the sketching in of the relationship between Scott and Zelda."

G561.   Manola, John E.   Review of *Correspondence of F. Scott Fitzgerald*, Asbury Park (N.J.) *Press*, May 7, 1980, p. B17.

F's "almost atheistic outlook, his expressed belief that life is totally without meaning or purpose, and his antipathy for any meaningful message that might come out of literature reduced his works to thin and superficial stories."

G562.   Mason, Philip A.   "Last Strains of the Jazz Age," Washington (D.C.) *Post*, August 10, 1980, "Book World" Section, pp. 5, 8.

"Both the filling in of the cracks in his literary life and the capturing of his humanity make this fourth collection of Fitzgerald's letters important for those interested in Fitzgerald and the literature of the '20s and '30s."

G563.   Meier, T. K.   Review of *Correspondence of F. Scott Fitzgerald*, *Studies in Short Fiction*, 18 (Spring 1981), 195–196.

"There is much here which illuminates the art and life of Fitzgerald, and he is a writer of such stature as to demand further investigation by the scholar as well as the general reader."

G564.   Merkin, Daphne.   "Life on a Dare," *New Leader*, 63 (May 19, 1980), 5–6.

"There are curious and beguiling things to be found here if one is willing to wade through the picayune details that make up much of the correspondence."

G565.   M[esic], P[enelope].   Review of *Correspondence of F. Scott Fitzgerald*, *The Booklist*, 76 (July 15, 1980), 1650.

"Because these letters give us the unresolved feeling of life, they are valuable humanly as well as for their completeness as a collection."

G566.   Michaelis, David.   "The Fitzgerald Mystique," *Quest/80*, 4 (June 1980), 76–77.

"With letters such as these now available, we can hope that the romantic legend of the Fitzgeralds will be humanized rather than hyped."

G567.   Milazzo, Lee.   "Thoughtful, Gossipy, Heart-Wrenching Fitzgerald Letters," Dallas *Morning News*, April 27, 1980, p. 3G.

Volume "can truly be recommended as one of the key books on the ever-fascinating Fitzgerald."

G568.   Millichap, Joe.   Review of *Correspondence of F. Scott Fitzgerald*, Tulsa *World*, May 25, 1980, Sec. F, p. 4.
"This is a well-edited volume providing considerable information about one of the most interesting of our Modern writers."

G569.   Nolte, William H.   Review of *Correspondence of F. Scott Fitzgerald, American Spectator*, 13 (December 1980), 38–39.
Although the "literary value" of these letters is "slight," "they tell us a great deal about a writer whose life was inextricably mingled with his art." Despite his "great talent, or genius," F was a "failure," because he produced only "two excellent novels and a handful of first-rate stories."

G570.   O'Leary, Theodore M.   "Personal Letters of F. Scott Fitzgerald: An Author's Artistry and Anguish," Kansas City *Star*, May 25, 1980, p. 1G.
"Some of the letters are of only scant interest, but most of them disclose new aspects of one of the most tragic American love stories and put on record revealing words by many distinguished participants in one of the most fertile of American literary periods—the 1920s and 1930s."

G571.   Peterson, Dick.   "Author's Career Documented By Correspondence," Charleston (S.C.) *Evening Post*, June 20, 1980, Sec. C, p. 7.
Descriptive review.

G572.   Spearman, Walter.   "The Literary Lantern," Durham (N.C.) *Sun*, June 14, 1980, p. 14-A.
"Even though too many of the extraneous letters in this new volume are incidental and hardly worth reading, there are bits of heart-breaking drama that come through in the Zelda-Scott correspondence."

G573.   Staley, Thomas F.   Review of *Correspondence of F. Scott Fitzgerald, Tulsa Home & Garden*, 4 (July 1980), 37.
"This extensive collection of letters by Fitzgerald provides a more ample portrait of the artist and offers letter after letter to a whole range of contemporaries, but of special interest in this volume are the letters of Zelda to Scott."

G574.   Stanley, Don.   "Book Review: Scott and Zelda: His Broken Heart, Her Broken Mind," Vancouver *Province*, June 15, 1980, Magazine, p. 13.
"The heart of an otherwise picked-over selection is 85 letters between Scott and Zelda which illuminate both their troubled courtship and the sad later years...."

G575.   Streissguth, Tom.   "The Book Score," Torrance (Calif.) *Daily Breeze*, April 25, 1980, p. E8.

"A landmark achievement—vital, fascinating, and invaluable for the scholar as well as the casual reader."

G576.   [Stuttaford, Genevieve?].   Review of *Correspondence of F. Scott Fitzgerald, Publishers' Weekly*, 217 (February 22, 1980), 98.

"Fitzgerald was not one of the great letter writers—he put his real talent into his fiction—but his letters abound in zest, immediacy and charm, and sometimes in wit."

G577.   Sullivan, Mary Rose.   "F. Scott Fitzgerald: The Dreadful Hemorrhage of Time," *San Diego Magazine*, 32 (July 1980), 77–78.

"There emerges in these letters a man whose self-esteem, along with a quaint sense of decorum and justice, and a desperate determination to find some meaning in the hopeless muddle of his life, survived the battering."

G578.   Tavernier-Courbin, Jacqueline.   Review of *Correspondence of F. Scott Fitzgerald, Library Journal*, 107 (February 15, 1980), 511.

"It constitutes an authoritative and fascinating biography of Scott and it provides massive documentary evidence."

*Vidal, Gore.   "Scott's Case," *NY Review of Books*, 27 (May 1, 1980), 12–20 [13–15].

"If the marvelous letters of Zelda do not make the project absolutely worthwhile, they at least provide some literary pleasure in the course of a correspondence which, on Fitzgerald's side, is pretty depressing." See G414.

Reprinted: Vidal (I355).

G579.   Whelan, Gloria.   "The Ruin of Scott and Zelda," Detroit *Free Press*, July 27, 1980, p. 6G.

"What is new in this volume is Fitzgerald's obsessive need to control the lives of his wife and daughter....The unique value of this book is in the letters written to, as well as by, Fitzgerald. The most memorable of these...are the letters from Zelda."

G580.   Whitman, Alden.   "The Scott-Zelda Letters: Intimacy and Vulnerability," Philadelphia *Inquirer*, April 20, 1980, p. 16-H.

"One thing to make clear about Fitzgerald's letters is that they are not consciously literary....It is this very quality of spontaneity that gives them their special charm. Reading them made me feel as if I were in the company of a wonderfully talented yet terribly vulnerable person."

The glow of his humanity radiates from these letters, and I felt warmed by it."

G581.   Wood, Ralph C.   "Grace in Failure," *Christian Century*, 97 (October 15, 1980), 982–983, 985.

"Much of the minutiae printed here will...be of interest to none but the most slavish devotee. However, this big book is worth reading if only for its stunning documentation of the Zelda and Scott story in all its wrenching tragedy."

G582.   Yardley, Jonathan.   "Fitzgerald: Many 'Orts,' a Few Gems," Washington (D.C.) *Sunday Star*, May 4, 1980, p. D–8.

"With the notable exception of a handful of the letters it publishes, this is a wholly unnecessary book." This review also appeared in Baltimore *News-American*, April 27, 1980, p. 9C; Miami (Fla.) *Herald*, April 27, 1980, p. 7N.

POEMS—1911–1940
(1981)

G583.   Anonymous.   Review of *Poems—1911–1940*, *American Literature*, 53 (January 1982), 757.

Very brief review which praises Dickey's Foreword (I105) and Bruccoli's editing.

G584.   ———.   Review of *Poems—1911–1940*, *Choice*, 19 (February 1982), 764.

"This past master of our prose goes slack when dealing with meter and rhyme, whether for light or serious emotions; the great poetry of, say, the last page of *Gatsby* never surfaces here."

G585.   Dunn, Douglas.   "Courtly Diversions," *Times Literary Supplement* (London), January 29, 1982, p. 101.

"One can hardly avoid the impression that while Fitzgerald possessed a deep and expert appreciation of poetry, its practice was, for him, an incidental and perhaps sentimental pastime."

G586.   Gates, John.   "The Book Stand—F. Scott Fitzgerald Was Bad to Verse," Charlotte *Observer*, October 11, 1981, "Book Week" Section, p. 7F.

"Fitzgerald was not a poet. This volume would never have been published without his reputation and popularity to support it. And yet, it has its moments."

G587.   Harris, Roger.   "Books—Scott in Verse," Newark (N.J.) *Sunday Star-Ledger*, September 20, 1981, "Leisure" Section, p. 20. "What this volume shows is that Fitzgerald has a masterful talent for light verse."

G588.   Lipari, Joseph A.   Review of *Poems—1911–1940*, *Library Journal*, 106 (October 15, 1981), 2032.

"The dedicated and patient Fitzgerald scholar may glean a small insight or two from this collection of juvenilia, song lyrics, personal banter, and doggerel, but clearly whatever interest or value these verses have lies exclusively in who wrote them."

G589.   Locklin, Gerald.   "Fitzgerald: Tender Is the Verse," Los Angeles *Times*, September 27, 1981, "Book Review" Section, p. 8.

"Except for the inspired Gatsby epigraph, quotation from these poems would not serve as an enticement.   The Fitzgerald lapses are too amply on display: silliness, insecurity, sentimentality."

H

Articles about
F. Scott Fitzgerald

This section includes material about Fitzgerald written in English and published in magazines and newspapers. It is arranged chronologically and alphabetically within each year. Anonymous items are listed alphabetically by title. It both updates and supplements Section B of *The Critical Reputation of F. Scott Fitzgerald.* As in the earlier book, less selectivity has been exercised with pieces published during Fitzgerald's lifetime than with those since 1940. In fact, scholarly study of and popular commentary on Fitzgerald has, in the past two decades, reached such proportions that to find every magazine and newspaper article is literally an impossibility. Presumably, no significant essay has been overlooked. In a very few instances, items listed in a bibliography or checklist could not be located for verification and annotation; these are listed without annotation and with an indication of the source of the bibliographical listing.

Reviews of the films made from Fitzgerald's works and of the stage and television adaptations of his fiction are included only when they mention Fitzgerald or the quality of the adaptation or if they are written by a recognizably significant critic, such as Edmund Wilson, Brooks Atkinson, Alexander Woollcott, Robert E. Sherwood, Joseph Wood Krutch, or George Jean Nathan.

Disproportions in the length of the annotations in this section do not, in most cases, reflect an estimate of the relative values of items; rather, longer annotations usually imply difficulty in briefly summarizing an essay's contents.

No attempt has been made to separate out the relatively few items in this section which deal with Zelda Fitzgerald and her writing because most of them relate her work to that of her husband. Anyone wishing to find these pieces can do so by consulting the index.

Articles reprinted in books or periodicals have this fact indicated following the annotation, with appropriate cross-referencing. For general articles which include mention of Fitzgerald, the page numbers of the full article are listed first followed by the pages on Fitzgerald, in brackets.

In several instances, for English-language articles in Japanese periodicals, transliterated journal names and essay titles have been supplied, as the names and titles are in Japanesse in the original.

In listing syndicated or widely reprinted articles in newspapers, no attempt has been made to locate all appearances; nor has there been any effort to verify all that are listed.

1913

H1.   "Tiger Out To-Morrow For First Airing of Year," *Daily Princetonian*, October 21, 1913, p. 3.

Notes that F will make his debut as *Tiger* contributor in October 22, 1913, issue.

1920

H2.   "Author and Leading Man Assist Viola Dana to Great Comedy Success," *Wid's Daily*, August 22, 1920, p. 3.

Review of Metro film, "The Chorus Girl's Romance," adapted from F's "Head and Shoulders," with brief mention of F's reputation as short story writer and of the original F story.

H3.   Butcher, Fanny. "Tabloid Book Review," Chicago *Sunday Tribune*, April 25, 1920, Part 1, p. 9.

Brief paragraph reporting that F "was married last week in New York to Rosalind" and recording several readers' responses to TSOP.

H4.   Collins, Seward B. "Editor's Table," *Nassau Literary Magazine*, 76 (November 1920), 161.

Notes that the first of two poems printed here is F's reaction or response to the other, "Princeton Asleep" by Aiken Reichner, which Reichner sent to F for criticism.

H5.   "Engagements," Montgomery *Journal*, March 28, 1920, p. 14.

Brief announcement of F's engagement to Zelda Sayre.

H6.   Kelley. "'The Chorus Girl's Romance'—Viola Dana in a Most Original Metro Feature," *Dramatic Mirror*, 82 (August 14, 1920), 295.

Review of film adapted from F's "Head and Shoulders": "To F. Scott Fitzgerald, the author of the original story from which the picture was adapted, must be given a large share of the credit for the general merit of the production."

H7.   "Our Writers—F. Scott Fitzgerald," *Christian Science Monitor*, October 6, 1920, p. 12.
Review of F's career to date, including comparison of TSOP with St. John Irvine's *Changing Winds*. "Surely as Fitzgerald goes on to work of a wider scope, he will polish off much of the roughness of his laborings."

H8.   Rosemon, Ethel. "The Chorus Girl's Romance," *Moving Picture Stories*, 16 (October 1, 1920), 6–9.
Scenario adaptation by Percy Heath of F's "Head and Shoulders," adapted by Ethel Rosemon into story form. Also lists cast of film.

H9.   "Storyless Comedy Has Some Effective 'Low' Scenes," *Wid's Daily*, September 5, 1920, p. 25.
Review of Fox film, "The Husband Hunter," adapted from F's "Myra Meets His Family." "The good comedy [in the film] is probably retained...from F. Scott Fitzgerald's original story...."

H10.   "Where Is He Now: No. 23 of a Series of Short Articles About St. Paul Men Who Have Won Fame Elsewhere—F. Scott Fitzgerald, Author," St. Paul *Daily News*, May 2, 1920, Magazine, p. 5.
Short biographical sketch of F who "seems to defy the old adage that there are no shortcuts on the road to Fame."

1921

H11.   Calhoun, Donald. "The Offshore Pirate," *Motion Picture Classic*, 12 (March 1921), 37–41, 76, 80.
"Fictionalized" version of Metro production of F's story.

H12.   Kelley. "'The Offshore Pirate'—Viola Dana in a Amusing Metro Romance," *Dramatic Mirror and Theatre World*, 83 (February 19, 1921), 337.
Review of film adaptation of F's story. "There is always a freshness and originality about the stories of F. Scott Fitzgerald that is most appealing. He doesn't go in for deep psychological development, but his characters ring true and his situations are never less than amusing. He seems the ideal type of story teller for film comedies."

H13.   Lardner, Ring W. "Bathing Made Painless," St. Paul *Sunday Pioneer Press*, October 23, 1921, Second Section, p. 12.
Brief mention of scene in B&D as starting point for essay on bathing.

1922

H14.   Ferri, Roger. "'The Beautiful and Damned,'" *Moving Picture World*, 59 (December 23, 1922), 774–775.

Review of B&D film which includes quite extensive discussion of differences between it and F's novel: "One who read the original story in book form, must admit that the picture is more convincing, more true to life."

H15.   "The New Order of Critical Values—In Which Ten of the Modern Critics of America Are Allowed to Substitute New Laurels For Old," *Vanity Fair*, 18 (April 1922), 40–41.

Heywood Broun, Henry McBride, H. L. Mencken, George Jean Nathan, Burton Rascoe, Paul Rosenfeld, Gilbert Seldes, Deems Taylor, Edmund Wilson, Jr., and Willard Huntington Wright rate various historical and contemporary persons, including F, on a scale from +25 to –25.

H16.   O'Donnell, John. "Fitzgerald Condemns St. Paul Flappers," St. Paul *Daily News*, April 16, 1922, Sec. I, pp. 1, 5.

Interview in which F gives his opinions of midwestern, southern, and eastern flappers.

H17.   Rascoe, Burton. "A Bookman's Day Book," NY *Tribune*, April 30, 1922, p. 6-IV.

Recounts an incident told to him by Frederick A. Stokes about F plucking hairs from Robert Bridges' beard.

H18.   "The Screen—Another Flapper Story," NY *Times*, December 11, 1922, p. 22.

Review of B&D film with some mention of F: "Whether F. Scott Fitzgerald is responsible, or whether those who made his novel, 'The Beautiful and Damned,' into a picture should be held to account, is a question which one unacquainted with the novel is not qualified to answer, but certainly somebody is to blame for a story that fails to satisfy as entertainment and means nothing, and yet fills several reels of film."

1923

H19.   "The Beautiful and Damned," *Moving Picture Stories*, 21 (January 19, 1923), 8–9.

Stills with captions from Warner Brothers production of "The Beautiful and Damned."

H20.   Lardner, Ring.   "In Regards to Geniuses," *Hearst's International*, 43 (May 1923), 28–29 [28].
Passing mention of F as "a prominent writer of the younger set."
Reprinted: Lardner (I216).

H21.   Marsh, Leo A.   "Fay Bainter Due Here in New Play Week of Dec. 14," NY *Morning Telegraph*, November 28, 1923, p. 4.
Brief mention that producer Sam H. Harris has decided to close the touring production of "The Vegetable" in Stamford on December 14, after which F plans to "rewrite the second act."

H22.   "Novelist Flays Drys, Exalting Our Flappers," NY *Daily News*, January 24, 1923, p. 18.
Quotes F's reactions to a raid on a Greenwich Village cabaret in the context of Prohibition and contemporary sexual morality: "'Half the young people who get drunk or go to shady cabarets do so simply because prohibition has made an adventure instead of a disgrace of such parties.'"

H23.   Rascoe, Burton.   "A Bookman's Day Book," NY *Tribune*, March 18, 1923, p. 26-VI.
Recounts Edmund Wilson's stories about F composing impromptu ridiculous songs.

H24.   S[herwood], R[obert] E.   "The Silent Drama," *Life*, 81 (January 11, 1923), 26.
Brief review of B&D film comments on how it differs from F's novel.

H25.   "'The Vegetable' for Holiday at Playhouse," Wilmington (Del.) *Sunday Morning Star*, November 25, 1923, p. 14.
Preview article about play, which opens following night.

H26.   Wilson, B. F.   "F. Scott Fitzgerald on 'Minnie McGluke,'" *Picture-Play*, 19 (October 1923), 83–84, 102.
Interview with F in which he discusses the motion pictures of the day, suggesting that they are made for a hypothetical creature, Minnie McGluke, "'half child, half woman, whose intelligence is just above that of an infant,'" and recommending that young writers and first-rate newspaper men be brought to Hollywood to improve the quality of the scripts. F also discusses his plans for the movie version of TSOP, "Grit" (the movie), and "The Vegetable," as well as his work in progress.

H27.   ———.   "F. Scott Fitzgerald Says: 'All Women Over Thirty-Five Should Be Murdered,'" *Metropolitan Magazine*, 58 (November 1923), 34, 75–76.

Interview in which F comments on flappers, Thackeray's *Henry Esmond*, Middle West girls, and the superiority of men over women. Reprinted (abridged): Bruccoli and Bryer, eds. (I59)

1924

H28.   Beebe, Lucius. "The Younger Generation As They See Themselves—A Short Consideration of the Novels of Four Young American Writers," Boston *Telegram*, April 8, 1924, p. 11.

F is "one of four novelists who have contributed serious material to the literature by which these socially hectic years will eventually be judged." TSOP "is still the standard work on undergraduate life at a great eastern university and will probably remain in unquestioned supremacy as the most brilliant story of its kind ever written in this day and generation." Also discusses Cyril Hume, Percy Marks, and James Gould Cozzens.

H29.   "Earns 31,000 By Pen, Yet Loses Out," Boston *Post*, April 4, 1924, p. 22.

Summary of F's article, "How to Live on 36,000 a Year," in April 5, 1924, *Saturday Evening Post*, concluding that F "came and saw and conquered."

H30.   Review of "Grit," *Film Daily*, 27 (January 6, 1924), 7.

Review of a "crook story that is far from being good even with F. Scott Fitzgerald's name attached to it." F is cited as "author" of this film and reviewer suggests that F's name is being exploited to reach audience.

H31.   Warren, Dale. "An Autumn Harvest of Princeton Books," *Princeton Alumni Weekly*, 25 (December 3, 1924), 217–221 [217, 218].

Passing mention of F as Princeton alumnus who is a novelist and short story writer.

1925

H32.   Broun, Heywood. "It Seems to Me," NY *World*, December 6, 1925, p. 3E.

Brief mention of GG, "a novel which has not yet had half the attention it deserves....It is a tale of the romantic tragedy of success in America, and the thing is done with an extraordinary combination of pace and beauty."

H33.   Lardner, Ring. "The Riviera," *Liberty*, 1 (February 28, 1925), 5, 7.

Brief account of visit with F and Zelda on Riviera which includes

comment that "Mr. Fitzgerald is a novelist and Mrs. Fitzgerald is a novelty."
Reprinted: Lardner (I216).

1926

H34.   Anderson, John.   "The Play," NY *Evening Post*, February 3, 1926, p. 14.
Review of GG play which comments briefly on the failure of the adaptation to capture the irony of F's novel.

H35.   ———.   "Two on the Aisle," NY *Evening Post*, February 6, 1926, Sec. 5, p. 6.
Review of GG play which includes passing mention of F and his novel.

H36.   Atkinson, J. Brooks.   "Drama For Adults—Franz Werfel's Perplexing 'Goat Song' in Colorful Performance—Qualities of 'The Great Gatsby,'" NY *Times*, February 7, 1926, Sec. 7, p. 1.
Review of GG play which includes discussion of the effectiveness of the adaptation: "Owen Davis' dramatization of 'The Great Gatsby' transposes F. Scott Fitzgerald's novel to the stage remarkably well, and retains not only the contours of the story, but the essence of the characterization."

H37.   ———.   "The Play—Careless People and Gatsby," NY *Times*, February 3, 1926, p. 22.
Review of GG play which praises both F's novel and the adaptation: "Both novel and play subordinate the meretricious cleverness inherent in this material to the task of telling a story and keeping the characters in true focus." The play, however, is sometimes "too faithful to the book," with the result that there is "much clumsiness in the ordering of the material, occasional bare spots and frequent confusing shifts of mood."

H38.   B., D. W.   "This American Scene in Vivid Dramatization," Boston *Evening Transcript*, April 2, 1926, p. 6.
Review of NY production of GG play which comments on the realism of the novel as well as the effectiveness of the adaptation: "...beneath its surface glamour as play or, better, as novel, one senses an understanding and a puissant mind at work."

H39.   Barretto, Larry.   "The New Yorker," *The Bookman* (NY), 63 (April 1926), 213–217 [216].
Review of GG play which praises the adaptation but concedes that "the book still remains greater than the play."

H40.   Benchley, Robert. "Drama—Red Meat," *Life*, 5 (March 4, 1926), 21.
Review of GG play. "'The Great Gatsby' keeps to the ironic spirit of the novel with a fidelity seldom found in dramatizations."

H41.   C., O. "The Current Cinema," *New Yorker*, 2 (November 27, 1926), 58.
Review of GG film, "a fairly true adaptation of the book that does not quite come off, but it is enough above the average picture to recommend."

H42.   Carb, David. "Seen on the Stage," *Vogue*, 67 (April 1, 1926), 94–95, 126, 134 [126].
Review of GG play which explains why reviewer felt initially that an adaptation of F's novel could not be successful but now concedes that the "play retains the spirit of the novel and is, besides, a good play."

H43.   Cassidy, Claudia. "Theaters: Backstage Chat at *The Great Gatsby*," *Chicago Journal of Commerce and La Salle Street Journal*, August 21, 1926, p. 10.
Interview with James Rennie who portrays Gatsby in GG play. Rennie reports that F has never seen the play and that Warner Baxter will play Gatsby in the forthcoming film. Also interviews actress who plays Jordan Baker in the film.

H44.   ———. "Theaters—Bori, Charnlee in Traviata," *Chicago Journal of Commerce*, July 29, 1926, p. 14.
Suggests that the stage adaptation of GG extracts "the meat" from the book "without losing a whit of its flavor" and tells the story of the play's "devious route to the stage."

H45.   ———. "Theaters—'Great Gatsby' Is a Great Show," *Chicago Journal of Commerce and La Salle Street Journal*, August 2, 1926, p. 14.
Review of Chicago production of GG play which includes brief discussion of adaptation: "It follows the book just as far as is expedient, then it makes a change or two for dramatic thrill."

H46.   ———. "Theaters—This and That of Theatre Interest," *Chicago Journal of Commerce and La Salle Street Journal*, July 31, 1926, p. 2.
Quotes from F letter to Owen Davis after NY opening of GG play as proof that F approves of adaptation.

H47.   The Conways. "Stage Set," *Town Topics*, 95 (April 1, 1926), 14.
Review of GG play with brief mention of adaptation: "It is a wild

play just as it was a wild story, and if it has not followed the book too closely, for dramatic purposes, it is more than adequate."

H48.   Crolius, Margaret Mann.   "Amusement Notes," Chicago *Daily News*, July 28, 1926, p. 17.
Brief account of how GG came to be adapted for the stage from producer William A. Brady's reading of F's novel through Owen Davis' writing the adaptation.

H49.   D., F.   "Theater—'The Great Gatsby,'" Chicago *Daily Tribune*, August 2, 1926, Part Three, p. 1.
Review of Chicago production of GG play which discusses adaptation at length. "As a dramatization of what Mr. Fitzgerald put into the best of his novels to-date, the piece is as good, I suspect, as any writer for the stage could have devised."

H50.   Dale, Virginia.   "James Rennie Leads Excellent Company in 'Great Gatsby,' First Play of Season," Chicago *Daily Journal*, August 2, 1926, p. 8.
Review of Chicago production of GG play which is primarily a plot summary. Calls adaptation "compact and effective."

H51.   ———.   "Speaking of Plays and Players," Chicago *Daily Journal*, August 14, 1926, p. 6.
Interview with James Rennie, actor portraying Gatsby in GG play, which includes comments on adaptation by Rennie and by Dale.

H52.   Dudley, Bide.   "The Stage—Fitzgerald Not Ill," NY *Evening World*, February 2, 1926, p. 20.
Reports that F cabled Edward H. Wever, a former member of Princeton's Triangle Club now playing Nick in GG play, wishing him good luck, and also that F is not ill, as had been rumored.

H53.   "Elliot Cabot Defends Tom Buchanan—Not a Mucker at All, Just Poor Weakling Deeply in Love With His Wife," NY *Herald/NY Tribune*, April 11, 1926, Sec. VI, p. 2.
Actor playing Tom Buchanan in GG play defends the character.

H54.   G., G. W.   "The Theatre," *New Yorker*, 1 (February 13, 1926), 22–23 [23].
Review of GG play which praises adaptation briefly.

H55.   Gabriel, Gilbert.   "Dramatizing 'The Great Gatsby,'" NY *Sun*, February 3, 1926, p. 16.
Review of GG play which briefly discusses how the play differs from F's novel, suggesting that though the play does differ in some respects it still is faithful to the original.

H56.   "Gatsby on Screen; What We Said," Great Neck (NY) *News*, June 19, 1926, p. 14.
Report on movie adaptation of GG which has begun production at Paramount's Long Island studio.

H57.   "The Great Gatsby," San Francisco *Examiner*, July 11, 1926, p. 7E.
Notes changes made in characters' names for GG film.

H58.   "'Great Gatsby' Is Done Into Drama," NY *Morning Telegraph*, February 3, 1926, p. 3.
Review of GG play which briefly discusses fidelity of adaptation.

H59.   "'The Great Gatsby' Is New Play," Chicago *Herald and Examiner*, August 1, 1926, Part Four, p. 1.
Primarily plot summary of GG play but mentions fidelity of play to F's novel.

H60.   "'Great Gatsby,' New Brady Play, Is Tense Drama," *Journal of Commerce and Commercial Bulletin* (NY), February 3, 1926, p. 22.
Review of GG play which is called a "reasonably good piece of work."

H61.   "'The Great Gatsby' Oozes Sentiment," NY *Commercial*, February 3, 1926, p. 9.
Review of GG play. "Those who read the book will know whether the playwright has adhered closely to the book."

H62.   Hammond, Percy. "'The Great Gatsby' Provides Recreation For the Adult Playgoer," NY *Herald*/NY *Tribune*, February 3, 1926, p. 14.
Review of GG play which praises adaptation as able and skillful.

H63.   ———. "Oddments and Remainders," NY *Herald*/NY *Tribune*, February 14, 1926, Sec. 5, p. 1.
Discusses effectiveness of Davis' adaptation of GG: "Mr. Davis's deft shifting of the book's essential episodes is a marvel of rearrangement and dovetailing.... 'The Great Gatsby' in the theater is at least half as satisfactory an entertainment as it is in the book."

H64.   Ibee. "The Great Gatsby," *Variety*, 81 (February 10, 1926), 26.
Review of GG play which is primarily a plot summary but includes some mention of F's novel and Davis' adaptation.

H65.   Krutch, Joseph Wood.   "Drama—Long Island Sentiment," *The Nation*, 122 (February 24, 1926), 211–212.

Review of GG play which characterizes F as "less the genuine historian of a phase of social development than one of the characteristic phenomena of that development itself, and his books are seen to be little more than documents for the study of the thing which they purport to treat." GG as a novel is a "naive and sentimental story"; Davis' adaptation has "the same elements of popularity as the book."

H66.   Lanigan, Hal W.   "'The Great Gatsby' Almost Bound to Hit," Great Neck (NY) *News*, January 30, 1926, p. 10.

Preview of GG play, about to open on Broadway, which comments briefly on the adaptation and notes that F wrote novel while he lived in Great Neck.

H67.   Leslie, Amy.   "'The Great Gatsby' Is Tragic, Thrilling," Chicago *Daily News*, August 2, 1926, p. 13.

Review of Chicago production of GG play with brief discussion of adaptation: It "brings out the poignant sentiment and melodrama with a violence which the author entirely lacks and needs for the stage."

H68.   "Literary Life in the Cotton Belt," *Brentano's Book Chat*, 5 (May-June 1926), 32–36 [35].

Brief mention of F in article on reading habits of Southerners: F's works are not read but he is known for his and Zelda's antics.

H69.   Mantle, Burns.   "'Great Gatsby' Fine Story Play; 'Matinee Girl' a Dancing Show," NY *Daily News*, February 3, 1926, p. 34.

Review of GG play. "Owen Davis has taken the Scott Fitzgerald story…and made it over into an interesting story play."

H70.   "Mr. Hornblow Goes to the Play," *Theatre Magazine*, 43 (April 1926), 15–16, 18, 64, 66, 72 [64, 66].

Review of GG play. Although it is "billed as a dramatization of a novel by F. Scott Fitzgerald,…previous acquaintance with the novel was by no means necessary for the enjoyment of the audience."

H71.   Nathan, George Jean.   "Judging the Shows," *Judge*, 90 (February 27, 1926), 18–19 [19].

Review of GG play which notes that "a measure of Fitzgerald's literary style—the leading asset of the novel—is missing, but that is something that might have been got into the play only…at the expense of its movement and drama."

H72.   ———. "The Theatre," *American Mercury*, 7 (April 1926), 500–505 [504–505].
Review of GG play. "Davis has made a dramatization which not only safeguards most of the virtues of the novel but which actually, in one instance, improves on the latter."

H73.   ———. "The Week in the Theatre," NY *Morning Telegraph*, February 14, 1926, Sec. 4, pp. 1, 8.
Review of GG play which praises casting—"Of all the dramatized novels before which I have deposited my critical person, none has been peopled with greater accuracy than this one,"—and the fidelity of Davis' adaptation of F's novel.

H74.   Osborn, E. W. "The New Plays—'The Great Gatsby'— 'Little Eyolf,'" NY *Evening World*, February 3, 1926, p. 18.
Review of GG play which comments that the adaptation is fairly faithful: "There are a few compromises of stage conveniences. There are small dramatic re-touchings at the hand of Owen Davis, playwright."

H75.   "Owen Davis' Style Changed in 'Gatsby,'" NY *American*, February 28, 1926, p. M–9.
Interview in which Davis discusses his difficulty in adapting GG because it was "against any training" he'd had "of the theatre," training "in a theatre of sentimentality." He characterizes F's novel as "entirely sophisticated," "sinful, wicked, hard, ironic."

H76.   "Plays and Players," *Town & Country*, 81 (March 1, 1926), 64, 94, 96 [64, 94].
Review of GG play which discusses some of the failures of the adaptation—not establishing "the basic frivolity of the characters," in particular—and concludes that those "who felt Fitzgerald had done something rather genuine in his book will not find 'The Great Gatsby' [as a play]...satisfying."

H77.   "Rennie in Title Role of New Drama," NY *American*, February 3, 1926, p. 10.
Review of GG play which is primarily plot summary but also suggests that the play "satisfactorily" follows F's novel.

H78.   "Rennie Mastered Gatsby From Novel," NY *American*, February 14, 1926, p. M–9.
Interview in which actor playing Gatsby in GG play reveals how his interpretation of the part is based on his reading of F's novel.

H79.   Review of GG play, *Drama Calendar*, 8 (February 15, 1926), 2

In "its dramatic form...it fails to penetrate with understanding and reveal the inner play of motives which propel the story's action. The author [Owen Davis] outlines a dramatic situation, but adds nothing in telling to intensify and interpret it."

H80.   Sargent, Epes. W.   "'The Great Gatsby,'" *Moving Picture World*, 83 (December 4, 1926), 365.

Brief discussion of GG film which also mentions GG play in passing.

H81.   "Sessue Hayakawa—'The Great Gatsby'—Roxy and His Gang," Great Neck (NY) *News*, January 16, 1926, p. 17.

Briefly comments on F's novel, community interest in it, and the stage adaptation which retains "the flavor, atmosphere, and color of the book, keeping the air of mystery and romance around Gatsby."

H82.   Sherwood, R[obert] E.   "The Silent Drama," *Life*, 88 (December 16, 1926), 24.

Review of GG film which is critical of the adaptation which "tried hard to do the right thing" by F's novel.

H83.   Skinner, R. Dana.   "The Play," *Commonweal*, 3 (February 24, 1926), 441–442 [441].

Review of GG play which praises fidelity of the adaptation but does not find the play "very stimulating," criticizing the plot of both play and novel—it "will probably please the sentimentalists, and retard by that much the progress of important drama. Its moral is politely but unquestionably wrong."

H84.   Small, Alex.   "Latin Quarter Notes," Chicago *Daily Tribune* (Paris edition), August 4, 1926, p. 3.

Notes that F and Zelda are in Juan-les-Pins and that F is working on a new novel.

Reprinted: Ford, ed. (I132)

H85.   Stevens, Ashton.   "Complete Hero Gone, Says Stevens—If You Don't Believe It Make the Acquaintance of 'The Great Gatsby,'" Chicago *Herald and Examiner*, August 8, 1926, Drama Section, pp. 1, 3.

Discusses the death of the hero and the preponderance of "bounders" in modern literature, citing the character of Jay Gatsby from the play (with brief mention of F's novel) as an example.

H86.   ———. "Rennie Rings a Real Crime," Chicago *Herald and Examiner*, August 2, 1926, p. 19.
Review of Chicago production of GG play which praises F's novel and the adaptation. "'The Great Gatsby' may not be a great play, but it is a great story that has been translated to the theater by Owen Davis not only with dramatic skill but with a certain literary persuasiveness, and it has been staged cannily and not without art by William A. Brady."

H87.   "Theater News," NY *Sun*, January 25, 1926, p. 20.
Announcement that GG play "will have its first performance to-night in Great Neck. It will open at the Ambassador next week."

H88.   Underhill, Harriette. "On the Screen—'The Great Gatsby,' at Rivoli, Good; 'Flaming Forest,' at Capitol, a Thriller," NY *Herald Tribune*, November 22, 1926, p. 14.
Review of GG film. "Perhaps 'The Great Gatsby' is no better than the book from which it was taken, but we find it much better than the play which Owen Davis built from F. Scott Fitzgerald's story. We never read the novel, but upon inquiring closely as to the temperaments of the persons involved, we find that the characters have been considerably softened."

H89.   "West Egg Not Us," Great Neck (NY) *News*, March 13, 1926, p. 18.
Report on the Great Neck preview and subsequent NY production of GG play which denies that it was inspired in part by Great Neck—"It's unfair of the New York critics to claim that Great Neck bears even the slightest resemblance to West Egg."

H90.   Wilson, Edmund. "Mürger and Wilde on Screen," *New Republic*, 46 (March 24, 1926), 144–145 [145].
Review of GG play which praises the adaptation as "very agreeable entertainment," adapted "adroitly, keeping as much of the original dialogue as possible and filling in the gaps with intelligence and happy invention." Sees F's novel as having "enchantment" and "vitality."

H91.   Woollcott, Alexander. "The Stage—Great Scott," NY *World*, February 3, 1926, p. 13.
Review of GG play which praises Davis' adaptation for having "carried the book over on to the stage with almost the minimum of spilling," adopting the novel's "substance without its sequence," and F's novel as "an engrossing book written with fine art."

1927

H92.   Gray, James. "The World of Art, Books and Drama," St. Paul *Dispatch*, February 7, 1927, p. 15.
Reports that F is in Hollywood taking screen test for possible role in Lois Moran's next film; also mentions F's next novel which reputedly will deal with a young man "not unlike...Richard Loeb" and "will deal with Americans in Europe."

H93.   ————. "The World of Art, Books and Drama," St. Paul *Dispatch*, April 6, 1927, p. 17.
Report on F's NY *World* interview with Harry Salpeter (B98), quoting extensively from F's remarks.

1928

H94.   "Down the Spillway," Baltimore *Sun*, July 27, 1928, p. 10.
Comments on popularity of works of F and Hemingway and conjectures on reasons for their success, what that success indicates, and what will be the future direction of American fiction.

H95.   Lanier, Henry Wysham. "Some Persons of Importance," *Golden Book*, 7 (February 1928), 6, 8, 10, 12 [6].
F "catalogued...mirthful modernity" in TSOP, F&P, B&D, and TJA; but in GG he "showed a disconcerting tendency to break bounds....I don't see how anyone could read that almost grotesque anecdotal little novel without adding somewhat to his comprehension of the emotional possibilities of men and women—and surely that is one of the main reasons for existence of the fiction-writer."

1929

H96.   Bald, Wambly. "La Vie de Boheme (As Lived on the Left Bank)," Chicago *Daily Tribune* and the *Daily News* (Paris edition), December 16, 1929, p. 5.
Interview with F who comments on his proposal for a fund "for indigent authors," money for which would be derived from selling famous writers' autographs for a fee, and on his forthcoming fourth novel.

H97.   "Fitzgerald Back From Riviera; Is Working on Novel," Chicago *Daily Tribune* and the *Daily News* (Paris edition), April 9, 1929, p. 8.
Notes that F has returned to Paris from Nice and reports his com-

ments on the Riviera, expatriates, and events in the U.S.
Reprinted: Ford, ed. (I132)

H98.   "Lenox Hill Players Seen in 'Vegetable'—Fitzgerald Play
Rap Against Man With No Ambition," NY *American*, April 11, 1929,
p. 17.
Descriptive announcement of Lenox Hill Players production of F's
play.

H99.   Stearns, Harold. "Apologia of an Expatriate," *Scribner's
Magazine*, 85 (March 1929), 338–341.
Letter, dated October 1, 1928, from Stearns to F critical of American society and explains why he remains an expatriate.

H100.   Uzzell, Thomas H. "The Story Without a Plot—In 'The
Original Follies Girl' the Fitzgeralds Give a Good Example of the Story
Which Confounds Beginning Writers," *Writer's Digest*, 9 (June 1929),
17–19.
Discussion cites F and Zelda's story as a successful example of a
"story without a plot" and explores its style and subject matter.

1932

H101.   Gray, James. "St. Paul's Family of Writers Have Almost
Scribner's Monopoly," St. Paul *Dispatch*, July 27, 1932, Sec. 1, p. 6.
Appreciation of Zelda's story "A Couple of Nuts," with observation
that there is "a similarity in the work that comes from the two desks in
the Fitzgerald studio."

H102.   "Hopkins Group to Denounce War," Baltimore *Evening
Sun*, November 4, 1932, p. 22.
F listed among speakers to appear at meeting denouncing war and
sponsored by the Johns Hopkins Liberal Club and the Baltimore
District of the National Students' League; F's topic announced as "How
the War Came to Princeton."

H103.   "Noted Author Chooses Suburb of City For Permanent
Home," Baltimore *Post*, November 4, 1932, p. 26.
Recounts reasons why F has chosen to establish residence in
Baltimore—his Maryland ancestry; the beauty of Maryland; Baltimore's achievements in medicine, education, and culture; eminent
Marylanders; the central location of Maryland; Maryland's beaches.

H104.   Pierce, Arthur D. "Recent Books in Review," Camden
(N.J.) *Post*, May 28, 1932, p. 8.
Announcement of forthcoming novel by Zelda, SMTW.

1933

H105. Dobbin, Beatrice D. "Heard About Town—Sculptress and Dancer Becomes Playwright," Baltimore *American*, June 25, 1933, p. 8-SS.
Biographical sketch of Zelda, with mention of SMTW and her stories, on occasion of opening (June 26, 1933) of her play "Scandalabra."

H106. "Fire Damages Home Occupied By Writer," Baltimore *Sun*, June 17, 1933, p. 15.
Short account of fire at La Paix on June 16, 1933.

H107. "Fitzgerald to Speak Today," Baltimore *Sunday Sun*, April 2, 1933, p. 15.
Announces that F will speak this day on the modern theater at the Vagabond Theater.

H108. Gray, James. "First Installment of Fitzgerald Novel Is Disappointment," St. Paul *Dispatch*, December 25, 1933, p. 8.
TITN is a disappointment and is compared here with GG.

H109. Root, Waverly Lewis. "Season's Most Brilliant Book Is Gertrude Stein's Biography," Chicago *Daily Tribune* and the *Daily News* (Paris edition), October 9, 1933, p. 2.
Review notes Stein's comment that F "was the only one of the younger writers who wrote naturally in sentences."
Reprinted: Ford, ed. (I132)

1934

H110. Cowley, Malcolm. "Good Reading," NY *Herald Tribune*, August 17, 1934, p. 11.
GG is included on Cowley's list of books "'that were generously praised, widely read, and deserved all their success, and more.'" F is called "'the poet of the American upper bourgeoisie, the only writer who ever succeeded in surrounding it with glamour.'"

H111. McBride, Mary Margaret. "Looking at Youth," NY *World-Telegram*, June 4, 1934, p. 21.
Interview with F and his daughter who discuss parent-child relationships and the differences between the youth of his generation and hers.

H112. Winsten, Archer. "Jazz Age Priestess Brings Forth Paintings," NY *Post*, April 3, 1934, p. 6.
Account of forthcoming exhibit of Zelda's paintings.

H113.   "Work of a Wife," *Time*, 23 (April 9, 1934), 42, 44.
Review of Zelda's NY painting exhibition—"The work of a brilliant introvert, they were vividly painted, intensely rhythmic."

1936

H114.   Coleman, Albert.   "Aren't We All?" *Esquire*, 5 (June 1936), 6.
Passing mention of F.

1937

H115.   Estcourt, Charles, Jr.   "New York Skylines," Baltimore *Evening Sun*, August 21, 1937, p. 7.
Recounts story told by Hemingway concerning his story "Fifty Grand." He deleted a line from the story because F claimed it was "an old line" he had heard before; but after the story appeared Hemingway realized that he himself had told F the line shortly after writing the story.

1938

H116.   "News of the Stage," NY *Times*, March 9, 1938, p. 21.
Brief mention that Cora Jarrett and Kate Oglebay have adapted TITN for the stage, with "no plans for immediate production."

1939

H117.   Hess, John D.   "Wanger Blends Abruptness With Charm in Personality," *The Dartmouth*, February 11, 1939, pp. 2, 13.
Interview with F and Walter Wanger on occasion of their visit to Dartmouth College in connection with planned motion picture "Winter Carnival."
Reprinted: Hess (H1185).

H118.   "News of the Screen," NY *Times*, February 10, 1939, p. 19.
Brief mention that F is going to Hanover, New Hampshire, to attend the Dartmouth Winter Carnival in preparation for writing the screenplay of "Winter Carnival."

1940

H119. "F. Scott Fitzgerald, Novelist, Dies—Heart Attack Fatal to Former St. Paulite," St. Paul *Pioneer Press*, December 23, 1940, pp. 1, 2.

Syndicated obituary notice, with added material on F's St. Paul background.

1941

H120. Carter, Jane. "Keeping Scott's Memory Green," *Esquire*, 16 (September 1941), 10.

Letter to the Editor which suggests that *Esquire* reprint an F piece at least once a year, observing, "Scott Fitzgerald was both one of the most revered and most maligned writers of our time."

H121. Parreño, Desiderio. "Keeping Scott's Memory Green," *Esquire*, 16 (August 1941), 10.

Letter to the Editor suggesting that "C-U" be published in book form and calling F's death "shockingly tragic" and "an incalculable blow to American letters....Many of us feel that anything that can be done to keep his memory green in the present (of the future we have no doubts) will be worthwhile."

H122. Welsh, Mary. "Is This Just a Subtle Hint?" *Esquire*, 15 (May 1941), 10.

Letter to the Editor: "Your recent editorials have been great—especially that last one on Fitzgerald [B188]."

1944

H123. Wilson, Edmund. "Thoughts on Being Bibliographed," *Princeton University Library Chronicle*, 5 (February 1944), 51–61 [51, 54].

Brief mention of F's premature death which bemoans loss of his influence and expresses sense of work left uncompleted; also notes F's aspiration to be "'one of the greatest writers who have ever lived.'"

1945

H124. Flandrau, Grace. "Fitzgerald Panegyric Inspires Some Queries," St. Paul *Pioneer Press*, September 9, 1945, Magazine, p. 6.

Reply to Lionel Trilling's high praise of F (A618), which criticizes GG and TITN as not worthy of Trilling's estimate.

H125.   Katkov, Norman.   "In Reply to Grace Flandrau—Calls
Fitzgerald 'A Great Writer,' " St. Paul *Pioneer Press*, September 30,
1945, Magazine, p. 8.
Elaborate and enthusiastic defense of F in answer to Flandrau's piece
(H124)

1946

H126.   "Cowan Back to Coast With 4 Pix on Sked," *Variety*, 162
(May 22, 1946), 11.
Announces that Lester Cowan will produce film adaptation of
"Babylon Revisited" in 1946–47.

H127.   " 'Gatsby' Freshened," *Variety*, 162 (May 22, 1946), 23.
Reports that script by Cyril Hume for GG film is finished and that
shooting is to begin the following week.

H128.   "Hy Kraft to Dramatize Scott Fitzgerald Novel," *Variety*,
162 (May 22, 1946), 2.
H. S. Kraft has acquired "sole dramatic rights" to LT which he plans
to adapt "in play form for Broadway production, completing the novel
at the same time."

H129.   "Knox Set for Lead in New RKO Film," NY *Times*, July
13, 1946, p. 12.
Brief report that David O. Selznick has acquired film rights to TITN
which he plans as "a probable vehicle for Dorothy McGuire."

H130.   Nathan, Paul S.   "Books Into Films," *Publishers'
Weekly*, 150 (October 26, 1946), 2491.
Passing mention that film censor's office has urged Paramount to
abandon GG film because of the "story's 'low moral tone.' "

H131.   ———.   "Books Into Films," *Publishers' Weekly*, 150
(November 23, 1946), 2932.
Gives censor's office's defense in GG film controversy. See H130.

1947

H132.   Brady, Thomas F.   "Redgrave Sought by RKO for
Picture," NY *Times*, February 28, 1947, p. 27.
Brief mention that Jennifer Jones will star in TITN film.

H133.   Calta, Louis.   "Premiere Tonight for 'It Takes Two,' "
NY *Times*, February 3, 1947, p. 23.

Reports that Martin Gabel has bought H. S. Kraft's stage adaptation of LT and that there is "a chance that the producer-director's wife, Arlene Francis, may be starred in it."

H134. Poore, Charles. "Books of the Times," NY *Times*, August 1, 1947, p. 15.

Review of Philip Van Doren Stern's anthology *Travelers in Time* which reprints F's "The Curious Case of Benjamin Button" which is called "as fresh and entertaining as when it appeared" in TJA.

1948

H135. "About Town—Hospital Fire Kindles Memory of Fitzgeralds," Minneapolis *Sunday Tribune*, March 14, 1948, Sec. W, p. 2.

Review of F's life and career on occasion of Zelda's death.

H136. Brady, Thomas F. "Nugent Replaces Farrow on Movie," NY *Times*, February 13, 1948, p. 26.

Announcement that Elliott Nugent has replaced John Farrow as director of GG film because "of a disagreement over casting with Richard Maibaum, producer of the picture." F's novel is characterized as depicting the "social aftermath of the first World War."

H137. Engle, William. "The Tragic Fitzgerald Story," Philadelphia *Sunday Bulletin*, June 13, 1948, "American Weekly" Section, pp. 16–17.

Widely syndicated review of F's life inspired by Zelda's death. "It was he who wrote, as no one else has ever written, of 'the jazz age' of the 1920s, peopled by 'the lost generation' and 'all the sad young men.' Over night he rose to fame, and he lived to be forgotten by the people who once idolized him."

H138. "Fire in Carolina Mental Hospital Kills 9 Women," NY *Herald Tribune*, March 12, 1948, p. 3.

Syndicated account of fire which also includes short obituary notice about Zelda.

H139. "9 Women Patients Die in Hospital Fire," NY *Times*, March 12, 1948, p. 33.

Syndicated account, with brief obituary notice of Zelda.

1949

H140. "Assignment in Hollywood," *Good Housekeeping*, 129 (August 1949), 10–11, 160–161 [10].

Review of GG film which comments briefly on F's novel and on the success of the adaptation.

H141.   Brady, Thomas F.   "Lana Turner Set for 'Abiding Vision,'" NY *Times*, February 14, 1949, p. 15.
Announces that F's story "Head and Shoulders" "will be remade by Metro as a talking picture."

H142.   Crowther, Bosley.   "The Screen in Review—'The Great Gatsby,' Based on Novel of F. Scott Fitzgerald, Opens at the Paramount," NY *Times*, July 14, 1949, p. 20.
Review of GG film which centers on the inadequacy of the adaptation and on Alan Ladd's poor portrayal of Gatsby: "Most of the tragic implications and bitter ironies of Mr. Fitzgerald's work have gone by the board in allowing for the generous exhibition of Mr. Ladd."

H143.   Farber, Manny.   "Films," *The Nation*, 169 (August 13, 1949), 162.
Review of GG film with brief mention of F's novel. This "limp translation" of the novel "captures just enough of the original to make it worth your while and rekindle admiration for a wonderful book."
Reprinted: Peary and Shatzkin, eds. (I284)

H144.   Hartung, Philip T.   "George and Jay," *Commonweal*, 50 (July 1, 1949), 295–296 [296].
Review of GG film which comments on F's novel and on why a screen adaptation of it cannot work: "The film lacks the necessary quality of action and seems more like a series of illustrations for the book than a true moving picture."

H145.   Hatch, Robert.   "Movies: Lost Generation," *New Republic*, 121 (July 25, 1949), 22–23 [22].
Review of GG film which includes discussion of F's novel and calls the screen adaptation "a quite literal transposition that manages to lose the whole book."

H146.   Hersey, John.   "Three Memorable Books of the Past 25 Years—'My Candidates,'" *NY Herald Tribune Weekly Book Review*, September 25, 1949, p. 10.
TITN is one of Hersey's three titles. "Besides being a genuinely tragic social commentary," it is "a marvel of construction and development" and a "richer and fuller novel" than GG.

H147.   McCarten, John.   "The Current Cinema—Not So Great Gatsby," *New Yorker*, 25 (July 23, 1949), 69.
Review of GG film which criticizes the adaptation as having boiled the novel down "to a simple description of the pursuit of a blue-blooded matron by a rich clodhopper."

H148. Maibaum, Richard. "The Question They Faced With 'Gatsby': Would Scott Approve?" NY *Daily Compass*, July 8, 1949, p. 19.

Producer and co-author of screenplay of GG film discusses problem of adapting F's novel to the screen, using as a guide the query "Would Scott approve?" and carefully explaining reasons for departing from the novel.

H149. "New Films," *Newsweek*, 34 (August 1, 1949), 64–66 [64].

Review of GG film which notes that the screenplay "follows the original with remarkable fidelity."

H150. "The New Pictures," *Time*, 54 (July 25, 1949), 78–80 [78].

Review of GG film which praises F's novel and suggests that the adaptation "misses many of its opportunities" to be "a fine motion picture....Like most second-rate copies, *Gatsby* captures much of the detail, but defaults on the grand design."

H151. Thurber, James. "Three Memorable Books of the Past 25 Years—'Three Out of All Those Thousands!'" *NY Herald Tribune Weekly Book Review*, September 25, 1949, p. 4.

Thurber includes GG, "one of the brightest American jewels on anybody's shelf."

H152. Voyeur. "The New Films," *Theatre Arts*, 33 (July 1949), 9–10 [9].

Review of GG film which notes that the adaptation preserves "all the clean excellence of the original."

H153. Zunser, Jesse. "New Films—F. Scott Fitzgerald's Classic Comes to Paramount," *Cue*, 18 (July 16, 1949), 19.

Review of GG film which comments on the theme and plot of F's novel and discusses the strengths and weaknesses of the adaptation.

1950

H154. Boal, Sam. "I Tell You True," *Park East*, 10 (December 1950), 18–19, 46–47 [47].

Profile-interview on Hemingway who comments briefly about F.

H155. "Book Notes—Golden Boy," NY *Herald Tribune*, October 18, 1950, p. 27.

Brief announcement of several winter and spring books by or about F.

H156.   Mason, Franklin. "Scott," *Decade of Short Stories*, 10 (Fourth Quarter 1950), 12–15.

Reminiscence of boyhood encounter with F in 1934, when he fell into a drunken sleep over some copies of TITN which Mason, working in the book department of a Baltimore store, had brought to F's house for him to autograph.

H157.   Thompson, Lawrance. Review of *The Disenchanted*, *Princeton Alumni Weekly*, 51 (November 17, 1950), "Good Reading" Supplement, p. 3.

Manley Halliday, "the pathetic hero," is "a fictional projection of F. Scott Fitzgerald. Although the yarn itself covers only one relatively brief sequence of episodes representing the final dipsomaniac degeneration of F. Scott...the flashbacks create an accurate and unflattering illumination of what made F. Scott run." See H163 and H158.

1951

H158.   Benziger, James, and Arthur Mizener. "The Fitzgerald Saga," *Princeton Alumni Weekly*, 51 (February 9, 1951), 3.

Letters to the Editor regarding Parreño's letter and Thompson's reply (H163). Both Benziger and Mizener praise F.

H159.   Gorman, Kathryn. "The Jazz Age and F. Scott Fitzgerald—St. Paul Author Lives Again In Book On an Era," St. Paul *Sunday Pioneer Press*, January 21, 1951, Second News Section, p. 1.

Extensive biographical piece, with emphasis on F's St. Paul ties, on occasion of publication of Mizener's biography (C110).

H160.   McNamara, Ed. "Fitzgerald Magic," *NY Times Book Review*, January 7, 1951, p. 21.

Letter to the Editor which disputes Budd Schulberg's portrait of F in *The Disenchanted* (C139) in light of the six completed chapters and the notes of LT.

H161.   Mayfield, John S. "A Jazz Ager Confesses a Crime," *Autograph Collectors' Journal*, 3 (Summer 1951), 55.

Reminiscence of having received a letter from F, text of which is here reprinted.

Mizener, Arthur. See Benziger (H158).

H162.   Prescott, Orville. "Books of The Times," *NY Times*, January 29, 1951, p. 17.

Overview of F's life and works, as part of a review of Mizener's biography (C110).

H163.   Parreño, Desiderio, and Lawrance Thompson. Letter to the Editor and reply, *Princeton Alumni Weekly*, 51 (January 19, 1951), 5.

Parreño's letter attacks Thompson's assertion that Schulberg's *The Disenchanted* is an accurate portrait of F; in reply, Thompson refers Parreño to Mizener's biography (C110). See Thompson's review of *The Disenchanted* (H157).

H164.   Shanley, J. P. "Krakeur to Offer Bush-Feteke Play," NY *Times*, August 14, 1951, p. 20.

Notes that planned Phoenix Theatre production of "The Vegetable" has been cancelled "due to an uncertainty as to which literary agency was authorized to lease production rights of the Fitzgerald play."

H165.   ———. "Oliver Smith Set to Do Bowles Play," NY *Times*, July 12, 1951, p. 22.

Notes that group of Cleveland Princeton alumni has offered to invest in proposed Hy Kraft stage adaptation of LT, planned for Broadway production in fall of 1951.

H166.   "Studios Warned on Fitzgerald Biography," *Variety*, 181 (February 14, 1951), 2.

Notes that, according to F's daughter, F's biography will not be filmed "without a fight."

H167.   Zolotow, Sam. "'Enemy of the People' Closes Tomorrow," NY *Times*, January 26, 1951, p. 19.

Notes that Dailey Paskman has obtained permission from F estate to produce his dramatization of TSOP.

H168.   ———. "Joan Greenwood Considering Role," NY *Times*, April 11, 1951, p. 35.

Announces that Sol Cornberg will produce Hy Kraft's dramatization of LT in NY.

1952

H169.   Calta, Louis. "'The Brass Ring' to Open Tonight," NY *Times*, April 10, 1952, p. 36.

Announces that "Josephine," Sally Benson's play based on F's Josephine stories, will open on Broadway on October 1, 1952, after tryout runs in New Haven, Boston, and Washington.

H170.   Funke, Lewis. "News and Gossip of the Rialto," NY *Times*, August 17, 1952, Sec. 2, p. 1.

Notes that title of Benson play may be changed from "Josephine" and that casting and rehearsals will begin immediately.

H171.   Shanley, J. P. "New Benson Play Near Completion," NY *Times*, July 26, 1952, p. 9.

Script of Benson's adaptation of Josephine stories is to be given to producer Leonard Key on July 28; play will be set in Chicago just before World War I.

1953

H172.   Carmody, Jay. "The Passing Show—Echoes of Many a Comedy Caught in 'Josephine,'" Washington (D.C.) *Evening Star*, January 13, 1953, p. A–12.

Review of Washington tryout production of Benson play with only passing mention of F stories on which it is based.

H173.   Coe, Richard L. "One on the Aisle—'Josephine' Delights at the Shubert," Washington (D.C.) *Post*, January 13, 1953, p. 14.

Review of Washington tryout production of Benson play which briefly discusses F's stories and the adaptation which retains "only isolated lines and observations."

H174.   Crosland, Phillip F. "'Josephine' Is Nostalgic," Wilmington (Del.) *Journal Every Evening*, January 9, 1953, p. 23.

Review of Wilmington tryout production of Benson play with only passing mention of F's stories.

H175.   Zolotow, Sam. "Miss Cornell Back on Stage Tonight," NY *Times*, December 16, 1953, p. 49.

Notes that Harry D. Squires is considering producing Dailey Paskman's adaptation of TSOP as "a dramatic reading with top names."

1954

H176.   "Cinema—The New Pictures," *Time*, 64 (November 22, 1954), 102, 104–105 [102, 104].

Review of "The Last Time I Saw Paris" film which includes brief criticism of its adaptation of F's "Babylon Revisited."

H177.   Crowther, Bosley. "Screen: 'The Last Time I Saw Paris'—Capitol's Film Inspired by Fitzgerald Story," NY *Times*, November 19, 1954, p. 20.

Review which includes mention of F's story: "Mr. Fitzgerald's cryptic story...has excited the picture-makers into an orgy of turning up the past and constructing a whole lurid flashback on the loving and lushing of the man and his wife before she died." Includes some detail on how adaptation differs from "Babylon Revisited."

H178.   Freeman, Marilla Waite.   "New Films From Books,"
Library Journal, 79 (December 15, 1954), 2438.
Review of "The Last Time I Saw Paris" which includes brief discus-
sion of how adaptation differs from "Babylon Revisited."

H179.   Funke, Lewis.   "Rialto Gossip," NY *Times*, May 30,
1954, Sec. 2, p. 1.
Reports that Wally Cox is negotiating to acquire "The Vegetable"
for summer tour prior to Broadway production; gives plot summary and
production history of F's play.   See A328 & A329.

H180.   Geor.   "Strawhat Reviews—The Last Tycoon," *Variety*,
196 (September 8, 1954), 70.
Review of Woodstock, N.Y., tryout of Hy Kraft stage adaptation of
LT.   Briefly comments on the novel and Kraft's "sparing" adaptation.

H181.   Hartung, Philip T.   "The Screen—Parasites in Paris
Sites," *Commonweal*, 61 (November 26, 1954), 223–224.
Review of "The Last Time I Saw Paris" which comments briefly on
"Babylon Revisited" and on the deviations the screenplay makes from
it, but concludes that the movie "has caught the sweet sad tone of the
original."

H182.   McCarten, John.   "The Current Cinema—Muddled Fitzgerald," *New Yorker*, 30 (December 4, 1954), 227–228.
Review of "The Last Time I Saw Paris" which criticizes the
"heavy-breathing efforts" of the adapters who have "reduced Fitzgerald's tale to a lachrymose shambles....the screen version of the story
plays fast and loose with the content and the style of the original in almost every possible way."

H183.   "New Films," *Newsweek*, 44 (November 22, 1954),
106–107.
Review of "The Last Time I Saw Paris" which calls the adaptation
"the movie corruption of some very good literature."

H184.   Rogow, Lee.   "SR Goes to the Movies—Three From the
Library," *Saturday Review*, 37 (November 20, 1954), 31.
Review of "The Last Time I Saw Paris" which is primarily a comparison of it and "Babylon Revisited" which suggests that the
"transmogrification" of the story to the film has produced "nothing
serviceable."

H185.   Thomas, Anne.   "'President Peepers,'" Boston *Post*, August 22, 1954, Magazine, p. 2.
Brief picture story on summer stock revival of "The Vegetable" starring Wally Cox, TV's Mr. Peepers (see A328 & A329).

H186.   Walsh, Moira.   "Films," *America*, 92 (December 4, 1954), 284–285 [285].
Review of "The Last Time I Saw Paris" which includes brief discussion of "Babylon Revisited" and the adaptation: The film "is a very long and lugubrious movie based on a very short short story by F. Scott Fitzgerald taken out of its context."

1955

H187.   Atkinson, Brooks.   "Theatre: Flirt With Ideas," NY *Times*, October 3, 1955, p. 23.
Review of NY production of Benson's "The Young and Beautiful" which "represents faithfully" F's "puritannical sense of the punishment that sin exacts from gay transgressors."

H188.   Chapman, John.   "'Young and Beautiful' Enjoyable; Lois Smith Is Gifted," NY *Daily News*, October 3, 1955, p. 47.
Review of NY production of Benson play which calls her adaptation of F's stories "skillful" but sees F's original stories as "repetitive."

H189.   Coleman, Robert.   "Robert Coleman's Theatre—Young and Beautiful Recalls Jazz Age," NY *Daily Mirror*, October 4, 1955, p. 8.
Review of NY production of Benson play which briefly discusses adaptation and F.

H190.   "Shows on Broadway," *Variety*, 200 (October 5, 1955), 64, 67.
Review of NY production of Benson play with only passing mention of F and his stories.

H191.   Taylor, Brian.   Review of "The Last Time I Saw Paris," *Films and Filming*, 1 (February 1955), 20.
Review which notes that this film "illustrates just how difficult an author he is to translate successfully to the screen."

1956

H192. Rice, Howard C. "Americans in Paris—Catalogue of an Exhibition—Princeton University Library—May 4–June 30, 1956," *Princeton University Library Chronicle*, 17 (Summer 1956), 191–259 [248–249].
Includes descriptions of a letter from Hemingway to F, a typescript of "Babylon Revisited," and a first edition of SMTW.

H193. "Scott Fitzgerald Heir, Sally Benson Quarrel Over Rival TV Bids," *Variety*, 202 (May 2, 1956), 2.
Reports that Benson and F's daughter are disputing over two TV offers for former's "The Young and Beautiful."

1957

H194. Biggs, John, Jr. "A Few Early Years—Recollections of F. Scott Fitzgerald and Princeton's Literary Past," *The Tiger* (Princeton University), 68 (January 1957), 14, 21.
Reminiscences of Biggs' first meeting with F and their subsequent friendship.

H195. Calta, Louis. "Sillman Reading English Comedy," *NY Times*, November 30, 1957, p. 13.
Reports possible musical version of GG, perhaps to be done by Joseph McCarthy, Victor Wolfson, and George Kleinsinger; and mentions Yale Dramatic Association musical version of GG and Owen Davis play.

H196. Crosby, John. "TV-Radio—'Last Tycoon' a Bit Sketchy," Chicago *Sun-Times*, March 19, 1957, p. 31.
Discusses virtues and defects of LT which were incorporated into Playhouse 90 TV adaptation.

H197. "Fitzgerald Book Issued," *NY Times*, December 1, 1957, p. 13.
Brief squib on publication of AofA.

H198. Godbout, Oscar. "'The Last Tycoon'—Fitzgerald's Novel About Movie Colony Is Readied for 'Playhouse 90' Show," *NY Times*, March 10, 1957, Sec. 2, p. 11.
Quotes Peter Kortner, story editor for Playhouse 90, on job of adapting F's novel for TV, with mention of changes made in F's novel: "'The essence we distilled, as it was with his novel, is in the dramatization of the story of a man with a fantastic drive to create.'"

H199.   Pryor, Thomas M.   "Film Will Depict Scott Fitzgerald,"
NY *Times*, October 5, 1957, p. 9.
Announces plans to film Graham's *Beloved Infidel* (C67).

H200.   S[hanley], J. P.   "TV Review—'Playhouse 90' Offers
Fitzgerald Story," NY *Times*, May 24, 1957, p. 51.
Review of Playhouse 90 TV adaptation of "Winter Dreams" which
briefly describes adaptation and F's story.

H201.   T[orre], M[arie].   "'The Last Tycoon,'" NY *Herald
Tribune*, March 15, 1957, p. 10.
Review of Playhouse 90 TV adaptation of LT which comments
briefly on effectiveness of adaptation.

H202.   Weiler, A. H.   "'Rich Boy' and Other Movie News," NY
Times, November 10, 1957, Sec. 2, p. 5.
Notes that Fred Coe has acquired film rights to F's story which is described as a "character study of a wealthy youth and his inability to con-
summate a decent emotional life."

1958

H203.   Coleman,   Robert.   "Robert   Coleman's   Theatre—
'Disenchanted' Too Artificial," NY *Mirror*, December 5, 1958, p. 35.
Review of "The Disenchanted" on stage which includes brief bio-
graphical discussion of F.

H204.   O'Hara, John.   "Novelist Likes the Film Translation,"
NY *Herald Tribune*, May 18, 1958, Sec. 4, p. 3.
Recounting of unsuccessful attempt in 1936 to buy movie rights to
GG in order to write talking-picture version—the price was quadrupled
as soon as O'Hara indicated his interest. Includes O'Hara's praise for
the silent version of GG.
Reprinted: O'Hara (I279).

H205.   Wisneski, Ken.   "Scott Fitzgerald Wrote 1st Novel at 599
Summit," St. Paul *Dispatch*, November 6, 1958, "Your Neighborhood
North Area" Section, p. 1.
Concerns house where F finished TSOP and its present occupant,
with brief mention of other places in St. Paul where F lived.

1959

H206.   Adams, Richard P.   "Sunrise Out of the Wasteland,"
Tulane Studies in English, 9 (1959), 119–131 [124–125].
Mention of GG in comparison with *The Waste Land* and *The Sun
Also Rises*: the structure of all three works is "a truncated version of the

death-and-rebirth cycle of the fertility myths, of the successful Grail quest, and of the typical pastoral elegy."

H207.   Gelb, Arthur.   "Producer Seeks Political Comedy," NY *Times*, March 16, 1959, p. 26.

Reports that F's daughter plans to write a "musical comedy about grass-roots politics" and mentions in passing that F is portrayed in Schulberg's *The Disenchanted*.

H208.   Higbee, Arthur.   "Golden Era of American Expatriates in Paris," St. Louis *Post-Dispatch*, September 8, 1959, p. 3D.

Brief mention of F in UPI syndicated discussion of American expatriate writers occasioned by exhibit of Sylvia Beach memorabilia at American Cultural Center in Paris.

H209.   Nichols, Lewis.   "In and Out of Books—FSF," *NY Times Book Review*, June 21, 1959, p. 8.

Brief description of the *Fitzgerald Newsletter*.

H210.   Schier, Ernie.   "A Talk With Sheilah Graham—Fitzgerald's 'Beloved Infidel' Explains Why She Wrote Book," Philadelphia *Sunday Bulletin*, March 1, 1959, Sec. 5, p. 8.

Interview with Sheilah Graham who reminisces about F.

H211.   Schumach, Murray.   "Wald Finds Many Knew Them When," NY *Times*, May 21, 1959, p. 36.

Interview with Jerry Wald, producer of film version of *Beloved Infidel* (C67), who discusses mail he has received about F and the film project.

1960

H212.   Nichols, Lewis.   "In and Out of Books—F.S.F.," *NY Times Book Review*, March 13, 1960, p. 8.

Announces publication of 6TJA and reprints lengthy quote from F's daughter's Introduction (C98).

1961

H213.   Archer, Eugene.   "Fitzgerald Story Planned For Film," NY *Times*, February 10, 1961, p. 21.

Announces plan for film of "The Rich Boy" starring Richard Burton and directed by Sidney Lumet, to be filmed in NY in June or July. Briefly discusses F's story, the earlier TV adaptation, and plans for the film version.

H214.   Esterow, Milton.   "Politics Is Topic of New Musical; Show By F. Scott Fitzgerald's Daughter Awaits Libretto," NY *Times*, August 5, 1961, p. 8.

Report of Scottie Fitzgerald Lanahan's completion of music and lyrics for "See How They Run" includes biographical account of her life and mention of F's connection with Triangle Club and "The Vegetable."

H215.   Roney, Betty.   "'You Can Sense It'—Where Dwells the Ghost of F. Scott Fitzgerald," St. Paul *Dispatch*, January 6, 1961, p. 22.

Interview with Alberta Gurtler who occupies apartment where F completed TSOP.

1962

H216.   Boardman, Kathryn.   "Scott Fitzgerald's St. Paul Days Relived," St. Paul *Dispatch*, March 7, 1962, p. 26.

Brief narrative about F's St. Paul years and mention of persons in St. Paul interviewed by Turnbull for his biography (C167). Includes brief remarks by Mr. and Mrs. Norris Jackson, both childhood friends of F.

H216a.   Connolly, Cyril.   "A Fitzgerald Entertainment," London *Sunday Times*, October 21, 1962, p. 32.

Review of Turnbull's *Scott Fitzgerald* (C167) largely composed of a comparison of Turnbull's and Mizener's accounts of F's meeting with Edith Wharton.

H217.   Consuela, Sister Mary, R.D.C.   "Babylon and All-American Boys: A Study of the Dream in Slow Motion," *Notre Dame English Journal*, 1 (No. 2, 1962), 12–13, 19.

Explicates the dreamquest and the cinematic images in "Babylon Revisited." Also includes brief mention of "May Day," "Crazy Sunday," "The Long Way Out," and "The Diamond as Big as the Ritz."

H218.   Crowther, Bosley.   "Screen: 'Tender Is the Night' Opens at 2 Theatres," NY *Times,* January 30, 1962, p. 13.

Review of TITN film which includes brief discussion of adaptation, noting that approximately the first third of the 1951 version of the novel has been cut in the movie.

H219.   "A Fatal Desire to Please," *Time*, 79 (January 26, 1962), 92.

Review of TITN film which calls F's novel "a miracle of literary chic" whose aspects other than style are "sort of a mess," and suggests that the "briars" of the original have been "leaped with resolute skill" by the screenwriter.

H220.   "Fitzgerald Made Simple," *Newsweek*, 59 (January 29, 1962), 81.
Review of TITN film which briefly comments on the lukewarm 1934 reception of F's novel and suggests that the adaptation has made "the main points so clear they have explained the life out of the story."

H221.   Fitzpatrick, Ellen.   "Tender Is the Night," *Films in Review*, 13 (February 1962), 106–107.
Review of TITN film which comments briefly on F's novel and on the failures of the adaptation.

H222.   Frazier, George.   "Show Me a Hero," Boston *Herald*, August 1, 1962, p. 14.
Discussion of Tomkins' *New Yorker* profile of the Murphys (B516) which includes discussion of whether or not Dick Diver is based on Gerald Murphy.

H223.   ————.   "Will the Real Dick Diver...," Boston *Herald*, July 31, 1962, p. 8.
Brief comments on TITN in discussion of Tomkins' *New Yorker* profile of the Murphys (B516).

H224.   Gill, Brendan.   "The Current Cinema—Lower Class, Upper Class," *New Yorker*, 37 (January 27, 1962), 82–84 [83–84].
Review of TITN film which suggests that the adaptation "attempts a likeness and achieves parody."

H225.   Hartung, Philip T.   "The Screen—But Cruel Is the Day," *Commonweal*, 75 (February 2, 1962), 493–495.
Review of TITN film which comments briefly on F's novel and discusses the success of the adaptation.

H226.   Hodgens, R. M.   "Entertainments," *Film Quarterly*, 15 (Spring 1962), 71–72 [72].
Review of TITN film which calls the adaptation "too faithful, too literal, and too tactful."

H227.   Kauffmann, Stanley.   "The Unadaptable Adapted," *New Republic*, 146 (February 12, 1962), 26–27 [26].
Review of TITN film which suggests that F's novel "is impossible to transpose to the screen...because its motion cannot be externalized" and calls this adaptation "a vulgarization."

H228.   Littlejohn, David.   "Fitzgerald's Grand Illusion," *Commonweal*, 76 (May 11, 1962), 168–169.

Review-essay on Turnbull's *Scott Fitzgerald* (C167) which surveys F's life and work, concluding that F's genius "was fully to understand the hopelessness, even the appalling viciousness of the romantic ideal he created."
Reprinted: Littlejohn (I221).

H229.   Taubman, Howard. "The Theatre: 'This Side of Paradise,'" NY *Times*, February 22, 1962, p. 19.
Review of Sydney Sloane's stage adaptation of F's novel which is criticized for its "failure to bend the materials of the novel into dramatic shape."

H230.   Watts, Richard, Jr. "Two on the Aisle—Play Based on Early Fitzgerald," NY *Post*, February 22, 1962, p. 10.
Review of Off-Broadway production of adaptation of TSOP by Sydney Sloane. The "wistful appeal of nostalgia" is its "best feature."

H231.   Wyndham, Francis. "Americans in Europe," *Sight and Sound*, 31 (Spring 1962), 92–93.
Review of TITN film which briefly notes how the movie has "tidied away" the "book's distinction."

1963

H232.   Addison, Eleanor B. "Random Notes—Why Follow the Same Pattern?" Columbus (Ohio) *Dispatch*, October 27, 1963, p. 4C.
Brief memories of a childhood acquaintanceship with Zelda.

H233.   Gould, Jack. "TV: F. Scott Fitzgerald—Robard's [*sic*] Reading of 'The Crack-Up' Is Marred By Cranial Calisthenics on 'Festival,'" NY *Times*, March 7, 1963, p. 8.
Review of local TV program "Festival of the Performing Arts" on which Jason Robards, Jr., read from F's essays.

Graham, Sheilah. See Turnbull (H237).

Mizener, Arthur. See Turnbull (H237).

H234.   Quemada, David V. "The Other Side of Paradise: Satire in F. Scott Fitzgerald," *Silliman Journal*, 10 (Third Quarter 1963), 272–288.
Study of F's use of satire which focuses on TSOP, GG, TITN, and LT and concludes, "Fitzgerald's satire is mixed with romance and served with love and grace."

H235.   "Three Stars Charioted," *The Courier* (Syracuse University Library Associates), 3 (June 1963), 4–7.
Reproduces F inscription to Sinclair Lewis in association copy of TITN.

H236. Tsuboi, Kiyohiko. "Terror in *The Beautiful and Damned*," *Okayama Daigaku Hōkei Tanki Daigakubu Kiyō: Bungaku Renshū*, 4 (December 1963), i-ix.

In English. Examines three scenes of terror in B&D in attempt to show that these scenes and other symbols in the novel suggest "the struggle of Anthony and Gloria to escape from this meaningless world to find a meaning to live" and thus contradict the expressed theme of the novel, "the meaninglessness of life."

H237. Turnbull, Andrew, Arthur Mizener, and Sheilah Graham. "Looking Back on Fitzgerald," *Famous Writers Magazine*, 1 (Winter 1963), 16–18, 44–51.

Reprinted "vignettes" from Turnbull's *Scott Fitzgerald* (C167), Mizener's *The Far Side of Paradise* (C110), and Graham's *Beloved Infidel* (C67).

H238. Yeiser, Frederick. "Total Unrecall," *Dimension: Cincinnati*, 1 (June 1963), 10–14.

Recollections of a personal friendship with F which began at Princeton in 1916 and extended to an encounter on the Riviera in 1924. Also includes discussion of TSOP, B&D, GG, and F's stories, as well as a description of F meeting Philip Barry in 1924.

1964

H239. Farrell, James T. Untitled Article on F, *Literary Times*, 3 (October 1964), 5.

Suggests that TSOP and B&D and F's early life must be considered in any attempt to understand F and his work.

H240. "Fitzgerald's Daughter Visits Area Birthplace," Minneapolis *Star*, October 27, 1964, p. 6C.

Account of F's daughter's visit to her birthplace in St. Paul and to homes of her parents' friends.

H241. Flanagan, Barbara. "Daughter of F. Scott Fitzgerald Visits Author's St. Paul Haunts," Minneapolis *Tribune*, October 27, 1964, pp. 15–16.

Account of F's daughter's visit to St. Paul landmarks associated with her parents.

H242. [Kuehl, John, ed.] "An Early Scott Fitzgerald Rediscovered," Washington (D.C.) *Post*, December 27 1964, p. E5.

Reprinting of Kuehl's comments on F's "The Pierian Springs and the Last Straw" (here reprinted) from Summer 1964 issue of *University* (B588).

H243.   La Barre, Harriet. "Scott's Daughter Scottie," *Cosmopolitan*, 156 (May 1964), 23.
Brief article about F's daughter's current activities and her taste in clothes.

H244.   La Camera, Anthony. "BesTView in Town: 'Dear Scottie' Notes Timely," Boston *Record American*, February 4, 1964, p. 19.
Review of half-hour local TV program based on readings of F's letters to his daughter delivered by actor Farley Granger.

H245.   "Newsmakers—Old School Tie," *Newsweek*, 63 (June 8, 1964), 62.
Brief mention that F's grandson, Tim Lanahan, who "hopes to be a writer," will attend Princeton.

1965

H246.   Beebe, Lucius. "Moriarity's Wonderful Saloon," *American Heritage*, 16 (August 1965), 65–69, 105–106.
Brief mention of F, not "a Moriarity regular." He "put in an occasional appearance" and "did not hold his liquor with the distinguished aplomb…considered necessary…and he was several times asked to take himself elsewhere."

H247.   Blackshear, Helen F. "Mama Sayre, Scott Fitzgerald's Mother-in-Law," *Georgia Review*, 19 (Winter 1965), 465–470.
Memoir of Zelda's mother which focuses on family history and includes Mrs. Sayre's comments on her son-in-law: "'He was a handsome thing, I'll say that for him. But he was not good for my daughter and he gave her things she shouldn't have. He was a selfish man. What he wanted always came first.'"

H248.   Clements, Robert J. "European Literary Scene," *Saturday Review*, 48 (July 17, 1965), 30–31.
Brief mention of first Russian translation of GG and of F's reputation in the Soviet Union.

H249.   Dundy, Elaine. "Some Highly Personal Thoughts on the Ideal Man in Legend, Myth, Literature and History," *Glamour*, 53 (June 1965), 84–85, 140–141, 169 [140–141].
Monroe Stahr is listed as one of several "ideal men" for his "univeral care and concern and perception."

H250. "The Fitzgerald Touch," *Newsweek*, 66 (November 15, 1965) 110.
Interview with and profile of F's daughter, who has just accepted a job covering the Washington social scene for the NY *Times*.
Funke, Lewis. See Hayes (H251).

H251. Hayes, Helen, with Lewis Funke. "A Gift of Joy," *McCall's*, 92 (September 1965), 73–75, 172–180 [173, 174].
Brief mention of F as friend of Charles MacArthur and includes poem F wrote for the MacArthurs' daughter Mary.
Reprinted: Hayes (I173).

H252. Hoffman, Frederick J. "The Scholar-Critic: Trends in Contemporary British and American Literary Study," *Modern Language Quarterly*, 26 (March 1965), 1–15 [5–6, 7].
Brief mentions of F's exploitation by the press and of the corrupt text of GG.

H253. Kauffmann, Stanley. "Literature of the Early Sixties," *Wilson Library Bulletin*, 39 (May 1965), 748–777 [767–770].
Excerpt from *The Great Ideas Today* (I200).

H254. Manning, Robert. "Hemingway in Cuba," *Atlantic Monthly*, 216 (August 1965), 101–108 [103].
Brief mention of Hemingway's jabs at F in *A Moveable Feast*.

H255. Shuttleworth, Jack. "John Held, Jr., and His World," *American Heritage*, 16 (August 1965), 28–31.
Brief mention of encounter with F and Held in NY restaurant.
Reprinted: Shuttleworth (H256).

H256. ————. "The Creation of the Jazz Age—An Editor Who Watched Its Birth Recalls Two of the Era's Foremost Exponents," Detroit *News*, November 29, 1965, p. 4-B.
Reprinting of Shuttleworth's *American Heritage* essay (H255).

1966

H257. Adkinson, R. V. "Novelist as Mythmaker: A View of Scott Fitzgerald," *Revue des Langues Vivantes* (Brussels), 32 (Summer 1966), 413–419.
Discussion of the mythical elements of GG and TITN, with emphasis on Jay Gatsby and Dick Diver, whose permanence as characters "lies in their rôle as representatives and victims of modern human experience."

H258. Angoff, Charles. "Reflections Upon Aspects of American Literature," *Literary Review*, 10 (Autumn 1966), 5–17 [14–15].

Brief suggestion that F is over-rated.

H259.   Calhoun, Lillian.   "Alcoholism Listed, Too—Links
Delinquency, Glandular Upset," Chicago *Sun-Times*, April 16, 1966,
p. 18.
F mentioned very briefly by Dr. F. L. Sullivan of Freeport, Illinois,
as a "'classic case of alcoholism due to hyper-insulinism [too much
insulin].'"

H260.   Doyno, Victor A.   "Patterns in *The Great Gatsby*,"
Modern Fiction Studies, 12 (Winter 1966–67), 415–426.
Study of various patterns in the novel—repetition of dialogue, ges-
ture, detail; juxtaposition of themes; use of analogous scene codas.
Reprinted: Piper, ed. (I286)

H261.   Graham, Sheilah.   "The Education of Lily Sheil,"
London *Sunday Times*, January 30, 1966, pp. 41–42; "What 'College
of One' Taught Me," London *Sunday Times*, February 6, 1966, pp.
42–43.
Excerpts from *College of One* (I159).

H262.   Harper, Gordon Lloyd.   "The Art of Fiction XXXVII—
Saul Bellow—An Interview," *Paris Review*, 36 (Winter 1966), 48–73
[53–54].
Bellow comments on F: "I like Fitzgerald's novels better [than
Hemingway's], but I often feel about Fitzgerald that he couldn't distin-
guish between innocence and social climbing. I am thinking of *The
Great Gatsby*."
Reprinted: Harper (I170).

H263.   Long, Robert Emmet.   "*The Great Gatsby* and the
Tradition of Joseph Conrad—Part II," *Texas Studies in Literature and
Language*, 8 (Fall 1966), 407–422.
Study of the parallels between GG and *Heart of Darkness* and of the
effect of Conrad's tradition—his "romantic interpretation of French
realism"—on F's novel. See F41 for Part I of this essay.

H264.   Mayes, Herbert R.   "Trade Winds," *Saturday Review*, 49
(August 6, 1966), 11.
Brief mention of an unpublished F story, "The Pearl and the Fur."

H265.   Mellard, James M.   "Counterpoint as Technique in *The
Great Gatsby*," *English Journal*, 55 (October 1966), 853–859.
Discussion of juxtapositions of characters, settings, and plot structures in counterpoint as the major technical device in GG, a device employed principally to demonstrate the moral change and ethical growth
of Nick Carraway.

H265a. Mizener, Arthur. Letter to the Editor, *Times Literary Supplement* (London), July 7, 1966, p. 595.

Letter includes copy of Roderick Coup's letter to Cyril Connolly which supports Mizener's version of the F-Wharton encounter.

H266. O'Hara, John. "Eunuchs in the Harem," *Holiday*, 40 (September 1966), 16, 20–21.

Very brief suggestion that Hemingway is being over-punished for his chapter on F in *A Moveable Feast*.

H267. Rice, Cy. "Stage Whispers—Echoes of Dead Reverberate," Milwaukee *Sentinel*, March 2, 1966, Part 3, p. 7.

Mention of Hemingway's treatment of F in *A Moveable Feast* in connection with a discussion of court decision allowing A. E. Hotchner to publish his Hemingway reminiscence-biography.

H268. Richardson, Jim. "Probably Not…—Did Writer Haunt Commodore Bar?" St. Paul *Life*, February 15, 1966, pp. 1, 8.

Account of F's St. Paul associations.

H269. Scheuerle, William H. "'The Valley of Ashes': Fitzgerald's Lost Paradise," *Iowa English Yearbook*, 11 (1966), 55–58.

Examination of the ironic parallel between F's description of "The Valley of Ashes" in GG and Milton's presentation of the Heavenly Muse in the opening prayer of *Paradise Lost*.

H270. "Scott Fitzgerald: Libretto Base," *Variety*, 241 (February 16, 1966), 3, 11.

Announces that composer Dominic Frontiere has acquired rights to B&D and "The Diamond as Big as the Ritz" for "initial presentation as musicals and eventual filming."

H271. Shulman, Robert. "Myth, Mr. Eliot, and the Comic Novel," *Modern Fiction Studies*, 12 (Winter 1966–67), 395–403 [395–399].

The "comic novel" explored here is GG, with *The Waste Land* providing a point of reference. In GG, F originally and comically transformed the "mythic patterns" Eliot "had used to structure and deepen his own *Waste Land*."

H272. Sisk, John P. "F. Scott Fitzgerald's Discovery of Illusion," *Gordon Review*, 10 (Fall 1966), 12–23.

Discussion of F's compulsion to discover illusion, most specifically in "Early Success" and GG, with the latter described as "a conflict of the legendary and historical views of reality."

H273.   Smith, William Jay. "F. Scott Fitzgerald: A Poet's View," *Hollins College Bulletin*, 16 (April 1966), 10–13.
Examination of the poetic qualities of GG.
Reprinted: Smith (I325).

H274.   "St. Paulites Who Made Good—Scott Fitzgerald Hated His St. Paul," St. Paul *Life*, August 17, 1966, pp. 9–10.
Brief biographical sketch which stresses F's residences in St. Paul and the dislike for the city evidenced in his writings.

H275.   Tressin, Deanna. "Toward Understanding," *English Journal*, 55 (December 1966), 1170–1174.
F's "The Freshest Boy" is one of four stories studied through psychological and thematic approaches to their characters and their problems.

H275a.   Turnbull, Andrew. Letter to the Editor, *Times Literary Supplement* (London), September 29, 1966, p. 899.
Turnbull refutes Mizener's version of the F-Wharton meeting partly by quoting a letter to himself from Theodore Chanler.

H276.   Warren, Virginia Lee. "Fitzgerald's Plaza Sheds Its Cobwebs," NY *Times*, December 25, 1966, p. 44.
Brief mention of F's love of the Plaza Hotel and his use of it in his fiction.

H277.   White, William. "Two Versions of F. Scott Fitzgerald's 'Babylon Revisited': A Textual and Bibliographical Study," *Papers of the Bibliographical Society of America*, 60 (Fourth Quarter 1966), 439–452.
List of anthologies reprinting the story and a close examination of the textual variants, the textual errors, and other discrepancies between different versions in an effort to arrive at an accurate text worthy of the story's artistry.

H278.   Wiggins, John R. "Impressions of F. Scott Fitzgerald," Ellsworth (Me.) *American*, December 28, 1966, p. 3.
Interview with Landon Raymond, F's classmate at Princeton and an F collector, who reminisces about F at Princeton and speaks of his F collection.

1967

H279.   Bensky, L. M. Sketch of Zelda Fitzgerald's life, NY *Times Book Review*, August 13, 1967, p. 32.
Brief account of Zelda's life and marriage.

H280.   Bjorkman, Carol.   "Carol," *Women's Wear Daily*, March 10, 1967, p. 6.
Interview with Sheilah Graham who discusses her relationship with F.   See also San Francisco *Sunday Examiner & Chronicle*, March 26, 1967, "Sunday Punch" Section, p. 4.

H281.   Boardman, Kathryn.   "Books—Manchester Advance Sale Brisk at $10 a Copy," St. Paul *Sunday Pioneer Press*, March 26, 1967, TV Tab and Lively Arts Section, p. 21.
Brief announcement of new edition of SMTW.

H282.   ———.   "Books—Manchester's Book Sells First 600,000," St. Paul *Sunday Pioneer Press*, June 11, 1967, TV Tab and Lively Arts Section, p. 25.
Another brief mention of reissue of SMTW.

H283.   Bontemps, Jacques, and Richard Overstreet.   "Measure for Measure: Interview With Joseph Mankiewicz," *Cahiers du Cinema in English*, 18 (February 1967), 28–41 [31].
Quotes Mankiewicz' response to criticism that he tampered with F's screenplay for "Three Comrades": "'I personally have been attacked as if I had spat on the American flag because it happened once that I rewrote some dialogue by F. Scott Fitzgerald.   But indeed it needed it!   The actors, among them Margaret Sullavan, absolutely could not read the lines.   It was very literary dialogue, novelistic dialogue that lacked all the qualities required for screen dialogue.   The latter must be "spoken." Scott Fitzgerald really wrote very bad spoken dialogue.'"

H284.   Burleson, Richard A.   "Color Imagery in GG," *Fitzgerald Newsletter*, No. 39 (Fall 1967), 13–14.
Examination of the color imagery shows that F "uses colors to refer to and heighten the meaning of people, places, and ideas, and that in doing so he makes a somewhat damning commentary on the American dream and the red, white, and blue."

H285.   Burt, Nathaniel.   "Outpost of Sensibility or the Literary Tradition of the Town of Princeton From Annis Stockton to John O'Hara," *Princeton University Library Chronicle*, 28 (Spring 1967), 156–170 [164, 165].
Brief mention of F, with material quoted from Turnbull's biography (C167).

H286.   Bush, Alfred L.   "Literary Landmarks of Princeton," *Princeton University Library Chronicle*, 29 (Autumn 1967), 31–33.
Brief mention of F presentation copy of TSOP.

H287.   Cabau, Jacques. "Reluctant Vogue," *NY Times Book Review*, May 14, 1967, pp. 4, 32, 34, 36 [4, 34].

Mention of F in discussion of reputations of American writers and writing in France; notes current popularity of F's works in France.

H288.   Callaghan, Morley. "Fitzgerald's Paris," *Saturday Review*, 50 (March 11, 1967), 50, 82, 84.

Excerpt from *That Summer in Paris* (C34).

H289.   "Checklist," *Fitzgerald Newsletter*, No. 36 (Winter 1967), 9–10; No. 37 (Spring 1967), 6–7; No. 38 (Summer 1967), 6–10; No. 39 (Fall 1967), 17–18.

Briefly annotated listings of recent material by and about F.

H290.   Cowley, Malcolm. "The Twenties in Montparnasse," *Saturday Review*, 50 (March 11, 1967), 51, 55, 98–101.

Memories of F and others in Paris in the Twenties.

H291.   D'Avanzo, Mario L. "Gatsby and Holden Caulfield," *Fitzgerald Newsletter*, No. 38 (Summer 1967), 4–6.

Examination of reasons for Holden's strong attraction to Gatsby which searches F's novel in order to illuminate Holden's character.

Ellis, James. See Stephens (H325).

H292.   Forrey, Robert. "Negroes in the Fiction of F. Scott Fitzgerald," *Phylon*, 28 (Third Quarter 1967), 293–298.

Traces F's depiction of negroes in his fiction, seeing a development from a racist view initially to a more tolerant one in his later works.

H293.   Foster, Richard. "Fitzgerald's Imagination: A Parable for Criticism," *Minnesota Review*, 7 (Numbers 1 & 2, 1967), 144–156.

Detailed examination of F as a conscious artist, whose "loyalty to the life of his imagination...makes him rare and moving in the role of artist in the twentieth century."

H294.   Friend, James. "In the Footsteps of F. Scott Fitzgerald: The Fictional Strides of Philip Roth," Chicago *Daily News*, August 12, 1967, "Panorama" Section, pp. 8–9.

Compares GG with *Goodbye, Columbus*, in attempt to show that Roth was influenced by F with respect to characters, symbolism, and incidents.

H295.   Gifford, Thomas. "The Fellow Who Went on So About Flappers, Wasn't He?" *Twin Citian*, 10 (October 1967), 20–24.

Biographical piece, with short discussions of TSOP, GG, TITN, and the Pat Hobby stories.

H296.   Gilroy,   Harry.   "Scribner's   Is   Giving   Archives   to Princeton," NY *Times*, March 31, 1967, p. 33.
Mentions that 468 F letters and 1248 F documents are included in archive.

H297.   Graham,   Sheilah.   "College   of   One,"   *NY   Times   Book Review*, April 2, 1967, p. 42.
Letter to the Editor in reply to Morley Callaghan's review of *College of One* (see I159ix).

H298.   Higgins,   George   V.   "F.   Scott   Fitzgerald: A   Reassessment," Boston *Sunday Herald*, March 26, 1967, "Show Guide" Section, p. 18.
Attempt to show the influence of F and GG on Mailer's *An American Dream* and Bourjaily's *The Man Who Knew Kennedy* as indications that F is a "great novelist" whose work deals with universal themes still relevant today.

H299.   Hogan,   William.   "Between the Lines—A Dusting-Off of the Zelda Fitzgerald Novel," San Francisco *Sunday Examiner & Chronicle*, June 18, 1967, "This World" Section, p. 40.
Announcement of forthcoming reissue of SMTW.

H300.   Jenkins,   Dan.   "Life   With   the   Jax   Pack,"   *Sports Illustrated*, 27 (July 10, 1967), 56–62 [61].
Brief mention that the dollhouse F mentions in LT is located on the grounds of the home of sportswear designer Jack Hanson (the house once belonged to Pola Negri).

H301.   Kent,   Beth.   "Fitzgerald—A Ghostly Figure of Another Time," *Twin Citian*, 10 (October 1967), 15–19.
Biographical account centering on F's life in St. Paul and drawn from reminiscences of friends and F letters.

H302.   Koenigsberg,   Richard A.   "F. Scott Fitzgerald: Literature and the Work of Mourning," *American Imago*, 24 (No. 3, 1967), 248–270.
Examines themes in a random sample of thirty F short stories in order to show that F's work "involves the attempt to bring into consciousness his fixation upon his mother, and simultaneously, to dissolve this fixation through the work of mourning."

H303.   La Hood, Marvin J.   "Sensuality and Asceticism in *Tender Is the Night*," *English Record*, 17 (February 1967), 9–12.
Views TITN as F's "masterpiece" and examines the characterization

of Dick, concluding that the "final index of the book's greatness is that in it the modern world is seen as one in which the only possibility is not tragedy but pathos."
Reprinted: La Hood, ed. (I213)

H304.   Lanahan, Scottie. "The Group and I," *McCall's*, 94 (July 1967), 59, 131.
F's daughter's memories of her days at Vassar and results of a twenty-five-year reunion questionnaire filled out by members of her class. Contains only passing mention of F.

H305.   ———. "Scott, Ernest, Arnold and Whoever," *Esquire*, 67 (March 1967), 159.
Tongue-in-cheek Letter to the Editor in which F's daughter responds with mock horror to Arnold Gingrich's characterization of her in an *Esquire* essay (F36) as "'supremely normal.'"

H306.   Light, Paul. "The Light Touch," St. Paul *Pioneer Press*, November 1, 1967, p. 17.
Mention of F's parody newspaper, the *Daily Dirge*, printed for the 1922 Cotillion Club Bad Luck Ball; includes extensive quotation from 1922 *Pioneer Press* story (B52).

H307.   ———. "The Light Touch—Poor Professor," St. Paul *Pioneer Press*, November 8, 1967, p. 17.
Reports that only known copy of the *Daily Dirge*, owned by W. Homer Sweney, will be donated to the Minnesota Historical Society rather than given to Professor Matthew J. Bruccoli, as previously reported (H306).

H308.   Lisca, Peter. "Nick Carraway and the Imagery of Disorder," *Twentieth Century Literature*, 13 (April 1967), 18–28.
Detailed examination of Nick's character and his function as narrator. Through Nick, F is "able to smuggle into the novel weighted descriptions and judgements with which to intensify the contrast between the order and disorder which is the novel's central axis, around which all other major meanings are oriented."

H309.   Long, Robert E[mmet]. "Dreiser and Frederic: The Upstate New York Exile of Dick Diver," *Fitzgerald Newsletter*, No. 37 (Spring 1967), 1–2.
Explores F's choice of the upstate NY region as the site for Dick's eclipse as representative of the character's "final submergence in a money culture, in conditions bleakly materialistic."

H310.   ———. "*Vanity Fair* and the Guest List in GG," *Fitzgerald Newsletter*, No. 38 (Summer 1967), 4.

Notes that F was familiar with Thackeray's comic guest list in
Vanity Fair, "the device which he used with great originality in GG."

H311.   Marsden, Donald. "F and the Princeton Triangle Club,
II," *Fitzgerald Newsletter*, No. 36 (Winter 1967), 1–4.
Brief historical account of the Triangle Club; conjectures on how important a role the Club played in F's decision to attend Princeton. For
Part I of this series, see F42.
Reprinted: Marsden (I246).

H312.   ———. "F and the Triangle Club (III)," *Fitzgerald
Newsletter*, No. 38 (Summer 1967), 1–3.
Partial account of F's first year in the Triangle Club which includes
parts of lyrics F wrote for Triangle Club shows in 1913 and 1914–15.
Reprinted: Marsden (I246).

H313.   ———. "F and the Triangle Club (IV)," *Fitzgerald
Newsletter*, No. 39 (Fall 1967), 8–11.
Brief discussion of "The Girl From 'Lazy J,'" "The Captured
Shadow," and "The Coward" (plays F wrote in St. Paul in the summers
while he was at Princeton), in order to show their similarities with "The
Pursuit of Priscilla," the first Triangle Club show with which F was
connected.
Reprinted: Marsden (I246).

H314.   Nestrick, William V. "F. Scott Fitzgerald's Types and
Narrators," *Revue des Langues Vivantes* (Brussels), 33 (No. 2, 1967),
164–184.
F's major works, GG and TITN, "both deal with the problem of
plucking the essential from the mass of individual idiosyncracies,
stripping the individuals of their faces to reveal the 'queerer' depths,
and justifying the author's own point of view."

H315.   Nichols, Lewis. "Down the Years in Cerfdom," *NY
Times Book Review*, May 7, 1967, pp. 36–37 [37].
Brief mention that Modern Library GG sold "about 700 copies a
year" in the 1930s; while the Scribner Library edition now sells
300,000 a year.

Overstreet, Richard. See Bontemps (H283).

H316.   Randall, John H., III. "Jay Gatsby's Hidden Source of
Wealth," *Modern Fiction Studies*, 13 (Summer 1967), 247–257.
Speculates that Gatsby's business transaction hinted at by Tom in
Chapter VII hotel scene may be more corrupt than bootlegging, suggesting that he may be involved in the Teapot Dome Affair.
Reprinted: Piper, ed. (I286)

H317.   Rice, Cy.   "Fitzmania: Happy Affliction," Milwaukee *Sentinel*, December 13, 1967, Part 3, p. 9.
Interview with and article on F collector Matthew J. Bruccoli; reprints two F inscriptions in presentation copies of TSOP and TITN.

H318.   ———.   "Stage   Whispers—The   Slight   Brigade," Milwaukee *Sentinel*, May 10, 1967, Part 3, p. 7.
Concerns poor treatment of F and his works by his contemporaries, especially Dos Passos, Wilson, Bishop, Millay, and Hemingway.

Richards, Chris. See Richards (H319).

H319.   Richards, Robert, and Chris Richards.   "Feeling in *The Great Gatsby*," *Western Humanities Review*, 21 (Summer 1967), 257–265.
Focus on teaching GG, with an emphasis on the "shifting, fleeting, ambiguous aspects of feeling in the book, presented in terms of time, lyric imagery, and of comedy."

H320.   Saal, Rollene W.   "Pick of the Paperbacks," *Saturday Review*, 50 (June 10, 1967), 46.
Brief paragraph on Southern Illinois University Press' "coup" in reissuing SMTW.

H321.   Sawyer, Paul.   "The   Schedule   in   GG," *Fitzgerald Newsletter*, No. 39 (Fall 1967), 4–8.
The schedule in GG, while it evidences F's lack of complete knowledge of his protagonist—by confirming the inconsistencies in Gatsby's characterization—it is imaginatively consistent with the theme of Gatsby's maturation process.

H322.   Slattery, Sister Margaret P.   "The Function of Time in GG and 'Babylon,'" *Fitzgerald Newsletter*, No. 39 (Fall 1967), 1–4.
A circular time pattern controls the structural design of the two works and functions to underline conflicts within the characters.

H323.   Slevin, James F.   "Water Images in GG," *Fitzgerald Newsletter*, No. 39 (Fall 1967), 12–13.
Motionless water images in the novel are associated with Gatsby's dreams about himself and Daisy; while moving water comes to represent the reality which disturbs and destroys these illusions.

H324.   Spencer, Benjamin T.   "Fitzgerald and the American Ambivalence," *South Atlantic Quarterly*, 66 (Summer 1967), 367–381.
From year to year, as F's own experiences and moods varied, "he shifted accordingly his record and assessment of human aspirations and defeats. Hence the ambivalence of his attitudes...."
Reprinted: Spencer (I331).

H325. Stephens, Robert O., and James Ellis. "Hemingway, Fitzgerald, and the Riddle of 'Henry's Bicycle,'" *English Language Notes*, 5 (September 1967), 46–49.

Cites an F letter to Maxwell Perkins as documentation that the phrase "like Henry's bicycle" in *The Sun Also Rises* alludes to Henry James' impotence. F's condoning Hemingway's allusion and commenting on James underlines the emotional distance between James' and Hemingway's expatriates.

H326. "Talk of the Town," *New Yorker*, 43 (June 17, 1967), 23.

Author muses on a poem by F about one of his flappers upon observing Julie Andrews in front of the Algonquin Hotel.

H327. Tamke, Alexander R. "Abe North as Abe Lincoln in TITN," *Fitzgerald Newsletter*, No. 36 (Winter 1967), 6–7.

Identifies a Ring Lardner-Abe North-Abe Lincoln linkage which indicates that F's parody "was inspired by Lardner's Lincolnesque appearance and manner."

H328. ———. "Basil Duke Lee: The Confederate F. Scott Fitzgerald," *Mississippi Quarterly*, 20 (Fall 1967), 231–233.

Sees F's use of the name Basil Duke Lee as "consciously contrived and entirely appropriate. A romantic echo of the Civil War generals Duke and Lee, it echoes as well the intensely romantic view of life which characterized the young Scott Fitzgerald."

H329. Taylor, Robert. "Gatsby Is Alive and in Boston," *Boston Sunday Globe*, November 5, 1967, "Sunday Magazine" Section, pp. 12–13, 15, 17–18, 20, 22.

Describes a Great Gatsby Ball given in Boston and draws parallels between the party and the novel.

H330. "Tips," *Publishers' Weekly*, 192 (September 25, 1967), 83–89 [84].

Paragraph on success of reissued SMTW.

H331. Trask, David F. "A Note on Fitzgerald's *The Great Gatsby*," *University Review*, 33 (March 1967), 197–202.

Views GG as a general critique of the "American dream" and "agrarian myth" and as "a powerful demonstration of their invalidity for Americans of Fitzgerald's generation and after."

Reprinted: Piper, ed. (I286)

H332. Turnbull, Andrew. "Speaking of Books: Perkins' Three Generals," *NY Times Book Review*, July 16, 1967, pp. 2, 25–27.

Details the interrelationship of F, Hemingway, and Wolfe—principally through Maxwell Perkins—with emphasis on their professional rivalries and on assistance given to F by the others during his decline.

H333. Wilson, Edmund. "Profiles—A Prelude—II—Landscapes, Characters, and Conversations From the Earlier Years of My Life," *New Yorker*, 43 (May 6, 1967), 52–54, 56, 59–60, 62, 64–66, 71–72, 74, 76–78, 81–82, 84, 86–88, 90, 95–96, 98, 100–102, 104, 107–108, 110, 112, 114, 119–120, 122, 124, 126, 129, 132–138, 140–149 [86].

Brief glimpse of F's Catholicism at Princeton and his later loss of it that left him "with nothing at all to sustain his moral standards or to steady him in self-discipline."
Reprinted: Wilson (I378).

H334. ———. "Profiles—A Prelude—III—Landscapes, Characters, and Conversations From the Earlier Years of My Life," *New Yorker*, 43 (May 13, 1967), 54–56, 58, 61–62, 64, 67–68, 70, 73–76, 78, 80, 85–86, 88, 91–93, 96, 98, 101–102, 104, 109–114, 116, 119–122, 125–128, 131–136, 138, 140–154, 157 [58].

Brief mention of reading TSOP and thinking its picture of Princeton "more or less preposterous" and then on later reflection realizing that he had shared F's infatuation with the school.
Reprinted: Wilson (I378).

H335. "Zelda's Book," London *Sunday Telegraph*, September 3, 1967, "Mandrake" Section, p. 5.

Mention of new American edition of SMTW and of forthcoming new English edition, and an account of how the novel came to be written.

1968

H336. "American Notebook: Potpourri," *NY Times Book Review*, February 11, 1968, p. 43.

Brief note on the suspension of the *Fitzgerald Newsletter*.

H337. Anderson, Hilton. "The Rich Bunch in *The Great Gatsby*," *Southern Quarterly*, 6 (January 1968), 163–173.

F was a critic of the rich, "concerned more with the effects of wealth on different individuals than with depicting an era." In GG and his other works, it is apparent that F objects to the rich; but it is also "obvious that he has no solution to offer for the problem other than to present and criticize it."

H338. Astro, Richard. "*Vandover and the Brute* and *The Beautiful and Damned*: A Search For Thematic and Stylistic Reinterpretations," *Modern Fiction Studies*, 14 (Winter 1968–69), 397–413.

Because F based B&D on Norris' novel, by defining the parallels between the two, "fresh insight may be shed on Fitzgerald's work, insight which enables the novel's value to be measured in terms of a new and more satisfying perspective."

H339.   Brockman, Zoe.   "'Save Me the Waltz' Has Become a Collector's Item," Gastonia (N.C.) *Gazette*, May 12, 1968, p. P4.

Description of SMTW and material about F and Zelda drawn primarily from Piper's biography (C128) and from Moore's introduction (I265).

H340.   [Bruccoli, Matthew J.] "The Different Rich Again," *Fitzgerald Newsletter*, No. 40 (Winter 1968), 19.

Notes that a Maxwell Perkins letter to Elizabeth Lemmon which is quoted in Andrew Turnbull's *Thomas Wolfe* indicates that Hemingway made the famous remark about the rich being different in a conversation with Molly Colum.

H341.   ———. "F on Joseph Conrad," *Fitzgerald Newsletter*, No. 40 (Winter 1968), 14.

Reprints F letter to Fanny Butcher of the Chicago *Tribune* in which he expresses admiration for Conrad's *Nostromo*.

H342.   ———. "Ghost," *Fitzgerald Newsletter*, No. 40 (Winter 1968), 18.

The by-line Edward Moore Gresham was not a collaboration of F, John Peale Bishop, and Edmund Wilson while they were at Princeton: "Gresham was Wilson, Bishop, and Alfred Bellinger of Yale."

H343.   ———. "TSOP and B&D Serials," *Fitzgerald Newsletter*, No. 40 (Winter 1968), 14–15.

Notes post-book publication serializations of F's first two novels in NY *Daily News* in 1923.

H344.   "Checklist," *Fitzgerald Newsletter*, No. 40 (Winter 1968), 15–18.

Occasionally annotated listing of recent materials by and about F.

H345.   Cohen, Richard. "The Inessential Houses of *The Great Gatsby*," *Husson Review*, 2 (November 1968), 48–57.

The "inessential houses" F created in GG not only provide settings for the novel but also function symbolically in that "each is representative of the personality, beliefs, character, and social status of the particular individual or individuals who occupy the dwellings."

H346.   Cowley, Malcolm. "American Writers and the First World War," *Proceedings of the American Academy of Arts and Letters*, 2nd series, No. 18 (1968), 25–50 [28–29, 30–31, 34, 35, 38].

Brief discussion of relationship between F and World War I.
Reprinted: Cowley (H347).

H347. ————. "'Apres la guerre finie,'" *Horizon*, 10 (Winter 1968), 112–119 [112, 114, 115, 117].
Reprinting of H346.

H348. Crim, Lottie R., and Neal B. Houston. "The Catalogue of Names in *The Great Gatsby*," *Research Studies*, 36 (June 1968), 113–130.
Examination of the title of the book, the major characters, the minor characters, and Gatsby's guest list in order to study the significance of names in the novel.

H349. DeBold, Betty. "From Flaming Youth to Cheerful Grandma—Star Recalls Films' Golden Age," Columbus (Ohio) *Citizen-Journal*, February 27, 1968, pp. 1, 2.
Interview with silent movie star Colleen Moore who mentions F briefly: "'I absolutely worshipped Scott. He was a nice guy, but his obsession with Zelda was strange. I never understood it....'"

H350. Edenbaum, Robert I. "'Babylon Revisited': A Psychological Note on F. Scott Fitzgerald," *Literature and Psychology*, 18 (No. 1, 1968), 27–29.
Suggests that F misremembered that he had had Charlie Wales leave the Peters' address for Duncan at the Ritz bar. This "slip" indicates F's own "unconscious self-destructive impulse" through "the medium of Charlie Wales."

H351. Foster, Richard. "Mailer and the Fitzgerald Tradition," *Novel*, 1 (Spring 1968), 219–230.
Parallels drawn between F's and Mailer's heroes and between their reactions to the drift of history away from tradition and order "toward anarchy and chaos." For both, "the beauties and ambiguities of the 'American Dream' have been...inescapable motifs."

H352. Gross, Barry. "The Dark Side of Twenty-five: Fitzgerald and *The Beautiful and Damned*," *Bucknell Review*, 16 (December 1968), 40–52.
In B&D, "we are in the presence of an imagination that could not really substantiate what it envisioned yet could not deny the truth of what it saw."

H353. ————. "Newman to Gatsby: This Side of Innocence," *Papers of the Michigan Academy of Science, Arts, and Letters*, 53 (1968), 279–289.
Response to Kermit Vanderbilt's assertion (see B642) that a moral

continuity exists between Gatsby and Christopher Newman of *The American.* Because Gatsby remains, "in spite of everything, on this side of innocence," GG "parts company with *The American.*"

H354.   Gross, Theodore L.   "F. Scott Fitzgerald: The Hero in Retrospect," *South Atlantic Quarterly,* 67 (Winter 1968), 64–77.

Examines the heroes of GG, TITN, and LT, novels in which F presents his stories retrospectively, concluding that F's awareness of those elements that "'will not come again into our time'" and the authority with which he writes "of being a man unable to find grandeur except in memories" give his work its special significance.
Reprinted: Gross (I165).

H355.   Hamblen, Abigail Ann.   "The Fitzgeralds' Coming of Age," *University Review,* 35 (Winter 1968), 157–160.

The painful struggles of F and Zelda's coming of age were depicted in his TSOP and her SMTW and are examined here.

H356.   Hill, John S.   "Henry James: F's Literary Ancestor," *Fitzgerald Newsletter,* No. 40 (Winter 1968), 6–10.

Views GG and *The Ambassadors* "in direct line of descent" in "their revelation that standard old beliefs were disappearing or were dead."

Houston, Neal B. See Crim (H348).

H357.   Kelley, David J. F.   "The Polishing of 'Diamond,'" *Fitzgerald Newsletter,* No. 40 (Winter 1968), 1–2.

Examines the substantive revisions F made in the story between its periodical publication and its collection in TJA as evidence of F's "craftsmanship."

H358.   Lanahan, Frances ("Scottie").   "When I Was Sixteen," *Good Housekeeping,* 167 (October 1968), 100–101.

Brief reminiscence by F's daughter, including an incident with her mother on a segregated bus in North Carolina.

H359.   Long, Robert Emmet.   "B&D: Nathan and Mencken as Maury Noble," *Fitzgerald Newsletter,* No. 40 (Winter 1968), 3–4.

Noble is one of F's composite characters; his "attitudes and prejudices at times suggest H. L. Mencken more strongly" than George Jean Nathan.

H360.   Marsden, Donald.   "F and the Princeton Triangle Club, V," *Fitzgerald Newsletter,* No. 40 (Winter 1968), 11–14.

Plot synopsis of "Assorted Spirits" suggests that F "had continued to explore...the poor rich, the *femme fatale,* and the *homme manque*; and he had begun to explore regional and class antagonisms."
Reprinted: Marsden (I246).

H361.   Natterstad, J. H.   "Fitzgerald's *The Great Gatsby*," *The Explicator*, 26 (April 1968), Item 68.

The opposition in the novel is not so much between East and West as it is "between wealthy, sophisticated urbanized life and its opposite."

H362.   Nolan, William F.   "Papa's Planet," *Playboy*, 15 (April 1968), 131, 182–183.

Humorous fictional fantasy about Hemingway and F set in 2068 on an eccentric millionaire's private planet somewhere in outer space. The planet is populated by robots of Hemingway and his friends, including F.

H363.   O'Hara, John.   "Hello Hollywood Good-Bye," *Holiday*, 43 (May 1968), 54–55, 125–129 [55, 125].

Brief mention of F and of O'Hara having read proof on TITN.

H364.   Rodda, Peter.   *"The Great Gatsby," English Studies in Africa*, 11 (September 1968), 95–126.

General survey which reveals that F harmoniously combines the roles of artist and moralist.

H365.   Schmidt, Paul.   Notes to F's translation of Rimbaud's "Voyelles," *Delos*, No. 2 (1968), 102–103.

Footnotes to F's translation (the original and F's translation appear on pp. 100 and 101, respectively) which are highly critical—in an amusing way—of F's talents as a translator.

H366.   Shroeder, John.   "'Some Unfortunate Idyllic Love Affair': The Legends of Taji and Jay Gatsby," *Books at Brown*, 22 (1968), 143–153.

Exploration of series of parallels between GG and Melville's *Mardi* which suggests possibility that it may have been the source for F's novel.

H367.   Tamke, Alexander R.   "The 'Gat' in *Gatsby*: Neglected Aspect of a Novel," *Modern Fiction Studies*, 14 (Winter 1968–69), 443–445.

Gat is "Prohibition era slang for revolver" and is apparently derived "from the similar appellation of the Gatling gun."

H368.   ———.   "Michaelis in GG: St. Michael in the Valley of Ashes," *Fitzgerald Newsletter*, No. 40 (Winter 1968), 4–5.

Views Michaelis performing three of the four traditional offices of the Biblical St. Michael as well as "playing the part of a kind of intercessor and mediator" who is, ultimately, unsuccessful because "he is but the twentieth-century common-man counterpart of the archangel and cannot triumph over the materialism and irreligion of modern society."

H369.   Tillotson, Dolph.   "Fitzgerald Biography—Miss May-field Writes About Zelda, Scott," Tuscaloosa (Ala.) *News*, April 5, 1968, "Fun" Section, p. 10.
Interview with Sara Mayfield who speaks of her friendship with Scott and Zelda and of her forthcoming book (I252).

H370.   Wadden, Anthony T.   "J. Hyatt Downing: The Chronicle of an Era," *Books at Iowa*, 8 (April 1968), 11–23 [11, 15].
Brief mention of Downing's correspondence with F and his friendship with F in St. Paul.

H371.   Young, Philip.   "Scott Fitzgerald on His Thirtieth Birthday Sends a Small Gift to Ernest Hemingway," *Modern Fiction Studies*, 14 (Summer 1968), 229–230.
The gift is a letter in which F parodies some of the sketches of *In Our Time*.

1969

H372.   Bahrenburg, Bruce.   "Fitzgerald's Princeton," Newark (N.J.) *Sunday News*, January 19, 1969, Magazine, pp. 4–10, 14–15.
Short essay on F and Princeton, illustrated by many photographs captioned with F quotations.

H373.   ———.   "'Jazz Age' Historian," Newark (N.J.) *Sunday News*, January 19, 1969, Magazine, p. 12.
Brief biographical sketch.

H374.   Bolton, Whitney.   "Theater—A Long Lost Story Is Found—Wanting," NY *Morning Telegraph*, August 21, 1969, p. 3.
Comments on "Dearly Beloved," reminiscences of F in Hollywood, and remarks about F's relationship with Hemingway.

H375.   Boyle, Thomas E.   "Unreliable Narration in *The Great Gatsby*," *Bulletin of the Rocky Mountain Modern Language Association*, 23 (March 1969), 21–26.
Calls Nick "shallow, confused, hypocritical, and immoral" and tries "to see Nick's unreliability as an integral part of the book by finding ways in which norms of the novel are conveyed independent of and in contradiction to the explanations Carraway offers."

H376.   Bufkin, E. C.   "A Pattern of Parallel and Double: The Function of Myrtle in *The Great Gatsby*," *Modern Fiction Studies*, 15 (Winter 1969–70), 517–524.
Parallels cited include age and conduct, relationship to the Buchanans, unrealistic outlook, and yearnings toward a higher world; Myrtle is "the device by which...we can truly gauge and evaluate"

Gatsby's greatness, for she is the road he has not taken.

H377.   Burhans, Clinton S., Jr.   "'Magnificently Attune to Life': The Value of 'Winter Dreams,'" *Studies in Short Fiction*, 6 (Summer 1969), 401–412.
Stresses differences between Dexter and Jay Gatsby: Dexter's dreams are "mundane and specific" and Judy Jones "is *part* of" his dreams; Daisy is "the *incarnation* of Gatsby's dreams."

H378.   ————.   "Structure and Theme in *This Side of Paradise*," *Journal of English and Germanic Philology*, 68 (October 1969), 605–624.
Although the flaws in TSOP mask many of the structural relationships, once sought, the latter "appear in surprising profusion."

H379.   Coren, Alan.   "Scott Fitzgerald—Refractions of a Strange Peter Pan," London *Daily Telegraph*, November 28, 1969, Magazine, pp. 66–67.
Survey of F's life and work on occasions of discovery of "Dearly Beloved" and first issue of the *Fitzgerald/Hemingway Annual*. Emphasis is on F as a man who never grew up, a "strange, sad Peter Pan who retained so much romantic adolescence right to the end."

H380.   Drake, Constance.   "Josephine and Emotional Bankruptcy," *Fitzgerald/Hemingway Annual*, 1 (1969), 5–13.
Examination of the Josephine stories for F's definition and fullest exploration of the causes of "emotional bankruptcy."

H381.   Gindin, James.   "Gods and Fathers in F. Scott Fitzgerald's Novels," *Modern Language Quarterly*, 30 (March 1969), 64–85.
In his earlier novels, F presented a "romantic hero" who wanted to be God, who wanted to "dominate through his own capacity," but "moral judgment demonstrates that no man, no matter how special in secular terms, can play God"; and, in his last two novels, this parable form "was less appropriate, less able to summarize and direct issues of the novel."
Reprinted: Gindin (I150).

H382.   Gross, Barry.   "*This Side of Paradise*: The Dominating Intention," *Studies in the Novel*, 1 (Spring 1969), 51–59.
F's first novel is not " 'a gesture of indefinite revolt' " but "a mature affirmation that, although all gods are dead, all wars fought, all faiths in man shaken, man can—must—struggle to guide and control life, foredoomed though it may be."

H383.   Hall, William F.   "T. J. Eckleburg: 'un dieu à l'américaine,'" *Fitzgerald/Hemingway Annual*, 1 (1969), 35–39.

Suggests a number of links between details in GG and outside sources and contends that the novel reflects the transformation of the concept of God from the European view of Nordic perfection to the imperfect democratic vision embodied by the Midwesterner.

H384.   Hart, Jeffrey.   "Men and Letters—Fitzgerald and Hemingway: The Difficult Friend," *National Review*, 21 (January 14, 1969), 29–31.

Explores F-Hemingway relationship as revealed through TITN and *A Moveable Feast* (C77), contending that, in TITN, F says that "though he himself possesses the true understanding, the rewards—wealth, glamor, success, love—will accrue to Hemingway."

H385.   Hurwitz, Harold.   *"The Great Gatsby* and *Heart of Darkness*: The Confrontation Scenes," *Fitzgerald/Hemingway Annual*, 1 (1969), 27–34.

Compares the interview scenes which occur at the ends of the two novels.

H386.   Kopf, Josephine Z.   "Meyer Wolfsheim and Robert Cohn: A Study of a Jewish Type and Stereotype," *Tradition: A Journal of Orthodox Jewish Thought*, 10 (Spring 1969), 93–104.

Wolfsheim is viewed as a stereotypical "villanous Jew" and Cohn as an inauthentic "shlemiel" type.

H387.   Kruse, Horst H.   "'Gatsby' and 'Gadsby,'" *Modern Fiction Studies*, 15 (Winter 1969–70), 539–541.

Points out parallels between Gatsby and the two men "'who put up at Gadsby's'" in Mark Twain's *A Tramp Abroad* and suggests that latter may have determined F's choice of a name for his character.

H388.   Latham, Aaron.   "Fitzgerald-Hemingway Letters," Washington (D.C.) *Post*, November 30, 1969, pp. F1, F3.

Discusses at length F's letter to Hemingway suggesting changes in *The Sun Also Rises* (H448) and, more briefly, F's suggestions for changes in *A Farewell to Arms* (I297) and the F-Hemingway friendship.

H389.   Long, Robert Emmet.   "Fitzgerald and Hemingway on Stage," *Fitzgerald/Hemingway Annual*, 1 (1969), 143–144.

Brief review of Trevor Reese's "Before I Wake," a play about the F-Hemingway relationship which opened at the Greenwich Mews Theatre in New York City in October 1968.

H390. ——. "The Vogue of Gatsby's Guest List," *Fitzgerald/Hemingway Annual*, 1 (1969), 23–25.

Contends that the guest list has become a literary vogue and has been emulated by William Styron in *Lie Down in Darkness* and by James Baldwin in *Tell Me How Long the Train's Been Gone*.

H391. McCarthy, Paul. "Daisy's Voice in *The Great Gatsby*," *Lock Haven Review*, 11 (1969), 51–56.

Argues that "not only does Daisy Buchanan's voice indicate aspects of her character, but it also suggests the nature and direction of Jay Gatsby's dream."

H392. "Newsmakers," *Newsweek*, 74 (September 1, 1969), 41.

Brief comment on "Dearly Beloved" and its publication in *Fitzgerald/Hemingway Annual*.

H393. Palmer, George. "Writing in Rome—A Fragment of Scott Fitzgerald," Cincinnati *Enquirer*, July 10, 1969, p. 24.

Interview with novelist Robert Westbrook, Sheilah Graham's son, with considerable mention of the Graham-F relationship.

H394. "People," *Time*, 94 (August 29, 1969), 30.

Comments briefly on "Dearly Beloved" and its publication in *Fitzgerald/Hemingway Annual*.

H395. Rao, E. Nageswara. "The Structure of *Tender Is the Night*," *Literary Criterion* (University of Mysore, India), 8 (Summer 1969), 54–62.

Examination of the structure of TITN as related to its theme; it is concerned "with the inner life of a man and a woman, the disintegration of an integrated personality and the integration of a split one." Thus, there "seems to be some peculiar appropriateness in the double version of this novel on schizophrenia and some inexplicable justification for the shifts in point of view in this novel of confused identities."

H396. Samsell, R. L. "Hollywood—It Wasn't All That Bad," *Fitzgerald/Hemingway Annual*, 1 (1969), 15–19.

Maintains that too much has been made of F's difficulties in Hollywood; F enjoyed some of the "golden age" of the film capital.

H397. Speer, Roderick S. "The Bibliography of Fitzgerald's Magazine 'Essays,'" *Fitzgerald/Hemingway Annual*, 1 (1969), 43–46.

Offers suggestions for reclassification of F's non-fictional prose in magazines and a list of errata in existing bibliographies.

H398. Wells, Elizabeth. "A Comparative Statistical Analysis of the Prose Styles of F. Scott Fitzgerald and Ernest Hemingway," *Fitzgerald/Hemingway Annual*, 1 (1969), 47–67.

Texts used are F's "The Rich Boy," parts 1 through 5, and Hemingway's "Big Two-Hearted River," part 1.

H399.   Whitman, Alden.   "The First Hemingway/Fitzgerald [*sic*] Annual," San Francisco *Sunday Examiner & Chronicle*, September 21, 1969, "This World" Section, p. 35.

Review of first issue of new periodical, with emphasis on "Dearly Beloved." This article also appeared in NY *Times*, August 20, 1969, p. 42; *International Herald Tribune* (Paris), August 21, 1969, p. 14; Louisville *Courier-Journal*, August 21, 1969, p. A5; London *Times*, August 21, 1969, p. 4; Toronto *Globe and Mail*, August 22, 1969, p. 13.

H400.   Winter, Keith.   "Artistic Tensions: The Enigma of F. Scott Fitzgerald," *Research Studies*, 37 (December 1969), 285–297.

Asserts that F "selected and arranged his fiction in terms of basic dualities because this was the habitual way he experienced life. As a result, there is a continual tension in his work. As an artist he was perpetually suspended over a gulf of ironic sensibility."

1970

H401.   Archerd, Army.   "Just for Variety," *Variety*, 147 (April 3, 1970), 2.

Reports that "Paul Newman and John Foreman met with Joe Mankiewicz to talk writing-directing Newman in 'The Great Gatsby.'"

H402.   Atkinson, Jennifer E.   "Fitzgerald's Marked Copy of *The Great Gatsby*," *Fitzgerald/Hemingway Annual*, 2 (1970), 28–33.

Comments on F's corrections, revisions, and alternative phrases pencilled into his first-printing copy of GG.

H403.   B[ruccoli], M[atthew] J.   "Editorial," *Fitzgerald/Hemingway Annual*, 2 (1970), 265.

Notes that the text of GG printed in the Scribner Research Anthology, *"The Great Gatsby": The Novel, The Critics, The Background* (I286), reprints the faulty Scribner's Library Edition text and adds further variants of its own.

H404.   ———.   "A Note on Jordan Baker," *Fitzgerald/Hemingway Annual*, 2 (1970), 232–233.

Since the Jordan was "a sporty car with a romantic image" and the Baker was "an electric car...in fact, an old lady's car," the name Jordan Baker suggests contradictory connotations which are appropriate to her characterization: conservative but careless as well.

H405. ———, ed. "Fitzgerald's List of Neglected Books," *Fitzgerald/Hemingway Annual*, 2 (1970), 229–230.

Reprints, with brief prefatory note, a portion of Malcolm Cowley's "Good Books That Almost Nobody Has Read" from the *New Republic* for April 18, 1934 (B122).

H406. ———, ed. "Six Letters to the Menckens From F. Scott Fitzgerald," *Fitzgerald/Hemingway Annual*, 2 (1970), 102–104 [102].

Brief prefatory note indicates that letters are located at Goucher College and the Enoch Pratt Free Library in Baltimore.

H407. ———, ed. "'Sleep of a University': An Unrecorded Fitzgerald Poem," *Fitzgerald/Hemingway Annual*, 2 (1970), 14–15.

Brief prefatory note records that this material first appeared in the November 1920, *Nassau Literary Magazine*.

H408. Cass, Colin S. "Fitzgerald's Second Thoughts About 'May Day': A Collation and Study," *Fitzgerald/Hemingway Annual*, 2 (1970), 69–95.

A collation of the magazine and TJA texts of the story provides insight into the ways in which F matured as a writer in the 1920s.

H409. "Checklist," *Fitzgerald/Hemingway Annual*, 2 (1970), 272–273.

Listing of recent material by and about F.

H410. Coleman, Tom C., III. "The Rise of Dr. Diver," *Discourse*, 13 (Spring 1970), 226–238.

The characterization of Dick Diver is analyzed: He is not "believable" as a psychiatrist but succeeds as an "innocent victim of false values, the romantic artist with too much lifetime left over after his life's work is completed." Includes some comparison with Gatsby.

Cowley, Malcolm. See Bruccoli (H405).

H411. Elmore, A. E. "Color and Cosmos in *The Great Gatsby*," *Sewanee Review*, 78 (Summer 1970), 427–443.

Demonstrates the intricate patterning in GG by focusing on F's use of color and light imagery.

H412. "The Elusiveness of Zelda Fitzgerald," *San Francisco Chronicle*, September 29, 1970, p. 25.

Interview with Nancy Milford in which she discusses her research for *Zelda* (I258) and gives her opinions of both Scott and Zelda.

H413. Eyles, Allen, and John Gillett. "Writing For the Movies—Donald Ogden Stewart," *Focus on Film*, No. 5 (Winter 1970), 49–57 [52].

Stewart speaks briefly of his friendship with F and of working with him in Hollywood.

Gillett, John. See Eyles (H413).

H414.   Gollin, Rita K.   "The Automobiles of *The Great Gatsby*," *Studies in the Twentieth Century*, No. 6 (Fall 1970), 63–83.

Discussion of F's use of the automobile in the novel; it is "the novel's most obvious yet subtle image of power and destruction."

H415.   Goodwin, Donald W.   "The Alcoholism of F. Scott Fitzgerald," *Journal of the American Medical Association*, 212 (April 6, 1970), 86–90.

Summarizes the facts about F's drinking to the extent that they are determinable and speculates about the relationship of the man and the writer to alcoholism, concluding that the "origin of his alcoholism is as inscrutable as the mystery of his writing talent."

H416.   Gross, Barry.   "'Our Gatsby, Our Nick,'" *Centennial Review*, 14 (Summer 1970), 331–340.

F's novel elicits nostalgia for a type of heroism: Gatsby "is the hero we need to acknowledge and affirm, but the hero we dare not be"; Nick, who is, "like us, within and without,...is the hero we can and must become."

H417.   ———.   "Scott Fitzgerald's *The Last Tycoon*: The Great American Novel?" *Arizona Quarterly*, 26 (Autumn 1970), 197–216.

Maintains that LT would have been F's best novel, a combination of the dramatic and psychological with a final affirmation of the human spirit.

H418.   Gross, Dalton.   "F. Scott Fitzgerald's *The Great Gatsby* and Oswald Spengler's *The Decline of the West*," *Notes and Queries*, 17 (December 1970), 467.

Suggests that an article in the July 1924, issue of the *Yale Review* outlining Spengler's theories in detail was F's source of information about the German philosopher rather than *The Decline of the West* itself.

H419.   Hubbell, Jay B.   "1922: A Turning Point in American Literary History," *Texas Studies in Literature and Language*, 12 (Fall 1970), 481–492 [482, 483, 487, 488, 490, 491].

Passing mention of F in discussion of the major American writers between the wars.

Reprinted: Hubbell (I189).

H420.   Johnson, Richard.   "The Eyes of Dr. T. J. Eckleburg Re-Examined," *American Notes & Queries*, 9 (September 1970), 20–21.

Sees F's emendation of the word "retinas" to "eyeballs" as making possible the definition of the "real subject of Fitzgerald's passage...the symbolic value of the eyes, not the description of them."

H421.   Latham, John Aaron.   "Performing Arts—A Day at the Studio—Scott Fitzgerald in Hollywood," *Harper's Magazine*, 241 (November 1970), 38–39, 41–42, 46, 48, 50.
Excerpt from *Crazy Sundays* (I218).

H422.   Lease, Benjamin.   "An Evening at the Scott Fitzgeralds': An Unpublished Letter of Ring Lardner," *English Language Notes*, 8 (September 1970), 40–42.
Prints a June 15, 1923, letter from Lardner to Francis Kitchell in which he describes what happened at a F party after Lardner left— "'Scott nearly killed'" one of the guests and, as a result, he is "'nursing a broken hand.'"

H423.   Lid, R. W.   "The Passion of F. Scott Fitzgerald," *Fitzgerald/Hemingway Annual*, 2 (1970), 43–59.
A discussion of narrative pattern in GG which suggests that F is working out a variety of selves through the narrative pattern he gives his characters; through "character and fable," F tests "a series of passionately held hypotheses about life."

H424.   Loos, Anita.   "Cocktail Parties of the Twenties," *Gourmet*, 30 (January 1970), 18–19.
Brief reminiscence of Scott and Zelda, "who would always compete with each other in bloodcurdling misbehavior."

H425.   Mackie, Elizabeth Beckwith.   "My Friend Scott Fitzgerald," *Fitzgerald/Hemingway Annual*, 2 (1970), 16–27.
Reminiscence of friendship with F in the summer of 1917, when he is remembered as sensitive, sexually naive, and reticent. From 1932–36, the author and F resumed their friendship; at their last meeting, F, despite being on a downward spiral, had "tragic grandeur."
Reprinted: Eble, ed. (I118)

H426.   Mangum, Bryant.   "The Reception of *Dearly Beloved*," *Fitzgerald/Hemingway Annual*, 2 (1970), 241–244.
Survey of the reprintings and reviews of the story after its first appearance in the 1969 *Fitzgerald/Hemingway Annual*. Accounts for interest shown in the story: That F "considered a Negro as suitable material for serious fiction in 1940 has mass appeal."

Mann, Charles W. See Young (H448).

H427.   Margolies, Alan.   "F. Scott Fitzgerald and *The Wedding Night*," *Fitzgerald/Hemingway Annual*, 2 (1970), 224–225.
A 1935 film, "The Wedding Night," written by Edwin H. Knopf,

was based on an earlier manuscript, "Broken Soil," in which many allusions suggest that Scott and Zelda were the models for the main characters in both scripts.

H428.   Martin, Judith.   "'Zelda'—Life and Legacy," Washington (D.C.) *Post*, July 7, 1970, pp. B1, B2.
Brief interview with Nancy Milford and news account of Scottie Fitzgerald's anger at Milford's use of Zelda's letters and medical records without permission to use them as Milford did.   This article also appeared in San Francisco *Sunday Examiner & Chronicle*, August 9, 1970, "This World" Section, p. 37; Portland *Oregonian*, August 5, 1970, Section Two, p. 4.

H429.   Mayfield, Sara.   "Scott and Zelda: Exiles From Paradise," *Atlanta*, 9 (January 1970), 49–50, 86, 88–90, 92, 94.
Excerpt from *Exiles From Paradise* (I252).

H430.   Milford, Nancy.   "Scott and Zelda: Their Wild Years Near Wilmington," Philadelphia *Inquirer*, December 13, 1970, Magazine, pp. 10–16.
Excerpt from *Zelda* (I258).

H431.   ———.   *"Zelda," Ladies' Home Journal*, 87 (June 1970), 117–121.
Excerpts from *Zelda* (I258).

H432.   Murari, Timeri.   "Bricktop: In Her Corner," Washington (D.C.) *Post*, December 21, 1970, pp. C1, C3.
Brief mention of fact that F was a frequenter of Bricktop's Paris nightclub.

H433.   Nason, Thelma.   "Afternoon (and Evening) of an Author," *Johns Hopkins Magazine*, 21 (February 1970), 2–15.
Account of F's life in Baltimore, drawn principally from "Afternoon of an Author," his stories and novels, and from F letters written while he lived in Baltimore.   Illustrated with pictures of his residences in Baltimore.

H434.   Pearson, Roger L.   "Gatsby: False Prophet of the American Dream," *English Journal*, 59 (May 1970), 638–642, 645.
Gatsby is not a "son of God" but a "perverted God; one who is dedicated to the physical rather than the spiritual world." He has "come to espouse the gospel of the corrupted American dream."

H435.   "A Positive Postscript," *Johns Hopkins Magazine*, 21 (October 1970), 9.
Brief mention that photograph of F's overturned gravestone in earlier article (H433) has provoked response and gravestone has now been permanently righted.

H436.   Powell, Anthony. "Hollywood Canteen—A Memoir of Scott Fitzgerald in 1937," London *Times*, October 3, 1970, p. 15.

Detailed memories of a lunch with F in the MGM commissary on July 20, 1937.

Reprinted: Powell (H507); Powell (I288).

H437.   Prigozy, Ruth. Letter to the Editor, *NY Times Book Review*, October 25, 1970, p. 48.

Criticism of Harry T. Moore's review of *Zelda* (see I258lxxi) which claims that much of what Moore suggests is new in the Milford book is in fact not. Moore replies briefly.

H438.   Samsell, R. L. "Won't You Come Home, Dick Diver?" *Fitzgerald/Hemingway Annual*, 2 (1970), 34–42.

Character study of Dick in which hearing a dramatization of TITN has changed the author's earlier positive assessment and has alerted him to Diver's "vanities, weaknesses and indulgences."

H439.   Smith, Susan Harris. "Some Biographical Aspects of *This Side of Paradise*," *Fitzgerald/Hemingway Annual*, 2 (1970), 96–101.

Interview with F's boyhood friend Norris Jackson as a basis for a clearer view of TSOP.

H440.   Stafford, Wm. T. "Fitzgerald's *The Great Gatsby*," *The Explicator*, 28 (March 1970), Item 57.

The ash-heap passage at the beginning of Chapter II contains a "double vision" in its suggestions of "peace and plenty, of honest rural toil, of sweet bountiful reward," as well as a description of a wasteland.

H441.   Stuttaford, Genevieve. "Flip 'Zelda'—and the Reluctant Biographer," San Francisco *Sunday Examiner & Chronicle*, December 6, 1970, "This World" Section, pp. 51, 60.

Interview with Nancy Milford who discusses her book and F's daughter's reaction to it.

H442.   Wagner, Paul. "'I Just Can't See Daylight...,'" *Fitzgerald/Hemingway Annual*, 2 (1970), 60–68.

Biographical sketch of Yale football star Ted Coy, whom F idolized and used as the model for the football hero in the Basil stories.

H443.   West, James L. W., III. "James Agee's Early Tribute to *Tender Is the Night*," *Fitzgerald/Hemingway Annual*, 2 (1970), 226–227.

Notes that Agee included F's name in the dedication to *Permit Me*

Voyage (1934) as one of the artists "whose work had informed his own." Since Agee could not have known GG well, his admiration for F must have stemmed from having read TITN.

H444. ———. "The Wrong Duel in *Tender Is the Night*," *Fitzgerald/Hemingway Annual*, 2 (1970), 231.
F's reference to a duel in "'a novel of Pushkin's'" is incorrect; the duel scene is in Lermontov's *A Hero of Our Own Times*, and F's error was probably unintentional.

H445. Wilkinson, Burke. "Andrew Turnbull, 1921–1970," *Fitzgerald/Hemingway Annual*, 2 (1970), 266–267.
Obituary tribute which cites Turnbull's close relationship to F and his "first-class" work on F.

H446. Wilson, W. Emerson. "Zelda's Ellerslie," Wilmington (Del.) *Evening Journal*, July 18, 1970, p. 21.
History of Ellerslie including Scott and Zelda's time there in 1927–29.

H447. "The Writer's Vice," *Time*, 96 (October 5, 1970), 59.
Column on high incidence of alcoholism among leading American writers of the modern period refers to F and to Goodwin's essay on F's drinking (H415).

H448. Young, Philip, and Charles W. Mann. "Fitzgerald's *Sun Also Rises*: Notes and Comment," *Fitzgerald/Hemingway Annual*, 2 (1970), 1–9.
Gives background to detailed criticism of *Sun Also Rises* which F offered Hemingway and which latter followed but never clearly admitted was F's doing.
Reprinted: Young and Mann (I389).

H449. "Zelda's Child Dislikes Books," Richmond (Va.) *News Leader*, August 4, 1970, p. 15.
Quotes Scottie on her disapproval of Milford's *Zelda* (I258).

1971

H450. Alexander, Archibald S. "Collecting Hemingway," *Fitzgerald/Hemingway Annual*, 3 (1971), 298–301 [300].
Description of a F letter to Boni and Liveright urging them to publish *Torrents of Spring* by Hemingway.

H451. Atkinson, Jennifer McCabe. "Lost and Unpublished Stories By F. Scott Fitzgerald," *Fitzgerald/Hemingway Annual*, 3 (1971), 32–63.
Description of nineteen unpublished F stories which also records

Harold Ober's reactions to them and his suggestions for revision and publication.

H452.   Bahnks, Jean.   Letter to the Editor, Galena (Ill.) *Gazette*, March 4, 1971, p. 4.

Gives details from the life of F's grandfather, Philip Francis McQuillen, who lived in Galena from 1843 to 1857 and who married his Galena sweetheart Louisa Allen in 1860 after he moved to St. Paul.

H453.   Bahrenburg, Bruce.   "Fitzgerald Failed as Film Scripter," Newark (N.J.) *Sunday News*, May 23, 1971, Sec. 6, p. 5.

A review of Latham's *Crazy Sundays* (I218) which also includes details about F in Hollywood, concluding that the "Hollywood years were a terrible waste for a superlative novelist who suffered from the dream that he could write movies."

H454.   Bakker, J.   "F. Scott Fitzgerald and the American Dream," *Levende Talen*, 283 (December 1971), 784–793.

Examines TSOP and GG in the context of the American dream of success and maintains that none of F's works dramatizes the insight that the weight of wealth and social position might be used to change the social structure as well as the configuration of self because F never stood outside of American society.

H455.   Banta, Martha.   "Benjamin, Edgar, Humbert, and Jay," *Yale Review*, 60 (June 1971), 532–549.

Uses *Lolita* and GG to assess two American dream traditions as originally defined and later put to creative use, the "Franklinian fable" and the "Poesque dream."

H456.   Boardman, Kathryn G.   "F. Scott Fitzgerald's Sister Annabell [*sic*] Makes Final Visit to Home City," St. Paul *Sunday Pioneer Press*, August 22, 1971, Lively Arts Section, pp. 27, 28.

Article-interview in which F's sister reminisces about him.

H457.   Bready, James H.   "Reading Mencken's Mail," Baltimore *Sun*, January 24, 1971, Magazine, pp. 4–5, 7.

Recently released Mencken materials include correspondence to and from F; F manuscripts, with changes in F's and Mencken's handwritings; and an Easter card painted by Zelda. The F-Mencken relationship was "recurrently artificial."

H458.   B[ruccoli], M[atthew] J.   "Boulevardier Ghost," *Fitzgerald/Hemingway Annual*, 3 (1971), 312.

Although F supposedly published in *The Boulevardier*, "a search of all the issues yields nothing."

H459. ———. "Fitzgerald's Marked Copy of *This Side of Paradise*," *Fitzgerald/Hemingway Annual*, 3 (1971), 64–69.

In his copy, F marked passages mentioned by reviewers, as well as passages he himself considered weak.

H460. ———, and J[ennifer] McC[abe] A[tkinson]. "F. Scott Fitzgerald's Hollywood Assignments, 1937–1940," *Fitzgerald/Hemingway Annual*, 3 (1971), 307–308.

List of film titles and dates F worked on them.

H461. Bryer, Jackson R. *"Fitzgerald-Hemingway Annual, 1970," Connecticut Review*, 4 (April 1971), 37–40.

Review, with brief evaluations of each piece.

H462. Burton, Mary E. "The Counter-Transference of Dr. Diver," *ELH*, 38 (September 1971), 459–471.

Maintains that Dick effects a "counter-transference" in the Freudian sense and becomes "morally infected with the dream he sought to break and cure." When he is finally released from the counter-transference by the removal of his love object and his own realization, he is released forever into the "liberty of the lost, and the loneliness of the self-knowing."

H463. Campbell, Lawton. "Scott and Zelda Were His Friends," *The Villager* (Bronxville, NY), 43 (April 1971), 8, 20.

Memories of a friendship with F and Zelda and of assistance given to F biographers Turnbull and Milford.

H464. Coleman, Tom C., III. "Nicole Warren Diver and Scott Fitzgerald: The Girl and the Egotist," *Studies in the Novel*, 3 (Spring 1971), 34–43.

Sees F as a misogynist who, like his characters, tends "to regard women as success symbols or as narcissistic mirrors." Nicole "does not fail in her role as American girl" but "in the romantic role which Dick has written for her."

H465. Dahlie, Hallvard. "Alienation and Disintegration in 'Tender Is the Night,'" *Humanities Association Bulletin*, 22 (Fall 1971), 3–8.

Focuses on Dick as tainted—willfully alienated and isolated from others (in particular Nicole)—even at the beginning of the novel. Dick's "actions and words are clear and unambiguous: he was a man who could not give of himself honestly and unselfishly, and he never did find it possible to move from his state of alienation into a whole-hearted commitment to the human condition."

H466.   Eldot, Paula. "Five Decades of Student Life: From
Fitzgerald to Savio," *Journal of General Education*, 22 (January 1971),
269–280 [269–272].

F's Amory Blaine and TSOP "symbolize the American undergraduate between the decline of progressivism and the fall of the stock
market."

H467.   Elmore, Albert E. "Nick Carraway's Self-Introduction,"
Fitzgerald/Hemingway Annual, 3 (1971), 130–147.

Examination of the opening paragraphs of GG. Nick is "an ideal narrator for a novel of this sort...for in addition to any strictly literary
skills and talents we may presume from his background, he has a certain detachment of temperament which allows him to observe the actions of others and of himself with a clear eye, at the same time he is
developing a firm and credible moral groundwork which allows (indeed
causes) him finally to make the necessary judgments he withholds
earlier."

H468.   Evans, Oliver H. "'A Sort of Moral Attention': The
Narrator of *The Great Gatsby*," *Fitzgerald/Hemingway Annual*, 3
(1971), 117–129.

Contends that Nick "fails to understand why Gatsby refuses to betray
Daisy and, on the basis of that misunderstanding, proceeds to turn
Gatsby into an ideal. Gatsby becomes for Nick what Daisy was for
Gatsby, an embodiment of an ideal, and Gatsby is as far removed in
reality from the ideal Nick imagines him to be as Daisy was far removed from what Gatsby imagined her to be." This is the ultimate
irony of the novel.

H469.   "Fitzgerald Checklist," *Fitzgerald/Hemingway Annual*, 3
(1971), 366–374.

Listing of recent materials by and about F.

H470.   Gent, George. "Mencken's Letters Displayed Today,"
NY *Times*, January 29, 1971, p. 20.

Mention that newly released Mencken papers at the NY Public
Library include letters from Scott and from Zelda.

H471.   Gere, Anne R. "Color in Fitzgerald's Novels,"
Fitzgerald/Hemingway Annual, 3 (1971), 333–339.

Concludes that F "uses color in a significant way in all of his novels
and...[the] color imagery in *The Great Gatsby* takes on new dimension
in light of the other novels." Color, often "used to show nature crossed
or distorted," is traced through TSOP, B&D, GG, and TITN.

H472.   Gollin, Rita K.   "Modes of Travel in *Tender is the Night*," *Studies in the Twentieth Century*, No. 8 (Fall 1971), 103–114.

A thematic pattern not previously noted in TITN is that "bicycles, cars, trains, and boats convey or propel characters through this 'story of the boom years'; they are crucial to the novel's structure of action and significance. They symbolize the values and dilemmas of the twenties, particularly Dick Diver's."

H473.   Gunter, Bradley.   "Wrong Impression," *Barron's*, 51 (October 18, 1971), 24.

Letter to the Editor noting that Nick Carraway was conscientious about "the business of bonds" and did not spend most of his time watching Gatsby, as was claimed in a recent mention of GG in a *Barron's* article (H486).

H474.   Hamill, Pete.   "From the Ruins," NY *Post*, August 26, 1971, p. 33.

Uses remarks by F on NY as point of departure for column on the city's need for federal assistance.

H475.   Hendrickson, Joe.   "Bow Wow!" Pasadena *Star-News*, December 1, 1971, p. B–2.

W. S. Wojkiewicz, former husband of Sheilah Graham, claims to have a trunkful of unpublished F stories and material on them "that nobody has seen." See H501.

H476.   Hoban, Brendan.   "'Breakdown' in the Novels of Scott Fitzgerald," *Zenith* (Dublin), 1 (1971), 51, 53–57.

Traces F's breakdown as reflected in the heroes of his first four novels, a breakdown precipitated by the conflict between a new world and older values.

H477.   Hoffman, Nancy Y.   *"The Great Gatsby: Troilus and Criseyde* Revisited?" *Fitzgerald/Hemingway Annual*, 3 (1971), 148–158.

F's novel and Chaucer's poem share similarities in structure and theme; both show that "all human endeavor comes to nothing when potential for greatness...is wasted on that which is unworthy of it."

H478.   Horan, Tom.   "Zelda Remembered Ere She Married Scott Fitzgerald," Dalton (Ga.) *Citizen-News*, July 14, 1971, p. 14.

Memories of Zelda by Dalton natives.

H479.   Johnston, Jill.   "Descent to Olympus," *Village Voice*, August 19, 1971, pp. 13–14 [14].

Compares and contrasts Zelda with Virginia Woolf.

H480.   ———.   "Zelda, Zelda, Zelda," *Village Voice*, August 26, 1971, pp. 20, 22, 30.

Reviews the Scott-Zelda relationship, concluding that F, her psychiatrist, and society were responsible for Zelda's insanity: "Zelda the wife mother daughter sister is still a relic of the law of chastity that dictated anonymity to women right through the 19th century and tolerates her publicity in the present only under the greatest duress."

H481.   ———.   "Serial Monogamy With Raisins & Honey," *Village Voice*, September 2, 1971, pp. 21–22.

Contends that "Zelda is an encyclopedia of the Western sexual tragedy. She played all the parts and they never added up to a whole." Explores Zelda's relationships with her mother and with her ballet teacher, Egorova.

H482.   ———.   "Quam Erroris Viam Apellamus," *Village Voice*, September 9, 1971, pp. 33, 42 [42].

Mentions Zelda in context of discussion of schizophrenia.

H483.   Kobayashi, Yoshitada.   "A Preliminary Note on the Structure of *The Great Gatsby* by F. Scott Fitzgerald," *Memoirs of the Wakayama Technical College*, 6 (December 1971), 113–118.

In English. Includes discussion of the Lost Generation, of F's life, and, in a very general way, of the structure of GG.

H484.   Latham, Aaron.   "The Making of 'Crazy Sundays,'" *Princeton Alumni Weekly*, 71 (June 1, 1971), 8–10.

Recounts details of research on *Crazy Sundays* (I218), with emphasis on account of the relationship between F and Charles ("Bill") Warren in Hollywood and on how Latham uncovered that.

H485.   ———.   "A Movie Scott Didn't Finish," Washington (D.C.) *Post*, February 28, 1971, pp. B1, B5.

Excerpt from *Crazy Sundays* (I218). This excerpt also appeared in Boston *Sunday Globe*, April 18, 1971, "Sunday Magazine" Section, pp. 38, 42–44; Greensboro (N.C.) *Daily News*, March 21, 1971, p. B3;, *Los Angeles Times*, March 28, 1971, "Calendar" Section, pp. 1, 23–26.

H486.   Lenzner, Robert.   "More Fetching Than Stocks? Bonds Have Given Investors Several Buying Opportunities," *Barron's*, 51 (August 23, 1971), 5, 17 [5].

Brief mention of Nick Carraway, F's fictional stockbroker, who "spent most of his time observing and chronicling the waning days of his neighbor, Jay Gatsby." For a response to this article, see H473.

H487. Llona, Victor. "Days and Nights in Paris With Scott Fitzgerald," *Voyages*, 4 (Winter 1971), 29–39.

Reminiscences of a friendship with F in Paris in 1926–27, when Llona was translating GG into French. Includes translation into English of Llona's 1927 essay, "Pourquoi j'ai traduit *Gatsby le magnifique*" (see D33); and an introductory note by Ernest Kroll, pp. 27–28.

H488. Long, Robert Emmet. "The Fitzgerald-Mencken Correspondence," *Fitzgerald/Hemingway Annual*, 3 (1971), 319–321.

New group of Mencken materials made available in January 1971 include fifty-seven separate letters exchanged between F and Mencken which throw new light on the F-Mencken friendship and confirm F's letters as "one of the most personal and touching achievements of his literary career."

H489. L[owes], B[ob]. "Fitzgerald Book Revival Seems Created By Author Himself," *Washington University Student Life* (St. Louis), 93 (December 10, 1971), 15–16.

Surveys the F revival from 1951 to 1971, concluding, "in regard to the exploitation of his poor writing and fine reputation methinks that success could easily ride a good Fitzgerald to death."

H490. ———. "Man With a Crack—A Biographical Note on F. Scott Fitzgerald," *Washington University Student Life* (St. Louis), 93 (December 10, 1971), 14, 16.

Biographical summary. F "did have a crack in him, a sentence that divided him into the observer and the observed, though the crack was delicate and both sides of him often touched."

H491. ———. "My Side of F. Scott Fitzgerald—Sometimes You Know a Person Too Well," *Washington University Student Life* (St. Louis), 93 (December 10, 1971), 13–16.

Recounting of a two-year addiction to F and his work and how it was cured.

H492. McCall, Dan. "'The Self-Same Song That Found a Path': Keats and *The Great Gatsby*," *American Literature*, 42 (January 1971), 521–530.

Concentrates on F's use of sensuous imagery, his use of Keatsian techniques, and on Gatsby's vision—his desire to reach into the past, to buy back a moment of pleasure and beauty, and his realization that "no present pleasure, realized and consummated, can fulfill the yearning for 'the orgiastic future'"—studied in comparison with "The Eve of St. Agnes," "Ode to a Nightingale," and "Ode on a Grecian Urn."

H493.   McCollum, Kenneth. "'Babylon Revisited' Revisited," *Fitzgerald/Hemingway Annual*, 3 (1971), 314–316.

Although there are numerous mistakes in logic and chronology in the story, F made no effort to correct them because he "was interested in words and their effect" and he "chose his words carefully and well."

H494.   McNally, John J. "Boats and Automobiles in *The Great Gatsby*: Symbols of Drift and Death," *Husson Review*, 5 (No. 1, 1971), 11–17.

Contends that F uses boats and water imagery "to emphasize the lack of stability of most of the novel's characters and to symbolize the anachronism inherent in the American Dream as typified by Jay Gatsby"; in the automobile, F found "a workable symbol, not only to illustrate the rampant carelessness so typical of the corrupt Easterners in the novel, but also to forbode injury as well as accidental and natural death."

H495.   ———. "Prefiguration of Incidents in *The Great Gatsby*," *University of Dayton Review*, 7 (Spring 1971), 39–49.

Examination of Chapter I in attempt to show how F prepares the reader "for the unfolding of the novel's larger design." Also includes a defense of Nick's character as consistent throughout.

H496.   Mann, Jona J. "Is There an Angel in the House?" *Iowa English Bulletin: Yearbook*, 21 (Fall 1971), 39–48 [39, 47, 49].

Brief mention of Daisy and other F women characters in discussion of role of women in the American novel.

H497.   Margolies, Alan. "The Dramatic Novel, *The Great Gatsby*, and *The Last Tycoon*," *Fitzgerald/Hemingway Annual*, 3 (1971), 159–171.

Discusses GG and LT as dramatic novels, contending that, in LT, F was returning to the successful dramatic format he had used in GG.

H498.   ———. "F. Scott Fitzgerald's Work in the Film Studios," *Princeton University Library Chronicle*, 32 (Winter 1971), 81–110.

Detailed examination of F's movie scripts—principally "Three Comrades," "Cosmopolitan," and "A Yank at Oxford"—which suggests that he "was not an exceptional screenwriter. But he worked seriously at his new craft." Also shows how he used similar procedures and techniques in his fiction and his film scripts.

H499.   Martin, Jay. "Fitzgerald Recommends Nathanael West For a Guggenheim," *Fitzgerald/Hemingway Annual*, 3 (1971),

302–304.

West's letter to F requesting a recommendation is printed, along with F's letter sponsoring West, who did not receive the award.

I1500.   Mayfield, Sara. "Exiles From Paradise," *McCall's*, 98 (July 1971), 64–65, 127–129, 131–132, 140.

Excerpt from *Exiles From Paradise* (I252).

H501.   Merchant, Larry. "Bow Wow," NY *Post*, November 10, 1971, p. 92.

Interview with W. J. Wojkiewicz, Sheilah Graham's ex-husband, who claims to have a trunkful of "unpublished short stories and things" by F and to be writing a book "on F. Scott Fitzgerald and Zelda in the wild twenties." See H475.

H502.   Moffat, Frances. "Who's Who—Memories of Fitzgerald," San Francisco *Chronicle*, September 15, 1971, p. 16.

The Ginevra King-F romance is recalled on occasion of her granddaughter's debut.

H503.   Murfin, James V. "The Fall of a Literary Light: The Last Days of F. Scott Fitzgerald," *Maryland*, 4 (Winter 1971), 20–23.

Brief account of F's ties to Maryland and of his burial in Rockville, Maryland.

H504.   "Never Knew Fitzgerald," Columbia (S.C.) *Record*, October 30, 1971, p. 8-B.

Actress Joan Blondell refutes description of a party in Hollywood in Latham's *Crazy Sundays* (I218) by saying, "'I never met Scott. I would have remembered if I had.'"

H505.   Nevius, Reverend R. C. "A Note on F. Scott Fitzgerald's Monsignor Sigourney Fay and His Early Career as an Episcopalian," *Fitzgerald/Hemingway Annual*, 3 (1971), 105–113.

Focuses on Fay's life prior to his conversion to Catholicism when he was a "brilliant and unstable" associate of Nashotah House, an Episcopalian seminary touched by the Anglo-Catholic influence of the Oxford Movement.

H506.   Perelman, S. J. "The Machismo Mystique, or Some Various Aspects of Masculinity, as Demonstrated by Ernest Hemingway, Mike Todd, F. Scott Fitzgerald, and a Sensuous Shrimp From Providence, Rhode Island," *McCall's*, 98 (February 1971), 88–89, 168–169 [169].

Brief mention of F's obsession with his sexual inadequacy and small literary output.

H507.   Powell, Anthony.   "Hollywood Canteen: A Memoir of Scott Fitzgerald in 1937," *Fitzgerald/Hemingway Annual*, 3 (1971), 71–80.

Reprinting of Powell's London *Times* article (H436). See I288.

H508.   Prigozy, Ruth.   "A Matter of Measurement: The Tangled Relationship Between Fitzgerald and Hemingway," *Commonweal*, 95 (October 29, 1971), 103–106, 108–109.

Examination of the F-Hemingway relationship. For F, Hemingway was "the embodiment for his dreams of personal heroism and physical superiority"; F was for Hemingway an alter ego, "a repository for his very real insecurities and sexual worries." Thus, "each writer began to act out the other's conception of himself, thereby attesting to the power of what psychologists call the 'self-fulfilling prophecy.'"

H509.   Reed, Kenneth T.   "East Egg, West Egg, All Around the Tower," *Fitzgerald/Hemingway Annual*, 3 (1971), 325.

Attempt to give the geographical location of GG a "psychoanalytical reading," pointing to the "urogenital imagery" in the novel.

H510.   Rodda, Peter.   *"The Last Tycoon," English Studies in Africa*, 14 (March 1971), 49–71.

Focuses on F's use of Hollywood as a "microcosm for at least an important part of the world."

H511.   Samsell, R. L.   "'The Falsest of the Arts,'" *Fitzgerald/Hemingway Annual*, 3 (1971), 173–176.

Discussion of biographical errata concerning the time and place of F's death.

H512.   Schmidt, Dolores Barracano.   "The Great American Bitch," *College English*, 32 (May 1971), 900–905.

F is one of several American writers discussed. He is concerned with "at what point does that charming hoyden [the flapper, the free and independent spirit] turn into the Great American Bitch?" and that question is at the center of all of F's work.

H513.   Shimomura, Noboru.   "A Study on 'This Side of Paradise,'" *Kure Kōgyō Kōtō Semmon Gakkō Kenkyū Hōkoku*, 7 (November 1971), 1–10.

In English. Primarily a plot summary which concludes that the novel's value lies in its "frank revelation" of contemporary society, its romanticism and lyricism, and its "atmosphere of restlessness."

H514.   Siegel, Daniel G.   "T. S. Eliot's Copy of *Gatsby*," *Fitzgerald/Hemingway Annual*, 3 (1971), 291–293.

Notes marginal comments in the copy of GG which F sent to Eliot; comments may or may not have been written by Eliot.

H515.   Sinick, Heidi.   "Where the Writer Lives," Washington (D.C.) *Post*, March 28, 1971, p. E3.

Records visit to F's daughter's house with mention of F first editions and Zelda's paintings found there.

H516.   Sivaramakrishna, M.   "The Problem of 'The Will to Believe' in Scott Fitzgerald's *This Side of Paradise* and *The Great Gatsby*," *Osmania Journal of English Studies*, 8 (No. 1, 1971), 37–51.

Examines Amory and Gatsby in terms of William James' concept of "the will to believe," concluding that "Amory's ideas and beliefs are relatively powerless for they have lost all connection with a will....Gatsby represents the supreme exercise of the will to believe under conditions of risk."

H517.   Stewart, Donald Ogden.   "Recollections of Fitzgerald and Hemingway," *Fitzgerald/Hemingway Annual*, 3 (1971), 177–188.

Memories of friendships with F and Hemingway from Stewart's autobiography-in-progress.

Reprinted: Stewart (I342).

H518.   Stewart, Lawrence D.   "Fitzgerald's Film Scripts of 'Babylon Revisited,'" *Fitzgerald/Hemingway Annual*, 3 (1971), 81–104.

Discussion of "what went wrong with the film scripts of 'Babylon Revisited'" which argues that F wanted to become an artistic screenwriter but that he was alienated from the Hollywood environment and produced in these scripts flat conventional characters unworthy of his talent.

H519.   Stouck, David.   "White Sheep on Fifth Avenue: *The Great Gatsby* as Pastoral," *Genre*, 4 (December 1971), 335–347.

Examination of Gatsby and Nick as representing two alternative responses to the dilemma of the pastoral dream and the ironic recognition of the impossibility of its fulfillment. Gatsby pursues the pastoral dream; Nick realizes the impossibility of realizing the pastoral dream and withdraws from the self-destructive holocaust at the end.

H520.   Sutton, Horace.   "Booked For Travel—In the Land of the Voluptuaries," *Saturday Review*, 54 (August 7, 1971), 34–35.

Travelogue of a trip to the Riviera includes references to TITN, F, the Murphys, and Tomkins' book (I348).

H521.   Tate, Allen. "Miss Toklas' American Cake," *Prose*, 3 (Fall 1971), 137–161 [157–158].
Reminiscences of life in Paris in the late 1920s includes memory of meeting F. See also H709.

H522.   Turlish, Lewis A. *"The Rising Tide of Color*: A Note on the Historicism of *The Great Gatsby*," *American Literature*, 43 (November 1971), 442–444.
Suggests that Theodore Lothrop Stoddard's book is the source for Tom's reference and that "the historical framework" of Stoddard's study is a source for the "decline and decay" historicism of GG.

H523.   Wood, Rob. "Hemingway Help," Washington (D.C.) *Post*, January 5, 1971, p. C6.
Report on the publication of F's letter to Hemingway about *The Sun Also Rises*. See H447. This syndicated article also appeared as follows: Worcester *Telegram*, January 5, 1971, p. 20; Durham (N.C.) *Morning Herald*, January 5, 1971, p. 4B; Newark (N.J.) *Evening News*, January 5, 1971; Toronto *Daily Star*, January 5, 1971, p. 18; Philadelphia *Inquirer*, January 6, 1971, p. 2; Los Angeles *Times*, January 5, 1971, p. 16; Kansas City *Times*, January 11, 1971, p. 3B; *Arizona Daily Star* (Tucson), January 5, 1971; Atlanta *Constitution*, January 5, 1971, p. 2-A; Omaha *World-Herald*, January 5, 1971, p. 25; Peoria *Journal Star*, January 6, 1971; Des Moines *Register*, January 5, 1971, p. 3-S; *Newsday* (Garden City, NY), January 6, 1971, p. 60A; Miami (Fla.) *News*, January 6, 1971; Mobile *Register*, January 5, 1971, p. 4-D; Chicago *Tribune*, January 6, 1971, Sec. 2, p. 7.

1972

H524.   Atkinson, Jennifer McCabe. "Indeed, 'Lo, the Poor Peacock!' " *Fitzgerald/Hemingway Annual*, 4 (1972), 283–285.
Describes cuts and emendations made in text of F's story for its September 1971 publication in *Esquire*.

H525.   Behrman, S. N. "People in a Diary—Part II," *New Yorker*, 48 (May 20, 1972), 39–95 [73, 86].
Brief mentions of F.
Reprinted: Behrman (I16).

H526.   Berry, Linda, and Patricia Powell. "Fitzgerald In Translation: A Checklist," *Fitzgerald/Hemingway Annual*, 4 (1972), 69–80.
Listing includes translations of TSOP, B&D, "The Vegetable," GG, TITN, LT, C-U, AofA, PH, *Letters*, and "Collections of Fitzgerald's Stories."

H527. Boardman, Kathryn. "Designated National Landmark— F. Scott Fitzgerald House Cited," St. Paul *Dispatch*, February 16, 1972, Sec. IV, p. 43.

F's house at 599 Summit Avenue in St. Paul has been designated a National Historic Landmark.

H528. Bowman, LaBarbara. "Famous Author's Obscure Grave," Washington (D.C.) *Post*, January 6, 1972, pp. G1, G3.

Description of circumstances surrounding F's burial and of site of his grave. This article also appeared in the Wilmington (Del.) *Morning News*, January 29, 1972, p. 11.

H529. Brogunier, Joseph. "An Incident in *The Great Gatsby* and *Huckleberry Finn*," *Mark Twain Journal*, 16 (Summer 1972), 1–3.

Notes parallels between passage in GG where Nick recalls Myrtle's death, imagining "some garrulous man telling over and over what happened," and the scene in Twain's novel where Huck watches a man act out Sherburn's shooting of Boggs.

H530. Brown, Dennis. "Books: Scottie Fitzgerald Smith," St. Louis *Post-Dispatch*, February 6, 1972, p. 4B.

Interview with F's daughter in which she discusses the F revival, her favorite F works, and her feelings about being the daughter of a legend.

H531. B[ruccoli], M[atthew] J. "Malcolm Lowry's Film Treatment for *Tender Is the Night*," *Fitzgerald/Hemingway Annual*, 4 (1972), 337.

Brief article about film script that Lowry and his wife did of TITN. See I228.

H532. ———, ed. "An Additional Lyric For 'It Is Art,'" *Fitzgerald/Hemingway Annual*, 4 (1972), 19–23 [19].

Short headnote indicates that F wrote this additional lyric to a song from the Triangle Club's "Safety First" for St. Paul friend Ruth Sturtevant.

H533. ———, ed. "The Catalogue of Zelda Fitzgerald's Paintings," *Fitzgerald/Hemingway Annual*, 4 (1972), 35–37 [35].

Introductory paragraph notes that Zelda's paintings exhibited in Cary Ross' gallery in 1934 (see H112, H113) are not locatable and requests information on them; includes two-page photostat of the exhibition program.

H534. ———, ed. "Fitzgerald to Roger Burlingame: A New Letter," *Fitzgerald/Hemingway Annual*, 4 (1972), 81–83 [81].

Introductory note dates the letter as 1925, despite F's dating it 1924, and indicates that it is F's response to a Burlingame letter regarding GG.

H535.   Buttitta, Anthony.   "Scott: One More Emotion," *Fitzgerald/Hemingway Annual*, 4 (1972), 25–34.
Pre-publication excerpts from Buttitta's reminiscences of F in Asheville in 1935. See I78.

H536.   Butwin, David.   "In the Days of the Ice Palace," *Saturday Review*, 55 (January 29, 1972), 55–56.
Memories of the St. Paul Winter Carnival of the 1940s, when the Ice Palace was at its center, with mention of F's use of the occasion in his story and of influence of St. Paul on F's work.

H537.   Casty, Alan.   "'I and It' in the Stories of F. Scott Fitzgerald," *Studies in Short Fiction*, 9 (Winter 1972), 47–58.
Traces the loss of "I" or self as the central thematic pattern in F's stories. The "recurrent pattern of relationship is the violation of the other in the mode of I and It, the end is always the violation of oneself, the loss of self, as well."

H538.   Chesler, Phyllis.   "Women & Madness," *Ms.*, 1 (July 1972), 109–113 [109–110].
Zelda is one of three women studied, whose "repressed energies eventually struggled free," demanding, however, the heavy prices of "marital and maternal 'disloyalty,' social ostracism, imprisonment, madness, and death." Some mention of F's role in Zelda's illness.

H539.   Curtiss, Thomas Quinn.   "Paris Theater: The Innocence of Fitzgerald's Twenties," *International Herald Tribune* (Paris), October 11, 1972, p. 6.
Review of French version of "The Vegetable," an "amusing period piece" which was "an artificial product originally and perhaps that quality has preserved it."

H540.   D[uggan], M[argaret] M., ed. "Edith Wharton's *Gatsby* Letter," *Fitzgerald/Hemingway Annual*, 4 (1972), 85–87 [85].
Introductory note indicates that letter was in response to F's sending Wharton a copy of GG.

H541.   Ellis, James.   "The 'Stoddard Lectures' in *The Great Gatsby*," *American Literature*, 44 (November 1972), 470–471.
Suggests that the Stoddard referred to in GG is John Lawson Stoddard, a public lecturer, rather than Theodore Lothrop Stoddard (see H522).

H542. Eyre, Richard. "'Scott,'" *The Scotsman* (Edinburgh), August 25, 1972, p. 8.

Unfavorable review of musical based on F's life and letters, written by John Kester James and Colin Sell and presented by and at Bristol University.

H543. "Fitzgerald Bibliography Presented to Library," *Library of Congress Information Bulletin*, 31 (December 8, 1972), 525.

Brief account of ceremony at which first copy of Bruccoli's F Bibliography (I40) was presented to Librarian of Congress.

H544. "Fitzgerald Bust," *Fitzgerald/Hemingway Annual*, 4 (1972), 425.

Brief note on copies of plaster (with bronze finish) portrait bust of F by sculptor Ron Tunnison which are available from the Gale Gallery in NY for $37.50.

H545. "Fitzgerald Checklist," *Fitzgerald/Hemingway Annual*, 4 (1972), 341–346.

Listing of recent materials by and about F.

H546. "Fitzgerald House Picked as 'Landmark,'" St. Paul *Pioneer Press*, February 11, 1972, p. 21.

Announces that F's birthplace, 599 Summit Avenue, St. Paul, has been designated as a national historical landmark. Includes brief comments on TSOP and on fact that it was written in St. Paul.

H547. "F. Scott Fitzgerald…'Nobody Ever Wrote Better Prose,'" Pittsburgh *Press*, November 19, 1972, "Roto" Section, p. 36.

Interview with Matthew J. Bruccoli on occasion of publication of his F Bibliography (I40).

H548. "F. Scott Fitzgerald's Copy of *Ulysses*," *Fitzgerald/Hemingway Annual*, 4 (1972), 5–7 [5–6].

Introduction explains F's first meeting with Joyce in 1928 and the references to it in F's inscribed copy of *Ulysses*; also notes F's annotations in his copy of Joyce's novel.

H549. Fujioka, Michiko. "A Study of F. Scott Fitzgerald," *Nagasaki Gaikokugo Tanki Daigaku Ronsō*, 14 (February 1972), 39–50.

In English. Study of romanticism in GG which includes brief discussion of F as member of the Lost Generation.

H550. Gent, George. "Hemingway's Letters Tell of Fitzgerald," NY *Times*, October 25, 1972, p. 38.

Description of contents of Hemingway letters to F biographer Arthur

Mizener due to be auctioned at Sotheby Parke Bernet; includes long excerpts from the letters.

H551.   Graham, D. B.   "Fitzgerald's Valley of Ashes and Frank Norris' 'Sordid and Grimy Wilderness,'" *Fitzgerald/Hemingway Annual*, 4 (1972), 303–306.
Traces the Valley of Ashes to material from Norris' *Vandover and the Brute*.

H552.   Graham, Sheilah.   "Scott Fitzgerald Legend a Bonanza For Literati Set," *Variety*, 265 (January 5, 1972), 5, 62.
Comments on the "errors and misconceptions" in recent books about F and Zelda and reports F's anger at Hemingway, his embarrassment at his own failure, his relationship with Zelda, and his use of Zelda and Graham as characters in his fiction. This material was incorporated into Graham's *The Real F. Scott Fitzgerald* (I160).

H553.   Hoffman, Nancy Y.   "The Doctor as Scapegoat," *American Medical Association Journal*, 220 (April 3, 1972), 58–61 [60].
Mention of Dick Diver, "both healer and scapegoat," who finds that in the process of healing Nicole he "loses his own identity as man and physician."

H554.   Hughes, G. I.   "Sub Specie Doctor T. J. Eckleburg: Man and God in 'The Great Gatsby,'" *English Studies in Africa*, 15 (September 1972), 81–92.
Contrasts Gatsby and Wilson, the only two characters in the novel who believe in anything, with all the others, who are characterized "either by irresponsible self-gratification...or by violent criminal acquisition...or by parasitic idleness." The "central moral irony" of GG is that because Gatsby and Wilson are "committed idealists in a world which admits only cynical alienation," they appear madmen.

H555.   K., E., ed.   "A Letter From Victor Llona to Fitzgerald," *Fitzgerald/Hemingway Annual*, 4 (1972), 287–288 [287].
Brief introductory note prefacing letter.

H556.   Keating, Micheline.   "A Keating Review—Rizzo's 'Stained Glass' Fascinating," Tucson *Daily Citizen*, October 25, 1972, "Focus" Section, p. 28.
Review of new play by Frank Rizzo based on episodes in lives of F and Zelda and presented by students at University of Arizona.

H557.   Kobayashi, Yoshitada.   "On American Dream and Its Truth in *The Great Gatsby* by F. Scott Fitzgerald," *Wakayama Kōgyō Kōtō Semmon Gakkō Kenkyū Kiyō*, 7 (December 1972), 77–82.

In English. Defines the American Dream and discusses F's use of the concept in GG.

H558.   Loftus, Margaret Frances. "John Keats in the Works of F. Scott Fitzgerald," *KIYO—Studies in English Literature (Notorudamu Seishin Joshi Daigaku Eibunka)*, 7 (March 1972), 17–26.
In English. Concentrates on the similarities between B&D and "La Belle Dame Sans Merci," with focus on the basic unresolved ambiguity of who is responsible for the male character's dissolution.

H559.   Long, Robert Emmet. "The Allusion to Gilda Gray in *The Great Gatsby*," *Fitzgerald/Hemingway Annual*, 4 (1972), 307–309.
Describes Gilda Gray as a "golden girl" who evoked the era of the Roaring Twenties, a "goddess in the flesh" similar to what Daisy meant to Gatsby.

H560.   ———. "The Image of Gatsby in the Fiction of Louis Auchincloss and C. D. B. Bryan," *Fitzgerald/Hemingway Annual*, 4 (1972), 325–328.
Notes influence on Auchincloss' *A World of Profit* and Bryan's *The Great Dethriffe*.

H561.   McCabe, Charles. "Fellow Feeling," San Francisco *Chronicle*, October 6, 1972, p. 41.
Column on sympathy uses Sara Murphy's assessment of F in *Living Well Is the Best Revenge* (I348) as a starting point and includes brief comments on F and his artistry.

H562.   McLean, John. "USC Team Specializes in Hemingway, Fitzgerald," Greenville (S.C.) *News*, July 23, 1972, p. 12C.
Extended interview with Matthew J. Bruccoli who talks of his twenty-one-year interest in F and of the *Fitzgerald/Hemingway Annual*.

H563.   McNalley, James. "A Hemingway Mention of *Gentlemen*," *Fitzgerald/Hemingway Annual*, 4 (1972), 333–334.
Suggests that Hemingway's reference to *Gentlemen* recorded in Lillian Ross' *New Yorker* profile refers to Stephen Vincent Benét's 1941 assessment of F (A566)—"You can take off your hats, now, gentlemen, and I think perhaps you had better."

H564.   MacPhee, Laurence E. "*The Great Gatsby*'s 'Romance of Motoring': Nick Carraway and Jordan Baker," *Modern Fiction Studies*, 18 (Summer 1972), 207–212.
Contends that F "employs the automobile as part of a pattern of images embodying the disorder of the Twenties and, particularly, the chaotic lives of the central characters," most notably Nick and Jordan.

H565.   Margolies, Alan. "F. Scott Fitzgerald's Prison Play," *Papers of the Bibliographical Society of America*, 66 (First Quarter 1972), 61–64.

Description of notes for a prison play found among F's papers at Princeton.

H566.   ———. "A Note on Fitzgerald's Lost and Unpublished Stories," *Fitzgerald/Hemingway Annual*, 4 (1972), 335–336.

Corrections of Jennifer McCabe Atkinson's listing (H451). Versions of three stories are not lost but are in the Fitzgerald Papers at Princeton; one of these, "Make Yourself at Home," was published as "Strange Sanctuary" in *Liberty* for December 9, 1939.

H567.   Martin, Judith. "The Importance of Being Ernest; Does Someone Who Has Killed '122 Sures' Still Have to Answer Those Probing Questions?" Washington (D.C.) *Post*, October 30, 1972, pp. B1, B2.

Description of and extensive quotes from Hemingway's letters about F written to F biographer Arthur Mizener and about to be auctioned.

H568.   Mathieson, Theodore. "The F. Scott Fitzgerald Murder Case," *Ellery Queen's Mystery Magazine*, 60 (November 1972), 85–97.

Fictional murder mystery in which F and Zelda and the Murphys are characters.

H569.   Milford, Nancy. "Gatsby, Where Are You?" *Lifestyle*, 1 (November 1972), 22–29.

This item, listed in the "Fitzgerald Checklist" (p. 352) in the 1973 *Fitzgerald/Hemingway Annual*, could not be located.

H570.   Monteiro, George. "James Gatz and John Keats," *Fitzgerald/Hemingway Annual*, 4 (1972), 291–294.

Suggests "The Eve of St. Agnes" as a source for GG, contending that the novel is an ironic inversion of the poem.

H571.   Morse, J. I. "Fitzgerald's *Sagitta Volante in Dei*: An Emendation and a Possible Source," *Fitzgerald/Hemingway Annual*, 4 (1972), 321–322.

F's failure to use the accusative form "Deum" after "in" in the passage from "Absolution" is probably one of his "notorious spelling errors" (he probably meant "in die," which suggests the Joycean irony of the rest of the story).

H572.   Moyer, Kermit W. "*The Great Gatsby*: Fitzgerald's Meditation on American History," *Fitzgerald/Hemingway Annual*, 4 (1972), 43–57.

Attempts to show how F "worked out his historical theme" in GG, noting that "Gatsby's urge is transcendental: his vision of life acknowledges neither time nor limit" and thus his attempt is to recapture not only the physical past but also "the moment when reality promised to realize the ideal." American pioneers have pursued this same dream across the entire continent.

H573.   "Names—Faces," *Arizona Republic* (Phoenix), December 6, 1972, p. A–14.

Brief mention that Zelda's home in Montgomery, Alabama, has been auctioned off for $200 and is to be torn down.

H574.   "Newsmakers," *Newsweek*, 80 (October 9, 1972), 56.

Brief mention of Hemingway's opinion of F as expressed in letters to Arthur Mizener about to be auctioned. See H550.

H575.   O'Donoghue, Michael. "The Zircon as Big as the Taft—Random Incidents in the Lives of the Jazz Babies," *National Lampoon*, 1 (May 1972), 46–47.

F parody.

Powell, Patricia. See Berry (H526).

H576.   Prigozy, Ruth. "Gatsby's Guest List and Fitzgerald's Technique of Naming," *Fitzgerald/Hemingway Annual*, 4 (1972), 99–112.

Discussion of F's use of names as "social indicators, symbolic reflectors of class status and even moral outlook," with emphasis on GG, TITN, and B&D.

H577.   Raymont, Henry. "Reprint Houses Vex Publishers," *NY Times*, March 21, 1972, p. 38.

Notes that Folcroft Press has been served notice by Scribner's that it is liable for copyright infringement for having issued facsimile editions of ATSYM, "The Vegetable," and TJA.

H578.   Robson, Vincent. "The Psychosocial Conflict and the Distortion of Time: A Study of Diver's Disintegration in *Tender is the Night*," *Language and Literature* (Copenhagen), 1 (Winter 1972), 55–64.

Asserts that F's protagonists pursue "values not found in their own social environment" and "transcend its confines, if only temporarily, and in so doing become transgressors seeking social treasures never meant for them." Diver is "unable to break out of his circular motion toward end and beginning; a motion which itself has no termination."

H579.   Rose, Alan Henry.   "Sin and the City: The Uses of Disorder in the Urban Novel," *Centennial Review*, 16 (Summer 1972), 203–220 [214–217].

Considers GG as one of several American novels in which rural innocence experiences initiation and maturity in the city; but contends that "Nick's barrenness upon leaving the city reflects the collapse of the archetypal pattern of the fall into urban experience as an effective initiation myth in America."

H580.   Samsell, R. L., ed.   "Six Fitzgerald Letters to Hunt Stromberg," *Fitzgerald/Hemingway Annual*, 4 (1972), 9–18 [9–12].

Introduction gives background on letters to Stromberg, identified by F as a "key man among the bosses" in Hollywood in 1937 with whom he tried to forge a friendship in order to establish himself as sole writer on a picture.

H581.   "Scandalabra Program," *Fitzgerald/Hemingway Annual*, 4 (1972), 97–98.

Discusses 1933 production of Zelda's play by Baltimore's Vagabond Junior Players (see H105) and notes F's cutting and revision of the script after the first performance; includes photostat of program.

H582.   Stark, John.   "The Style of *Tender Is the Night*," *Fitzgerald/Hemingway Annual*, 4 (1972), 89–95.

Studies the style of the novel in which F glorifies imagination and the magical world of the resort, while implying that "the materialistic world, fascinating though it is, will crush imagination."

H583.   Stavola, Thomas J.   "Crisis in American Identity—Erik Erikson, Scott and Zelda Fitzgerald," *New Jersey Psychologist*, 22 (Summer 1972), 24–27.

Suggests that American identity, according to Erikson and the Fitzgeralds, is anchored in the emotional myth of the Garden of Eden: loss, conflict, struggle, and imperfect love. This essay is incorporated into Stavola's *Scott Fitzgerald: Crisis in an American Identity* (I335).

H584.   Stevenson, Laura Lee.   "New York Magazine Competition," *New York*, 5 (October 16, 1972), 95.

F parody submitted in *New York* competition.

H585.   Stone, Edward.   "More About Gatsby's Guest List," *Fitzgerald/Hemingway Annual*, 4 (1972), 315–316.

Gatsby's guest list suggests "the aimlessness of American life after World War I," as well as its "triviality and comedy." It also echoes the fifth section of James' "The Aspern Papers" and possibly inspired Wolfe in Chapter 14 of *Look Homeward, Angel*.

H586. Sullivan, Scott. "Remembering Ernest, Scott and Zelda," Baltimore *Sun*, July 16, 1972, p. K–5.

Report on Paris conference on F and Hemingway which quotes from papers given and discussions held. See H605, H608, H610, H623, H644, H647, H656

H587. Tasaka, Takashi. "The Ethic and Aesthetic Aspects in *Tender is the Night*," *Studies in American Literature*, No. 8 (March 1972), 15–23.

In English. Sees theme of the novel as the "tragedy of Dick Diver who fails to create the ideal life which is, in a way, an amalgamation of the 'ethic' and 'aesthetic' elements of life."

H588. Tochiyama, Michico. "F. S. Fitzgerald's American Hero—A Study of *The Last Tycoon*," *Otani Joshi Daigaku Kiyō*, 6 (August 1972), 13–35.

In English. Suggests, using F's affinities with Spengler, that LT is "the history of America and of himself [F] projected in Monroe Stahr and...affirms the greatness of the youth both of man and the nation."

H589. Trower, Katherine B. "Visions of Paradise in *The Great Gatsby*," *Renascence*, 25 (Autumn 1972), 14–23.

Attempts to uncover the flaws inherent in Gatsby's idea of earthly paradise (symbolized in Daisy), rather than to emphasize his lack of self-knowledge.

H590. West, James L. W., III. "F. Scott Fitzgerald's Contributions to *The American Credo*," *Princeton University Library Chronicle*, 34 (Autumn 1972), 53–58.

F's marked copy of Mencken and Nathan's *The American Credo* (1920) indicates that 12 of the 488 credos which "poke fun at the cherished beliefs of the American mind" are F's.

H591. Williams, Harry. "An Epistle to Gatsby: On the Use of Riches," *Fitzgerald/Hemingway Annual*, 4 (1972), 61–65.

Suggests that Pope's "*Moral Epistles* on riches and *Gatsby* show by comparison...a strikingly similar approach by their authors to the use of money, to the user, and to the inherent moral question and its inevitable resurrection in terms of nature, society, and the individual."

H592. Willis, Martee. "A Writer Who Sought Peace in Florida's Backwoods," St. Petersburg *Times*, September 24, 1972, "Floridian" Section, pp. 28–30 [28–29].

Article on Marjorie Kinnan Rawlings mentions her friendship with and a visit paid to F in Asheville, North Carolina.

H593.   Wood, Rob.   "USC Professor Probes Writer's Past," Columbia (S.C.) *State*, November 14, 1972, p. 5-B.
Discusses Matthew J. Bruccoli's F collection and notes presentation of first copy of Bruccoli's F Bibliography to Library of Congress (see H543).

H594.   "Zelda's Play By Vagabond Players," Baltimore *Sunday Sun*, September 10, 1972, p. D 10.
Announcement of revival of "Scandalabra."

1973

H595.   Alderman, Taylor.   "The Begetting of Gatsby," *Modern Fiction Studies*, 19 (Winter 1973–74), 563–565.
Brief notes on the two names "Jay" and "Gatsby," which include Howells' use of "jay" as social climber in *The Landlord at Lion's Head*.

H596.   Aldridge, John W.   "Afterthoughts on the 20's," *Commentary*, 56 (November 1973), 37–41 [38–39, 40, 41].
Passing mention of GG, TSOP, TITN, and "Babylon Revisited."

H597.   Allen, Joan M.   "The Myth of Fitzgerald's Proscription Disproved," *Fitzgerald/Hemingway Annual*, 5 (1973), 175–179.
Contends that F was not refused burial in the Catholic cemetery in Rockville, Maryland, because his books were proscribed but purely because he was not a practicing Catholic.

H598.   Alpert, Hollis.   "Scott, Zelda and the Last of the Southern Belles," *Saturday Review/World*, 1 (November 20, 1973), 52–54.
Descriptive preview of upcoming TV special, "F. Scott Fitzgerald and 'The Last of the Belles,'" calling it "the best and most faithful capturing of the Fitzgerald mood and quality."

H599.   "Announcements," *Fitzgerald/Hemingway Annual*, 5 (1973), 367–372.
Brief notes on forthcoming publications and recent events related to F or Hemingway.   Includes a list of "Recent Princeton Library Acquisitions" of F materials (p. 371).

H600.   Banning, Margaret Culkin.   "Scott Fitzgerald in Tryon, North Carolina," *Fitzgerald/Hemingway Annual*, 5 (1973), 151–154.
Reminiscences of F in the mid–1930s.

H601.   Barbour, Brian M.   "*The Great Gatsby* and the American Past," *Southern Review*, n.s. 9 (Spring 1973), 288–299.
The novel dramatizes the fundamental American conflict embodied

in two American dreams stemming from two American thinkers—"The Franklinian dream" of "self-validating materialism" seen in the Buchanans; and the Emersonian dream whose power "lies in its promise to free the ordinary self from the materialism, stagnancy, and moral complacency of the enacted Franklinian dream," as seen in Gatsby (who repudiated the Franklinian dream of his youth).

H602.   "Briefs on the Arts—'The Last Tycoon' to be a Movie," NY *Times*, June 19, 1973, p. 30.

Announcement that producer Sam Spiegel has bought film rights to F's novel and is negotiating with Mike Nichols to direct it.

H603.   "Brooklin Resident Gives Rich Fitzgerald Lode to Princeton," Ellsworth (Me.) *American*, November 8, 1973, p. 20.

Gives details of Landon Raymond's gift of his Class of 1917 collection of papers to Princeton University; collection includes "a major 'Fitzgeraldiana' archive."

H604.   B[ruccoli], M[atthew] J. "Bruccoli Addenda," *Fitzgerald/Hemingway Annual*, 5 (1973), 339–346.

Listing of material either omitted from or appearing since Bruccoli's F Bibliography (I40).

H605.   ——. Introduction to "Fitzgerald and Hemingway in Paris: Conference Proceedings," *Fitzgerald/Hemingway Annual*, 5 (1973), 3–4.

Brief note describing the conference and introducing papers given.

H606.   ——. "The SCADE Series: Apparatus for Definitive Editions," *Publications of the Bibliographical Society of America*, 67 (Fourth Quarter 1973), 431–435.

Introduces series which will give "apparatus only, without the text, for a definitive edition of a work in copyright—or of a work that is not feasible to republish" and presents brief explanation of post-publication history of GG, showing how badly text was corrupted. This material was incorporated into Bruccoli's *Apparatus for F. Scott Fitzgerald's "The Great Gatsby"* (I38).

H607.   Buntain, Lucy M. "A Note on the Editions of *Tender is the Night*," *Studies in American Fiction*, 1 (Autumn 1973), 208–213.

Comparison of 1934 edition with Cowley's 1951 edition suggests that F wanted to write two novels: The original edition fulfills his plan "to expose the sham and superficiality of the expatriate life"; while the revised edition fulfills his later desire to tell of the "spoiled priest." Neither is obviously superior and they indicate F's "painful indecision about what the novel should ultimately mean."

H608.   Chamson, André.   "Remarks By André Chamson," *Fitz-gerald/Hemingway Annual*, 5 (1973), 69–76.

Text of talk at Paris Conference by F's closest friend in the French literary world; recalls their friendship in Paris in the 1920s.

H609.   Chard, Leslie F., II.   "Outward Forms and the Inner Life: Coleridge and Gatsby," *Fitzgerald/Hemingway Annual*, 5 (1973), 189–194.

Comparison between GG and Coleridge's "Dejection: An Ode" which sees "Dejection" as "Coleridge's lament for the personal loss of "'My shaping spirit of Imagination'" and GG as F's expression of a similar but greater tragedy: man's loss of "'something commensurate to his capacity for wonder.'" The difference is that "Coleridge's speaker is aware of the futility of continued striving, just as he is aware of the difference between valid and false ideals, whereas Gatsby and his world will continue to seek their false gods."

H610.   Cody, Morrill.   "Remarks By Morrill Cody," *Fitzgerald/ Hemingway Annual*, 5 (1973), 39–42 [39, 42].

Text of talk at Paris Conference; includes brief mention of friendship with F in Paris in 1920s.

H611.   Crosby, John.   "The 'Nonsense' About 'E.H.,'" San Francisco *Sunday Examiner & Chronicle*, December 2, 1973, "This World" Section, p. 23.

Brief assessment of F-Hemingway relationship as well as of their respective careers and personae.

H612.   Crowther, Frank.   "The Day I Didn't Have Cancer," *Village Voice*, October 25, 1973, p. 19.

Humorous essay in which author recounts his attempt to remember name of Dr. T. J. Eckleburg on day he learns he hasn't got cancer; quotes from the novel are interspersed.

H613.   Daniels, Thomas E.   "Pat Hobby: Anti-Hero," *Fitzger-ald/Hemingway Annual*, 5 (1973), 131–139.

Concludes that "perhaps the major significance of" the Pat Hobby stories is F's "ability here to create a character quite different from what he had done in the past, and then to present Hobby in a very objective way. His portrait of a rogue who is likeable and worthless is most effective...."

H614.   Donaldson, Scott.   "'No, I Am Not Prince Charming': Fairy Tales in *Tender is the Night*," *Fitzgerald/Hemingway Annual*, 5 (1973), 105–112.

Examines F's frequent references to fairy tales in TITN which

"provide a gloss on his characters" and "suggest the drastic consequences in failure of perception and in moral corruption of swallowing
whole the sentimentalized view of the world implicit in this kind of
fiction. But the frequent references...also function to distance these
sentimental writers from Fitzgerald himself."

H615. ⸻. "Scott Fitzgerald's Romance With the South,"
Southern Literary Journal, 5 (Spring 1973), 3–17.
Explores F's ambivalent attitude toward the South, as shaped principally by Zelda and his father. Traces the Zelda-like Southern belle
figure from warm and charming in "The Ice Palace" to vicious and
cruel in "The Last of the Belles"; F's father, however, lived up to his
son's ideal of the polite aristocrat of the Old South.

H616. Donnelly, Tom. "'Infidelity': A Screenplay By Fitzgerald," Washington (D.C.) *Post*, December 2, 1973, pp. K1, K8.
Description and assessment of F's screenplay, published for the first
time in the December *Esquire*. "Authentic Fitzgerald glamour gleams
in [the script] and...it's great fun in 1973 to read a drama that takes
place in sumptuous apartments and 'palatial country houses' and is populated by hordes of servants and their imperial employers."

H617. Duggan, Margaret M. "Fitzgerald Checklist," *Fitz-
gerald/Hemingway Annual*, 5 (1973), 349–354.
Listing of recent materials by and about F.

H618. ⸻. "Fitzgerald in Translation," *Fitzgerald/Heming-
way Annual*, 5 (1973), 355–356.
Brief supplement to Berry and Powell listing (H526).

H619. Farrell, James T. "F. Scott Fitzgerald and His
Romanticism," *Thought*, 25 (May 5, 1973), 15–17.
Brief overview of F's fiction for Indian readers which discusses
TSOP, B&D, GG, and TITN and suggests that F was betrayed by
romanticism which by his time had "decayed."

H620. "Filming of 'Gatsby' Could Stimulate Movie-Making in
Newport," Newport (R.I.) *Daily News*, April 2, 1973, p. 21.
Account of history of Rosecliff, mansion being used as Gatsby's
house in GG film.

H621. "The Fitzgerald Hemingway Epoch," *Esquire*, 80
(October 1973), 139.
Introduction to F and Hemingway pieces reprinted here from earlier
issues of *Esquire*; calls "C-U" essays "brilliant" and briefly sketches details of F's relationships with Hemingway and with *Esquire*.

H622.   Gidley, M. "Notes on F. Scott Fitzgerald and the Passing of the Great Race," *Journal of American Studies*, 7 (August 1973), 171–181.

Cites Madison Grant's *The Passing of the Great Race* along with Stoddard's *The Rising Tide of Color* as sources for Tom Buchanan's remark about Goddard's *The Rise of the Colored Empires*.

H623.   Gilliam, Florence. "Remarks By Florence Gilliam," *Fitzgerald/Hemingway Annual*, 5 (1973), 43–48 [44].

Text of talk at Paris Conference; includes story about F.

H624.   Gingrich, Arnold. "Scott, Ernest and Whoever," *Esquire*, 80 (October 1973), 151–154, 374–380.

Reprinting of essay from December 1966 issue of *Esquire* (F36).

H625.   Gorman, Herbert. "Glimpses of F. Scott Fitzgerald," *Fitzgerald/Hemingway Annual*, 5 (1973), 113–118.

Reminiscences of three encounters with F—in Cannes (1926), with Joyce in Paris (1928 or 1929), and in New York (1929).

H626.   "Great Scott?" *Newsweek*, 81 (March 26, 1973), 61.

Brief discussion of impact of GG movie on current fashion.

H627.   Griffith, Ann. "Brick Top Shared Life With Famous," Bergen (N.J.) *Evening Record*, September 10, 1973, p. A-14.

Paris cabaret singer of the 1920s remembers F and Zelda and disputes claim that Zelda was jealous of F's success.

H628.   Gross, Barry. "Back West: Time and Place in *The Great Gatsby*," *Western American Literature*, 8 (Spring and Summer 1973), 3–13.

Points out that if GG were a 19th century novel, the West would be the geographical and psychological direction of the future and the East that of the past; but in F's novel "West is past, East future" and it is "in this sense that the characters are Westerners and their common deficiency is their inability to live in the future."

H629.   ———. "Fitzgerald in the Fifties," *Studies in the Novel*, 5 (Fall 1973), 324–335.

Accounts for the F revival in the 1950s by identifying the 1950s generation with Nick Carraway—a "little solemn," a "little complacent, avoiding entanglements but also restless for involvement and excitement and romance." Also relates Gatsby to John F. Kennedy—"We responded to Kennedy as Nick responded to Gatsby, [in] that Kennedy fulfilled a need of ours as Gatsby fulfilled a need of Nick's."

H630.   Gruber, Michael P.   "Fitzgerald's 'May Day': A Prelude to Triumph," *Essays in Literature* (University of Denver), 2 (No. 1, 1973), 20–35.

Sees "May Day" as prelude to F's greatest works and as exploring the same themes—"the mystique of wealth, the pedestal under the woman, the relentlessness of Time." These themes are examined in the story.

H631.   Gunn, Giles.   "F Scott Fitzgerald's *Gatsby* and the Imagination of Wonder," *Journal of the American Academy of Religion*, 41 (June 1973), 171–183.

Views novel as "a story about Gatsby's poetry of desire, his imagination of wonder that Americans have lost" because "we can no longer be so vulnerable." Gatsby's attempt to make a religion of his wonder is not without vulgarity; but in the end, even though it "can never overcome the current, cannot even resist the current," it "is the poetry of beating on that counts."

H632.   Hartford, G. F.   "Reflections and Affinities: Aspects of the American Past, the American Dream, and 'The Great Gatsby,'" *English Studies in Africa*, 16 (March 1973), 23–36.

Uses James Truslow Adams' original definition of the American Dream as basis for examining GG in which the same "business materialism" which destroyed the American Dream of Adams destroys Gatsby's dream.

H633.   Hills, Rust.   "Fiction," *Esquire*, 80 (October 1973), 68P–74 [74].

Brief mention of GG in discussion of "point-of-view characters" in fiction.

H634.   Howard, Leon.   "Raymond Chandler's Not-So-Great Gatsby," *Mystery & Detection Annual*, 2 (1973), 1–15.

Compares GG and *The Long Goodbye* with respect to parallel characters and plot, noting also differences between Nick and Philip Marlowe as narrators and between Chandler's antipathy for wealth and F's more ambivalent attitude.

H635.   Hunt, Jan, and John M. Suarez.   "The Evasion of Adult Love in Fitzgerald's Fiction," *Centennial Review*, 17 (Spring 1973), 152–169.

Contends that F portrays women either as "monsters of virtue" or "monsters of bitchery" and that his heroes "actually need, however unconsciously, to perceive such images of women, even if they must distort reality in order to do so." A comparison of F's life and those of his heroes indicates that he "may have used his fiction as a vehicle for projecting his own need to avoid adult love."

H636.   Inge, M. Thomas.   "Fitzgerald's *Great Gatsby*: It's THE Great American Novel," Richmond (Va.) *Times-Dispatch*, June 24, 1973, p. F–5.

"The style is sensitive, almost poetic in its meaningful succinctness; the characters are striking and unforgettable; and it incorporates themes of significance to American traditions and culture."

H637.   Irish, Carol.   "The Myth of Success in Fitzgerald's Boyhood," *Studies in American Fiction*, 1 (Autumn 1973), 176–187.

Suggests that F "grew up in a *milieu* which hymned 'the earnest worship of and respect for riches as the first article of its creed' and encouraged fierce competition among its young. In his efforts to meet the standards of his community, Fitzgerald sought to typify the ideals of his contemporaries long before he became the symbol of the flamboyant generation of the 1920's."

H638.   Judge, Frank.   "Judging It," Detroit *News*, June 25, 1973, p. 12-A.

Notes planned TV special, "F. Scott Fitzgerald and 'The Last of the Belles,'" which "could well turn out to be one of next season's most rewarding shows."

H639.   Kent, Beth.   "Fitzgerald's Back in Town," *The Grand Gazette* (St. Paul), 1 (August 1973), 1, 6–7.

Biographical account of F's associations with St. Paul which includes quotes from unidentified F friends.

H640.   [Kohler, Vincent].   "Somewhere West of Laramie, On the Road to West Egg: Automobiles, Fillies, and the West in *The Great Gatsby*," *Journal of Popular Culture*, 7 (Summer 1973), 152–158.

Notes how cars used by characters in GG reflect the characters and how Jordan Baker's name is compounded of the names of two makes of automobile; also discusses permeating influence of the West. This essay is incorrectly attributed to R[obert] A. Corrigan in the journal and in bibliographical listings.

H641.   Korb, David M.   "'Gatsby' Leaves Droll Anecdotes," Newport (R.I.) *Daily News*, July 16, 1973, p. 12.

Variety of anecdotes concerning filming of GG film in Newport recounted.

H642.   Langman, F. H.   "Style and Shape in *The Great Gatsby*," *Southern Review* (University of Adelaide, Australia), 6 (March 1973), 48–67.

Uses detailed examples from the text of GG to show that we read it "for the sake of its distinctive voice, or voices, for the way in which it puts things, at least as much as for the significance of the episodes it recounts."

H643.   Larsen, Erling.   "The Geography of Fitzgerald's Saint Paul," *Carleton Miscellany*, 13 (Spring-Summer 1973), 3–30.
Detailed view of St. Paul as it was when F lived there at different points in his life and examination of how the city is depicted in F's work.

H644.   Le Vot, André.   "Fitzgerald in Paris," *Fitzgerald/Hemingway Annual*, 5 (1973), 49–68.
Text of talk at Paris Conference; detailed year-by-year account of F's life in Paris which assesses "the extent to which the streets and the monuments, the mood and the atmosphere of Paris play a part in Fitzgerald's work."

H645.   Lewis, William F.   "Masculine Inferiority Feelings of F. Scott Fitzgerald," *Medical Aspects of Human Sexuality*, 7 (April 1973), 60–73.
Uses biographical details, with emphasis on the F-Hemingway relationship, to support the thesis that "basic instability, lack of discipline, and strong feelings of masculine inferiority were partly responsible for [F's] tragic life, inconsistent literary output, and suffering at the hands of women."

H646.   Lockwood, Allison.   "A Day For Scott," *Princeton Alumni Weekly*, 73 (May 22, 1973), 10, 14.
Account of F's funeral and description of the gravesite in Union Cemetery, Rockville, Maryland.

H647.   Loeb, Harold.   "Remarks By Harold Loeb," *Fitzgerald/Hemingway Annual*, 5 (1973), 33–38 [34].
Text of talk at Paris Conference; includes brief recollections of F in Paris in the 1920s.

H648.   McCabe, Bruce.   "'Gatsby'—Rendezvous in Newport," Boston *Globe*, March 3, 1973, p. 6.
Interview with Jack Clayton, director of GG film, who discusses the novel and the making of the movie.

H649.   McCooey, Meriel.   "Gatsby the Third," London *Sunday Times*, October 14, 1973, Magazine, pp. 58–66, 68, 71–72, 74.
Account of shooting of film version of GG which includes brief interviews with actresses who played Daisy in the 1926 and 1949 movie adaptations.

H650.   McMaster, John D.   "As I Remember Scott (Memoir),"
Confrontation, No. 7 (Fall 1973), 3–11.
Former editor of *Princeton Tiger* reminisces about F at Princeton.
Reprinted: McMaster (H781).

H651.   Maibaum, Richard.   "*Great Gatsby* Employs Two Generations of Farrows," Los Angeles *Times*, July 15, 1973, "Calendar"
Section, pp. 14, 38–39, 41–42.
Account of planning and making of the 1949 film version of GG by
its producer and screenwriter; mentions that father of Mia Farrow was
originally chosen to direct the 1949 film.

H652.   Maimon, Elaine P.   "F. Scott Fitzgerald's Book Sales: A
Look at the Record," *Fitzgerald/Hemingway Annual*, 5 (1973), 165–
173.
Detailed examination of the annual sales of F's books from 1936 to
1968 as a means of documenting "the phenomenon of the Fitzgerald
revival."

H653.   Martin, Robert A.   "'Gatsby and the Dutch Sailors,'"
American Notes & Queries, 12 (December 1973), 61–63.
Suggests that if the paragraph about the Dutch sailors is restored to
its original position at the end of Chapter I, it becomes the "source for a
number of subsequent references scattered throughout the novel in
which Gatsby is closely associated with water and nautical objects connected with water."

H654.   Mayo, Travis.   "Monroe Native Author of Nostalgic
Literary Work," Monroe (La.) *News-Star*, July 4, 1973, p. 13-A.
Preview of Buttitta's forthcoming *After the Good Gay Times* (I78)
which quotes extensively from a letter from Buttitta to his sister in
Monroe describing the book and the friendship with F which it depicts.

H655.   Monteiro, George.   "The Limits of Professionalism: A
Sociological Approach to Faulkner, Fitzgerald and Hemingway,"
Criticism, 15 (Spring 1973), 145–155 [148–149].
Uses Talcott Parsons' concept of "affective neutrality" in the role of
the physician in society in examining TITN, *The Wild Palms*, and three
Hemingway stories; in each, "an individual fails, and in each case the
failure is one of professional objectivity—a failure of affective
neutrality."

H656.   "The Montparnasse of Fitzgerald and Hemingway," *Fitz-
gerald/Hemingway Annual*, 5 (1973), 5–9.
Map of Montparnasse section of Paris keyed with numbers to indi-

cate "those places...which were significant in the lives of Fitzgerald, Hemingway and their friends." Each numbered spot is identified and its significance briefly described.

H657.   Morsberger, Robert E.   "The Romantic Ancestry of *The Great Gatsby*," *Fitzgerald/Hemingway Annual*, 5 (1973), 119–130.
Suggests variety of sources in romantic fiction as potential influences on F and GG—Scott, Doyle, Dumas, Kingsley, Anthony Hope, Justin Huntly M'Carthy, London, Jeffrey Farnol, Rafael Sabatini, and, in greatest detail, Brontë's *Wuthering Heights*.

H658.   Murphy, George D.   "The Unconscious Dimension of *Tender Is the Night*," *Studies in the Novel*, 5 (Fall 1973), 314–323.
Sees Dick Diver's collapse as a foreshadowing of F's own breakdown in 1935–36 and concludes that F "proved as unable to portray explicitly this dysfunction in Dick's personality [his super-ego's failure 'to come effectively to terms with the disruptive, libido-charged impulses of his id and ego'] as he was unable to confront directly its symptoms in his own."

H659.   Namba, Tatsuo.   "Stylistic Devices in F. Scott Fitzgerald's *The Last Tycoon*," *Yasuda Joshi Daigaku Kiyō*, 3 (October 1973), 83–90.
In English.   Examines first person narration, colloquial tone, metaphor, simile, symbolism, sentence structure, cinematic description, oxymoron, allusion, and irony.

H660.   Nemy, Enid.   "Those Extras on 'Gatsby' Set Weren't Doing It For the $20," NY *Times*, July 11, 1973, p. 36.
Article on Newport society people who performed as extras in party scenes of GG film.

H661.   Oliver, Ruth Hale.   "F. Scott and Zelda Fitzgerald—A Sad Story From the Jazz Age," *American Federation of Astrologers Bulletin*, 35 (April 3, 1973), 17–24.
Analysis of F's and Zelda's personalities based on a reading of their astrological charts.

H662.   Omarr, Sydney.   "Tomorrow's Horoscope—Libra Proper For Fitzgerald," Washington (D.C.) *Evening Star and Daily News*, May 26, 1973, "Weekender" Magazine, p. 18.
Brief astrological analysis of F who was "both sensitive and stubborn."

H663.   Parker, David.   "*The Great Gatsby*: Two Versions of the Hero," *English Studies*, 54 (February 1973), 37–51.
Sees Gatsby as the hero of the romance, "an idealist loyal to some

transcending object, and relentless in his quest for it," and compares him to Browning's Childe Roland; and views Nick as the hero of the novel of "sentimental education" and briefly compares him to the narrator of *Wuthering Heights*.

H664.   Peden, William.   "The American Short Story During the Twenties," *Studies in Short Fiction*, 10 (Fall 1973), 367–371.
Passing mention of F and of prices his stories commanded.

H665.   Peeples, Edwin A.   "Twilight of a God: A Brief, Beery Encounter With F. Scott Fitzgerald," *Mademoiselle*, 78 (November 1973), 170–171, 209–212.
Memories of a July 1935 afternoon and evening spent with F at the Grove Park Inn in Asheville, North Carolina.

H666.   Podis, Leonard A.   *"The Beautiful and Damned*: Fitzgerald's Test of Youth," *Fitzgerald/Hemingway Annual*, 5 (1973), 141–147.
Sees B&D as F's "first major attempt...to reconcile his romantic faith in the magic of youth with his morally ingrained suspicions that life wasn't 'the reckless business' for which he and his young creatures had been taking it." In B&D, "uninformed by parental values," youth fails its "first serious moral test"; but "it was only by isolating youth from a mature, conventional morality that Fitzgerald could administer the test."

H667.   Powers, J. F.   "Dealer in Diamonds and Rhinestones," *Commonweal*, 99 (November 16, 1973), 191–193.
Reprinting of article-review from August 10, 1945, *Commonweal* (A613).

H668.   Randall, John H., III.   "Romeo and Juliet in the New World: A Study in James, Wharton, and Fitzgerald 'Fay ce que vouldras,'" *Costerus*, 8 (1973), 109–175.
Examines GG with *Daisy Miller* and *The House of Mirth* as all employing the Romeo and Juliet legend in order to write about freedom—"or, to put it differently, they write tales of romantic love and freight them with meanings that are, in the broad sense, political....The political meaning of these love stories suggests...the tragi-comic tension in our nation between the aspirations of our founding fathers...and our social customs and modes of behavior, which all too often give those ideals the lie."

H669.   Ring, Frances, and R. L. Samsell. "Sisyphus in Hollywood: Refocusing F. Scott Fitzgerald," *Fitzgerald/Hemingway Annual*, 5 (1973), 93–104.

F's secretary in Hollywood (Ring) presents personal recollections and the statements of "percipient witnesses" in order to show that although the "continuing drain on his resources—physical and financial—must have taken its toll," F is remembered "with great affection" by those who knew him in Hollywood and had a positive perspective—"he was always looking ahead, working up new dreams, firing up new hopes, planning one project after another."

H670.   Rosenbaum, Ron. "The Corpse as Big as the Ritz," *Esquire*, 80 (August 1973), 57–61, 148–159 [153–155].

Account of life of David Whiting who died under mysterious circumstances in February 1973 and who was obsessed with F and had a relationship with F's granddaughter Eleanor.

Samsell, R. L. See Ring (H669).

H671.   Sanford, Robert. "American Writers: A Boozy Muse?" St. Louis *Post-Dispatch*, October 14, 1973, p. 1G.

Article on American writers and drinking briefly mentions research of Dr. Donald W. Goodwin of Washington University on F and alcoholism (see H415).

H672.   Scanlon, Paul A. "*The Great Gatsby*: Romance and Realism," *Work in Progress* (Zaria), 2 (1973), 207–214.

This item, listed in the 1973 *PMLA* Bibliography (no. 9998), could not be located.

H673.   Schulte, F. G. F. "Technical Potential and Achievement in *Tender Is the Night*," *Dutch Quarterly Review of Anglo-American Letters*, 3 (No. 2, 1973), 49–55.

Attempts to "reconcile" the two views of the novel—that F "had lost his power of clarity and control" and that "he had mastered his medium in a perfect way." Contends that the novel ultimately fails because F suppresses knowledge of the flaws in Dick's character and does not clearly or completely define the power of the forces working against him.

H674.   Sheed, Wilfrid. "Fitzgerald: Once Again in Fashion," *Harpers Bazaar*, 106 (January 1973), 80–81.

Comments on the F revivals of the 1950s and 1970s and speculates on the cultural and historical reasons for them.

Reprinted: Sheed (I318).

H675.   Slater, Peter Gregg.   "Ethnicity in *The Great Gatsby*," *Twentieth Century Literature*, 19 (January 1973), 53–62.

Focuses on Nick's "ethnocentric interpretation of the American dream" in showing that "a heightened awareness of ethnic differences does constitute a significant element in the book."

H676.   Smith, Scottie.   "Christmas as Big as the Ritz," Washington (D.C.) *Post*, December 23, 1973, "Potomac" Magazine, pp. 7–8.

F's daughter's memories of Christmases with her parents: "Christmas was always the time...when I allowed my parents to give full vent to their romantic imaginations and throw themselves whole-heartedly into fantasy."

H677.   Starr, Roger.   "The City as a Work of Art: F. Scott Fitzgerald and Robert Moses," *New York Affairs*, 1 (No. 1, 1973), 60–69.

Discussion of F's Valley of Ashes in GG as one of "the more memorable novelistic uses of New York scenery to elucidate the human condition." F believed that green America had vanished forever into ashes; but the ash heap he wrote about was transformed into Flushing Meadow Park by Commissioner of Parks Robert Moses.
Reprinted (abridged): Starr (H678).

H678.   ———.   "F. Scott Fitzgerald and Robert Moses," *Intellectual Digest*, 4 (October 1973), 76–77.

Excerpt from article in Summer 1973 *New York Affairs* (H677).

H679.   Stewart, Donald Ogden.   "An Interview," *Fitzgerald/Hemingway Annual*, 5 (1973), 83–89 [85, 89].

Brief memories of his acquaintance with F in Paris in the 1920s.

H680.   Stewart, Lawrence D.   "'Absolution' and *The Great Gatsby*," *Fitzgerald/Hemingway Annual*, 5 (1973), 181–187.

Contends that the story and the novel are "basically irreconcilable," though "they share a few superficial similarities": "The short story's alleged Gatsby-as-boy is a child who has no awareness of Father Schwartz's dilemma and who uses the priest's behavior for developing quite different notions."

H681.   ———.   "The Dust Jackets of *The Great Gatsby* and *The Long Goodbye*," *Mystery & Detection Annual*, 2 (1973), 331–334.

Points out similarities in dust jackets of the two novels but also notes differences: "Fitzgerald's wrapper seems to have been designed to help him, fortuitously, in the creation of his book; Chandler's, to help the reader in his reading."

Suarez, John M. See Hunt (H635).

H682.   Tillotson, Jery.   "Some Call It Lousy...But Fans Cherish Zelda's Art Works," Montgomery *Advertiser*, February 3, 1973, p. 13.

Description of three of Zelda's paintings owned by Montgomery Museum of Fine Arts; also includes short biographical summary of F and Zelda and comments on F revival.

H683.   Toor, David.   "Guilt and Retribution in 'Babylon Revisited,'" *Fitzgerald/Hemingway Annual*, 5 (1973), 155–164.

Examines story in attempt to show that it is not "about the inability of the world to forgive and forget, or even about a man drawn back to the past and therefore unable to come to terms with the present," but rather "about self-destruction, about the human mind's ability to delude itself into thinking that what it does is based on logic and reason."

H684.   Towne, Oliver.   "The Oliver Towne Column—The Plaque 'Goes There!'" St. Paul *Dispatch*, September 5, 1973, Sec. 3, p. 31.

Miss Ethel Cline, current owner of the house at 599 Summit Avenue, St. Paul, is interviewed on the house and its association with F and his works.

H685.   "U.S. Portrait Gallery Gets What F. Scott Wanted," St. Paul *Sunday Pioneer Press*, March 4, 1973, Metropolitan Section, p. 11.

News item on recent acquisition by National Portrait Gallery in Washington, D.C., of only known life portrait of F, by David Silvette.

H686.   Vandersee, Charles.   "*Gatsby* in Kiev," *NY Times Book Review*, September 9, 1973, p. 51.

Letter to the Editor which reports seeing stacks of copies of GG on sale in Kiev for 55 cents and quotes from preface to the edition.

H687.   Watts, Richard.   "Random Notes," *NY Post*, October 23, 1973, p. 52.

Brief favorable mention of recent publication of B&J.

H688.   Wenglin, Barbara.   "Zelda's Montgomery," Montgomery *Advertiser-Journal*, April 29, 1973, Magazine, pp. 4–5, 14–15.

Descriptive tour of places relating to Zelda in Montgomery; also includes biographical information on F and Zelda.

H689.   West, James L. W., III.   "The Corrections Lists for F. Scott Fitzgerald's *This Side of Paradise*," *Studies in Bibliography*, 26 (1973), 254–264.

Traces various lists of corrections in first printing of TSOP submitted to Scribner's by F, Perkins, Robert Bridges, and F. P. Adams, and how, in general, Scribner's did not heed them so that, as of 1960, some of those corrections still had not been made.

H690.   ———.   "F. Scott Fitzgerald to Arnold Gingrich: A Composition Date for 'Dearly Beloved,'" *Publications of the Bibliographical Society of America*, 67 (Fourth Quarter 1973), 452–454.

A February 23, 1940, F letter to *Esquire* editor Gingrich (printed here for the first time) fixes composition date as February or January 1940.

H691.   ———.   "Notes on the Text of F. Scott Fitzgerald's 'Early Success,'" *Resources for American Literary Study*, 3 (Spring 1973), 73–99.

Detailed examination and comparison of the typescript drafts and published version of F's 1937 autobiographical essay, followed by the "newly edited" text of the essay and a list of "Emendations in the Copy-Text."

H692.   Wheelock, Alan S.   "Paradise Regained: Fitzgerald on Campus," *Gypsy Scholar*, 1 (Fall 1973), 60–63.

Speculations on the reasons for "the phenomenal resurgence in popularity" of F on college campuses: sympathy for F's theme of "the good times that were but are no more"; the "images of form, grace, and beauty" undergraduates find in F's works; and F's "pervading sense of disillusionment" which makes a success out of not succeeding.

1974

H693.   Allen, Joan M.   "The Better Fathers: The Priests in Fitzgerald's Life," *Fitzgerald/Hemingway Annual*, 6 (1974), 29–39.

Biographical information on four priests who, along with Father Fay, "significantly touched" F's life: Reverend Michael Fallon of Holy Angels in Buffalo; Thomas Delihant, a Jesuit F met when he was at the Newman School; Father William Hemmick, Father Fay's assistant at Newman School; and Father Joseph Thomas Barron, a priest in St. Paul.

H694.   Arakawa, Fumio.   "F. Scott Fitzgerald: In Search of Order," *Eigo Ei-Bei Bungaku*, 14 (March 1974), 1–19.

In English. Discusses GG as the "culmination and synthesis" of F's effort to deal with the conflict of opposites ("success and failure and wealth and poverty").

H695. Atkins, Irene Kahn. "In Search of the Greatest Gatsby," *Literature/Film Quarterly*, 2 (Summer 1974), 216–228.

Comparison of 1949 and 1974 GG films which describes 1949 version in great detail and stresses its anachronistic sets and music and its alterations in F's story and praises 1974 movie for its faithfulness to the novel and care taken with details such as costumes and music.

H696. Atkinson, Jennifer McCabe. "The Discarded Ending of 'The Offshore Pirate,'" *Fitzgerald/Hemingway Annual*, 6 (1974), 47–49.

Discarded ending is printed here for first time; speculation is that F's agent advised the revision and a comparison of the two endings suggests that F was wise to make the change.

H697. Bachrach, Judy. "Sheilah Graham: Memories of Scott," Washington (D.C.) *Post*, October 22, 1974, pp. C1, C3.

Interview in which Sheilah Graham speaks of her memories of F.

H698. Bacon, James. "Hollywood's Monument to F. Scott Fitzgerald—'The Great Gatsby,'" *Coronet*, 12 (May 1974), 9–14.

Discusses the genesis, casting, production, script, direction, and promotion of GG film and concludes with brief description of F in Hollywood and assessment of his reputation and art.

H699. Barnes, Clive. "Theater: Hunter's 'Scott and Zelda,'" NY *Times*, January 8, 1974, p. 27.

Review of Paul Hunter's play "Scott and Zelda," prefaced by biographical assessments of F and Zelda: "They were bright lights too quickly snuffed out."

H700. Beale, Betty. "Glamorous Joan Can Be Serious," Durham (N.C.) *Morning Herald*, February 24, 1974, p. 6B.

Brief mention in syndicated gossip column that F's daughter is preparing *The Romantic Egoists* (I324) with Matthew J. Bruccoli. This item also appeared in Washington (D.C.) *Star-News*, February 24, 1974, p. D–2; Birmingham (Ala.) *News*, February 24, 1974, p. 1-D.

H701. Benét, William Rose. "Fitzgerald—THE GREAT GATSBY," *Saturday Review/World*, 1 (August 10, 1974), 68.

Reprinting—in Golden Anniversary Issue of the *Saturday Review*— of Benét's review of GG from the May 9, 1925, issue (A350).

H702. Berry, Linda. "Fitzgerald in Translation II," *Fitzgerald/Hemingway Annual*, 6 (1974), 313–315.

Supplements 1972 and 1973 listings (see H526, H618).

H703. Bohen, Mike. "Fitzgerald: Asheville—Summer of '35," *Greensboro Sun* (Greensboro, N.C.), 3 (September 1974), 9.

Interview with Tony Buttitta who reminisces about his friendship with F on occasion of publication of his *After the Good Gay Times* (I78). This article also appeared in *New South Writing*, 1 (April 1976), 50–52.

H704.   "Book Ends—Scott," *NY Times Book Review*, April 21, 1974, p. 45.
Brief report on upsurge in sales of F's books as result of GG movie.

H705.   Brasch, James D.   "Some Tourists in Gatsby's America: A Review Essay," *Modernist Studies: Literature and Culture 1920–1940*, 1 (No. 2, 1974), 51–57 [52, 55].
Review of five new books on American fiction of the 1920s and 1930s mentions F and GG in passing.

H706.   "Brooklin Man Former Classmate of Fitzgerald," Ellsworth (Me.) *American*, October 31, 1974, Sec. II, p. 10.
Briefly notes display of GG materials at Princeton University Library and local resident Landon T. Raymond's gift of his Princeton Class of 1917 collection to the library.

H707.   Brower, Nancy.   "Highland Happenings—Fitzgerald's Friend Revisits the Scene," Asheville (N.C.) *Times*, July 10, 1974, p. 1.
Interview with Tony Buttitta who speaks of his friendship with F and of how he came to write *After the Good Gay Times* (I78).

H708.   B[ruccoli], M[atthew] J.   "Bruccoli Addenda II," *Fitzgerald/Hemingway Annual*, 6 (1974), 275–283.
Lists material either omitted from Bruccoli's F Bibliography (I40) or which has appeared after it was published.

H709.   ———.   "Interview With Allen Tate," *Fitzgerald/Hemingway Annual*, 6 (1974), 101–113.
Memories of a brief acquaintance with F in Paris in 1929.   See H521.

H710.   Buttitta, Tony.   "Former Resident Authors Book on Scott Fitzgerald," Monroe (La.) *News-Star*, June 24, 1974, p. 6-A.
Background on writing of *After the Good Gay Times* and memories of relationships with F and with Faulkner.

H711.   Canby, Vincent.   "A Lavish 'Gatsby' Loses Book's Spirit," *NY Times*, March 28, 1974, p. 32.
Review of GG film which discusses failure of the adaptation which is attributed to "the all-too-reverential attitude" toward the novel.

H712. ————. "They've Turned 'Gatsby' to Goo," NY *Times*, March 31, 1974, Sec. 2, pp. 1, 3.

Suggests that "the substance of the novel has largely vanished" from GG film, gives a brief overview of film and TV adaptations of "Babylon Revisited," TITN, and "Winter Dreams," and briefly explicates F's novel.

H713. Carmody, John. "For Whom the Belle Tolled," Washington (D.C.) *Post*, January 7, 1974, pp. B1, B9.

Review of "F. Scott Fitzgerald and 'The Last of the Belles'" TV special which includes some discussion of F's life.

H714. Carson, Andrea. "Inside Story From Producer David Merrick—Tensions and Heartaches With Mia Farrow and Robert Redford Filming The Great Gatsby," *Modern Screen*, 68 (June 1974), 49–51, 58, 60.

Gossipy account of filming of GG movie.

H715. Casey, J. C. "On Fitzgerald—Former Monroyan Publishes Memoir," Monroe (La.) *Morning World*, November 3, 1974, p. 14-C.

Extended interview with Tony Buttitta who reminisces about his friendship with F and discusses how he came to write *After the Good Gay Times* (I78).

H716. Chadwick, Bruce. "Princeton Does Not Need Any Revival of Fitzgerald," NY *Daily News*—N.J. Supplement, March 31, 1974, pp. J1, J2.

Not seen; listed in "Fitzgerald Checklist," *Fitzgerald/Hemingway Annual*, 7 (1975), 343.

H717. Champlin, Charles. "It's Authentic 'Gatsby,' But Is It Great?" Los Angeles *Times*, March 31, 1974, "Calendar" Section, pp. 1, 36, 37.

Review of GG film with brief comment on F's novel and on the fidelity of the adaptation.

H718. Christiansen, Richard. "Golden Gatsby—A Beautiful Book, Reborn in Triumph," Chicago *Daily News*, March 30–31, 1974, "Panorama" Section, p. 4.

Appreciation of GG: "It is Fitzgerald's dual view, expressed in Gatsby's hopeful romanticism and Nick Carraway's skeptical analysis, that gives 'The Great Gatsby' its sad beauty and irony."

H719. Collin, Dorothy. "People," Chicago *Tribune*, December 1, 1974, Sec. 1, p. 25.

F's daughter attributes "misconceptions about her parents" to women's liberation.

H720.   Collins, Thomas.   "Fitzgerald's 'Gatsby' Just as He Wrote It," *Newsday* (Garden City, NY), January 31, 1974, pp. 3A, 17A.

Description of GG facsimile edition, with background on novel's composition and several examples of revisions F made in the text. This article also appeared in Toronto *Star*, March 2, 1974, p. C7; Hong Kong *Standard*, March 9, 1974, p. 7.

H721.   Cowley, Malcolm.   "The Fitzgerald Revival, 1941–1953," *Fitzgerald/Hemingway Annual*, 6 (1974), 11–13.

Brief review of publishing activities related to books by and about F, with emphasis on Cowley's own role in helping restore F's reputation.

H722.   Crafton, Jean.   "The Fitzgeralds' Daughter Explodes Some Myths," NY *Daily News*, April 1, 1974, p. 40.

Interview with Scottie Smith who comments on her parents and on forthcoming book *The Romantic Egoists* (I324).   This article also appeared in Ft. Lauderdale (Fla.) *News*, April 3, 1974; Detroit *Free Press*, April 3, 1974, p. 2-C; Des Moines *Tribune*, April 2, 1974.

H723.   Crosland, Andrew.   "Sleeping and Waking—The Literary Reputation of *The Great Gatsby*, 1927–1944," *Fitzgerald/Hemingway Annual*, 6 (1974), 15–24.

Brief survey of comment on GG up to 1944, followed by unannotated listing of material.

H723a.   Davis, Russell.   "The Hole in Gatsby's Heart." *The Observer* (London), April 14, 1974, p. 30.

Review of GG film which includes brief discussion of the novel and of the problems of adapting it to the screen.

H724.   De Vries, Peter.   "The Good But Not Great Gatsby," *Playboy*, 21 (May 1974), 109, 184–185.

Humorous parody of GG.

H725.   Doar, Harriet.   "Contempo Was Born Fast and Didn't Die Slowly," Charlotte *Observer*, July 7, 1974, p. 4B.

Interview with Tony Buttitta who reminisces, in part, about his friendship with F.

H726.   Drawbell, James.   "To Alabama and the Scott and Zelda Fitzgeralds," *Scottish Field*, 121 (March 1974), 26–28.

Reminiscences of Zelda's childhood friend, Eugenia Tuttle; memories of F; and review of F's career and of F revival.

H727. Duggan, Margaret M. "Fitzgerald Checklist," *Fitzgerald/Hemingway Annual*, 6 (1974), 317–322.
Listing of recent materials by and about F.

H728. ———. "Reprintings of Fitzgerald," *Fitzgerald/Hemingway Annual*, 6 (1974), 285–311.
Listing of "all located reprintings of work by Fitzgerald—including letters"; includes stories, essays, poems, and letters in anthologies or collections other than those entirely by F.

H729. Duke, Maurice. "Fitzgerald Revival Caution: Books Better Than Films, TV," Richmond (Va.) *Times-Dispatch*, January 20, 1974, p. F–3.
Review of TV program, "F. Scott Fitzgerald and 'The Last of the Belles,'" which advises interested viewers to read F's works as well as see the various movies and TV programs about him.

H730. Eble, Kenneth. *"The Great Gatsby," College Literature*, 1 (Winter 1974), 34–47.
Finds sources of novel's "greatness" in three areas: its theme, "one which illuminates the American past and present but which also has the power of myth to convey meaning independent of time, place, and the particulars of the narrative"; its design, which was the result of considerable revision in structure and arrangement; and its style.

H731. "Echoes of the Jazz Age," *Georgetowner* (Washington, D.C.), 29 (April 17–30, 1974), 2.
Brief paragraph summarizing F's life and works as introduction to reprinting of excerpts from "Echoes of the Jazz Age."

H732. Eisiminger, Sterling K. "Gatsby's Bluff and Fitzgerald's Blunders," *Fitzgerald/Hemingway Annual*, 6 (1974), 95–98.
Finds several factual errors in GG: there was no Earl of Doncaster between 1919 and 1922; the Montenegrin *Orderi de Danilo* medal "cannot be inscribed on either side because of its ceramic coating"; and if "Gatsby did all he said he did [in the war], his war exploits would certainly have been known."

H733. Elliott, David. "Golden Gatsby—A Super-Money Movie and Its Unsung Director," Chicago *Daily News*, March 30–31, 1974, "Panorama" Section, pp. 2–3.
Discussion of GG film, with peripheral attention to F's novel.

H734. Fabricant, Florence. "Sound Chef—Guests Languished at Zelda's Table But Scott's Characters Furnished Some Tasty Ideas," *On the Sound*, 4 (April 1974), 50–52.

Gives eight recipes characteristic or popular in the 1920s but notes that neither F nor Zelda "gave a damn about food."

H735.   Farrell, James T.   "The 1920's in American Life and Literature," *Fitzgerald/Hemingway Annual*, 6 (1974), 115–128 [119, 125].
Brief passing mention of F's themes and of his failure to read much of the political writing of the 1920s.

H736.   Fedo, Michael W.   "St. Paul: A Visit to Fitzgerald Country," Los Angeles *Times*, May 19, 1974, Sec. XI, p. 11.
Visit to F's St. Paul neighborhood which includes interviews with present owner of 599 Summit Avenue (house where F lived) and with F's friends Xandra Kalman and Norris and Betty Jackson.   An earlier version of this article appeared in *Minnesota—AAA—Motorist*, March 1974, pp. 6–7.

H737.   "The Fitzgerald 'Magic' Intrigues Class," *Campus Report* (Emory University, Atlanta, Ga.), 26 (July 29, 1974), 2.
Interview with F scholar James L. W. West III, who is teaching summer course at Emory on F and Hemingway.

H738.   Fitzgerald, Zelda.   "Zelda Fitzgerald's Tribute to F. Scott Fitzgerald," *Fitzgerald/Hemingway Annual*, 6 (1974), 3–7.
Previously unpublished obituary tribute found in holograph manuscript form in F papers at Princeton.

H739.   Fitzpatrick, Tom.   "Zelda, Scott and Scottie—Pictures From a Family Album," Chicago *Sun-Times*, December 6, 1974, p. 58.
Accounts of interviews with F's daughter conducted by Studs Terkel and Robert Cromie during promotional tour for *The Romantic Egoists* (I324).

H740.   Fowler, Jane Pecinovsky.   "Being Kin to a Legend Keeps Scottie Fitzgerald Smith Busy," Kansas City *Star*, February 17, 1974, pp. 1C, 4C.
Interview with F's daughter who comments on her childhood, on GG film, and on *The Romantic Egoists* (I324).

H741.   Frazier, George.   "Scott Fitzgerald: The Gatsby Legend," *Saturday Evening Post*, 246 (May 1974), 60–62, 141.
Re-examination of F's life and career on occasion of the "brouhaha" over GG film. "There is something about Fitzgerald that is part Gatsby, because of all American heroes,...Jay Gatsby may well be the noblest."

H742.   Friskey, Elizabeth.   "Visiting the Golden Girl," *Princeton Alumni Weekly*, 75 (October 8, 1974), 10–11.
Interview with former Ginevra King who reminisces about F.

H743.   Gale, Bill.   "Getting 'Gatsby' Garbed," *Gentlemen's Quarterly*, 44 (March 1974), 52–55, 134, 138, 140–142.

Discusses clothes designed for GG film and the rivalry between Ralph Lauren and Theonie Aldredge.

H744.   Gallo, William.   "Fitzgerald in the Halls of Ivy," *Rocky Mountain News* (Denver), March 31, 1974, "Now" Section, pp. 19, 33.

Interviews with college literature teachers who comment on F's popularity with students.

H745.   ———.   "Fitzgeralds Are Diluted in Two-Hour TV Special," *Rocky Mountain News* (Denver), January 9, 1974, pp. 70, 72.

Harsh criticism of TV special, "F. Scott Fitzgerald and 'The Last of the Belles,'" for portraying F's work and life as "one and the same."

H746.   Gardner, Paul.   "Making the Movie—Transplanted From the Sound, Gatsby Comes Alive in Newport," *On the Sound*, 4 (April 1974), 22–24.

Tells of attempts of those involved in GG film to locate mansion to serve as Gatsby's house in the movie.

H747.   Gilliatt, Penelope.   "The Current Cinema—Courtly Love's Last Throw of the Dice," *New Yorker*, 50 (April 1, 1974), 93–98.

Review of GG film with considerable mention of F and his works, especially "Winter Dreams," B&D, "The Rich Boy," and "The Diamond as Big as the Ritz."

H748.   Goldhurst, William.   "The *F. Scott Fitzgerald and His Contemporaries* Correspondence," *Fitzgerald/Hemingway Annual*, 6 (1974), 89–93.

Describes letters Goldhurst received while he was doing research for his book (C66) and his dissertation (E10).

H749.   Graham, Sheilah.   "The Scott Fitzgerald I Knew," Chicago *Sun-Times*, March 24, 1974, Sec. 2, pp. 1, 2; March 25, 1974, p. 51; March 26, 1974, pp. 43, 56; March 27, 1974, p. 73; March 28, 1974, p. 85.

Memories of F later incorporated into her *The Real F. Scott Fitzgerald* (I160). Some of this material also appeared in *Rocky Mountain News* (Denver), March 31, 1974, "Now" Section, pp. 6, 11, 12.

H750.   Greenspun, Roger. "Films—American Dreams," *Penthouse*, 5 (July 1974), 36.
Review of GG film which contends that F's novel "was approached as if it were a tomb."

H751.   Greiff, Louis K. "Perfect Marriage in *Tender is the Night*: A Study in the Progress of a Symbol," *Fitzgerald/Hemingway Annual*, 6 (1974), 63–73.
Views the Divers' marriage as F's "effort as a writer to reconcile the ideal with the real, to merge them through his central characters in the expectation that contrary elements will yield a new and perfected whole," and sees this as an Emersonian union of spirit and reality, a union which is celebrated in Book I and whose destruction is traced through the remainder of the novel.

H752.   Hamill, Pete. "Irwin Shaw: Talk With a Not So Young Lion," *Village Voice*, December 23, 1974, pp. 49–50.
Shaw indicates that F has been an influence on his work, especially TITN which he calls a "masterpiece."

H753.   Hanscom, Leslie. "The Fitzgeralds: A Daughter's View," *The State* (Columbia, S.C.), December 29, 1974, p. 4-E.
Interview with Scottie Smith who comments on her parents. This article also appeared in *Newsday* (Garden City, NY), December 15, 1974.

H754.   Hayden, Bill. "Fitzgerald Elegy—Du Pont Reverie," Wilmington (Del.) *Evening Journal*, January 7, 1974, Sec. 2, p. 19.
Brief article which discusses F's life at Ellerslie outside of Wilmington and previews "F. Scott Fitzgerald and 'The Last of the Belles,'" upcoming TV special.

H755.   Hemming, Jan. "Fitzgerald's Daughter—Scottie Remembers Spirit of Jazz Age," New Haven *Register*, November 16, 1974, pp. 1, 2.
Reminiscences by F's daughter and by Reverend Erdman Harris, F's classmate at Princeton.

H756.   Henry, Bill. "Writer Recalls Good Times With Great Gatsby Author," Gastonia (N.C.) *Gazette*, July 21, 1974, p. 6-B.
Interview with Tony Buttitta on occasion of publication of *After the Good Gay Times* (I78).

H757.   Hicks, Granville. "Behind the Gatsby Phenomenon," *The American Way*, 7 (May 1974), 14–18.
Summarizes the plot and explains the novel's success: "The portrait of Jay Gatsby is a masterpiece....[F] not only found the form that

would make us see Gatsby and feel his impact; symbol and image deepened his narrative, so that a somewhat sordid story speaks to us of the human condition."

H758.   Higgins, Jim, and Shirley Rose Higgins.   "Retracing Fitzgerald's Steps Through France," Chicago *Tribune*, July 14, 1974, Sec. 4, p. 13.
Brief recounting of F and Zelda's life on the Riviera and in Paris.

H759.   Hirsch, Foster.   "Why Are They Being So Mean to 'The Great Gatsby?'" NY *Times*, May 19, 1974, Sec. 2, p. 13.
Defense of GG film which is "just the sort of property that movies are equipped to handle" and is quite faithful to F's novel—it is "a graceful and intelligent complement to the novel."

H760.   Hoffman, Steve.   "Monday's 'Last of Belles' Visually Superb," Cincinnati *Enquirer*, January 5, 1974, p. 14.
Preview of upcoming TV special which includes interview with star Richard Chamberlain.

H761.   Hogan, William.   "World of Books—Fitzgerald and the Men's Room," San Francisco *Chronicle*, June 18, 1974, p. 37.
Discusses the genesis of *After the Good Gay Times* (I78) and quotes F's opinion on press agents.

H762.   Houston, Penelope.   "Gatsby," *Sight and Sound*, 43 (Spring 1974), 78–79.
Discussion of GG film which notes changes made from action of the novel.

H763.   Howe, Irving.   "Literature of the Latecomers: A View of the Twenties," *Saturday Review/World*, 1 (August 10, 1974), 32–43 [38–42].
Discusses writers of the 1920s as descendants of Emerson and latecomers to the explosion of cultural modernism and sees F as having "understood instinctively that romanticism is the American fate."

H764.   Humma, John B.   "Edward Russell Thomas: The Prototype for *Gatsby*'s Tom Buchanan?" *Markham Review*, 4 (February 1974), 38–39.
Cites striking parallels between Tom and Daisy Buchanan and Edward Russell Thomas and Linda Lee Thomas (later to become Mrs. Cole Porter).

H764a.   Irving, Clive.   "Backcloth to Gatsby," London *Daily Telegraph*, April 5, 1974, Magazine, pp. 36–39, 41.
Brief discussion of GG included in article on Newport mansions used as settings for GG film.

H765.   Isaac, Dan.   "The Other Scott Fitzgerald," *The Nation*, 219 (September 28, 1974), 282–284.

Uses Buttitta's book (I78) as point of departure for discussion of "the other F. Scott Fitzgerald—the Fitzgerald who was desperately striving to become a serious historical and political writer, and took a final shot at writing a proto-Marxist novel with *The Last Tycoon*."

H766.   Isaacs, Stan.   "The Gatsby Garage," *Newsday* (Garden City, NY), October 24, 1974, p. 11.

Description of house in Great Neck, Long Island, NY, where F lived when he wrote GG and of room above garage where he actually worked on the novel. Calls on citizens of Great Neck to do something to memorialize this spot which has become an attraction for scholars and curiosity-seekers.

H767.   Jones, Edward T.   "Green Thoughts in a Technicolor Shade: A Revaluation of *The Great Gatsby*," *Literature/Film Quarterly*, 2 (Summer 1974), 229–236.

Study of 1974 GG film which praises it for its faithfulness to the novel, especially its depiction of F's "characterization by gesture" and "scenic narration," and for the care and detail it gives to the minor characters, and attributes some of differences between film and novel to differences between the media.

H768.   Karon, Joseph.   "Adapting Gatsby," *Atlantic Monthly*, 233 (June 1974), 102, 104, 106, 108.

Review of GG film which attributes its failure to the fact that "it is almost religiously faithful to its source material and yet not like it at all....The terrible irony of all this misplaced fidelity to the original...is that it prevents the movie from doing much in its own right."

H769.   Katterjohn, William.   "An Interview With Theodora Gager, Fitzgerald's Private Nurse," *Fitzgerald/Hemingway Annual*, 6 (1974), 75–85.

Interview with F's nurse for about a month early in 1935 at La Paix outside Baltimore: "In most ways, he was a very ordinary man, sweet and appealing until he became intoxicated and then he was wild."

H770.   Kelly, Frederic.   "F. Scott Fitzgerald: His Baltimore Years," Baltimore *Sunday Sun*, July 14, 1974, Magazine, pp. 14–15, 17–19, 22, 24–25; July 21, 1974, Magazine, pp. 10, 12–13, 15.

Detailed account of F's years in and around Baltimore in 1932–36 which includes interview with Mrs. Gaylord Estabrook, resident manager of the Cambridge Arms apartment building when F lived there.

H771. Kenner, Hugh. "The Promised Land," *Bulletin of the Midwest Modern Language Association*, 7 (Fall 1974), 14–33.

Discussion of the myth of America as a "promised land" and relation of that myth to the writings of Horatio Alger, Jr., which includes mention of GG and TITN.
Reprinted: Kenner (I204).

H772. Kissel, Howard. "The Fitzgerald Scrapbook, By One Who Knows," *Women's Wear Daily*, December 5, 1974, p. 20.

Extended interview with Scottie Smith who reminisces about her parents and speaks of revival of interest in their lives and works.

H773. Layman, Richard. "Fitzgerald and Horace McCoy," *Fitzgerald/Hemingway Annual*, 6 (1974), 99–100.

Brief suggestion of possible friendship between F and author of *They Shoot Horses, Don't They?*

H774. Lee, Lawrence. "Tender Was the Man: Memories of F. Scott Fitzgerald," Pittsburgh *Press*, July 14, 1974, Magazine, p. 5.

Recollections of F—in Montgomery and Charlottesville, Virginia—during the early 1930s.

H775. Lerman, Leo. "Scene/Seen—Scott, Zelda and Scottie by Zelda," *Mademoiselle*, 78 (March 1974), 168–169, 196.

Text accompanying publication of first pictures of a paper doll family complete with outfits which Zelda made for Scottie: "This paper doll family is fascinating not only because Zelda Fitzgerald created them but because they really look like the people represented and so constitute an extraordinary autobiographical document."

H776. Lerner, Max. "Gatsby," NY *Post*, April 1, 1974, p. 41.

Comments on F, on the 1920s, and on GG, on the occasion of opening of GG film.

H777. "Literature of the 20's," *The Georgetowner* (Washington, D.C.), 29 (April 17–30, 1974), 2.

Brief overview of major writers and works of the 1920s mentions F and GG.

H778. Lucid, Robert F. "Three Public Performances: Fitzgerald, Hemingway, Mailer," *American Scholar*, 43 (Summer 1974), 447–466.

Examines how work of each of these three writers gives off a "crucial quality," an "element of personal presence" that the reader can feel; in F's case, "our need to wonder has terribly to do with our need to be strong enough to survive the experience of personal failure....The fiction hinted that Fitzgerald could claim the strength that came with such experience."

H779.   McCabe, Charles.   "Himself—Princeton and the Irish,"
San Francisco *Chronicle*, May 3, 1974, p. 57.
F discussed as one of several Irish-American writers who were fas-
cinated by Princeton University.

H780.   McLendon, Winzola.   "Scott & Zelda," *Ladies' Home
Journal*, 91 (November 1974), 58, 60, 62, 170–171.
Extended interview with Scottie Smith who reminisces about her
childhood and about her parents' marriage. This material also appeared, abridged, in Chicago *Tribune*, December 4, 1974, Sec. 4, pp.
1, 4; Portland *Oregonian*, December 14, 1974, Sec. B, p. 1.

H781.   McMaster, John D.   "As I Remember Scott," *Nassau
Literary Review*, Winter 1974, pp. 54–60.
Reminiscences by F's Princeton friend which are essentially the
same as those in *Confrontation* for Fall 1973 (H650).

H782.   Margolies, Alan.   "'The Camel's Back' and *Conductor
1492*," *Fitzgerald/Hemingway Annual*, 6 (1974), 87–88.
Shows that story bears no resemblance to the film, despite F's note
in his Ledger that he had sold movie rights to Warner Brothers and that
they had made it into "Conductor 1492."

H783.   Martin, Robert A.   "The Hot Madness of Four O'Clock in
Fitzgerald's 'Absolution' and *Gatsby*," *Studies in American Fiction*, 2
(Autumn 1974), 230–238.
Examines structural similarities between story and novel which indicate that "some of the original links that would have tied 'Absolution'
to *Gatsby* as prologue to novel are still visible beneath the surfaces and
that the two works are, in fact, linked by numerous parallels that reflect
Fitzgerald's original conception of the novel as an extended treatment
of Jimmy Gatz's metamorphosis and career as Jay Gatsby."

H784.   Maslin, Janet.   "The Day They Shot 'The Great Gats-
by,'" *New Ingenue Magazine*, 2 (May 1974), 35–36, 61.
Examines one day of shooting of GG film at Rosecliff Manor in
Newport, Rhode Island.

H785.   Mass, Roslyn.   "A Linking of Legends: *The Great
Gatsby* and *Citizen Kane*," *Literature/Film Quarterly*, 2 (Summer
1974), 207–215.
Cites parallels between F's novel and Welles' movie—use of narrator figures, similarities between Kane and Gatsby as figures of
"legendary proportions," the use of the automobile to bring an
"awareness of mortality" in both, and the circular form of both in that
"we end where and how we begin."

H786. Messenger, Christian. "Tom Buchanan and the Demise of the Ivy League Athletic Hero," *Journal of Popular Culture*, 8 (Fall 1974), 402–410.
Shows how in depicting Tom as embodying all the disagreeable aspects of a former Ivy League athlete F was completely reversing the praise lavished on the Ivy League athlete by a generation of writers like London, Crane, Santayana, and Richard Harding Davis.
Reprinted (expanded): Messenger (I255).

H787. Michener, Charles. "Cooling the Jazz Age," *Newsweek*, 83 (April 1, 1974), 72.
Review of GG film which discusses reasons for failure of adaptation.

H788. ———. "The Great Redford," *Newsweek*, 83 (February 4, 1974), 44–50 [44–47, 50].
Feature article on GG film and its star includes discussion of F's novel and its title character.

H789. Mizener, Arthur. "Scott and Zelda in Great Neck Where Gatsby Was Born in a Room Over the Garage," *On the Sound*, 4 (April 1974), 25–29.
Biographical account of F and Zelda's years in New York City and Great Neck.

H790. Monteiro, George. *"McNaught's Monthly*: Addenda to the Bibliographies of Cather, Dickinson, Fitzgerald, Ford, Hemingway, Hergesheimer and Machen," *Papers of the Bibliographical Society of America*, 68 (First Quarter 1974), 64–65.
Lists reviews of GG and ATSYM.

H791. Moses, Edwin. "F. Scott Fitzgerald and the Quest to the Ice Palace," *CEA Critic*, 36 (January 1974), 11–14.
Studies the false quest motif of the story and its North-South opposition, pointing out that neither is the answer—"What is really needed is a synthesis of the feminine qualities of the South and the masculine ones of the North. But Sally Carrol is hardly the girl to achieve such a synthesis. It is an ideal, after all, which better Fitzgerald characters than she never achieved."

H792. Moyer, Kermit W. "Fitzgerald's Two Unfinished Novels: The Count and the Tycoon in Spenglerian Perspective," *Contemporary Literature*, 15 (Spring 1974), 238–256.
Cites parallels based on Spenglerian motifs between LT and the four published sections of F's incomplete novel "Count of Darkness," stressing how "images of death and rebirth—reflecting the consonance

of historical decline and renewal—are of central importance" in LT.

H793.   O'Connor, John J.   "TV: A Stylized Portrait of Fitzgerald," NY *Times*, January 7, 1974, p. 63.
Review of "F. Scott Fitzgerald and 'The Last of the Belles'" which characterizes the adaptation of F's story as "charming but rather insubstantial" and the material on F's life as "less realized than suggested."

H794.   "Off the Screen: Mia's Back and Gatsby's Got Her," *People*, 1 (March 4, 1974), 32–33.
Pictorial essay on GG film with passing mention of F and the novel.

H795.   O'Flaherty, Terrence.   "Tender Is the Night," San Francisco *Chronicle*, January 9, 1974, p. 40.
Review of "F. Scott Fitzgerald and 'The Last of the Belles'" TV program which calls it "immensely stylish."

H796.   ———.   "Views TV—Scott Fitzgerald, Is That You?" San Francisco *Chronicle*, May 20, 1974, p. 42.
Recollection of June 26, 1958, "Playhouse 90" TV adaptation of GG: "The only things left intact by the Martin Manulis production were the names. Everything else had been changed to protect the innocent." The 1974 film is much more faithful.

H797.   O'Hara, John.   "John O'Hara's Remarks on the Silent *Gatsby*," *Fitzgerald/Hemingway Annual*, 6 (1974), 25–27.
Reprinting of May 18, 1958, NY *Herald Tribune* column (H204).

H798.   Oleksy, Walter, and Cynthia Scheer.   "F. Scott Fitzgerald's America," *Discovery*, 14 (Autumn 1974), 9–13.
Biographical information and contemporary views of St. Paul, Lake Geneva, New York City, Louisville, and Southern California, juxtaposed with descriptions of these places from F's fiction, concluding, "Few American writers can match Fitzgerald as a travel writer. In a few, well chosen words he captured the mood and reality of place."

H799.   Owett, Trudy.   "The Greater Gatsby," *Ladies' Home Journal*, 91 (March 1974), 72–75.
F's granddaughter models contemporary versions of the clothes of the Jazz Age and comments very briefly on the clothes and on the lifestyles of the 1920s and the 1970s.

H800.   Pitts, Stella.   "Exploring New Orleans—F. Scott Fitzgerald Once Stayed at House on Prytania," New Orleans *Times-Picayune*, June 30, 1974, Sec. II, p. 4.
Describes house in which F spent a few weeks in early 1920 and gives biographical details about that period of his life.

H801.   Prigozy, Ruth. "The Unpublished Stories: Fitzgerald in His Final Stage," *Twentieth Century Literature*, 20 (April 1974), 69–90.

Plot summaries and brief analyses of seven unpublished F stories, three of which are also included in Atkinson's essay (H451).

H802.   Pritchard, Billy. "The Fitzgeralds in Asheville: The Tragic Years," Asheville (N.C.) *Citizen-Times*, April 28, 1974, p. 1C.

Detailed account of F and Zelda's years in North Carolina based primarily on published sources but including also an interview with Ulysses G. Johnson, bell captain at the Grove Park Inn during F's stay there, and much information about the fire in which Zelda died. This article also appeared in Raleigh *News and Observer*, June 9, 1974, Sec. 1, p. 8.

H803.   Rainer, Peter. "Novels Into Film," *National Review*, 26 (August 30, 1974), 983–984 [984].

The GG film is "probably the greatest demonstration ever of how one can be faithful in all particulars and yet still completely miss the boat."

H804.   "Ready or Not, Here Comes Gatsby," *Time*, 103 (March 8, 1974), 82–91.

Cover story on the making and promotion of GG film.

H805.   Reddy, John. "F. Scott Fitzgerald: The Last Romantic," *Reader's Digest*, 104 (June 1974), 193, 195–196, 198–202.

Review of F's life and career and comment on various manifestations of the recent revival of interest in his works and personality.

H806.   Reed, Rex. "Two Talented People Who Are Worshipped and Damned," San Francisco *Sunday Examiner & Chronicle*, January 6, 1974, "Date Book" Section, p. 22.

Review of "F. Scott Fitzgerald and 'The Last of the Belles'" TV program, a "distinguished, heartfelt and beautifully realized evocation of the time, place, mood, atmosphere and temperament of the Fitzgeralds."

H807.   Rinaldi, Ann. "In Search of F. Scott Fitzgerald," Trenton *Trentonian*, April 15, 1974, pp. 41, 44.

Interviews with Scottie Smith, with Alexander Clark and Wanda Randall of the Princeton University Library, with Graham Johnston (classmate of F's at Princeton), and with the three Princeton undergraduates currently living in F's room in Little Hall.

H808.   Romine, Dannye.   "Tryon Revisited," *Mountain Living Magazine*, 5 (Fall 1974), 59–61.
Gives details of F's stay in Tryon, N.C., at the Oak Hall Hotel through the reminiscences of several people who knew him there, and also gives other information about F's life.

H809.   Runyon, Keith.   "If You Visit Montgomery," Louisville *Courier-Journal & Times*, March 24, 1974, p. G14.
Describes places in Montgomery, Alabama, associated with F and Zelda.

H810.   ———.   "Montgomery Is Now Home for 'Scottie,' " Louisville *Courier-Journal & Times*, March 24, 1974, p. G15.
Interview with F's daughter who discusses *The Romantic Egoists* (I324), her relationships with her parents, her income from F's books, and the reasons for F's popularity.

H811.   ———.   "Scott and Zelda Fitzgerald's Montgomery, Ala.," Louisville *Courier-Journal & Times*, March 24, 1974, pp. G1, G14.
Gives details of Zelda's life in Montgomery and includes interviews with one of her sisters and a childhood friend.

Scheer, Cynthia.   See Oleksy (H696).

H812.   Schickel, Richard.   "Debunking the Myth-Making About F. Scott Fitzgerald," Chicago *Sun-Times*, April 28, 1974, "Showcase" Section, p. 3.
Reprinting of article from April 1974 issue of *More* (H813).

H813.   ———.   "Further More—What's So Great About Gatsby?" *More*, 4 (April 1974), 22–23.
Review and estimate of the F revival which suggests that "Fitzgerald was his own greatest creation and what we have been doing this past quarter century is writing in our heads the great American pop novel he never quite managed, using him, as the protagonist in this group enterprise, which now it is time to abandon."
Reprinted: Schickel (H812).

H814.   Schulberg, Budd.   "F. Scott Fitzgerald," *TV Guide*, 22 (January 5, 1974), 23–25.
Memories of F in Hollywood in 1939–40 and thoughts on the revival of interest in his life and works.

H815.   "Searching the Coast for Jay Gatsby's Palace," *On the Sound*, 4 (April 1974), 37.
Pictures four Long Island estates one of which may have served as the model for Gatsby's mansion.

H816.   "7 White Bear Houses on Tour," St. Paul *Sunday Pioneer Press*, July 28, 1974, Family Life Section, p. 3.
Brief mention of house where F and Zelda spent summer of 1921, with picture of house and its present owners.

H817.   Severo, Richard. "For Fitzgerald's Works, It's Roaring 70's," NY *Times*, March 20, 1974, p. 36.
Discusses financial success of F's works in the 1970s and quotes Matthew J. Bruccoli on contrast between sales of F's books in 1920s and 1930s and in the 1970s.

H818.   Seward, William W., Jr. "F. Scott Fitzgerald's Associations With Norfolk and Virginia Beach," *Fitzgerald/Hemingway Annual*, 6 (1974), 41–46.
Concerns F's visits to his cousin Cecilia Taylor ("Ceci") in Norfolk while he was at Newman and Princeton and in later years and to the Cavalier Hotel in Virginia Beach. Includes reminiscences by Cecilia Taylor's daughters.

H819.   Shaffer, John. "Zelda: 'Parfois la folie est la sagesse,'" *The Chronicle* (Duke University), 70 (October 25, 1974), 12.
Review of exhibit of Zelda's paintings at the Montgomery (Ala.) Museum of Fine Arts which suggests that had she had less talent in writing and dancing she might have developed "greatness" as a painter. Includes photographs of some of the works in the exhibit.

H820.   Sheppard, Eugenia. "Inside Fashion—Inside Scott and Zelda," NY *Post*, December 5, 1974, p. 49.
Interview with Scottie Smith who talks of *The Romantic Egoists* (I324) and of her parents. This article also appeared in Seattle *Times*, December 10, 1974, p. B1.

H821.   Simon, John. "Films," *Esquire*, 82 (July 1974), 144, 146, 149 [144, 146].
Review of GG film which includes discussion of shortcomings of screenplay as adaptation of F's novel.

H822.   Sloane, Leonard. "Advertising: Gatsby Bandwagon," NY *Times*, February 15, 1974, p. 52.
Discusses advertising campaigns to be launched by various manufacturers capitalizing on GG film.

H823.   [Smith, Frances Scott Fitzgerald].   "Mia Is the Daisy
Father Had in Mind," *People*, 1 (March 4, 1974), 34.

F's daughter comments on her father and his relationship to GG, on
her mother, on the suitability of Mia Farrow and Robert Redford for
their roles, on the screenplay of GG film, and on contemporary movies
in general.

H824.   ———.   "Notes About My Now-Famous Father,"
Family Circle, 84 (May 1974), 118, 120.

F's daughter notes the F revival (GG sold 448,420 copies in the U.S.
in 1968), and contends that reasons for it are not either nostalgia for the
Jazz Age or appreciation of his talent but rather that "People read him
now for clues and guidelines, as if by understanding him and his beautiful and damned period, they could see more clearly what's wrong [in
their own]."

H825.   ———.   "Now Scottie Pays a Tribute to Her Famous
Parents," Chicago *Sun-Times*, December 1, 1974, Sec. 1-C, p. 7.
Excerpt from Introduction to *The Romantic Egoists* (I324).

H826.   Speer, Roderick S.   "*The Great Gatsby*'s 'Romance of
Motoring' and 'The Cruise of the Rolling Junk,'" *Modern Fiction
Studies*, 20 (Winter 1974–75), 540–543.
Notes similar sense of disappointment lurking beneath the idealism
in GG and in F's essay about his and Zelda's motor trip from Westport,
Conn., to Montgomery, Ala., published early in 1924, and also serious
themes of GG fermenting in the essay.

H827.   Stark, Bruce R.   "The Intricate Pattern in *The Great
Gatsby*," *Fitzgerald/Hemingway Annual*, 6 (1974), 51–61.
Suggests through examples that "the words in *The Great Gatsby* par-
ticipate in a multitude of complex patterns that link images, anomalous
minor scenes, and even rather large units to one another in a variety of
complex and subtle ways."

H827a.   Stewart, Bruce.   "Gatsby in Camera," *Month*, 7 (June
1974), 616.
Review of GG film which discusses problems of adapting the novel
for the screen.

H828.   Stoner, Carroll.   "F. Scott Fitzgerald's Star Is Rising
Again," Philadelphia *Inquirer*, April 7, 1974, pp. K1, K6.
Discussion of America's "romantic infatuation with F. Scott
Fitzgerald" which emphasizes GG and the psychological and cultural
reasons why there is renewed interest in F and his themes.

H829.   Thorpe, Day.   "The 'Other' Fitzgerald as Writer,"
Washington (D.C.) *Star-News*, May 12, 1974, p. G5.
Account of writing of SMTW and estimate of its worth—"not a

great book, but...one that mirrors its author—a human being with blood in her veins."

H829a.　Tynan, Kenneth.　"Gatsby and the American Dream," *The Observer* (London), April 14, 1974, p. 25.
Summary of plot and analysis of GG.　"Gatsby represents a nation at the peak of its pride and self-confidence, tainted by corruption but still reaching for the stars."

H830.　"Understanding Fitzgerald," *The Georgetowner* (Washington, D.C.), 29 (April 17–30, 1974), 2, 9.
Recounts elements of F legend and asserts his value as an artist: "The right elements of his legend were...not only his charm, his recklessness, and his love of pleasure and prestige, but also his unique talent, his violated conscience, and, above all, his actual achievement."

H831.　"Update: Fitzgerald's 'Golden Girl,'" *Newsweek*, 84 (December 2, 1974), 13.
Interview with former Ginevra King, now Mrs. John T. Pirie, Jr., 74, who reminisces about her relationship with F.

H832.　Voorhees, John.　"A.B.C. Special Rings Belles," Seattle *Times*, January 7, 1974, p. A8.
Review of "F. Scott Fitzgerald and 'The Last of the Belles'": "Not only is it one of the most distinguished productions to be seen on TV this year but it is also one of the most romantic, a brilliant evocation of both a great American author and the dramatization of one of his works."

H833.　Watson, Jerry.　"The Fabulous Fitzgerald and the Last Woman in His Life," London *Evening News*, April 15, 1974, p. 8C.
Interview with Sheilah Graham who discusses F's death, his works, and her relationship with him.

H834.　Wayne, Leslie.　"Fitzgerald Daughter—Setting the Record Straight," Los Angeles *Times*, December 6, 1974, Part IV, p. 32.
Interview with Scottie Smith who speaks of her parents.　This article also appeared in Washington (D.C.) *Star-News*, December 1, 1974, p. G–4.

H835.　Weinberg, Nancy.　"The Gold Coast: The Battlements of Wealth and Privilege That Gatsby Tried to Conquer," *On the Sound*, 4 (April 1974), 30, 35–36.
Describes the origins of Long Island's Gold Coast at the turn of the century consisting of tycoons who made money on World War I and newly wealthy show business people, and its fading away gradually after the 1929 stock market crash.

H836.   Wells, Robert.   "Princeton's Impact on Fitzgerald," *Rocky Mountain News* (Denver), March 31, 1974, pp. 19, 33.

Compares and contrasts impact of Princeton on F and on himself and focuses on attitudes towards status, nature, and women.

H837.   West, James L. W., III.   "Mencken's Review of *Tales of the Jazz Age*," *Menckeniana*, 50 (Summer 1974), 2–4.

Reprints—with brief introduction—hitherto unlisted review of TJA from *Smart Set* for July 1923 (G9).

H838.   White, Linda.   "Neville Warns Against Nostalgia," Bangor (Me.) *Daily News*, May 27, 1974, pp. 1, 3.

Account of commencement address by President Howard R. Neville of University of Maine in Orono in which he cited GG as an "example of what the graduates must avoid as they move into a new phase of their lives....Gatsby's desperate gamble for an unattainable goal had its reasons rooted in the past and therefore he failed."

H839.   Wilkinson, Burke.   "Gatsby Re-visited: Film Shadows and Substance," *The Georgetowner* (Washington, D.C.), 29 (April 17–30, 1974), 1–2.

Review of GG film. "There is enough stardust here to make it worth seeing." Includes extensive quotations from Wilkinson's December 24, 1950, NY *Times* article (B246).

H840.   Williams, Susan.   "On the Campus," *Princeton Alumni Weekly*, 74 (May 14, 1974), 7.

Interviews with current Princeton undergraduates concerning their feelings about F and his work and with Alexander Clark and Wanda Randall, curators of F papers in Princeton University Library.

H841.   Worsnop, Richard L.   "The F. Scott Mystique Is Still Unflappable," Miami (Fla.) *Herald*, January 26, 1974, p. 7A.

Brief discussion of the F revival noting that F's "star continues to blaze brighter than those of his contemporaries."

H842.   Wycherley, H. Alan.   "The Fitzgerald Fad," *CEA Critic*, 36 (January 1974), 29–30.

Laments the sentimental appraisers of F who try "to blurb into immortality a writer of limited talent and scope."

H843.   Yardley, Jonathan.   "'The Great Gatsby' and the Real Fitzgerald," Miami (Fla.) *Herald*, April 14, 1974, pp. 1G, 7G.

Separates F's "real" life from the current myth, noting, "Fitzgerald's life had many low moments, but it was a good life. He was not the dashing romantic of legend though occasionally he played at the role, but a quiet and sensitive man of inordinate decency."

1975

H844.　"Acceptable For Burial," *The Nation,* 221 (October 25, 1975), 390.
Brief mention that F and Zelda will be reburied in St. Mary's Cemetery.

H845.　Adams, Val.　"Radio Roundup," NY *Sunday News,* August 17, 1975, p. TV8.
Brief mention that National Public Radio hopes to produce 52 half-hour dramas based on F short stories and that an adaptation of "The Ice Palace" by Arch Oboler and narrated by William Shriver, a Baltimore actor-radio announcer who has obtained rights to the stories from F's daughter, is already taped.

H846.　Alderman, Taylor.　*"The Great Gatsby* and *Hopalong Cassidy," Fitzgerald/Hemingway Annual,* 7 (1975), 83–87.
Although F's use of *Hopalong Cassidy* is anachronistic because the book was not published until 1910, four years after young Jimmy Gatz used it, F's choice of it is appropriate as it is "the account of a Western hero who ironically parallels Gatsby by succeeding where Gatsby fails—in love, and, in his career; [and] a novel which portrays the violent and morally ambiguous American society similar in many ways to the America which ultimately destroys Jay Gatsby."

H847.　"Baltimore," *Boxoffice,* 108 (November 3, 1975), E–7.
Brief mention of impending F reburial and of recent death of Sara Murphy.

H848.　Berry, Linda.　"The Text of *Bits of Paradise," Fitzgerald/Hemingway Annual,* 7 (1975), 141–145.
Listing of variants between magazine texts of stories in *Bits* and the book texts (the 1974 American edition is a reprint of the 1973 English edition and uses the same texts).

H849.　Browne, Joseph.　"The Greening of America: Irish-American Writers," *Journal of Ethnic Studies,* 2 (Winter 1975), 71–76 [71].
Article on new and young Irish-American writers whose works deal with the Irish-American experience mentions F in passing.

H850.　[Bruccoli, Matthew J.] "Bruccoli Addenda," *Fitzgerald/Hemingway Annual,* 7 (1975), 337–339.
Material updating and supplementing Bruccoli's F Bibliography (I40).

H851.   ————.   "Fitzgerald's St. Paul Academy Publications: Possible Addenda," *Fitzgerald/Hemingway Annual*, 7 (1975), 147–148.

Reprints five unsigned limericks about his schoolmates from the *Now & Then* which F pasted in his scrapbook, possibly because he wrote them.

H852.   ————.   "'How Are You and the Family Old Sport?'—Gerlach and Gatsby," *Fitzgerald/Hemingway Annual*, 7 (1975), 33–36.

Speculations about presence on Long Island in 1923–24 of a man named Gerlach whom F knew and who used the expression "old sport."

————.   See Smith (H918).

H853.   Carringer, Robert L.   *"Citizen Kane, The Great Gatsby* and Some Conventions of American Narrative," *Critical Inquiry*, 2 (Winter 1975), 307–325.

Cites similarities between Kane and Gatsby, between the green light and the little glass globe (both symbolize "the loss of a woman, child-hood innocence versus adult experience, and the ideal West versus the corrupt East"), and between the narrator figures Nick and Thompson. Also shows parallels between GG and "American," the first draft screenplay of "Citizen Kane," much of which was deleted from final movie.

H854.   Chadwick, Bruce.   "Fitzgerald's Works Nourished in Jersey," NY *Sunday News*—New Jersey Edition, August 31, 1975, p. J34.

Summary of F's school days in New Jersey—at Newman School and Princeton—and remarks on the "Fitzgerald boom" precipitated by recent GG film.

H855.   Christy, Marian.   "Scottie Remembers Scott & Zelda," Boston *Sunday Globe*, March 2, 1975, p. A–20.

Extended interview with F's daughter.

H856.   Coe, Richard L.   "New Play About Zelda," Washington (D.C.) *Post*, June 13, 1974, p. B13.

Review of "The Amateur: Reflections of Zelda" by Leslie Jacobson and produced by the Washington Area Feminist Theater: "a resourceful, absorbing play."

H857.   Crosland, Andrew.   *"The Great Gatsby* and *The Secret Agent*," *Fitzgerald/Hemingway Annual*, 7 (1975), 75–81.

Cites parallels: two characters named Michaelis, two characters named Tom, similarities between Gatsby and Stevie, similar functions of the police in both novels, and similarities between Daisy and Winnie Verloc.

H858. Drabble, Margaret. "The Beautiful Couple," *Radio Times* (BBC Radio Brighton), 207 (April 26-May 2, 1975), 60, 63.
Brief assessment of F's marriage on occasion of BBC2 program "A Dream of Living" about a crucial period in F and Zelda's lives: "Whatever the causes of their collapse they remain a warning of the danger of achieving one's heart's desire."

H859. Dudley, Juanita Williams. "Dr. Diver, Vivisectionist," *College Literature*, 2 (Spring 1975), 128–134.
Uses passage about Dick wanting to give a "bad party" as basis for seeing him as a "specious hero," a man "given to using people for his own purposes, whether diversionary or downright sadistic," and the novel as "the chronicle of a brilliant and promising young man who connived at his own destruction by forces representing wealth and power."

H860. Duggan, Margaret M. "Fitzgerald Checklist," *Fitzgerald/Hemingway Annual*, 7 (1975), 341–350.
Listing of recent material by and about F.

H861. "F. Scott Fitzgerald to Get His Wish," Washington (D.C.) *Star*, October 12, 1975, p. A–3.
Syndicated (AP) report on plans to rebury F and Zelda.

H862. Fain, J. T. "Recollections of F. Scott Fitzgerald," *Fitzgerald/Hemingway Annual*, 7 (1975), 133–139.
Memories of a newsman who knew F in North Carolina in 1935–36, with emphasis on his drinking, his Marxism, his charm, and his frequent mention of a Catholic Church with which he had broken ties.

H863. Foster, Richard. "Time's Exile: Dick Diver and the Heroic Idea," *Mosaic*, 8 (Spring 1975), 89–108.
Sees TITN as ending in a "late Emersonian…note of affirmation" and stresses its epic qualities, comparing Dick to Hamlet and contending that Dick is a "tragic hero because he found himself cut off, finally, from both his duty and his fulfillment in it."

H864. Franklin, Ben A. "'Happy Thought' for the Fitzgeralds," NY *Times*, November 8, 1975, p. 29.
Account of reburial of F and Zelda. Abridged versions of this article also appeared in Boston *Herald-American*, November 8, 1975, p. 21; San Francisco *Chronicle*, November 8, 1975, p. 15; Raleigh *News and Observer*, November 12, 1975, p. 19.

H865.   Giannetti, Louis.   "The Gatsby Flap," *Literature/Film Quarterly*, 3 (Winter 1975), 13–22.

Defends 1974 GG film by focusing on effectiveness of the adaptation which is "merely a flawed but highly intelligent attempt to adapt an understated, deceptively complex literary masterpiece into another medium of generally greater aesthetic complexity."

H866.   Gill, Brendan.   "Profiles: The Dark Advantage," *New Yorker*, 51 (September 15, 1975), 42–92 [49–54].

Profile of playwright Philip Barry which also discusses F, John O'Hara, and Eugene O'Neill as three other Irish-American writers. Emphasis on F's sense of being an outsider, a poor boy in a rich man's school, but, like Gatsby, having an "extraordinary gift for hope." Reprinted: Gill (I147).

H867.   Gorney, Cynthia.   "Fitzgerald Reburied in Simple Ceremony," Washington (D.C.) *Post*, November 8, 1975, pp. A 15, A 28.

Detailed account of F reburial.

H868.   Hamilton, Ruth.   "The Crazily Charmed Life of Donald Ogden Stewart," New Haven *Register*, December 21, 1975, pp. 1D, 4D.

Interview with Stewart on occasion of publication of his autobiography *By a Stroke of Luck!* (I342) includes passing mention of his friendship with F.

H869.   Hart, Stan.   "The Great Gasbag," *Mad Magazine*, 172 (January 1975), 4–10.

Cartoon parody which purports to explain how the movie killed the "Gatsby look."

H870.   Hendrickson, Paul.   "'He had come a long way to this blue lawn...,'" *National Observer*, November 22, 1975, p. 20.

Account of F reburial.

H871.   Higgins, Brian, and Hershel Parker.   "Sober Second Thoughts: The 'Author's Final Version' of Fitzgerald's *Tender Is the Night*," *Proof*, 4 (1975), 111–134.

After reviewing critical comment on both 1934 and 1951 texts, offers considerable criticism of Cowley's editing procedures, principally that rearrangement could not be undertaken without callously destroying "the effects Fitzgerald elaborately calculated" and concludes that therefore 1934 edition is superior.

H872.   Hobhouse, Janet.   "The Literary Lions of Paris Had Some Sharp Teeth—In the World of Hemingway, Stein, Anderson and Fitzgerald, One Had to Be Careful," Milwaukee *Journal*, December 2, 1975, p. 12.
Passing mention of F's relationships with Gertrude Stein and Hemingway in Paris in the 1920s.

H873.   Hogan, William.   "World of Books—Budd Schulberg's 'The Disenchanted,'" San Francisco *Chronicle*, April 11, 1975, p. 43.
Review of paperback reissue of Schulberg's novel (C139) with discussion of F as Manley Halliday.

H874.   Iida, Tomo.   "'Babylon Revisited' and F. Scott Fitzgerald," *Kinran Tanki Daigaku Kenkyū Shi*, 6 (April 1975), 29–37.
In English. Primarily a biographical reading of the story focusing on the drinking of F and Charlie Wales.

H875.   Isaacs, Stan.   "Fitzgerald to Truex Gets Quite a Play," *Newsday* (Garden City, NY), November 4, 1975, p. 7A.
Account of how F scholar Matthew J. Bruccoli acquired a copy of *The Vegetable* inscribed by F to actor Ernest Truex fifteen years after having seen it in a Boston bookstore.

H876.   ———.   "Schulberg, Fitzgerald and 'The Disenchanted,'" *Newsday* (Garden City, NY), September 2, 1975, p. 7A.
Interview with Budd Schulberg who reminisces about F and talks about *The Disenchanted* (C139) and the F revival.

Kerr, Joan P. See Smith (H918).

H877.   Kishi, Masaaki.   "Great Gatsby or, the Career of an Unsuccessful Alger Hero," *Newsboy* (Horatio Alger Society, Kalamazoo, Mich.), 13 (March-April 1975), 3–6.
Although F was "consistently critical of the Alger philosophy," GG "was not intended to caricature the Alger hero" but rather "mirrors 'the economic fantasies of the twenties.'" This essay originally appeared in *Kyushu American Literature*, No. 8 (1965).

H878.   Korenman, Joan S.   " 'Only Her Hairdresser...': Another Look at Daisy Buchanan," *American Literature*, 46 (January 1975), 574–578.
Notes that F describes Daisy in contradictory ways, as a blonde and as a brunette, and cites her affinities with both the fair-haired heroines of the Romantic tradition and with "the knowledgeable experienced dark women" of the Romanticists, concluding that the "character that results is both cool innocent princess and sensual *femme fatale*, a combination that further enhances Daisy's enigmatic charm."

H879.   ———. "A View From the (Queensboro) Bridge," *Fitzgerald/Hemingway Annual*, 7 (1975), 93–96.

Detailed study of passage in which Nick and Gatsby drive across the Queensboro Bridge on their way to New York City as a "splendid illustration of Fitzgerald's mastery of patterning and his use of irony" and "especially important for what it has to say about Gatsby and the American dream."

H880.   Lang, Sylvia. "Determined, Dusty Families Tackle Laurel Renovation," St. Paul *Sunday Pioneer Press*, July 13, 1975, City Life Section, p. 2.

Article on renovation of house where F was born.

H881.   Lawry, J. S. "Green Light or Square of Light in *The Great Gatsby*," *Dalhousie Review*, 55 (Spring 1975), 114–132.

Examination of two of the most effective images in GG, "those of a line leading to a green light, and a flat white light fixed and bounded in a square." The line signifies " 'romantic readiness' " and moves "freely and yearningly across space and time"; the square, sought out or inhabited by the Buchanans, "attempts to freeze, flatten, or contain space and time."

H882.   Lewis, Janet. "Fitzgerald's 'Philippe, Count of Darkness,' " *Fitzgerald/Hemingway Annual*, 7 (1975), 7–32.

Detailed close study of the composition, reworking, and plans for projected novel, as well as of the four published sections. Relates style to the "tough guy" fiction of the 1930s and sees Philippe as fictional rendering of Hemingway.

H883.   Littleton, Taylor. "A Letter From Zelda Fitzgerald," *Fitzgerald/Hemingway Annual*, 7 (1975), 3–6.

First printing—with brief introductory note—of Zelda letter about F, written in 1944 or 1945 to childhood friend.

H884.   Long, Robert Emmet. "The Opening Three Chapters of 'The Great Gatsby,' " *English Record*, 26 (Fall 1975), 85–94.

Examination to show how opening chapters "work together as a single unit" revealing characters through settings, intimating the events of the plot to follow, and expressing the theme of the novel (the corrupting effect of money). This material is incorporated into Long's *The Achieving of "The Great Gatsby"* (I224).

H885.   Lueders, Edward. "Revisiting Babylon: Fitzgerald and the 1920's," *Western Humanities Review*, 29 (Summer 1975), 285–291.

Personal memories of the 1920s and of the era as pictured by F and by Carl Van Vechten.

H886. McCabe, Bruce. "Ernest's Wild Ride With Scott and Zelda," Boston *Globe*, March 14, 1975, p. 31.

Describes four-page Hemingway piece on F in the Kennedy Library which Hemingway "originally intended to publish in 'A Moveable Feast' but which he subsequently decided not to include for reasons that are not clear" and which depicts F as a capricious drunk.

H887. Makurath, Paul A., Jr. "Another Source for 'Gatsby,'" *Fitzgerald/Hemingway Annual*, 7 (1975), 115–116.

Suggests source for name as character named "Gadsby" in George Eliot's *The Mill on the Floss*.

H888. Marder, Daniel. "Exiles at Home in American Literature," *Mosaic*, 8 (Spring 1975), 49–75 [51, 52].

Passing mention of F and of "Babylon Revisited."

H889. Margolis, Jon. "Dissecting Today's Trends—The America of the Future Is Before Your Eyes," Chicago *Tribune*, June 29, 1975, Sec. 2, p. 8.

Brief mention of end of GG in article on trend among Americans to move often.

H890. Miura, Yachiyo. "F. Scott Fitzgerald: The Tragic Hero of the Jazz Age," *Aichi Daigaku Bungaku Ronshū*, 53 (March 1975), 1–34.

In English. Discusses "Winter Dreams," "The Rich Boy," and GG to illustrate F's desire for wealth, his attraction/distrust attitude toward the rich, and his "bafflement" at not being able to achieve success and entrance into the wealthy class.

H891. Nance, William L. "Eden, Oedipus, and Rebirth in American Fiction," *Arizona Quarterly*, 31 (Winter 1975), 353–365 [354–355, 360, 361, 364–365].

Mention of GG as providing the "classic example of Oedipal rebuff" in discussion of pastoral and erotic-regressive modes in American literature; also mentions "The Curious Case of Benjamin Button" and "The Diamond as Big as the Ritz."

H892. "New Burial Site Chosen For Fitzgerald," Washington (D.C.) *Post*, October 12, 1975, p. A18.

Article announcing F reburial plans.

H893. Oakes, Philip. "The Way They Were," London *Sunday Times*, October 12, 1975, p. 35.

Memories of F and Zelda recounted by Bijou O'Connor, who knew them in Paris in 1920s.

H894.   Ower, John. "A Thematic Reference to *The Rubaiyat of Omar Khayyam* in *The Great Gatsby*," *Fitzgerald/Hemingway Annual*, 7 (1975), 103–105.

Nick's use of word "caravansary" in Chapter VII alludes to Stanza 17 of *The Rubaiyat* and suggests range of similarities, some quite ironic, between F's novel and the poem.

Parker, Hershel. See Higgins (H871).

H895.   Parrott, Jennings. "Newsmakers—'They Shall Melt Guns Into Crosses...,'" Los Angeles *Times*, October 13, 1975, Part I, p. 2.

Brief paragraph on upcoming F reburial.

H896.   "People," St. Louis *Post-Dispatch*, November 9, 1975, p. 5A.

Brief account of F reburial.

H897.   "People," *Time*, 106 (November 17, 1975), 63.

Brief paragraph giving reactions of cast of film version of LT.

H898.   Pinsker, Sanford. "Seeing *The Great Gatsby* Eye to Eye," *College Literature*, 3 (Winter 1975), 69–71.

Examination of the symbol of Dr. Eckleburg's eyes, which observes that, although F wrote the image into the novel as an afterthought (after seeing a book jacket), it is not an ineffective symbol but rather part of "a pattern of inter-locking images."

H899.   "Programs—Libraries & Culture: Writers, Art & Music," *Library Journal*, 100 (September 15, 1975), 1594–1595.

Notes that F was the "focal figure" in the Great Neck (NY) Public Library's "recent exhibit and lecture series about area celebrities from the 1920s."

H900.   Qualls, Barry V. "Physician in the Counting House: The Religious Motif in *Tender Is the Night*," *Essays in Literature* (Western Illinois University, Macomb), 2 (Fall 1975), 192–208.

Contends that "the novel's structure, both paralleling and inverting the Christ story, has presented a modern pilgrim's progress to nothingness....Richard Diver is homeless, physically and metaphorically, condemned by his own illusions and his nation's to wander forever in a materialistic morass and psychic hell of his own making."

H901.   Raeburn, John. "Hemingway in the Twenties: 'The Artist's Reward,'" *Rocky Mountain Review of Language and Literature*, 29 (Autumn 1975), 118–146 [118, 122, 133, 141, 144–145].

Passing mention of F in discussion of development of Hemingway's public personality in the 1920s.

H902. Rees, John O. "Fitzgerald's Pat Hobby Stories," *Colorado Quarterly*, 23 (Spring 1975), 553–562.

Essentially summaries of the stories which admit their unevenness but also contends that they deserve "to be better known."

H903. Reinhold, Robert. "Hemingway Papers Open For Study In a Setting That Belies Their Vitality," NY *Times*, January 31, 1975, pp. 35, 66 [35].

Includes brief mention of F's critiques of *The Sun Also Rises* and *A Farewell to Arms*.

H904. Rhodes, Jack. "Fitzgerald Home Restoration Attracts Buyers to the Hill," St. Paul *Pioneer Press*, March 17, 1975, p. 19.

Article on restoration of F's birthplace.

H905. Robillard, Douglas. "The Paradises of Scott Fitzgerald," *Essays in Arts and Sciences* (University of New Haven), 4 (May 1975), 64–73.

Discussion of TSOP, GG, and TITN, and, more briefly, several short stories. Both TSOP and TITN deal with the "paradise of the romantic egoist"; while the "chief difficulty" of GG is that it is "often read as though Gatsby were at the center," when, actually, the domination of the novel by Nick gives it "a texture inappropriate to tragedy."

H906. Robinson, Jeffrey. "Fitzgerald's Riviera—'disappeared with time,'" *Christian Science Monitor*, April 8, 1975, p. 19.

Memories of the Murphys' Villa America—the basis of the Villa Diana in TITN—by Marie Revello, caretaker with her husband since 1926, and Edmund Uher, the owner since 1950.

H907. Rodewald, F. A. "Faulkner's Possible Use of *The Great Gatsby*," *Fitzgerald/Hemingway Annual*, 7 (1975), 97–101.

Examination of similarities between GG and *Absalom, Absalom!* which focuses on parallels between Gatsby and Sutpen.

H908. Roulston, Robert. "*This Side of Paradise*: The Ghost of Rupert Brooke," *Fitzgerald/Hemingway Annual*, 7 (1975), 117–130.

Notes references to Brooke and tries to account for Amory Blaine's and F's fascination with him, concluding that it leads to two opposing motifs in the novel: "In his struggles first to emulate then to disassociate himself from Rupert Brooke, Amory finds himself striving, usually without success, to reconcile vestiges of nineteenth century romanticism with the twentieth century, middle class and Catholic sexual morality with amoral eroticism, traditional culture with newer modes of thought and expression, and a yearning for a patrician manner with a left-of-center egalitarianism."

H909.   Salloch, Roger.   "Ernest & Scott in Paris," NY *Times*, October 5, 1975, Sec. 10, pp. 1, 14.
Retraces trip F and Hemingway took from Paris to Lyon and back, filling in details through the account in *A Moveable Feast*.

H910.   Sanders, Barbara Gerber.   "Structural Imagery in *The Great Gatsby*: Metaphor and Matrix," *Linguistics in Literature*, 1 (Fall 1975), 53–75.
Uses a "linguistic-oriented" technique based on "the arrangement and choice of words" to discover in GG "preliminary evidence" of a "complex matrix or overall plan of some sort about the subject of birth," specifically in the verb sentences at the end of each chapter and in the subject of the last paragraph of each chapter. This "birth matrix" is then used to interpret Gatsby, Nick, and the Buchanans.

H911.   Savage, David.   "Who Is 'Owl Eyes' in *The Great Gatsby*?" *American Notes & Queries*, 13 (January 1975), 72–74.
Contrasts Owl Eyes with Dr. T. J. Eckleburg, seeing the former as typifying "the American capacity for compassion" and associated with "the best in moral and conservative America."

H912.   Schulberg, Budd.   "The Best Gatsby," *NY Times Book Review*, May 18, 1975, p. 55.
Study of the recently published GG manuscript facsimile (I48) which emphasizes the care F took in revising the novel and points to several examples of the judiciousness with which he did it.

H913.   Schwartz, Tony.   "The Word—So We Beat On (and Then One Fine Day...)," *New Times*, 5 (November 14, 1975), 15.
Brief note on F reburial.

H914.   Scott, Robert Ian.   "A Sense of Loss: Entropy vs. Ecology in *The Great Gatsby*," *Queen's Quarterly*, 82 (Winter 1975), 559–571.
Suggests that GG illustrates concretely the second law of thermodynamics: Time and wealth disorganize and destroy the "green breast of the new world" the Dutch sailors saw, the reality on which human relationships and hope depend. Also points out the many forms of entropy in the world of GG—boredom, confusion, a sense of loss (particularly of the past).

H915.   [Sharbutt, Eve].   "Fitzgerald Scrapbooks—Scottie Recalls Scott and Zelda," Atlanta *Journal and Constitution*, January 12, 1975, p. 8-C.

Syndicated (AP) interview with F's daughter on occasion of publication of *The Romantic Egoists* (I324) in which she reminisces about her parents. This article also appeared as follows: Richmond (Va.) *Times-Dispatch*, January 12, 1975; Lynchburg (Va.) *News*, January 12, 1975, p. A–8; Columbus (Ohio) *Dispatch*, January 12, 1975; Kalamazoo *Gazette*, January 12, 1975; Los Angeles *Times*, January 12, 1975; Houston *Post*, January 12, 1975; Burlington (N.C.) *Times-News*, January 10, 1975; Palm Beach (Fla.) *Post*, January 13, 1975; Bridgeport (Conn.) *Sunday Post*, January 12, 1975; Newport News (Va.) *Daily Press*, January 12, 1975; Florence (Ala.) *Times*, January 26, 1975; Providence *Sunday Journal*, January 12, 1975, p. E–2; Great Bend (Kan.) *Tribune*, January 17, 1975; Sedalia (Mo.) *Capital*, January 18, 1975; Huntington (W.Va.) *Herald-Advertiser*, January 12, 1975, p. 30; Poughkeepsie *Journal*, January 12, 1975; Huntsville (Ala.) *Times*, January 12, 1975; Vicksburg (Miss.) *Post*, February 1, 1975; Fresno *Bee*, January 12, 1975; New Orleans *Times-Picayune*, January 12, 1975, Sec. 2, p. 8; Lowell (Mass.) *Sunday Sun*, January 12, 1975; Wichita *Eagle and Beacon*, January 12, 1975, p. 4G; Cleveland *Plain Dealer*, January 12, 1975, p. 2-E; Allentown (Pa.) *Sunday Call-Chronicle*, January 12, 1975; St. Petersburg *Times*, January 12, 1975; Mansfield (Ohio) *News-Journal*, January 31, 1975.

H916.   Sheffield, R. Michael. "The Temporal Location of Fitzgerald's Jay Gatsby," *Texas Quarterly*, 18 (Summer 1975), 122–130.

Distinguishes between the "quantitative time" and the "qualitative time" of Gatsby's life: The period of his life between his meeting Daisy and leaving her is the "qualitative period which eventually became the center of his entire being" and because Gatsby never discovered the "nothingness" in his life he never "found what he had given of his 'self'" and never "regained consciousness with reality."

H917.   Sherwood, John. "Scott and Zelda: The Final Chapter— Very Tender Was the Day," Washington (D.C.) *Star*, November 8, 1975, pp. A1, A8.

Detailed account of F reburial which includes some biographical details.

H918.   Smith, Scottie Fitzgerald, Matthew J. Bruccoli, and Joan P. Kerr, eds. "The Romantic Egoists," *Book Digest Magazine*, 2 (April 1975), 131–145.

Excerpts from *The Romantic Egoists* (I324).

H919.   Taylor, David. "Passing Through," *Punch*, 269 (August 27, 1975), 336.

Interview with Sheilah Graham who reminisces about F.

H920.   Tenenbaum, Ruth Betsy.   "'The Gray-Turning, Gold-Turning Consciousness' of Nick Carraway," *Fitzgerald/Hemingway Annual*, 7 (1975), 37–55.

Contends that Nick has a "double vision," his "'everyday consciousness'" and his "'poetic consciousness,' " and examines images manifested by each: The former is manifested in descriptions of settings and characters, details of the action, and reporting of conversations; the latter in images of "disorder" and "homogeneity," images which are indices of Nick's "subjective feeling," and in images which undercut the despair of the novel "by their very exuberance and charm."

H921.   Thornton, Lawrence.   "Ford Madox Ford and *The Great Gatsby*," *Fitzgerald/Hemingway Annual*, 7 (1975), 57–74.

Suggests that a close reading of GG and Ford's *The Good Soldier* "reveals similarities in narrative techniques, impressionistic form and romantic theme" and examines these parallels in detail.

H922.   Webb, Dorothy M.   "Fitzgerald on El Greco: A View of *The Great Gatsby*," *Fitzgerald/Hemingway Annual*, 7 (1975), 89–91.

Detailed examination of El Greco's "View of Toledo" which finds similarities between the painting and details in GG.

H923.   Wheelock, Alan S.   "As Ever, 'Daddy's Girl': Incest Motifs in *Day for Night*," *Gypsy Scholar*, 2 (Spring 1975), 69–75.

Contends that Truffaut uses TITN in an effort to make his movie "resonate with the force of an older, literary excursion into" the "murky region" of incest.

H924.   Whitman, Alden.   "Sara Murphy, Patron of Writers and Artists in France, 91, Dead," NY *Times*, October 11, 1975, p. 34.

Obituary which includes several paragraphs on the similarities between the Murphys and Dick and Nicole Diver of TITN and comment on the friendship between the Murphys and the Fitzgeralds.

H925.   Wilson, B. W.   "The Theatrical Motif in *The Great Gatsby*," *Fitzgerald/Hemingway Annual*, 7 (1975), 107–113.

Comments on "Gatsby's dual role as performer and impresario and the significance such a role has for our understanding of the novel."

H926.   Winkel, Gabrielle.   "Fitzgerald's Agge of Denmark," *Fitzgerald/Hemingway Annual*, 7 (1975), 131–132.

Speculations on who the character of Prince Agge of Denmark in LT might be based upon.

H927.   Young, Philip.   "In Search of a Lost Generation," *Kansas Quarterly*, 7 (Fall 1975), 127–134 [129, 130].

Brief passing mention of F.

1976

H928.　Alpert, Hollis. "Fitzgerald, Hollywood, and *The Last Tycoon*," *American Film*, 1 (March 1976), 8–14.
Some mention of F's desire to become successful screenwriter in article mainly devoted to LT film.

H929.　————. "Hollywood Daze," *American Film*, 1 (March 1976), 13.
Mentions TV program "F. Scott Fitzgerald and 'The Last of the Belles,'" Latham's *Crazy Sundays* (I218), and Graham's *Beloved Infidel* (C67), suggesting that F would be better served on TV by a dramatization of his screenplay of "Babylon Revisited."

H930.　Baba, Hirotoshi. "*The Last Tycoon*—Fitzgerald's Tragic Vision of America," *Bungei to Shisō*, 40 (February 1976), 39–54.
In English. F's "tragic vision of American culture and history" in LT is revealed in "Stahr's decline, Hollywood's debasement of the past values, and the nation's ignorance of the cultural heritage."

H931.　Baker, Russell. "Sunday Observer—The Golden Apple," *NY Times Magazine*, March 14, 1976, p. 7.
Brief mention of F and Zelda in humorous fantasy about NY.

H932.　[Brock, Mark]. "In Search of F. Scott Fitzgerald," *Carolinian* (University of South Carolina, Columbia), 1 (Summer 1976), 1–2.
Extended interview with Matthew J. Bruccoli who discusses origins and extent of his interest in F.

H933.　Brown, James. "F. Scott Fitzgerald to Be Put to Test," Los Angeles *Times*, December 19, 1976, "Calendar" Section, pp. 118–119.
Discusses proposed National Public Radio series "The World of F. Scott Fitzgerald," quoting producer-director William Shriver, F scholar Matthew J. Bruccoli, and Arch Oboler who has adapted "One Trip Abroad" for the pilot program.

H934.　[Bruccoli, Matthew J.] "Bruccoli Addenda," *Fitzgerald/ Hemingway Annual*, 8 (1976), 251–253.
Supplements and updates Bruccoli's F Bibliography (I40).

H935.　————. "A Great Neck Friendship," NY *Times*, November 7, 1976, Long Island Weekly Section, pp. 3, 16.
Detailed account of F-Ring Lardner relationship.

H936. ———, ed. "'Ballet Shoes': A Movie Synopsis," *Fitzgerald/Hemingway Annual*, 8 (1976), 3–7 [3–4].

Brief introductory note gives background and significance of F movie synopsis printed here for first time: "Like Boxley in *The Last Tycoon*, Fitzgerald was still thinking of movies in terms of cheap stories."

H937. Canby, Vincent. "'Tycoon' Echoes 30's Hollywood," NY *Times*, November 18, 1976, p. 59.

Review of LT film which sees adaptation of F's "very complete satisfying fragment" as preserving "the original feeling and intelligence" of F's work.

H938. Cary, Meredith. "*Save Me the Waltz* as a Novel," *Fitzgerald/Hemingway Annual*, 8 (1976), 65–78.

Detailed examination of the novel, especially the characterization of Alabama Beggs, which reveals it to be "a thoughtful and carefully balanced study of a search for individuality, social relevance, and order" whose "avoidance of oversimplification" is the "key" to its "power."

H939. Champlin, Charles. "Fitzgerald's 'Last Tycoon' on Screen," Los Angeles *Times*, November 18, 1976, Part IV, pp. 1, 21.

Review of LT film which notes that F "was probably the most sensitive eyewitness the [movie] industry has ever had," so that the failure of this film is "unusually disappointing and angering" and can be attributed to Pinter's lack of congeniality with F's material.

H940. Cocks, Jay. "Babylon Revisited: The Last Tycoon," *Time*, 108 (December 6, 1976), 87–88.

Review of LT film which "shares roughly the strengths and weaknesses of the novel."

H941. Cooper, Ashley. "Doing the Charleston," Charleston (S.C.) *News and Courier*, November 3, 1976, Sec. B, p. 1.

Article on opening of new section of interstate highway includes quotes from Clara Edwards, who runs the Oak Hall Hotel in Tryon, North Carolina, and Ted King, dining room captain at the hotel, regarding F's stays there.

H942. Corso, Joseph. "One Not-Forgotten Summer Night: Sources for Fictional Symbols of American Character in *The Great Gatsby*," *Fitzgerald/Hemingway Annual*, 8 (1976), 8–33.

Explores possible sources for characters of Gatsby (F himself, novelist Edvart Rölvaag, Robert C. Kerr, Jr., and Long Island bootlegger Max Gerlach) and Dan Cody ("Buffalo Bill" Cody, Dan Cody of

Montgomery, Alabama, and Major Edwin R. Gilman), as well as of other details in novel.

H943.   C[ousins], N[orman].   "Editor's Page—The Hemingway Letters," *Saturday Review*, n.s. 4 (October 2, 1976), 4–6.

Describes Hemingway's letters about F written to F biographer Arthur Mizener and owned by the University of Maryland Library.

H944.   Crist, Judith.   "The Movies—Murder in the Reverential Degree," *Saturday Review*, n.s. 4 (December 11, 1976), 77–78.

Review of LT film which includes discussion of the fragmentary state of F's novel and of Harold Pinter's inadequate screen adaptation.

H945.   Curry, Ralph, and Janet Lewis.   "Stephen Leacock: An Early Influence on F. Scott Fitzgerald," *Canadian Review of American Studies*, 7 (Spring 1976), 5–14.

Traces Leacock's influence on F in prep school and college writings, especially "Jemina," and in "The Cruise of the Rolling Junk."

H946.   Daniels, Thomas E.   "English Periodical Publications of Fitzgerald's Short Stories: A Correction of the Record," *Fitzgerald/Hemingway Annual*, 8 (1976), 124–129.

Corrects errors in Bruccoli's F Bibliography in dates for first appearances of F stories in English periodicals and one error in a title for a first English publication.

H947.   "Dialogue on Film/Elia Kazan," *American Film*, 1 (March 1976), 33–48.

Interview with director of LT film which includes comments on the movie.

H948.   Duggan, Margaret M.   "Editorial: A New Edition of Gatsby," *Fitzgerald/Hemingway Annual*, 8 (1976), 303.

A "spot investigation" of the newly reset Scribner Library paperback edition of GG "reveals that it is indeed more corrupt than the preceding Scribner Library edition." A brief list of new errors is appended.

H949.   ———.   "Fitzgerald Checklist," *Fitzgerald/Hemingway Annual*, 8 (1976), 254–259.

Listing of recent material by and about F.

H950.   ———.   "Sara Sherman Wiborg Murphy (1883-1975)," *Fitzgerald/Hemingway Annual*, 8 (1976), 306–307.

Brief obituary tribute.

H951.   Eder, Richard.   "A Critic's Jottings: On Being Gripped Versus Being Touched," NY *Times*, November 28, 1976, Sec. 2, pp. 17, 44 [17].

Film of LT is "a decent and intelligent tribute to F. Scott Fitzgerald's burning fragment" which avoids "defacing it."

H952.   "Famous Mothers—Fitzgerald's 'Old Peasant,'" San Francisco *Chronicle*, September 3, 1976, p. 19.

Short account of Mollie Fitzgerald's influence on her son.

H953.   Farber, Stephen. "Film—Hollywood Takes on 'The Last Tycoon,'" NY *Times*, March 21, 1976, p. D 15.

Lengthy account of problems involved in making of LT film: "The real-life dramas of the people making the movie are inextricably bound up with the story that Fitzgerald wrote."

H954.   Fujitani, Seiwa. "On the Tragic Sense of Love in the Novels of F. Scott Fitzgerald—Chiefly in the Case of *The Last Tycoon*," *Otemon Gakuin Daigaku Bungakubu Kiyō*, 10 (December 1976), 65–73.

In English. Discusses how treatment of love in LT differs from that in GG and TITN; in latter two novels, the protagonists deteriorate through love affairs, while in LT, F shows a type of "tragic and wise" love which is suitable for a "rationalist's point of view."

H955.   "Go to Work on an Egg," *Times Literary Supplement* (London), May 28, 1976, p. 644.

Review of the 1975 *Fitzgerald/Hemingway Annual* which is cynically critical of some of the F articles.

H956.   Good, Dorothy Ballweg. "'A Romance and a Reading List': The Literary References in *This Side of Paradise*," *Fitzgerald/Hemingway Annual*, 8 (1976), 35–64.

Very briefly annotated listing of literary titles and authors and works quoted from in TSOP.

H957.   Graham, Don. "The Common Ground of *Goodbye, Columbus* and *The Great Gatsby*," *Forum* (Houston), 13 (Winter 1976), 68–71.

Claims that Philip Roth's novel "echoes, modifies, reverses the themes of Fitzgerald's much more hopeful fiction" and is a "retelling of the Gatsby fable, an interim report on the American Dream fifty years after Fitzgerald's analysis."

H958.   Graham, Sheilah. "Fitzgerald's Plans for Completing 'Tycoon,'" NY *Times*, November 14, 1976, Sec. 2, pp. 1, 15.

Text, with brief introduction, of March 6, 1941, letter Graham wrote Edmund Wilson outlining F's plans for finishing LT.

H959.   ———. "The Most Interesting Men I've Ever Known,"
Family Weekly, March 7, 1976, pp. 4–5.
Men discussed are J. Paul Getty, Howard Hughes, Noel Coward,
Michael Caine, and F who is described as "simply the most interesting
human being I ever knew."

H960.   [Grant, Annette]. "John Cheever—The Art of Fiction
LXII," *Paris Review*, 67 (Fall 1976), 39–66 [56].
Interview in which Cheever briefly discusses F as a "documentary
novelist."
Reprinted: Grant (I163).

H961.   Grey, M. Cameron. "Miss Toklas Alone," *Virginia
Quarterly Review*, 52 (Autumn 1976), 687–696.
Passing mention of F and Zelda in personal reminiscence of Alice B.
Toklas.

H962.   Gross, Dalton H. "The Death of Rosy Rosenthal: A Note
on Fitzgerald's Use of Background in *The Great Gatsby*," *Notes and
Queries*, 221 (January 1976), 22–23.
Meyer Wolfsheim's reference to the murder of Rosy Rosenthal is an
allusion to an actual gangland murder in 1912 and for Nick and the
reader is "a chillingly realistic introduction to Gatsby's world."

H963.   Hackl, Lloyd. "Fitzgerald in St. Paul: An Oral History
Portrait," *Fitzgerald/Hemingway Annual*, 8 (1976), 117–122.
Description of oral history project of interviews with F's St. Paul
contemporaries being conducted by Minnesota Historical Society and
account of 1975 interview with Mrs. C. O. (Xandra) Kalman, a lifelong
friend of F.

H964.   Hampton, Riley V. "Owl Eyes in *The Great Gatsby*,"
American Literature, 48 (May 1976), 229.
Brief note suggesting that Ring Lardner who was dubbed "Owl
Eyes" by a fellow sportswriter at the 1919 World Series might be the
"real-life prototype" for the character in GG.

H965.   Hart, Jeffrey. "Reconsideration—*The Great Gatsby* By
F. Scott Fitzgerald," *New Republic*, 174 (April 17, 1976), 31–33.
Claims that a "sense of strange transformation pervades" GG in
which Gatsby, as divinity, changes his name, appearance, and
dwelling—all through the magic power of the dollar; but he cannot an-
nihilate time and thus proves a "false Christ," a "great doomed magi-
cian, a heresiarch in his relationship to reality."

H966.   Hogan, William.   "A Hard Look at Movie-Making—'Last Tycoon' Captures the Essence of Fitzgerald," *San Francisco Chronicle*, December 22, 1976, p. 39.

Review of LT film, "an honest interpretation of Fitzgerald" and "thoroughly absorbing," with some mention of the novel which "no doubt would have been his finest work if completed."

H967.   Johnson, Christiane.   "Daughter and Father: An Interview With Mrs. Frances Scott Fitzgerald Smith—Washington, D.C., August 29, 1973," *Études Anglaises*, 29 (January-March 1976), 72–75.

F's daughter speaks of her father's difficulties with TITN, of his love of place, his sense of history, his disappointment with "the lack of intellectualism in American life," his enthusiasm about Roosevelt, and of the F revival.

H968.   ———.   "*The Great Gatsby*: The Final Vision," *Fitzgerald/Hemingway Annual*, 8 (1976), 108–115.

Close reading of the last page of GG which suggests that it depicts man's endless aspiration "toward the past, toward a lost paradise. His continual quest for the future can only lead him into the past. But there is grandeur in his constant quest in spite of his helplessness."

H969.   Kael, Pauline.   "The Current Cinema—Stallone and Stahr," *New Yorker*, 88 (November 29, 1976), 154, 157–160, 163 [157–160, 163].

Review of LT film with comments on the novel and on the problems of adapting an unfinished work.
Reprinted: Kael (I198).

H970.   Kane, Patricia.   "F. Scott Fitzgerald's St. Paul: A Writer's Use of Material," *Minnesota History*, 45 (Winter 1976), 141–148.

Shows, through discussion of GG, "The Ice Palace," "Winter Dreams," and the Basil stories, how F's St. Paul "is more symbolic than actual" and how, while his "use of the city corresponds in part to his experience of it," he "freely altered or reinterpreted his perceptions to suit the characters and themes of his fiction."

H971.   Kauffmann, Stanley.   "Stanley Kauffmann on Films—The Last Tycoon," *New Republic*, 175 (December 4, 1976), 20–21.

Review of LT film which attributes failure of Pinter's adaptation to his attempts to make a unified whole from a fragment.

H972.   Kaufman, Bill.   "TV Film About Fitzgerald," *Arizona Republic* (Phoenix), May 16, 1976, p. N–6.

Preview of upcoming TV special "F. Scott Fitzgerald in Hollywood."

H973. Kazin, Alfred. "'The Giant Killer': Drink & the American Writer," *Commentary*, 61 (March 1976), 44–50 [45–46].

Mention of F's drunkenness—which was "involved in his need to be picturesque, to ease the money and sexual strains in his life, to keep up with his crazy wife Zelda."

H974. Knodt, Kenneth S. "The Gathering Darkness: A Study of the Effects of Technology in *The Great Gatsby*," *Fitzgerald/Hemingway Annual*, 8 (1976), 130–138.

Discusses cars, the railroad, telephones, and guns as symbols of technology, a technology which "extracts Nick and Gatsby from their more comfortable, secure worlds," is "a means of transacting wider, not deeper, relationships," and is "ultimately responsible for killing two characters and seriously upsetting several other characters' lives" and thereby for destroying "a simpler, easier, pastoral world."

H975. Kroll, Jack. "Falling Stahr," *Newsweek*, 88 (November 22, 1976), 107–110.

Review of LT film with comments on F and the novel: The "cadence of Fitzgerald's quixotic voyage toward the ideal through tawdry seas is what you miss in this elegant film."

H976. LaHurd, Ryan. "'Absolution': *Gatsby*'s Forgotten Front Door," *College Literature*, 3 (Spring 1976), 113–123.

Knowing that F originally designed "Absolution" as a prologue to GG, we see that, "compelled by his environment into adolescent isolation, Gatsby has formed an *alter ego* and a puzzle of perfection. He has a characteristic 'honesty of imagination,' and in matters of his life of illusion he is answerable only to his imagination rather than to God."

H977. Latham, Aaron. "What Would F. Scott Think of 'Fitzgerald in Hollywood?'" NY *Times*, May 16, 1976, pp. D29–D30.

Negative review of TV special which also discusses F's Hollywood experience and his fascination with the movies. For a response to this review, see H1006.

H978. Levin, Eric. "TV Teletype: New York," *TV Guide*, 24 (February 14, 1976), 28.

Brief report of Sheilah Graham's response to upcoming TV special on "F. Scott Fitzgerald in Hollywood."

Lewis, Janet. See Curry (H945).

H979. Lindley, Tom. "Henderson, Ky., Woman F. Scott Fitzgerald's Nurse," Evansville (Ind.) *Sunday Courier and Press*, January 11, 1976, p. 2B.

Interview with Theodora Gager who was F's nurse at La Paix in 1932.

H980.   Mann, Charles.   "F. Scott Fitzgerald's Critique of *A Farewell to Arms*," *Fitzgerald/Hemingway Annual*, 8 (1976), 141–152.

Prefaces first publication of F's notes on a late typescript of Hemingway's novel with discussion of significance of F's critique; also supplies notes identifying passages which F referred to in his memo.

H981.   Marcotte, Edward.   "Fitzgerald and Nostalgia," *Midwest Quarterly*, 17 (Winter 1976), 186–191.

Cites several "evocations" of nostalgia ("a fixation on the past—but the past evoked in a special way") in GG and in F's Notebooks and draws parallels with Thomas Wolfe and Marcel Proust.

H982.   Martin, Marjory.   "Fitzgerald's Image of Woman— Anima Projections in *Tender Is the Night*," *English Studies Collections*, 1 (September 1976), 1–17.

Contends that the women in TITN, "while somewhat two-dimensional if viewed as realistic characters, become multi-dimensional and aesthetically valid creations if examined from a Jungian archetypal point of view" and as anima projections of Dick Diver.

H983.   Marx, Samuel.   "The Last Writes of the 'Eminent Authors,'" Los Angeles *Times*, June 13, 1976, "Book Review" Section, pp. 3, 12 [3].

Memories of F in Hollywood by former story editor at MGM.

H984.   Matters, Marion.   "Grandmother's House—F. Scott and the Riddle of the McQuillan Residence," *The Grand Gazette* (St. Paul), 3 (April 1976), 2–3.

Examines documentary evidence on the homes F's grandmother McQuillan occupied in St. Paul, concluding that F's memories are not entirely consistent with the facts.

H985.   Mayer, Stanley Dehler.   "'A Fine and (Too) Private Place,'" Pittsburgh *Press*, June 20, 1976, Magazine, pp. 3, 11.

Account of a trip to see F's original grave in the Union Cemetery and of the difficulties encountered in locating it.

H986.   Melebeck, Paul.   "Time and Time Structure in *The Great Gatsby*," *Revue des Langues Vivantes*, 42 (U.S. Bicentennial Issue, 1976), 213–224.

Dates events in GG to provide a precise schedule and shows how the time structure of the first three chapters sets up different classes of society which will conflict with each other. Sees F as stressing that time is double in nature—it is material and visible and also psychological and internal—and, ultimately, the novel is what Gatsby could not achieve—control of the past, an order and meaning imposed only by art.

H987.   Mencken, H. L. "Newspapers, Women, and Beer," *Harper's Magazine*, 253 (September 1976), 41–48 [43].

Selection of Mencken letters excerpted from forthcoming collection includes his April 3, 1920, letter to F.

Reprinted: Bode, ed. (I29)

H988.   Miller, Linda Patterson. "'As a Friend You Have Never Failed Me': The Fitzgerald-Murphy Correspondence," *Journal of Modern Literature*, 5 (September 1976), 357–382.

Nineteen letters and three telegrams from the Murphys to F prefaced by introduction—"These...letters display in vivid and sympathetic terms the crucial role that Gerald and Sara Murphy played in confronting Fitzgerald, as man and artist, with himself"—and interspersed with biographical commentary.

H989.   Mitgang, Herbert. "In Search of The Great Gatsby— Retracing Fitzgerald's Footsteps," NY *Times*, February 22, 1976, Long Island Weekly, pp. 1, 17–18.

Details of a visit to house F rented while working on GG and search for possible prototype of Gatsby's mansion.

H990.   Monteiro, George. "Henry James and Scott Fitzgerald: A Source," *Notes on Contemporary Literature*, 6 (March 1976), 4–6.

Examines the ways in which *Daisy Miller* "might be seen to bear on" the episode in TITN in which Dick Diver, "bicycling through Europe, unexpectedly runs into Nicole Warren, his young patient in Switzerland": "What Fitzgerald learned from James was how to manage the narration of a scene between two young people who are not lovers, but who might well appear to be, and an older suitor who stumbles upon them in a more or less compromising situation."

H991.   Moorehead, Caroline. "Scott Fitzgerald: The Man Behind the Twenties Myths," London *Times*, October 9, 1976, p. 12.

Profile of and interview with Sheilah Graham on occasion of English publication of *The Real F. Scott Fitzgerald* (I160).

H992.   Moorty, S. S. "Frank Norris and Scott Fitzgerald: Two Sides of the Same Coin," *Proceedings of the Utah Academy of Sciences, Arts, and Letters*, 53 (Part 2, 1976), 29–34.

Discussion of the influence of Norris' theme of degeneration and realistic technique on F's works which sees F and Norris as "the obverse and reverse of the same coin," although "their works reflect a few common moral principles."

H993.   Myers, Andrew B. "'I Am Used to Being Dunned': F. Scott Fitzgerald and the Modern Library," *Columbia Library Columns*, 25 (February 1976), 28–39.

Account of publication of GG in Modern Library which focuses on exchanges of letters (here reproduced) between F and Bennett Cerf and Donald Klopfer of Random House.

H994. Nicholas, Charles A. "The G-G-Great Gatsby," *CEA Critic*, 38 (January 1976), 8–10.

Examines often overlooked stylistic device of alliteration in the novel: "Gatsby, his green light, and the gray land, linked by their sharing the letter G, all contribute to the novel's movement toward the *grotesque*."

H995. O'Flaherty, Terrence. "Not So Tender Is the Night," San Francisco *Chronicle*, May 17, 1976, p. 34.

Review of "F. Scott Fitzgerald in Hollywood" TV special.

H996. "People," *Time*, 107 (February 9, 1976), 49.

Brief mention of Tuesday Weld's and Jason Miller's preparations for filming "F. Scott Fitzgerald in Hollywood."

H997. Perlmutter, Ruth. "Malcolm Lowry's Unpublished Filmscript of *Tender Is the Night*," *American Quarterly*, 28 (Winter 1976), 561–574.

Stresses "the remarkable affinities between Lowry and Fitzgerald in life and work" and discusses the script which is "not only a brilliant amplification of Fitzgerald's intent in the novel," but also "a culmination of Lowry's own aspirations, of his lifelong interest in films and the impact of film on his own fiction."

H998. Pottorf, Michael. "*The Great Gatsby*: Myrtle's Dog and Its Relation to the Dog-God of Pound and Eliot," *American Notes & Queries*, 14 (February 1976), 88–90.

Contends that "sightless eyes incorporated within a dog-God motif was a metaphor common to Eliot, Fitzgerald, and others [who used it] as a vehicle to the perception of the materialistic demise and the moral disintegration of the jazz age."

H999. Prigozy, Ruth. " 'Poor Butterfly': F. Scott Fitzgerald and Popular Music," *Prospects*, 2 (1976), 41–67.

Traces F's use of movies, musical comedy, and popular music in his fiction, suggesting "a relationship between his musical heritage, his prose style, and the expression of his ideas." Includes a list of popular songs referred to in F's works.

H1000. "Reburial of the Fitzgeralds," *Fitzgerald/Hemingway Annual*, 8 (1976), 305–306.

Brief account followed by texts of words of F's and Zelda's read at the reinterment service.

H1001. Romine, Dannye. "Figments of F. S. Fitzgerald: 'Please, Just Call Me Scott,'" Charlotte *Observer*, May 30, 1976, p. 5F.
Visit to the Oak Hall Hotel in Tryon, North Carolina, where F stayed during the winter and spring of 1937, prompts a long imaginary conversation with F.

H1002. Rosenberg, Howard. "Scott Fitzgerald in Hollywood," Louisville *Times*, May 15, 1976, "TV Scene" Section, p. 2.
Preview of upcoming TV special on "F. Scott Fitzgerald in Hollywood" which includes some biographical information about F.

H1003. Scanlon, Paul A. "The Great Gatsby: Romance and Realism," *Antigonish Review*, 27 (Autumn 1976), 37–41.
Brief discussion of Gatsby as medieval chivalric knight who rises from mysterious origins, changes his name, wins fame in combat, gains wealth and kingdom, and follows his grail, exhibiting prowess, liberality, courtesy, and especially loyalty to his beloved, in the best tradition of courtly love.

H1004. Seay, James. "The Wicked Witch of North Carolina," *Esquire*, 86 (October 1976), 116–117, 161–165.
Account of seance at Grove Park Inn in Asheville, when medium Joann Denton tried to raise the spirit of F.

H1005. Seshachari, Neila. *"The Great Gatsby*: Apogee of Fitzgerald's Mythopoeia," *Fitzgerald/Hemingway Annual*, 8 (1976), 96–107.
Sees GG as "polysemous in mythic overtones," with Gatsby himself seeming "a minor avatar of the truly great mythic heroes of the stature of Theseus, Jason, Karna, and others"; points out that "there are basic generic differences between the traditional American Dream and Gatsby's own personal quest" and that GG "is a critique of the American Dream and a criticism of its material values, but this criticism somehow never touches Gatsby's own personality," just as the "death of a mythic hero is a tragedy only for the people; it is always a triumph or ultimate victory for the hero himself."

H1006. Sheed, Wilfrid. "Letter—But Scott and Zelda Were Wordy," NY *Times*, May 30, 1976, p. D19.
Letter to the Editor which takes issue with Aaron Latham's criticism (H977) of "F. Scott Fitzgerald in Hollywood" TV special, calling it "the kind of literate television that some of us had been praying for."

H1007. Simon, John. "Stallone's Ring of Truth," *New York*, 9 (November 29, 1976), 69–72 [70–72].
Review of LT film which characterizes the adaptation as "an honor-

able failure" in which most of the changes made to the novel for the film are "unfelicitous."

H1008.   "Television," *Playboy*, 23 (May 1976), 30.
Review of "F. Scott Fitzgerald in Hollywood" TV special which includes comments from Sheilah Graham calling it "'the one good thing that's ever been done about Scott Fitzgerald in any medium.'"

H1009.   Thomas, Bob. "Wily Producer Aims to Cut String of F. Scott Fitzgerald Flops," Boston *Sunday Globe*, March 14, 1976, p. A13.
Syndicated (AP) interview with LT film producer Sam Spiegel who talks of the making of the movie. This article also appeared in *Bergen County Record* (Hackensack, N.J.), January 12, 1976, p. A–13; Seattle *Times*, February 9, 1976.

H1010.   Tsuboi, Kiyohiko. "Fitzgerald's Revision of 'Tarquin of Cheapside,'" *Persica (Journal of the English Literary Society of Okayama)*, No. 3 (December 1976), 123–137.
In English. Compares original version of story (as reprinted in AF) and revised version (as reprinted in TJA), concluding that F "seemed to have concentrated his effort chiefly on expansion and elaboration for the purpose of making it more plausible, realistic, and dramatic."

H1011.   Voorhees, John. "Big Weekend for TV Flicks," Seattle *Times*, May 15, 1976, p. B4.
Review of "F. Scott Fitzgerald in Hollywood" TV special which calls it "a tremendously well-done and exciting dramatization of the latter portion of the American writer's life."

H1012.   Warga, Wayne. "Good Years in the Sun—The Not So Disenchanted," Los Angeles *Times*, August 13, 1976, Part IV, p. 1.
Cites Tom Dardis' *Some Time in the Sun* (I100) as evidence that F was happy and successful in Hollywood.

H1013.   West, James L. W., III. "The Mencken-Fitzgerald Papers: An Annotated Checklist," *Princeton University Library Chronicle*, 38 (Autumn 1976), 21–45.
Checklist of available materials, published and in libraries, which document personal relationship between F and Mencken, preceded by introduction which details and analyzes the relationship.

H1014.   Whitman, Alden. "Elia Kazan: 'The Movie We Made Is Realistic Hollywood,'" NY *Times*, November 14, 1976, Sec. 2, pp. 1, 15–16.
Discussion of LT film which includes remarks by Kazan, biographical background on F, factual information on LT, and mention of how

the film departs from the novel.

H1015. Wilt, Judith. "The Spinning Story: Gothic Motifs in *Tender Is the Night*," *Fitzgerald/Hemingway Annual*, 8 (1976), 79–95.
Explores "three major strands from the tradition of Gothic fiction" in TITN and traces "their weave in this novel": They are "that peculiarly Gothic narrative strategy...of drawing in, often through two or three loops of storytellers, towards the unthinkable act, the unsayable desire, the unbearable bargain, the 'unhuman' mystery that generates the story"; the theme of "complicity" ("the desire of the forbidden, desire of the evil, desire of the unnatural, desire of the destructive, the rotten, the dying, desire of death"); and the "Gothic setting, the madhouse, transmuted during the nineteenth century into the laboratory,...with its cast of attendant victim-ghouls, and its ambiguously dreadful presiding spirit, the scientist, and above all its constant nightmare dissolving of the boundaries of madness and reason."

H1016. Yost, Barbara. "The Importance of Being Ernest...Or Walt, Or Scott," Phoenix *Gazette*, March 6, 1976, "Marquee" Section, p. 15.
Biographical sketch of F on occasion of airing of "F. Scott Fitzgerald in Hollywood" TV special.

H1017. ———. "Scott Fitzgerald: Brownie in a Fantasy World," Phoenix *Gazette*, May 15, 1976, "Marquee" Section, p. 5.
Interview with Sheilah Graham on occasion of airing of "F. Scott Fitzgerald in Hollywood" TV special.

1977

H1018. Adams, Michael. "Dick Diver and Constance Talmadge," *Fitzgerald/Hemingway Annual*, 9 (1977), 61–62.
Although F's reference to Constance Talmadge's film "Breakfast at Sunrise" in TITN is anachronistic (the reference is to events in 1925; the film didn't appear until 1927), F may have used the title because it fit in with the "Life and death" contrasts presented in the scene.

H1019. ———. "Fitzgerald Filmography," *Fitzgerald/Hemingway Annual*, 9 (1977), 101–109.
Listing of "the directors, screenwriters, producers, and casts for all the theatrical movies made from the works of F. Scott Fitzgerald....between 1920 and 1976."

H1020. Alderman, Taylor. "Fitzgerald, Hemingway, and *The Passing of the Great Race*," *Fitzgerald/Hemingway Annual*, 9 (1977), 215–217.

Suggests that Hemingway's subtitle for *The Torrents of Spring, A Romantic Novel in Honor of the Passing of a Great Race*, could have resulted from conversations with F and from the latter's use of Madison Grant's *The Passing of the Great Race* in GG.

H1021.   Anderson, W[illiam] R[ichard, Jr.] "Rivalry and Partnership: The Short Fiction of Zelda Sayre Fitzgerald," *Fitzgerald/Hemingway Annual*, 9 (1977), 19–42.

Surveys the stories with two objectives—"to trace Zelda Fitzgerald's progress as she moved from her first tentative efforts in fiction through a series of increasingly more ambitious undertakings toward her novel *Save Me the Waltz*"; and "to explore the interrelationship between her writing and the literary career of her husband."

H1022.   Arnold, Edwin T. "The Motion Picture as Metaphor in the Works of F. Scott Fitzgerald," *Fitzgerald/Hemingway Annual*, 9 (1977), 43–60.

Discusses F's use of the cinema metaphor as embodying the theme of reality vs. illusion and examines the two "ideal symbols" he found in movies, "personifications of two possible attitudes toward life"—the actor, who "enters the illusion and is controlled by it"; and the director, who "dominates the cheap and the mundane around him." Deals with TSOP, B&D, GG, "Jacob's Ladder," TITN, PH, and LT.

H1023.   "Artie Shaw Gets $118,200, From Par, Merrick, Ober Re 'Gatsby,'" *Variety*, 287 (June 29, 1977), 4.

Notes that Shaw received the money because he had gotten the rights to produce a stage version of GG from F's daughter in 1969, an agreement which she terminated when she was offered $350,000 by David Merrick and Paramount Pictures.

H1024.   Atkins, Irene Kahn. "Hollywood Revisited: A Sad Homecoming," *Literature/Film Quarterly*, 5 (Spring 1977), 105–111.

Surveys the history of LT film and reviews it, calling it "faithful neither to Fitzgerald's fascination and love-hate relationship with Hollywood or the movies of the '30's themselves."

H1025.   Baer, William, and Steven McLean Folks. "Language and Character in *The Great Gatsby*," *The Language of Poems*, 6 (December 1977), 18–25.

Two graduate papers which investigate how F manipulates reader's sympathies for Daisy and Tom "by means of the language that he gives those characters to say." Baer analyzes Daisy's language closely, concluding that F "attempted to draw a character who was so charming that her superficiality would not make Gatsby's obsession an absurdity" and that she is "simultaneously real and ideal"; Folks examines Tom's language in his first appearance, suggesting that his social identity, personality, and ultimate destiny are developed through his language in this scene.

H1026.   Bandy, B. B. "Fitzgerald's 'Vegetable' Flourishes at Cerritos," *Daily Southeast News* (Los Angeles), January 24, 1977, Sec. B, p. 4.
Review of undergraduate production at Cerritos College.

H1027.   Barron, James. "On the Trail of the Fitzgerald Legend," NY *Times*, July 31, 1977, New Jersey Weekly, pp. 1, 4.
Syndicated (NY Times) account of connections with New Jersey in F's life and works which includes interviews with Robert Crawford, F's friend at Princeton who may have served as the model for Kerry Holliday in TSOP, and Gregg Daugherty, another Princeton friend of F's and later a professor there. This article also appeared in Cleveland *Plain Dealer*, August 29, 1977, pp. 8B–9B; Chicago *Tribune*, August 13, 1977, Sec. I, pp. 9–10; San Francisco *Chronicle*, August 12, 1977, p. 27.

H1028.   Bodeen, DeWitt. "F. Scott Fitzgerald and Films," *Films in Review*, 28 (May 1977), 285–294.
Discussion of film adaptations of F's works which asserts that, after first four adaptations—"A Chorus Girl's Romance" ("Head and Shoulders"), "The Off-Shore Pirate," "The Husband Hunter" ("Myra Meets His Family"), and B&D—"every screen version of a Fitzgerald story has been flawed by miscasting and a direful misunderstanding of the story itself." In this category, discusses three GG films, "The Last Time I Saw Paris" ("Babylon Revisited"), LT, and "Bernice Bobs Her Hair." Also briefly considers "The Vegetable" and stage versions of GG and TITN.

H1029.   "Book Ends," *NY Times Book Review*, March 6, 1977, p. 37.
Brief mention of filmscript of B&D recently completed by Christopher Isherwood and Don Bachardy.

H1030.   Brown, James. "PBS Probes the Short Story," Los Angeles *Times*, April 5, 1977, Part IV, p. 10.
Reviews first two stories in TV series on "The American Short Story," one of which is "Bernice Bobs Her Hair": "The dialogue is rich and witty and the central characters...are never less than appropriate inhabitants of Fitzgerald's world."

H1031.   B[ruccoli], M[atthew] J. "Bruccoli Addenda," *Fitzgerald/Hemingway Annual*, 9 (1977), 247–249.

Listing of material either omitted from or appearing since the publication of Bruccoli's F Bibliography (I40).

H1032.   ———, ed. " 'The Feather Fan,' " *Fitzgerald/Hemingway Annual*, 9 (1977), 3–8 [3].

Brief introductory note preceding a "two-page outline and three-page treatment for what appears to have been a projected movie" entitled "The Feather Fan."

H1033.   Christon, Lawrence. " 'Vegetable' at Cerritos College," Los Angeles *Times*, January 21, 1977, Part IV, p. 18.

Review of undergraduate production which calls the play "hopeless,...dated in its prototypes, mixed up in its conventions and sophomoric in its dialogue."

H1034.   Combs, Richard. *"The Last Tycoon," Sight and Sound*, 46 (Spring 1977), 124.

Review of film which includes extensive commentary on F's novel and suggests that the adaptation of this "minor classic of wishful thinking" is "the cruellest trick played by Hollywood on Fitzgerald."

Connelly, Mary. See Greaves (H1050).

Corliss, Mary. See Silver (H1079).

H1035.   Curry, Steven, and Peter L. Hays. "Fitzgerald's *Vanity Fair*," *Fitzgerald/Hemingway Annual*, 9 (1977), 63–75.

Traces and measures the extent of influence of Thackeray's novel on GG. Points out similarities in "narrative technique, parallels between the major characters in both works...and parallels between the settings," and in facts that "both make significant thematic use of time, the past, and history, especially war" and that each "contains an indictment of the materialism and superficiality of its respective age, yet each lacks a moral center itself."

H1036.   Daniels, Thomas E. "The Texts of 'Winter Dreams,' " *Fitzgerald/Hemingway Annual*, 9 (1977), 77–100.

Comparison of American magazine, English magazine, and American collection (ATSYM) texts of the story which argues for using the American magazine text as the copy-text with emendations to be made from the other two versions.

H1037.   ———. "Toward a Definitive Edition of F. Scott Fitzgerald's Short Stories," *Publications of the Bibliographical Society of America*, 71 (Third Quarter 1977), 295–310.

Criticizes existing reprint editions of F's stories for not attempting to discover if the "'collected text' was the most desirable [to choose as copy-text], was different from the original text, or whether or not the changes made in the collected editions were authorial" and urges for each story trying "to discover whether or not a holograph manuscript, typescript, or proof sheets exist" and then using them "in connection with the relevant texts involved....to provide texts as close to Fitzgerald's intention as possible." For a response to this essay, see H1099.

H1038.   Dardis, Tom.   "Justice Done F. Scott in Film 'Last Tycoon,'" Phoenix *Gazette*, January 27, 1977, Sec. D, p. 8.
Résumé of films made from F's works and praise for LT movie, "remarkably faithful to Fitzgerald's unfinished book."

H1039.   DiBattista, Maria.   "The Aesthetic of Forbearance: Fitzgerald's *Tender Is the Night*," *Novel*, 11 (Fall 1977), 26–39.
Discusses TITN in the context of the aesthetic of forbearance—"a suppression of narrative information" which "demands a canny narrative treatment of history, of character, and of appropriate generic and mythic material to insure that the ironic mystery of its fable is protected against sentimental moralistic readings"—and as F's *Odyssey*, "a novelistic treatment of an epic theme—the odyssey of acculturation and adjustment undertaken in the Vanity Fair of the mechanical age."

H1040.   Ditsky, John.   "F. Scott Fitzgerald and the Jacob's Ladder," *Journal of Narrative Technique*, 7 (Fall 1977), 226–228.
Examines ladder images in B&D and GG and contrasts Jacob's ladder in Genesis with F's, concluding that F's "insight into the nature of human experience" is the "taking of a horizontal progress to be a climbing upward to the stars."

H1041.   Duggan, Margaret M.   "Fitzgerald Checklist," *Fitzgerald/Hemingway Annual*, 9 (1977), 250–254.
Listing of recent material by and about F.

H1042.   ———.   "A New Fitzgerald Book Review: *The Boy Grew Older*," *Fitzgerald/Hemingway Annual*, 9 (1977), 9–10.
Brief introduction to reprinting (pp. 11–12) of F review of 1922 Heywood Broun novel, an unlocated clipping of which exists in F's scrapbook; gives background to F-Broun relationship.

H1043.   Dunn, William.   "Limited Books, Limitless Authors," NY *Times*, May 22, 1977, p. F7.
Survey of history and operation of Bruccoli-Clark Books which includes comments on their edition of F's *Ledger*.

H1044.   Ferguson, Sally.   "Short Stories: Wonderfully Loving Transpositions," *Humanities*, 7 (April 1977), 1–3.

Review of "The American Short Story" TV series with passing mention of "Bernice Bobs Her Hair" production.

H1045.   Flor.   "À l'Ombre de Gatsby (In Gatsby's Shadow)," *Variety*, 287 (June 1, 1977), 70, 74.

Review of play about F and Zelda by Belgian writer Jeannine Monsieur.

Folks, Steven McLean. See Baer (H1025).

H1045a.   Foley, Charles.   "The Stuff That Dreams Are Made Of," *The Observer* (London), January 30, 1977, pp. 25, 27.

Although primarily concerned with LT film, article includes brief discussion of the novel.

H1046.   Fraser, Lady Antonia.   "Immortal Love Letters," *NY Times Magazine*, February 13, 1977, pp. 16–18 [18].

Selection includes one from Zelda to F from Spring 1919, previously printed in *Zelda* (I258).

H1047.   Gill, Brendan.   "Brendan Gill on THE LAST TYCOON," *Film Comment*, 13 (January-February 1977), 44–45.

Review of LT film includes passing mention of GG and LT as novels.

H1048.   Gow, Gordon.   "*The Last Tycoon,*" *Films and Filming*, 23 (March 1977), 41–42.

Review of LT film which includes some discussion of the effectiveness of the adaptation: "The spare and sensitive adaptation by Harold Pinter is respectful to the source material."

H1049.   Grant, Sister Mary Kathryn, R.S.M.   "The Search For Celebration in *The Sun Also Rises* and *The Great Gatsby*," *Arizona Quarterly*, 33 (Summer 1977), 181–192.

Discusses use and function of dancing and the dance as a metaphor in the two novels: "Hemingway reflects the tension between meaningful ritual dancing in the bullfight and meaningless, social dancing in the *bal musette* and in the streets....Fitzgerald limns the tension between the deep inner need for affirmation and celebration and the 'glimmering' illusory world which proffers only false feasts and surrogate celebrations."

H1050.   Greaves, William, and Mary Connelly.   "'Gatsby': Scottie Fitzgerald Gets a Stay," NY *Post*, April 29, 1977, p. 81.

F's daughter wins court order temporarily barring arbitration of claim that she breached contract with bandleader Artie Shaw for exclusive rights to adapt GG.

H1051.   Greenspun, Roger.   "Films—Star Billings," *Penthouse*, 8 (February 1977), 37–39 [37–38].

Review of LT film with brief mention of the screenplay as "by far the best film adaptation of a Fitzgerald novel ever made (and the most faithful)."

H1052.   Hartl, John.   "'The Last Tycoon' Is Still Unfinished," Seattle *Times*, March 11, 1977, "Tempo" Section, p. 6.

Review of LT film which asserts that "the problem with the movie is the problem with the book: it thins out as the love story begins to take over, and there is no satisfactory ending."

H1053.   Hays, Peter L.   *"Gatsby*, Myth, Fairy Tale, and Legend," *Southern Folklore Quarterly*, 41 (1977), 213–223.

Contends that GG "combines characteristics of the fairy tale with those of the legend," showing how Gatsby "has several qualifications of a fairy tale hero," how setting and incidents in GG are also appropriate to fairy tale, and also how "Gatsby also lives in the world of local legend, where miracles are rare and the protagonist is stifled by time and convention." Concludes that F uses fairy tale and legend in GG "to mock the American dream, to show that it is no more than legend to those who believe in it, and a fairy tale, in the most pejorative sense, for most of us."

————. See Curry (H1035).

Inge, J. Barclay. See West (H1086).

H1054.   Laird, David.   "Hallucination and History in *The Great Gatsby*," *South Dakota Review*, 15 (Spring 1977), 18–27.

Sees GG as both a "city novel," in which "the hero tries to establish himself or herself in an urban environment, undergoing some kind of re-examination of values and attitudes which had prompted an earlier break with an impoverished or provincial past," and, embedded within it, a "pastoral romance." The "interweaving of the two modes" gives "incandescent expression to the struggle of the individual to impose his or her attitudes or goals upon the rush of events, indeed, to bend that rush in a direction which will reclaim a remembered past and thus to transcend time and history."

H1055.   LeGates, Charlotte.   "Dual-Perspective Irony and the Fitzgerald Short Story," *Iowa English Bulletin: Yearbook*, 26 (1977), 18–20.

Examines "The Diamond as Big as the Ritz," "The Rich Boy," "May Day," " 'I Didn't Get Over,' " and other F stories as examples of his ability to "convey, simultaneously, two diametrically opposed views" and thus make "a significant advance in the use of irony in the short story."

H1056.   Levin, Bernard.   "Welcome to the Aspirin Age," London *Times*, January 14, 1977, p. 16.

A first reading of GG prompts a reading of all F's published works and an assessment of his achievement: F "wrote about the heart of man" and "the bitter truths or falsehoods Fitzgerald provides will remain alive though not one grain of dust from the world in which he set them survives."

H1057.   Lhamon, W. T., Jr.   "The Essential Houses of *The Great Gatsby*," *Markham Review*, 6 (Spring 1977), 56–60.

Examines the Buchanans' house, Myrtle's apartment in NY, and Gatsby's mansion in attempt to show that "the houses of *The Great Gatsby* manifest at a subtle, structural level the seeming variety but underlying undimensionality that the novel postulates....nearly everyone in the society subscribes to a single set of values."

H1058.   McBride, Margaret.   "The Divine Dick Diver," *Notes on Modern American Literature*, 1 (Fall 1977), Item 28.

Explores symbolic connotations of name Diver which suggests both a "tragic fall" and a "god" and stresses Dick as a Christ figure.

H1059.   McElfresh, Tom.   "F. Scott and Films Still Don't Mix," Cincinnati *Enquirer*, March 10, 1977, p. B–8.

Review of LT film which includes considerable mention of F's novel.

H1060.   McIlvaine, Robert M.   "Thomas Parke D'Invilliers and Villiers de L'Isle-Adam," *Notes on Modern American Literature*, 1 (Summer 1977), Item 19.

Suggests that F intended to associate D'Invilliers in TSOP with Jean-Marie Villiers de L'Isle-Adam and "thus heighten the *fin de siècle* atmosphere that pervades the Princeton section of the novel."

H1061.   McNicholas, Mary Verity, O.P.   "Fitzgerald's Women in *Tender Is the Night*," *College Literature*, 4 (Winter 1977), 40–70.

Examines Mrs. Abrams, Violet McKisco, Kaethe Gregorovius, Mary North, Mrs. Elsie Speers, Baby Warren, Rosemary Hoyt, and Nicole Warren Diver, and suggests that they "exist primarily as sources of delight and admiration, and/or faces of destruction in terms of the influence they have upon, or the power they wield over, Dick Diver."

H1062.   McQuiston, John T.   "Russell Patterson Is Dead at 82; Set the Fashions For Flapper Era," NY *Times*, March 19, 1977, p. 22.

Obituary of "illustrator, cartoonist and designer whose slick, sophisticated drawings created many of the fashions of the flapper and collegiate eras of the 1920s" mentions that Patterson told an interviewer that he "'started' the flapper...for no other reason than he had read F. Scott Fitzgerald...and wanted to create a different type."

H1063.   Martin, Robert A.   "Gatsby's 'Good Night' in Chapter III of *The Great Gatsby*," *CEA Critic*, 39 (May 1977), 12–16.

Close study of five "good nights" Gatsby says which asserts that they are directed at Nick rather than at guests at the party and are seen as evidence of Gatsby's deliberate and aggressive attempts "to cultivate Nick's friendship to the exclusion of everyone else 'clustered' around him" so that Nick can help arrange a meeting between Gatsby and Daisy.

H1064.   Mazzella, Anthony J.   "The Tension of Opposites in Fitzgerald's 'May Day,'" *Studies in Short Fiction*, 14 (Fall 1977), 379–385.

Detailed examination which discusses "the title's rich allusiveness," "the story's structural and imagistic opposites, and its paradoxes of form," and its theme—"Life may reward its privileged few and defeat its hapless many, but art is better than life because it is invulnerable to it."

H1065.   Moses, Edwin.   "Tragic Inevitability in *The Great Gatsby*," *College Language Association Journal*, 21 (September 1977), 51–57.

Sees in the first chapter of GG a "sense of tragic inevitability ...concerned with nemesis," the "inevitable convulsive righting of a balance in nature which the tragic hero has disturbed." Gatsby "looses chaos into the world and invites nemesis" when he leaves "his own milieu" and lures Daisy from hers.

H1066.   Nelson, Eric.   "Commitment and Insight in *The Great Gatsby*," *Revue des Langues Vivantes*, 43 (Summer 1977), 142–152.

Suggests that the "defeat of Nick, the man of insight, and Gatsby, the man of commitment, at the end of Fitzgerald's novel suggests that in modern America these qualities stand separate and vulnerable."

H1067.   Neuhaus, Ron.   "Gatsby and the Failure of the Omniscient 'I,'" *University of Denver Quarterly*, 12 (Spring 1977), 303–312.

Contends that GG "begins with first person narration, but Fitzgerald will not accept the limitation of this self-imposed restriction and constantly strains toward an 'omniscient I' through diction, flashback, and reconstructed events," because "the moral authority of first person narrative was not adequate" for "a world which could not provide the fulfillment" of the "the desire for moral security."

H1068.   "Notes From Broadcast Markets in the U.S. and Abroad," *Variety*, 288 (September 28, 1977), 54.
Brief mention that National Public Radio has commissioned the All-Media Dramatic Workshop to adapt seven of F's short stories.

H1069.   O'Connor, John J.   "TV: 'The American Short Story' Impresses," NY *Times*, April 5, 1977, p. 66.
Review of TV adaptation of "Bernice Bobs Her Hair" which praises production and acting.

H1070.   Pace, Eric.   "The Lure—and Allure—of a White Suit," NY *Times*, July 24, 1977, p. 38.
Article on wearing of white suits by men includes comments by Matthew J. Bruccoli on use of color white in GG.

H1071.   Peterman, Michael A.   "A Neglected Source for *The Great Gatsby*: The Influence of Edith Wharton's *The Spark*," *Canadian Review of American Studies*, 8 (Spring 1977), 26–35.
Shows similarities in details, point of view, narrative mood and tone, central characters, and structural technique, and claims that *The Spark* "stimulated" F while he was writing GG.

H1072.   Podis, Leonard A.   "'The Unreality of Reality': Metaphor in *The Great Gatsby*," *Style*, 11 (Winter 1977), 56–72.
Detailed examination of three types of metaphors used by F in GG—"clichéd and dead metaphors [which] surround Nick with an aura of conversational naturalness [and] suggest a straightforward, objective way of viewing experience"; "rationally analogical metaphors [which] suggest that Nick is a sensitive but straightforward young man"; and "highly subjective, surreal" metaphors which take place "in the contexts of what seem to be nearly surreal excursions." Taken together, the metaphors in GG "reveal a divided narrative vision which corresponds to, because it is instrumental in helping to create, the sense of ideological division that exists at the book's thematic level."

H1073.   Polek, Fran James.   "From Renegade to Solid Citizen: The Extraordinary Individual and the Community," *South Dakota Review*, 15 (Spring 1977), 61–72.
Examines GG, *Absalom, Absalom!*, and *The Godfather* as "circular dramas....structured around the dynamic of a young self-proclaimed extraordinary person ('marked,' somehow), who makes a conscious de-

cision to leave the traditional ethnic, political or religious community because of its rigidity or final capacity to desensitize or eliminate the non-conforming individual....Paradoxically, however, the motivation to 'make it' by moving initially toward renegade status without benefit of traditional community is tempered by a repressed but equally strong motivation to eventually rejoin the traditional community as a fully accepted leader or power figure."

H1074. Roulston, Robert. *"The Beautiful and Damned*: The Alcoholic's Revenge," *Literature and Psychology*, 27 (No 3, 1977), 156–163.

Sees B&D as the only one of F's works to offer "an across the board, all-out assault upon his boyhood years, the two decades preceding World War I, and obliquely upon values embodied by his own parents—in fact, upon those forces which had shaped his character and aroused expectations which recent events had shattered....in 1920 and 1921 the demons he had identified with Edward and Mollie Fitzgerald drove him to excoriate in *The Beautiful and Damned* everything he could connect with his father and mother....the very existence of the neurosis which was making Fitzgerald ever more dependent upon alcohol indicates that he had legitimate complaints against his parents, just as conditions in the United States during the Prohibition era suggest that he and his contemporaries had valid complaints against pre-war America for having engendered those conditions."

H1075. Rusch, Frederic E. "Addenda to Bruccoli: Four Fitzgerald Dust Jackets," *Fitzgerald/Hemingway Annual*, 9 (1977), 13–18.

Facsimiles and bibliographical transcriptions of dust jackets for English editions of TSOP, F&P, B&D, and TJA, newly located in University Library, Cambridge, England.

H1076. Serlen, Ellen. "The American Dream: From F. Scott Fitzgerald to Herbert Gold," *Midamerica*, 4 (1977), 122–137 [122–123].

Brief comments on GG in article largely devoted to Gold.

H1077. Shales, Tom. "'Stories': Television Treasures," Washington (D.C.) *Post*, April 5, 1977, pp. B1, B9.

Preview of upcoming TV adaptation of F's "Bernice Bobs Her Hair" which makes passing reference to difficulties of transfering the story to television.

H1078. Siegel, Joel E. "The Last Tycoon," *Film Heritage*, 12 (Spring 1977), 39–41.

Review of LT film which includes assessment of F's works and themes.

H1079.   Silver, Charles, and Mary Corliss.   "Hollywood Under Water: Elia Kazan on *The Last Tycoon*," *Film Comment*, 13 (January-February 1977), 40–44.
Interview which includes Kazan's interpretation and opinion of the novel.

H1080.   Starr, Kevin.   "Fitzgerald in Tinseltown," San Francisco *Examiner*, January 3, 1977, p. 22.
Examines F's life in Hollywood and sees reason for F revival: "because he tells us how vulnerable we are to the destructive side of our own best myths."

H1081.   Stern, Daniel.   "An Ambitious New Series Brings the American Short Story to TV," NY *Times*, April 3, 1977, Sec. 2, p. 33.
Background on "The American Short Story" which includes mention of "Bernice Bobs Her Hair" adaptation.

H1082.   Tasaka, Takashi.   "The Meaning of Oxymoron in *The Great Gatsby*," *Yasuda Joshi Daigaku Kiyō*, 6 (November 1977), 31–39.
In English. Examines oxymorons in GG which "suggest and foreshadow the matured 'moral point of view' of Nick" as well as aiding in understanding "the personality and background of each character."

H1083.   Tochiyama, Michiko.   "What the Fitzgeraldian Romantic Egoist Pursues," *Gendai Eigo Bungaku Kenkyū*, 5 (November 1977), 1–15.
In English. Discusses Monroe Stahr as F romantic egotist in tradition of Amory Blaine, Anthony Patch, Jay Gatsby, and Dick Diver, and points out that Stahr's failure, unlike that of the others, "is failure in spite of him."

H1084.   Wasserstrom, William.   "The Goad of Guilt: Henry Adams, Scott and Zelda," *Journal of Modern Literature*, 6 (April 1977), 289–310.
Assesses influence of Adams' views of politics and the politics of sex on F: "Adams furnished Fitzgerald with the rationale which justified disgrace of sex, of love, of marriage." Also discusses F-Zelda relationship and its influence on their literary works—they were united to each other in "a synergy of self-realization and ruin."

H1085.   Weiler, A. H.   "'All the President's Men' Wins Critics' Award," NY *Times*, January 4, 1977, p. 22.
Passing mention that Harold Pinter was runner-up for NY Film Critics' Circle award for best screenplay for LT film.

H1086. West, James L. W., III, and J. Barclay Inge. "F. Scott Fitzgerald's Revision of 'The Rich Boy,'" *Proof*, 5 (1977), 127–146.

Traces compositional history of the story, comparing the successive versions, and uses this information to show the changes F made in the way the narrator of the story views Anson Hunter.

H1087. Westerbeck, Colin L., Jr. "The Lost Tycoon," *Commonweal*, 104 (January 21, 1977), 51–52.

Review of LT film which discusses incomplete state of F's novel, its effects on a reader, and the shortcomings of Pinter's screen adaptation.

H1088. Wilson, Edmund. "Edmund Wilson's Letters: To and About F. Scott Fitzgerald," *NY Review of Books*, 24 (February 17, 1977), 3–4, 6, 8.

First printing of fourteen Wilson letters between 1919 and 1951 which include critiques of TSOP, GG, TITN, and considerable comment on Mizener's F biography (C110).

Reprinted: Wilson, ed. (I381)

H1089. Wilson, Raymond J. "Henry James and F. Scott Fitzgerald: Americans Abroad," *Research Studies*, 45 (June 1977), 82–91.

Discusses "startling similarities" between *Daisy Miller*, *The American*, and TITN in "how they describe their settings and their main characters; in the situations that challenge their characters; in the alternatives their characters cannot take; and, not only in the success or failure of their characters, but even in the very criteria by which they expect us to judge success or failure."

H1090. Yardley, Jonathan. "Harmony in Great Neck: The Friendship of Ring Lardner and F. Scott Fitzgerald," *Saturday Review*, n.s. 4 (July 9, 1977), 23–25, 36.

Pre-publication excerpt from Yardley's Lardner biography (I387) which focuses on the F-Lardner relationship between 1922 and 1924, notes the "profound differences" between them, but stresses their similarities, especially the "real foundation" of their friendship, a shared realization that they were both "outsiders" in Great Neck because they were writers and "serious men."

1978

H1091. Adams, Michael. "*Gatsby, Tycoon, Islands*, and the Film Critics," *Fitzgerald/Hemingway Annual*, 10 (1978), 297–306.

Surveys reviews of GG and LT films and quotes extensively from several of them.

H1092.   Aldrich, Ross.   "Jay Gatsby Breaks His Maiden," *Fitzgerald/Hemingway Annual*, 10 (1978), 181–182.

Brief note on thoroughbred race horse named Jay Gatsby winning his first race after seventeen previous races.

H1093.   Arora, V. N.   "*The Great Gatsby*: The Predicament of the Dual Vision," *Indian Journal of American Studies*, 8 (January 1978), 1–9.

Sees GG as universal because in it "the dream retains all its grandeur, while in the growth of Nick's tragic awareness, which has acquired a haunting quality, Fitzgerald implies an ironic comment on that dream....Since the two—the dream and the tragic awareness—cannot be reconciled, the book projects this human predicament most vividly and powerfully through the double vision of Nick Carraway."

H1094.   Berg, A. Scott.   "The Man Who Discovered Fitzgerald—How Max Perkins Persuaded Scribners to Take a Chance on an Unconventional Author," *Princeton Alumni Weekly*, 79 (October 23, 1978), 15–20.

Excerpt from Berg's *Max Perkins—Editor of Genius* (I20) which traces the F-Perkins relationship from its beginnings through the selection by Perkins of stories included in F&P.

H1095.   Bird, Christine M., and Thomas L. McHaney.   "*The Great Gatsby* and *The Golden Bough*," *Arizona Quarterly*, 34 (Summer 1978), 125–131.

Concludes that the "images of vegetation in the novel, coupled with the figurative deification of Gatsby, 'son of god'...with a short summer's reign, provide striking parallels to *The Golden Bough* ....Gatsby, then, is ultimately no Adonis, but a counterpart to Adonis and the other vegetation gods, seen as he would have to be in a modern valueless world."

H1096.   Brady, James.   "All About Mankiewicz," *Advertising Age*, 49 (November 27, 1978), 18, 84.

Brief mention of F-Mankiewicz disagreement over "Three Comrades" in review of Kenneth L. Geist's *Pictures Will Talk* (I145).

H1097.   ———.   "A Plaque for Scott Fitzgerald," *Advertising Age*, 49 (September 11, 1978), 53.

Musings about F occasioned by visit to St. Paul including biographical details (some inaccurate) and call for a memorial to F in St. Paul or New York City.

H1098.   Bruccoli, Matthew J.   "'An Instance of Apparent Plagiarism': F. Scott Fitzgerald, Willa Cather, and the First *Gatsby* Manuscript," *Princeton University Library Chronicle*, 39 (Spring 1978), 171–178.

Cites and prints letter from F to Cather enclosing two pages from working manuscript of GG in which F apologized to Cather for inadvertently echoing her description of Marian Forrester in *A Lost Lady* in his evocation of Daisy's voice. Reprints passages referred to from both novels as well as the pages from the working manuscript—which are cited as "the only known pages from the working draft that preceded the complete 1924 manuscript now in the Princeton University Library."

H1099. ———. Letter to the Editor, *Papers of the Bibliographical Society of America*, 72 (First Quarter 1978), 143–144.

Response to Thomas E. Daniels' "Toward a Definitive Edition of F. Scott Fitzgerald's Short Stories" (H1037) which contends that Daniels errs in claiming textual significance for the English magazine versions of F's stories.

H1100. ———. "The Perkins/Wilson Correspondence About Publication of *The Last Tycoon*," *Fitzgerald/Hemingway Annual*, 10 (1978), 63–66.

Summarizes contents of thirty letters exchanged between January and September 1941 which were unavailable to Bruccoli when he was preparing *"The Last of the Novelists"* (I49) and which show that the "preparation of *The Last Tycoon* for publication was Edmund Wilson's sole responsibility. There is no evidence that Maxwell Perkins or anyone else collaborated on editing Fitzgerald's drafts."

H1101. ———, ed. "Lipstick," *Fitzgerald/Hemingway Annual*, 10 (1978), 3–35 [3–4].

Brief historical and biographical note precede first printing of 1927 screenplay F wrote for Constance Talmadge.

H1102. Bryer, Jackson R. "Notes Toward a Corrected Edition of *Dear Scott/Dear Max*," *Fitzgerald/Hemingway Annual*, 10 (1978), 177–180.

Listing of the corrections in the first American edition which were sent to Scribner's for insertion in the English and paperback reprintings which were only partially incorporated, and then only in the paperback.

H1103. Burton, W. C. "Literary Lore," Greensboro (N.C.) *Daily News*, September 3, 1978, Sec. D, p. 5.

Discussion of F's associations with North Carolina which includes anecdote about F buying copies of Wolfe's novels for the Asheville Public Library and the reminiscences of Robroy Farquhar, who acted in "Scandalabra" in Baltimore, about F's revisions of the script.

H1104.   Callahan, John.   "The Unfinished Business of *The Last Tycoon*," *Literature/Film Quarterly*, 6 (Summer 1978), 204–213.

Largely a review of the LT film with some mention of F's intention in the novel "to project a way of looking at the movies and their world operationally *and* in terms of values" and of the "newness" of his "examination, using techniques of film and the novel, of that 'instability of the balance' between an American individual of talent and the arena of popular culture."

H1105.   Campbell, C. Lawton.   "The Fitzgeralds Were My Friends," *Fitzgerald/Hemingway Annual*, 10 (1978), 37–54.

Memories of F at Princeton in 1913–14, of Zelda in Montgomery in 1919, and of both F and Zelda in the 1920s in NY and Paris.

H1106.   Creesy, Charles L.   "From Senior Thesis to Best-Selling Biography," *Princeton Alumni Weekly*, 79 (October 23, 1978), 14.

Account of genesis of A. Scott Berg's *Max Perkins—Editor of Genius* (I20) beginning with his interest in F as an undergraduate at Princeton.

H1107.   Davis, L. J.   "Keeper of the Flame—and the Foul Papers," Chicago *Tribune*, December 24, 1978, "Book World" Section, p. 2.

Article on and interview with F scholar-collector Matthew J. Bruccoli who explains reasons for his interest in F.

H1108.   Devlin, James E.   "Fitzgerald's Discovery of Erskine Caldwell," *Fitzgerald/Hemingway Annual*, 10 (1978), 101–103.

Notes F's role in bringing Caldwell's work to attention of Maxwell Perkins.

H1109.   Ellis, James.   "The Shadow-Figure Behind *The Great Gatsby*: James, Duke of Monmouth," *Fitzgerald/Hemingway Annual*, 10 (1978), 171–175.

Suggests that Nick's reference to himself as descended from "the Dukes of Buccleuch" and Gatsby's picture of himself with "the Earl of Doncaster" show "how consciously and subtly Fitzgerald used the device of the double in creating his Carraway-Gatsby relationship" because both titles were created for the same man, James, Duke of Monmouth (1649–1685).

H1110.   Epstein, Joseph.   "Grey Eminence With a Blue Pencil," *Times Literary Supplement* (London), July 28, 1978, pp. 834–836.

Review of Berg's *Max Perkins—Editor of Genius* (I20), with considerable mention of F.

H1111. Forczek, Deborah A. "Fitzgerald and Hemingway in the Academy: A Survey of Dissertations," *Fitzgerald/Hemingway Annual*, 10 (1978), 351–385.

Listing preceded by analysis and classification of dissertations done on F and Hemingway with respect to works studied, aspect stressed, topics most frequently used.

H1112. "Goodwin Sale," *Fitzgerald/Hemingway Annual*, 10 (1978), 467.

Brief note on 1977–78 sale of Jonathan Goodwin collection at Sotheby Parke Bernet gallery, with prices for which top F items sold.

H1113. Grenberg, Bruce L. "Fitzgerald's 'Figured Curtain': Personality and History in *Tender Is the Night*," *Fitzgerald/Hemingway Annual*, 10 (1978), 105–136.

Sees F as a "'moral' historical novelist, intent on comprehending and explaining in rational terms the motives and implications of human events, viewed simultaneously as personal experience and public phenomena," and relates events and characters in TITN to historical and cultural events in the 1920s and 1930s. Thus, Nicole's "experience and her suffering typify rather than merely illustrate the experience and suffering of an immature America in the opening decades of the twentieth century"; and Dick, in his failure to cure Nicole, illustrates "the tragic failure of American idealism in the twentieth century."

H1114. Hoffman, Madelyn. "*This Side of Paradise*: A Study of Pathological Narcissism," *Literature and Psychology*, 28 (Number 3 & 4, 1978), 178–185.

Charts Amory Blaine's abortive attempts to connect himself with charismatic others—Darcy, Isabelle, Dick Humbird, Clara Page, Rosalind, and Eleanor—and speculates that this pattern implies "the narcissistic personality's weakness for charisma in others [which] represents a quest for re-union with the original narcissistic charismatic parent."

H1115. Ishikawa, Akiko. "From 'Winter Dreams' to *The Great Gatsby*," *Persica (Journal of the English Literary Society of Okayama)*, No. 5 (January 1978), 79–92.

In English. Discusses development of F's art by comparing and contrasting "Winter Dreams" and GG. "The author strived to refine the romantic view and justify it theoretically and, as a result, found out that it is inevitable that one who lives truly for a romantic dream will be defeated in reality."

H1116. Johnston, Carol. "Fitzgerald Checklist," *Fitzgerald/Hemingway Annual*, 10 (1978), 437–447.
Listing of recent material by and about F.

H1117. Johnston, Kenneth. "Fitzgerald's 'Crazy Sunday': Cinderella in Hollywood," *Literature/Film Quarterly*, 6 (Summer 1978), 214–221.
Focuses on Joel Coles as an unreliable narrator whose "blunted and uncertain perception...is responsible for the inconsistent portrayal of character, the blurred relationships and motivations, and the 'structural disharmony.' These 'shortcomings' reflect flaws in his own character and, thus, they eventually lead one to the thematic center of the story" which is Joel's "inability to distinguish between appearance and reality."

H1118. Jones, Daryl E. "Fitzgerald and Pulp Fiction: From Diamond Dick to Gatsby," *Fitzgerald/Hemingway Annual*, 10 (1978), 137–139.
Examines F's story "Diamond Dick and the First Law of Woman" and finds in its "frequent allusions to a series of pulp Westerns issued at the turn of the century, and through its assignment of values espoused in these Westerns to a female prototype of Gatsby" an "additional source for Gatsby's naive romantic idealism and exaggerated notions of virtue and chivalry."

H1119. Joy, Neill R. "Fitzgerald's Retort to Hemingway's 'Poor Scott Fitzgerald,'" *Notes on Modern American Literature*, 2 (Spring 1978), Item 13.
Examines Brimmer-Stahr fight scene in LT as F's "mutation" of the "Eastman-Hemingway imbroglio" in Maxwell Perkins' office in 1937 and as F's retaliation to Hemingway's slur in "The Snows of Kilimanjaro."

H1120. Kawachino, Hiromi. "*The Great Gatsby* as a Story of America," *Kyushu American Literature* (Fukuoka, Japan), 19 (May 1978), 73–76.
In English. Explores GG as a history of the decline of the American Dream into materialism, with the East seen as "corrupted" and the West as "only an old world without a possibility."

H1121. Keen, William P. "*The Great Gatsby* and 'The Golden Windows,'" *Notes on Modern American Literature*, 3 (Winter 1978), Item 5.
Suggests that passage in GG describing "French windows, glowing now with reflected gold," implies a connection with Laura Richards' popular children's story "The Golden Windows" (1903).

H1122.   Kolbenschlag, Madonna C.   "Madness and Sexual My-
thology in Scott Fitzgerald," *International Journal of Women's Studies*,
1 (May/June 1978), 263–271.

Uses Freud's and Laing's theories on madness and sex role behavior
in examining F's heroines and plots, with an emphasis on TITN and its
relationship to F's own marriage. Suggests that "Zelda and Nicole are
the archetypal examples of the pattern of recurring mental illness which
marks the lives of a dispropriate number of contemporary women" and
notes that TITN implies—"perhaps without the author's intending it—
that in an insane and oppressive social structure, the 'cured' are the
ones who are really confined."

H1123.   Kuhnle, John H.   *"The Great Gatsby* as Pastoral Elegy,"
Fitzgerald/Hemingway Annual, 10 (1978), 141–154.

Examines GG in detail as "the prose equivalent of a pastoral elegy,"
under the headings of form, pastoralism, biography, and resolution,
concluding that GG is "in form, convention, and theme...a pastoral elegy emphasizing Nick's interpretation of the life and death of Gatsby
and their effect on the survivors."

H1124.   Lewis, Janet.   "'The Cruise of the Rolling Junk'—The
Fictionalized Joys of Motoring," *Fitzgerald/Hemingway Annual*, 10
(1978), 69–81.

Examines "The Cruise of the Rolling Junk" as "fictionalized
autobiography" to see "how Fitzgerald has altered or blurred facts to
enhance his narrative," concluding that it is "an entertaining and rewarding part of Fitzgerald's writing" and "a series that he worked on
with care and real interest, a genuine attempt to bridge autobiography
and storytelling."

H1125.   "Literary Renaissance of the 20's Is Discussed," *Among
Friends of LBJ* (LBJ Library, Austin, Tex.), No. 18 (December 15,
1978), 7, 12.

Excerpts from talk given by Matthew J. Bruccoli at LBJ Library include material on F.

H1126.   McCabe, Charles.   "Himself—Muse in the Bottle?" San
Francisco *Chronicle*, December 6, 1978, p. 51.

Mention of F in article on possible relationship between writing and
drinking.

McHaney, Thomas L. See Bird (H1095).

H1127.   Martin, Robert K.   "Sexual and Group Relationships in
'May Day': Fear and Longing," *Studies in Short Fiction*, 15 (Winter
1978), 99–101.

Suggests that F, in the character of Gordon, is "treating, albeit covertly and perhaps unconsciously, the problems faced by the repressed homosexual when he is forced to leave a place of relative happiness and security, such as the military or a men's college, and take up a place in a heterosexual world which he fears."

H1128.   Monroe, H. Keith. "Gatsby and the Gods," *Renascence*, 31 (Autumn 1978), 51–63.

Contends that there are "several layers" to the parallel between Gatsby and Jesus Christ and that what "has, at first glance, seemed a desultory ironic linking...seems, on closer examination, to be an expression of a philosophical dualism that recognizes the chasm between the material vegetative world and the imaginative ideal world."

H1129.   Paulson, A. B. *"The Great Gatsby*: Oral Aggression and Splitting," *American Imago*, 35 (Fall 1978), 311–330.

Discusses the novel's tendency "to double its characters and imagery in terms of a notion Freud employed to understand certain perversions of genital sexuality: the notion of splitting."

H1130.   Person, Leland S., Jr. "'Herstory' and Daisy Buchanan," *American Literature*, 50 (May 1978), 250–257.

Interprets Daisy as the "female double" of Gatsby who is "both anima and Doppelgänger,...*The Great Gatsby* is finally the story of the failure of a mutual dream"; thus, Gatsby "is as much an ideal to Daisy as she is to him" and neither Nick nor Gatsby "realize (and communicate) the essence of Daisy's meaning....[They] progressively devitalize Daisy's symbolic meaning until she exists as a vulgar emblem of the money values which dominate their world" when, in fact, she is "victimized by a male tendency to project a self-satisfying, yet ultimately dehumanizing, image on woman."

H1131.   Peterson, Gerald L. "An Unpublished Letter From F. Scott Fitzgerald," *Fitzgerald/Hemingway Annual*, 10 (1978), 82–83 [82].

Brief explanatory note prefacing F letter to translator John Myers O'Hara thanking him for copy of his translation of Sappho's poems.

H1132.   Roulston, Robert. "Dick Diver's Plunge Into the Roman Void: The Setting of *Tender Is the Night*," *South Atlantic Quarterly*, 77 (Winter 1978), 85–97.

Examines five chapters of TITN set in Rome as "the narrative and thematic focal point of the novel"; Rome is "a reflection of Dick Diver's fears and longings,...a place full of historical resonances and modern object lessons" and "a perfect microcosm of all that has become debased in Western civilization. [It] provides an inimitable framework within which Dick Diver...can plunge into the vortex of his own self-hatred—a modern Everyman hurtling toward destruction enveloped by ageless emblems of humanity's failure."

H1133. ———. "Slumbering With the Just: A Maryland Lens for *Tender Is the Night*," *Southern Quarterly*, 16 (January 1978), 125–137.

Views TITN against a background of F's attitude toward Maryland, the state in which he wrote most of it and the state from which his father's family came. F "regarded Maryland both as a personal haven for himself, his wife and daughter and as a reminder of what America at its best once had been—a place where socially useful work had been done within the framework of benign tradition....an evanescent embodiment of an ancestral memory and a fading example of what a civilized society should be."

H1134. ———. "Tom Buchanan: Patrician in Motley," *Arizona Quarterly*, 34 (Summer 1978), 101–111.

Sees Tom as "one of the great comic characters in literature" in the tradition of Falstaff, inspiring "laughter that blends compassion with disapproval, comprehension with scorn," and serving as a vehicle to express F's hatred of the leisure class, his bitterness over his failure at football, as well as functioning as a moral scapegoat for himself. But Tom is also "the wise fool" who "most clearly grasps the major point about society—that it is in disarray."

H1135. Scharnhorst, Gary. "Scribbling Upward: Fitzgerald's Debt to Horatio Alger, Jr.," *Fitzgerald/Hemingway Annual*, 10 (1978), 161–169.

Examines TSOP, *The Vegetable*, GG, and "Forging Ahead" for evidence of F's satirization of the Alger myth and its conventions which served as a vehicle "for his condemnation of the elusive, seductive Bitch-goddess."

H1136. Schmid, Hans. "The Switzerland of Fitzgerald and Hemingway," *Fitzgerald/Hemingway Annual*, 10 (1978), 261–271.

Recounts the factual details of F's stay in Switzerland between May 1930 and September 1931 and notes his use of his experiences and observations in "One Trip Abroad," "The Hotel Child," "Indecision," "Flight and Pursuit," and TITN, and compares F's portrayal of Switzerland with Hemingway's.

H1137. Sojka, Gregory S. "The American Short Story Into Film," *Studies in Short Fiction*, 15 (Spring 1978), 203–204.

Review of "The American Short Story" TV series includes mention of "Bernice Bobs Her Hair" adaptation.

H1138.   Tanner, Stephen L.   "Fitzgerald: 'What to Make of a Diminished Thing,'" *Arizona Quarterly*, 34 (Summer 1978), 153–161.

Sees all of F's work as "composed of two parts, the second growing naturally and inevitably out of the first." The first is "Romantic Promise" ("the complex of hope, dream, yearning, aspiration, expectation, idealism, mystery, confidence and future possibility characteristic of so many of his characters"); the second is the "Diminished Thing" ("the unavoidable aftermath of Romantic Promise: hopes and dreams thwarted, the mystery and excitement become commonplace, the future devoid of expectation and possibility").

H1139.   Trower, Katherine B.   "The Fitzgeralds' Letters to the Hoveys," *Fitzgerald/Hemingway Annual*, 10 (1978), 55–60 [55–56].

Brief explanatory note preceding first publication of eight letters from F or Zelda to either Carl Hovey, the editor of *Metropolitan Magazine*, or his wife, screenwriter Sonya Levien.

H1140.   Tsuboi, Kiyohiko.   "*Philippe, Count of Darkness* by F. Scott Fitzgerald," *Persica (Journal of the English Literary Society of Okayama)*, 5 (January 1978), 25–33.

In English. Sees the four published sections of the proposed novel as evidence of F's "hard struggle and effort to find out new materials and new methods to create a new type of hero in the days of his deterioration."

H1141.   Twitchell, James B.   "'Babylon Revisited': Chronology and Characters," *Fitzgerald/Hemingway Annual*, 10 (1978), 155–160.

Examines the chronology and characters to support assertions that "Charlie has indeed reformed, but...in this scurvy world 'moral reformation may not be enough'" and that Charlie should be exonerated "from the charge of being a conscious or unconscious co-conspirator in his ultimate disappointment."

H1142.   Tyler, Ralph.   "The Muse in the Bottle," *Bookviews*, 2 (September 1978), 14–16, 18–19 [14, 15, 16].

Passing mention of F in discussion of relationship between alcohol and American writers.

H1143.   West, James L. W., III.   "The Bantam 'Gatsby,'" *Book Collector's Market*, 3 (November/December 1978), 15–18.

Studies the covers and jackets of the Bantam Books paperback impressions of GG issued in 1945, 1946, 1949, and 1951, concluding that "an author's image is reflected by *all* forms in which his work is presented to the public and...even such items as cheap paperback printings are collectible because of the information they reveal about an author's reputation."

H1144. West, Suzanne. "Nicole's Gardens," *Fitzgerald/Hemingway Annual*, 10 (1978), 85–95.

Explores F's use of flower imagery to reveal and develop Nicole Diver's character in TITN, noting her association with the rose and emphasizing F's "development of Nicole's character by associating her with three different gardens"—the one at Dr. Dohmler's sanitarium ("a romantic Eden"), the one at the Villa Diana ("an enclosed refuge that Dick establishes for his half-cured bride"), and a metaphorical garden that Nicole creates herself.

H1145. White, Ray Lewis. "Ben Hecht on *The Vegetable*: A Lost Chicago Review," *Fitzgerald/Hemingway Annual*, 10 (1978), 97–98.

Reprints and comments on review here attributed to Hecht but in fact written by Maxwell Bodenheim (see G15).

H1146. Winslow, Richard. "Fitzgerald's 'Favorite Story,'" *Fitzgerald/Hemingway Annual*, 10 (1978), 67.

Reprints from the April 8, 1923, NY *Herald* an English drinking tale which F chose.

H1147. Yost, Barbara. "Professor Extricates Authors From Rumor Mill," Phoenix *Gazette*, June 3, 1978, "Marquee" Section, p. 15.

Interview with Matthew J. Bruccoli on occasion of publication of *Scott and Ernest* (I54).

1979

H1148. Anderson, William R[ichard, Jr.] "Fitzgerald After *Tender Is the Night*: A Literary Strategy For the 1930s," *Fitzgerald/Hemingway Annual*, 11 (1979), 39–63.

Studies heroes of F's post-TITN fiction, especially Philippe, Pat Hobby, and Monroe Stahr, for evidence of development of a different type of character and a new philosophy in tune with the 1930s—a "capacity to continue functioning in the face of the breakdown of order, harmony, and established values."

H1149. Baker, Carlos. "The Sun Rose Differently," *NY Times Book Review*, March 18, 1979, pp. 7, 28.

Recounts F's role in pruning the original opening of *The Sun Also Rises* in June 1926 and asserts that "Scott saved Ernest a very probable drubbing by reviewers for the insouciance of that original opening."

H1150.   Bennett, Elizabeth.   "Scottie Fitzgerald Smith—For a Writer, Being the Daughter of a Literary Giant Can Be 'A Terrible Block,'" Houston *Post*, November 11, 1979, p. 3BB.

Interview with F's daughter who comments on her parents.

H1151.   Bennett, Warren.   "Prefigurations of Gatsby, Eckleburg, Owl Eyes, and Klipspringer," *Fitzgerald/Hemingway Annual*, 11 (1979), 207–223.

Demonstrates a pattern of ocular imagery in GG and shows how this imagery had its genesis in "Absolution," "The Diamond as Big as the Ritz," " 'The Sensible Thing,'" TSOP, and B&D.

H1152.   Berman, Jeffrey.   *"Tender Is the Night*: Fitzgerald's *A Psychology for Psychiatrists," Literature and Psychology*, 29 (No. 1/2, 1979), 34–48.

Explores F's knowledge of "the theoretical and clinical intricacies of tranference-love," Dick Diver's disregard of medical ethics in becoming romantically involved with Nicole, and F's allowing Nicole to recover and Dick to fall.

H1153.   Bizzell, Patricia.   "Pecuniary Emulation of the Mediator in *The Great Gatsby," Modern Language Notes*, 94 (May 1979), 774–783.

Argues, using theories of Thorstein Veblen and René Gerard, that GG "exposes the absence of an authentic orthodoxy in American capitalist democratic ideology," that American ideology "attempts to make the material world itself a bridge to the abstract world," and that "getting money replaces heroic achievement as a way of living morally in the world." Gatsby's death, in this context, seems the inevitable result of following such an ideology.

H1154.   Bolch, Jennifer.   "Scottie Fitzgerald Recalls Life With a Famous Father," Dallas *Times-Herald*, November 11, 1979, pp. H–1, H–3.

Interview with F's daughter who reminisces about her parents.

H1155.   Bordewyck, Gordon.   "Gatsby: The Figure of the Host," *American Notes & Queries*, 17 (May 1979), 141–143.

Examines three images associated with the Eucharist which appear in Chapter III of GG and relates them to F's depiction of Gatsby as "a priest of romantic idealism."

H1156.   Brady, James.   "Scott Fitzgerald and Romantic Memory," NY *Post*, March 12, 1979, p. 22.

Muses about reverence for F and his works.

H1157. Bruccoli, Matthew J. "Bennett Cerf's Fan Letter on *Tender Is the Night*: A Source for Abe North's Death," *Fitzgerald/Hemingway Annual*, 11 (1979), 229–230.

Quotes from 1934 Cerf letter to Maxwell Perkins in which Cerf cites 1928 death of Princeton alumnus (Class of 1918) Cornelius R. Winant in a speakeasy brawl as possible source for North's death in TITN.

H1158. ———. "The Education of Dorothy Richardson," *Fitzgerald/Hemingway Annual*, 11 (1979), 227–228.

Prints list of Modern Library titles F prepared in 1936 for his nurse in Asheville, North Carolina.

H1159. ———. "Epilogue: A Woman, a Gift, and a Still Unanswered Question," *Esquire*, 91 (January 30, 1979), 67.

Recounts F's meeting and subsequent friendship with Bert Barr (Bertha Weinberg Goldstein), who has donated typescripts and proofs of 39 F *Esquire* stories and articles and other F materials to Princeton, and notes parallels between story "On Your Own" and their relationship.

H1160. ———. "Zelda Fitzgerald's Lost Stories," *Fitzgerald/Hemingway Annual*, 11 (1979), 123–126.

Gives synopses, located in the files of F's agent Harold Ober, of eight Zelda short stories written between 1930 and 1932 which were never published and for which there are no manuscripts.

H1161. ———, ed. "Arnold Gingrich Writes to F. Scott Fitzgerald," *Fitzgerald/Hemingway Annual*, 11 (1979), 233.

Prints, with very brief introductory note, piece of 1934 letter which notes Mencken's and Alfred A. Knopf's opinions of TITN.

H1162. Carroll, E. Jean. "The Hemingway-Fitzgerald Literary Intelligence Text," *Esquire*, 91 (January 2–16, 1979), 81–82.

Quiz on F and Hemingway which requires thorough knowledge of them both in order to score well.

H1163. Cheatham, David W. "Owen Davis's Dramatization of *The Great Gatsby*," *Fitzgerald/Hemingway Annual*, 11 (1979), 99–113.

Detailed description and analysis of 1926 stage adaptation of GG which fails ultimately because the "settings contribute almost nothing,…plot conflicts with characterization," because "Davis treated the supporting characters superficially, so that we essentially see only one alternative to Gatsby's character and goal…[and] therefore cannot view his pursuit of the ideal as a necessary response to life; neither do we find his response admirable," and because "the play's Gatsby is not heroic: his sentimentality undercuts his dignity; his ruthlessness as a criminal undercuts his compassion; and his failure to act at crucial points undercuts his commitment to his dream."

H1164.   Coburn, Randy Sue. "Scott & Matthew—An Obsession as Big as the Ritz," Washington (D.C.) *Sunday Star*, February 4, 1979, pp. E–1, E–2.

Extensive profile of and interview with F scholar-collector Matthew J. Bruccoli.

H1165.   Crosland, Andrew. "Sources for Fitzgerald's 'The Curious Case of Benjamin Button,'" *Fitzgerald/Hemingway Annual*, 11 (1979), 135–139.

Locates remark in Albert Bigelow Paine's *Mark Twain: A Biography* which may have given F inspiration for his story, as well as passage in Samuel Butler's *Note-Books* in which, after completing the story, F found a similar plot.

H1166.   Cushman, Keith. "Scott Fitzgerald's Scrupulous Meanness: 'Absolution' and 'The Sisters,'" *Fitzgerald/Hemingway Annual*, 11 (1979), 115–121.

Examines "borrowings" from Joyce's story in F's: Both "turn on the relationship between an innocent young protagonist and a priest who has lost his vocation"; in each, "the experience with the priest teaches the boy something about life"; and, in the story's communion scene, F uses Joyce's technique of "'scrupulous meanness'" in which the language "is packed with implication, suggestion, and symbol."

H1167.   Davison, Richard Allan. "*The Great Gatsby* and *Hopalong Cassidy*, Fitzgerald's Anachronism?" *Fitzgerald/Hemingway Annual*, 11 (1979), 155–157.

Refutes Taylor Alderman's assertion (see H846) that F's use of Hopalong Cassidy in GG is anachronistic by noting that Cassidy's adventures were serialized in *The Outing Magazine* beginning in 1905, and that while young Jimmy Gatz could not have had a bound copy of *Hopalong Cassidy*, "the reference to the character is not" anachronistic.

H1168.   Deegan, Thomas. "Dick Diver's Childishness in *Tender Is the Night*," *Fitzgerald/Hemingway Annual*, 11 (1979), 129–133.

Explores F's use of "two symbolic motifs to delineate Dick's incompleteness": the "childlike aspect of Dick's character" which suggests "his longing for his lost innocence and his escape into a limited but intact world of his own making"; and "the contrast in Dick's mind between light and darkness" which shows that, when he is under strain, "Dick wishes to withdraw from the bright light of human contact into the tender night of his illusions."

H1169.   Dessner, Lawrence Jay.   "Photography and *The Great Gatsby*," *Essays in Literature* (Western Illinois University, Macomb), 6 (Spring 1979), 79–90.

Examines references to photography and cinematography in GG, concluding that "photography expresses and affects the ways its characters think" and reinforces "their assumptions about the nature of reality and time."

H1170.   Donaldson, Scott.   "F. Scott Fitzgerald, Princeton '17," *Princeton University Library Chronicle*, 40 (Winter 1979), 119–154.

Detailed examination of F at Princeton and of his relationship to it, in his life and in his works after he left it which suggests that F's attitudes towards class and his desire to become a big man on campus were at odds with Princeton's own view of itself and its alumni.

H1171.   Dorn, Norman K.   "Fitzgerald's One and Only," San Francisco *Sunday Examiner & Chronicle*, April 22, 1979, "Datebook" Section, p. 16.

Discussion of F's screenplay for "Three Comrades," on occasions of opening of revival of movie at a local theater and of publication of screenplay (see I37).

H1172.   Doughty, Peter.   "The Seating Arrangement in *Tender Is the Night*," *Fitzgerald/Hemingway Annual*, 11 (1979), 159–161.

Notes that Rosemary Hoyt is left out of the seating arrangement described in the Villa Diana dinner scene and suggests that this may be the result "of Fitzgerald's confusing his character's perspective with his own."

H1173.   Duke, Maurice.   "Fitzgerald Stories Basis for Series on Public Radio," Richmond (Va.) *Times-Dispatch*, July 1, 1979, p. G–5.

Preview of radio series "The World of F. Scott Fitzgerald" which summarizes the content of each of the eight segments to be broadcast.

H1174.   Elstein, Rochelle S.   "Fitzgerald's Josephine Stories: The End of the Romantic Illusion," *American Literature*, 51 (March 1979), 69–83.

Examines the Josephine stories as revealing a metamorphosis which F had undergone in that he "worked and reworked the same elements until he arrived at a formulation which was antithetical to the original construct of the 'genteel romantic heroine.'"

H1175.   Evans, T. Jeff.   "For Whom the Earth Moves: A Fitzgerald Parody of Hemingway," *American Notes & Queries*, 17 (April 1979), 127–128.

Notes F's parody of the love scene in *For Whom the Bell Tolls* in LT when Kathleen and Stahr visit site of his new home: "Specifically, Fitzgerald parodies Hemingway's affected use of Spanish to infuse tenderness into the love affair...and the excessive solipsistic image of the earth shifting to express the physical love experience"; more generally, F "parodies the immaturity...and the overall sentimentality of Hemingway's portrayal."

H1176.   Fairey, Wendy. *"The Last Tycoon*: The Dilemma of Maturity for F. Scott Fitzgerald," *Fitzgerald/Hemingway Annual*, 11 (1979), 65–78.

Examines LT as evidence of the dilemma of F's view of maturity, concluding that to "see fatigue as the crucial development of maturity is a limitation of vision that may have been as destructive as time itself— a self-fulfilling prophecy, aborting his own development and denying life's full drama."

H1177.   Fenstermaker, J. J. "The Literary Reputation of F. Scott Fitzgerald 1940–1941: Appraisal and Reappraisal," *Fitzgerald/Hemingway Annual*, 11 (1979), 79–90.

Studies the shift in F's literary reputation between December 1940 and December 1941 through three stages: "the commentary immediately following his death, the reminiscence-appraisals, and...the reviews of " LT.   Credits the upsurge in F's reputation partly to LT but also to writers for *Esquire* and *New Republic*, who, as early as spring 1941, were "declaring and justifying the need for a reappraisal."

H1178.   Ferguson, Robert A.   "The Grotesque in the Novels of F. Scott Fitzgerald," *South Atlantic Quarterly*, 78 (Autumn 1979), 460–477.

Explores F's employment of the grotesque in his completed novels as a "chronological gauge for evaluating his growing power and rapid development as a novelist in the early 1920's" and concludes that such a study helps explain why GG is superior to TITN.

H1179.   Fraser, Keath.   "Another Reading of *The Great Gatsby*," *English Studies in Canada*, 5 (Autumn 1979), 330–343.

Discusses the sexual ambiguity in GG, noting evidence of the "theme of impotence and bisexuality" in F's novel as "discoverable in *The Satyricon* of Petronius," and drawing parallels between Encolpios as narrator of *The Satyricon* and Nick: The corruption of GG "originates not merely in Gatsby's shady business connections, but also in Nick Carraway's disingenuous sexuality."

H1180.   Fulkerson, Tahita N.   "Ibsen in 'The Ice Palace,'" *Fitzgerald/Hemingway Annual*, 11 (1979), 169–171.

Claims that "the direct references to Ibsen and to *Peer Gynt* along with the similarity between Sally Carrol's ideas and Nora's suggest Fitzgerald's debt to Ibsen in 'The Ice Palace.'"

H1181. "Gatsby Gala to Benefit Radio Theater for Blind," Portland *Oregonian*, May 24, 1979, p. C3.
Announces planned Gatsby Gala to be held in Portland to benefit local radio theater and to mark beginning of Public Radio series "The World of F. Scott Fitzgerald."

H1182. Greenwald, Fay T. "Fitzgerald's Female Narrators," *Mid-Hudson Language Studies*, 2 (1979), 116–133.
Discusses Rosemary Hoyt of TITN and Cecilia Brady of LT, contending that F's "attempts at constructing a female narrative point of view both as technique and as characters were failures" which nevertheless "tell us something about the roles of men and women in America."

H1183. Gross, Barry. "Fitzgerald's Midwest: 'Something Gorgeous Somewhere'—Somewhere *Else*," *Midamerica*, 6 (1979), 111–126.
Examines the two views of the Midwest in F's work—"the secure and stable country of Basil Duke Lee and Nick Carraway and Amory Blaine" and the "narrow and constricted country of Rudolph Miller and Dexter Green and Jimmy Gatz." Includes discussion of "Bernice Bobs Her Hair," "The Camel's Back," "The Ice Palace," "Absolution," "Winter Dreams," and GG.

H1184. Hemenway, Robert. "Two New Fitzgerald Letters," *Fitzgerald/Hemingway Annual*, 11 (1979), 127–128.
Prints, with introductory note, two letters from 1921 and 1922 to writer-journalist-diplomat John Franklin Carter.

H1185. [Hess, John D.] "Fitzgerald at the Winter Carnival," *Fitzgerald/Hemingway Annual*, 11 (1979), 35–36.
Reprinting, with brief explanatory note, of interview from February 11, 1939, issue of *The Dartmouth* (see H117).

H1186. Hill, Michael. "TV-Radio—At 7 p.m., Forsake TV for Public Radio," Baltimore *Evening Sun*, June 11, 1979, p. B6.
Review of Public Radio series "The World of F. Scott Fitzgerald" which praises it as the "type of stimulation and entertainment many seek from television, but rarely find."

H1187. Johnston, Carol. "Fitzgerald Checklist," *Fitzgerald/Hemingway Annual*, 11 (1979), 453–461.
Listing of recent published material by and about F.

H1188.   Kirkby, Joan. "Spengler and Apocalyptic Typology in F. Scott Fitzgerald's *Tender Is the Night*," *Southern Review* (University of Adelaide, Australia), 12 (November 1979), 246–261.

Discusses the employment of the historical type provided by Spengler's *The Decline of the West* and the crisis archetype (or apocalyptic typology) used in TITN, arguing that the novel "bodies forth without resolving (and therby diminishing) the conflicting demands of its [personal and historical] typologies." Also briefly discusses apocalyptic typology of F's other novels.

H1189.   Lardner, Ring W. "'Great Neck Is Like a Cemetery': Ring Lardner to Thomas Boyd," *Fitzgerald/Hemingway Annual*, 11 (1979), 231–232.

Letter of May 18, 1924, which mentions that F and Zelda have recently left Great Neck.

H1190.   ———. "Ring Lardner on *The Beautiful and Damned*," *Fitzgerald/Hemingway Annual*, 11 (1979), 225.

Reprinting of section of Lardner's October 23, 1921, syndicated newspaper column, with mention of F (see H13).

H1191.   Levith, Murray J. "Fitzgerald's *The Great Gatsby*," *The Explicator*, 37 (Spring 1979), Item 7.

Discusses sexual imagery in GG to illuminate the "central issues"— "absence of fertility, faith, and love in our modern 'valley of ashes.'"

H1192.   Lewis, Roger. "Ruth Sturtevant and F. Scott Fitzgerald (1916–1921)," *Fitzgerald/Hemingway Annual*, 11 (1979), 3–21.

Prints, with brief introduction giving details of F's friendship with Ruth Sturtevant in 1915–17 and the early 1920s, ten previously unpublished F letters to her written between July 1915 and April 1917.

H1193.   Maddocks, Melvin. "Fitzgerald's Green Light—A Half Century Later," *Christian Science Monitor*, January 29, 1979, p. 30.

Evaluation of "On Your Own"—"a rather naive example of would-be-slick magazine fiction." This article also appeared in *Rocky Mountain News* (Denver), March 4, 1979, "Now" Section, p. 4; Seattle *Times*, February 4, 1979, Sec. M, p. 2.

H1194.   Mark, Carolyn Bengston. "Scottie Brings Back the '20s," Austin (Tex.) *Citizen*, November 2, 1979, p. 1.

Interview with F's daughter, in Austin for the "Roaring Twenties" exhibit at the LBJ Library.

H1195.   Marshall, Jane P. "Gift of Fan Recalls Memories of Fitzgeralds' Flamboyancy," Fort Worth *Star-Telegram*, November 16, 1979, Sec. E, p. 1.

Interview with F's daughter who has donated fan belonging to her mother to "Roaring Twenties" exhibit at LBJ Library.

H1196.   Messina, Lynne.   "Scottie's Memories—F. Scott Fitzgerald's Daughter Keeper of Family Flame," Austin (Tex.) *American-Statesman*, November 7, 1979, p. C1.

Interview with F's daughter who speaks of her parents.

H1197.   Morrison, Bill.   "F. Scott Fitzgerald's Bittersweet Life Is on Radio," Raleigh *News and Observer*, June 6, 1979, p. 11.

Review of Public Radio series on F which "promises a portrait of the man far more lucid and intelligent than the anemic television films based on his madcap and quite mad relationship with Zelda."

H1198.   Morrison, Gail Moore.   "Faulkner's Priests and Fitzgerald's 'Absolution,'" *Mississippi Quarterly*, 32 (Summer 1979), 461–465.

Notes verbal parallels between Faulkner's "The Priest" and F's story and the more general parallels between "Absolution" and Faulkner's "Mistral."

H1199.   Nagaoka, Sadao.   "Fitzgerald Bibliographical Center in Japan," *Fitzgerald/Hemingway Annual*, 11 (1979), 145–146.

Describes founding of and holdings in the Fitzgerald Bibliographical Center at Yamanashi University.

H1200.   Perlis, Alan.   "The Narrative Is All: A Study of F. Scott Fitzgerald's *May Day*," *Western Humanities Review*, 33 (Winter 1979), 65–72.

Studies the story's structure and identifies F's narrative techniques and handling of point of view, suggesting that the recurrent pattern of removal of the author's sympathies for the characters implies that "the narrative is all: the characters' mutual indifference forces the story's own voice to become more and more hollow, its stance the drained efforts toward compassion."

H1201.   Pleasants, Ben.   "West View—Remembering Fitzgerald on a Hollywood Side Street," Los Angeles *Times*, April 22, 1979, "Book Review" Section, p. 3.

Memories of seeing house on which Gatsby's mansion is based and of the apartment in which F died and a call for the city of Los Angeles to place a brass plate on the door of the apartment indicating its importance.   Includes text of letter from Budd Schulberg to Pleasants supporting idea of the brass plate.

H1202.   Powell, Caroline.   "Fitzgerald Remembered," *Daily Texan* (University of Texas, Austin), November 9, 1979, p. 17.

Account of talks about F given at LBJ Library by Matthew J. Bruccoli and Scottie Fitzgerald Smith.

H1203.   Rusch, Frederic E.   "Fitzgerald in Competition," *Fitzgerald/Hemingway Annual*, 11 (1979), 151–153.
Describes contest held by Wm. Collins Sons, publishers of English edition of TSOP, in which readers were asked to decide which of four first novels in Collins' "First Novel Library" series " 'shows the greatest promise' " and reprints advertisement in which results were announced and TSOP was declared the winner, indicating that TSOP "was favorably received by the reading public in England even though the novel never achieved the great success it enjoyed in America."

H1204.   Sanders, Donald.   "Saga of Author Starts on Radio," Phoenix *Gazette*, June 8, 1979, Sec. D, p. 17.
Preview of upcoming Public Radio series of dramatizations of F stories.

H1205.   Saposnik, Irving S.   "The Passion and the Life: Technology as Pattern in *The Great Gatsby*," *Fitzgerald/Hemingway Annual*, 11 (1979), 181–188.
Studies use and abuse of cars, trains, and other forms of modern technology in GG as reflecting "a severe imbalance between outward form and inner dislocation" in that Gatsby "pursues the outward forms as if they were inner fountains, convinced that the trappings of his twentieth-century society will allow him to recapture a time past but not lost."

Schulberg, Budd. See Pleasants (H1201).

H1206.   Shepherd, Allen.   "Dick Diver in Nashville: A Note on Robert Penn Warren's *A Place to Come To*," *Fitzgerald/Hemingway Annual*, 11 (1979), 173–175.
Studies influence of TITN on Warren's novel, especially similarities between Dick Diver and J. Lawford Carrington and in the language chosen to portray each character.

H1207.   Smith, Cassandra L.   "Longstanding Inaccuracy," Los Angeles *Times*, June 24, 1979, "Book Review" Section, p. 2.
Letter to the Editor noting that in June 10, 1979, book review F was incorrectly cited as source of remark that "the rich are very different from you and me" which was made by Hemingway. For a reply, see H1208.

H1208.   Smith, Smitty.   "Papa, Fitzgerald's Rich," Los Angeles *Times*, July 8, 1979, "Book Review" Section, p. 2.

Letter to the Editor in reply to Cassandra L. Smith's letter (H1207) which cites passage in F's *Notebooks* indicating that F did make the comment about the rich.

H1209.　Sullivan, Victoria.　"An American Dream Destroyed: Zelda Fitzgerald," *CEA Critic*, 41 (January 1979), 33–35, 37–39. Discusses SMTW which is "unique and worthy of critical attention" because of "its poetic style; its ironic evocation of scene and of personality; and its subject matter, both the detailed description of the creation of a ballet dancer and the brutal, lyrical portrait of a woman destroyed in her efforts to achieve autonomy."

H1210.　Tavernier-Courbin, Jacqueline.　"Art as Woman's Response and Search: Zelda Fitzgerald's *Save Me the Waltz*," *Southern Literary Journal*, 11 (Spring 1979), 22–42. Examines the F-Zelda relationship and analyzes SMTW which is "simultaneously a response and a search: a response to a personal situation..., to the social role its author was expected to play..., and to the universal condition that comes from simply being a woman. It is a search for identity, a justification of the self, and an affirmation of it. It is finally the *cri du coeur* of a woman who wants to exist on her own terms and who is claiming her life experience as her own material."

H1211.　Thornton, Patricia Pacey.　"Sexual Roles in *The Great Gatsby*," *English Studies in Canada*, 5 (Winter 1979), 457–468. Explores major characters of GG in order to examine patterns of sexual confusion, role reversal, and exchange of one stereotyped role for another, contending that the genders of F's couples "seem inextricably confused; they are more like twins than lovers." Sees three sets of twins representing the three dominant types of sexual roles: the he-man and the traditional fair heroine (Tom and Daisy), the self-made man and the flapper (Gatsby and Myrtle), and the androgynous twins (Nick and Jordan).

H1212.　Tritten, Larry.　"Loose Leaves—(Some Pages Left Out of the New Edition of The Notebooks of F. Scott Fitzgerald)," *New Yorker*, 54 (February 12, 1979), 28. Parody of F's *Notebooks*.

H1213.　Trouard, Dawn.　"Fitzgerald's Missed Moments: Surrealistic Style in His Major Novels," *Fitzgerald/Hemingway Annual*, 11 (1979), 189–205. Traces through TSOP, GG, TITN, and LT "a motif of missed moments—the nightmarish idealization of that golden dream"—in attempt to show that "'the heightened sensitivity' in each novel is not solely the product of a tragic-romantic theme but a skillful reinforcement of content by a surrealistic style."

H1214.   Tsuboi, Kiyohiko.   "The Reception of F. Scott Fitzgerald in Japan," *Fitzgerald/Hemingway Annual*, 11 (1979), 141–143.

Overview of F's reception includes historical account of his growing acceptance, names of works translated into Japanese, elements in F which appeal to the Japanese, and a brief summary of F scholarly activity in Japan.

H1215.   Valenti, Peter.   "Gatsby: Franklin and Hoppy," *Notes on Modern American Literature*, 3 (Fall 1979), Item 23.

Refutes Callahan's (I79) interpretation of the Hopalong Cassidy allusion in GG, noting that "Hoppy was simply a cowboy who faced bravely the challenges of a dirty, brutal, and demanding lifestyle." On the other hand, "D. H. Lawrence's evaluation of Franklin as a crafty courtier determined to make good regardless of means, while maintaining external rectitude, comes far closer to young Gatsby's desires than the thoroughly American but thoroughly uncultured cowboy."

H1216.   Vanderwerken, David L.   "Who Killed Jay Gatsby?" *Notes on Modern American Literature*, 3 (Spring 1979), Item 12.

Suggests that George Wilson is a surrogate for Gatsby's original identity, James Gatz, and that Wilson's murder of Gatsby demonstrates "the ideal self's inability to control the moral self's anarchic passions." Also draws parallels between Gatsby and Wilson and Thomas Sutpen and Wash Jones in Faulkner's *Absalom, Absalom!*

H1217.   Wagner, Joseph B.   "*Gatsby* and John Keats: Another Version," *Fitzgerald/Hemingway Annual*, 11 (1979), 91–98.

Cites parallels between GG and *Endymion* in basic situation—"both Gatsby and Endymion fall in love with inaccessible ideals, and their respective narratives tell how they single-mindedly pursue their loves through arduous and fantastic quests"—and in "the extensive use of moon imagery," suggesting that GG is "a modern, ironic version of the Endymion myth."

H1218.   West, James L. W., III.   "The Second Serials of *This Side of Paradise* and *The Beautiful and Damned*," *Publications of the Bibliographical Society of America*, 73 (First Quarter 1979), 63–74.

Examines second serializations of TSOP and B&D in four major American cities, the advertising leading up to these appearances, and the accuracy of the serialized texts, concluding that "the manner in which his fiction was advertised and the way in which his texts were treated surely played a significant role in shaping his image as a popular writer in his own time." Includes facsimiles of advertisements.

H1219.   Westbrook, Wayne W.   "Portrait of a Dandy in *The Beautiful and Damned*," *Fitzgerald/Hemingway Annual*, 11 (1979), 147–149.

Biographical sketch of Ward McAllister, "a real-life society figure in New York during the 1870s and 1880s" who served as the model for Adam Ulysses Patch, Anthony's father, in B&D and is briefly alluded to in TITN.

H1220.   White, Ray Lewis.   "*The Pat Hobby Stories*: A File of Reviews," *Fitzgerald/Hemingway Annual*, 11 (1979), 177–180.

Lists with annotations eleven reviews of PH not previously listed.

H1221.   ———.   "Zelda Fitzgerald's *Save Me the Waltz*: Collection of Reviews From 1932–1933," *Fitzgerald/Hemingway Annual*, 11 (1979), 163–168.

Annotated list of twelve reviews not included in 1932 *Book Review Digest*.

H1222.   Young, Perry Deane.   "This Side of Rockville," Washington (D.C.) *Post*, January 14, 1979, Magazine, pp. 8–15.

Detailed discussion of "how and why the golden couple of the Jazz Age come to be buried" in Rockville, Maryland, which includes descriptions of original burials in 1940 and 1948 and the 1975 reburials.

H1223.   Zibart, Eve.   "Fitzgerald's World—F. Scott Fitzgerald—Inventor of 'Jazz Age,'" *Rocky Mountain News* (Denver), June 4, 1979, p. 46; "Fitzgerald's World—Champagne, Frivolity and Life in N.Y.," *Rocky Mountain News* (Denver), June 5, 1979, p. 42; "Fitzgerald's World—In France, Fitzgerald Began 'Going to Ruin,'" *Rocky Mountain News* (Denver), June 6, 1979, p. 66; "Fitzgerald's World—A Man Who Outlived His Reputation," *Rocky Mountain News* (Denver), June 7, 1979, pp. 99, 100.

Four-part series of articles examining F, "his times and his works, based on the new National Public Radio series 'The World of F. Scott Fitzgerald,'" and which is largely a detailed biographical account.

1980

H1224.   Anderson, David D.   "Midwestern Writers and the Myth of the Search," *Georgia Review*, 34 (Spring 1980), 131–143 [131–133, 139–141].

Discusses F's life and GG as illustrating his "determination to move, to seek a measure of fulfillment in [his] own life, and to use the experience and its significance" in his work.

H1225.   Audhuy, Letha.   *"The Waste Land*: Myth and Symbolism in *The Great Gatsby*," *Études Anglaises*, 33 (January-March 1980), 41–54.

Explores the setting, social criticism, elemental and seasonal symbols, and the moral theme of GG to support contention that F "consciously and unconsciously drew upon *The Waste Land* as a whole, to the point of making it the informing myth of his novel."

H1226.   Bagchee, Shyamal.   *"The Great Gatsby* and John Fowles's *The Collector*," *Notes on Contemporary Literature*, 10 (September 1980), 7–8.

Compares and contrasts GG and *The Collector* in order to suggest that the latter is "a remarkably clever inversion or distortion of *The Great Gatsby*."

H1227.   Bremer, Sidney H.   "American Dreams and American Cities in Three Post-World War I Novels," *South Atlantic Quarterly*, 79 (Summer 1980), 274–285 [275, 278–281, 284–285].

Discusses *The Age of Innocence*, GG, and *Miss Lonelyhearts* as "historical reflections of a deep postwar pessimism" and as "metaphoric reflections upon the reasons for and consequences of that pessimism, which they dramatize as a crisis in dreams and dreaming." GG "blames the disintegration of both communalism and individualism in urban America upon the primary failure of the pastoral dream of possibility."

H1228.   Bryer, Jackson R.   "Four Decades of Fitzgerald Studies: The Best and the Brightest," *Twentieth Century Literature*, 26 (Summer 1980), 247–267.

Surveys F studies since 1940 and points out the best research and criticism in each of several areas—biography, bibliography and textual study, criticism of individual novels and stories.

H1229.   Buckley, Peter.   "Tennessee Williams' New Lady," *Horizon*, 23 (April 1980), 66–71.

Discussion of Williams' "Clothes For a Summer Hotel" which includes brief biographical summaries of F and Zelda and analysis of Zelda character in the play as another of Williams' "lost Southern ladies."

H1230.   Cass, Colin S.   "'Pandered in whispers': Narrative Reliability in *The Great Gatsby*," *College Literature*, 7 (Spring 1980), 113–124.

Examines F's "attempts to establish the reliability of his narrator," "the technical necessity of doing so in order to conceal unavoidable implausibilities," and "the transparent difficulties [he] had with his plot and narrative convention" in order to show that Nick is not a pander but rather a "believable human with normal faults," "an upright man."

H1231. Cowley, Malcolm. "Selection—Echoes of the Jazz Age," *NY Times Book Review*, January 13, 1980, pp. 7, 28.
Excerpt from Cowley's *The Dream of the Golden Mountains* (I91).

I11232. Crane, Joan, "The True 'True Story of Appomattox': A Fitzgerald Fable Verified," *American Book Collector*, 1 (September/October 1980), 8–11.
Gives account of the July 1934 incident involving F, Maxwell Perkins, and Elizabeth Lemmon which resulted in "The True Story of Appomattox," a fictional account in which Grant surrenders to Lee, which F wrote and published as a joke.

H1233. Crumpler, David. "Ashley Hall Teacher Co-Edits Collection of Fitzgerald Letters," Charleston (S.C.) *News & Courier-Evening Post*, June 22, 1980, p. 6-E.
Interview with Margaret Duggan who speaks of her work editing F's *Correspondence* with Matthew J. Bruccoli.

H1234. Donaldson, Scott. "The Crisis of Fitzgerald's 'Crack-Up,'" *Twentieth Century Literature*, 26 (Summer 1980), 171–188.
Explores the reactions to, the circumstances leading to the composition of, and the art of the three "C-U" articles, suggesting that their subject is F's misanthropy and the self-hatred behind it; the essays do "not measure up to the best confessional writing," but they "had something of the same therapeutic effect on the man who set" them down on paper.

H1235. Evans, Elizabeth. "Opulent Vulgarity: Ring Lardner and F. Scott Fitzgerald," *Notes on Contemporary Literature*, 10 (January 1980), 2–3.
Suggests that the "shirt scene" in GG may have been prefigured in a scene from Lardner's *The Big Town*.

H1236. Evans, T. Jeff. "F. Scott Fitzgerald and Henry James: The Raw Material of American Innocence," *Notes on Modern American Literature*, 4 (Spring 1980), Item 8.
James' use of the word "raw" at the conclusion of *Daisy Miller* suggests a "cultural sensibility" that reappears in GG in that both "use 'raw' to dramatize the attempted Violation of an established order...by American innocence and idealism."

H1237. Fedo, David. "Women in the Fiction of F. Scott Fitzgerald," *Ball State University Forum*, 21 (Spring 1980), 26–33.
Discusses relationship between what F discovered about women and how he characterized them in Gloria Gilbert, Daisy Buchanan, and Nicole Warren Diver. F "sees them as weak, frail creatures, unfit for the spell of their beauty....But Fitzgerald never excuses their inadequacies, always pointing to the romantic ideal."

H1238.   Gervais, Ronald J.   "The Snow of Twenty-nine: 'Babylon Revisited' as *ubi sunt* Lament," *College Literature*, 7 (Winter 1980), 47–52.

Suggests that F's story "belongs to the generic convention known as the *ubi sunt* lament" and is "organised around allusions to one of the most famous of such works, François Villon's 'Ballade of Dead Ladies'"; both story and "Ballade" are "farewells to lost ladies, who represent the lost values of love, youth, and beauty that exist now only in the imagination."

H1239.   ———.   "The Trains of Their Youth: The Aesthetics of Homecoming in 'The Great Gatsby,' 'The Sun Also Rises' and 'The Sound and the Fury,'" *Americana—Austriaca Beitrage zur Amerikakunde*, 5 (1980), 51–63 [51–56, 58, 62–63].

Analyzes homecoming scenes in the three novels, noting that "Homecoming emerges in these passages not just as a longing for a lost unity, but as a vital essence, a primal act of art, a return to the source of existence and creativity." Nick seeks "memory, not reality" in his homecoming; he seeks to return home to find out who he is, "identity through community."

H1240.   Gery, John.   "The Curious Grace of Benjimin [*sic*] Button," *Studies in Short Fiction*, 17 (Fall 1980), 495–497.

Contends that F's story, in addition to conveying a "satiric view of the Gilded Age," also suggests the "underlying American social ideal of the unique power of individualism."

H1241.   Hagemann, E. R.   "'Small *Latine*' in the Three Printings of F. Scott Fitzgerald's 'Absolution,'" *Notes on Modern American Literature*, 4 (Spring 1980), Item 7.

Points out errors in the Latin of the *American Mercury* and ATSYM printings of "Absolution" and notes that one of these errors still remains in the corrected version in *Babylon Revisited and Other Stories*. Also gives correct readings and translations for the Latin in the story.

H1242.   Haywood, Lynn.   "Historical Notes for *This Side of Paradise*," *Resources for American Literary Study*, 10 (Autumn 1980), 191–208.

Identifies and explains obscure references—mostly literary ones—in TSOP: persons, literary works, fictional characters, primarily.

H1243.   Horne, Lewis B.   "The Gesture of Pity in 'Jude the Obscure' and 'Tender Is the Night,'" *Ariel*, 11 (April 1980), 53–62.

Compares Jude in Hardy's novel with Dick Diver; they both "suffer the advent of a new era inimical to the qualities with which each man was born and nurtured. In the life of each is dramatized the waning effectiveness of the altruistic impulse."

H1244. Kakutani, Michiko. "'Ghosts' of the Fitzgeralds Rehearse Under Williams's Watchful Eye," NY *Times*, January 8, 1980, p. C9.

Article on progress of rehearsals for "Clothes for a Summer Hotel" includes comments on F and Zelda by Tennessee Williams and actress Geraldine Page.

H1245. ———. "Williams and Quintero Build a 'Summer Hotel,'" NY *Times*, March 23, 1980, Sec. 2, pp. 1, 26.

Article on occasion of Broadway opening of "Clothes for a Summer Hotel" gives details of how Williams came to write play, noting that he saw parallels between his life and F's and that much of play is based on Milford's *Zelda* (I258).

H1246. Kessler, Pamela. "Scott and Zelda Come to Visit," Washington (D.C.) *Post*, June 6, 1980, "Weekend" Section, p. 5.

Brief description of F exhibit opening at the National Portrait Gallery.

H1247. Kilker, Marie J. "'Some Clews' to the Source of Doctor Eckleburg's Eyes and *The Great Gatsby*," *Publications of the Missouri Philological Association*, 5 (1980), 44–48.

Cites similarities between Henry Clews, Jr.'s *Mumbo Jumbo* (1923) and GG, suggesting that F probably read Clews' book and was subtly influenced by it, especially by the description of the billboard in it.

H1248. Kriebel, Charles. "An Afternoon in Gray With Tennessee Williams," *After Dark*, 11 (April 1980), 39, 76–77.

Interview which includes some mention of F and Zelda.

H1249. Lehan, Richard. "F. Scott Fitzgerald and Romantic Destiny," *Twentieth Century Literature*, 26 (Summer 1980), 137–156.

Explores Spenglerian elements in GG, TITN, "Philippe, Count of Darkness," and LT, concluding that, "In Fitzgerald's fiction, a sense of romantic possibility plays itself out in a cultural wasteland. Fitzgerald's sense of opportunity warred with a Spenglerian sense of destiny; and if Fitzgerald found in Spengler a historian whose idea of the modern augmented his own,...he also brought to Spengler a sense of romantic possibility that challenged these historical assumptions at the outset."

H1250. Lunde, Erik S. "Return to Innocence?: The Value of Nick Carraway's Midwestern Perspective in F. Scott Fitzgerald's *The Great Gatsby*," *Society for the Study of Midwestern Literature Newsletter*, 10 (Summer 1980), 14–23.

Contends that Nick's "midwestern perspective, with its critical, moralistic, agrarian overtones,...gives Nick the detachment necessary to make judgements on the activities of Eastern compatriots" and concludes that by viewing GG from this perspective it can be seen as "a triumph of intellectual retrospection, a promise of rebirth."

H1251.   McElwaine, Sandra.   "Reception for Scott and Zelda," Washington (D.C.) *Star*, June 6, 1980, pp. D–9, D–10.

Description of National Portrait Gallery's F exhibit and of party opening it, including brief interview with F's daughter.

H1252.   McLellan, Joseph.   "The Jazz Age Revisited—Notables and Potables at the Portrait Gallery," Washington (D.C.) *Post*, June 7, 1980, pp. B1, B2.

Account of party opening National Portrait Gallery's F exhibit which includes brief interview with F's daughter regarding her parents.

H1253.   ———.   "Relics of Paradise—The Portrait Gallery's Fitzgerald Exhibit," Washington (D.C.) *Post*, June 6, 1980, p. B1.

Description of National Portrait Gallery's F exhibit.

H1254.   M[andelbaum], P[aul].   "The Highballed Boy," *The Diamondback* (University of Maryland, College Park), December 9, 1980, "Christmas Classics" Section, p. 13.

Short story parody of F's style and subject matter.

H1255.   ———.   "Tender is My Nose," *Calvert Review* (University of Maryland, College Park), Spring 1980, pp. 48–51.

Short story parody of style and subject matter of several F novels and short stories.

H1256.   Michelson, Bruce.   "The Myth of Gatsby," *Modern Fiction Studies*, 26 (Winter 1980–81), 563–577.

Argues that GG is "a modern myth" and draws parallels between it and the classical myth of Phaeton, noting that Nick "experiences it as a myth, and tells it as a myth of the classic kind."

H1257.   Micklus, Carla.   "Fitzgerald's Revision of *The Great Gatsby*: The Creation of a Textual Anomaly," *American Notes & Queries*, 19 (October 1980), 21–24.

Shows how Nick's use of phrase "'men who had cared for her'" to describe Daisy is an anomaly left over from F's original versions in which an omniscient narrator was to tell story and then a narrator who knew the Buchanans well; but is inappropriate for the Nick of the final version who knows them only slightly.

H1258.   Morsberger, Robert E.   "Trimalchio in West Egg: *The Great Gatsby* Onstage," *Prospects*, 5 (1980), 489–506.

Discusses changes in structure, plot, character, dialogue, and other details which Owen Davis made to GG in his 1926 stage adaptation and also briefly outlines the history of the NY production of the play.

H1259. Perosa, Sergio. "Fitzgerald Studies in the 1970s," *Twentieth Century Literature*, 26 (Summer 1980), 222–246.
Surveys and evaluates approximately twenty major books by and about F published in the 1970s.

H1260. Podis, Leonard A. "Fitzgerald's *The Great Gatsby*," *The Explicator*, 38 (Summer 1980), 10–11.
Explores the ambivalence of Nick's decision to return West after Gatsby's death—indicating both his realistic approach to life as well as his romanticism.

H1261. Prigozy, Ruth. "From Griffith's Girls to *Daddy's Girl*: The Masks of Innocence in *Tender Is the Night*," *Twentieth Century Literature*, 26 (Summer 1980), 189–221.
Traces F's "debt to the 'daddy's girls' in real life and in popular culture, particularly in silent films of Griffith and others," and addresses some of the questions still raised by TITN, concluding that popular culture "provided the metaphor capable of sustaining [F's] most searching exploration of American history in the twentieth century."

H1262. Roulston, Robert. "Traces of *Tono-Bungay* in *The Great Gatsby*," *Journal of Narrative Technique*, 10 (Winter 1980), 68–76.
Shows parallels between point of view, structure, characters, plot, and themes of GG and Wells' novel to support contention that F's evolution as an artist was a process of accretion in which he retained the best aspects of many of the writers who influenced him to forge his art.

H1263. ———. "Whistling 'Dixie' in Encino: *The Last Tycoon* and F. Scott Fitzgerald's Two Souths," *South Atlantic Quarterly*, 79 (Autumn 1980), 355–363.
Detailed study of Chapter 1 of LT in which F "seems to be setting up the Old South as a paradigm for the patterns of disintegration which he would later depict as operating upon...Hollywood."

H1264. Ryan, Lindel. "F. Scott Fitzgerald and the Battle of the Sexes," *LiNQ (Literature in North Queensland)*, 8 (No. 3, 1980), 84–94.
Examines the battle between men and women as portrayed in TSOP, GG, B&D, TITN, "A Woman With a Past," and "First Blood." F depicted women as "destroyers" because he held his society's outmoded views of women.

H1265. Schroeder, Chris. "The Oculist, the Son, and the Holy Owl Eyes," *American Notes & Queries*, 18 (February 1980), 89–90.
Suggests that the oculist who paid for the billboard of Dr. T. J. Eckleburg, Dr. Eckleburg, and Owl Eyes constitute a Holy Trinity in GG.

H1266.   Stavola, Thomas J.   "Scott Fitzgerald: A Survivor of the American Dream," *Fairleigh Dickinson University Magazine*, 7 (Spring 1980), 25–27.

Summary of F's life and of its effect on his work. See I335.

H1267.   Steinbrink, Jeffrey.   "'Boats Against the Current': Mortality and the Myth of Renewal in *The Great Gatsby*," *Twentieth Century Literature*, 26 (Summer 1980), 157–170.

Sees GG as an "attempt to explore the past and the present in the hope of discovering a sense of balance between giddiness and despair capable of sustaining a man without delusion as he enters life's long decline"; it "exhorts those of us who would be reconciled with the future to see the past truly, to acknowledge its irrecoverability, and to chasten our expectations in view of our slight stature in the world of time and our ever-diminishing store of vitality."

H1268.   Stem, Thad, Jr.   "The Ninety and the Nine," *Pembroke Magazine*, No. 12 (1980), 155–159.

Facile survey of F's life and works with errors of facts and even titles of works (TSOP is *The Far Side of Paradise*; B&D is *The Beautiful and the Damned*; "The Last of the Belles" is "Taps at Reveille.")

H1269.   Weatherby, W. J.   "Scott and Zelda Relive the Jazz Age," London *Sunday Times*, March 30, 1980, p. 38.

Article on "Clothes for a Summer Hotel" which focuses on Williams' manipulation of the facts of F's and Zelda's lives: "We are in the mind not of the Fitzgeralds but of Tennessee Williams brooding over one of America's most romantic literary legends."

1981

H1270.   Bakker, Jan.   "Parallel Water Journeys Into the American Eden in John Davis's *The First Settlers of Virginia* and F. Scott Fitzgerald's *The Great Gatsby*," *Early American Literature*, 16 (Spring 1981), 50–53.

Sees an episode near the end of Davis' work as "a precursor to Fitzgerald's elegaic water journey" at the end of GG and contends that both works also share the "tragic theme of lost innocence, of a lost hope for a renewal of mankind in the New World" and protagonists who "have a dream of regaining an earthly paradise that was lost irretrievably in some mythic past." Both water journeys contrast "a pastoral, Edenic hope of regeneration with a grim, tragic reality of postlapsarian loss and death."

H1271.   Bawer, Bruce.   "'I Could Still Hear the Music': Jay Gatsby and the Musical Metaphor," *Notes on Modern American*

Literature, 5 (Fall 1981), Item 25.
Studies the use of musical metaphor in GG to contrast Gatsby's romanticism with the world's reality.

H1272.   Baxter, Charles.   "De-Faced America: *The Great Gatsby* and *The Crying of Lot 49*," *Pynchon Notes*, 7 (October 1981), 22–37.
Discusses the presentation of the disjunction between past ideals and present actuality in GG and Thomas Pynchon's *The Crying of Lot 49*. "In both these novels, certain themes and preoccupations having to do with history, culture, and 'reading' coincide...around a central image: the face." Traces echoes of GG in Pynchon's novel and concludes that the vision of GG is a "deeply disturbed and embryonically schizoid vision of America" which is further developed in Pynchon's novel into one of "wrecked and merged identities" from which there is no escape.

H1273.   Brown, Chip.   "F. Scott Fitzgerald's Gravesite: An Uneasy Marriage With Present," Washington (D.C.) *Post*, February 18, 1981, pp. C1, C7.
Discusses the irony of the commercial encroachments on F's Rockville, Maryland, gravesite and the parallels that situation evokes with GG.

H1274.   Bruccoli, Matthew J.   "Some Sort of Epic Grandeur, 1: by Matthew J. Bruccoli—Scott Fitzgerald and the Last Resort," London *Times*, August 10, 1981, p. 6; "Some Sort of Epic Grandeur, 2: by Matthew J. Bruccoli—Off the Wagon, With Faded Dreams," London *Times*, August 11, 1981, p. 6; "Some Sort of Epic Grandeur, 3: by Matthew J. Bruccoli—The Wise and Tragic Sense of Life," London *Times*, August 12, 1981, p. 7; "Some Sort of Epic Grandeur, 4: by Matthew J. Bruccoli—'Last of the Novelists for a Long Time Now,'" London *Times*, August 13, 1981, p. 7; "Some Sort of Epic Grandeur, 5: by Matthew J. Bruccoli—In a Small Way I Was an Original...," London *Times*, August 14, 1981, p. 7.
Excerpts from Bruccoli's F biography (I55).

H1275.   Donaldson, Scott.   "The Political Development of F. Scott Fitzgerald," *Prospects*, 6 (1981), 313–355.
Chronicles F's political development as divided into three periods: 1913–1931, "The Growth of Doubt"; 1932–1935, "The Pink Period"; 1937–1940, "Final Reflections." Includes discussions of TSOP, "May Day," "Lo, the Poor Peacock!," TITN, "Gods of Darkness," "A Patriotic Short," and LT.

H1276.   Gervais, Ronald J.   "A Miracle of Rare Device: Fitzgerald's 'The Ice Palace,'" *Notes on Modern American Literature*, 5 (Summer 1981), Item 21.

Sees F's story as "a parable of artistic creativity, an attempt to establish in art a unity that life does not possess." F does not create a reconciliation of "'northern' understanding" and "'southern' imagination" in the story, but the story itself achieves unity "as a verbal enactment of the creative process." Uses Coleridge's "Kubla Khan" as a point of reference and comparison.

H1277. ———. "'Sleepy Hollow's Gone': Pastoral Myth and Artifice in Fitzgerald's *The Beautiful and Damned*," *Ball State University Forum*, 22 (Summer 1981), 75–79.

Views B&D as "a re-working of the pastoral for people who have lost the American pastoral vision as public myth but want it back again as private fantasy....Fitzgerald's modern pastoral seeks an ordering of landscape which captures a fixed and static fantasy, a still point of the individual imagination." The "primary symbols" of B&D are "pastoral landscapes of artificial preservation"; and because it lacks a detached interpreting viewpoint, "Anthony's pastoral dream seems finally childish."

H1278. Howell, John M. "Dr. Tom Rennie and *Tender is the Night*," *ICarbS*, 4 (Spring-Summer 1981), 111–115.

Suggests that F's confusion of Dr. Thomas Rennie, one of Zelda's psychiatrists, and James Rennie, the actor who played Gatsby on stage, may have contributed to the unconvincing portrayal of psychiatrist Dick Diver in TITN.

H1279. Lardner, James. "Flimsy 'Scott & Zelda,'" Washington (D.C.) *Post*, April 18, 1981, p. D3.

Review of Washington, D.C.'s Source Theatre production of "Scott and Zelda" by Rosemary Walsh and John Pruessner, based on material from their fiction and correspondence.

H1280. Lynn, Kenneth S. "More Facts!—One Sort of Scholarship," *Harper's Magazine*, 263 (December 1981), 58–61.

Harsh review of Matthew J. Bruccoli's *Some Sort of Epic Grandeur* (I55) which indicts "the Bruccoli cottage industry" in general and the biography specifically, "an awful book, because it is built on the impoverishing assumption that the heaping up of facts is what biographical writing is all about, and that historical scene-setting, literary interpretation, evaluation of personality, and every other sort of analytical activity are dispensable extras." Also rebukes Bruccoli for not examining further if F had any "hidden sexual secret," because "some sexually abnormal imagination surely informs his fiction."

H1281. Murphy, Garry N., and William C. Slattery. "The Flawed Text of 'Babylon Revisited': A Challenge to Editors, a Warning to Readers," *Studies in Short Fiction*, 18 (Summer 1981), 315–318.

Notes presence in latest editions of text of story in TAR of paragraph which F wanted deleted because he had used it in TITN.

H1282. Nelson, Raymond S. Review of *Fitzgerald/Hemingway Annual 1979* and *The Foreign Critical Reputation of F. Scott Fitzgerald*, *Modern Fiction Studies*, 27 (Summer 1981), 362–364.

Includes short comment on David Kerner's *Annual* article on "A Clean, Well-Lighted Place"; Nelson asserts that F had previously used the device of anti-metronomic dialogue—which Kerner sees as Hemingway's innovation—in TSOP and in his short stories. For Kerner's reply, see H1299.

H1283. "Notes on People—Letters From Fitzgerald to Be Sold at Auction," NY *Times*, November 27, 1981, p. D26.

Mention that F's letters to eleven-year-old Florida author Horace Wade are to be auctioned by Charles Hamilton Galleries on December 10, 1981, with brief quotes from one letter.

H1284. Ogunsanwo, Olatubosun. "George Meredith and F. Scott Fitzgerald: Literary Affinities: Narrative Indirectness and Realism," *Neohelicon*, 8 (No. 2, 1981), 191–216.

Discusses Meredith's *One of Our Conquerors* and GG in order to show "how both novelists avoid a straightforward method of character-drawing, in search of a narrative method that will allow for both moral realism and romantic temperament." Both novels "avoid a fixed moral viewpoint and a fixed narrative point of view, while consistently pre-serving an artistic distance and an intellectual control that demonstrate the entirety of their creative moral vision and their intrinsic integrity."

H1285. Parr, Susan Resneck. "Individual Responsibility in *The Great Gatsby*," *Virginia Quarterly Review*, 57 (Autumn 1981), 662–680.

Explores the implications of the contradictions in Nick's narrative and concludes that in the 1920s F was much like Nick in that both "were concerned with the question of individual responsibility" but "neither was willing or able to confront fully its implications in terms of both America's myths and her realities."

H1286. Piacentino, Edward J. "The Illusory Effects of Cynthian Light: Monroe Stahr and the Moon in *The Last Tycoon*," *American Notes & Queries*, 20 (September/October 1981), 12–16.

Examines "the recurring moon imagery—one of the novel's key and functional image patterns"—which "serves to emphasize the magic, the fantasy, and above all the mystique that invades Stahr's dreams, dreams that clearly go beyond the physical reality of common-place existence, and that emanate from the highest and most irresistible lunar light."

H1287.   Searles, George J. "The Symbolic Function of Food and Eating in F. Scott Fitzgerald's *The Beautiful and Damned*," *Ball State University Forum*, 22 (Summer 1981), 14–19.

Contends that F's use of food imagery in B&D reinforces characterization and theme: "The device reinforces the fundamental judgmental, censorious tone of the book, while lending to it an additional artistic dimension."

H1288.   Sherer, Tim. "Midwestern Influences in F. Scott Fitzgerald's *The Great Gatsby*," *Society for the Study of Midwestern Literature Newsletter*, 11 (Summer 1981), 9–22.

Discusses midwestern attributes and affinities shared by F and Gatsby: perseverance, individuality, and optimism.

H1289.   Sherwood, John. "Tender Was the Night—Remembering Scott and Zelda Fitzgerald's Tragic Baltimore Years," Washington (D.C.) *Post*, September 14, 1981, pp. C1, C3.

Account of party at Baltimore's Belvedere Hotel which includes brief interview with Isabel Owen, F's secretary while he lived in Baltimore.

Slattery, William C. See Murphy (H1281).

H1290.   Starr, William M. "Scott Fitzgerald: Clearing Mists of Time Away," *The State* (Columbia, S.C.), November 8, 1981, pp. 11-B, 13-B.

Interview with Matthew J. Bruccoli who discusses F and his F biography (I55), the value of F's short stories, and common myths about F.

H1291.   Tanner, Stephen L. "Fitzgerald's Lost City," *Rocky Mountain Review of Language and Literature*, 35 (Number 1, 1981), 55–62.

Suggests that in "My Lost City" F blends literary art with autobiography, using his characteristic themes of "Romantic Promise" and "Diminished Thing," as well as other literary devices such as selection, imagery, symbolism, and myth. Calls the essay "a skillfully wrought parable of just ten pages...[which] expresses the essence of Fitzgerald's artistic vision."

H1292.   White, Richard L. "F. Scott Fitzgerald: The Cumulative Portrait," *Biography*, 4 (Spring 1981), 154–168.

Surveys portrait of F which emerges in biographies by Mizener (C110), Turnbull (C167), Buttitta (I78), Graham (C67, I159, I160), Latham (I218), Milford (I258), and Mayfield (I252) and suggests that F's "accessibility" is represented in all of them.

H1293.   Willis, Lonnie L.   *"Brautigan's The Hawkline Monster:* As Big as the Ritz," *Critique—Studies in Modern Fiction,* 23 (Winter 1981–82), 37–47.

Explores similarities between Richard Brautigan's *The Hawkline Monster* and "The Diamond as Big as the Ritz"—a sense of futility, organization, and theme. F's story provides "a sense of tradition for Brautigan's skepticism and a source for his 'monster.'"

1982

H1294.   Brondell, William J.   "Structural Metaphors in Fitzgerald's Short Fiction," *Kansas Quarterly,* 14 (Spring 1982), 95–112.

Analyzes the structural metaphors which inform the superstructures and deep structures of "Absolution," "The Freshest Boy," and "Babylon Revisited." F portrays "accurately and convincingly the inner life of the characters who inhabit the stories"; to control the motion of the "souls" of the characters, he "has created a deep structure which traces the characters' most profound thoughts and emotions; and in these stories, he has provided a map, the structural metaphor, so that the reader may follow the motion of these souls."

H1295.   Donaldson, Scott.   "The Wooing of Ernest Hemingway," *American Literature,* 53 (January 1982), 691–710.

Recounts the wooing of Hemingway to Scribner's by F and Maxwell Perkins between February 1925 and February 1927 and includes discussion of F's editorial suggestions about Hemingway's "Fifty Grand" and of F's and Perkins' "near-conspiratorial relationship...where Hemingway was concerned."

H1296.   Edwards, Duane.   "Who Killed Myrtle Wilson?—A Study of *The Great Gatsby,*" *Ball State University Forum,* 23 (Winter 1982), 35–41.

Examines Nick, Gatsby, and the Gatsby-Nick relationship in order to determine who killed Myrtle, concluding that Gatsby killed her, based on the unreliability of statements made by Nick and Gatsby and on Nick's close identification with Gatsby.

H1297.   Gervais, Ronald J.   "The Socialist and the Silk Stockings: Fitzgerald's Double Allegiance," *Mosaic,* 15 (June 1982), 79–92.

Uses F's fiction and correspondence in discussing his ambivalence towards Marxism and bourgeois capitalism: "He could incorporate Marxism into the moral standpoint from which he examined and con-

Marxism into the moral standpoint from which he examined and condemned his American plutocrats, and yet not be blinded by its ideology from seeing and wondering at their beauty and heroism." Includes discussions of TSOP, "May Day," TITN and LT.

H1298.   Hebert, Hugh.   "That Side of Paradise," *Manchester Guardian*, February 1, 1982, p. 11.

Interview with Matthew J. Bruccoli on occasion of publication of his F biography (I55).

H1299.   Kerner,   David.   "Correspondence—Fitzgerald   vs. Hemingway: The Origins of Anti-Metronomic Dialogue," *Modern Fiction Studies*, 28 (Summer 1982), 247–250.

Disputes Raymond S. Nelson's claim (H1282) that anti-metronomic dialogue turns up "repeatedly" in F's work, especially TSOP and the stories, by pointing out there are actually very few examples of pure anti-metronomic dialogue in F's works.

H1300.   Michaels, I. Lloyd.   "Auteurism, Creativity, and Entropy in *The Last Tycoon*," *Literature/Film Quarterly*, 10 (April 1982), 110–119.

Analyzes the LT film as a work of cinematic art with "a dialectical impulse for creation and entropy" and discusses the roles of Harold Pinter, Elia Kazan, Sam Spiegel, and Robert DeNiro in its creation. Includes brief discussion of the controversy over whether the novel is "unfinished" or "unformed."

H1301.   Nettels, Elsa.   "Howells's 'A Circle in the Water' and Fitzgerald's 'Babylon Revisited,'" *Studies in Short Fiction*, 19 (Summer 1982), 261–267.

Explores the similarities in plot, situation, and character in these two stories. "The stories also highlight the different outlooks of the two writers and help to explain why Fitzgerald rejected Howells as a literary mentor."

H1302.   Quirk, Tom.   "Fitzgerald and Cather: *The Great Gatsby*," *American Literature*, 54 (December 1982), 576–591.

Discusses possible influence of Cather's work on F, with specific reference to Cather's "Paul's Case" and F's "Absolution" and to Cather's *Alexander's Bridge* and GG.

H1303.   Roberts, Ruth E.   "Nonverbal Communication in *The Great Gatsby*," *Language and Literature*, 7 (Nos. 1–3, 1982), 107–129.

Analyzes the nonverbal aspects of Daisy and Gatsby's interactions—body language, tone of voice, and "interactional

Gatsby." Also includes briefer discussions of Tom Buchanan, Jordan Baker, and Myrtle Wilson.

H1304.   Symons, Julian.   "A Gift for Hope," *Times Literary Supplement* (London), February 26, 1982, pp. 221–222.

Review of Bruccoli's *Some Sort of Epic Grandeur* (155), which is called "indispensable" despite the gracelessness of its style, but primarily an assessment of F as artist which sees him as three different men—the "pure artist," the man "concerned about his position on the writing ladder," and the man "who was interested above all in the sound of the cash register," as well as a "moral censor" who "brooded over all three Fitzgeralds." TSOP and B&D perhaps "cannot be called anything but very bad," but behind their "absurdities lie a readiness to experiment and an eagerness to excel"; GG is an unquestioned success; TITN is an "interesting failure"; LT is a "half-finished work that might have been a fine novel"; and his shorter pieces are "brilliant bits ...which don't weigh heavily in the scales beside the best of the novels."

H1305.   Wagner, Linda W.   "A Note on Zelda Fitzgerald's *Scandalabra*," *Notes on Contemporary Literature*, 12 (May 1982), 4–5.

Compares Zelda's play with SMTW, citing differences in motivation and tone: "Rather than treat her ostensible subject with the seriousness that it held for her, she turned it [in the play] to bitter banter among people who were only—and then at best—caricatures."

1983

H1306.   Desruisseaux, Paul.   "Fitzgerald and Faulkner in Hollywood—Literary Scholars Are Analyzing the Art and Craft of Scriptwriting," *Chronicle of Higher Education*, 25 (February 2, 1983), 7–8.

Reports comments on Fitzgerald and Faulkner as screenwriters made at Modern Language Association convention session in Los Angeles by Tom Dardis, Alan Margolies, and Bernard F. Dick. F's Hollywood experience was "life-saving" financially, but he failed to become an "accomplished" screenwriter because he didn't "fully" understand "the medium for which he was writing."

H1307.   Davison, Richard Allan.   "F. Scott Fitzgerald and Charles G. Norris," *Journal of Modern Literature*, 10 (March 1983), 40–54.

Attempts "to lay the groundwork for further clarification, examination, and discussion" of the relationship between F and Charles G. Norris. Includes discussion of parallels between Norris' *Brass* and *Salt*

Norris. Includes discussion of parallels between Norris' *Brass* and *Salt* and GG and "May Day."

H1308. Mansfield, Stephanie. "Growing Up Living Well," Washington (D.C.) *Post*, January 27, 1983, pp. D1, D11 [D11]. Interview with Honoria Murphy Donnelly on occasion of publication of her book on her parents (I112) includes memories of F and Zelda.

I
Books and Book Sections
about F. Scott Fitzgerald

This section includes references to Fitzgerald in books printed in English. They are arranged alphabetically by author or editor; unsigned listings are grouped together under "Anonymous." As in the other sections of this volume, this section both updates and supplements *The Critical Reputation of F. Scott Fitzgerald.* Most sketches in biographical dictionaries, introductory notes in anthologies, and passing references in literary histories have been omitted, except in instances where these are extensive enough to warrant their inclusion, are the work of a major critic, or were written at a time when comment of any kind on Fitzgerald was significant.

Titles of books entirely or primarily about Fitzgerald are listed in capital letters. For these books, first American and English (where applicable) publisher and date of publication and number of pages have been listed. Information about English or other foreign publishers is not, in general, included for other books in this section, except in instances where the foreign publication preceded the American one or when a relatively obscure publisher issued the book originally and it has been subsequently reprinted in more widely available form.

Following the annotations for books entirely or primarily about Fitzgerald are listings of reviews of these books. These listings are based on information available in standard reference works and in publishers' files—when the latter could be obtained—and thus can only be regarded as representative. No attempt has been made to locate or verify all appearances of syndicated reviews; those few which were found are included, sometimes with only partial citations. Important reviews of books about Fitzgerald—important either because they are review-essays or because they are written by major Fitzgerald scholars—are marked with an asterisk and are occasionally listed and annotated in the Articles section of this volume. In general, only English-language reviews are included; the few exceptions are marked as such.

Where the material in a book is reprinted from another source, no annotation is given. A notation of the original place of publication is given, with appropriate cross-indexing to the item's original appearance as listed either in this volume or in the first edition of this work. Unlike the arrangement in *The Critical Reputation of F. Scott Fitzgerald,* in instances when a single book includes several relevant essays by different individuals, the book is listed once, under the name(s) of the editor(s); and the individual pieces, their authors, and their page numbers are listed thereunder. If the piece is reprinted, no annotation is given but rather a cross-reference number is included. If the piece is original, it is annotated and its author's name is also listed alphabetically in the section, with a cross-reference to the editor of the collection where the annotated full reference can be found. The one exception to this rule is the unlocated reviews found in Fitzgerald's scrapbooks and reprinted in *F. Scott Fitzgerald—The Critical Reception* (I73). Although these are, strictly speaking, reprintings, they are annotated under the listing for the collection—because their original appearances cannot be determined and hence are not listed elsewhere in this volume or in its predecessor—and their authors' names (when known) are listed alphabetically in the section with a cross-reference to the collection.

I1.   Alberts, Robert C. *Connoisseur's Haven.* Pittsburgh: Privately printed for the Pittsburgh Bibliophiles, 1967. Unpaged.
Quotes F's flyleaf inscription to Mencken in Hemingway's *Men Without Women* in which he calls Hemingway "a great writer, since [Sherwood] Anderson's collapse the best we have I think."

I2.   Aldridge, John W. "The Life of Gatsby." In his *Time to Murder and Create—The Contemporary Novel in Crisis.* NY: David McKay, 1966. Pp. 192–218.
Reprinting of 1958 essay from Shapiro collection (C4).

I3.   ———. "The Life of Gatsby: A Preamble." In his *The Devil in the Fire—Retrospective Essays on American Literature and Culture—1951–1971.* NY: Harper's Magazine Press, 1972. Pp. 101–105; see also pp. 6–7, and *passim.*
Reprinting of 1958 essay from Shapiro collection (C4) and scattered mention of F in other reprinted essays in collection.

I4.   Allen, Joan M. CANDLES AND CARNIVAL LIGHTS:
THE CATHOLIC SENSIBILITY OF F. SCOTT FITZGERALD. NY:
New York University Press, 1978. 163 pp.

Discusses F's "profound moralism" and how his "Roman Catholic
early education and family experience, the complexities of a Catholic
upbringing in an atmosphere of inadequate paternity and oppressive
maternity and ambivalence about money, formed his moral consciousness." Documents the facts of F's Catholicism and reads his
fiction for evidence of Catholic elements.

REVIEWS:

i.   Anonymous. Review of *Candles and Carnival Lights:
The Catholic Sensibility of F. Scott Fitzgerald, Choice,* 15 (September
1978), 862.

ii.   ————. Review of *Candles and Carnival Lights: The
Catholic Sensibility of F. Scott Fitzgerald, Queen's Quarterly,* 86
(Winter 1979/80), 739.

iii.   *Anderson, W[illiam] R[ichard, Jr.] Review of *Candles
and Carnival Lights: The Catholic Sensibility of F. Scott Fitzgerald,
Fitzgerald/Hemingway Annual,* 11 (1979), 429–433.

iv.   Astro, Richard. Review of *Candles and Carnival Lights:
The Catholic Sensibility of F. Scott Fitzgerald, Modern Fiction Studies,*
26 (Summer 1980), 325–327.

v.   Lodge, David. "The Fear of the Flesh," *Times Literary
Supplement* (London), August 25, 1978, p. 944.

vi.   Martin, Terence. Review of *Candles and Carnival
Lights: The Catholic Sensibility of F. Scott Fitzgerald, American
Literature,* 50 (January 1979), 664–665.

vii.   Tavernier-Courbin, Jacqueline. Review of *Candles and
Carnival Lights: The Catholic Sensibility of F. Scott Fitzgerald,
Library Journal,* 103 (February 15, 1978), 462.

I5.   Allen, Walter. *The Short Story in English.* NY: Oxford
University Press, 1980. Pp. 131, 141–146, 173, 201, 394.

Suggests that F's stories show that he "was never taken in by the
glitter; he was always aware of the presence of the Furies, even though
others were not." Includes discussions of "Babylon Revisited" and
"May Day."

I5a.   ————. *The Urgent West—The American Dream and
Modern Man.* NY: E. P. Dutton, 1969. Pp. 9–11, 110, 200–201.

Brief discussion of GG includes assessment that it is a "poetic celebration of the American dream, and a comment, pessimistic maybe,
upon it."

Anderson, Sherwood.   See White, ed. (I369)

I6.   Anonymous. "Famous Faces of the Twenties: F. Scott Fitzgerald." In Ralph K. Andrist, *et al*. *The American Heritage History of the '20s and '30s*. NY: American Heritage, 1970. Pp. 162–163; see also pp. 80, 81, 310.
Biographical essay on F and review of his career as spokesman for and "typical product" of the 1920s.

I7.   ————. *Fiestas, Moveable Feasts and "Many Fêtes" in Their Time/1920–1940—An Exhibition at the University of Virginia Library—December 1977-March 1978*. Bloomfield Hills, Mich., and Columbia, S.C.: Bruccoli Clark, 1977. Pp. [7, 9–10, 12–14, 15, 17–18, 21, 24, 36, 41, 65, 66–69, 74, 77].
Catalogue descriptions and photographs of and notes on letters, personal belongings, and presentation copies pertaining to F included in the exhibition.

I8.   ————. "'The Roaring Twenties.'" In *Building the Future From Our Past—A Report on the Saint Paul Historic Hill District Planning Program*. St. Paul: Old Town Restorations, 1975. Pp. 60–61.
Brief mention of F and Zelda in St. Paul in the 1920s.

I9.   Astro, Richard, and Jackson J. Benson, eds. *Hemingway in Our Time*. Corvallis: Oregon State University Press, 1974.

I.   George Wickes, "Sketches of the Author's Life in Paris in the Twenties," pp. 25–38 [28–33].
Discussion of *A Moveable Feast* which notes the facts, fabrications, and omissions in Hemingway's material about F and speculates on reasons for them.

II.   Peter L. Hays, "Hemingway and Fitzgerald," pp. 87–97.
Detailed comparison of *The Sun Also Rises* and GG in terms of their narrator figures, their influence by "The Waste Land," their use of sports as a metaphor for life, their use of frustrated patterns of initiation, and their theme of the quest for meaning and personal standards in the wasteland of contemporary society.

III.   Faith G. Norris, "*A Moveable Feast* and *Remembrance of Things Past*: Two Quests for Lost Time," pp. 99–111 [104, 105, 107–108].
Passing mention of sketches of F and Zelda in *A Moveable Feast*.

I10.   Auchincloss, Louis.   *Three "Perfect Novels" and What They Have in Common.* Bloomfield Hills, Mich., and Columbia, S.C.: Bruccoli Clark, 1981. Pp. 1, 10–15.

Discusses *The Scarlet Letter, Wuthering Heights,* and GG as "perfect" novels because they are timeless and almost "myths" which "have something to say to everybody." In GG, F shows that creating illusion "may be the only thing worth doing in this vale of constant disillusionment."

Babcock, Muriel. See Bruccoli and Bryer, eds. (I59)

I11.   Bahrenburg, Bruce.   FILMING "THE GREAT GATSBY." NY: Berkley, 1974. 254 pp.

Detailed diary of the shooting of the 1974 GG film which includes the screenwriter's and actors' explications of F's novel as well as quotes from and allusions to other F works.

REVIEWS:

i.   Anonymous.   "Originals," *Publishers' Weekly,* 205 (March 4, 1974), 77.

ii.   McCormick, Edith.   "Bringing Off Gatsby," *American Libraries,* 5 (May 1974), 234.

I12.   Baker, Carlos.   *Ernest Hemingway—A Life Story.* NY: Charles Scribner's, 1969. Pp. 144–146, 157–165, 169–171, 198–199, 201–202, 206–207, 273–274, 295–296, 539–540, 580–581, 588–589, and *passim.*

Scattered but detailed and extensive discussion of Hemingway's relationship with F personally and professionally.

————. See Bryer, ed. (I74)

I13.   ————, ed.   *Ernest Hemingway—Selected Letters 1917–1961.* NY: Charles Scribner's, 1981. Pp. 140, 160, 162–163, 165–166, 172, 176–177, 178, 180–185, 191, 195–197, 199–205, 212, 214–218, 225, 228, 231–233, 237–239, 246, 248–250, 260–262, 267–270, 273, 276–277, 285, 287–291, 293, 299, 304–307, 308–311, 312–315, 318–320, 339–340, 347, 351, 356, 364–365, 368, 376–377, 388, 407–409, 423, 424–425, 427–429, 433, 437–438, 440, 444, 483, 523, 527–529, 532–533, 553, 556–557, 594–595, 657–658, 668, 678–679, 688–690, 694–696, 701, 716–719, 726, 743, 746, 751, 758, 772, 793–794, 800, 805, 834–836, 862, 863, 896–897, 918.

Includes Hemingway's letters to F and his comments about F in letters to others, principally Maxwell Perkins and F biographer Arthur Mizener.

I14.   Baritz, Loren, ed. *The Culture of the Twenties*. Indianapolis: Bobbs-Merrill, 1970. Pp. xvi, xvii, xix, xxxii, xxxvii, xl, xlviii–1, 272, 300–301, 314–315, 413.
Brief comments on F as spokesman and philosopher of the 1920s.

I15.   Behlmer, Rudy, ed. *Memo From David O. Selznick*. NY: Viking Press, 1972. Pp. xviii, 72, 184, 443–468.
Includes Selznick's recollections of F in Hollywood and his detailed explication of TITN for two screenwriters adapting it for the 1962 film, as well as all of Selznick's correspondence about that project.

I16.   Behrman, S. N. *People in a Diary*. Boston: Little, Brown, 1972. Pp. 140, 158.
Memories of F in Hollywood. This material originally appeared in *New Yorker* (H525).

I17.   Bell, Millicent. *Marquand—An American Life*. Boston: Little, Brown, 1979. Pp. 89, 106, 122, 136–137, 153, 156, 281, 286, 347, 400.
Brief passing mentions of Marquand's admiration of F's work and of Marquand's meeting F in Paris.

I18.   Bellman, Samuel I. *Marjorie Kinnan Rawlings*. Twayne's United States Authors Series, No. 241. NY: Twayne, 1974. Pp. 21–22.
Brief mention of Rawlings' meeting F in Asheville in 1936 and of her impressions of him.

I19.   Bennett, George N. *The Realism of William Dean Howells, 1889–1920*. Nashville: Vanderbilt University Press, 1973. Pp. 147–148.
Briefly compares GG with Howells' *The Landlord at Lion's Head*.

I20.   Berg, A. Scott. *Max Perkins—Editor of Genius*. NY: E. P. Dutton, 1978. Pp. 3, 4, 6–7, 12–22, 40–53, 60–71, 77–79, 82–86, 87–97, 111–116, 119–122, 151–154, 161–163, 186–191, 198–202, 228–234, 245–247, 302–308, 326–328, 340–342, 368–371, 382–386, 387–395, and *passim*.
Detailed account of F's relationships with his only editor and publisher and with other Scribner's authors, especially Hemingway.

I21.   Bernstein, Burton. *Thurber—A Biography*. NY: Dodd, Mead, 1975. Pp. 213, 216–217, 345.
Brief mentions of Thurber's memories and opinions of F, expressed in a letter to Malcolm Cowley and in a 1951 essay (B287) and in a review of LT (A589).

I22. Bewley, Marius. "Scott Fitzgerald: The Apprentice Fiction." In his *Masks & Mirrors—Essays in Criticism*. London: Chatto & Windus, 1970. Pp. 154–159.

Reprinting of Bewley's *NY Review of Books* review-essay (A1014).

I23. Bigelow, Gordon E. *Frontier Eden—The Literary Career of Marjorie Kinnan Rawlings*. Tallahassee: University of Florida Press, 1966. Pp. 28–34, 137, and *passim*.

Gives Rawlings' account of her September 1936 meeting with F in Asheville, as well as other passing references to F and his works.

Bigsby, C. W. E. See Bradbury and Palmer, eds. (I32)

I24. Birmingham, Frederic Alexander. *The Writer's Craft*. NY: Hawthorn Books, 1958. Pp. 14, 67, 79–81, 101, 216–217.

Brief passing mention of F and of "Shaggy's Morning" and "The Night Before Chancellorsville."

Bishop, John Peale. See Raymond (I292).

———. See Young and Hindle, eds. (I390)

Blacker, Irwin R. See Bruccoli, ed. (I37)

I25. Blake, Nelson M. "The Pleasure Domes of West Egg and Tarmes." In his *Novelist's America: Fiction as History, 1910–1940*. Syracuse, NY: Syracuse University Press, 1969. Pp. 45–74.

Relates TSOP and F's Princeton experiences to the social and sexual mores of the day and discusses F's portraits of the very rich in America (GG) and in Europe (TITN), noting that he was "an insecure member of the leisure class" who was neither completely of it nor outside it.

I26. Blotner, Joseph. *Faulkner—A Biography*. NY: Random House, 1974. Pp. 368, 410, 429, 450, 457, 1005, 1107, 1109, 1140, 1142–1143, 1356, 1522, 1547.

Brief passing mentions of Faulkner's acquaintance with F and opinions of F's fiction.

I27. ———, ed. *Selected Letters of William Faulkner*. NY: Random House, 1977. Pp. 168–169, 172.

Brief references in letters to Harold Ober, agent for both F and Faulkner, of Faulkner's interest in adapting F's story "The Curious Case of Benjamin Button" as a play and as a screenplay.

I28. Bode, Carl. *Mencken*. Carbondale: Southern Illinois University Press, 1969. Pp. 74, 146, 176–177, 185, 280.

Brief references to F's contributions to *Smart Set*, his relationship with Mencken, and his respect for Mencken's opinions.

I29.   ————, ed. *The New Mencken Letters*. NY: Dial Press, 1977. Pp. 122–123, 139–140, 208–209, 211, 356, 474–475, 560, 563, 565.

Four Mencken to F letters are published and F is referred to in several other Mencken letters, principally one to Jim Tully (pp. 474–475) shortly after F's death.

I30.   Bourjaily, Vance. "Fitzgerald Attends My Fitzgerald Seminar." In his *Now Playing at Canterbury*. NY: Dial Press, 1976. Pp. 100–116.

Reprinting of Bourjaily's fictional fantasy, slightly revised, from *Esquire* (B562).

I31.   Boylan, James, ed. *"The World" and the 20's*. NY: Dial Press, 1973.

I.   "F. Scott Fitzgerald's Latest a Dud," p. 192.

Reprinted review of GG (A333).

II.   "Fitzgerald, Spenglerian" by Harry Salpeter, pp. 233-236.

Reprinting of 1927 interview (B98).

I31a.   Bradbury, Malcolm. *Possibilities—Essays on the State of the Novel*. London: Oxford University Press, 1973. Pp. 89, 120, 184, 185, 206.

Includes brief assessments of F and discussion of his affinities with Malcolm Lowry and C. P. Snow.

I32.   ————, and David Palmer, eds. *The American Novel and the Nineteen Twenties*. London: Edward Arnold, 1971.

I.   Malcolm Bradbury. "Style of Life, Style of Art and the American Novelist in the Nineteen Twenties," pp. 11–35 [29–34 and *passim*].

Discusses TSOP, GG, and TITN, contending that F, more than any other writer of the 1920s, reflects the "intensity of modern American life, as well as the euphoria to trauma to slump process that was the pattern of the decade."

II.   Henry Dan Piper, "Social Criticism in the American Novel in the Nineteen Twenties," pp. 59–83.

Suggests that Faulkner, F, and Hemingway differed from other novelists of the 1920–1940 period in using tragedy to dramatize conflicts between the individual and society and in doing so they achieved greater art than the naturalists; also notes Anderson's and Dreiser's significance for F.

III. Howell Daniels, "Sinclair Lewis and the Drama of Dissociation," pp. 85–106 [90].

Notes presence of the "depriving of sexual relationship of meaning by reducing it to an infantile level" in F's work and in Lewis'.

IV. C. W. E. Bigsby, "The Two Identities of F. Scott Fitzgerald," pp. 129–149.

Sees F as one of the artists Trilling defines as containing "a large part of the dialectic within themselves...the very essence...the yes and no of their culture" and contends that the problem in F's early writing was "that he could never quite bring himself to face his essential pessimism"; only in TITN did he finally bring "himself to face the full implications of his vision and to establish the irrevocable connection between personal tragedy and cultural decline which formed the basis of his dialectic."

V. Jonathan Raban, "A Surfeit of Commodities: The Novels of Nathanael West," pp. 215–231, [217, 230–231].

Brief comments on F's transition from the 1920s to the 1930s as illustrated in GG and TITN.

VI. Eric Mottram, "The Hostile Environment and the Survival Artist: A Note on the Twenties," pp. 233–262 [249–252 and *passim*].

Sees F as having learned to combine knowledge gleaned from Freud and Marx and defining the ability "to function" as being "able to see that things are hopeless and yet be determined to make them otherwise."

I33. [Brannum, Mary]. "Frances Scott Fitzgerald Lanahan." In her ed. *When I Was 16*. NY: Platt & Munk, 1967. Pp. 200–221.

Interview, preceded by brief introductory note, in which F's daughter speaks of attitudes toward women when she was sixteen and mentions F's role as a father.

I34. Brooks, Cleanth. "The American 'Innocence' in James, Fitzgerald and Faulkner." In his *A Shaping Joy—Studies in the Writer's Craft*. NY: Harcourt Brace Jovanovich, 1971. Pp. 181–197.

Reprinting of 1964 essay from *Shenandoah* (B563).

I35. Brophy, Brigid, Michael Levey, and Charles Osborne, eds. *Fifty Works of English [and American] Literature We Could Do Without*. London: Rapp & Carroll, 1967. P. 150.

F is not listed but is rated above Faulkner and Hemingway; latter is called "an appendix to the biography of the great novelist Fitzgerald."

I36.   Brown, Eve. *The Plaza—Its Life and Times.* NY: Meredith Press, 1967. Pp. 67–68.
Brief mention of F's love of the Plaza Hotel and of his depiction of it in GG.

I37.   Bruccoli, Matthew J. "Afterword." In his ed. *F. Scott Fitzgerald's Screenplay for "Three Comrades" by Erich Maria Remarque.* Preface by Irwin R. Blacker. Carbondale: Southern Illinois University Press, 1978. Pp. 255–269.
Gives history and background of F's involvement with the script of "Three Comrades," drawing extensively on F's correspondence with producer Joseph Mankiewicz and collaborator E. F. ("Ted") Paramore. Blacker's "Preface" (pp. ix-xi) is a brief overview and evaluation of F's screenplay. This volume also includes a list of the revisions made in F's original screenplay by others (pp. 270–289), which prints sequences as F originally wrote them and also as they were revised; and a list of F's "Movie Work" (p. 290).

I38.   ———. APPARATUS FOR F. SCOTT FITZGERALD's "THE GREAT GATSBY" [UNDER THE RED, WHITE, AND BLUE]. South Carolina Apparatus for Definitive Editions. Columbia: University of South Carolina Press, 1974. 140 pp.
Contains history of composition of GG; textual notes; editorial emendations in the copy-text; Fitzgerald's marked copy of the first printing; collation of the revised galleys against the first printing; historical collation; plate alterations in the second printing; collation of the Scribner Library edition; end-of-the-line hyphenation in the copy-text; pedigree of editions and printings; and explanatory notes. Intention is to "provide a do-it-yourself kit for converting the best available edition [the first printing in 1925]...into a definitive edition."

REVIEWS:

i.   Anonymous. Review of *Apparatus for F. Scott Fitzgerald's "The Great Gatsby," American Reference Books Annual,* 6 (1975), 601–602.
ii.   Daniels, Thomas. Review of *Apparatus for F. Scott Fitzgerald's "The Great Gatsby," Journal of Modern Literature,* 4 (Supplement 1975), 1038–1039.
iii.   Davison, Peter. Review of *Apparatus for F. Scott Fitzgerald's "The Great Gatsby," The Library,* 31 (March 1976), 83–85.

iv.   Isaacson, David. Review of *Apparatus for F. Scott Fitzgerald's "The Great Gatsby," Library Journal,* 99 (November 1, 1974), 2831.

v.   Nordloh, David J. Review of *Apparatus for F. Scott Fitzgerald's "The Great Gatsby," Fitzgerald/Hemingway Annual,* 6 (1974), 257–260.

vi.   Smith, Denzell S. "The Glossing of Gatsby," *Times Literary Supplement* (London), September 5, 1975, pp. 1002–1003.

vii.   *West, James L. W., III. "The SCADE *Gatsby*: A Review Article," *Proof,* 5 (1975), 237–256.

viii.   White, William. "Apparatus for 'Gatsby,'" *American Book Collector,* 26 (September-October 1975), 2–3.

ix.   ———. "Collecting Fitzgerald?" *American Book Collector,* 25 (July-August 1975), 7.

I39.   ———. "F. Scott Fitzgerald." In Margaret A. Van Antwerp, ed. *Dictionary of Literary Biography, Documentary Series: An Illustrated Chronicle. Volume One.* Detroit: Gale Research, 1982. Pp. 239–290

Includes bibliography (pp. 239–240) and the following reprinted articles about F:

I.   Harry Hansen, "Whew! How That Boy Can Write!" (A34), p. 240.

II.   Robert C. Benchley, "Books and Other Things" (A24), pp. 241, 244–245.

III.   Heywood Broun, "Books" (B24), pp. 245–246.

IV.   H. L. Mencken, Review of *Flappers and Philosophers* (A79), p. 246.

V.   Frederick James Smith, "Fitzgerald, Flappers and Fame: An Interview with F. Scott Fitzgerald" (B45), pp. 246–249.

VI.   Thomas Alexander Boyd, "Literary Libels—Francis Scott Key Fitzgerald" (B49), pp. 250–256.

VII.   Zelda Sayre [Fitzgerald], "Friend Husband's Latest" (A186), pp. 256–257.

VIII.   Stephen Vincent Benét, "Plotting an Author's Curve" (A230), pp. 257–258.

IX.   Edmund Wilson, Jr., "A Selection of Bric-a-Brac" (A326), p. 259.

x.   Gilbert Seldes, Review of *The Great Gatsby* (A380), pp. 262–263.

xi.   Thomas Caldecot Chubb, "Bagdad-on-Subway" (A353), pp. 263–265.

xii.   William Rose Benét, "Art's Bread and Butter" (A414), pp. 266–267.

xiii.   John Chamberlain, "Books of The Times" (A446), pp. 267, 270–271.

xiv.   ————, "Books of The Times" (A447), p. 271.

xv.   Malcolm Cowley, "Breakdown" (A451), pp. 273–275.

xvi.   John Chamberlain, "Books of The Times" (A511), pp. 275–278.

xvii.   Michel Mok, "The Other Side of Paradise" (B138), pp. 278–281.

xviii.   "F. Scott Fitzgerald Dies at 44; Chronicler of 'Lost Generation'" (B162), pp. 284–286.

xix.   "Notes and Comment" (B193), p. 286.

xx.   Stephen Vincent Benét, "Fitzgerald's Unfinished Symphony" (A566), pp. 286–287.

xxi.   James Thurber, "Taps at Assembly" (A589), pp. 287–289.

140.   ————. F. SCOTT FITZGERALD—A DESCRIPTIVE BIBLIOGRAPHY. Pittsburgh Series in Bibliography. Pittsburgh: University of Pittsburgh Press, 1972. 369 pp.
     Includes listings of separate publications; first-appearance contributions to books and pamphlets; appearances in magazines and newspapers; material quoted in catalogues; interviews; articles that include material by F; dust-jacket blurbs by F; keepsakes; and Zelda's publications. Appendices include: English-language editions of story collections published in Japan; unlocated clippings; published plays by others based on F stories; unpublished plays by F produced in St. Paul; mimeographed film scripts by F; F's movie-writing assignments; movies made from F's work; publications by F in Braille; contracts; and a listing of principal works about F.

REVIEWS:

i.   Anonymous. "Finding Fitzgerald," *Times Literary Supplement* (London), March 30, 1973, p. 360.

ii   ———. Review of *F. Scott Fitzgerald—A Descriptive Bibliography, AB Bookman's Weekly,* 50 (December 11, 1972), 1902.

iii.   ———. Review of *F. Scott Fitzgerald—A Descriptive Bibliography, The Book Exchange* (London), No. 306 (September 1973), 25.

iv.   ———. Review of *F. Scott Fitzgerald—A Descriptive Bibliography, Choice,* 10 (May 1973), 430.

v.   ———. Review of *F. Scott Fitzgerald—A Descriptive Bibliography, Journal of Modern Literature,* 3 (February 1974), 600.

vi.   ———. Review of *F. Scott Fitzgerald—A Descriptive Bibliography, Publishers' Weekly,* 202 (November 27, 1972), 29.

vii.   Anderson, David D. Review of *F. Scott Fitzgerald—A Descriptive Bibliography, Society for the Study of Midwestern Literature—Newsletter,* 3 (Fall 1973), 15.

viii.   Bryer, Jackson R. Review of *F. Scott Fitzgerald—A Descriptive Bibliography, Fitzgerald/Hemingway Annual,* 5 (1973), 331–334.

ix.   Horwitz, Carey. Review of *F. Scott Fitzgerald—A Descriptive Bibliography, Library Journal,* 97 (March 1, 1972), 905.

x.   Pastoureau, Mireille. Review of *F. Scott Fitzgerald—A Descriptive Bibliography, Bulletin des Bibliothèques de France,* 18 (June 1973), 482. In French.

xi.   Perosa, Sergio. Review of *F. Scott Fitzgerald—A Descriptive Bibliography, Annali di Ca'Foscari,* 13 (No. 2, 1974), 530–531. In Italian.

xii.   Raymond, Landon. "Books—A Fitzgerald Bibliography," *Princeton Alumni Weekly,* 73 (May 22, 1973), 11.

xiii.   Unger, Willy. Review of *F. Scott Fitzgerald—A Descriptive Bibliography, Deutsche Literaturzeitung für Kritik der Internationalen Wissenschaft,* 95 (April 1974), 309. In German.

xiv.   Welker, Robert L. Review of *F. Scott Fitzgerald—A Descriptive Bibliography, American Reference Books Annual,* 4 (1973), 494–495.

xv.   *West, James L. W., III. "Matthew J. Bruccoli's *F. Scott Fitzgerald: A Descriptive Bibliography,*" *Costerus,* n.s. 1 (1974), 165–176.

xvi.   White, William. Review of *F. Scott Fitzgerald—A Descriptive Bibliography, Library Journal,* 97 (July 1972), 2374.

I41. ———. "F. Scott Fitzgerald 1896–1940." In his *et al.*, eds. *First Printings of American Authors—Contributions Toward Descriptive Checklists*. Detroit: Gale Research, 1977. Volume 1, pp. 131–134.

Lists the first American printings and the first English printings of F's books; intended as a guide for collectors.

I42. ———. "Introduction." In his ed., with the assistance of Jennifer M. Atkinson. *As Ever, Scott Fitz—: Letters between F. Scott Fitzgerald and His Literary Agent, Harold Ober—1919–1940*. Philadelphia: J. B. Lippincott, 1972. Pp. xvii–xxii; "Foreword" by Scottie Fitzgerald Smith, pp. xi–xvi.

Bruccoli's "Introduction" includes discussion of the F-Ober relationship, a short biographical sketch of Ober, and an explanation of the physical form of the originals of the letters and of the editorial principles used in the collection. Smith's "Foreword" is a personal reminiscence of Ober.

I43. ———. "Introduction." In his and Margaret M. Duggan, eds., with the assistance of Susan Walker. *Correspondence of F. Scott Fitzgerald*. NY: Random House, 1980. Pp. xv–xvii.

Explains the scope of the volume and the rationale for publishing it: "In addition to providing documentary evidence, these letters reveal the qualities of a finely sensitive literary mind." Volume also includes numerous letters to F, most notably from Zelda, Shane Leslie, John Peale Bishop, H. L. Mencken, Ring Lardner, and Gerald and Sara Murphy, and an "Editorial Note," pp. xix–xx, and "Chronology," pp. xxi–xxx.

I44. ———. "Introduction." In F. Scott Fitzgerald. *The Cruise of the Rolling Junk*. Bloomfield Hills, Mich., and Columbia, S.C.: Bruccoli Clark, 1976. Unpaged.

Very brief (one-page) discussion of the details of composition and publication of this serial and assessment of its value: It is a "document in social history" and a "valuable view of the underside of the American Twenties."

I45. ———. "Introduction." In his ed. *F. Scott Fitzgerald's Ledger—A Facsimile*. Washington, D.C.: Bruccoli Clark/NCR Editions, 1973. Unpaged.

Brief (two-page) discussion of the *Ledger,* "the most useful bio-bibliographical document for Fitzgerald," of its composition history, and of its significance—it "demonstrates Fitzgerald's sense of his importance" and it was "a professional tool for Fitzgerald—a source for material."

I46. ———. "Introduction." In his ed. *The Notebooks of F. Scott Fitzgerald.* NY: Harcourt Brace Jovanovich/Bruccoli Clark, 1978. Pp. vii-x.

Discussion of the background and significance of F's *Notebooks.* Volume also includes "Editorial and Explanatory Notes," pp. 341–359, which identify persons and places mentioned in the *Notebook* entries, as well as indicating where F used the entries in his fiction.

I47. ———. "Introduction." In his ed. *The Price Was High—The Last Uncollected Stories of F. Scott Fitzgerald.* NY: Harcourt Brace Jovanovich/Bruccoli Clark, 1979. Pp. xi-xx.

Overview of F's career as a short story writer which provides the number of stories he wrote, the income he derived from their sale, and the variety of magazines in which they appeared. The stories collected in this volume show F "as a professional writer earning his living in a highly competitive market by meeting certain standards of quality and satisfying commercial requirements." Bruccoli also provides a brief introduction to each of the stories, giving background information on its composition and a suggestion of its significance in F's career.

I48. ———. "Introduction—'Something Extraordinary and Beautiful and Simple & Intricately Patterned.'" In his ed. *"The Great Gatsby"—A Facsimile of the Manuscript.* Washington, D.C.: Microcard Editions, 1973. Pp. xiii-xxxv.

Detailed study and discussion of the composition process of GG, with emphasis on the changes and revisions F made as he rewrote the novel. This volume also includes specimen galleys corrected in F's hand (pp. 305–308); a list of "False Starts on Versos" (p. 311); "Paper Stock for Inserts" (p. 313); "Markings on Galley Proofs and Inserts Attached to Galleys" (p. 315); and a list of "Erasures in the Manuscript" (pp. 317–336).

I49. ———. "THE LAST OF THE NOVELISTS"—F. SCOTT FITZGERALD AND "THE LAST TYCOON." Carbondale: Southern Illinois University Press, 1977. 163 pp.

Detailed reconstruction of the successive drafts of LT, with extensive quotations used to illustrate the changes F made as he revised, and considerable background on the circumstances surrounding the novel's composition, as well as literary analysis of it. Concludes that Edmund Wilson's 1941 edition "obscures the gestational nature of Fitzgerald's work and misleads readers into judging work-in-progress as completed stages."

REVIEWS:

i.   Anonymous. Review of *"The Last of the Novelists"—F. Scott Fitzgerald and "The Last Tycoon,"* The Booklist, 74 (November 1, 1977), 451.

ii.   ————. Review of *"The Last of the Novelists"—F. Scott Fitzgerald and "The Last Tycoon,"* Chicago Tribune, November 13, 1977, "Book World" Section, p. 2.

iii.   ————. Review of *"The Last of the Novelists"—F. Scott Fitzgerald and "The Last Tycoon,"* Choice, 14 (December 1977), 1357.

iv.   Baker, William. Review of *"The Last of the Novelists"—F. Scott Fitzgerald and "The Last Tycoon,"* University Times (Wright State University, Dayton, Ohio), October 29, 1979, p. 6.

v.   Dirda, Michael. "An Orderly Account of the Last Work—Fragments of Fitzgerald," Chronicle of Higher Education, 15 (October 31, 1977), 15.

vi.   Gollata, James A. Review of *"The Last of the Novelists"—F. Scott Fitzgerald and "The Last Tycoon,"* Library Journal, 102 (November 1, 1977), 2262.

vii.   Hartman, Zella. "Fitzgerald, Unfinished," Oklahoma City Sunday Oklahoman, February 26, 1978, "Showcase" Section, p. 12.

viii.   [Johnston, Albert H.] Review of *"The Last of the Novelists"—F. Scott Fitzgerald and "The Last Tycoon,"* Publishers' Weekly, 211 (June 27, 1977), 102, 104.

ix.   Landino, Bob. "Wide-Eyed in Lotus Land," The Clock (Plymouth, N.H.), March 30, 1978, p. 8.

x.   Miller, James E., Jr. Review of *"The Last of the Novelists"—F. Scott Fitzgerald and "The Last Tycoon,"* American Literature, 50 (November 1978), 505–506.

xi.   Moodey, J. S. Review of *"The Last of the Novelists"—F. Scott Fitzgerald and "The Last Tycoon,"* Fresno Bee, December 18, 1977, p. B6.

xii.   Oldsey, Bernard. Review of *"The Last of the Novelists"—F. Scott Fitzgerald and "The Last Tycoon,"* Modern Fiction Studies, 24 (Summer 1978), 274–275.

xiii.   Ring, Frances. Review of *"The Last of the Novelists"—F. Scott Fitzgerald and "The Last Tycoon,"* Fitzgerald/Hemingway Annual, 10 (1978), 411–413.

xiv.   Sermon, Charles. "A Closer Look at 'The Last Tycoon,'" The State (Columbia, S.C.), December 4, 1977, p. 4-E.

xv.   Wells, Robert W. "Between the Lines," Milwaukee *Journal*, September 11, 1977, Part 5, p. 5.
xvi.   Whitman, Alden. "Books: 'Last Tycoon' Revisited," NY *Times*, October 5, 1977, p. 32.

I50.   ———. THE MERRILL CHECKLIST OF F. SCOTT FITZGERALD. Columbus, Ohio: Charles E. Merrill, 1970. 39 pp.
Unannotated and selective listing of works by and about F.

I51.   ———. " 'A Might Collation': Animadversions on the Text of F. Scott Fitzgerald." In Francess G. Halpenny, ed. *Editing Twentieth Century Texts*. Toronto: University of Toronto Press, 1972. Pp. 28–50.
Detailed discussion of the textual errors and problems in editions of GG, TITN, LT, and the texts of F's letters in C-U, with contention that these come from F's carelessness, Maxwell Perkins' role in handling F's proofs, and F's publisher's failure to produce definitive texts. Includes an appendix of historical collation for the novels.

I52.   ———. *The O'Hara Concern—A Biography of John O'Hara*. NY: Random House, 1975. Pp. 91–95, 99–101, 115–116, 137–138, 159–160, 180–181, and *passim*.
Includes extensive quotations from O'Hara's letters to and published reminiscences of F and brief accounts of their friendship, in NY and in Hollywood.

I53.   ———. "On F. Scott Fitzgerald and 'Bernice Bobs Her Hair.' " In Calvin Skaggs, ed. *The American Short Story*. NY: Dell, 1977. Pp. 219–222.
Relates "Bernice Bobs Her Hair" to F's ability to deal with the "concerns of youth with seriousness" and to his "achievement as a social historian" and briefly discusses history of its composition and its source in F's detailed instructions to his sister on how to be popular. Although "not one of Fitzgerald's greatest stories," its characters "are convincing; the social details are right; there is a current of ideas; and the prose is wonderfully readable."

I54.   ———. SCOTT AND ERNEST—THE AUTHORITY OF FAILURE AND THE AUTHORITY OF SUCCESS. NY: Random House, 1978. 169 pp.; London: Bodley Head, 1978. 167 pp.
Detailed description and discussion of the personal and professional relationship between F and Hemingway, based on letters (some previously unpublished), interviews with their contemporaries, published autobiographical accounts, and published research.

REVIEWS:

i.   Anonymous. "Odd Pair," *The Economist,* 269 (October 28, 1978), 126.

ii.   ————. Review of *Scott and Ernest—The Authority of Failure and the Authority of Success, The Booklist,* 74 (March 15, 1978), 1158, 1160.

iii.   ————. Review of *Scott and Ernest—The Authority of Failure and the Authority of Success, Choice,* 15 (October 1978), 1046.

iv.   ————. Review of *Scott and Ernest—The Authority of Failure and the Authority of Success, Kirkus,* 46 (February 1, 1978), 144.

v.   ————. Review of *Scott and Ernest—The Authority of Failure and the Authority of Success, Queen's Quarterly,* 86 (Winter 1979/80), 739.

vi.   ————. " 'Scott and Ernest' and Memories of a Painful Literary Friendship," Washington (D.C.) *Sunday Star,* April 23, 1978, p. G–22.

vii.   Alexander, Glenda. "'Scott and Ernest' Destroys Myths," Winston-Salem *Journal,* April 16, 1978, p. C4.

viii.   Algren, Nelson. "Hemingway: His Misadventures With Fitzgerald," Chicago *Tribune,* April 2, 1978, "Book World" Section, p. 3. Reprinted in *Washington Book Review,* 1 (May 1979), 16, 12.

ix.   Astro, Richard. Review of *Scott and Ernest—The Authority of Failure and the Authority of Success, Modern Fiction Studies,* 26 (Summer 1980), 327–328.

x.   Baker, Mary M. "Literary Friendship That Faded," Wilmington (Del.) *Sunday News Journal,* April 23, 1978, Sec. D, p. 8.

xi.   Barsotti, Joseph. "Press Bookshelf—Fitzgerald, Hemingway Tie Weak," Pittsburgh *Press,* August 10, 1978, p. B–9.

xii.   Biederman, Patricia Ward. " 'Scott and Ernest'—Minor Episodes in a Continuing Soap Opera," Buffalo *Courier-Express,* April 16, 1978, p. F–8.

xiii.   Bonham, Roger. "Study Traces Friendship of Legendary Authors," Columbus (Ohio) *Dispatch,* May 21, 1978, p. K–9.

xiv.   *Bradbury, Malcolm. "The Wound and the Bow," *New Statesman,* n.s. 96 (October 27, 1978), 549.

xv.   Brady, Charles A. "Not So Odd Couple: Scott and Ernest," Buffalo *News,* May 28, 1978, p. G–4.

xvi.   Brownson, Cathy. "Book Review—Debunking Myths Around Fitzgerald and Hemingway," Oshawa (Canada) *Times,* October 6, 1978, p. 3.

xvii.   Broyard, Anatole. "Books of The Times—A Farewell to F. Scott," NY *Times*, April 8, 1978, p. 21. See also *Arkansas Gazette* (Little Rock), April 16, 1978, p. 12E; Seattle *Post-Intelligencer*, July 23, 1978.

xviii.   Bunke, Joan. "Image and Imagination," Des Moines *Sunday Register*, April 16, 1978, p. 4B.

xix.   Clarke, Margaret. "Literary Myths and Facts in Friendship of These Two Giants," Sydney (Australia) *Sun Herald*, January 21, 1979, p. 55.

xx.   Donaldson, Scott. Review of *Scott and Ernest—The Authority of Failure and the Authority of Success, Fitzgerald/Hemingway Annual*, 10 (1978), 403–405.

xxi.   ———. " 'We're Not Tragic Characters...All We Are Is Writers,' " Minneapolis *Tribune*, April 23, 1978, p. 12D.

xxii.   Drake, Anstiss. "Scott Versus Ernest, Sadly," Chicago *Sun-Times*, April 23, 1978, "Show" Section, p. 11.

xxiii.   Duhamel, P. Albert. "I've Been Reading—New Looks at Nelson, Scott and Hemingway," Boston *Herald-American*, April 23, 1978, p. E6.

xxiv.   Duncan, Ben. "Just Good Friends," *Gay News*, No. 155 (November 16–29, 1978), 25.

xxv.   Forster, Margaret. "A Hero and His Admirer," London *Evening Standard*, November 7, 1978, p. 20.

xxvi.   Fox, Thomas. "A Long and Painful Friendship," Memphis *Commercial Appeal*, April 23, 1978, Sec. G, p. 6.

xxvii.   Frank, Michael R. " 'Scott and Ernest': Odd Couple," *Daily Bruin* (University of California, Los Angeles), April 27, 1978, pp. 19, 22.

xxviii.   Friedman, Robert. "Two Cult Writers Analyzed," NY *Post*, June 8, 1978, p. 28.

xxix.   Gault, Webster. "Trying Friendship," Hartford *Courant*, May 7, 1978, p. 9G.

xxx.   Gohn, Jack Benoit. "Scott and Ernest: Just Good Friends," Baltimore *Sunday Sun*, May 14, 1978, p. D7.

xxxi.   Grumbach, Doris. Review of *Scott and Ernest—The Authority of Failure and the Authority of Success, NY Times Book Review*, April 23, 1978, p. 16.

xxxii.   Hagemann, E. R. "Fitzgerald Minus Hemingway," Louisville *Courier-Journal*, June 4, 1978, p. D5.

xxxiii.   Hanscom, Leslie. " 'Scott and Ernest' Probes Friendship of 2 Writers," Atlantic City *Sunday Press*, June 18, 1978, Sec. C, p. 18. See also *Newsday* (Garden City, NY), May 21, 1978, "Ideas" Section, p. 18; *Arizona Republic* (Phoenix), June 4, 1978, p. N–9.

xxxiv.   H[arrison], K[eith].   Review of *Scott and Ernest—The Authority of Failure and the Authority of Success, Carleton Miscellany*, 17 (Spring 1979), 247.

xxxv.   Higgens, Alison.   "Odd Friends: Hemingway, Fitzgerald," Sacramento *Bee*, May 28, 1978, "Forum" Section, p. 6.

xxxvi.   Higgins, George.   "The Column: Prolific Professor's Book on Fitzgerald, Hemingway Relationship 'Required Reading,'" Boston *Herald-American*, May 9, 1978, p. 2.

xxxvii.   Homberger, Eric.   "A Literary Friendship," *The Tablet*, 232 (November 25, 1978), 1141–1142.

xxxviii.   Houston, Levin.   "The Tragic Writers," Fredericksburg (Va.) *Free Lance-Star*, April 29, 1978, "Town and Country" Magazine, p. 6.

xxxix.   Jaynes, Roger.   "Strange Case of Scott and Ernie," Milwaukee *Journal*, April 23, 1978, "Lively Arts" Section, p. 5.

xl.   [Johnston, Albert H.] Review of *Scott and Ernest—The Authority of Failure and the Authority of Success, Publishers' Weekly*, 213 (February 13, 1978), 120.

xli.   Kapsidelis, Tom.   "Two Volumes Deal With 1920s Writers," *The State* (Columbia, S.C.), May 28, 1978, p. 4-E.

xlii.   Kelly, Robert.   "Scott Awed By Ernest's Aggression," Fort Wayne *News-Sentinel*, May 13, 1978, p. 14W.

xliii.   Kennedy, John S.   "Friends—At Least for Awhile," *Catholic Transcript* (Hartford, Conn.), April 28, 1978, p. 5.

xliv.   Kennedy, Joseph.   "Poor Scott," *Hibernia*, November 9, 1978, p. 16.

xlv.   Kerr, C. Douglas.   "'Scott and Ernest': Profile Proves Interesting Reading," Orlando *Sentinel-Star*, June 11, 1978, p. 8-H.

xlvi.   Kirsch, Robert.   "The Book Report—Scott, Ernest: Best Enemies," Los Angeles *Times*, June 5, 1978, Part IV, p. 2.

xlvii.   Klise, Thomas S.   Review of *Scott and Ernest—The Authority of Failure and the Authority of Success, Commonweal*, 105 (August 18, 1978), 542–543.

xlviii.   *Koch, C. J.   "Fitzgerald and Hemingway," *Quadrant*, 145 (August 1979), 60–62.

xlix.   L., V. J.   "Booktalk," *Fair Lady*, 15 (August 1, 1979), 31.

l.   Ludwig, Richard M.   "Book Review—Friendship and Estrangement," *Daily Princetonian* (Princeton University), April 25, 1978, p. 6.

li.   McLeod, Colin.   Review of *Scott and Ernest—The Authority of Failure and the Authority of Success, Library Journal*, 103 (April 1, 1978), 752.

lii.   Manning, Margaret. "A Farewell to Friendship," Boston *Sunday Globe*, April 16, 1978, p. A18.

liii.   Mellors, John. "Prickly People," *London Magazine*, 18 (March 1979), 83–86.

liv.   Milazzo, Lee. "The Stormy Scott-Ernest Relationship," Dallas *Morning News*, April 23, 1978, p. 4 G.

lv.   Miller, James E., Jr. Review of *Scott and Ernest—The Authority of Failure and the Authority of Success, American Literature,* 51 (January 1980), 574–575.

lvi.   Monteiro, George. Review of *Scott and Ernest—The Authority of Failure and the Authority of Success, New Republic,* 178 (June 3, 1978), 33–35.

lvii.   Mysak, Joe. "Scott & Ernest—Hold! Enough! and Enough Mysak For a Summer," *Summer Spectator* (Columbia University), August 10, 1978, p. 8.

lviii.   Nye, Robert. "Scott and Ernest: Just Good Friends," *The Scotsman* (Edinburgh), November 4, 1978, "Weekend Scotsman" Section, p. 3.

lix.   Paschall, Douglas D. Review of *Scott and Ernest—The Authority of Failure and the Authority of Success,* Chattanooga *Times,* March 4, 1979, p. D4.

lx.   Pintarich, Paul. "Writers' Friendship Complex," Portland *Sunday Oregonian*, June 11, 1978, p. B4.

lxi.   Rowse, A. L. "Literary Squalor," *Books and Bookmen,* 24 (December 1978), 16–18 [16–17].

lxii.   Sheppard, R. Z. "The Far Side of Friendship," *Time,* 111 (April 3, 1978), 89–90.

lxiii.   Sheridan, Victoria. "Scott and Ernest," Newport News (Va.) *Daily Press,* May 14, 1978, "Panorama" Section, p. 11.

lxiv.   Shone, Richard. "Crack-up," *The Spectator,* 241 (November 25, 1978), 23.

lxv.   Stewart, Ian. Review of *Scott and Ernest—The Authority of Failure and the Authority of Success, Country Life,* 164 (December 7, 1978), 2024.

lxvi.   Tucker, John. "The Saga of Hemingway v Fitzgerald," Pretoria (South Africa) *News,* March 2, 1979, p. 12.

lxvii.   Tyler, Ralph. Review of *Scott and Ernest—The Authority of Failure and the Authority of Success, Bookviews,* 1 (May 1978), 61.

lxviii.   Vogel, Jim. "Voice of a Failed Genius vs. Titan's Bellow: Weighing the Fitzgerald-Hemingway Ties," Memphis *Press-Scimitar,* May 6, 1978, p. 6.

lxix.   Walch, Bob. "Fitzgerald, Hemingway Characters Are Studied," Monterey (Calif.) *Sunday Peninsula-Herald,* May 7, 1978, p. 8C.

lxx. Warthen, Brad. "Scott, Ernest: The Facts," Jackson (Tenn.) *Sun,* August 13, 1978, p. 4A.
lxxi. Waters, Gregory. "The Bookshelf—Drinking Buddies: Scott and Ernest," Flint *Journal,* June 4, 1978, p. C-4.
lxxii. Wilkinson, Burke. "Scott and Ernest: What Are Friends For?" *Christian Science Monitor,* June 14, 1978, p. 30.
lxxiii. Wukas, Mark. "Friends or Enemies—Fitzgerald-Hemingway Relations Explored Impartially, Documented," *Daily Illini* (University of Illinois), May 6, 1978, "Spectrum" Section, p. 8.
lxxiv. Yardley, Jonathan. "Fitzgerald and Hemingway: The Decline of Friendship," Miami (Fla.) *Herald,* April 16, 1978, p. 7E. See also Macon *Telegraph & News,* April 23, 1978; Austin (Tex.) *American-Statesman,* April 23, 1978, p. D6.
lxxv. Y[ork], D[avid] W[inston]. "Scott and Ernest," *West Coast Review of Books,* 4 (July 1978), 33.

155. ———. SOME SORT OF EPIC GRANDEUR—THE LIFE OF F. SCOTT FITZGERALD. NY: Harcourt Brace Jovanovich, 1981; London: Hodder and Stoughton, 1982. 624 pp. "The Colonial Ancestors of Francis Scott Key Fitzgerald" by Scottie Fitzgerald Smith, pp. 496–509.

Detailed biography which attempts to "focus on Fitzgerald as writer by tracing the ontogeny of his major work while providing a detailed account of his career as a professional author." Presents much new evidence which has surfaced since last F biography in 1962, with thesis that F "was a hero with many flaws, but a hero. His life was a quest for heroism." Emphasis on F's own words, on reminiscences of friends, and on previous biographical accounts.

REVIEWS:

i. Anonymous. "Another Side of Paradise," *The Economist,* 282 (February 6–12, 1982), 91.
ii. ———. Review of *Some Sort of Epic Grandeur—The Life of F. Scott Fitzgerald, Journal of Modern Literature,* 9 (December 1982), 446.
iii. ———. Review of *Some Sort of Epic Grandeur—The Life of F. Scott Fitzgerald, Kirkus,* 49 (August 15, 1981), 1046.
iv. ———. Review of *Some Sort of Epic Grandeur—The Life of F. Scott Fitzgerald, New Yorker,* 57 (January 4, 1982), 90.
v. Bold, Alan. "Fitzgerald: Drunkard as Hero," *The Scotsman* (Edinburgh), February 13, 1982, "Weekend Scotsman" Section, p. 5.

vi.   Broyard, Anatole. "Books of The Times—The Sad Young Man," NY *Times,* November 7, 1981, p. 12.
vii.   Burgess, Anthony. "The Party and the Hangover," *The Observer* (London), February 7, 1982, p. 28.
viii.   Caesar, Daniel A. "F. Scott Fitzgerald: A Life Reconsidered," Chattanooga *Times,* November 14, 1981, p. B4.
ix.   Campbell, James. "Second Best," *New Stateman,* n.s. 103 (February 12, 1982), 21–23.
x.   Cohen, George. Review of *Some Sort of Epic Grandeur—The Life of F. Scott Fitzgerald, The Booklist,* 77 (July 15/August 1981), 1419.
xi.   Curtis, Anthony. "Scott Plain," *Financial Times* (London), January 30, 1982, p. 8.
xii.   Fremont-Smith, Eliot. Review of *Some Sort of Epic Grandeur—The Life of F. Scott Fitzgerald, Saturday Review,* n.s. 8 (November 1981), 78, 80.
xiii.   Haugen, Peter. "Stunning Portrait of Tragic Literary Genius," Fresno *Bee,* December 20, 1981, p. E6.
xiv.   H[olleran], A[ndrew]. Review of *Some Sort of Epic Grandeur—The Life of F. Scott Fitzgerald, New York,* 14 (December 7, 1981), 142, 144.
xv.   Leon, Philip W. "Biography of Fitzgerald Grand," *The State* (Columbia, S.C.), November 8, 1981, p. 13-B.
xvi.   Lord, Graham. "Just an Epic Bore," London *Sunday Express,* January 31, 1982, p. 6.
    *Lynn, Kenneth S. "More Facts—One Sort of Scholarship," *Harper's Magazine,* 263 (December 1981), 58–61. See H1280.
xvii.   McCaffery, Larry. "F. Scott Fitzgerald—Matters of Fact," San Diego *Union,* December 20, 1981, "Currents in Books" Section, pp. 1, 7.
xviii.   Manning, Margaret. "F. Scott Fitzgerald—The Story of His Life Was the Story of His Marriage," Boston *Sunday Globe,* November 29, 1981, pp. A22, A23.
xix.   Powell, Anthony. "The World of Gatsby," London *Daily Telegraph,* February 4, 1982, p. 12.
xx.   Prescott, Peter S. "Fitzgerald Without Tears," *Newsweek,* 98 (November 23, 1981), 110.
xxi.   Reefer, Mary M. "F. Scott Fitzgerald's Life Torn By Illusions and Hard Truths," Kansas City *Star,* December 20, 1981, p. 1F.
xxii.   Rovit, Earl. Review of *Some Sort of Epic Grandeur—The Life of F. Scott Fitzgerald, Library Journal,* 106 (September 1, 1981), 1631.

xxiii.   Schulberg, Budd. "F. Scott Fitzgerald, Sunlit and Night-Shadowed," *Newsday* (Garden City, NY), January 31, 1982, "Ideas" Section, pp. 20, 17. See also Buffalo *News*, February 21, 1982, p. F–7.

xxiv.   Stuttaford, Genevieve. Review of *Some Sort of Epic Grandeur—The Life of F. Scott Fitzgerald, Publishers' Weekly,* 220 (August 28, 1981), 386.

xxv.   Sullivan, Mary. "Scottie's Way," London *Sunday Telegraph,* February 7, 1982, p. 12.

*Symons, Julian. "A Gift For Hope," *Times Literary Supplement* (London), February 26, 1982, pp. 221–222. See H1304.

xxvi.   Wagner, Linda W. Review of *Some Sort of Epic Grandeur—The Life of F. Scott Fitzgerald, American Literature,* 54 (May 1982), 304–306.

xxvii.   Weeks, Robert P. Review of *Some Sort of Epic Grandeur—The Life of F. Scott Fitzgerald, Modern Fiction Studies,* 28 (Summer 1982), 295–298.

xxviii.   Wilkinson, Burke. "Thorough Biography of F. Scott Fitzgerald Corrects Many of the Myths," *Christian Science Monitor,* November 25, 1981, p. 21.

xxix.   Williamson, J. N. "New Look at F. Scott Fitzgerald," Indianapolis *News,* January 23, 1982, "Free Time" Section, p. 22.

xxx.   Yardley, Jonathan. " 'More Facts': Scott Fitzgerald and His Biographer," Washington (D.C.) *Post,* October 11, 1981, "Book World" Section, pp. 3, 4. See also Los Angeles *Herald Examiner,* October 25, 1981, "Book Week" Section, pp. F–5, F–6; *Manchester Guardian Weekly,* November 15, 1981, p. 18.

I56.   ———. SUPPLEMENT TO F. SCOTT FITZGER-ALD—A DESCRIPTIVE BIBLIOGRAPHY. Pittsburgh Series in Bibliography. Pittsburgh: University of Pittsburgh Press, 1980. 220 pp.

Corrects and updates *F. Scott Fitzgerald—A Descriptive Bibliography* (I40) and adds two new sections—translations; and re-publications of F's stories, poems, essays, and letters.

REVIEWS:

i.   Anonymous. Review of *Supplement to F. Scott Fitzgerald—A Descriptive Bibliography, Choice,* 18 (February 1981), 772.

ii.   Bassett, Charles. Review of *Supplement to F. Scott Fitzgerald—A Descriptive Bibliography, American Book Collector,* 2 (September/October 1981), 68–70.

iii.   Kelly, Richard J. Review of *Supplement to F. Scott Fitzgerald—A Descriptive Bibliography, Library Journal*, 105 (September 1, 1980), 1720.

———. See Moore (I265).

———. See Smith (I324).

I57.   ———, comp. PROFILE OF F. SCOTT FITZGER-ALD. Columbus, Ohio: Charles E. Merrill, 1971. 122 pp.

I.   M[atthew] J. B[ruccoli], "Preface," p. iii. Very brief statement of volume's intentions.

II.   John O'Hara, "Introduction to *The Portable F. Scott Fitzgerald*" (C123), pp. 11–20.

III.   John Kuehl, "Scott Fitzgerald's Critical Opinions" (B464), pp. 21–39.

IV.   John Kuehl, "Scott Fitzgerald's Reading" (B465), pp. 40–73.

V.   G. Thomas Tanselle and Jackson R. Bryer, "*The Great Gatsby*—A Study in Literary Reputation" (B608), pp. 74–91.

VI.   Matthew J. Bruccoli, "*Tender is the Night*—Reception and Reputation" (C30), pp. 92–106.

VII.   Vance Bourjaily, "Fitzgerald Attends My Fitzgerald Seminar" (B562), pp. 107–122.

I58.   ———, ed. *Selected Letters of John O'Hara*. NY: Random House, 1978. Pp. 50, 75–76, 78–79, 90, 92–93, 109–110, 115–117, 118, 164, 194, 224, 225, 251, 266, 278–280, 295, 300, 329, 375, 380, 401–402, 428–429, 432–433, 471, 492.

Frequent scattered mention throwing light on F's relationship with O'Hara, on F's influence on O'Hara, as well as his assistance to and encouragement of O'Hara, and on O'Hara's opinions regarding F's works and F's decline in reputation.

I59.   ———, and Jackson R. Bryer, eds. F. SCOTT FITZGERALD IN HIS OWN TIME: A MISCELLANY. Kent, Ohio: Kent State University Press, 1971. 481 pp.

I.   Matthew J. Bruccoli and Jackson R. Bryer, "Foreword," pp. vii-x.

Brief explanation of volume's arrangement and contents and justification for its publication.

II.   Frederick James Smith, "'I'm Sick of the Sexless Animals Writers Have Been Giving Us'" (B45), pp. 243–245.

III.   Thomas A. Boyd, " 'Hugh Walpole Was the Man Who Started Me Writing Novels'" (B49), pp. 245–254.

IV.   Marguerite Mooers Marshall, "'Our American Women Are Leeches'" (B63), pp. 255–258.

V.   "'Home Is the Place to Do the Things You Want to Do'—An Interview With Mr. and Mrs. F. Scott Fitzgerald" (B78), pp. 258–262.

VI.   B. F. Wilson, "'All Women Over Thirty-Five Should Be Murdered'" (H27), pp. 263–266.

VII.   Charles C. Baldwin, "'I Am a Pessimist, a Communist (With Nietschean Overtones), Have No Hobbies Except Conversation—And I am Trying to Repress That'" (C13), pp. 267-270.

VIII.   Muriel Babcock, "'America Is the Place Where Everybody Is Always Going to Have a Good Time Tomorrow,'" pp. 271-273.
Interview with correspondent for unidentified Los Angeles newspaper (a clipping of this item is in F's scrapbook) in 1927 in which F comments on his favorite books at different stages of his life and on his thoughts about America upon returning from France.

IX.   Harry Salpeter, "'The Next Fifteen Years Will Show How Much Resistance There Is in the American Race'" (B98), pp. 274–277.

X.   Margaret Reid, "'Flappers Are Just Girls With a Splendid Talent For Life'" (B97), pp. 277–281.

XI.   Charles G. Shaw, "F. Scott Fitzgerald" (C145), pp. 281–284.

XII.   Walling Keith, "'In Ideals I Am Somewhat of a Communist'" (B106), pp. 284–286.

XIII.   "'The American People Are Just Beginning to Wake Up to the Fact That Success Comes Hard'" (B113), pp. 286–288.

XIV.   Ed G. Thomas, "'This Is a Very Cautious Generation in a World So Full of Alarm'" (B132), pp. 289–292.

XV.   Anthony Buttitta, "'The Less the Parents of Today Try to Tell Their Children, the More Effective They Can Be in Making Them Believe in a Few Old Truths'" (B126), pp. 292–294.

XVI.   Michel Mok, "'A Writer Like Me Must Have an Utter Confidence, an Utter Faith in His Star'" (B138), pp. 294–299.

XVII.   "Apprentice Work Done at Princeton" (excerpts from B5, B7, B14, B12, B13, B11), pp. 301–304.

XVIII.   Burton Rascoe, "*This Side of Paradise*: A Youth in the Saddle" (A42), pp. 305–306.

XIX.   David W. Bailey (Harvard) and R. F. McPartlin (Dartmouth), "*This Side of Paradise*: Two Undergraduate Views" (A22 & A38), pp. 306–309.

XX.   "*This Side of Paradise*: With College Men" (A7), pp. 310–311.

XXI.   H. L. Mencken, "*This Side of Paradise*: Books More or Less Amusing " (A39), pp. 311–312.

XXII.   "*This Side of Paradise*: The Dangerous Teens" (A1), pp. 312–313.

XXIII.   "*This Side of Paradise*" (A49), pp. 313–315.

XXIV.   "*Flappers and Philosophers*" (A61), pp. 315–317.

XXV.   Henry Seidel Canby, "*The Beautiful and Damned*: The Flapper's Tragedy" (A157), pp. 317–319.

XXVI.   John Peale Bishop, "*The Beautiful and Damned*: Mr. Fitzgerald Sees the Flapper Through" (A152), pp. 320–324.

XXVII.   "*The Beautiful and Damned*: Reveals One Phase of Jazz-Vampire Period" (A131), pp. 324–326.

XXVIII.   Carl Van Doren, "*The Beautiful and Damned*" (A189), pp. 327–328.

XXIX.   Gilbert Seldes, "*The Beautfiul and Damned*: This Side of Innocence" (A187), pp. 329–331.

XXX.   Zelda Sayre, "*The Beautiful and Damned*: Friend Husband's Latest" (A186), pp. 332–334.

XXXI.   Mary M. Colum, "*The Beautiful and Damned*" (A160), pp. 334–336.

XXXII.   Henry Beston, "*The Beautfiul and Damned*" (A151), pp. 336–337.

L.   Henry Seidel Canby, "*Tender Is the Night*: In the Second Era of Demoralization" (A445), pp. 370–372.

LI.   John Chamberlain, "*Tender Is the Night*" (A446 & A447), pp. 372–375.

LII.   Clifton Fadiman, "*Tender Is the Night*" (A454), pp. 376–378.

LIII.   J. Donald Adams, "*Tender Is the Night*: Scott Fitzgerald's Return to the Novel" (A438), pp. 379–380.

LIV.   Peter Quennell, "*Tender Is the Night*" (A475), p. 381.

LV.   "*Tender Is the Night*: A New Fitzgerald" (A433), p. 382.

LVI.   Philip Rahv, "*Tender Is the Night*: You Can't Duck Hurricane Under a Beach Umbrella" (A476), pp. 383–384.

LVII.   William Troy, "*Tender Is the Night*: The Worm i' the Bud" (A481), pp. 385–387.

LVIII.   Malcolm Cowley, "*Tender Is the Night*: Breakdown" (A451), pp. 387–390.

LIX.   "*Tender Is the Night*" (A434), pp. 390–392.

LX.   Elizabeth Hart, "*Taps at Reveille*: F. Scott Fitzgerald, Looking Backward" (A516), pp. 393–395.

LXI.   Edith H. Walton, "*Taps at Reveille*: Scott Fitzgerald's Tales" (A526), pp. 395–396.

LXII.   William Troy, "*Taps at Reveille*: The Perfect Life" (A524), pp. 397–399.

LXIII.   Frances Newman, "*This Side of Paradise*" (B43), pp. 401–403.

LXIV.   Edmund Wilson, "F. Scott Fitzgerald" (B67), pp. 404–409.

LXV.   "Two Editorials on Fitzgerald" (B54 & B53), pp. 410–412.

LXVI.   "The Future of Fitzgerald" (B56), pp. 413–414.

LXVII.   B. F. Wilson, "Notes on Personalities: F. Scott Fitzgerald" (B81), pp. 414–420.

LXVIII.   Edmund Wilson, "The Delegate From Great Neck" (B82), pp. 421–431.

LXIX.   Paul Rosenfeld, "F. Scott Fitzgerald" (C135), pp. 431–435.

LXX.   Harvey Eagleton, "Prophets of the New Age: F. Scott Fitzgerald and *The Great Gatsby*" (A357), pp. 436–439.

LXXI.   Heywood Broun, "*The Great Gatsby*: It Seems to Me" (B85), pp. 439–441.

LXXII.   John Chapin Mosher, "That Sad Young Man" (B91), pp. 442–445.

LXXIII.   Shirley Spencer, "Handwriting Reveals Character: F. Scott Fitzgerald" (B131), pp. 445–446.

LXXIV.   Dorothy Parker, "Once More Mother Hubbard—As Told by F. Scott Fitzgerald" (B44), pp. 447–448.

LXXV.   Donald Ogden Stewart, "The Courtship of Miles Standish—In the Manner of F. Scott Fitzgerald" (C150), pp. 449–454.

LXXVI.   Edward Anthony, "Impious Impressions: F. Scott Fitzgerald" (B48), pp. 455–456.

LXXVII.   Christopher Ward, "Paradise Be Damned! by F. Scott Fitzjazzer" (C173), pp. 456–464.

LXXVIII.   H. W. H., "The Rubaiyat of Amory Khayyam As Translated by F. Scott Fitzgerald," pp. 464–465.
Humorous poetic parody found as unidentified newspaper or magazine clipping in F's scrapbook.

LXXIX.   James Gray, "A Last Salute to the Gayest of Sad Young Men" (B169), pp. 467–469.

LXXX.   "Not Wholly 'Lost'" (B173), pp. 469–470.

LXXXI.   "F. Scott Fitzgerald" (B152), pp. 470–472.

LXXXII.   Westbrook Pegler, "Fair Enough" (B174), pp. 472–473.

LXXXIII.   "Talk of the Town: F. Scott Fitzgerald" (B193), p. 474.

LXXXIV.   Amy Loveman, "Fitzgerald and the Jazz Age" (B191), pp. 475–476.

LXXXV.   Arnold Gingrich, "Salute and Farewell to F. Scott Fitzgerald" (B188), pp. 477–481.

REVIEWS: See G86–G107.

I60.   ———, and C. E. F[razer] C[lark, Jr.], eds. F. SCOTT
FITZGERALD AND ERNEST M. HEMINGWAY IN PARIS—AN
EXHIBITION AT THE BIBLIOTHÈQUE BENJAMIN FRANKLIN
IN CONJUNCTION WITH A CONFERENCE AT THE INSTITUT
D'ÉTUDES AMÉRICAINES 23–24 JUNE 1972—1, PLACE DE
L'ODÉON—PARIS, FRANCE. Bloomfield Hills, Mich., and
Columbia, S.C.: Bruccoli-Clark, 1972. Unpaged.
Exhibition catalogue which includes Frances Scott Fitzgerald
Smith's "Où Sont Les Soleils d'Antan? Françoise 'Fijeralde'?"—her
memories of life with her parents in Paris.
REVIEW:

i.   Meriwether, James B. Review of *F. Scott Fitzgerald and
Ernest M. Hemingway in Paris, Fitzgerald/Hemingway Annual*, 5
(1973), 335–336.

I61.   Bryer, Jackson R. THE CRITICAL REPUTATION OF
F. SCOTT FITZGERALD—A BIBLIOGRAPHICAL STUDY. Ham-
den, Conn.: Archon Books, 1967. 434 pp.
Annotated listing of works about F through early 1966, with sections
of reviews of books by F; articles about F; books and book sections
about F; foreign books and articles about F; graduate research (masters
essays and doctoral dissertations) on F; and detailed index to the entries.
REVIEWS:

i.   Anonymous. "The Reputation of Fitzgerald," Baltimore
Sunday Sun, October 8, 1967, Sec. D, p. 5.
ii.   ———. "Reputations," *Times Literary Supplement*
(London), August 1, 1968, p. 826.
iii.   ———. Review of *The Critical Reputation of F. Scott
Fitzgerald—A Bibliographical Study, American Literature*, 40 (March
1968), 112.
iv.   ———. Review of *The Critical Reputation of F. Scott
Fitzgerald—A Bibliographical Study, Choice*, 5 (July-August 1968),
607.
v.   ———. Review of *The Critical Reputation of F. Scott
Fitzgerald—A Bibliographical Study, Modern Fiction Studies*, 13
(Winter 1967–68), 526.
vi.   ———. Review of *The Critical Reputation of F. Scott
Fitzgerald—A Bibliographical Study, Reference Quarterly*, 7 (Fall
1967), 86.

vii. ———. Review of *The Critical Reputation of F. Scott Fitzgerald—A Bibliographical Study*, *Wilson Library Bulletin*, 42 (February 1968), 626.

viii. Cameron, John A. Review of *The Critical Reputation of F. Scott Fitzgerald—A Bibliographical Study*, *Amherst Alumni News*, 20 (Winter 1968), 32.

ix. French, Warren G. Review of *The Critical Reputation of F. Scott Fitzgerald—A Bibliographical Study*, *Midcontinent American Studies Journal*, 10 (Spring 1969), 90–91

x. Katz, Joseph. "The Critical Reputation of F," *Fitzgerald Newletter*, No. 39 (Fall 1967), 14–15.

xi. Kuehl, John. Review of *The Critical Reputation of F. Scott Fitzgerald—A Bibliographical Study*, *Modern Language Journal*, 52 (April 1968), 233.

xii. Menn, Thorpe. Review of *The Critical Reputation of F. Scott Fitzgerald—A Bibliographical Study*, *Kansas City Star*, October 29, 1967, p. 6F.

xiii. Perosa, Sergio. Review of *The Critical Reputation of F. Scott Fitzgerald—A Bibliographical Study*, *Annali di Ca' Foscari*, 7 (Part I, 1968), 204. In Italian.

xiv. Thompson, Lawrence S. "Scott Fitzgerald," *American Book Collector*, 18 (December 1967), 7.

xv. Wolfe, Peter. "Between Book Ends—First-Rate Reference on Scott Fitzgerald," St. Louis *Post-Dispatch*, November 2, 1967, p. 2E.

I62. ———. "Fitzgerald and Hemingway." In J. Albert Robbins, ed. *American Literary Scholarship—An Annual—1971*. Durham, N.C.: Duke University Press, 1973. Pp. 120–145.
Critical survey of the year's work in F studies.

I63. ———. "Fitzgerald and Hemingway." In J. Albert Robbins, ed. *American Literary Scholarship—An Annual—1972*. Durham, N.C.: Duke University Press, 1974. Pp. 131–152.
Critical survey of the year's work in F studies.

I64. ———. "Fitzgerald and Hemingway." In James Woodress, ed. *American Literary Scholarship—An Annual—1973*. Durham, N.C.: Duke University Press, 1975. Pp. 150–176.
Critical survey of the year's work in F studies.

I65. ———. "Fitzgerald and Hemingway." In James Woodress, ed. *American Literary Scholarship—An Annual—1974*. Durham, N.C.: Duke University Press, 1976. Pp. 139–164.
Critical survey of the year's work in F studies.

I66. ————. "Fitzgerald and Hemingway." In James Woodress, ed. *American Literary Scholarship—An Annual—1975*. Durham, N.C.: Duke University Press, 1977. Pp. 167–200.
Critical survey of the year's work in F studies.

I67. ————. "Fitzgerald and Hemingway." In J. Albert Robbins, ed. *American Literary Scholarship—An Annual—1976*. Durham, N.C.: Duke University Press, 1978. Pp. 141–166.
Critical survey of the year's work in F studies.

I68. ————. "Fitzgerald and Hemingway." In James Woodress, ed. *American Literary Scholarship—An Annual—1977*. Durham, N.C.: Duke University Press, 1979. Pp. 163–186.
Critical survey of the year's work in F studies.

I69. ————. "Fitzgerald and Hemingway." In J. Albert Robbins, ed. *American Literary Scholarship—An Annual—1978*. Durham, N.C.: Duke University Press, 1980. Pp. 153–178.
Critical survey of the year's work in F studies.

I70. ————. "F. Scott Fitzgerald." In his ed. *Fifteen Modern American Authors—A Survey of Research and Criticism*. Durham, N. C.: Duke University Press, 1969. Pp. 211–238.
Bibliographical essay, partially drawn from 1963 *Texas Studies in Literature and Language* article (B530), surveying the editions and reprintings of and the scholarship and criticism on F from the earliest reviews of his college fiction to the books and essays of the F revival in the 1950s and 1960s.
Reprinted: Bryer (I71).

I71. ————. "F. Scott Fitzgerald." In his ed. *Sixteen Modern American Authors—A Survey of Research and Criticism*. Durham, N.C.: Duke University Press, 1974. Pp. 277–321.
Reprinting of I70 with "Supplement" (pp. 304–321) which updates the survey and includes comment on work by and about F from 1969 through 1972.

I72. ————. "F. Scott Fitzgerald (1896–1940)." In Gerald Nemanic, ed. *A Bibliographical Guide to Midwestern Literature*. Iowa City: University of Iowa Press, 1981. Pp. 211–215.
Brief sketch of F's critical reputation, with emphasis on material about his midwestern background, followed by selective unannotated listing of works by and about him.

———— . See Bruccoli (I59).

————. See Kuehl (I211).

I73.   ————, ed. F. SCOTT FITZGERALD—THE CRIT-
ICAL RECEPTION. NY: Burt Franklin, 1978. 386 pp.

I.   Jackson R. Bryer, "Introduction," pp. xi-xxvi.
Overview and analysis of reviewers' responses to F's books as they
appeared from TSOP in 1920 to LT in 1941.

II.   Harry Hansen, "Whew! How That Boy Can Write!"
(A34), pp. 1–2.

III.   "Good Afternoon! Have You a Little P.D. in Your
Home?" (A5), pp. 2–3.

IV.   Burton Rascoe, "A Youth in the Saddle" (A42), pp.
3–5.

V.   "F. Scott Fitzgerald Is Writer Worth Watching" (A3),
pp. 5–6.

VI.   N. B. C., "Old and New Standards in First Novels"
(A29), pp. 6–7.

VII.   [Harry E. Dounce], "The New Youth Finds a Voice in
Fiction" (A8), pp. 7–8.

VIII.   J[ohn] B[lack], "A Good First Novel: Vigorous,
Amusing and Independent" (A25), pp. 8–9.

IX.   Heywood Broun, "Paradise and Princeton" (A27), pp.
9–11.

X.   R. S. L., "Ernest Poole and Tarkington at Their Best"
(A36), p. 11.

XI.   "A Remarkable Young American Writer" (A12), pp.
12–13.

XII.   "Novels for Various Tastes" (A10), p. 13.

XIII.   Robert C. Benchley, "Books and Other Things" (A24),
pp. 14–15.

XIV.   R. F. M[cPartlin], "Princeton Scene of Novel—'This
Side of Paradise' Is True-to-Life Novel" (A38), p. 16.

XV.   "Reforms and Beginnings" (A11), pp. 16–17.

XVI.   William Huse, "This First Book Has Real Merit" (A35),
pp. 17–19.

xvii.   D[avid] W. B[ailey], "A Novel About Flappers for Philosophers" (A22), pp. 19–20.

xviii.   "With College Men" (A7), p. 21.

xix.   E[dwin] F[rancis] E[dgett], "A Young Novelist Defies Tradition" (A30), pp. 21–22.

xx.   R. V. A. S., Review of *This Side of Paradise* (A44), pp. 22–23.

xxi.   C. B., "'This Side of Paradise' Marked by Individuality" (A21), pp. 23–24.

xxii.   Review of *This Side of Paradise* (A16), p. 25.

xxiii.   Review of *This Side of Paradise* (A13), p. 25.

xxiv.   Margaret Emerson Bailey, "A Chronicle of Youth by Youth" (A23), pp. 26–27.

xxv.   "Youth Will Be Served" (A19), pp. 27–28.

xxvi.   H. L. Mencken, Review of *This Side of Paradise* (A39), p. 28.

xxvii.   "The Dangerous Teens" (A1), pp. 28–29.

xxviii.   Maud Davis Walker, *"This Side of Paradise"* (A46), pp. 30–31.

xxix.   S[trafford] P. R[iggs], Review of *This Side of Paradise* (A43), p. 31.

xxx.   Mary S. Hogg, Review of *This Side of Paradise*, pp. 31–32.
Unidentified clipping found in F's scrapbook. "Mr. Fitzgerald is a young man of ability. There is no reason to believe that with a few more years of experience he will not contribute to American literature something of far greater value."

xxxi.   Sibyl Vane, *"Flappers and Philosophers"* (A80), p. 35.

xxxii.   "Sic Transit" (A62), pp. 35–36.

xxxiii.   William Huse, "Stories by F. Scott Fitzgerald" (A74), pp. 36–37.

xxxiv.   Review of *Flappers and Philosophers* (A60), pp. 37–38.

xxxv.   Fanny Butcher, Review of *Flappers and Philosophers* (A68), pp. 38–39.

xxxvi.   "Flappers" (A56), pp. 39–40.

xxxvii.   "Stories by Fitzgerald" (A63), p. 40.

xxxviii.   "Fitzgerald Again" (G2), p. 24.

xxxix.   C. B., "Fitzgerald's New Book is Disappointing" (A66), p. 42.

xl.   "A Young Man's Fancy" (A64), p. 42.

xli.   David Coyle, "Short Stories by Scott Fitzgerald" (A69), pp. 43–44.

xlii.   Review of *Flappers and Philosophers* (A59), p. 44.

xliii.   Review of *Flappers and Philosophers* (A55), pp. 44–45.

xliv.   Heywood Broun, "Books" (G4), pp. 45–46.

xlv.   I. W. L., "Flappers and Others" (A75), pp. 46–47.

xlvi.   Charles H. Shinn, "Fitzgerald Does It Again" (A79), p. 47.

xlvii.   H. L. Mencken, Review of *Flappers and Philosophers* (A76), p. 48.

xlviii.   Alexander Boyd, "Mostly Flappers" (G3), pp. 48–49.

xlix.   "Recent Fiction" (A61), pp. 49–51.

l.   "Youth Insurgent" (A65), pp. 51–52.

li.   Russell Gore, "F. Scott Fitzgerald—Flapper-Philosopher" (A71), pp. 52–53.

lii.   The Ringmaster, Review of *Flappers and Philosophers*, pp. 53–54.
Unidentified clipping found in F's scrapbook. F's "photographs from life are inimitable, the flapper vocabulary, the flapper standards, the practicality underlying the thin varnish of romance, for he is one with those he writes of, at home in his own *milieu*, an insider not an outlander."

liii.   A. L. S. W[ood?], "'Flappers and Philosophers,'" pp. 54–55.
Unidentified clipping found in F's scrapbook. The "most interesting

studies" in F's book "are his sketches of girls. Probably no more recent pieces of writing are as truthful and as characteristic."

LIV.   Review of "Flappers and Philosophers," pp. 55–56.
Unidentified clipping found in F's scrapbook. F's stories are "the most brilliant, enjoyable, worth while assortment...published in the past year." These eight "reveal a superlative excellence of plot originality" and "of distinctive and individual treatment."

LV.   Review of *Flappers and Philosophers*, p. 57.
Unidentified clipping found in F's scrapbook. "Mr. Fitzgerald's chief value lies in the fact that he deals with contemporary life, in a rapidly moving manner, with a viewpoint peculiarly his own."

LVI.   "Fitzgerald—One of the Most Promising American Writers of Fiction of the Present Day," pp. 57–58.
Unidentified clipping found in F's scrapbook. This collection proves that F "can do more than write about youth. He writes of adults and their problems as well as he writes of the buoyancy and bustle of the love-making of boys and girls in their late teens and early twenties."

LVII.   M[ary] B[elle] S[wan], "Author of *This Side of Paradise* Writes Biting Satire on Modern Life" (G8), pp. 61–62.

LVIII.   T[homas] C[aldecot] C[hubb], Review of *The Beautiful and Damned* (A158), pp. 62–63.

LIX.   Henry Seidel Canby, "The Flapper's Tragedy" (A157), pp. 63–65.

LX.   N. P. Dawson, "'The Beautiful and Damned'" (A162), pp. 65–67.

LXI.   Burns Mantle, "Speaking of Books" (A178), pp. 67–68.

LXII.   John V. A. Weaver, "Better than 'This Side of Paradise'" (A191), pp. 68–70.

LXIII.   "F. Scott Fitzgerald in New Novel Reverses Horatio Alger Formula" (A135), pp. 70–71.

LXIV.   John Peale Bishop, "Mr. Fitzgerald Sees the Flapper Through" (A152), pp. 71–74.

LXV.   Fanny Butcher, Review of *The Beautiful and Damned* (A156), pp. 74–75.

LXVI.   Louise Maunsell Field, Review of *The Beautiful and Damned* (A165), pp. 76–77.

LXVII.   E. W. Osborn, "Fitzgerald's Joy-Riders 'Beautiful and Damned' " (A182), p. 78.

LXVIII.   Edward N. Teall, "Trumpets Herald Scott Fitzgerald" (A188), pp. 78–79.

LXIX.   Nathaniel Burton Paradise, Review of *The Beautiful and Damned* (A183), pp. 79–80.

LXX.   P. B., "Young Married Crowd Is Trivial as the Flappers, According to Fitzgerald" (A150), pp. 80–81.

LXXI.   Edwin Francis Edgett, *"The Beautiful and Damned"* (A163), pp. 81–82.

LXXII.   John Clair Minot, "Mr. Fitzgerald" (G7), pp. 82–83.

LXXIII.   "'The Beautiful and Damned' Reveals One Phase of Jazz-Vampire Period in Gilded Panorama of Reckless Life" (A131), pp. 83–85.

LXXIV.   Samuel Abbott, "A Man and a Maid Tread the Maze of Modern Life" (A149), pp. 85–87.

LXXV.   P[hil] A. Kinsley, "Two in Swift Descent on Life's Toboggan" (A174), pp. 87–89.

LXXVI.   Review of *The Beautiful and Damned* (A145), pp. 89–90.

LXXVII.   Harry Hansen, "'The Beautiful and Damned'" (A170), pp. 90–92.

LXXVIII.   Carl Van Doren, "The Roving Critic" (A189), pp. 92–93.

LXXIX.   William Huse, "Fitzgerald" (A173), pp. 93–95.

LXXX.   "New Novels" (A140), pp. 95–96.

LXXXI.   L. C. G., "Fitzgerald's Flapper Grows Up" (A166), pp. 96–97.

LXXXII.   A. L. S. Wood, "Agates and Migs" (A194), pp. 97–99.

LXXXIII.   *"The Beautiful and Damned"* (A124), pp. 99–100.

LXXXIV.   Robert F. Rogan, "A Cocktail Party in Every Chapter" (A185), pp. 100–101.

LXXXV.   John S. Cohen, Jr., "Books I Like Best" (A159), pp. 101–102.

LXXXVI.   Nancy Barr Mavity, "Alcoholic Atmosphere Hangs Heavy Over 'The Beautiful and Damned'" (A179), pp. 102–103.

LXXXVII.   "*The Beautiful and Damned*" (A128), pp. 103–104.

LXXXVIII.   "Portraits of Modern Type" (A141), p. 105.

LXXXIX.   "'The Beautiful and Damned'" (A123), pp. 105–106.

XC.   H. L. Mencken, "Fitzgerald and Others" (A180), pp. 106–107.

XCI.   Vivian Shaw [Gilbert Seldes], "This Side of Innocence" (A187), pp. 107–109.

XCII.   Zelda Sayre [Fitzgerald], "Friend Husband's Latest" (A186), pp. 110–111.

XCIII.   W. E. W., "Startling Picture of 'Idle Rich Class'" (A190), p. 112.

XCIV.   "'The Beautiful and Damned'" (A126), pp. 112–114.

XCV.   Review of *The Beautiful and Damned* (A144), p. 114.

XCVI.   Catherine Myers, "This Is What Happens to Naughty Flappers" (A181), pp. 114–115.

XCVII.   William Curtis, "Some Recent Books" (A161), pp. 115–117.

XCVIII.   N. B. L., "Fitzgerald's Latest Not for All Palates" (A175), pp. 117–118.

XCIX.   H. W. Boynton, "Flashlight and Flame" (A155), pp. 118–119.

C.   Mary M. Colum, "Certificated, Mostly" (A160), pp. 119–121.

CI.   Burton Rascoe, "Novels from the Younger Set" (A184), p. 121.

CII.   "*Beautiful and Damned* by F. S. Fitzgerald" (A130), p. 122.

CIII.   "How Can We Tell What Effect a Book Will Have?" (A137), pp. 122–123.

CIV.   Robert Littell, "*The Beautiful and Damned*" (A177), pp. 123–125.

CXXII.   Margaret Culkin Banning, "Uneven Work of a Genius" (A229), pp. 147–148.

CXXIII.   "Fitzgerald's Short Stories" (A214), p. 148.

CXXIV.   "Scott Fitzgerald Scores One More" (A223), pp. 148–149.

CXXV.   Review of *Tales of the Jazz Age* (A222), p. 149.

CXXVI.   Hildegarde Hawthorne, Review of *Tales of the Jazz Age* (A238), pp. 149–151.

CXXVII.   "'Tales of the Jazz Age'" (A227), pp. 151–152.

CXXVIII.   Edmund Wilson, Jr., "The Jazz King Again" (A251), pp. 152–153.

CXXIX.   G[orham] B. M[unson], Review of *Tales of the Jazz Age* (A244), p. 153.

CXXX.   M[ary] B[elle] S[wan], "*Tales of the Jazz Age* Caviar for Jaded Taste" (G10), pp. 153–154.

CXXXI.   John Gunther, "Fitzgerald 'Collects'" (A237), pp. 154–155.

CXXXII.   Stephen Vincent Benét, "Plotting an Author's Curve" (A230), pp. 155–156.

CXXXIII.   "F. Scott Fitzgerald Puffs as Jazz Age Outpaces Him" (A215), p. 157.

CXXXIV.   Review of *Tales of the Jazz Age* (A221), pp. 157–158.

CXXXV.   Woodward Boyd, "The Fitzgerald Legend" (B50), pp. 158–161.

CXXXVI.   "'Tales of the Jazz Age'" (A226), pp. 161–162.

CXXXVII.   "Too Much Fire Water" (A228), pp. 162–163.

CXXXVIII.   I. E. L., Review of *Tales of the Jazz Age* (A240), p. 163.

CXXXIX.   H. L. Mencken, Review of *Tales of the Jazz Age* (G9), p. 163.

CXL.   H. B. D., "Clever Stories of the Jazz Age by Fitzgerald," pp. 163–164.
Unidentified clipping found in F's scrapbook. "No one—not even Tarkington—has recorded the dialogues of this generation with more

fidelity than" F. "And yet an air of the specially recreated hangs about them all, a selective and soundly inventive reporting."

CXLI.   A. A. White, "The Jazz Age in Story," pp. 164–166. Unidentified clipping found in F's scrapbook. Volume "does not offer the same material for recondite critical argument that made 'The Beautiful and Damned' such a widely discussed book, but it is certainly full of popular interest...."

CXLII.   E. W. Osborn, "'The Vegetable' by F. Scott Fitzgerald" (A316), p. 169.

CXLIII.   Burton Rascoe, "A Bookman's Day Book" (A317), pp. 169–170.

CXLIV.   "Eminent Novelist Turns to Comedy" (A269), pp. 170–171.

CXLV.   Harry Hansen, "About Eggs, Yokels and Just Folks" (A303), pp. 171–172.

CXLVI.   P[hil] A. Kinsley, "'The Vegetable' Proves Bird When Right Post Is Found" (A310), pp. 172–173.

CXLVII.   John Clair Minot, "*The Vegetable*" (A313), pp. 173-174.

CXLVIII.   Frederic F. Van de Water, "Books and So Forth" (A321), pp. 174–175.

CXLIX.   R. F., "The Day's Best Book" (G16), p. 175.

CL.   Howard Weeks, "F. S. Fitzgerald" (A324), pp. 175–176.

CLI.   "Fitzgerald Writes a Play" (A274), pp. 176–177.

CLII.   "'The Vegetable' Is Clever Play" (A291), pp. 177–178.

CLIII.   Review of *The Vegetable* (A286), p. 178.

CLIV.   J. W. Rogers, "F. Scott Fitzgerald's Brilliance Like Too Many Diamonds or Too Much Cake Icing; Needs Tempering" (A318), pp. 179–180.

CLV.   "*The Vegetable*" (A289), pp. 180–181.

CLVI.   A. Donald Douglas, "An Enchanted Vegetable" (A300), pp. 181–182.

CLVII.   Edmund Wilson, Jr., "A Selection of Bric-a-Brac" (A326), p. 182.

CLVIII.   "Fitzgerald's 'The Vegetable'" (A272), pp. 182–183.

CLIX.   "Fitzgerald as a Dramatist" (A270), pp. 183–184.

CLX.   John F Carter, Jr., "Scott Fitzgerald's Play" (A297), pp. 184–185.

CLXI.   Hamilton Thornton, "New Novel [*sic*] Called Three-Act Hybrid of Farce and Flippancy" (A320), p. 186.

CLXII.   [Anna L. Hopper], "Scott Fitzgerald as Dramatist" (A307), p. 187.

CLXIII.   L[isle] B[ell], Review of *The Vegetable* (A294), p. 187.

CLXIV.   Review of *The Vegetable* (A284), p. 188.

CLXV.   Anna Hazelton, "'The Vegetable'" (A304), pp. 188-189.

CLXVI.   Duncan Aikman, "Fitzgerald Comedy a Satire on Modern System of Democracy" (A293), p. 189.

CLXVII.   "New Comedy at Shore" (A327), p. 193.

CLXVIII.   "F. Scott Fitzgerald's Latest a Dud" (A333), p. 195.

CLXIX.   Ruth Snyder, "A Minute or Two with Books—F. Scott Fitzgerald Ventures" (A381), pp. 195–196.

CLXX.   Fanny Butcher, "New Fitzgerald Book Proves He's Really a Writer" (A352), pp. 196–197.

CLXXI.   Ruth Hale, "The Paper Knife" (A360), p. 197.

CLXXII.   Hunter Stagg, "Scott Fitzgerald's Latest Novel Is Heralded as His Best" (A382), pp. 198–199.

CLXXIII.   Edwin Clark, "Scott Fitzgerald Looks into Middle Age" (A354), pp. 199–200.

CLXXIV.   Isabel Paterson, "Up to the Minute" (A375), pp. 200–202.

CLXXV.   Review of *The Great Gatsby* (A342), pp. 202–203.

CLXXVI.   Review of *The Great Gatsby* (A346), p. 203.

CLXXVII.   Laurence Stallings, "The First Reader—Great Scott" (A383), pp. 203–205.

CLXXVIII.   Ralph Coghlan, "F. Scott Fitzgerald" (A355), pp. 205–206.

CLXXIX.   Phil A. Kinsley, "Man of Mystery Reigned Where Life Was Riotous" (A367), pp. 207–208.

CLXXX.   Baird Leonard, Review of *The Great Gatsby* (A368), p. 208.

CLXXXI.   E. K., Review of *The Great Gatsby* (A365), pp. 208–209.

CLXXXII.   Herbert S. Gorman, "Scott Fitzgerald's Novel" (A359), pp. 209–211.

CLXXXIII.   H. L. Mencken, "As H. L. M. Sees It" (A370), pp. 211–214.

CLXXXIV.   Walter Yust, "Jazz Parties on Long Island Beach—But F. Scott Fitzgerald Is Growing Up" (A386), pp. 214–216.

CLXXXV.   Review of *The Great Gatsby* (A341), p. 216.

CLXXXVI.   Clifford Trembly, "Gatsby, Esq." (A384), pp. 216–217.

CLXXXVII.   "Fitzgerald Has New Jazz Novel" (A331), p. 217.

CLXXXVIII.   H. B., "Books on Our Table" (A349), pp. 218–219.

CLXXXIX.   William Rose Benét, "An Admirable Novel" (A350), pp. 219–221.

CXC.   "Fitzgerald Squeezes Out a Tale of Brawlish Drinking" (A332), pp. 221–222.

CXCI.   Harvey Eagleton, "Prophets of the New Age—III. F. Scott Fitzgerald" (A357), pp. 222–224.

CXCII.   Lillian C. Ford, "The Seamy Side of Society" (A358), pp. 224–225.

CXCIII.   [Anna L. Hopper], "*The Great Gatsby*" (A363), p. 225.

CXCIV.   "Incorruptible Yegg" (A337), p. 226.

CXCV.   William Curtis, "Some Recent Books" (A356), pp. 226–228.

CXCVI.   Carl Van Vechten, "Fitzgerald on the March" (A385), pp. 229–230.

CXCVII.   Review of *The Great Gatsby* (A343), p. 230.

CXCVIII.   Harry Hansen, "Lots of Good Things" (A361), pp. 230–231.

CXCIX. Review of *The Great Gatsby* (A340), p. 23.

CC. John McClure, "Literature—and Less" (A369), pp. 232–233.

CCI. Isabel Paterson, "Rags to Riches in New Novels" (G61), pp. 233–234.

CCII. "Society and the Fringe" (A348), p. 234.

CCIII. John M. Kenny, Jr., Review of *The Great Gatsby* (A366), pp. 234–235.

CCIV. Gretchen Mount, "And So This is Fitzgerald!" (A372), pp. 235–237.

CCV. Review of *The Great Gatsby* (A344), p. 237.

CCVI. Thomas Caldecot Chubb, "Bagdad-on-Subway" (A353), pp. 237–239.

CCVII. William Lyon Phelps, Review of *The Great Gatsby* (A376), p. 239.

CCVIII. Gilbert Seldes, "Spring Flight" (A380), pp. 239–241.

CCIX. Grant Overton, "Have You Read—?" (A374), pp. 241–242.

CCX. Gilbert Seldes, Review of *The Great Gatsby* (A379), pp. 242–243.

CCXI. Conrad Aiken, Review of *The Great Gatsby* (A389), pp. 243–244.

CCXII. McAlister Coleman, "The Gin Age," p. 244.
Unidentified clipping found in F's scrapbook. "No author, alive or dead, can surpass this amazing young man when he sits down to write about flappers and gin and balked youth."

CCXIII. Walter K. Schwinn, "Mr. Fitzgerald Grows Older," pp. 245–246.
Unidentified clipping found in F's scrapbook. The "chief superiority" of GG is "the masterly organization of the narrative" and, in general, GG is "a stride" forward for F.

CCXIV. Edward Shenton, "*The Great Gatsby* Establishes Scott Fitzgerald as an Artist," pp. 246–247.
Unidentified clipping found in F's scrapbook. GG is "a mature conception, adroitly planned, executed with great cunning, incredibly alive, written with economy, with subtle feeling for beauty."

ccxv.   "F. Scott Fitzgerald: Artist," pp. 247–248.
Unidentified clipping found in F's scrapbook. GG is "a work of art.
Impersonal, almost Olympian in its detachment,...excellently taken and
sustained without flaw throughout. The tragedy and the irony of the
end surpasses pity and one is left with a sense of satisfaction, of a resolution of conflicting elements that is right, that is practically
inevitable."

ccxvi.   "A Remarkable Feat," pp. 248–249.
Unidentified clipping found in F's scrapbook. "In 'The Great
Gatsby' Scott Fitzgerald has achieved what he has been hinting at all
the time."

ccxvii.   Henry F. Pringle, "F. Scott Fitzgerald Grows Older and
Serene In His Book of Stories" (A428), pp. 253–254.

ccxviii.   James Gray, "The World of Art, Books and Drama"
(A420), pp. 254–255.

ccxix.   Harry Hansen, "The Boy Grows Older" (A421), pp.
255–256.

ccxx.   George Currie, "Passed in Review" (A417), pp.
256–257.

ccxxi.   "Scott Fitzgerald Turns a Corner" (A408), pp. 257–258.

ccxxii.   "Stories About 'All the Sad Young Men'" (A410), pp.
258–259.

ccxxiii.   E. C. Beckwith, "Volume of F. Scott Fitzgerald Stories
in Which 'Absolution' Reigns Supreme" (A413), pp. 260–261.

ccxxiv.   "Short Stories by Fitzgerald" (A409), p. 261.

ccxxv.   "'All the Sad Young Men' Is Scott Fitzgerald's Latest"
(A394), pp. 261–262.

ccxxvi.   Review of All the Sad Young Men (A405), pp. 262–263.

ccxxvii.   [Osman C. Hooper], Review of All the Sad Young Men
(A422), p. 263.

ccxxviii.   R. Ellsworth Larsson, "The Young, Sad Years" (A423),
pp. 263–265.

ccxxix.   "Pierrot Penseroso" (A399), p. 265.

ccxxx.   Louise Maunsell Field, "Three Exhibits of Drifting
Americans" (A418), pp. 266–267.

CCXXXI. Baird Leonard, Review of *All the Sad Young Men* (A424), p. 267.

CCXXXII. William Rose Benét, "Art's Bread and Butter" (A414), pp. 267–268.

CCXXXIII. John McClure, "Literature and Less" (A426), p. 269.

CCXXXIV. Frances Newman, "One of the Wistful Young Men" (A427), pp. 270–271.

CCXXXV. Malcolm Cowley, Review of *All the Sad Young Men* (G62), pp. 271–272.

CCXXXVI. "The Best of His Time" (A395), p. 272.

CCXXXVII. Review of *All the Sad Young Men* (A401), p. 273.

CCXXXVIII. Bellamy Partridge, "Some Good Short Stories" (G63), p. 273.

CCXXXIX. Review of *All the Sad Young Men* (A406), pp. 273–274.

CCXL. Clarence Gaines, Review of *All the Sad Young Men* (A419), p. 274.

CCXLI. Review of *All the Sad Young Men* (A403), pp. 274–275.

CCXLII. Leon Whipple, Review of *All the Sad Young Men* (A431), p. 275.

CCXLIII. Conrad Aiken, Review of *All the Sad Young Men* (A411), pp. 275–276.

CCXLIV. Brooks Cottle, "Books and Their Authors," pp. 276–277.
Unidentified clipping found in F's scrapbook. "The best of the stories in" ATSYM reveal "more of the same satire and artistic economy that marked" GG. F "has disciplined himself."

CCXLV. Clyde B. Davis, Review of *All the Sad Young Men*, pp. 277–278.
Unidentified clipping found in F's scrapbook. "There is...less of the prodigy and more of the mature artist in this volume than in his previous work." "Absolution" is a "masterpiece."

CCXLVI. M. H. K., "'All the Sad Young Men,'" pp. 278–279.
Unidentified clipping found in F's scrapbook. "All the stories are intensely human and all are realism of the sort that belongs to life in this third decade of the twentieth century."

CCXLVII.   "Jeunesse Doree," pp. 279–280.
Unidentified clipping found in F's scrapbook. "The Rich Boy" is
"the best piece of work the author has ever done" because it "has a
touch of a universal and timeless comment on human experience."

CCXLVIII.   Mary M. Colum, "The Psychopathic Novel" (A450),
pp. 283–286.

CCXLIX.   Burton Rascoe, Review of *Tender Is the Night* (A477),
pp. 286–287.

CCL.   Edward Weeks, Review of *Tender Is the Night* (A486),
p. 287.

CCLI.   Katherine McClure Anderson, "Today's Book" (A439),
pp. 287–288.

CCLII.   James Gray, "Scott Fitzgerald Re-enters, Leading
Bewildered Giant" (A459), pp. 288–290.

CCLIII.   Harry Hansen, "The First Reader" (A461), pp.
291–292.

CCLIV.   Gilbert Seldes, "True to Type—Scott Fitzgerald Writes
Superb Tragic Novel" (A480), pp. 292–293.

CCLV.   Hal Borland, "'Of Making Many Books—'" (A441),
pp. 293–294.

CCLVI.   John Chamberlain, "Books of The Times" (A446), pp.
294–296.

CCLVII.   Lewis Gannett, "Books and Things" (A456), pp.
296–297.

CCLVIII.   Clyde Beck, "The Doctor and the Movie Star" (A440),
p. 298.

CCLIX.   Fanny Butcher, "New Fitzgerald Book Brilliant; Fails as
Novel" (A444), pp. 298–299.

CCLX.   Henry Seidel Canby, "In the Second Era of Demoralization" (A445), pp. 300–301.

CCLXI.   Clifton Fadiman, "F. Scott Fitzgerald" (A454), pp.
301–303.

CCLXII.   Edith H. Walton, "Stale; Unprofitable" (A485), pp.
303–304.

CCLXXXII.   C. Hartley Grattan, Review of *Tender Is the Night* (A457), pp. 326–328.

CCLXXXIII.   Gertrude Diamant, "Child Prodigy" (A453), pp. 328–331.

CCLXXXIV.   Review of *Tender Is the Night* (A434), pp. 331–332.

CCLXXXV.   William Soskin, Review of *Tender Is the Night*, pp. 332–334. Unidentified clipping found in F's scrapbook. "Mr. Fitzgerald has applied his admirable ability to state meanings in terms of character and incident to this book, but I find both his characters and incidents often blurred, sometimes melodramatically forced and overwritten."

CCLXXXVI.   James Gray, "Scott Fitzgerald Brilliance Bared in Short Stories" (A513), pp. 337–338.

CCLXXXVII.   Arthur Coleman, "Stories by F. Scott Fitzgerald Are Merely Entertaining" (A512), pp. 338–339.

CCLXXXVIII.   P. H., "Three New Books From Fictioneers of Varied Merit" (A515), pp. 339–340.

CCLXXXIX.   John Chamberlain, "Books of The Times" (A511), pp. 340–342.

CCXC.   Elizabeth Hart, "F. Scott Fitzgerald, Looking Backward" (A516), pp. 342–343.

CCXCI.   Edith H. Walton, "Scott Fitzgerald's Tales" (A526), pp. 344–345.

CCXCII.   "Mr. Fitzgerald Grows Up" (A502), pp. 345–346.

CCXCIII.   N. H., "Short Stories" (A514), pp. 346–347.

CCXCIV.   T. S. Matthews, Review of *Taps at Reveille* (A518), p. 347.

CCXCV.   William Troy, "The Perfect Life" (A524), pp. 347–349.

CCXCVI.   Joan Nourse, "Better Short Stories by Fitzgerald" (A519), pp. 350–351.

CCXCVII.   Anne Perry, Review of *Taps at Reveille* (A521), pp. 351–352.

CCXCVIII.   Howard Baker, Review of *Taps at Reveille* (A509), p. 352.

CCXCIX.   Roger Pippett, "Last Book Is a Credit to F. Scott Fitzgerald" (A584), pp. 355–356.

CCC.   Milton Rugoff, Review of *The Last Tycoon* (A586), pp. 356–358.

CCCI.   James Gray, "Epitaph for Fitzgerald: Fascination and Faulty [*sic*]" (A575), pp. 358–360.

CCCII.   "Unfinished Life" (A561), pp. 360–361.

CCCIII.   Robert J. Conklin, "F. Scott Fitzgerald's Last Novel Unfinished" (A569), pp. 361–362.

CCCIV.   Joseph Henry Jackson, "Scott Fitzgerald's Posthumous Novel Limns U.S. Transition" (A578), pp. 362–363.

CCCV.   Margaret Marshall, "Notes by the Way" (A582), pp. 363–364.

CCCVI.   W. M. R., "Fitzgerald's Tragedy of Hollywood" (A585), pp. 364–366.

CCCVII.   J. Donald Adams, "Scott Fitzgerald's Last Novel" (A562), pp. 366–368.

CCCVIII.   Clifton Fadiman, "Fitzgerald, McFee, and Others" (A572), pp. 368–369.

CCCIX.   John T. Appleby, "Post-Mortem Findings" (A563), pp. 369–371.

CCCX.   Louis Nicholas, "F. Scott Fitzgerald's Novel an Anatomy of Hollywood" (A583), pp. 371–372.

CCCXI.   Roger Dow, "Books and Authors" (A570), pp. 372–373.

CCCXII.   Arnold Gingrich, "F. Scott Fitzgerald's Final Novel of a Bygone Era" (A573), pp. 373–374.

CCCXIII.   Stephen Vincent Benét, "Fitzgerald's Unfinished Symphony" (A566), pp. 374–376.

CCCXIV.   Millen Brand, "Fitzgerald's Last Novel" (A567), pp. 376–377.

CCCXV.   Robert Littell, Review of *The Last Tycoon* (A579), p. 377.

cccxvi.   Edward Weeks, Review of *The Last Tycoon* (A591), pp. 377–379.

cccxvii.   Ray Gould, "The Last Novel of Scott Fitzgerald; A Great, Unfinished Masterpiece" (A574), pp. 379–380.

cccxviii.   James Thurber, "Taps at Assembly" (A589), pp. 380–382.

REVIEWS:

i.   Ellis, James. Review of *F. Scott Fitzgerald—The Critical Reception*, *Southern Humanities Review*, 15 (Spring 1981), 173–174.

ii.   Seiters, Dan. Review of *F. Scott Fitzgerald—The Critical Reception*, *Fitzgerald/Hemingway Annual*, 11 (1979), 443–445.

iii.   Staley, Thomas F. Review of *F. Scott Fitzgerald—The Critical Reception*, *Tulsa Home & Garden*, 3 (December 1978), 96.

I74.   ———, ed. THE SHORT STORIES OF F. SCOTT FITZGERALD—NEW APPROACHES IN CRITICISM. Madison: University of Wisconsin Press, 1982. 384 pp.

I.   [Jackson R. Bryer], "Introduction," pp. xi-xviii.
Cites critical and scholarly neglect of F's stories as justification for collection of new essays and briefly describes value of several of the essays in the collection.

II.   Richard Lehan, "The Romantic Self and the Uses of Place in the Stories of F. Scott Fitzgerald," pp. 3–21.
Groups F's stories around F's novels which are contemporaneous with them and discusses how his sense of place and of the romantic self changes in the course of his career, citing many specific stories in the discussion.

III.   Lawrence Buell, "The Significance of Fantasy in Fitzgerald's Short Fiction," pp. 23–38.
Surveys the use of the fantastic in F's stories, with emphasis on "The Diamond as Big as the Ritz."

IV.   Kenneth E. Eble, "Touches of Disaster: Alcoholism and Mental Illness in Fitzgerald's Short Stories," pp. 39–52.
Discussion of how F "treated alcoholism and mental illness in his fiction," with emphasis on "A New Leaf," "An Alcoholic Case," the

"C-U" essays, and on Dr. Donald Goodwin's research on F's alcoholism.

v.   C. Hugh Holman, "Fitzgerald's Changes on the Southern Belle: The Tarleton Trilogy," pp. 53–64.

Discusses role the South played in F's life and work, with emphasis on "The Ice Palace," "The Jelly-Bean," and "The Last of the Belles," and on their depiction of the Southern belle.

vi.   Alan Margolies, "'Kissing, Shooting, and Sacrificing': F. Scott Fitzgerald and the Hollywood Market," pp. 65–73.

Examines several of F's stories to show that they were "written with an eye on sales to Hollywood," containing in them "visual effects important to the movies" as well as allusions to film-making. Emphasizes "The Offshore Pirate" and "Dice, Brass Knuckles & Guitar."

vii.   Scott Donaldson, "Money and Marriage in Fitzgerald's Stories," pp. 75–88.

Traces how F's stories "reveal his changing attitudes toward money and marriage," dividing them into those which depict "the success, or seeming success, of the poor young man in wooing the rich girl," and those in which "the young man is rejected in his quest or subsequently disapointed."

viii.   Joseph Mancini, Jr., "To Be Both Light and Dark: The Jungian Process of Individuation in Fitzgerald's Basil Duke Lee Stories," pp. 89–110.

Traces through the Basil stories Jung's process of individuation, in which "the individual learns to distinguish himself from two modes of collective life, the unconscious realm or ground of all being, and the conscious world of society."

ix.   Ruth Prigozy, "Fitzgerald's Short Stories and the Depression: An Artistic Crisis," pp. 111–126.

Discusses stories F wrote between 1929 and 1935 as indices to his "artistic crisis when his subjects were as serious as his and the nation's trials demanded, but his plots were outworn, stale, mechanical" and to his struggles with plot and style. Emphasizes "Babylon Revisited" and "Crazy Sunday."

x.   Robert A. Martin, "Hollywood in Fitzgerald: After Paradise," pp. 127–148.

Traces F's associations with Hollywood biographically and in his fiction, with emphasis on "The Diamond as Big as the Ritz," "Our Own Movie Queen," "Jacob's Ladder," "Magnetism," and "Crazy Sunday."

XI.   James L. W. West III, "Fitzgerald and *Esquire*," pp. 149–166.

Outlines F's relationship with *Esquire* and its editor Arnold Gingrich and examines "Three Acts of Music" and "The Lost Decade" as stories which "employ a compressed, understated method which is quite unusual in Fitzgerald's fiction."

XII.   John Kuehl, "Psychic Geography in 'The Ice Palace,'" pp. 169–179.

Discusses "The Ice Palace" as exemplary of the significance of the North and South of F's psyche and cites the contrasts and oppositions present in the story.

XIII.   James W. Tuttleton, "Seeing Slightly Red: Fitzgerald's 'May Day,'" pp. 181–197.

Examines "May Day" as a story which "combines with uncommon adroitness the social and the psychological, the public and the private tensions of Fitzgerald the man and the historical moment, the year 1919," and as presenting "nearly all of the themes" of F's "major and more mature stories." Stresses influence of Mencken, F's "lifelong sympathy with the ideology of socialism," and the story's "rather confused and ambivalent" treatment of socialism.

XIV.   Neil D. Isaacs, "'Winter Dreams' and Summer Sports," pp. 199–207.

Finds in F's fascination with and use of sports and sports figures in his fiction "a potential clue to an enriched understanding" of "Winter Dreams," as well as an approach which tells us "something that is central to Fitzgerald's work in general and...a primary element in accounting for the persistence of his strong following among young contemporary audiences."

XV.   Irving Malin, "'Absolution': Absolving Lies," pp. 209–216.

Detailed explication of "Absolution" as a story which "asks whether art itself—that is, imagination, dream, romance—can be as sufficient, helpful, and necessary as religious belief. Is faith in the other world enough to help us live here and now? What is the connection between artistic 'lies' and religious 'truths?'"

XVI.   Victor Doyno, "'No Americans Have Any Imagination': 'Rags Martin-Jones and the Pr-nce of W-les,'" pp. 217–225.

Uses stylistic, folkloristic, thematic, structural, genetic, and contextual critical approaches to illuminate different facets of "Rags Martin-Jones and the Pr-nce of W-les."

XVII.   Christiane Johnson, "Freedom, Contingency, and Ethics in 'The Adjuster,'" pp. 227–240.

Examines "The Adjuster" in detail as a story without "a clear focus" and with a "contrived" conclusion, but also as a story which "touches on most of the themes deal to the author and foreshadows concerns that he developed in his later work, especially in *Tender Is the Night.*"

XVIII.   Peter Wolfe, "Faces in a Dream: Innnocence Perpetuated in 'The Rich Boy,'" pp. 241–249.

Explicates "The Rich Boy" with respect to its theme, structure, use of a narrator, and characterizations.

XIX.   Melvin J. Friedman, "'The Swimmers': Paris and Virginia Reconciled," pp. 251–260.

Examines the French-American elements of "The Swimmers" in effort to show that it "somehow becomes a better story when viewed in terms of its 'transatlantic refraction.'"

XX.   James J. Martine, "Rich Boys and Rich Men: 'The Bridal Party,'" pp. 261–268.

Examines "The Bridal Party" in context with "May Day" and "Magnetism" to show that F's "understanding of the rich, the human situation, and the processes of male maturity" is deeper in it than in the earlier two stories.

XXI.   Carlos Baker, "When the Story Ends: 'Babylon Revisited,'" pp. 269–277.

Discusses "Babylon Revisited" in terms of its "double theme of freedom and imprisonment, of locking out and locking in," and also examines details of F's later life in Hollywood which reinforce this theme.

XXII.   Sheldon Grebstein, "The Sane Method of 'Crazy Sunday,'" pp. 279–289.

Examines the "subtle and controlled method" of "Crazy Sunday," focusing on its "'crazy'" motif, its "emphasis upon the artificiality and theatricality" of the Hollywood party scene as a "microcosm," and its use of eye imagery and images of seeing.

XXIII.   George Monteiro, "Two Sets of Books, One Balance Sheet: 'Financing Finnegan,'" pp. 291–299.

Suggests that "Financing Finnegan" presents in the narrator (F) and Finnegan (Hemingway) F's answer to Hemingway's "poor Scott" remark by portraying Finnegan-Hemingway as the same sort of scapegoat that Hemingway made F in "The Snows of Kilimanjaro."

xxiv.   Jackson R. Bryer, "The Short Stories of F. Scott Fitzgerald: A Checklist of Criticism," pp. 303–377.

Unannotated listing which includes collections containing F short stories; books on F's work containing discussion of the short stories; dissertations containing discussion of F's short stories; general books containing discussion of several F short stories; general articles containing discussion of several F short stories; reviews of F short story collections; and criticism, explication, and commentary on individual stories, listed by story—including specific articles, segments from books on F's work, and segments from general books.

I75.   ————, and John Kuehl. "Introduction." In F. Scott Fitzgerald. *The Basil and Josephine Stories*. NY: Charles Scribner's, 1973. Pp. vii-xxvi.

Gives background to the composition of the stories, notes F's original plan to publish them as a novel, and justifies printing them in full together on the basis of an increased appreciation of their themes and characters which is gained by such an arrangement. Devotes considerable attention to tracing recurrent themes, techniques, characters, and structural patterns through the stories.

Bryson, Lyman. See Trilling (I350).

Buell, Lawrence. See Bryer, ed. (I74)

I76.   Bulhof, Francis. *"Le Grand Meaulnes* and *The Great Gatsby."* In Ferdinand van Ingen, Elrud Kunne-Ibsch, Hans de Leeuwe, and Frank C. Maatje, eds. *Dichter und Leser: Studien zur Literatur*. Groningen: Wolters-Noordhoff, 1972. Pp. 276–286.

Compares and contrasts the two novels which share as their "two main motifs" the "problem of the past and the question of honesty," as well as similarities in the use of the narrator, in the emphasis on the "desolation of everyday life," and in the conflict between big city and countryside.

I77.   Burgess, Anthony. *Ernest Hemingway and His World*. NY: Charles Scribner's, 1978. Pp. 19, 43, 45, 57, 68, 70, 83, 115, 116.

Brief mentions of Hemingway's personal and professional relationships with F.

I78.   Buttitta, Tony. AFTER THE GOOD GAY TIMES— ASHEVILLE—SUMMER OF '35—A SEASON WITH F. SCOTT FITZGERALD. NY: Viking Press, 1974. 173 pp.

Memoir of friendship with F based on F's visits to Buttitta's bookstore, notes on which he "jotted down at the time on the fly-leaves of about sixty books, many of which are still in my library." These notes record, often in F's words, "a record of visits, events, encounters, phone calls that took place between" F, Buttitta, "and a few others"; they are supplemented by articles and reviews Buttitta wrote then and later, letters, and by the files of *Contempo* magazine.

REVIEWS:

i.   Anonymous. Review of *After the Good Gay Times— Asheville—Summer of '35—A Season With F. Scott Fitzgerald, The Booklist*, 70 (June 15, 1974), 1125.

ii.   ————. Review of *After the Good Gay Times— Asheville—Summer of '35—A Season With F. Scott Fitzgerald, Choice*, 11 (November 1974), 1304.

iii.   ————. Review of *After the Good Gay Times— Asheville—Summer of '35—A Season With F. Scott Fitzgerald, Journal of Modern Literature*, 4 (Supplement 1975), 1039.

iv.   ————. Review of *After the Good Gay Times— Asheville—Summer of '35—A Season With F. Scott Fitzgerald, Kirkus*, 42 (April 1, 1974), 395.

v.   ————. "Writer Draws Portrait of Scott Fitzgerald's Affinity with Asheville," Asheville (N.C.) *Citizen-Times*, June 23, 1974, p. 16B.

vi.   Alexander, John. "Book, etcetera—Summer Books, Good and Bad," Charlotte *News*, July 8, 1974, p. 12A.

vii.   Avant, Julia K. "Guide to Good Reading—Tony Buttitta's Book Received By Library," Monroe (La.) *Morning World*, September 22, 1974, p. 14-A.

viii.   Baker, Carlos. "And Reliving Fitzgerald's 'Sensational' Summer of '35," Chicago *Tribune*, July 14, 1974, "Book World" Section, p. 3.

        Bohen, Mike. "Fitzgerald: Asheville—Summer of '35," *Greensboro Sun* (Greensboro, N.C.), 3 (November 1974), 9. See also *New South Writing*, 1 (April 1976), 50–52.

ix.   Brown, Adger. "Fitzgerald Book: A Nostalgic View," *The State* (Columbia, S.C.), July 28, 1974, p. 4-E.

x.   Brown, Michael. "F. Scott on the Way Down," San Francisco *Chronicle*, August 25, 1974, "This World" Section, p. 31.

xi.   Burton, W. C. "Scott Fitzgerald in Tar Heel Country," Greensboro (N.C.) *Daily News*, September 17, 1978, p. C3.

xii.   DePriest, Joe. "Fitzgerald—Lonely, Aging, He Found a Listener in Asheville," Shelby (N.C.) *Daily Star*, July 13, 1974, p. 12B.

xiii.   Doar, Harriet. "Heat-Lightning: Asheville's Incredible
Summer of '35 Relived in Reminiscence of Fitzgerald," Charlotte
Observer, June 30, 1974, p. 4B.

xiv.   Eason, Henry. "Buttitta Captures Fitzgerald's Unknown
Side," Greenville (S.C.) *News*, July 20, 1974, p. 11.

xv.   Eichelbaum, Stanley. "A Revealing Memoir of Fitzgerald's 'Crack-up,'" San Francisco *Examiner*, July 29, 1974, p. 25.

xvi.   Gaines, C. B. "UNC Grad Writes Memoirs; Recalls
Fitzgerald's Loves," *Daily Tar Heel* (University of North Carolina,
Chapel Hill), July 16, 1974, p. 5.

xvii.   Gregson, Lillian. "Books 'n Stuff," DeKalb (Ga.) *New
Era*, July 25, 1974, p. 2B.

xviii.   H[all], E[lizabeth]. Review of *After the Good Gay
Times—Asheville—Summer of '35—A Season With F. Scott Fitzgerald, Psychology Today*, 8 (January 1975), 96.

xix.   Hodges, Betty. "Betty Hodges' Book Nook," Durham
(N.C.) *Morning Herald*, July 14, 1974, Sec. D, p. 3.

xx.   Houston, Levin. "Fitzgerald: By a Friend," Fredericksburg (Va.) *Free Lance-Star*, September 7, 1974, "Town &
Country" Section, p. 7.

     *Isaac, Dan. "The Other Scott Fitzgerald," *The Nation*,
219 (September 28, 1974), 282–284. See H765.

xxi.   [Johnston, Albert H.] Review of *After the Good Gay
Times—Asheville—Summer of '35—A Season With F. Scott Fitzgerald, Publishers' Weekly*, 205 (April 29, 1974), 46.

xxii.   Jordan, Enoch P. Review of *After the Good Gay Times—
Asheville—Summer of '35—A Season With F. Scott Fitzgerald,
Southern Humanities Review*, 11 (Winter 1977), 68–69.

xxiii.   Kirsch, Robert. "The Book Report—A Footnote to
Fitzgerald," Los Angeles *Times*, July 17, 1974, Part IV, p. 7.

xxiv.   Lee, R. W. "The Bookshelf," El Paso *Herald-Post*,
August 24, 1974, Sec. A, p. 4.

xxv.   McFadden, Jewel. Review of *After the Good Gay
Times—Asheville—Summer of '35—A Season With F. Scott Fitzgerald, Sacramento Bee*, July 21, 1974, p. P5.

xxvi.   McMurtry, Larry. "Ernest and Scott in the Land of
Misery," Washington (D.C.) *Post*, June 17, 1974, p. B4. See also NY
Post, July 17, 1974, p. 17.

xxvii.   McQueen, Debbi. "Decline and Fall of the Great Fitzgerald," Cleveland *Press*, July 26, 1974, "Showtime" Section, p. 23.

xxviii.   Mayo, Michael. "F. Scott Fitzgerald at a Sad, Bad
Time," Roanoke *Times*, August 4, 1974, Sec. H, p. 4.

xxix. Meacham, Harry M. "The Summer of '35: Fitzgerald Went to Asheville in Attempt to Lay Off Booze," Richmond (Va.) *News Leader*, July 3, 1974, p. 15.

xxx. Meehan, James. "'After the Good Gay Times': Scott Fitzgerald in Asheville," Raleigh *News and Observer*, June 30, 1974, Sec. IV, p.7.

xxxi. Monfried, Walter. "After the Age of Gatsby," Milwaukee *Journal*, July 28, 1974, Part 5, p. 4.

xxxii. M[oody], M[innie] H[ite]. "Fitzgerald Talked and Tony Listened," Columbus (Ohio) *Dispatch*, July 21, 1974, p. I–9.

xxxiii. Nathan, Robert S. "With Fitzgerald in Asheville (1935)," Greensboro (N.C.) *Daily News*, August 4, 1974, p. B3.

xxxiv. Nye, Robert. "Hero of a Lost Generation," *Christian Science Monitor*, July 31, 1974, p. 11. See also Minneapolis *Tribune*, August 11, 1974, p. 8D.

xxxv. Perosa, Sergio. Review of *After the Good Gay Times—Asheville—Summer of '35—A Season With F. Scott Fitzgerald*, *Annali di Ca' Foscari*, 13 (No. 2, 1974), 533–534. In Italian.

xxxvi. Reising, Dr. R. W. "Asheville, 1935, and the Private Depression of F. Scott Fitzgerald," *The Robesonian* (Lumberton, N.C.), July 14, 1974, p. 6B.

xxxvii. Shatzkin, Roger. Review of *After the Good Gay Times—Asheville—Summer of '35—A Season With F. Scott Fitzgerald*, *Library Journal*, 99 (June 1, 1974), 1538.

xxxviii. Spearman, Walter. "The Literary Lantern—Fitzgerald's Season of Discontent," Chapel Hill (N.C.) *Weekly*, July 14, 1974, Sec. B, p. 6. See also Greensboro (N.C.) *Record*, July 22, 1974, p. A17.

xxxix. Tanselle, G. Thomas. Review of *After the Good Gay Times—Asheville—Summer of '35—A Season With F. Scott Fitzgerald*, *American Literature*, 47 (March 1975), 131–132.

xl. Taylor, Robert. "Book of the Day—Fitzgerald Is Sacrified [*sic?*]," Boston *Evening Globe*, July 2, 1974, p. 11.

xli. Thompson, Richard J. Review of *After the Good Gay Times—Asheville—Summer of '35—A Season With F. Scott Fitzgerald*, *Best Sellers*, 34 (August 1, 1974), 216.

xlii. Teitel, Nathan. "Burnt Out in Asheville," *Newsday* (Garden City, NY), July 28, 1974, "Ideas" Section, p. 19.

xliii. Toledano, Ben C. "Books—Summer Notes on a Man and an Era," New Orleans *States-Item*, August 17, 1974, "Lagniappe" Section, p. 19.

xliv. Waters, Greg. "The Bookshelf—A Different F. Scott Fitzgerald in 'After the Good Gay Times,'" Flint *Journal*, July 7, 1974, p. F–1.

I79.   Callahan, John F. THE ILLUSIONS OF A NATION—
MYTH AND HISTORY IN THE NOVELS OF F. SCOTT FITZ-
GERALD. Urbana: University of Illinois Press, 1972. 221 pp.
Interdisciplinary study which views F as a "novelist who captured
the complexity of the American idealist, the frailty of his historical and
psychic awareness together with his 'willingness of the heart,'" and devotes individual chapters to GG and (briefly) to LT and approximately
two-thirds of the book to a study of TITN.

REVIEWS:

i.   Anonymous. Review of *The Illusions of a Nation—Myth
and History in the Novels of F. Scott Fitzgerald, Choice*, 9 (January
1973), 1445.

ii.   Barfoot, C. C. Review of *The Illusions of a Nation—
Myth and History in the Novels of F. Scott Fitzgerald, English Studies*,
54 (August 1973), 369.

iii.   Hoenisch, Michael. Review of *The Illusions of a
Nation—Myth and History in the Novels of F. Scott Fitzgerald,
Kritikon Litterarum*, 5 (Heft 1, 1976), 64–66.

iv.   Huberman, Edward. Review of *The Illusions of a
Nation—Myth and History in the Novels of F. Scott Fitzgerald, CEA
Critic*, 35 (November 1972), 41.

v.   Jordan, Enoch P. Review of *The Illusions of a Nation—
Myth and History in the Novels of F. Scott Fitzgerald, Southern
Humanities Review*, 11 (Winter 1977), 70.

vi.   Mann, Charles W., Jr. Review of *The Illusions of a
Nation—Myth and History in the Novels of F. Scott Fitzgerald, Library
Journal*, 97 (September 15, 1972), 2842.

vii.   Monaghan, David. Review of *The Illusions of a
Nation—Myth and History in the Novels of F. Scott Fitzgerald,
Dalhousie Review*, 52 (Summer 1972), 325–327.

viii.   Perosa, Sergio. Review of *The Illusions of a Nation—
Myth and History in the Novels of F. Scott Fitzgerald, Annali di
Ca'Foscari*, 13 (No. 2, 1974), 535–536. In Italian.

ix.   S[parks], D[ouglas]. "Illusions of a Nation," Murfreesboro (Tenn.) *Daily News-Journal*, April 30, 1973.

x.   Van Arsdol, Ted. Review of *The Illusions of a Nation—
Myth and History in the Novels of F. Scott Fitzgerald*, Vancouver
(Wash.) *Columbian*, March 4, 1973, Sec. 3, p. 28.

xi.   Waldmeir, Joseph J. Review of *The Illusions of a
Nation—Myth and History in the Novels of F. Scott Fitzgerald, Journal
of Popular Culture*, 6 (Fall 1972), 439.

180.   Callow, James T., and Robert J. Reilly. *Guide to American Literature From Emily Dickinson to the Present.* NY: Barnes & Noble, 1977. Pp. 121–124, 239–241.
Brief biographical introduction, plot summaries of F's major books, and a selected bibliography ot works by and about F.

181.   Canby, Henry S. *American Memoir.* Boston: Houghton Mifflin, 1947. Pp. 263, 301, 340.
Passing mention of F and of TSOP.

182.   Carter, Paul A. *Another Part of the Twenties.* NY: Columbia University Press, 1977. Pp. ix, xi, 1, 31, 113, 126, 128, 141, 159, 197, 207.
Brief passing mention of F, Zelda, and TSOP.

183.   ———. *The Twenties in America.* NY: Thomas Y. Crowell, 1968. Pp. 3, 4, 15–16, 25, 59.
Brief references to F and the 1920s.

184.   Caruthers, Clifford M., ed. *Ring Around Max—The Correspondence of Ring Lardner & Max Perkins.* Dekalb: Northern Illinois University Press, 1973. Pp. ix, x-xi, xiii, xviii, xix, xx, xxi, 1–6, 9, 12–13, 17, 19, 21, 24, 26, 35–36, 40, 43–45, 49–50, 52, 56, 58–59, 66, 68, 72–73, 76, 78, 80–81, 87–88, 90–92, 99–100, 110–113, 116, 120–121, 123–124, 135, 139, 141–147, 150, 155–156, 158–163.
References to F in the Lardner-Perkins correspondence include those to "The Vegetable," "Absolution," the composition process of GG and Lardner's role in it, the F-Hemingway relationship, TITN, ATSYM, the stage version of GG, F's health, Zelda's health, and SMTW.

185.   Cawelti, John G. *Apostles of the Self-Made Man.* Chicago: University of Chicago Press, 1965. Pp. 230–231.
Brief consideration of Jay Gatsby, with Thomas Sutpen and Willie Stark, as examples of the "archetypal self-made man of the twentieth century."

186.   Cerf, Bennett. *At Random—The Reminiscences of Bennett Cerf.* NY: Random House, 1977. Pp. 96, 97, 102, 148, 196, 203.
Brief passing mention of F.

Chandler, Raymond. See MacShane, ed. (I236)

187.   Cheever, John. "F. Scott Fitzgerald." In Louis Kronenberger, ed. *Atlantic Brief Lives—A Biographical Companion to the Arts.* Boston: Little, Brown, 1971. Pp. 275–276.

Brief overview of F's life and achievement. "His greatest innovation was to use social custom, clothing, overheard music, not as history but as an expression of his acute awareness of the meaning of time."

I88.   Chesler, Phyllis. "Women in Asylums: Four Lives." In her *Women and Madness*. Garden City, NY: Doubleday, 1972. Pp. 5–25 [7–9, 13]; see also pp. 30–31, 75.

Asserts that F "was extremely jealous of and threatened by Zelda's considerable literary talent" and that Zelda was "desperately and defiantly at odds with the female role....[She] attempted to escape its half-life by 'going crazy,'" and thus was "superficially freed from [her] female role as private social loser, as wife and mother."

I89.   Churchill, Allen. "Flappers and Philosophers—Scott and Zelda Fitzgerald" and "The Ever-Delayed Departure for Great Neck—Scott and Zelda Fitzgerald." In his *The Literary Decade*. Englewood Cliffs, N.J.: Prentice-Hall, 1971. Pp. 65–78 and 114–129; see also pp. 191–192, and *passim*.

Anecdotal biographical account, with emphasis on the legendary and eccentric aspects of F's life. Includes some summaries of the novels, especially B&D.

Clark, C. E. Frazer. See Bruccoli, ed. (I60)

I90.   Coindreau, Maurice Edgar. *The Time of William Faulkner: A French View of Modern American Fiction*. Tr. and ed. by George McMillan Reeves. Columbia: University of South Carolina Press, 1971. Pp. 104, 164, 179.

Brief comments on TSOP and TITN, as well as brief assessment of F's career.

Coleman, McAlister. See Bryer, ed. (I73)

Cottle, Brooks. See Bryer, ed. (I73)

I90a.   Connolly, Cyril. "A Fitzgerald Entertainment," "Scott Fitzgerald and Edith Wharton," "F. Scott Fitzgerald," and "Scott and Zelda Fitzgerald." In his *The Evening Colonnade*. NY and London: Harcourt Brace Jovanovich, 1975. Pp. 262–264, 264–268, 269–272, 273–276.

Reprinting of Connolly's reviews of *Scott Fitzgerald* (H216a), *Letters* (A922), *Zelda* (I258xxx), and SMTW (K72) which originally appeared in the London *Sunday Times*. Also reprints from the *Times Literary Supplement* Mizener's (H265a) and Turnbull's (H275a) responses to Connolly's review of *Scott Fitzgerald*.

I91.   Cowley, Malcolm.   "Echoes of the Jazz Age." In his *The Dream of the Golden Mountains—Remembering the 1930s.* NY: Viking Press, 1980. Pp. 177–191 [187–191]; see also pp. 33, 40, 111. Reprinting of Cowley's 1964 *Saturday Review* essay (B576).

I92.   ———.   "Fitzgerald—The Romance of Money." In his *A Second Flowering—Works and Days of the Lost Generation.* NY: Viking Press, 1973. Pp. 19–47; see also pp. vii, viii, 7–8, 10, 11, 13, 53, 55–56, 59, 60, 61, 75, 97, 101, 115, 119, 120, 121, 124, 132, 168, 187, 190, 201, 227, 233, 234, 235–236, 237, 238, 239, 240, 242, 247, 249–250, 252, 253, 254–255.
Reprinting of Cowley's 1953 *Western Review* essay (B305) and considerable scattered mention of F as a member of the "lost generation" of American writers in Paris in the 1920s.

I93.   ———.   "Fitzgerald's Goodbye to His Generation." In Henry Dan Piper, ed. *Think Back on Us...: A Contemporary Chronicle of the 1930's.* Carbondale: Southern Illinois University Press, 1967. Pp. 225–228.
Reprinting of Cowley's *New Republic* review of TITN (A451).

I94.   ———.   "A Ghost Story of the Jazz Age." In Martin Levin, ed. *The "Saturday Review" Sampler of Wit and Wisdom.* NY: Simon and Schuster, 1966. Pp. 59–62.
Reprinting of Cowley's 1964 *Saturday Review* essay (B576).

I95.   ———.   "*Tender Is the Night*." In Gilbert A. Harrison, ed. *The Critic as Artist: Essays on Books 1920–1970.* NY: Liveright, 1972. Pp. 86–90.
Reprinting of Cowley's *New Republic* review of TITN (A451).

I96.   Critoph, Gerald E.   "The Flapper and Her Critics." In Carol V. R. George, ed. *"Remember the Ladies"—New Perspectives on Women in American History.* Syracuse, NY: Syracuse University Press, 1975. Pp. 145–160 [147, 148, 155].
Cites F's descriptions of flappers in TSOP, "The Offshore Pirate," and "The Ice Palace."

I97.   Crosland, Andrew T.   A CONCORDANCE TO F. SCOTT FITZGERALD'S "THE GREAT GATSBY." Detroit: Gale/Bruccoli Clark, 1975. 425 pp.
Concordance is keyed to the 1925 first-printing text as emended in Bruccoli's *Apparatus* (I38) and includes: a list of words for which only location is given in the concordance; the concordance itself; a word frequency list in alphabetical order; a word frequency list in numerical order; and a pagination conversion table which enables one to convert

page references to the scarce 1925 first printing of GG to the pagination in the Scribner Library edition.

REVIEWS:

i.   Anonymous. Review of *A Concordance to F. Scott Fitzgerald's "The Great Gatsby," Book Exchange*, No. 328 (July 1975), 5.

ii.   ———. Review of *A Concordance to F. Scott Fitzgerald's "The Great Gatsby," Choice*, 12 (July/August 1975), 660.

iii.   ———. Review of *A Concordance to F. Scott Fitzgerald's "The Great Gatsby," Reference Book Review*, 1 (November 1976), 36.

iv.   ———. Review of *A Concordance to F. Scott Fitzgerald's "The Great Gatsby," Reference Services Review*, 3 (April/June 1975), 142.

v.   *Bickman, Martin. Review of *A Concordance to F. Scott Fitzgerald's "The Great Gatsby," Computers and the Humanities*, 10 (March/April 1976), 124–125.

vi.   Duggan, Margaret M. Review of *A Concordance to F. Scott Fitzgerald's "The Great Gatsby," Fitzgerald/Hemingway Annual*, 7 (1975), 329–330.

vii.   Fried, Lewis. Review of *A Concordance to F. Scott Fitzgerald's "The Great Gatsby," American Reference Books Annual*, 7 (1976), 596–597.

viii.   Olevnik, Peter P. Review of *A Concordance to F. Scott Fitzgerald's "The Great Gatsby," Library Journal*, 100 (July 1975), 1306.

ix.   Perosa, Sergio. Review of *A Concordance to F. Scott Fitzgerald's "The Great Gatsby," Annali di Ca'Foscari*, 13 (No. 2, 1974), 530. In Italian.

x.   *Shillingsburg, Miriam J. "A Rose Is a Four-Letter Word; or, The Machine Makes Another Concordance," *Costerus*, 4 (1975), 137–147 [142–147].

xi.   *Smith, John B. Review of *A Concordance to F. Scott Fitzgerald's "The Great Gatsby," Style*, 10 (Summer 1976), 303–305.

xii.   Thiébeauld, Sylvie B. Review of *A Concordance to F. Scott Fitzgerald's "The Great Gatsby," Bulletin des Bibliothèques de France*, 21 (September-October 1976), 806. In French.

xiii.   Willingham, John R. Review of *A Concordance to F. Scott Fitzgerald's "The Great Gatsby," CEA Forum*, 6 (October 1975), 14.

I98.   Crunden, Robert M. *From Self to Society—1919–1941*.
Englewood Cliffs, N.J.: Prentice-Hall, 1972. Pp. 72–75.
Brief survey of F's career which focuses on him as the embodiment
and depicter of the Twenties.

I99.   Cummings, J. Cicott. *The Higher Journalism*. Mt.
Vernon, NY: Golden Eagle Press, 1936. Unpaged.
One-page parody of F, p. [1].

> Daniels, Howell. See Bradbury and Palmer, eds. (I32)

I100.   Dardis, Tom. "F. Scott Fitzgerald: What Do You Do
When There's Nothing to Do?" In his *Some Time in the Sun*. NY:
Charles Scribner's, 1976; Harmondsworth: Penguin, 1981. Pp. 18–77.
Detailed account of F's years in Hollywood which tries to dispel the
myth that those years in F's life were entirely bleak—he was able to
pay off his debts; he sustained a relationship with Sheilah Graham; he
wrote LT. LT "is undeniable proof that Fitzgerald enjoyed a second
brief, brilliant rebirth in Hollywood." Paperback edition includes, in
footnotes to F chapter (pp. 259–269), "additional letters, telegrams,
and studio memoranda."

I101.   Davidson, Marshall B., and the editors of *American
Heritage*. *The "American Heritage" History of the Writer's America*.
NY: American Heritage, 1973. Pp. 329–331.
Brief survey of F's career.

> Davis, Clyde B. See Bryer, ed. (I73)

I102.   Davis, Owen. *I'd Like to Do It Again*. NY: Farrar &
Rinehart, 1931. Pp. 186–188.
Personal reminiscences of Davis' stage version of GG, which he
calls "really good and moderately successful."

I103.   Day, Douglas. *Malcolm Lowry—A Biography*. NY:
Oxford University Press, 1973. P. 417.
Brief mention of the Lowrys' interest in TITN.

I104.   Dekle, Bernard. "F. Scott Fitzgerald (1896–1940)—
'The Roaring Twenties.'" In his *Profiles of Modern American Authors*.
Rutland, Vt.: Charles E. Tuttle, 1969. Pp. 102–107.
Biographical sketch which focuses on F as spokesman for the
"Roaring Twenties."

I105.   Dickey, James. "F. Scott Fitzgerald's Poetry: The
Unreflecting Shield." In Matthew J. Bruccoli, ed. F. Scott Fitzgerald.
Poems 1911–1940. Bloomfield Hills, Mich., and Columbia, S.C.:
Bruccoli Clark, 1981. Pp. xi–xv.

Discusses the generally low quality of F's poetry, his "lyric insight" (primarily evident in his fiction), and the reasons why F's poetry is worth considering: "Beneath everything here, even the most trivial, there is the flicker of a fine unmistakable consciousness, and one could do worse—a lot worse—than to give each item the attention reserved for the inimitable."

I106.   Dolmetsch, Carl R. *"The Smart Set"—A History and Anthology.* NY: Dial Press, 1966. Pp. 82–83.
Contends that *The Smart Set*'s "discovery...of F. Scott Fitzgerald...must rank among the magazine's finest accomplishments" and gives details of F's association with the magazine.

I107.   Donald, Miles. "The Traditional Novel." In his *The American Novel in the Twentieth Century.* London: David & Charles; NY: Barnes & Noble, 1978. Pp. 13–72 [13–27]; see also pp. 8, 10, 11, 29, 43, 46, 47, 105, 163, 176, 199, 200.
Focuses on GG, with some brief discussions of TSOP and B&D. GG is *"the* American novel" because it "concentrates with the utmost intensity on the greatest American myth—that America is a place where dreams come true." Concludes that F "makes the twentieth-century American novel possible, for he shows that the twentieth century is here and America must learn to make the best of it, and American literature the best *with* it."

I108.   Donaldson, Scott. "Fitzgerald and Hemingway." In James Woodress, ed. *American Literary Scholarship—An Annual—1979.* Durham, N.C.: Duke University Press, 1981. Pp. 155–176.
Critical survey of the year's work in F studies.

I109.   ———. "Fitzgerald and Hemingway." In J. Albert Robbins, ed. *American Literary Scholarship—An Annual—1980.* Durham, N.C.: Duke University Press, 1982. Pp. 173–191.
Critical survey of the year's work in F studies.

I110.   ———. "F. Scott Fitzgerald." In James J. Martine, ed. *Dictionary of Literary Biography. Volume 9—American Novelists, 1910–1945, F. Scott Fitzgerald—O. E. Rölvaag.* Detroit: Gale, 1981. Pp. 3–18.
Biographical and critical overview of F's life and writing career.

I111.   ———. "Scott Versus Ernest." In his *By Force of Will— The Life and Art of Ernest Hemingway.* NY: Viking Press, 1977. Pp. 201–215; see also pp. 28, 36, 38–40, 52, 53, 64, 97, 101, 132, 135, 148, 165, 170, 185, 195, 219, 220, 226, 249, 251, 255, 259.
Explores the F-Hemingway relationship, using letters and *A Moveable Feast* (C77) to trace their friendship from F's early sponsor-

ship of Hemingway to Scribner's to Hemingway's later fictional and non-fictional attacks on F in print and tries to account for the virulence of these attacks. Also includes much passing mention of F in discussion of Hemingway's life and works.

———. See Bryer, ed. (I74)

I112.   Donnelly, Honoria Murphy, with Richard N. Billings. *Sara & Gerald—Villa America and After*. NY: Times Books, 1982. Pp. 3–5, 20–23, 26–28, 37–39, 43–44, 59–60, 100–101, 148–151, 156–164, and *passim*.

Memories of F and Zelda by the Murphys' daughter, as well as extensive quotations from F's and Zelda's letters to the Murphys and the latter's opinions of TITN.

I113.   Doody, Terence. "Clyde and Jephson, Gatsby and Nick." In his *Confession and Community in the Novel*. Baton Rouge: Louisiana State University Press, 1980. Pp. 101–132; see also pp. 9, 14, 96, 98, 146.

Comparison of GG and *An American Tragedy* which focuses on the confessions of the two protagonists, Jay Gatsby and Clyde Griffiths, and the significance of their respective confessors, suggesting that GG is pessimistic in its evasion "of the responsibility to form." Short discussions of "Absolution" and the three "C-U" essays are also included.

Dos Passos, John. See Ludington, ed. (I229)

Doyno, Victor. See Bryer, ed. (I74)

I114.   Durham, Philip. "Jay Gatsby and Hopalong Cassidy." In Ray B. Browne and Donald Pizer, eds. *Themes and Directions in American Literature—Essays in Honor of Leon Howard*. Lafayette, Ind.: Purdue University Studies, 1969. Pp. 163–170.

Discusses the East vs. West theme in GG as illustrating that moving East is mortally destructive to a Westerner like Gatsby. Gatsby's daring would have been appropriate in the mythic West of Hopalong Cassidy, but Cassidy would never have had anything to do with Gatsby's Ben Franklin-like "General Resolves."

I115.   Dyson, A. E. "Faith Among the Ashes: Scott Fitzgerald's *The Great Gatsby*." In his *Between Two Worlds—Aspects of Literary Form*. NY: St. Martin's Press, 1972. Pp. 100–113.

Reprinting of Dyson's 1961 *Modern Fiction Studies* essay (B458).

I116.   Earnest, Ernest. *Expatriates and Patriots—American Artists, Scholars, and Writers in Europe*. Durham, N.C.: Duke University Press, 1968. Pp. 260, 261, 264–266, 267, 268, 272, 273, 275, 277, 280.

Discusses F's escapades in Europe in the 1920s, based on anecdotes of his cronies, and attempts to find links between these anecdotes and characters and events in GG, TITN, and "Babylon Revisited."

I117.   Eble, Kenneth. F. SCOTT FITZGERALD. Twayne's United States Authors Series, No. 36. Revised edition. Boston: Twayne, 1977. 187 pp.

Reprinting of Eble's 1963 survey of F's life and work (C55), with a new "Preface" (unpaginated), an updated "Selected Bibliography" (pp. 169–182), "minor changes here and there in the text," and a new final chapter—"Final Assessment" (pp. 152–161)—which includes a brief review of F criticism and a defense of F's skill as a writer.

————. See Bryer, ed. (I74)

I118.   ————, ed. F. SCOTT FITZGERALD. Contemporary Studies in Literature. NY: McGraw-Hill, 1973. 152 pp.

I.   Kenneth E. Eble, "Introduction," pp. 1–6.

Brief review and general assessment of F scholarship and criticism and explanation of criteria used in selecting material for this collection.

II.   Elizabeth Beckwith MacKie, "My Friend Scott Fitzgerald" (H425), pp. 7–18.

III.   Donald A. Yates, "The Road to 'Paradise': Fitzgerald's Literary Apprenticeship" (B484), pp. 19–33.

IV.   Sy Kahn, "This Side of Paradise: The Pageantry of Disillusion" (F39), pp. 34–47.

V.   Sergio Perosa, "The Beautiful and Damned" (C127), pp. 48–59.

VI.   Robert Ornstein, "Scott Fitzgerald's Fable of East and West" (B338), pp. 60–66.

VII.   John W. Bicknell, "The Waste Land of F. Scott Fitzgerald" (B310), pp. 67–80.

VIII.   Kenneth E. Eble, "The Craft of Revision: The Great Gatsby" (B577), pp. 81–92.

IX.   J. Albert Robbins, "Fitzgerald and the Simple, Inarticulate Farmer" (B514), pp. 93–98.

X.   Arthur Mizener, "Scott Fitzgerald and the 1920s" (B470), pp. 99–111.

XI. William E. Doherty, *"Tender Is the Night* and the 'Ode to a Nightingale'"* (F57), pp. 112–126.

XII. Michael Millgate, *"The Last Tycoon*" (C108), pp. 127–134.

XIII. Midge Decter, "Fitzgerald at the End" (B407a), pp. 135–142.

XIV. [Kenneth E. Eble], "Selected Bibliography," pp. 143–152. Unannotated listing of works by and about F.

REVIEW:

i. Perosa, Sergio. Review of *F. Scott Fitzgerald, Annali di Ca'Foscari*, 13 (No. 2, 1974), 534. In Italian.

I119. Emmitt, Robert J. "Love, Death and Resurrection in *The Great Gatsby*." In Donna G. Fricke and Douglas C. Fricke, eds. *Aeolian Harps—Essays in Literature in Honor of Maurice Browning Cramer*. Bowling Green, Ohio: Bowling Green University Press, 1976. Pp. 273–289.

Suggests that F used the Grail legend, the waste land myth, and "the ancient Semitic and Egyptian resurrection myths" as a "central armature around which he modeled the novel, as well as a resource for much of the elaborative symbolism which adorns it." Focuses on F's choice of symbolic color words and character names, his use of the death and rebirth pattern, and the novel's symbols of seasonal change.

I120. Epstein, Joseph. *Ambition—The Secret Passion*. NY: E. P. Dutton, 1980. Pp. 203–211 and *passim*.

Contends that F has become a mythic figure and gives biographical information to illustrate this claim.

I121. Evert, Walter H. "Coadjustors of Oppression: A Romantic and Modern Theory of Evil." In George Bornstein, ed. *Romantic and Modern—Revaluations of Literary Tradition*. Pittsburgh: University of Pittsburgh Press, 1977. Pp. 29–52 [46–47].

Brief discussion of the "degradation of the divine idea in mortal action" in GG which "consistently turns good into its evil opposite in the novel."

I122. Fahey, William A. F. SCOTT FITZGERALD AND THE AMERICAN DREAM. NY: Thomas Y. Crowell, 1973. 179 pp.

Volume in Crowell's Twentieth-Century American Writers series intended for high school and junior college students. Presents a primarily biographical approach, with a chapter on each of the novels and one on the short stories.

REVIEWS:

    i.   Anonymous. Review of *F. Scott Fitzgerald and the American Dream, Bulletin of the Center for Children's Books,* 27 (December 1973), 63.

    ii.   ————. Review of *F. Scott Fitzgerald and the American Dream, Journal of Modern Literature,* 4 (November 1974), 322.

I123.   Farr, Finis. *O'Hara.* Boston: Little, Brown, 1973. Pp. 187–188, 271–272, and *passim.*

Includes brief discussions of "C-U," "May Day," GG, and LT, as well as mentions of the F-O'Hara relationship and of the similarities between the two writers.

I124.   Fass, Paula S. *The Diamond and the Beautiful— American Youth in the 1920's.* NY: Oxford University Press, 1977. Pp. 17, 25–29, 51, 128, 373.

Briefly discusses F's impact on his generation and his role as a model for the youth of his day, with emphasis on TSOP and GG.

    Faulkner, William. See Blotner, ed. (I27)

I125.   Fetterley, Judith. *"The Great Gatsby*—Fitzgerald's *droit de seigneur."* In her *The Resisting Reader: A Feminist Approach to American Fiction.* Bloomington: Indiana University Press, 1978. Pp. 72–100.

Sees GG as "another American 'love story' centered in hostility to women and the concomitant strategy of the scapegoat" in which Daisy is "the object of the novel's hostility" and the love battle "is here played out as a struggle for power in an elaborate pattern of advantage and disadvantage in which romance is finally but a strategy for male victory." Traces patterns of "investment/divestment" and "advantage/disadvantage" through the novel.

I126.   Finney, Ben. *Feet First.* NY: Crown, 1971. Pp. 26–31. Personal reminiscences of F and Zelda on the Riviera.

I127.   Flahiff, F[rederick] T. *"The Great Gatsby*: Scott Fitzgerald's Chaucerian Rag." In Diane Bessai and David Jackel, eds. *Figures in a Ground: Canadian Essays on Modern Literature Collected in Honor of Sheila Watson.* Saskatoon: Western Producer Prairie, 1978. Pp. 87–98.

Compares and contrasts GG and *Troilus and Criseyde* to support contention that F's novel is a "sequel" to Chaucer's poem.

I128.   Flanner, Janet. *Paris Was Yesterday 1925–1939*. Irving Drutman, ed. NY: Viking Press, 1972. Pp. xviii–xix, 176

Brief references to Flanner's memories of F.

I129.   Foltinek, Herbert. "A Hero Born to Be Hanged: A Comparative Study." In Sy M. Kahn and Martha Raetz, eds. *Interculture—A Collection of Essays and Creative Writing Commemorating the Twentieth Anniversary of the Fulbright Program at the Institute of Translation and Interpretation, University of Vienna (1955–1974)*. Vienna: Wilhelm Braumuller, 1975. Pp. 179–187 [185].

Brief mention of GG and "Winter Dreams" in study of young men with humble beginnings who rise.

I130.   Ford, Corey. *Time of Laughter*. Boston: Little, Brown, 1967. Pp. 163–165.

Memories of F in Hollywood in the late 1930s, when he was writing LT and "on the wagon."

I131.   Ford, Hugh. *Published in Paris—American and British Writers, Printers, and Publishers in Paris, 1920–1939*. NY: Macmillan, 1975. Pp. 154–155 and *passim*.

Brief mention of F's introduction of Morley Callaghan's work to Maxwell Perkins, as well as other passing references to F.

I132.   ————, ed. *The Left Bank Revisited: Selections From the Paris "Tribune" 1917–1934*. University Park: Pennsylvania State University Press, 1972.

I.   Alex Small, "Latin Quarter Notes" (H84), pp. 106–107.

II.   "Fitzgerald Back From Riviera; Is Working on Novel" (H97), p. 115.

III.   Waverly Lewis Root, "Season's Most Brilliant Book Is Gertrude Stein's Biography" (H109), pp. 277–280 [279].

IV.   Wambly Bald, "The Sweet Madness of Montparnasse," pp. 284–289 [284].

Brief mention of encounter with F in Paris.

I133.   Forgue, Guy J., ed. *Letters of H. L. Mencken*. NY: Alfred A. Knopf, 1961; Boston: Northeastern University Press, 1981. Pp. 194–195, 229, 236, 245, 279, 291, 345, 375–376, 390.

Includes letters to and about F, with brief mentions of and allusions to TSOP, B&D, F&P, GG, and TITN.

I134.   Foster, Richard. "The Way to Read *Gatsby*." In Brom Weber, ed. *Sense and Sensibility in Twentieth Century Writing—A Gathering in Memory of William Van O'Connor*. Carbondale: Southern Illinois University Press, 1970. Pp. 94–108.
Sees GG as "a deft masterpiece of affirmative romantic imagination" and focuses on Nick as "an object within the purview" of F's intelligence. Tested "by the norms of that intelligence, Nick's moral vision is at best of an uncertain purity, and his harsh, poignant, gross, beautiful, and always engaging recreations of it in words, are a kind of siren song whose seductions are quite clearly discerned and definitely to be resisted."

I135.   Frank, Charles P. *Edmund Wilson*. Twayne's United States Authors Series, No. 152. NY: Twayne, 1970. Pp. 13, 18, 84, 86, 101, 104, 115, 136, 143, 157, 186, 192, 194, 196.
Passing references to the F-Wilson relationship.

I136.   Frank, Waldo. *Memoirs of Waldo Frank*. Alan Trachtenberg, ed. Amherst: University of Massachusetts Press, 1973. Pp. 146, 239.
Brief mentions of F and GG.

I137.   Friedman, Melvin J. "Fitzgerald, F(rancis) Scott (Key)." In Wolfgang B. Fleischman, ed. *Encyclopedia of World Literature in the 20th Century*. NY: Frederick Ungar, 1967. Vol. 1, pp. 387–388.
Biographical sketch and brief critical assessment.

————. See Bryer, ed. (I74)

I138.   Friedman, Norman. "Pluralism Exemplified: *Great Expectations* and *The Great Gatsby*." In his *Form and Meaning in Fiction*. Athens: University of Georgia Press, 1975. Pp. 21–41; see also pp. 106–111, 150–151, 177–178, and *passim*.
Reprinting, slightly revised, of Friedman's 1954 *Accent* essay (B312). Other references include discussions of B&D, TITN, LT, "Babylon Revisited," and "Winter Dreams," and a six-page comparison of GG and *1984* (pp. 106–111).

I139.   Friedrich, Otto. *Going Crazy—An Inquiry Into Madness in Our Time*. NY: Simon and Schuster, 1976. Pp. 21, 98, 170–179.
Describes and discusses the breakdowns of F and Zelda; calls their story "one of our most popular folk tales—the brilliant young novelist and the Southern belle, spoiled darlings of the Jazz Age, outliving their time and descending into drunkenness and madness."

I140.   Gaines, James R. *Wit's End—Days and Nights of the Algonquin Round Table*. NY: Harcourt Brace Jovanovich, 1977. Pp. 103–106, 160–162, and *passim*.

Passing references to F's relationship with the regulars at the Round Table, expecially Lardner and Dorothy Parker.

I141.   Gallo, Rose Adrienne. F. SCOTT FITZGERALD. Modern Literature Monographs. NY: Frederick Ungar, 1978. 166 pp.

General survey which includes biographical chapter, chapter on each novel, chapter on the short stories, and a chapter on "The Vegetable" and stage and film adaptations of F's works.

REVIEWS:

i.   Anonymous. Review of *F. Scott Fitzgerald, Choice*, 15 (December 1978), 1367.

ii.   B[utscher], E[dward]. Review of *F. Scott Fitzgerald, The Booklist*, 75 (October 1, 1978), 270–271.

I142.   Geismar, Maxwell. "Fitzgerald, F. Scott." In *Collier's Encyclopedia*. NY: Macmillan Educational Corporation, 1971. Vol. X, pp. 32–33.

Biographical summary.

I143.   ———. *Rebels and Ancestors—The American Novel, 1890–1915*. Boston: Houghton Mifflin, 1953. Pp. 5, 9, 25, 37, 51, 55, 58, 198, 199, 225, 237, 299, 342, 353, 390, 391, 408, 413.

Brief passing mentions of affinities F shares with Frank Norris, Jack London, Ellen Glasgow, and Theodore Dreiser in longer discussions of these writers.

I144.   ———. *Ring Lardner and the Portrait of Folly*. NY: Thomas Y. Crowell, 1972. Pp. 1, 46, 49, 72, 99, 100, 102, 103, 104.

Volume in Crowell's Twentieth-Century American Writers series intended for high school and junior college students.   Includes brief passing mention of F-Lardner relationship.

I145.   Geist, Kenneth L. *Pictures Will Talk—The Life and Films of Joseph L. Mankiewicz*. NY: Charles Scribner's, 1978. Pp. 90–92 and *passim*.

Brief account of F's work on the script of "Three Comrades."

I146.   Gessner, Robert. *The Moving Image—A Guide to Cinematic Literacy*. NY: E. P. Dutton, 1968. Pp. 240–248.

Detailed comparison of "Babylon Revisited" and "Cosmopolitan," the screenplay adaptation which F wrote of his story, which concludes that an excessive number of scene climaxes in the film script lessen the impact of plot and character.

I147.   Gill, Brendan. "The Dark Advantage." In his ed. *States of Grace—Eight Plays By Philip Barry.* NY: Harcourt Brace Jovanovich, 1975. Pp. 3–47 [13–15].
Reprinting of Gill's 1975 *New Yorker* essay (H866).

I148.   ———. *Here at the "New Yorker."* NY: Random House, 1975. Pp. 47, 61, 157, 227, 256–258, 259, 262, 289, 335.
Passing references to F, longest of which deals with Edmund Wilson's ultimately successful attempts to get C-U published.

I149.   Gilmer, Walker. *Horace Liveright Publisher of the Twenties.* NY: David Lewis, 1970. Pp. 33, 122, 123, 124, 125.
Brief mention of role F played in getting Hemingway to move to Scribner's.

I150.   Gindin, James. "Fitzgerald." In his *Harvest of a Quiet Eye—The Novel of Compassion.* Bloomington: Indiana University Press, 1971. Pp. 237–257.
Slightly revised reprinting of Gindin's 1969 *Modern Language Quarterly* essay (H381).

I151.   Gingrich, Arnold. "The Cut of My Jib." In his *Toys of a Lifetime.* NY: Alfred A. Knopf, 1966. Pp. 3–34 [17–18].
Quotes F briefly as praising Gingrich's clothes.

I152.   ———. *Nothing But People—The Early Days at "Esquire"—A Personal History 1928–1958.* NY: Crown, 1971. Pp. 136–137, 241–244, 252–253, 283–289, 309–310, and *passim.*
Memories of F prior to publication of "C-U" essays and of the F-Hemingway relationship.

I153.   Girgus, Sam B. "Beyond the Diver Complex: The Dynamics of Modern Individualism in F. Scott Fitzgerald." In his *The Law of the Heart—Individualism and the Modern Self in American Literature.* Austin: University of Texas Press, 1979. Pp. 108–128; see also pp. 6, 18, 170–171.
Examines TITN and LT for evidence of F's commitment, "in the midst of rapid cultural change," to the idea of "the integrity of self." Asserts that F moved from the egotism and self-pity of Dick Diver, which results in the ultimate isolation from society through a flight into false and meaningless liberty, to democratic idealism as epitomized by

Monroe Stahr, who "reaffirms the idea of our responsibility for our own destiny" through his belief in work as a means of salvation.

I154.   Glassco, John. *Memoirs of Montparnasse.* Toronto and NY: Oxford University Press, 1970. Pp. 88, 90, 154.
Passing mention of F's associations with Paris.

I155.   Glicksberg, Charles I. "Fitzgerald and the Jazz Age." In his *The Sexual Revolution in Modern American Literature.* The Hague: Martinus Nijhoff, 1971. Pp. 58–67.
Discusses F as "the chief spokesman of the jazz age....the coryphaeus of its orgiastic dance, the articulate symbol of its heady aspirations, and, later, after the spree was over, the disillusioned recorder of the reasons for the collapse of its wildly romantic hopes." Includes brief discussions of TSOP, B&D, GG, TITN, and "Echoes of the Jazz Age," with emphasis on their "tug of war" between "the hedonistic and the ascetic" in F.

I156.   Going, William T. "Zelda Sayre Fitzgerald and Sara Haardt Mencken." In his *Essays on Alabama Literature.* University: University of Alabama Press, 1976. Pp. 114–141 [114, 116–127, 129–131, 139–141]; see also pp. 7, 42, 49–50, 53, 54, 85, 92.
Discusses Zelda's life and literary works and includes good deal of comment and information about F's works. Chapter 3 also includes a brief description and discussion of F's "Family in the Wind."

I157.   Goldstein, Malcolm. *George S. Kaufman—His Life, His Theater.* NY: Oxford University Press, 1979. P. 155.
Brief mention of F and Zelda's 1928 visit to the Kaufmans' villa on the Riviera.

I158.   Goldstone, Richard H. *Thornton Wilder: An Intimate Portrait.* NY: Saturday Review Press/E. P. Dutton, 1975. Pp. 6, 30, 31, 35, 53, 58–59, 64–65, 70, 101, 103, 156, 187, 188.
Passing references to the F-Wilder friendship.

I159.   Graham, Sheilah. COLLEGE OF ONE. NY: Viking Press, 1967; London: Weidenfeld and Nicholson, 1967. 245 pp.; Harmondsworth: Penguin, 1969. 187 pp.
Description of and reminiscence about course of study F designed for Sheilah Graham, with considerable quotation from comments by F written in books used in the course. Also prints as appendices facsimiles of the curriculum F typed out for Graham and a short story by Graham, "Beloved Infidel," corrected in F's hand.

REVIEWS:

i.   Anonymous. "Fitzgerald's Pupil," *Times Literary Supplement* (London), June 29, 1967, p. 576.

ii.   ————. Review of *College of One, The Booklist,* 63 (April 1, 1967), 817.

iii.   ————. Review of *College of One, Choice,* 5 (March 1968), 48, 50.

iv.   ————. Review of *College of One, Kirkus,* 34 (December 15, 1966), 1318.

v.   ————. Review of *College of One, Modern Fiction Studies,* 13 (Summer 1967), 276.

vi.   ————. Review of *College of One, The Observer* (London), November 30, 1969, p. 31.

vii.   Bryer, Jackson R. "How Fitzgerald Taught Sheila [*sic*]," Baltimore *Sunday Sun,* April 30, 1967, Sec. D, p. 5.

viii. Byatt, A. S. "Punch and Judy," *New Statesman,* n.s. 74 (July 14, 1967), 52–53.

ix.   *Callaghan, Morley. Review of *College of One, NY Times Book Review,* March 5, 1967, pp. 6–7.

x.   Christiansen, Richard. "The School Days of Scott and Sheilah," Chicago *Daily News,* March 11, 1967, "Panorama" Section, p. 8.

xi.   Coffey, Warren. Review of *College of One, Commonweal,* 86 (April 14, 1967), 132–133.

xii.   Coleman, Janet. "Teacher's Pet," *Book Week* (NY *World Journal Tribune,* Washington [D.C.] *Post,* Chicago *Sun-Times*), March 5, 1967, p. 6.

xiii. Coughlin, Francis. "An Inspired Teacher, a Devoted Student," Chicago *Tribune,* March 5, 1967, "Books Today" Section, pp. 1, 3.

xiv.   Duchene, Anne. "At School With Scott Fitzgerald," *Manchester Guardian Weekly,* June 22, 1967, p. 10.

xv.   Hogan, William. "World of Books—Scott Fitzgerald as 'Pygmalion,'" San Francisco *Chronicle,* February 6, 1967, p. 41.

xvi.   Holsinger, Robert. "There Was Only One Teacher, One Student," Columbus (Ohio), *Sunday Dispatch,* April 2, 1967, "Tab" Section, p. 6.

xvii. Hopkinson, Shirley L. Review of *College of One, Library Journal,* 92 (January 15, 1967), 241–242.

xviii. Kitching, Jessie. Review of *College of One, Publishers' Weekly,* 190 (December 12, 1966), 54.

xix.   Lehan, Richard.   "...More Than Kiss-and-Tell," Boston *Sunday Herald*, March 26, 1967, "Show Guide" Section, p. 18.
xx.   Marguerite, Sister M., R.S.M.   Review of *College of One, Best Sellers*, 26 (March 1, 1967), 424–425.
xxi.   Nordell, Roderick.   "General Education at Fitzgerald U.," *Christian Science Monitor*, March 23, 1967, p. 11.
xxii.   Schmidt, Sandra.   "Boobs and Charades," *Newsweek*, 69 (February 20, 1967), 94, 96.
xxiii.   Trevor, William.   "Tender Teacher," *The Listener*, 77 (June 1, 1967), 724.
xxiv.   *Turnbull, Andrew.   "Fitzgerald as Teacher," *Harper's Magazine*, 234 (February 1967), 106.

I160.   ———.   THE REAL F. SCOTT FITZGERALD— THIRTY-FIVE YEARS LATER. NY: Grosset & Dunlap, 1976. 287 pp.; London: W. H. Allen, 1976. 290 pp.
Compendium of information and reminiscence about F, divided into sections on Zelda, F as father, F as drinker, F as lover, F as writer, LT, F as educator, F's death, the F revival, and the GG film in 1974. Appendices include "Dame Rumor," script of an unpublished play by F and Graham, and facsimile of "Not in the Script," an unpublished short story by Graham, corrected in F's hand.

REVIEWS:

i.   Anonymous.   "All About F. Scott," Springfield (Mo.) *Saturday News and Leader*, July 24, 1976, "View" Section, p. 14.
ii.   ———.   "Quick Guide," London *Times*, October 21, 1976, p. 17.
iii.   ———.   Review of *The Real F. Scott Fitzgerald— Thirty-Five Years Later*, *The Booklist*, 72 (July 1, 1976), 1503.
iv.   ———.   Review of *The Real F. Scott Fitzgerald— Thirty-Five Years Later*, *Choice*, 13 (October 1976), 980.
v.   Allen, Wallace.   "A Few More Words From Sheilah Graham on...Guess What?" Minneapolis *Tribune*, May 23, 1976, p. 12D.
vi.   Barkham, John.   "Sheilah Graham Telling It Again," Youngstown *Vindicator*, March 21, 1976, p. B–12. See also Victoria (Tex.) *Advocate*, April 25, 1976.
vii.   Barnes, Jim.   "Some Life Stories—From Senator Sam to Dame Margot to Scott, et al.," Raleigh *News and Observer*, July 18, 1976, p. 6-IV.
viii.   Bauer, Malcolm.   "Bauer With Books—Light Shed on Lives of Great Writers Shared By Hollywood," Portland *Sunday Oregonian*, July 11, 1976, p. E4.

ix.   Bowers, Pat. "After 35 Years—Look Into the Past By Sheilah Graham Changes the Picture," Baton Rouge *Sunday Advocate,* July 4, 1976, p. 2-E.
x.   Brown, Dennis. "Parading the Fitzgerald Myth," St. Louis *Post-Dispatch,* May 16, 1976, p. 4D.
xi.   Clarey, Kathey. Review of *The Real F. Scott Fitzgerald—Thirty-Five Years Later,* Fresno *Bee,* July 4, 1976, p. J5.
xii.   Corley, Edwin. Review of *The Real F. Scott Fitzgerald—Thirty-Five Years Later,* Auburn (Ala.) *Bulletin,* January 2, 1977, Sec. B, p. 6. See also Sparta (Tenn.) *Expositor,* November 21, 1978; Brookfield (Conn.) *Journal,* December 9, 1976; Alexandria Bay (NY) *Thousand Islands Sun,* December 23, 1976; Amenia (NY) *Harlem Valley Times,* April 28, 1977; Crestline (Calif.) *Courier,* January 7, 1977; Conyers (Ga.) *Rockdale Citizen,* December 9, 1976; Bethel (Conn.) *Home News,* December 8, 1976; New Milford (Conn.) *Times,* December 9, 1976.
xiii.   Daniell, Constance. "Scott and Sheilah—Again," Milwaukee *Journal,* May 23, 1976, Part 5, p. 4.
xiv.   Davies, Russell. "Last Good-Bye?" *The Observer* (London), October 31, 1976, p. 29.
xv.   Donson, Naomi. "Book Scene—3½ Years With 'the Real' F. Scott Fitzgerald," Louisville *Times,* August 12, 1976, p. A15.
xvi.   Durham, John R. "No Gossip Ever Dies Away," St. Louis *Globe-Democrat,* June 5–6, 1976, p. 4F.
xvii.   Earl, Pauline J. Review of *The Real F. Scott Fitzgerald—Thirty-Five Years Later, Best Sellers,* 36 (September 1976), 195–196.
xviii.   Hall, Joan Joffe. Review of *The Real F. Scott Fitzgerald—Thirty-Five Years Later,* Houston *Post,* June 17, 1976, p. 3D.
xix.   Hill, Derrick. "A Sober Scott," Liverpool *Daily Post,* October 16, 1976, p. 7.
xx.   Hand, Judson. "Scraping the Bottom," NY *Sunday News,* April 11, 1976, "Leisure" Section, p. 19.
xxi.   Hogan, William. "World of Books—The Red Tinsel," San Francisco *Chronicle,* March 17, 1976, p. 47.
xxii.   Huff, Tom E. "Sheila [*sic*] Graham's Memoirs Going From Bed to Worse," Fort Worth *Morning Star-Telegram,* April 4, 1976, Sec. H, p. 8.
xxiii.   K., R. Review of *The Real F. Scott Fitzgerald—Thirty-Five Years Later,* Chicago *Sun-Times,* May 30, 1976, "Show" Section, p. 7.

xxiv.   Kinnaird, Clark.   Review of *The Real F. Scott Fitzgerald—Thirty-Five Years Later*, Ferndale (Mich.) *Gazette-Times*, May 27, 1976, Sec. 2, p. 10.

xxv.   Kogan, Rick.   "Miss Graham Adds to Lore of Fitzgerald," Huntsville (Ala.) *Times*, June 6, 1976, p. 28. See also Binghamton (NY) *Evening Press*, August 3, 1976, Sec. B, p. 4.

xxvi.   Land.   "More on F. Scott Fitzgerald," *Variety*, 284 (August 11, 1976), 62.

xxvii.   Leonard, John.   "Doing Time in Hollywood," NY *Times*, June 25, 1976, p. C25.

xxviii.   Lomax, Deane.   "The 'Real' Fitzgerald According to Graham," Charlotte *Observer*, August 29, 1976, p. 2F.

xxix.   Long, Fern.   "More Fitzgerald By Scott's Second Wife," Cleveland *Press*, June 25, 1976, p. 20.

xxx.   Luke, K. McCormick.   "'The Real F. Scott Fitzgerald' By Sheilah Graham Really Not So Hot," Denver *Post*, July 11, 1976, "Roundup" Section, p. 22.

xxxi.   McDonald, Emily.   Review of *The Real F. Scott Fitzgerald—Thirty-Five Years Later*, Chattanooga *Times*, July 18, 1976, p. B4.

xxxii.   McMurtry, Larry.   "Once More Into the Fitzgerald Myth," Washington (D.C.) *Post*, June 14, 1976, p. B4.

xxxiii.   McNaughton.   "New Titles," *Arizona Republic* (Phoenix), May 9, 1976, Sec. N, p. 9.

xxxiv.   Mason, Franklin.   "The Fitzgerald Assembly Line," Baltimore *Sun*, July 11, 1976, p. D5.

xxxv.   Moody, Minnie Hite.   "Fitzgerald Revisited Third Time," Columbus (Ohio) *Dispatch*, June 27, 1976, p. I–8.

Moorehead, Caroline.   "Scott Fitzgerald: The Man Behind the Twenties Myths," London *Times*, October 9, 1976, p. 12. See H991.

xxxvi.   O'Leary, Theodore M.   "Reviewing the Lives of Giants," Kansas City *Star and Times*, June 13, 1976, p. 7D.

xxxvii.   Paley, Maggie.   Review of *The Real F. Scott Fitzgerald—Thirty-Five Years Later*, *Bookletter*, 2 (August 2, 1976), 3.

xxxviii.   Scott, Ellen.   "A Truer Light on Her 'Beloved Infidel'— Graham's Fitzgerald Objective," Albany (NY) *Times-Union*, May 30, 1976, p. 7.

xxxix.   Sherman, Carl R.   "The Woman Misses the Myth," Boston *Sunday Herald Advertiser*, June 27, 1976, Sec. 6, p. A21.

xl.   Shroyer, Frederick.   "Laughton Story Needs No Subtitle to Impress," Los Angeles *Herald Examiner*, July 18, 1976, p. E–7.

xli.   Sullivan-Daly, Tess. "Relationship Explored," Worcester *Telegram*, May 16, 1976, p. 10E.
    xlii.   Tennant, Emma. "Fitzgerald's Zen Garden," *The Listener*, 96 (November 25, 1976), 681.
    xliii.   White, Edward M. "Sheilah's Later Look at Scott Fitzgerald," Los Angeles *Times*, August 8, 1976, "Book Review" Section, p. 14.
    xliv.   White, John B. "Books," Peabody (Mass.) *Times*, July 10, 1976, "North Shore" Section, p. 16.
    xlv.   Y[ork], D[avid] W[inston]. Review of *The Real F. Scott Fitzgerald—Thirty-Five Years Later*, West Coast Review of Books, 2 (August 1976), 38.

I161.   ———. "The Real Thing." In her *A State of Heat*. NY: Grosset & Dunlop, 1972. Pp. 137–152.
Account of F-Graham romance, with emphasis on the romantic and sexual aspects.

I162.   ———. "Scott." In her *The Garden of Allah*. NY: Crown, 1970. Pp. 154–174; see also pp. 59–60, 108–109, and *passim*.
Memories of F in Hollywood, with emphasis on his residence at the Garden of Allah bungalow hotel.

Grebstein, Sheldon. See Bryer, ed. (I74)

I163.   [Grant, Annette.] "6. John Cheever." In George Plimpton, ed. *Writers at Work—The "Paris Review" Interviews—Fifth Series*. NY: Viking Press, 1981. Pp. 113–135 [128].
Reprinting of 1976 *Paris Review* interview (H960).

I164.   Gross, Barry. "'Would 25-Cent Press Keep *Gatsby* in the Public Eye—Or Is the Book Unpopular?'" In Louis Filler, ed. *Seasoned Authors For a New Season: The Search For Standards In Popular Writing*. Bowling Green, Ohio: Bowling Green University Popular Press, 1980. Pp. 51–57.
Suggests that GG is two novels "combined...in one": "a novel for the young...about the dreams ahead and the orgastic" and "a novel for the...not-so-young about the 'future that recedes before us' and the dreams that lie behind." Also discusses importance of GG to the generation which grew up in the 1950s.

I165.   Gross, Theodore L. "F. Scott Fitzgerald: The Hero in Retrospect." In his *The Heroic Ideal in American Literature*. NY: Free Press, 1971. Pp. 221–239.
Slightly revised reprinting of Gross' 1968 *South Atlantic Quarterly* essay (H354).

I166. Guiles, Fred Lawrence. *Hanging On In Paradise.* NY: McGraw-Hill, 1975. Pp. 40–45, 83–84, 148–159, 166–175, 176–179, and *passim.*

Account of F's stays in Hollywood, with considerable attention to the scripts he worked on and I.T

I167. Hall, Donald, ed. *The Oxford Book of American Literary Anecdotes.* NY: Oxford University Press, 1981. Pp. 156–157, 199, 255–264, 269–270, 276–278, 290, 294.

Anecdotes about F reprinted from Swanberg's *Dreiser* (I345), Burlingame's *Of Making Many Books* (C32), Turnbull's *Scott Fitzgerald* (C167), Callaghan's *That Summer in Paris* (C34), Hemingway's *A Moveable Feast* (C77), Cowley's *The Dream of the Golden Mountains* (I91), Latham's *Crazy Sundays* (I218), Hellman's *An Unfinished Woman* (I174), Goldstone's *Thornton Wilder* (I158), Turnbull's *Thomas Wolfe* (I352), and Harwell's *Margaret Mitchell's "Gone With the Wind" Letters* (I172).

I168. Hardwick, Elizabeth. "Zelda." In her *Seduction and Betrayal—Women and Literature.* NY: Random House, 1974. Pp. 87-103.

Slightly revised version of Hardwick's *NY Review of Books* review of Milford's *Zelda* (I258xlviii). Zelda's life is interesting because of the "heroism of her efforts and the bitterness of her defeats."

I169. Harmon, Robert B., comp. THE FIRST EDITIONS OF F. SCOTT FITZGERALD. Los Altos, Calif.: Hermes, 1978.

Pocket-sized guide designed for book collectors which includes brief biographical sketch, alphabetical list of F's works with pertinent bibliographical information, and chronological list of F's works.

I170. Harper, Gordon Lloyd. "Saul Bellow." In *Writers at Work—The "Paris Review" Interviews—Third Series.* NY: Viking Press, 1967. Pp. 175–196 [181].

Reprinting of *Paris Review* interview with Bellow (H262).

I171. Harting, Emilie C. *A Literary Tour Guide to the United States: NORTHEAST.* NY: William Morrow, 1978. Pp. 51–52, 147, 171, 173.

Brief discussions of F's associations with Princeton, the Biltmore Hotel in NY, and the apartment in NY where he struggled to become a writer in 1919, and a longer discussion of F's burial site in Rockville, Md., focusing on his burial and reburial.

I172.   Harwell, Richard, ed. *Margaret Mitchell's "Gone With the Wind" Letters, 1936–1949.* NY: Macmillan, 1976. Pp. 50, 250, 270.

Mitchell comments on her admiration for F's novels and speculates that she and her mother may have given him a ride to Atlanta when he was at Camp Gordon.

I173.   Hayes, Helen, with Lewis Funke. *A Gift of Joy.* NY: M. Evans, 1965. Pp. 23, 28–29, 192–193, 194–195.

Mentions of F, most of which are reprinted from 1965 *McCall's* article (H251).

Hays, Peter L. See Astro and Benson, eds. (I9)

I174.   Hellman, Lillian. *An Unfinished Woman—A Memoir.* Boston: Little, Brown, 1969. Pp. 63–64, 67–69, 71, 77.

Includes comment on LT, recollection of an incident in Hollywood involving F and Hemingway, Dashiell Hammett's opinion of F, and remarks about the Murphys as models for the Divers in TITN.

Hemingway, Ernest. See Baker, ed. (I32)

I175.   Hemingway, Gregory H. *Papa—A Personal Memoir.* Boston: Houghton Mifflin, 1976. P. 103.

Hemingway's son quotes his father as having high regard for GG and TITN and contempt for TSOP and B&D.

I176.   Herbst, Josephine. "A Language Absolutely Unliterary." In Ring Lardner. *Gullible's Travels, Etc.* Chicago: University of Chicago Press, 1965. Pp. v–xiv [vii, viii–ix].

Brief mention of F-Lardner friendship.

I177.   Hicks, Granville. "Writers in the Thirties." In Rita James Simon, ed. *As We Saw the Thirties—Essays on Social and Political Movements of a Decade.* Urbana: University of Illinois Press, 1967. Pp. 78–101 [95–96].

Suggests that F's "radicalism doesn't influence his fiction...in any overt way," although TITN "is in part an experiment in social criticism" and F's having once considered having Dick Diver "denounce the whole capitalistic system and go to Russia" is "significant and typical of the times."

I178.   Higgins, John A. F. SCOTT FITZGERALD: A STUDY OF THE STORIES. Jamaica, NY: St. John's University Press, 1971. 212 pp.

Examines F's entire canon of short fiction chronologically, evaluating their art and relating them to F's novels. Shows how many little-known stories are important apprentice work for a better-known story or a novel and discusses the ways in which the big magazines influenced F's stories, "which of conflicting scholarly judgments on his stories are valid, and how perceptive a judge Fitzgerald was of his own work."

REVIEWS:

i.   Gertzman, Jay A. Review of *F. Scott Fitzgerald: A Study of the Stories, Studies in Short Fiction*, 11 (Summer 1974), 316–317.

ii.   McAleer, John J. Review of *F. Scott Fitzgerald: A Study of the Stories, America*, 125 (October 23, 1971), 327.

iii.   *Mangum, Bryant. Review of *F. Scott Fitzgerald: A Study of the Stories, Fitzgerald/Hemingway Annual*, 4 (1972), 411–415.

iv.   Perosa, Sergio. Review of *F. Scott Fitzgerald: A Study of the Stories, Annali di Ca'Foscari*, 10 (Nos. 1–2, 1971), 317. In Italian.

v.   Piper, Henry Dan. Review of *F. Scott Fitzgerald: A Study of the Stories, American Literature*, 43 (November 1971), 468.

I179.   Higgs, Robert J. "Apollo." In his *Laurel & Thorn—The Athlete in American Literature*. Lexington: University Press of Kentucky, 1981. Pp. 22–90 [35–39]; see also pp. 18, 23, 30–31, 69, 81.

Discusses Tom Buchanan as an example of the "sporting gentleman," a sub-species of the Apollonian type in American literature which attempts "to embody or uphold some concept or code of the unity of body and self" but "fails or is made to appear either ridiculous or in some way autocratic." Tom is "a surface hero" who has "everything but soul and intelligence."

I180.   Highet, Gilbert. *Talents & Geniuses*. NY: Meridian, 1959. Pp. 186, 219, 235.
Passing mention of LT and GG.

I181.   Hilfer, Anthony Channell. *The Revolt From the Village, 1915–1930*. Chapel Hill: University of North Carolina Press, 1969. P. 237.
Quotes F's disillusionment with Sherwood Anderson's novels.

Hindle, John J. See Young (I390).

I182.   Hindus, Milton. F. SCOTT FITZGERALD—AN INTRODUCTION AND INTERPRETATION. American Authors and Critics Series. NY: Holt, Rinehart and Winston, 1968. 129 pp.

General critical survey which includes a short biographical sketch, chapters on each of the novels, a chapter on the "C-U" essays, a chapter on the short stories, and a chapter on F's style. Attempts to "measure" F's achievement "more or less precisely and without falling into the errors of excess or niggardliness which have characterized some of the past critical studies of him" and sees him as "being part of the second wave or backwash of that romantic movement, the first wave of which crested in the early decades of the nineteenth century."

REVIEWS:

i.   Anonymous. Review of *F. Scott Fitzgerald—An Introduction and Interpretation*, *Virginia Quarterly Review*, 44 (Summer 1968), cxii.

ii.   [Bruccoli, Matthew J.] "Hindus Book Bad," *Fitzgerald Newsletter*, No. 40 (Winter 1968), 19–20.

iii.   Perosa, Sergio. Review of *F. Scott Fitzgerald—An Introduction and Interpretation*, *Annali di Ca'Foscari*, 10 (Nos. 1–2, 1971), 313. In Italian.

I183.   Hobhouse, Janet. *Everybody Who Was Anybody—A Biography of Gertrude Stein*. NY: G. P. Putnam's, 1975. Pp. 126-127, 128, 167, 189, 217.
Passing references to F-Stein friendship and to Stein's admiration of F's work.

I184.   Hoffman, Frederick J. "Hemingway and Fitzgerald." In James Woodress, ed. *American Literary Scholarship—An Annual— 1965*. Durham, N.C.: Duke University Press, 1967. Pp. 90–103.
Critical survey of the year's work in F studies.

I185.   ———. "Hemingway and Fitzgerald." In James Woodress, ed. *American Literary Scholarship—An Annual—1966*. Durham, N.C.: Duke University Press, 1968. Pp. 85–94.
Critical survey of the year's work in F studies.

Hogg, Mary S. See Bryer, ed. (I73)

I186.   Holman, C. Hugh. *Windows on the World—Essays on American Social Fiction*. Knoxville: University of Tennessee Press, 1979. Pp. 148–149, 170–171, 186–188, and *passim*.
Passing references to F, including (pp. 186–188) discussion of GG as one of several novels which are "a peculiarly American form of the *Bildungsroman*" in which a "narrator or the viewpoint character witnesses the action of the protagonist in the main story, and from this observation gains an insight into the nature of the experience."

————. See Bryer, ed. (I74)

I187.   Hoopes, Roy. *Cain.* NY: Holt, Rinehart and Winston, 1982. Pp. 96, 285, 323, 376–377, 466, 470–471.
Biography of James M. Cain includes Cain's account (p. 285) of meeting F in Hollywood and mention (pp. 376–377) of Cain's abortive attempt to adapt GG for the movies.

I188.   Horodowich, Peggi Maki. "Linguistics and Literary Style: Deriving F. Scott Fitzgerald's Linguistic Contours." In Donald M. Lance and Daniel E. Gulstad, eds. *Papers From the 1977 Mid-America Linguistics Conference.* Columbia: Linguistics Area Program, University of Missouri, 1978. Pp. 461–472.
Applies a tagmemic-generative model of grammar to TSOP, B&D, GG, TITN, and LT, and analyzes the results with respect to GG and LT, concluding that the "evocative quality" of GG is partially attributable to F's "preference for...fluid process verbs and dependent and independent adjectival and adverbial time clauses"; while the "bareness we find at the end of Fitzgerald's writing career, exhibited in *The Last Tycoon*, results...from a decline of adjectival clauses" and motion clauses towards "an increased trend to dramatize (in narration and dialogue)."

I189.   Hubbell, Jay. *Who Are the Major American Writers?* Durham, N.C.: Duke University Press, 1972. Pp. 167, 209, 214, 217, 221, 224, 226, 227, 280, 281, 282, 283, 284, 303, 313–314, 319.
Passing references to F in study of the changing stature of American writers as reflected in critical polls, literary histories, anthologies, literary prizes, reviews, and elections to the American Academy. Some of this material is reprinted from Hubbell's 1970 *Texas Studies in Literature and Language* essay (H419).

I190.   Hunter, Paul. "An Interview With F. Scott Fitzgerald." In Stanley Richards, ed. *The Best Short Plays 1972.* Philadelphia: Chilton, 1972. Pp. 323–352.
One-act play, preceded by brief introductory note by Richards, which dramatizes Michel Mok's 1936 NY *Post* interview with F (B138), quoting from the interview and from the "C-U" essays.

I191.   Huonder, Eugen. THE FUNCTIONAL SIGNIFICANCE OF SETTING IN THE NOVELS OF FRANCIS SCOTT FITZGERALD. Bern: Herbert Lang, 1974. 128 pp.
Focuses on F's use of setting as a means of creating atmosphere, character, meaning, and symbol in TSOP, B&D, GG, and TITN, in order to investigate the development of F's visual imagination.

I192.   Iacone, Salvatore J.   "Inscribed Books and Literary Scholarship." In H. George Fletcher, ed. *A Miscellany for Bibliophiles*. NY: Grastorf & Lang, 1979. Pp. 47–65 [49–52, 58, 64].

Reprints F's inscriptions found in presentation copies of GG, TITN, TSOP, and B&D to illustrate how literary scholars can use such inscriptions.

Isaacs, Neil D.   See Bryer, ed. (I74)

I193.   Jenkins, Alan.   *The Thirties*. London: William Heinemann, 1976. P. 175.

Brief mention of TITN and of "C-U" essays.

Johnson, Christiane.   See Bryer, ed. (I74)

I194.   Jones, Howard Mumford.   *The Bright Medusa*. Urbana: University of Illinois Press, 1952. Pp. 4–5, 8–14, 79–80, and *passim*.

Brief discussion of TSOP as a revolt of youth "in the name of art against contemporary culture." The novel's importance as well as that of F lies in the "typicality of both."

I195.   Joost, Nicholas.   *Ernest Hemingway and the Little Magazines: The Paris Years*. Barre, Mass.: Barre Publishers, 1968. P. 165.

Brief mention of Hemingway's defense of F against Gilbert Seldes' review of GG (A380).

I196.   Josephson, Matthew.   "Going West: The Lost Ones of Hollywood." In his *Infidel in the Temple*. NY: Alfred A. Knopf, 1967. Pp. 437–455 [446–450, 451, 454–455]; see also pp. 30, 122, 422–423.

Recounts recollections of meeting F in Hollywood in February 1938.

I197.   ———.   *Life Among the Surrealists—A Memoir*. NY: Holt, Rinehart and Winston, 1962. Pp. 17, 35, 250, 351, 365, 366, 373.

Quotes F on how Josephson's book on Zola influenced him in the completion of TITN, and contends that F "in his stories of the debacle of the Jazz Age was really writing a romantic elegy on the passing of his own gilded youth."

I198.   Kael, Pauline.   "Stallone and Stahr." In her *When the Lights Go Down*. NY: Holt, Rinehart and Winston, 1980. Pp. 213-219 [216–219].

Reprinting of Kael's 1976 *New Yorker* review of LT film (H969).

I199.   Karlinsky, Simon, ed.   *The Nabokov-Wilson Letters—Correspondence Between Vladimir Nabokov and Edmund Wilson 1940–1971*. NY: Harper & Row, 1979. Pp. 17, 114–115, 157.

Brief reference in Karlinsky's Introduction of Nabokov's "accepting view" of F; and two brief mentions in the letters themselves of Wilson's edition of C-U.

I200.   Kauffmann,   Stanley.   "Literature."   In   Robert   M. Hutchins, *et al*, eds. *The Great Ideas Today—1964.* Chicago: Encyclopaedia Britannica, 1964. Pp. 181–223 [207–210].
Assesses F and his work in context of Turnbull's *Letters* volume and Hemingway's *A Moveable Feast* (C77).

I201.   Kazin, Alfred.   "A Dream of Order—Hemingway." In his *Bright Book of Life—American Novelists and Storytellers From Hemingway to Mailer*. Boston: Little, Brown, 1971. Pp. 3–20.
Considerable passing mention of F and the F-Hemingway relationship.

I202.   Keats,   John.   *You Might As Well Live—The Life and Times of Dorothy Parker*. NY: Simon and Schuster, 1970. Pp. 71, 97, 107–108, 109, 112, 114, 154, 183.
Passing mention of Parker's friendship with F—in NY, Paris, Hollywood, and Cap d'Antibes.

I203.   Kennedy, Roger G.   "F. Scott Fitzgerald—William Gray Purcell." In his *Men on the Moving Frontier*. Palo Alto, Calif.: American West Publishing, 1969. Pp. 152–189 [152–169]; see also pp. 11, 15, 16, 179.
Suggests that F is a midwestern realist rather than a romantic and contrasts him with architect Purcell who, rather than F, "stands in the great romantic tradition." Examines F "as an observer and reporter of aspects of the midwestern experience that preceded the Jazz Age," with emphasis on his fascination with "money used for spending," his "special interest" in the "peculiar beauty" and "doom" of the rich, and the recurring theme in his work of "the tragedy of the fortunate."

I204.   Kenner, Hugh.   "The Promised Land." In his *A Homemade World—The American Modernist Writers*. NY: Alfred A. Knopf, 1975. Pp. 20–49; see also pp. xiii, xiv, xv, xvi, xvii, 13, 14, 15, 19, 84, 120, 121, 128, 130, 133, 139, 195, 218.
Reprinting of Kenner's 1974 essay from *Bulletin of the Midwest Modern Language Association* (H771).

Kinahan, Frank. See Madden, ed. (I238)

I205.   Kinney, Arthur F.   *Dorothy Parker*. Twayne's United States Authors Series, No. 315. Boston: Twayne, 1978. Pp. 38, 43, 50–51, 54, 63, 73, 131, 139, 165, 177.
Brief mention of Parker's association with F and Zelda and of her lit-

erary debts to F's works. Specific mention of "Bernice Bobs Her Hair" and "A Woman With a Past."

I206.   Klinkowitz, Jerome. *"Gatsby* as Composition." In his *The Practice of Fiction in America—Writers From Hawthorne to the Present*. Ames: Iowa State University Press, 1980. Pp. 49–54; see also pp. vii, 5–6, 62, 98.

Brief discussion of the flaw of composition in TSOP followed by more extensive discussion of the successful compositional manner of GG.

I207.   Koblas, John J. F. SCOTT FITZGERALD IN MINNESOTA—HIS HOMES AND HAUNTS. St. Paul: Minnesota Historical Society Press, 1978. 50 pp.

Brief biographical introduction followed by descriptions of 35 locations in and near St. Paul with F associations, with discussion of how they are related to F and his works. Appendix lists "houses, schools, churches, clubs, and other buildings in St. Paul and White Bear Lake that are known to have F. Scott Fitzgerald connections." These include some of the 35 discussed at length and others. A map keyed to the descriptions is provided; and photographs of the 35 major buildings and of some of the others are included.

REVIEWS:

i.   Donaldson, Scott. Review of *F. Scott Fitzgerald in Minnesota—His Homes and Haunts, Modern Fiction Studies*, 26 (Summer 1980), 334.

ii.   Hackl, Lloyd. Review of *F. Scott Fitzgerald in Minnesota—His Homes and Haunts, Fitzgerald/Hemingway Annual*, 11 (1979), 436–437.

I208.   Koenig, Linda Lee. *The Vagabonds—America's Oldest Little Theater*. Rutherford, N.J.: Fairleigh Dickinson University Press, 1983. Pp. 69–71, 111, 112.

Account of 1933 Vagabonds production of Zelda's "Scandalabra" which includes reminiscences by Zack Maccubin who acted in it; and briefer mention (p. 111) of 1972 revival.

I209.   Kolodny, Annette. "Making It With Paradise—The Twentieth Century." In her *The Lay of the Land—Metaphor as Experience and History in American Life and Letters*. Chapel Hill: University of North Carolina Press, 1975. Pp. 138–160 [138–139, 144].

Brief reference to GG: Gatsby's illusion "stands, at the end of the novel, as a kind of miniature of American history itself, with its pastoral longings both to return to and to master the beautiful and bountiful femininity of the new continent."

I210. Kraft, Stephanie. "F. Scott Fitzgerald in St. Paul: On the Threshold of the Jazz Age." In her *No Castles on Main Street—American Authors and Their Homes.* Chicago: Rand McNally, 1979. Pp. 203–206.
Brief sketch of F's associations with and life in St. Paul.

I211. Kuehl, John. "Characterization, Structure, & Symbolism." In his *Write and Rewrite—A Study of the Creative Process.* NY: Meredith, 1967. Pp. 131–166.
Brief explanation (p. 131) describes the physical form of the holograph draft of Chapter I of GG and notes important changes F made before the first edition. Juxtaposes (pp. 132–162) the texts of the draft and the first edition of Chapter I; and analyzes (pp. 163–166) the importance and effects of the changes F made. The paperback edition of this book is entitled *Creative Writing & Rewriting—Contemporary American Novelists at Work.* NY: Appleton-Century-Crofts, 1967, with the same pagination.

————. See Bryer (I75).

————. See Bryer, ed. (I74)

I212. ————, and Jackson [R.] Bryer. "Introduction." In their ed. *Dear Scott/Dear Max—The Fitzgerald-Perkins Correspondence.* NY: Charles Scribner's, 1971. Pp. 1–15.
Account and analysis of the F-Perkins relationship, with emphasis on Perkins as a man and as an editor.

I213. LaHood, Marvin J., ed. "TENDER IS THE NIGHT"—ESSAYS IN CRITICISM. Bloomington: Indiana University Press, 1969. 208 pp.

I. Marvin J. LaHood, "Introduction," pp. ix-xi.
Brief defense of Dick Diver as a character and TITN as a novel, with comparisons drawn with GG and with Yeats.

II. John Kuehl, "Scott Fitzgerald: Romantic and Realist" (B414), pp. 1–19.

III. G. C. Millard, "F. Scott Fitzgerald: *The Great Gatsby, Tender is the Night, The Last Tycoon*" (B635), pp. 20–47.

IV. Kent & Gretchen Kreuter, "The Moralism of the Later Fitzgerald" (B463), pp. 48–60.

v.   Richard D. Lehan, "*Tender Is the Night*" (F63), pp.
61–85.

vi.   James E. Miller, Jr., "*Tender Is the Night*" (C106), pp.
86–101.

vii.   Arthur Mizener, "*Tender Is the Night*" (I261), pp.
102–116.

viii.   Eugene White, "The 'Intricate Destiny' of Dick Diver"
(B483), pp. 117–126.

ix.   James Ellis, "Fitzgerald's Fragmented Hero: Dick Diver" (B622a), pp. 127–137.

x.   A. H. Steinberg, "Fitzgerald's Portrait of a Psychiatrist"
(B328), pp. 138–143.

xi.   William F. Hall, "Dialogue and Theme in *Tender is the
Night*" (B461), pp. 144–150.

xii.   Marvin J. LaHood, "Sensuality and Asceticism in
Tender Is the Night" (H303), pp. 151–155.

xiii.   Robert Stanton, "'Daddy's Girl': Symbol and Theme in
Tender is the Night" (B388), pp. 156–164.

xiv.   Lee M. Whitehead, "*Tender Is the Night* and George
Herbert Mead: an 'Actor's' Tragedy" (B644), pp. 165–178.

xv.   John Grube, "*Tender Is the Night*: Keats and Scott
Fitzgerald" (B625a), pp. 179–189.

xvi.   William E. Doherty, "*Tender Is the Night* and The 'Ode
to a Nightingale'" (F57), pp. 90–206.

I214.   Lambert, Gavin. *GWTW—The Making of "Gone With
the Wind."* Boston: Little, Brown, 1973. Pp. 48, 71–73, 145, 170,
197.
    Mention of F's work on the script for the film.

I215.   Land, Myrick. *The Fine Art of Literary Mayhem—A
Lively Account of Famous Writers and Their Feuds.* NY: Holt,
Rinehart and Winston, 1963. Pp. 195–197.
    Brief mention of F in account of Hemingway-Callaghan boxing
match.

Landor, Mikhail. See Proffer, ed. (I289)

I216.   Lardner, Ring. "The Other Side" and "In Regards to Genius." In his *What Of It?* NY: Charles Scribner's, 1925. Pp. 3–38 [18–20] and 114–120 [115–116]. Reprintings of Lardner's 1923 *Hearst's International* (H20) and 1925 *Liberty* (H33) essays.

————. See Caruthers, ed. (I84)

I217.   Lardner, Ring, Jr. *The Lardners—My Family Remembered.* NY: Harper & Row, 1976. Pp. 153–155, 161–168, and *passim.* Account of how F introduced Lardner to Scribner's through Maxwell Perkins and remarks and reminiscences about the Lardners' friendship with F and Zelda.

I218.   Latham, Aaron. CRAZY SUNDAYS—F. SCOTT FITZGERALD IN HOLLYWOOD. NY: Viking Press, 1971; London: Secker & Warburg, 1972. 308 pp. Detailed account of F's stays in Hollywood, based on interviews with persons who knew him and on unpublished sources—including the scripts on which F worked—as well as on previously published biographical accounts. Some attention is also given to F's use of the movies and drama in his fiction and to analyses of the scripts F worked on, especially during the last three years of his life, as well as to LT and its relation to F's work in Hollywood.

REVIEWS:
i.   Anonymous. "Cash Without Credit," *Times Literary Supplement* (London), October 6, 1972, p. 1193.
ii.   ————. Review of *Crazy Sundays—F. Scott Fitzgerald in Hollywood, The Booklist*, 67 (July 15, 1971), 925.
iii.   ————. Review of *Crazy Sundays—F. Scott Fitzgerald in Hollywood, Choice*, 8 (October 1971), 1015.
iv.   ————. Review of *Crazy Sundays—F. Scott Fitzgerald in Hollywood, Hemingway Notes*, 1 (Fall 1971), 23.
v.   ————. Review of *Crazy Sundays—F. Scott Fitzgerald in Hollywood, Kirkus*, 39 (January 15, 1971), 91.
vi.   ————. Review of *Crazy Sundays—F. Scott Fitzgerald in Hollywood, Playboy*, 18 (April 1971), 26.
vii.   Adams, Phoebe. Review of *Crazy Sundays—F. Scott Fitzgerald in Hollywood, The Atlantic*, 227 (April 1971), 104.
*Adams, Robert M. "Attis Adonis Osiris Fitzgerald & Co.," *NY Review of Books*, 17–18 (January 27, 1972), 26–29 [27]. See G91.

viii.   Alldridge, John. "Picture of Hollywood," Manchester (England) *Evening News*, May 18, 1972, p. 12.

ix.   Allen, Wallace. "Scott Fitzgerald...a Foreigner in the World of Andy Hardy," Minneapolis *Tribune*, April 11, 1971, p. 6E.

x.   Avant, John Alfred. Review of *Crazy Sundays—F. Scott Fitzgerald in Hollywood*, *Library Journal*, 96 (March 15, 1971), 952.

Bahrenberg, Bruce. "Fitzgerald Failed as Film Scripter," Newark, (N. J.) *Sunday News*, May 23, 1971, Sec. 6, p. 5. See H453.

xi.   Benasutti, Marion. "Books—Fitzgeralds and Murphys: Two Contrasting Stories," *Catholic Star Herald* (Camden, N.J.), July 30, 1971, p. 9.

xii.   Bryer, Jackson R. Review of *Crazy Sundays—F. Scott Fitzgerald in Hollywood*, *American Literature*, 43 (January 1972), 667–668.

xiii.   ———. "The Years of Frustration," *New Republic*, 164 (May 29, 1971), 29–30, 34.

xiv.   Champlin, Charles. "Fitzgerald's Life and Times in Hollywood," Los Angeles *Times*, March 28, 1971, "Book Review" Section, pp. 1, 9.

xv.   Clemons, Walter. "Books of The Times—The Signal Was Growing Faint," NY *Times*, March 22, 1971, p. 31. See also Nashville *Tennessean*, April 11, 1971, p. 10-F; Dayton *Daily News*, April 4, 1971, "Dayton Leisure" Section, p. 29.

xvi.   Cocks, Jay. "Writer's Gauntlet," *Time*, 97 (April 26, 1971), 94.

xvii.   Connolly, Cyril. "Period Pieces," London *Sunday Times*, May 14, 1972, p. 40.

xviii.   Davis, Paxton. "Scott and Zelda, Zelda and Scott," Roanoke *Times*, July 11, 1971, Sec. C, p. 12.

xix.   Dick, Kay. "Self-Imposed Purgatory," London *Times*, May 18, 1972, p. 14.

xx.   Dignan, Josef. "Fitzgerald's Nightmarish Years in Hollywood," Louisville *Courier-Journal & Times*, May 16, 1971, p. E5.

xxi.   Donadio, Stephen. "F. Scott at the Movies," Washington (D.C.) *Post*, April 25, 1971, "Book World" Section, pp. 10–11. See also Chicago *Tribune*, April 25, 1971, "Book World" Section, pp. 12–13.

xxii.   Gallo, William. "Notes From the Mule—The Last Crack-Up of Scott Fitzgerald," *Rocky Mountain News* (Denver), April 18, 1971, "Startime" Section, p. 18.

xxiii.   Garmel, Marion Simon. "Wide, Wide World of Books—Hollywood Bested Mr. Fitzgerald, But It Educated Him Nonetheless," *National Observer*, April 26, 1971, p. 21.

xxiv. Goldman, Arnold. "Orestes in Dreamland," Manchester *Guardian*, May 18, 1972, p. 18. See also *Manchester Guardian Weekly*, June 3, 1972, p. 22.

xxv. Graham, Beverly. "Ill-Fated Novelist in Filmland," Columbus (Ohio) *Sunday Dispatch*, April 25, 1971, "Tab" Section, p. 15.

xxvi. Harrell, Don. "Fitzgerald—Gin and Innocence Revisited," Houston *Chronicle*, April 11, 1971, "Zest" Section, p. 13.

xxvii. Hill, William B., S.J. Review of *Crazy Sundays—F. Scott Fitzgerald in Hollywood*, *Best Sellers*, 31 (July 15, 1971), 185.

xxviii. Hogan, William. "World of Books—The Far Side of Paradise," San Francisco *Chronicle*, March 15, 1971, p. 35.

xxix. ———. "World of Books—'Write Hard, Mr. Fitzgerald,'" San Francisco *Chronicle*, March 16, 1971, p. 31.

xxx. *Hughes, William. "The Ventriloquist and the Doll," *The Nation*, 212 (June 28, 1971), 821–823.

xxxi. James, Clive. "Scott's Inferno," *The Observer* (London), April 30, 1972, p. 36.

xxxii. [Johnston, Albert]. Review of *Crazy Sundays—F. Scott Fitzgerald in Hollywood*, *Publishers' Weekly*, 199 (January 4, 1971), 57.

xxxiii. Keister, Don A. "Fitzgerald Finale," Cleveland *Plain Dealer*, April 4, 1971, p. 14-F.

xxxiv. Kennedy, William. "Looking at Books: Dear Scott, You're Not a Poor S.O.B. Anymore," *Look*, 35 (April 6, 1971), 12.

*Lambert, Gavin. "Scott Fitzgerald in Hollywood," *Books and Bookmen*, 17 (August 1972), 55–56. See G200.

xxxv. Long, Robert Emmet. Review of *Crazy Sundays—F. Scott Fitzgerald in Hollywood*, *Saturday Review*, 54 (July 24, 1971), 39.

xxxvi. *Margolies, Alan. Review of *Crazy Sundays—F. Scott Fitzgerald in Hollywood*, *Fitzgerald/Hemingway Annual*, 3 (1971), 362–365.

xxxvii. Marshall, Arthur. "Misfitz," London *Sunday Telegraph*, May 14, 1972, p. 16.

xxxviii. *Mizener, Arthur. "Astonishing Achievement," Washington (D.C.) *Post*, March 22, 1971, pp. B1, B12.

xxxix. Morley, Sheridan. "Books," *Films & Filming* (London), 18 (June 1972), 66.

xl. Morrison, Bill. "Scott in Lotus Land," Raleigh *News and Observer*, April 18, 1971, p. 6-IV.

xli.   Muir, Alexander. "Anyone For Strip Tennis?" London *Daily Mirror*, May 18, 1972, "Book" Section, p. 23.

xlii.   Nye, Robert. "A Man Drawn in White Chalk," *The Scotsman* (Edinburgh), May 13, 1972, "Week-end Scotsman" Section, p. 3.

xliii.   Perosa, Sergio. Review of *Crazy Sundays—F. Scott Fitzgerald in Hollywood*, *Annali di Ca'Foscari*, 10 (Nos. 1–2, 1971), 316–317. In Italian.

xliv.   Powell, Anthony. "Romantic in Hollywood," London *Daily Telegraph*, May 18, 1972, p. 8.

xlv.   Rogers, W. G. "The Literary Scene," NY *Post*, March 12, 1971, p. 20.

xlvi.   *Schulberg, Budd. "F. Scott the Scriptwriter," *Life*, 70 (March 19, 1971), 9.

xlvii.   Shapiro, Morton. "Fitzgerald Never Stood a Chance in Hollywood," Charlotte *Observer*, April 11, 1971, p. 5F.

xlviii.   Silberberg, Elliot. "Hollywood's High Price," St. Louis *Post-Dispatch*, May 23, 1971, p. 4C.

xlix.   Taylor, Robert. "Scott Fitzgerald vs. Hollywood," Boston *Globe*, March 26, 1971, p. 22.

l.   Tuttleton, James W. Review of *Crazy Sundays—F. Scott Fitzgerald in Hollywood*, *Journal of Modern Literature*, 3 (February 1974), 602–604.

li.   Werry, Richard R. "Turning Off the Stars—F. Scott Fitzgerald's Hollywood Fiasco," Detroit *Sunday News*, March 28, 1971, p. 5-E.

lii.   Wolff, Geoffrey. "Crack-up in Babylon," *Newsweek*, 77 (April 5, 1971), 95–96.

Lehan, Richard. See Bryer, ed. (I74)

———. See Madden, ed. (I238)

I219.   Le Vot, André. F. SCOTT FITZGERALD—A BIOG-RAPHY. Tr. by William Byron. NY: Doubleday, 1983. 393 pp.

Detailed biographical account with emphasis on F's residences in Europe—in Paris, on the Riviera, and in Switzerland. Includes some critical discussions of the novels, especially GG, and of the "C-U" essays. This book originally appeared in French in 1979, published by Julliard.

REVIEWS:

    i.   Anonymous. Review of *F. Scott Fitzgerald, Kirkus Reviews*, 51 (February 1, 1983), 162.

    ii.   Anonymous. Review of *F. Scott Fitzgerald, Publishers' Weekly*, 223 (February 11, 1983), 60.

    iii.   Kakutani, Michiko. "Books of The Times," NY *Times*, March 29, 1983, p. C13.

    iv.   Pritchard, William H. "Fitzgerald Frenchified," NY *Times Book Review*, April 3, 1983, pp. 8–9, 13.

    v.   Tavernier-Courbin, Jacqueline. Review of *F. Scott Fitzgerald, Library Journal*, 108 (April 1, 1983), 744.

    vi.   Wilkinson, Burke. "Fitzgerald from a Frenchman's View," *Christian Science Monitor*, May 4, 1983, p. 9.

    vii.   Yardley, Jonathan. "F. Scott Fitzgerald From a French Perspective." Washington (D.C.) *Post*, April 10, 1983, "Book World" Section, pp. 3, 11.

I220.   Lewis, R. W. B. *Edith Wharton—A Biography*. NY: Harper & Row, 1975. Pp. 467–468.

Brief mention of Wharton's admiration of GG and of F's celebrated visit to her Paris apartment.

I221.   Littlejohn, David. "Three Glimpses of F. Scott Fitzgerald." In his *Interruptions*. NY: Grossman, 1970. Pp. 93–105.

Reprinted reviews of Turnbull's biography (C167), of Turnbull's edition of F's *Letters* (A936), and of AF (A1024).

I222.   Litz, A. Walton. "Maxwell Perkins: The Editor as Critic." In Wm. J. Howard, ed. *Editor, Author and Publisher*. Toronto: University of Toronto Press, 1969. Pp. 96–112.

Discusses Perkins' editorial methods, suggesting "ways in which his work was symptomatic of a general departure from the traditional relationship of author, editor and publisher," and mentioning his adept criticism of GG and his correspondence with F.

I223.   Lockridge, Ernest H, ed. TWENTIETH CENTURY INTERPRETATIONS OF "THE GREAT GATSBY"—A COLLECTION OF CRITICAL ESSAYS. Englewood Cliffs, N.J.: Prentice-Hall, 1968. 119 pp.

    i.   Ernest H. Lockridge, "Introduction," pp. 1–18.

Biographical overview and analysis of GG which focuses on the meaning of F's affirmation: GG "asserts the value of human order in defiance of all which defeats it."

II.   James E. Miller, Jr., "Boats Against the Current" (C106), pp. 19–36.

III.   Marius Bewley, "Scott Fitzgerald's Criticism of America" (B309), pp. 37–53.

IV.   Robert Ornstein, "Scott Fitzgerald's Fable of East and West" (B338), pp. 54–60.

V.   Thomas A. Hanzo, "The Theme and the Narrator of *The Great Gatsby*" (B349), pp. 61–69.

VI.   Gary J. Scrimgeour, "Against *The Great Gatsby*" (F48), pp. 70–81.

VII.   David L. Minter, "Dream, Design, and Interpretation in *The Great Gatsby*," pp. 82–89.
Contends that Gatsby is "great" because of "the beauty of his dream and the heroism of his effort to move beyond it"; but because his dreams give way to ugly reality, "he can be made great only through [Nick's] reconstituting interpretation, reordering art."
Reprinted: Minter (I260).

VIII.   W. J. Harvey, "Theme and Texture in *The Great Gatsby*" (B350), pp. 90–100.

IX.   Maxwell Perkins, "Letter to F. Scott Fitzgerald" (C179), pp. 101–103.

X.   Conrad Aiken, "F. Scott Fitzgerald" (C2), pp. 103–104.

XI.   Peter Quennell, "*The Great Gatsby*" (B196), pp. 104–105.

XII.   Edith Wharton, "Letter to F. Scott Fitzgerald" (C191), pp. 106–107.

XIII.   Richard Chase, "From 'Three Novels of Manners'" (C37), pp. 107–108.

XIV.   Lionel Trilling, "F. Scott Fitzgerald" (C162), pp. 110–113.

I224.   Long, Robert Emmet. THE ACHIEVING OF "THE GREAT GATSBY"—F. SCOTT FITZGERALD, 1920–1925. Lewisburg, Pa.: Bucknell University Press, 1979. 226 pp.
Studies F's apprenticeship leading to GG, focusing on TSOP, B&D, "The Diamond as Big as the Ritz," "Winter Dreams," and "Absolution"; Conrad's influence on GG, stressing parallels between GG

and *Almayer's Folly* (this chapter is a reprinting with revision of Long's 1966 essay in *Texas Studies in Literature and Language* [F4 & H263]; the art and "aesthetic strategies" of GG, with emphasis on the duality of F's "imagination, which accomodates both social satire and tragic myth and reconciles a strong sense of alienation with a deep sense of involvement" (some of this chapter is drawn from Long's 1975 *English Record* essay [H884]); and places GG "in the context of the American literary milieu of the early twenties." An Appendix traces "the growth of Fitzgerald's conception as it is revealed in the manuscript versions of" GG.

REVIEWS:

i.   Anonymous. Review of *The Achieving of "The Great Gatsby"—F. Scott Fitzgerald, 1920–1925*, *Choice*, 17 (April 1980), 222.

ii.   B[utscher], E[dward]. Review of *The Achieving of "The Great Gatsby"—F. Scott Fitzgerald, 1920–1925*, *The Booklist*, 76 (November 1, 1979), 422.

iii.   Donaldson, Scott. Review of *The Achieving of "The Great Gatsby"—F. Scott Fitzgerald, 1920–1925*, *Modern Fiction Studies*, 26 (Summer 1980), 332–333.

I225.   Longstreet, Stephen. "Scott." In his *We All Went to Paris—Americans in the City of Light: 1776–1971.* NY: Macmillan, 1972. Pp. 369–372.

Brief consideration of F's days in Paris which concludes that "if Paris helped many Americans write or paint or compose with more ease, it helped ruin both Fitzgeralds."

I226.   Loos, Anita. *Cast of Thousands.* NY: Grosset & Dunlap, 1977. Pp. 40, 74, 113, 126–129, 130.

Autobiographical recollections of F in Great Neck and Hollywood.

I227.   ———. *Kiss Hollywood Good-by.* NY: Viking Press, 1974. Pp. 34, 119, 120–124, 175.

Memories of F and Zelda in Paris, on the Riviera, in Great Neck, and in Hollywood.

I228.   Lowry, Malcolm, and Margerie Bonner Lowry. NOTES ON A SCREENPLAY FOR F. SCOTT FITZGERALD'S "TENDER IS THE NIGHT." Bloomfield Hills, Mich., and Columbia, S.C.: Bruccoli Clark, 1976. 84 pp.

Volume includes an "Introduction" (pp. v-xix) by Paul Tiessen which gives the background and history of the Lowrys' writing a screenplay adaptation of TITN and includes excerpts from their correspondence concerning the project, as well as noting some of the changes the Lowrys made in F's original plot and technique; a "Letter to [MGM producer] Frank Taylor" from the Lowrys which accompanied the manuscript of the screenplay when it was mailed in 1950; and the Lowrys' "Notes on a Screenplay for *Tender Is the Night*" which contains the Lowrys' observations on and interpretations of TITN, as well as their principles and rationales in making the adaptation. The volume does not include the text of the screenplay.

REVIEW:

i.   Dunlap, Benjamin B. Review of *Notes on a Screenplay for F. Scott Fitzgerald's "Tender Is the Night,"* *Fitzgerald/Hemingway Annual*, 8 (1976), 283–288.

Lowry, Margerie Bonner. See Lowry (I228).

I229.   Ludington, Townsend. *John Dos Passos—A Twentieth Century Odyssey.* NY: E. P. Dutton, 1980. Pp. 216, 218, 221, 222–223, 228, 234, 241, 254, 264, 280, 286, 293, 316, 332, 357, 365, 407, 424.
Passing references to Dos Passos' contacts with F in NY, on the Riviera, in Paris, and in Baltimore, and to mentions of F in letters to and from Dos Passos.

I230.   ——, ed. *The Fourteenth Chronicle—Letters and Diaries of John Dos Passos.* Boston: Gambit, 1973. Pp. 336, 353, 377, 383, 385, 398–399, 408, 424, 429, 445, 448, 483, 488, 507, 533, 534, 553, 570, 575, 627.
Scattered mention of F in letters from Dos Passos to friends and associates and several letters to F.

I231.   Lueders, Edward. *Carl Van Vechten.* Twayne's United States Authors Series, No. 75. NY: Twayne, 1965. Pp. 19, 35, 52, 56, 60, 64, 72, 89, 105–106, 113, 116, 135, 145–146.
Passing references to F and Zelda include sections of their letters to Van Vechten and comparisons of Van Vechten's works with F's.

I232.   McAlmon, Robert. *Being Geniuses Together.* Revised by Kay Boyle. Garden City, NY: Doubleday, 1968. Pp. 181, 226, 347.
Brief mention of F as referee of Hemingway-Callaghan boxing match; and F quoted as "thinking that most of his books will not be interesting to later generations."

I233.   McCormick, John. *The Middle Distance—A Comparative History of American Imaginative Literature: 1919–1932.* NY:

Free Press, 1971. Pp. 28–41.

Sees F's theme, "the sentimental education with its allied depiction of the character's failure to grasp the disparity between youthful illusion and the world's mauling of that illusion in maturity," as suitable for "the moralist and satirist" F was. Emphasis on GG. This book appeared in England under the title *American Literature, 1919–1932: A Comparative History*.

I234.   McDowell, Margaret B. *Edith Wharton*. Twayne's United States Authors Series, No. 265. Boston: Twayne, 1976. Pp. 108, 143.
Brief mention of Wharton's famous letter to F in praise of GG.

I235.   MacShane, Frank. *The Life of John O'Hara*. NY: E. P. Dutton, 1980. Pp. 31, 35, 59, 63, 64, 66, 67, 75, 76, 78, 81, 82, 83, 84, 102, 104–105, 127–128, 132, 157, 177, 184, 237.
Passing mention of the F-O'Hara relationship, including O'Hara's debt to F in *Appointment in Samarra* and O'Hara's opinions on F's progress on LT.

I236.   ———. *The Life of Raymond Chandler*. NY: E. P. Dutton, 1976. P. 150.
Brief mention of Chandler's admiration of LT.

I237.   ———, ed. *Selected Letters of Raymond Chandler*. NY: Columbia University Press, 1981. P. 239.
Reference to F in Chandler letter of 1950 to Dale Warren: "He had one of the rarest qualities in all literature….charm—charm as Keats would have used it."

I238.   Madden, David, ed. *American Dreams, American Nightmares*. Carbondale: Southern Illinois University Press, 1970.

I.   Richard Lehan, "Focus on F. Scott Fitzgerald's *The Great Gatsby*," pp. 106–114.
Explores the theme of the "betrayed promise" of the American dream in GG and links the novel and this theme with Henry James, Henry Adams, and Mark Twain who also contrasted "the values of modern America with those of the past."

II.   Frank Kinahan, "Focus on F. Scott Fitzgerald's *Tender Is the Night*," pp. 115–128.
Discusses the tension between dream and reality and how this theme is developed "primarily in terms of the personality of Dick Diver….the contradictions inherent in his character are the same as those of the Dream as a whole; the Dream evaporates and Dick dies [*sic*] for much the same reasons and much the same inevitability."

I239.   Madison,   Charles   A.   "The   Commercialization   of
Literature: 1900–1945—Charles Scribner's Sons." In his *Book Publishing in America.* NY: McGraw-Hill, 1966. Pp. 196–217
[207–210].
Tells of F-Perkins relationship from Shane Leslie's letter introducing
submission of first version of TSOP through F's death.

I240.   ———.   "Maxwell Perkins & F. Scott Fitzgerald." In his
Irving to Irving: Author-Publisher Relations 1800–1974. NY: R. R.
Bowker, 1974. Pp. 152–167.
Primarily a biographical account of F, relating the facts of his life to
his fiction, with some discussion of the F-Perkins relationship.

I241.   Magny, Claude-Edmonde.   *The Age of the American
Novel—The Film Aesthetic of Fiction Between the Two Wars.* Tr. by
Eleanor Hochman. NY: Frederick Ungar, 1972. Pp. 146, 225–229,
232.
Attributes premature deaths of some American writers including F to
the lack of cultural tradition and the lack of a stable and homogeneous
audience.

I242.   Mailer, Norman.   "The Third Presidential Paper—The
Existential Hero." In his *The Presidential Papers.* NY: G. P.
Putnam's, 1963. Pp. 25–61 [54].
Notes that the style of the Kennedy supporters who demonstrated on
the floor of the 1960 Democratic convention was reminiscent of F's
works.

Malin, Irving. See Bryer, ed. (I74)

Mancini, Joseph, Jr. See Bryer, ed. (I74)

I243.   Mangione, Jerre.   *The Dream and the Deal—The Federal
Writer's Project, 1935–1943.* Boston: Little, Brown, 1972. P. 31.
Brief mention of TITN, a "casualty" of the "prolitarian" literary order of the 1930s, which was "dismissed by the book reviewers as socially insignificant because instead of dealing with workers and the
class struggle it dealt with 'superficial Americans living on the
Riviera.'"

I244.   Marcell, David W.   "Poor Richard: Nixon and the
Problem of Innocence." In John A. Hague, ed. *American Character
and Culture in a Changing World: Some Twentieth-Century
Perspectives.* Westport, Conn.: Greenwood Press, 1979. Pp. 325–337
[329–331, 334, 335, 336].
Calls GG "the most powerful twentieth-century exploration of
innocence" and examines the similarities between Jay Gatsby and

Richard Nixon whose respective dreams were but "narcissistic projections" of themselves.

I245.   Margolies, Alan.   "Introduction." In his ed. *F. Scott Fitzgerald's St. Paul Plays—1911–1914.* Princeton: Princeton University Library, 1978. Pp. 3–10.

Outlines F's interest in the theatre during his youth and gives facts surrounding his writing and performing the four plays collected in this edition. Each play is also preceded by a brief note (pp. 13, 23–24, 57–58, 89) which points out its strengths and weaknesses and its relation to other F works. Appended to the volume is "Textual Apparatus" (pp. 121–166).

————.   See Bryer, ed. (I74)

I246.   Marsden, Donald.   *The Long Kickline—A History of the Princeton Triangle Club.* Princeton: Princeton University Press, 1968. Pp. 90–94, 98–99, 101, 103–105, 123, 240.

Discusses F's contributions to three Triangle Club shows; this material originally appeared in the *Fitzgerald Newsletter* (F42, H311–H313, H360).

I247.   Martin, Jay.   *Nathanael West—The Art of His Life.* NY: Farrar, Straus and Giroux, 1970. Pp. 7, 11, 48, 75, 186, 254, 286, 323, 353, and *passim*.

Scattered mention of the West-F relationship.

Martin, Robert A.   See Bryer, ed. (I74)

Martine, James J.   See Bryer, ed. (I74)

I248.   Marx, Leo.   "The Puzzle of Anti-Urbanism in Classic American Literature." In Michael C. Jaye and Ann Chalmers Watts, eds. *Literature & the Urban Experience: Essays on the City and Literature.* New Brunswick, N.J.: Rutgers University Press, 1981. Pp. 63–80 [75–78].

Discusses GG as an example of the "pastoral romance of manifest failure" and compares it to *The Scarlet Letter*; both novels expose "the glorious impracticality of the alternative each has posed to urban reality."

I249.   Marx, Samuel.   *Mayer and Thalberg: The Make-Believe Saints.* NY: Random House, 1975. Pp. 182–184, 222–223.

Brief mentions of F's unsuccessful attempt to write a scenario for "Red-Headed Woman" and of his offering TITN to Thalberg as a potential starring vehicle for Norma Shearer.

Maslin, Janet.   See Peary and Shatzkin, eds. (I284)

I250.   May, Ernest R., and the editors of TIME-LIFE BOOKS.
The "Life" History of the United States, Volume 10: 1917–1932, Boom and Bust. NY: Time-Life Books, 1974. Pp. 117, 119, 131.
Brief mentions of F as the "beacon of 'flaming youth'" and as the embodiment of the Jazz Age.

I251.   Mayfield, Sara. *The Constant Circle—H. L. Mencken and His Friends.* NY: Delacorte Press, 1968. Pp. 5–6, 30–33, 35–38, 39–40, 41–44, 58–59, 95–96, 125–126, 205–208, 247–248, and *passim*.
Recounts events in the F-Mencken friendship, with emphasis on Mencken's opinions of F's works and on Mayfield's opinion of F's use of Zelda in his works.

I252.   ————. EXILES FROM PARADISE—ZELDA AND SCOTT FITZGERALD. NY: Delacorte Press, 1971. 309 pp.
Focuses on Zelda and the author's forty-year friendship with her to give a very personal biographical account which is heavily dependent on personal reminiscence and on personal interviews with friends of F and Zelda. Includes chapter on SMTW which is seen as better written than TITN and claims that F was jealous of Zelda's talents as a writer and consistently thwarted her attempts to dance and to write.

REVIEWS:

i.   Anonymous. "Fitzgeraldiana—Two Sides of Paradise," *Family Digest*, 27 (November 1971), 60.

ii.   ————. Review of *Exiles From Paradise—Zelda and Scott Fitzgerald, The Booklist*, 68 (November 15, 1971), 266.

iii.   ————. Review of *Exiles From Paradise—Zelda and Scott Fitzgerald, Journal of Modern Literature*, 3 (February 1974), 604.

iv.   ————. Review of *Exiles From Paradise—Zelda and Scott Fitzgerald, Kirkus*, 39 (January 15, 1971), 92–93.

v.   ————. Review of *Exiles From Paradise—Zelda and Scott Fitzgerald, New Yorker*, 47 (August 14, 1971), 88.

vi.   *Aaron, Daniel. "The Legend of the Golden Couple," *Virginia Quarterly Review*, 48 (Winter 1972), 157–160.

*Adams, Robert M. "Attis Adonis Osiris Fitzgerald & Co.," *NY Review of Books*, 17–18 (January 27, 1972), 26–29 [26]. See G91.

vii.   Allen, Wallace. "Poor, Poor Zelda...Married to a 'Monster' Like Scott," Minneapolis *Tribune*, July 25, 1971, p. 9D.

viii. Avant, John Alfred. Review of *Exiles From Paradise—Zelda and Scott Fitzgerald*, *Library Journal*, 96 (July 1971), 2306.

ix. Bauer, Malcolm. "Bauer With Books—Two Fresh Looks at the World of Fitzgerald," Portland *Oregonian*, July 18, 1971, p 6F

x. Beezer, Phil. "New Viewpoint on Fitzgeralds," Philadelphia *Inquirer*, August 29, 1971, Sec. 7, p. 8.

xi. Bergman, B. A. "Cover to Cover—Zelda to the Life," Philadelphia *Bulletin*, March 14, 1971, Sec. 2, p. 3.

xii. Berthelsen, John. "More About Zelda, Scott," Sacramento *Bee*, August 8, 1971, "Leisure" Section, p. 13.

xiii. Bolger, Eugenie. "Behind Every Great Man...," *New Leader*, 54 (September 20, 1971), 20–21.

xiv. Brown, Dennis. "'Everything But Happiness,'" St. Louis *Post-Dispatch*, July 11, 1971, p. 4D.

xv. Bryer, Jackson R. "A Planned Campaign to Exonerate Zelda," Baltimore *Sunday Sun*, September 26, 1971, Sec. D, p. 6.

xvi. Buchan, Bliss S. "Old Neighbor Speaks Up for Zelda Fitzgerald," New Orleans *Times-Picayune*, July 18, 1971, Sec. 3, p. 2.

xvii. Bunke, Joan. "Staunch Defender of Zelda," Des Moines *Sunday Register*, August 1, 1971, p. 9-T.

xviii. Chapin, Don. "Zelda's Friend Too Close For Objective Account," Huntsville (Ala.) *Times*, July 25, 1971, p. 58.

xix. Conklin, Richard W. "Zelda and Scott—Fitzgeralds Placed Under New Light," South Bend (Ind.) *Tribune*, August 29, 1971, "Michiana" Section, p. 10.

xx. Conroy, Jack. "'Exiles': It High-Rates Zelda and Throws the Book at Scott," Chicago *Daily News*, July 24, 1971, "Panorama" Section, p. 8.

xxi. Cooper, Arthur. "A Brief for Zelda," *Newsweek*, 78 (July 12, 1971), 84, 86–87.

xxii. Coyle, William. "Exiles From Paradise—American Morality Play," Miami (Fla.) *Herald*, July 25, 1971, p. 7-H.

  Davis, Paxton. "Scott and Zelda, Zelda and Scott," Roanoke *Times*, July 11, 1971, Sec. C, p. 12. See I218xviii.

xxiii. Deutsch, James I. "Fitzgerald 'Biography' Misses Mark," Indianapolis *Star*, August 1, 1971, Sec. 8, p. 7.

xxiv. Donnelly, Tom. "The Jazz Age Was a Guilty Party," Washington (D.C.) *News*, August 27, 1971, p. 28.

xxv. Drewry, John E. "New Book News—F. Scott Fitzgerald Subject of New Books," Athens (Ga.) *Banner-Herald*, July 6, 1972, p. 4.

xxvi.   Firkins, Arlyn.   Review of *Exiles From Paradise—Zelda and Scott Fitzgerald*, *Fitzgerald/Hemingway Annual*, 3 (1971), 348–351.

xxvii.   Flora, Doris P.   "Exiles From Paradise: Miss Mayfield Proves Once Again Fact Is Stranger Than Fiction," Tuscaloosa (Ala.) *News*, August 15, 1971, Sec. D, p. 4.

xxviii.   Frazer, Jan.   "Book Review," Bar Harbor (Me.) *Times*, September 2, 1971, p. 3.

xxix.   Gilreath, James.   "Paradise Lost—So Did the Fitzgeralds," Cleveland *Press*, July 30, 1971, "Showtime" Section, p. 18.

xxx.   Greenwood, Walter B.   "Biased Look at Scott and Zelda," Buffalo *Evening News*, July 10, 1971, p. B–8.

xxxi.   Gregson, Lillian.   "Books 'n Stuff," DeKalb (Ga.) *New Era*, October 14, 1971, p. 5A.

xxxii.   G[riscom], I[sobel].   "Personal Glimpses," Chattanooga *Times*, January 2, 1972, p. B4.

xxxiii.   Gump, Marilynn.   "Zelda Glorified By Fond Admirer," Wichita *Eagle and Beacon*, July 25, 1971, p. 3C.

xxxiv.   Hall, Randy.   "Zelda and Scott—Sara Mayfield's Biography Excellent," Anniston (Ala.) *Star*, July 4, 1971, p. 8B.

xxxv.   Harriss, R. P.   "Zelda and Scott and 'Scandalabra,'" Baltimore *News-American*, July 25, 1971, p. 2-G.

xxxvi.   Hill, William B., S.J.   Review of *Exiles From Paradise—Zelda and Scott Fitzgerald*, *Best Sellers*, 31 (July 15, 1971), 185.

xxxvii.   Hofmann, Virginia C.   "Disintegration of a Marriage Told in Book on Fitzgeralds," Dayton *News*, August 22, 1971, "Dayton Leisure" Section, p. 8.

xxxviii.   Hood, Ronald C.   "Recollects Fitzgerald Friendship," Lumberton (N.C.) *Robesonian*, July 25, 1971, p. 5A.   See also High Point (N.C.) *Enterprise*, August 15, 1971; Ada (Okla.) *News*, September 19, 1971; Orangeburg (S.C.) *Times-Democrat*, July 25, 1971; Troy (NY) *Record*, July 31, 1971; Shelby (N.C.) *Star*, July 24, 1971; Sioux City (Iowa) *Journal*, July 25, 1971; Hanover (Pa.) *Evening Sun*, July 21, 1971; Haysville (Kan.) *Daily Reporter*, July 29, 1971; Niagara Falls (NY) *Gazette*, August 1, 1971; Alma (Mich.) *Record-Leader*, July 26, 1971; East St. Louis (Ill.) *Metro-East Journal*, August 1, 1971; Derby (Kan.) *Daily Reporter*, July 29, 1971; Tulsa *World*, August 1, 1971, "Your World" Section, p. 9; Menominee (Mich.) *Herald-Leader*, July 27, 1971; Fayetteville (N.C.) *Observer*, July 25, 1971; Monroe (Mich.) *News*, August 2, 1971; Merrill (Wis.) *Herald*, August 4, 1971; Midland (Mich.) *News*, July 31, 1971; Syracuse (NY) *Herald-American*, July 25, 1971; Lewistown (Pa.)

Sentinel, July 26, 1971; Scranton *Times*, July 25, 1971; Allentown (Pa.) *Call-Chronicle*, July 25, 1971; Billings (Mont.) *Morning Gazette*, July 25, 1971; Middletown (Ohio) *Journal*, July 25, 1971; Lansdale (Pa.) *North Penn Reporter*, July 22, 1971; Poughkeepsie *Journal*, July 25, 1971; Framingham (Mass.) *News*, July 25, 1971; Oxnard (Calif.) *Press-Courier*, July 25, 1971; Tiffin (Ohio) *Advertiser*, July 26, 1971; San Angelo (Tex.) *Standard-Times*, August 29, 1971; Waycross (Ga.) *Journal Herald*, July 26, 1971; New Brunswick (N.J.) *Home News*, July 25, 1971; Tuscaloosa (Ala.) *News*, August 22, 1971; Baton Rouge *State Times*, July 20, 1971; Michigan City (Ind.) *News-Dispatch*, July 22, 1971; Key West *Citizen*, October 11, 1971; Durham (N.C.) *Morning Herald*, August 22, 1971; Austin (Tex.) *American-Statesman*, August 22, 1971; Van Wert (Ohio) *Times-Bulletin*, August 25, 1971; Elyria (Ohio) *Chronicle-Telegram*, August 29, 1971; Shreveport *Times*, September 5, 1971; Harrisonburg (Va.) *News-Record*, August 14, 1971; Chester (Pa.) *Times*, July 26, 1971; Charlottesville (Va.) *Progress*, September 5, 1971; Albany (NY) *Times-Union*, July 25, 1971.

xxxix.   Horan, Tom. "Zelda Remembered Ere She Married Scott Fitzgerald," Dalton (Ga.) *Citizen-News*, July 14, 1971, p. 14.

xl.   Hosie, Ron. "Skewered in the Night," Riverside (Calif.) *Press*, August 1, 1971, Sec. C, p. 4.

xli.   Howes, Victor. "The Party Had to Stop," *Christian Science Monitor*, July 8, 1971, p. 11.

xlii.   [Johnston, Albert]. Review of *Exiles From Paradise— Zelda and Scott Fitzgerald*, *Publishers' Weekly*, 199 (February 22, 1971), 144.

xliii.   Keister, Don A. "My Friend, Zelda," Cleveland *Plain Dealer*, July 4, 1971, p. 7-E.

xliv.   Kennedy, Msgr. John S. Review of *Exiles From Paradise—Zelda and Scott Fitzgerald*, *Witness* (Dubuque, Iowa), August 26, 1971, p. 12. See also *Catholic Observer* (Springfield, Mass.), August 27, 1971; *Catholic Transcript* (Hartford, Conn.), August 20, 1971; *Our Sunday Visitor* (Ottawa, Canada), August 29, 1971.

    Kennedy, William. "Looking at Books—Dear Scott: You're Not a Poor S.O.B. Anymore," *Look*, 35 (April 6, 1971), 12. See I218xxxiv.

xlv.   Keown, Don. "The Scott Fitzgeralds, By a Zelda Partisan and Friend," San Rafael (Calif.) *Independent-Journal*, July 10, 1971, p. M15.

xlvi.   Kirsch, Robert. "Lost Generation, With All Its Legends, Revisited," Los Angeles *Times*, July 11, 1971, "Calendar" Section, p. 44. See also Watertown (NY) *Times*, July 17, 1971; Newark (N.J.)

Star-Ledger, July 18, 1971; Rochester (NY) *Democrat & Chronicle*, July 25, 1971; Biloxi-Gulfport (Miss.) *Herald*, July 18, 1971.

    Latham, Aaron. "Scott's Editor, Zelda's Friend," *Book World* (Washington [D.C.] *Post*, Chicago *Tribune*), December 19, 1971, p. 15. See G160.

xlvii.   Long, Robert Emmet. Review of *Exiles From Paradise—Zelda and Scott Fitzgerald*, *Saturday Review*, 54 (July 24, 1971), 40.

xlviii.   McKenzie, Alice. "Bookshelf," Clearwater (Fla.) *Sun*, July 11, 1971, Sec. F, p. 9.

xlix.   Mather, Bobby. "Scott's the Heavy—This One Favors Zelda Fitzgerald," Macon *Telegraph and News*, July 4, 1971, p. 7B. See also Detroit *Free Press*, June 27, 1971, p. 5-B.

l.   Moody, Minnie Hite. "Four Special People In Nostalgic Memoirs," Columbus (Ohio) *Sunday Dispatch*, July 25, 1971, "Tab" Section, p. 14.

li.   Norris, Hoke. "Death in Life—Appraisals of Tragic Fitzgeralds," Chicago *Sun-Times*, July 11, 1971, "Book Week" Section, p. 17. See also Phoenix *Gazette*, July 24, 1971; Baltimore *News-American*, July 18, 1971; Corpus Christi *Caller*, July 18, 1971; Salt Lake City *Tribune*, August 1, 1971; San Francisco *Examiner*, July 16, 1971; Long Island (NY) *Press*, July 18, 1971; Memphis *Commercial Appeal*, July 18, 1971.

lii.   Osborne, Lorraine. "Gentle Defense of Zelda From a Life-Long Friend," Bridgeport (Conn.) *Sunday Post*, September 19, 1971, p. C–4.

liii.   Perley, Maie E. "The Book Scene—New Light Is Shed on Scott and Zelda," Louisville *Times*, July 15, 1971, p. A 11.

liv.   Perosa, Sergio. Review of *Exiles From Paradise—Zelda and Scott Fitzgerald*, *Annali di Ca'Foscari*, 10 (Nos. 1–2, 1971), 314. In Italian.

lv.   Perpich, Mary. "'Exiles From Paradise'—'Zelda Knew Too Much'—So Scott Locked Her Up to Keep Her Quiet," Lansing (Mich.) *Journal*, July 10, 1971, p. D–9.

lvi.   Piel, Candida. "'Exiles From Paradise,'" *Women's Wear Daily*, July 13, 1971, p. 22.

lvii.   Piper, Henry Dan. Review of *Exiles From Paradise—Zelda and Scott Fitzgerald*, *American Literature*, 44 (November 1972), 512–513.

lviii.   Powell, Larry. "More About Scott and Zelda," Savannah *News-Press*, August 1, 1971, Magazine, p. 9.

lix.   Pugel, Robert J. "Fitzgeralds Explored Again By Mayfield—Scott and Zelda: The Golden Dream Rekindled," *Rocky Mountain News* (Denver), November 14, 1971, "Startime" Section, p. 13.

lx.   Raines, Howell. "Friend Tracks Comet's Flight of Zelda, Scott," Birmingham (Ala.) *News*, July 11, 1971, p. E–7.

lxi.   Rogers, W. G. "The Literary Scene," NY *Post*, July 7, 1971, p. 28. See also Youngstown *Vindicator*, July 4, 1971, p. B–8.

lxii.   Roman, Camille. Review of *Exiles From Paradise—Zelda and Scott Fitzgerald*, Quincy (Mass.) *Patriot Ledger*, September 2, 1971, "Limelight" Section, p. 34.

lxiii.   Rose, Ruth G. "Literary Guidepost," *The Scrantonian* (Scranton, Pa.), August 29, 1971, Sec. II, p. 27.

lxiv.   Russ, Margaret. "Scott and Zelda—They Were Doomed," Buffalo *Courier-Express*, July 18, 1971, "Focus" Section, p. 10.

lxv.   S., D. "Exiles From Paradise," Murfreesboro (Tenn.) *News-Journal*, July 18, 1971, p. 8.

lxvi.   Sanders, Leonard. "Scott, Zelda Studied Again," Fort Worth *Star-Telegram*, July 25, 1971, Sec. F, p. 7.

lxvii.   Shackelford, Arn. "Marriage on the Rocks," Grand Rapids *Press*, July 11, 1971, p. 2-E.

lxviii.   Shapiro, Morton. "Zelda Fitzgerald's Talent Touted at Scott's Expense," Charlotte *Observer*, July 25, 1971, p. 5F.

lxix.   Talbot, Virgil. "Two Victims of Extremes," *Northwest Arkansas Times* (Fayetteville), September 10, 1971, p. 9.

lxx.   Terry, Barbara A. "In This Account, Scott Is the Villain," Greensboro (N.C.) *News*, November 28, 1971, p. B3.

lxxi.   Thorpe, Day. "Books: The Case For Seeing Zelda as Co-Author," Washington (D.C.) *Star*, July 11, 1971, p. D–12.

lxxii.   Waldron, Ann. "Books...Light Biographies Replace the Hammock Novel," Houston *Chronicle*, July 4, 1971, "Zest" Section, p. 24.

lxxiii.   Wellejus, Ed. "Scott and Zelda," Erie (Pa.) *Daily Times*, October 5, 1971, p. 5-A.

lxxiv.   Wharton, Will. "Scott and Zelda, A Backyard View," St. Louis *Globe Democrat*, June 26–27, 1971, p. 4C.

lxxv.   Williams, Mary. Review of *Exiles From Paradise—Zelda and Scott Fitzgerald*, Sioux Falls *Argus-Leader*, June 27, 1971, Sec. C, p. 11.

lxxvi.   Wilson, W. Emerson. "Books in the News," Wilmington (Del.) *Morning News*, August 18, 1971, p. 25.

I253.   Mellow, James R.   *Charmed Circle—Gertrude Stein &
Company.*   NY: Praeger, 1974. Pp. 249, 272, 274–277, 324, 352,
394–395.
Recounts meetings between F and Stein and includes Stein's assessment of F's talent, quoting from letters.

I254.   Mencken, H. L.   "Two Years Too Late" and "A Step
Forward." In William H. Nolte, ed. *H. L. Mencken's "Smart Set"
Criticism.* Ithaca, NY: Cornell University Press, 1968. Pp. 286–288.
Reprintings of Mencken's reviews of F&P (A76) and B&D (A180).

————. See Bode, ed. (I29)

————. See Forgue, ed. (I133)

I255.   Messenger, Christian.   "Fitzgerald: The School Sports
Hero." In his *Sport and the Spirit of Play in American Fiction—
Hawthorne to Faulkner.* NY: Columbia University Press, 1981. Pp.
180–207; see also pp. 177–178, 208–211, 218–219, 224–227, 311-
312, and *passim.*
Contends that F "inherited the rhetoric of the boys' school sports sto-
ry and reshaped it through romantic wonder and sadness at the School
Sports Hero and through realistic deflation of the figure," and discusses
TSOP, the Basil stories, Tom Buchanan and Jordan Baker of GG, and
Dick Diver of TITN, with a brief mention of Lardner's influence on F.
Some of this material first appeared in Messenger's 1974 *Journal of
Popular Culture* essay (H786).

I256.   Meyers, Jeffrey.   "Scott and Zelda Fitzgerald: The Artist
and the Model." In his *Married to Genius.* NY: Barnes & Noble,
1977. Pp. 190–210.
Account of the F-Zelda relationship and how it influenced F's writing career, with considerable attention paid to TITN and SMTW.

I257.   Milbank, Kitty.   "I Remember Scott Fitzgerald." In her
Miscellanea. NY: Privately Printed, 1965. Pp. 3–7.
Recollections of F by a St. Paul friend.

I258.   Milford, Nancy.   ZELDA—A BIOGRAPHY.   NY: Harper & Row, 1970. 425 pp. ZELDA FITZGERALD—A BIOG-
RAPHY. London: Bodley Head, 1970. 440 pp.
Detailed account of Zelda's life and writing career, drawing heavily
on unpublished letters, records, and interviews, with considerable emphasis on the interdependence of F and Zelda in their marriage.
Includes chapter on SMTW, and a great deal of material on Zelda's
breakdown.

REVIEWS:

i.   Anonymous. "Book Reviews," *Jewish Chronicle* (London), No. 5304 (December 18, 1970), 12.

ii   ———. "In a Nutshell," Birmingham (England) *Evening Mail*, January 8, 1971, p. 14.

iii.   ———. "Jazz Age Priestess," *The Economist*, 237 (October 10, 1970), 57.

iv.   ———. "Not So Tender Was the Night," *Time*, 95 (June 13, 1970), 99.

v.   ———. "Putting Zelda Back Centre of Stage," *Times Literary Supplement* (London), January 1, 1971, p. 8.

vi.   ———. Review of *Zelda—A Biography*, *The Booklist*, 67 (October 1, 1970), 125.

vii.   ———. Review of *Zelda—A Biography*, *Kirkus*, 38 (April 1, 1970), 430–431.

viii.   ———. Review of *Zelda—A Biography*, *New Yorker*, 46 (July 25, 1970), 80.

ix.   ———. Review of *Zelda Fitzgerald—A Biography*, *Top of the News*, 27 (November 1970), 93.

     *Aaron, Daniel. "The Legend of the Golden Couple," *Virginia Quarterly Review*, 48 (Winter 1972), 157–160. See I252vi.

x.   Adelman, Maurice, Jr. Review of *Zelda—A Biography*, *America*, 123 (November 28, 1970), 467–468.

xi.   Allen, Wallace. "The Lady Lived on the Far Side of Paradise," Minneapolis *Tribune*, June 21, 1970, pp. 8E, 9E.

xii.   Allsop, Kenneth. "The Glittering Goofos," London *Evening News*, October 8, 1970, p. 14.

xiii.   Avant, John Alfred. "Zelda in Extraordinarily Evocative Prose," *Library Journal*, 95 (April 15, 1970), 1470.

xiv.   Barkham, John. "The Literary Scene," NY *Post*, June 10, 1970, p. 60. See also Dallas *Morning News*, June 14, 1970, p. 7C.

xv.   Barrett, Mary Ellin. Review of *Zelda—A Biography*, *Cosmopolitan*, 169 (July 1970), 10.

xvi.   Bartek, Zenka. "A Genius Who Might Have Been?" London *Daily Telegraph*, October 8, 1970, p. 6.

xvii.   Beer, Patricia. "Loved Her, Hated Him," *The Listener*, 84 (October 22, 1970), 554–555.

xviii.   Boardman, Kathryn G. "Zelda—Fitzgerald and Wife Bad For Each Other," St. Paul *Sunday Pioneer Press*, June 14, 1970, "Tab and Lively Arts" Section, p. 30.

xix.   Bradbury, Malcolm. "The Beautiful and Damned," Manchester *Guardian*, October 8, 1970, p. 8. See also *Manchester Guardian Weekly*, October 17, 1970, p. 18.

xx.   Brittain, Victoria. Review of *Zelda Fitzgerald—A Biography, Illustrated London News*, 257 (October 24, 1970), 18.

xxi.   Broderick, John. "The Beautiful and Damned," *Irish Times* (Dublin), October 24, 1970, p. 10.

xxii.   Bryer, Jackson R. "'A Pair Whose Fantasies Matched,'" Baltimore *Sunday Sun*, June 14, 1970, Sec. D, p. 5.

xxiii.   Buchan, Bliss S. "New Details Are Added to Story of a Tragic Love," New Orleans *Times-Picayune*, June 21, 1970, Sec. 3, p. 6.

xxiv.   Bunke, Joan. "A Sad, Mad Melodrama Excruciatingly Lived," Des Moines *Sunday Register*, June 14, 1970, p. 7-T.

xxv.   Burroway, Janet. "Reckless Driving," *New Statesman*, n.s. 80 (October 9, 1970), 460–461.

xxvi.   Byrd, James W. "A Yankee Author and Montgomery's Reaction," *Southwest Review*, 57 (Spring 1972), 167–168.

xxvii.   Campbell, Mary. "Those Madcap Fitzgeralds," Tulsa *Sunday World*, July 19, 1970, "Your World" Section, p. 14.

xxviii.   Carter, Lane. "Zelda Biography Tells of Frustrated Talent," Birmingham (Ala.) *News*, June 14, 1970, p. 7-E.

xxix.   Clark, Alastair. "Zelda's Hell," *The Scotsman* (Edinburgh), October 17, 1970, "Week-end Scotsman" Section, p. 3.

xxx.   Connolly, Cyril. "The Missing Magic," London *Sunday Times*, October 11, 1970, p. 41. Reprinted: Connolly (I90a).

xxxi.   Copeland, James D., Jr. "Meet the Original Flapper Girl," Pittsburgh *Press*, June 24, 1970, p. 83.

xxxii.   Coxhead, Elizabeth. "Hard Times," *The Lady* (London), 172 (November 5, 1970), 749.

xxxiii.   Crinklaw, Don. "Fitzgerald's Heroine—His Wife," St. Louis *Post-Dispatch*, June 7, 1970, p. 4C.

xxxiv.   Cross, Leslie. "Zelda, Who Made the '20s Roar, Makes Her Full Story Heard at Last," Milwaukee *Journal*, June 14, 1970, Part 5, p. 4.

xxxv.   Delehanty, James. "Not-so-Good Companions," *Irish Press* (Dublin), November 7, 1970, p. 12.

xxxvi.   Dick, Kay. "Books," *The Queen* (London), 436 (October 22, 1970), 98.

xxxvii.   ———. "Love at First Sight, and a Common Passion For Notoriety," London *Times*, October 8, 1970, p. 14.

xxxviii.   *Donadio, Stephen. "An American Dream," *Commentary*, 50 (August 1970), 54–60.

xxxix.   Drawbell, James. "The Couple Who Destroyed Each Other...," Edinburgh *Evening News*, October 17, 1970, p. 7.

xl. Duke, Maurice. "Fascinating Portrait Pictures Zelda and Scott Fitzgerald," Richmond (Va.) *Times-Dispatch*, June 28, 1970, p. F–5.

xli. Forster, Jonathan. "Marriage of the Jazz Age," Oxford (England) *Mail*, October 15, 1970, "Books" Section, p. 10.

xlii. French, Philip. "Scott's Wife," *Financial Times* (London), October 15, 1970, p. 30.

xliii. Fuller, Edmund. "The Bookshelf—The Apotheosis of the Twenties," *Wall Street Journal*, June 25, 1970, p. 12.

xliv. Gingrich, Arnold. "'Zelda': Tortured Flapper or Jazz Age Heroine?" Minneapolis *Star*, July 4, 1970, p. 5A. See also Newark (N.J.) *Sunday Star-Ledger*, June 21, 1970, Sec. 4, p. 9; Omaha *Sunday World-Herald*, July 19, 1970, Sec. I, p. 31.

xlv. Grosvenor, Peter. "Zelda—A Voice of Inspiration...," London *Daily Express*, October 8, 1970, p. 13.

xlvi. Hall, Angus. "A Make-Believe Genius," *Books and Bookmen*, 16 (December 1970), 30–31.

xlvii. Hall, Wade. "Zelda Sayre Fitzgerald: A Pathetic Love Story," Louisville *Courier-Journal & Times*, July 12, 1970, p. E5.

xlviii. *Hardwick, Elizabeth. "Caesar's Things," *NY Review of Books*, 15 (September 24, 1970), 3–4, 6. Reprinted: Hardwick (I168).

xlix. Hill, William B., S.J. Review of *Zelda—A Biography*, *Best Sellers*, 30 (June 15, 1970), 114.

l. Hopper, Lynn. "Was Zelda F. Scott's Tragedy, Or He Hers?" Indianapolis *Star*, June 28, 1970, Sec. 9, p. 11.

li. Horgan, Paul. "'No Caprice Was Too Idiotic, No Binge Too Protracted For These Golden Children,'" *Book-of-the-Month Club News*, May 1970, pp. 1–6.

lii. Igoe, W. J. "Far Side of Fitzgerald," *The Tablet*, 224 (October 10, 1970), 977.

liii. *Janeway, Elizabeth. Review of *Zelda—A Biography*, *Saturday Review*, 53 (June 13, 1970), 30–31.

liv. [Johnston, Albert]. Review of *Zelda—A Biography*, *Publishers' Weekly*, 197 (March 30, 1970), 60.

lv. Keister, Don A. "A New View of Zelda," Cleveland *Plain Dealer*, June 14, 1970, p. 8-H.

lvi. Kirsch, Robert. "Biography Tells Zelda's Side of Story," Los Angeles *Times*, July 5, 1970, "Book Review" Section, pp. 2, 11.

lvii. Kitchen, Paddy. "The Role of Women," London *Tribune*, January 15, 1971, Literary Section, p. 11.

lviii. Koenenn, Connie. "Bonds That Linked the Fitzgeralds," Raleigh *News and Observer*, June 21, 1970, p. 6-IV.

lix.   Lehan, Richard.   "The Troubled Life of the Troubled Wife of F. Scott Fitzgerald," Boston *Sunday Herald Traveler*, July 12, 1970, "Book Guide" Section, p. 3.

lx.   Lehmann-Haupt, Christopher.   "Books of The Times— The Other Half of F. Scott Fitzgerald's Life," NY *Times*, June 8, 1970, p. 35. See also *Arizona Republic* (Phoenix), June 14, 1970, p. N–9; Seattle *Post-Intelligencer*, June 21, 1970, "Northwest Today" Section, p. 16; Dayton *Daily News*, June 21, 1970, "Dayton Leisure" Section, p. 5.

lxi.   Long, Robert Emmet.   "The Beautiful and the Damned," *Commonweal*, 92 (July 24, 1970), 370–371.

lxii.   Loving, Jane Parker.   "Opulent Living and Optimistic Dreams Characterized Zelda and Scott's Life," Richmond (Va.) *News-Leader*, August 5, 1970, p. 13.

lxiii.   McAleer, John J.   "The Riddle of Zelda Fitzgerald," Boston *Globe*, July 28, 1970, p. 13.

lxiv.   McPherson, William.   "'Zelda,'" Washington (D.C.) *Post*, June 12, 1970, pp. B1, B4.

lxv.   Manners, Guy.   "20th Century History," *Investors Chronicle & S.E.G.*, 14 (November 13, 1970), 599.

lxvi.   Mannes, Marya.   "Book of the Week: Biography as Fever Chart," *New York*, 3 (May 25, 1970), 53.

lxvii.   Manning, Mary.   "Two American Women," *Hibernia*, October 9, 1970, p. 10.

lxviii.   Mayfield, Sara.   Review of *Zelda—A Biography*, *Fitzgerald/Hemingway Annual*, 2 (1970), 260–262.

lxix.   *Mizener, Arthur.   "F. Scott's Doomed Princess," *Life*, 68 (June 12, 1970), 24.

lxx.   Moody, Minnie Hite.   "Tender Is Right Word For Superb Biography," Columbus (Ohio) *Sunday Dispatch*, June 21, 1970, "Tab" Section, p. 16.

lxxi.   *Moore, Harry T.   "Zelda," NY *Times Book Review*, June 14, 1970, pp. 1, 10, 12, 14, 16, 18.

lxxii.   Muggeridge, Malcolm.   "Books," *Esquire*, 75 (January 1971), 14.

lxxiii.   Murphy, Reverend Harold B.   "Current Trends in Biography," *Catholic Library World*, 42 (March 1971), 429–432 [430–431].

lxxiv.   O'Leary, Theodore M.   "The Great Fitzgeralds—Lyrical Lives and Tragedy," Kansas City *Star*, June 21, 1970, p. 3E.

lxxv.   Parker, Dorothy L.   "The Fitzgerald That Might Have Been," *Christian Science Monitor*, June 18, 1970, p. 13.

lxxvi.   Perosa, Sergio.   Review of *Zelda—A Biography, Annali di Ca'Foscari*, 10 (Nos. 1–2, 1971), 313–314. In Italian.

lxxvii.   Polk, Peggy.   "Fitzgerald's Heroine," Houston *Post*, July 12, 1970, "Spotlight" Section, p. 12.

lxxviii.   Pollock, Duncan.   "Milford Biography of Zelda's Light and Darkness—Victim of the Jazz Age," *Rocky Mountain News* (Denver), July 5, 1970, "Startime" Section, p. 10.

lxxix.   Potts, Paul.   "Zelda and Scott," *Times Educational Supplement* (London), November 13, 1970, "Review" Section, p. 24.

lxxx.   Pryce-Jones, Alan.   "How Two Beautiful People Loved and Then Destroyed," Philadelphia *Inquirer*, June 14, 1970, Sec. 7, p. 6. See also Detroit *Sunday News*, June 28, 1970, p. 5-E.

lxxxi.   Pulson, Diana.   "A Tragic Marriage of the Jazz Age," Liverpool *Daily Post*, October 7, 1970, p. 6.

lxxxii.   Reeve, F. D.   "The Rise and Fall of a Love Affair," *Book World* (Washington [D.C.] *Post*, Chicago *Tribune*), June 28, 1970, pp. 4–5.

lxxxiii.   Rumley, Larry.   "Zelda and Scott," Seattle *Times*, July 26, 1970, p. E4.

lxxxiv.   S., A.   "The Jazz Age," *Church Times* (London), November 13, 1970, p. 6.

lxxxv.   S., C.   "The Over-Full Heart," Glasgow *Herald*, October 10, 1970, p. 14.

lxxxvi.   S., C. M.   "Zelda's Life," *Southern Evening Echo* (Southampton, England), October 24, 1970, p. 8.

lxxxvii.   Sainsbury, Ian.   "The Southern Belle and the Poor Boy From St. Paul," Sheffield (England) *Morning Telegraph*, October 10, 1970, p. 13.

lxxxviii.   *Samuels, Charles Thomas.   "A Woman's Place," *New Republic*, 162 (June 27, 1970), 24–27.

lxxxix.   *Schorer, Mark.   "Zelda; Or, What's in a Name?" *The Atlantic*, 226 (August 1970), 104–106.

xc.   Shapiro, Morton.   "Zelda: The Golden Girl of the Flapper Age," Charlotte *Observer*, June 14, 1970, p. 7F.

xci.   Shultz, Kathy.   "Fitzgerald's Story One of Destruction," Indianapolis *News*, June 6, 1970, p. 32.

xcii.   Simon, Marion.   "Wide, Wide World of Books—'Zelda' Lived and Loved With a Mad Earnestness," *National Observer*, June 15, 1970, p. 19.

xciii.   Sklar, Robert.   "Belle's Hell," *The Nation*, 211 (August 17, 1970), 123–124.

xciv.   Stevenson, Reba.   "Tragic Zelda 'Unlike Any Other Woman,'" Nashville *Tennessean*, June 21, 1970, p. 21-D.

xcv.   Stix, Fredrick W.   "Star Crossed Lives," Cincinnati *Enquirer*, June 18, 1970, p. 34.

xcvi.   Stockwood, Jane.   "Focus," *Harpers Bazaar* (London), October 1970, p. 28.

xcvii.   Sudler, Barbara.   "Biography of Zelda Fitzgerald Confirms Novelist's Theory," Denver *Sunday Post*, June 21, 1970, "Roundup" Section, p. 17.

xcviii. Thomas, Sidney.   "Dixie Belle's Life Mirrors Jazz Age," Atlanta *Journal and Constitution*, June 14, 1970, p. 8-D.

xcix.   Toynbee, Philip.   "Dance of Death," *The Observer* (London), October 11, 1970, p. 33.

c.   W[aldron], A[nn].   "The Fitzgeralds Have Been Lucky With...Their Biographers," Houston *Chronicle*, June 14, 1970, "Zest" Section, p. 35.

ci.   Walker, Alexander.   "Cruel Is the Night—The Madness in the American Dream," Birmingham (England) *Post*, October 10, 1970, Saturday Magazine, p. II.

cii.   Warren, Clifton.   "Scott Wrote of His Wife in Novels," Oklahoma City *Sunday Oklahoman*, June 28, 1970, "Showcase" Section, p. 8.

ciii.   Washburn, Beatrice.   *"Zelda*—Restless and Reckless, a Symbol of Her Day," Miami (Fla.) *Herald*, June 14, 1970, p. 7-G.

civ.   Watkins, Geoffrey.   "Creative Cocteau Bridged the Chasm of Class," *Western Mail* (Cardiff, Wales), December 12, 1970, p. 8.

cv.   Weldon, Jill.   "Distractions," *Vogue* (London), 127 (October 1, 1970), 55, 59–60 [59].

cvi.   West, Rebecca.   "The Symbol Kids," London *Sunday Telegraph*, October 11, 1970, p. 16.

cvii.   Wiseman, Thomas.   Review of *Zelda Fitzgerald—A Biography*, Manchester *Guardian*, October 27, 1970, p. 8.

cviii.   Wood, Michael.   "The Real Crack-Up," *New Society* (London), 16 (October 22, 1970), 741.

cix.   Woods, Eddie.   "Tragic Taps From Old Papa's Drum," London *Morning Star*, November 19, 1970, p. 4.

cx.   Yardley, Jonathan.   "About Books," Greensboro (N.C.) *Daily News*, June 7, 1970, p. B 3.

cxi.   Zaiman, Mildred.   "Short Days of Youth," Hartford *Courant*, July 26, 1970, "Sunday" Section, p. 22.

cxii.   Zimmerman, Paul D.   "Beautiful and Damned," *Newsweek*, 75 (June 15, 1970), 102, 104.

I259.   Miller, James E., Jr. "Fitzgerald's *Gatsby*: The World as Ash Heap." In Warren French, ed. *The Twenties: Fiction, Poetry, Drama*. Deland, Fla.: Everett/Edwards, 1975. Pp. 181–202.

Focuses on novel's "meaning, its themes, its moral implications," comparing first two chapters with "The Waste Land," especially Eliot's and F's use of the world as ash heap imagery; discusses its use of what Henry James called the "solidity of specification," details from the 1920s which enable F to dramatize his era rather than state it as Lewis does; and deals with the novel's theme of the corruption of the American dream and its universality.

Miller, Perry. See Trilling (I350).

I260.   Minter, David L. "Extension of the Form: Henry James, and Fitzgerald's *The Great Gatsby*." In his *The Interpreted Design as a Structural Principle in American Prose*. New Haven, Conn.: Yale University Press, 1969. Pp. 161–190 [179–190].

Slightly augmented reprinting of Minter's essay from Lockridge's *Twentieth Century Interpretations of "The Great Gatsby": A Collection of Critical Essays* (I223).

————. See Lockridge, ed. (I223)

Mitchell, Margaret. See Harwell, ed. (I72)

I261.   Mizener, Arthur. "Arthur Mizener on F. Scott Fitzgerald." In Charles F. Madden, ed. *Talks With Authors*. Carbondale: Southern Illinois University Press, 1968. Pp. 23–38.

Brief F biography and discussion of conflict for F between his "old dream of being an entire man in the Goethe, Byron, Shaw tradition with an opulent American touch" and the insensitive, exploitive habits brought on by wealth, and how this conflict is dramatized in Dick Diver of TITN.

I262.   ————. "F. Scott Fitzgerald 1896–1940—*Tender Is the Night*—1934." In his *Twelve Great American Novels*. NY: New American Library, 1967. Pp. 104–119.

Sees that "the tension between [F's] unescapable commitment to the inner reality of his imagination and his necessary respect for the outer reality of the world is what gives his fiction its peculiar charm." Focuses on TITN and Dick Diver as a man of imagination who sees what opportunities wealth presents to people and who is contrasted with the insensitive rich who point up his own sensitivity.

Reprinted: LaHood, ed. (I213)

I263.   ———.   SCOTT FITZGERALD AND HIS WORLD.
London: Thames and Hudson; NY: G. P. Putnam's, 1972. 128 pp.
Essentially biographical account, with large number of photographs—of F, of places where he lived or visited, of friends and ac-
quaintances, of his family, of places depicted in his fiction, and of persons and places typical of the 1920s and 1930s.

REVIEWS:

i.   Anonymous. Review of *Scott Fitzgerald and His World*,
Best Sellers, 32 (February 1, 1973), 498.
ii.   ———. Review of *Scott Fitzgerald and His World*, *The
Booklist*, 69 (April 15, 1973), 788.
iii.   ———. Review of *Scott Fitzgerald and His World*,
Choice, 10 (May 1973), 459.
iv.   ———. Review of *Scott Fitzgerald and His World*,
Journal of Modern Literature, 3 (February 1974), 604.
v.   ———. Review of *Scott Fitzgerald and His World*,
London *Times*, October 19, 1972, p. 10.
vi.   ———. Review of *Scott Fitzgerald and His World*, *Times
Literary Supplement* (London), November 3, 1972, p. 1349.
vii.   Curley, Arthur. Review of *Scott Fitzgerald and His
World*, *Library Journal*, 98 (July 1973), 2108.
viii.   Lipsius, Frank. Review of *Scott Fitzgerald and His
World*, *Books and Bookmen*, 18 (February 1973), 88–89.
ix.   Perosa, Sergio. Review of *Scott Fitzgerald and His
World*, *Annali di Ca' Foscari*, 13 (No. 2, 1974), 534. In Italian.

Monteiro, George. See Bryer, ed. (I74)

I264.   Moore, Colleen. *Silent Star*. Garden City, NY: Doubleday, 1968. P. 141.
Brief anecdote about F and Zelda crashing Samuel Goldwyn's party
for Norma and Constance Talmadge.

I264a.   Moore, Geoffrey. "F. Scott Fitzgerald (1896–1940)." In
his ed. *American Literature—A Representative Anthology of American
Writing From Colonial Times to the Present*. London: Faber and Faber,
1962. Pp. 1092–1095.
Brief biographical and critical assessment of F and his work.
Includes a short bibliography.

I265.   Moore, Harry T. "Preface." In Zelda Fitzgerald. *Save
Me the Waltz*. Carbondale: Southern Illinois University Press, 1967.
Pp. vii-xi.
Gives biographical and historical background on F and Zelda, his-
torical background on SMTW, and some mention of the relationship

between TITN and SMTW. Volume also includes, pp. 239–255, "A Note on the Text" by Matthew J. Bruccoli, which includes a brief summary of the circumstances surrounding the composition and publication of SMTW and a long listing of "Emendations in the Copy-Text."

I266.   Moorty, S. S. "Norris and Fitzgerald as Moralists." In Jagdish Chander and Narindar S. Pradhan, eds. *Studies in American Literature—Essays in Honour of William Mulder.* Delhi: Oxford University Press, 1976. Pp. 119–126.

Contends that "If Norris represented the bright moral energy of American society in his time, Fitzgerald represented the moral wasteland and the spiritual decay of American society in his....Laxity in personal morals is detested by both the novelists....And both Norris and Fitzgerald viewed with concern American life and experience in an era that saw the rise of commerce and industry, resulting in wealth that affected immensely the mores, manners and morals of a great majority of American society."

I267.   Mordden, Ethan. *That Jazz!* NY: G. P. Putnam's, 1978. Pp. 12, 34, 46, 48, 52, 54, 55, 83, 86, 94, 108, 112, 163–164, 165, 176, 221, 283, 287.

Passing mention of F, TSOP, and GG, with a brief discussion (pp. 163–164) of "The Diamond as Big as the Ritz."

I268.   Morgan, Wanda. "Fitzgerald's Babylon." In Robert J. Owens, Jr. and Barbara E. Hamm, eds. *Increase in Learning: Essays in Honor of James G. Van Buren.* Manhattan, Kan.: Manhattan Christian College, [c. 1979]. Pp. 37–42.

More a general essay on F's life and technique than a study of "Babylon Revisited," although the themes and style of the story are discussed.

I269.   Moseley, Edwin M. F. SCOTT FITZGERALD—A CRITICAL ESSAY. Contemporary Writers in Christian Perspective. Grand Rapids, Mich.: William B. Eerdmans, 1967. 47 pp.

Views F's works in a Christian perspective, with individual sections on TSOP, B&D, GG, TITN, and LT. Concludes that F "showed impressive sensitivity to what religion is all about and even an emotional attachment to the dramatizing color and ritual which he intellectually mocked and criticized."

REVIEW:

i.   Bryer, Jackson R. "Review: *F—A Critical Essay*," *Fitzgerald Newsletter*, No. 39 (Fall 1967), 15–16.

Mottram, Eric. See Bradbury and Palmer, eds. (I32)

I270.   Murray, Edward. "F. Scott Fitzgerald, Hollywood, and *The Last Tycoon.*" In his *The Cinematic Imagination—Writers and the Motion Pictures.* NY: Frederick Ungar, 1972. Pp. 179–205.

Discusses F's interest in, associations with, and use of film in his works and life, with emphasis on cinematic techniques in his fiction, on his three trips to Hollywood (especially the third), on the films made from his works, and on LT as "one of the most striking applications of the cinematic imagination to a literary subject that has yet been written."

Nabokov, Vladimir. See Karlinsky, ed. (I199)

I271.   Nahal, Chaman. *The Narrative Pattern in Ernest Hemingway's Fiction.* Rutherford, N.J.: Fairleigh Dickinson University Press, 1971. Pp. 196–197.

Brief mention of F's critique of the opening pages of the original version of *The Sun Also Rises.*

I272.   Nelson, Gerald B. "Dick Diver." In his *Ten Versions of America.* NY: Alfred A. Knopf, 1972. Pp. 43–60.

Contrasts Dick with Hemingway's Jake Barnes, and discusses the Puritan basis for "what Dick's father could offer him...how to act toward others, how to be nice."

I273.   Newby, Peter T. "Literature and the Fashioning of Tourist Taste." In Douglas C. D. Pocock, ed. *Humanistic Geography and Literature: Essays on the Experience of Place.* London: Croom Helm; Totowa, N.J.: Barnes & Noble, 1981. Pp. 130–141 [135–136, 140].

Attributes popularizing of the summer season on the Riviera to F's vacations there and to TITN.

I274.   Newlove, Donald. *Those Drinking Days: Myself and Other Writers.* NY: Horizon Press, 1981. Pp. 18, 94, 127–129.

Brief discussion of F's alcoholism with mention of TITN and LT.

I275.   Niven, David. *Bring on the Empty Horses.* NY: G. P. Putnam's, 1975. Pp. 99–103.

Memories of F in Hollywood, while he was writing "Raffles" for Samuel Goldwyn, a movie in which Niven was starring.

I276.   Noble, David W. "The Lost Generation." In his *The Eternal Adam and the New World Garden—The Central Myth in the American Novel Since 1830.* NY: George Braziller, 1968. Pp. 135-160 [152–160].

Connects GG with *The Scarlet Letter, Moby-Dick,* and *The American,* noting that F "sensed that the myth of the American Adam and the American Eden was bankrupt, had indeed always been morally indefensible, even though he was unable to find another faith to live by." Sees GG as "a document of the Lost Generation" which is "self-criticism without constructive purpose."

I277.   Nolte, William H. *H. L. Mencken—Literary Critic.* Middletown, Conn.: Wesleyan University Press, 1966. Pp. 107–108, 240–241, 256.
Brief allusions to Mencken's reviews of F's works and to F's admiration of Mencken.

Norris, Faith G. See Astro and Benson, eds. (I9)

I278.   Nugent, Elliott. *Events Leading Up to the Comedy.* NY: Trident Press, 1965. Pp. 69, 87.
Brief mention of effect of TSOP on readers of the early 1920s, especially Nugent and his friend James Thurber, who were jealous of F's success.

I279.   O'Hara, John. "On F. Scott Fitzgerald." In Matthew J. Bruccoli, ed. *"An Artist Is His Own Fault"—John O'Hara on Writers and Writing.* Carbondale: Southern Illinois University Press, 1977. Pp. 135–154; see also pp. 45, 61, 62, 75, 76, 77, 78, 157, 164, 198, 199.
Reprinting of O'Hara's 1941 *New Republic* reminiscence of F (B195), of his 1945 *NY Times Book Review* review of C-U (A611), and of his Introduction to *The Portable F. Scott Fitzgerald* (C123), as well as scattered mention of F in other reprinted essays and reviews.

————. See Bruccoli, ed. (I58)

I280.   O'Neill, William L. *The Last Romantic—A Life of Max Eastman.* NY: Oxford University Press, 1978. Pp. 121, 122, 178–179, 265, 266.
Suggests that F was the first to make Eastman "sense he was out of touch with things" when he treated Eastman's novel *Venture* as an "historical document"; and asserts that F's use of the Eastman-Hemingway fight in Maxwell Perkins' office as the model for the Brimmer-Stahr fight in LT is F's subtle "revenge" for Hemingway's slighting reference to him in "The Snows of Kilimanjaro."

I281.   Ousby, Ian. "The Lost Generation." In his *A Reader's Guide to Fifty American Novels.* London: Heinemann; NY: Barnes & Noble, 1979. Pp. 205–276 [208–227].
Brief biographical sketch and critical overview of F's career, with extended summaries and critical assessments of TSOP, GG, and TITN.

I282.   Patmore, Derek. *Private History—An Autobiography.*
London: Jonathan Cape, 1960. Pp. 98–99, 109, 150.
Brief references to F and his writings.

Pattilo, Edward. See Smith (I323).

I283.   Paul, Sherman. *Edmund Wilson—A Study of Literary
Vocation in Our Time.* Urbana: University of Illinois Press, 1965.
Pp. 13, 14, 16, 19, 20, 28, 29, 34, 38, 43–44, 48, 52, 67, 68, 104,
143, 145.
Passing mentions of the F-Wilson relationship, with conjecture that
Simon Delacy of Wilson's "The Crime in the Whistler Room" is
"modelled on" F.

I284.   Peary, Gerald, and Roger Shatzkin, eds. *The Classic
American Novel and the Movies.* NY: Frederick Ungar, 1977.

I.   Manny Farber, "East Egg on the Face: Gatsby 1949"
(H143), pp. 257–260.

II.   Janet Maslin, "Ballantine's Scotch, Glemby Haircuts,
White Suits, and White Teflon: Gatsby 1974," pp. 261–267.
Review of 1974 GG film which notes that the "single most intriguing
aspect of the movie remained its maverick stupidity; the film is neither
faithful enough to qualify as even a run-of-the-mill screen adaptation,
nor is it guided by even the faintest glimmer of adaptive imagination."

Perkins, Maxwell. See Caruthers, ed. (I84)

I285.   Petrie, Dennis W. "Portrait of the Author as a Man or
Woman." In his *Ultimately Fiction—Design in Modern American
Literary Biography.* West Lafayette, Ind.: Purdue University Press,
1981. Pp. 111–145 [124–138]; see also pp. 2, 25, 61, 73, 120,
205–206.
Examines and evaluates Turnbull's *Scott Fitzgerald* (C167) as an ex-
ample of "the portrait type of modern American literary biography."
Also includes passing references to other F biographies, principally
Mizener's (C10 & F66).

I286.   Piper, Henry Dan, ed. FITZGERALD'S "THE GREAT
GATSBY": THE NOVEL, THE CRITICS, THE BACKGROUND.
Scribner Research Anthologies. NY: Charles Scribner's, 1970. 235 pp.

I.   Henry Dan Piper, "Introduction," pp. 1–2.
Brief explanation of and justification of the types of material included in this anthology.

II.   Henry Dan Piper, "The Untrimmed Christmas Tree: The Religious Background of *The Great Gatsby*" (C128), pp. 93–100.

III.   Kenneth Eble, "The Craft of Revision: *The Great Gatsby*" (B577), pp. 110–117

IV.   H. L. Mencken, "The Great Gatsby" (A370), pp. 121–123.

V.   John M. Kenny, Jr., "The Great Gatsby" (A366), p. 124.

VI.   Gilbert Seldes, "New York Chronicle" (A379), pp. 125–126.

VII.   Arthur Mizener, "[The Great Gatsby]" (C110), pp. 127–132.

VIII.   Malcolm Cowley, "The Romance of Money" (C61), pp. 133–140.

IX.   John Henry Raleigh, "F. Scott Fitzgerald's *The Great Gatsby*: Legendary Bases and Allegorical Significances" (B354), pp. 141–144.

X.   Daniel J. Schneider, "Color Symbolism in *The Great Gatsby*" (B605), pp. 145–150.

XI.   Charles Thomas Samuels, "The Greatness of 'Gatsby'" (F47), pp. 151–159.

XII.   Victor A. Doyno, "Patterns in *The Great Gatsby*" (H260), pp. 160–167.

XIII.   Henry Dan Piper, "[The Fuller-McGee Case]" (C128), pp. 171–175.

XIV.   John H. Randall III, "Jay Gatsby's Hidden Source of Wealth" (H316), pp. 190–197.

XV.   Floyd C. Watkins, "Fitzgerald's Jay Gatz and Young Ben Franklin" (B317), pp. 201–202.

XVI.   David F. Trask, "[The End of the American Dream]" (H331), pp. 213–217.

————. See Bradbury and Palmer, eds. (I32)

I287.   Porter, Carolyn. "William Faulkner: Innocence Historicized." In her *Seeing and Being—The Plight of the Participant Observer in Emerson, James, Adams, and Faulkner*. Middletown,

Conn.: Wesleyan University Press, 1981. Pp. 205–276 [238–240]; see also pp. 218, 282–283.
Compares and contrasts characters, themes, and designs of GG and *Absalom, Absalom!*

I288.   Powell, Anthony. "North Palm Drive." In his *To Keep the Ball Rolling—The Memoirs of Anthony Powell. Volume III—Faces in My Time.* London: William Heinemann, 1980. Pp. 46–71 [48, 61–68].
Slightly revised reprinting of Powell's 1970 London *Times* F reminiscence (H436).

Prigozy, Ruth. See Bryer, ed. (I74)

I289.   Proffer, Carl R., ed. and tr. *Soviet Criticism of American Literature in the Sixties—An Anthology.* Ann Arbor, Mich.: Ardis, 1972.

I.   A. Startsev, "Fitzgerald's Bitter Fate," pp. 97–109.
Sees F as the talented victim of the "destructive influences of bourgeois civilization," giving a biographical sketch which stresses the failures of his personal fortunes, morals and talents because of his involvement in a corrupt capitalistic society, discussing GG, whose theme is the "'American way of life' as a trap for Western man," and placing F alongside those writers whose fiction reflected the "class struggle and Marxist" ideas of the 1930s. This essay originally appeared in Russian in *Foreign Literature*, No. 2, 1965.

II.   Mikhail Landor, "Gift of Hope," pp. 111–115.
Discusses GG and explains why it is so widely appreciated: "At the basis of the novel's dynamic plot lies a romantic story which touches even those who do not appreciate all the complexities of the author's conception." This essay originally appeared in Russian in *Novyi Mir*, No. 10, 1965.

I290.   Randall, David A. "Wolfe and Fitzgerald." In his *Dukedom Large Enough.* NY: Random House, 1969. Pp. 242–259 [253–259].
Account of Princeton University's refusal, in 1941, to buy F's library for anything more than $750. Also includes texts of several of F's letters to Maxwell Perkins.

Raban, Jonathan. See Bradbury and Palmer, eds. (I32)

I291.   Rao, B. Ramachandra. "Scott Fitzgerald." In his *The American Fictional Hero: An Analysis of the Works of Fitzgerald, Wolfe, Farrell, Dos Passos and Steinbeck.* Chandigarh: Bahri, 1979. Pp. 13–27; see also pp. 9, 10, 82.
Discusses the quests of the heroes of F's five novels as following a

pattern of "alienation and involvement, of withdrawal and return," in which, after his wanderings, the hero "comes back to a disenchanting realisation of the impossibility of translating one's ideals into reality....It is only in the refuge of the past that Fitzgerald's hero is able to find sustenance and strength."

I292.   Raymond, Landon T. "1917 in Print." In Edward Durell, Harvey Smith, and David Tibbot, eds. ...*1917—Fifty Years in the Wide, Wide World.* Princeton: Class of 1917, 1967. Pp. 303–304; see also pp. 7, 279, 305.

Fifty Year Reunion book of F's class at Princeton includes Raymond's description of his collection of books by and about members of the class, including F. Volume also contains reprinting of John Peale Bishop's 1941 poem for F (B184) and excerpts from F's essay on Princeton.

I293.   Reese, Lee. "What? No Characters?" In his *The Horse on Rodney Square.* Wilmington, Del.: News-Journal Co., 1977. Pp. 161-181 [165, 173–178].

Memoir of years 1900–1940 in Wilmington includes chapter on John Biggs, Jr., F's Princeton roommate and executor, with section giving Biggs' accounts of drinking with F during Prohibition, the opening of "The Vegetable" in Atlantic City, F's life at Ellerslie, and F's will.

I294.   Reid, Margaret. "Has the Flapper Changed?" In Harry M. Geduld, ed. *Authors on Film.* Bloomington: Indiana University Press, 1972. Pp. 267–272.

Reprinting of Reid's 1927 *Motion Picture* F interview (B97).

I295.   ———. "Has the Flapper Changed?" In George C. Pratt. *Spellbound in Darkness.* Rochester, NY: University of Rochester School of Liberal and Applied Studies, 1966. Pp. 385–386; *Spellbound in Darkness—A History of the Silent Film.* Greenwich, Conn.: NY Graphic Society, 1973. Pp. 453–456.

Reprinting of Reid's 1927 *Motion Picture* F interview (B97).

I296.   Reid, Randall. "*Miss Lonelyhearts*: The Dead Redeemer." In his *The Fiction of Nathanael West—No Redeemer, No Promised Land.* Chicago and London: University of Chicago Press, 1967. Pp. 41–105 [98–99].

Discusses the similarities and differences between GG and *Miss Lonelyhearts*; asserts his belief that "West learned from" F.

Reilly, Robert J. See Callow (I80).

I297.   Reynolds, Michael S. *Hemingway's First War—The Making of "A Farewell to Arms."* Princeton: Princeton University Press, 1976. Pp. 17, 18–19, 49–50, 75, 77–78, 83, 139, 275.

Scattered references to the F-Hemingway artistic relationship, with emphasis on F's critique of the typescript of *A Farewell to Arms*.

I298.   Reynolds, Paul R.   *The Middle Man—The Adventures of a Literary Agent*. NY: Morrow, 1972. Pp. 17, 18, 202.

Brief passing references to F as a client of the Reynolds agency.

I299.   Rhodes, Robert E.   "F. Scott Fitzgerald: 'All My Fathers.'" In his and Daniel J. Casey, eds. *Irish-American Fiction*. NY: AMS Press, 1979. Pp. 29–51; see also pp. x, xi, xii.

Traces F's treatment of the Irish in TSOP, B&D, GG, and TITN, with brief mention of LT: "At the end Fitzgerald was extending the range of his Irish characters,...he was no longer motivated primarily by considerations of class, and...if they are not at center stage, neither are they bit-players hovering in the wings."

I300.   Robbins, Jhan.   *Front Page Marriage*. NY: G. P. Putnam's, 1982. Pp. 104, 186.

Biography of Helen Hayes and Charles MacArthur includes mention of birthday poem F wrote for their daughter and reference to fact that F "put [MacArthur] in *Tender Is the Night*."

I301.   Rose, W. K.   "Remembering Nancy." In Hugh Ford, ed. *Nancy Cunard: Brave Poet, Indomitable Rebel—1896–1965*. Philadelphia: Chilton, 1968. Pp. 316–319 [317].

Brief mention of F.

I302.   Rosenthal, Alan.   "The Dream Divided." In his *The New Documentary in Action: A Casebook in Film Making*. Berkeley: University of California Press, 1971. Pp. 176–185.

Interview with Fred Burnley who discusses his 1969 BBC documentary on F and Zelda, "The Dream Divided."

I303.   Ross, Ishbel.   "Hemingway and Fitzgerald." In his *The Expatriates*. NY: Thomas Y. Crowell, 1970. Pp. 255–266 [255, 257–263]; see also pp. 6, 180, 223, 234, 236, 242–244, 246.

Gives details of F's expatriate experience, with emphasis on the F-Hemingway relationship.

I304.   Rota, Anthony.   "F. Scott Fitzgerald Appraises His Library." In Matthew J. Bruccoli and C. E. Frazer Clark, eds. *Pages: The World of Books, Writers, and Writing—Volume 1*. Detroit: Gale Research, 1976. Pp. 83–89.

Prints a facsimile of a list of part of his library which F drew up—probably sometime in the 1930s—with the thought of raising money, with F's estimates of the values of individual titles. Also notes that the books are worth about twenty times what F estimated in present market.

I305.   Sandeen, Ernest R. "F. Scott Fitzgerald's Summit Avenue." In his *St. Paul's Historic Summit Avenue*. St. Paul: Living Historical Museum, Macalester College, 1978. Pp. 91–94.
Gives brief biographical account of F's St. Paul associations, quotes from F's writings on Summit Avenue, and includes a map and guide for a walking tour of principal surviving sites of F's youth.

I306.   Sanford, John. "F. Scott Fitzgerald—Seven Bucks Found In a Toilet." In his *A More Goodly Country—A Personal History of America*. NY: Horizon Press, 1975. Pp. 272–273.
Brief impressionistic memoir of F.

I307.   Sann, Paul. "F. Scott Fitzgerald—Paradise and Zelda." In his *The Lawless Decade—A Pictorial History of a Great American Transition: From the World War I Armistice and Prohibition to Repeal and the New Deal*. NY: Crown, 1957. Pp. 115–118; see also pp. 50, 66.
Short biographical overview and brief commentary on the novels; includes several inaccuracies, most glaring of which is to date Zelda's death as 1939, before F's.

I308.   Sarotte, Georges-Michel. "Francis Scott Fitzgerald: Self-Virilization and Its Failure." In his *Like a Brother, Like a Lover: Male Homosexuality in the American Novel and Theater*. Garden City, NY: Doubleday, 1978. Pp. 212–228; see also pp. ix, 16, 38–40, 45, 61–62, 67, 177, 238, 253, 262, 276, 285, 290, 294, 299, 301.
Explores latent homosexuality in F and his novels, suggesting that in his life and his art F used women in order to bring himself and his protagonists "closer to their heroes."

I309.   Schorer, Mark. "Some Relationships: Gertrude Stein, Sherwood Anderson, F. Scott Fitzgerald, and Ernest Hemingway." In his *The World We Imagine*. NY: Farrar, Straus and Giroux, 1968. Pp. 299–382 [324–330, 332, 337–341, 342–344, 349–350, 351–353, 356–364, 365, 366–368, 374–380].
Much-expanded version of Schorer's essay in *Major Writers of America* (C137), which dwells at length on F's relationships with Anderson, Ring Lardner, Edmund Wilson, Stein, and particularly Ernest Hemingway, and comments on TSOP ("cynical, witty, overwritten, very romantic"), "Babylon Revisited" ("one of Fitzgerald's most moving stories"), TITN ("it has endured until now with ever increasing prestige"), and "C-U" ("a beautiful and moving confession").

I310.   Schulberg, Budd. "Introduction." In his *The Disen-chanted*. NY: Viking Press, 1975. Pp. v-xii.
Suggests that his observation of F was not only of the man but also of "the Scott Fitzgerald TYPE. Or syndrome. Or wound. A deep American gash in the creative spirit," and that Manley Halliday in *The Disenchanted* is "Scott...and Red Lewis, and Johnnie Weaver, and 'Mank,' and Vinnie, and Eddie Mayer, and my old man. And me."

I311.   ———. *Moving Pictures—Memories of a Hollywood Prince*. NY: Stein and Day, 1981. Pp. 121, 125, 155.
Includes (p. 121) comparison of B&D and B. P. Schulberg's movie "The Beauty Market": "Both Fitzgerald and the creators of *The Beauty Market* were striken with a double vision and a double morality, glorifying the society they were so heatedly exposing, exposing the society they could not resist glorifying."

I312.   ———. "Old Scott—The Myth, the Masque, the Man." In his *The Four Seasons of Success*. Garden City, NY: Doubleday, 1972. Pp. 89–143.
Reprinting of Schulberg's 1961 *Esquire* essay (B473).

I313.   Schwartz, Nancy Lynn. *The Hollywood Writers' Wars*. Completed by Sheila Schwartz. NY: Alfred A. Knopf, 1982. Pp. 76, 80, 133, 145–146, 152, 170, 293n.
Brief references to F's activities in Hollywood in the late 1930s, with emphasis on his portrait of Irving Thalberg in LT, on his Dartmouth Winter Carnival experience with Budd Schulberg, and on his Leftist leanings.

Schwinn, Walter K. See Bryer, ed. (I73)

I314.   Scribner, Charles, III. "Introduction." In F. Scott Fitzgerald. *The Vegetable or From President to Postman*. NY: Charles Scribner's, 1976. Pp. v-xx.
Gives account of the composition of F's play, and includes extensive quotations from F's correspondence with Maxwell Perkins and from F's notes on the play.

I315.   See, Carolyn. "The Hollywood Novel—The American Dream Cheat." In David Madden, ed. *Tough Guy Writers of the Thirties*. Carbondale: Southern Illinois University Press, 1968. Pp. 199–217 [199, 200, 201].
Passing mention of F and GG.

Selznick, David O. See Behlmer, ed. (I15)

I316. Shahane, Vasant A. "F. Scott Fitzgerald's Dual Vision in *The Great Gatsby.*" In M. K. Naik, S. K. Desai, and S. Mokashi-Punekar, eds. *Indian Studies in American Fiction.* Delhi: Karnatak University, Dharwar and Macmillan India, 1974. Pp. 153–162.

Sees the dual vision in GG as the abstract or spiritual and the con crete or physical; it is embodied in Gatsby's "Romantic Quest" for both beauty and money, in Gatsby's "sense of commitment to the ideal as well as his subtle awareness of the inevitable failure of that ideal," and in the paradox that his "dream destroys him but at the same time it gives him a new lease on life."

I317. Shain, Charles E. "F. Scott Fitzgerald—1896–1940." In Leonard Unger, ed. *American Writers—A Collection of Literary Biographies.* NY: Charles Scribner's, 1974. Volume II, pp. 77–100.

Slightly revised and updated reprinting of Shain's Minnesota Pamphlet on F (C142).

I318. Sheed, Wilfrid. "F. Scott Fitzgerald." In his *The Good Word & Other Words.* NY: E. P. Dutton, 1978. Pp. 243–247.

Reprinting of Sheed's 1973 *Harpers Bazaar* article (H674).

Shenton, Edward. See Bryer, ed. (I73)

I319. Shirer, William L. *20th Century Journey—A Memoir of a Life and the Times. The Start 1904–1930.* NY: Simon and Schuster, 1976. Pp. 17, 44–45, 108, 168, 231–234, 258, 271, 279, 301, 346, 445, 455, 456, 458.

Memories of an encounter with a drunken F in the newsroom of the Paris edition of the Chicago *Tribune* in the fall or winter of 1925 or 1926, as well as scattered references to Shirer's admiration of F and his works.

I320. Simon, Linda. *The Biography of Alice B. Tolkas.* Garden City, NY: Doubleday, 1977. Pp. 125–126, 148, 169, 222, 223, 231.

Brief mentions of incidents in the Toklas-Gertrude Stein-F relationship and of Toklas' opinions of F and his works.

I321. Sklar, Robert. F. SCOTT FITZGERALD—THE LAST LAOCOÖN. NY: Oxford University Press, 1967. 376 pp.

Suggests that F, the last of the important American novelists "to grow up believing in the genteel romantic ideals that pervaded late nineteenth-century American culture," overcame the genteel tradition by criticizing it, "adapting it, and finally transforming its values," and creating "an alternative vision of order, an Apollonian vision of moral order and measured beauty." Includes material on successive literary influences to which F was subject, as well as substantial sections on TSOP, B&D, GG, TITN, and LT, and brief discusions of many short stories.

REVIEWS:

i.   Anonymous. Review of *F. Scott Fitzgerald—The Last Laocoön, The Booklist*, 64 (September 1, 1967), 39.

ii.   ———. Review of *F. Scott Fitzgerald—The Last Laocoön, Choice*, 4 (October 1967), 836.

iii.   ———. Review of *F. Scott Fitzgerald—The Last Laocoön, Kirkus*, 35 (March 1, 1967), 326.

iv.   ———. Review of *F. Scott Fitzgerald—The Last Laocoön, Modern Fiction Studies*, 13 (Summer 1967), 276.

v.   ———. Review of *F. Scott Fitzgerald—The Last Laocoön, The Nation*, 205 (July 3, 1967), 26.

vi.   ———. Review of *F. Scott Fitzgerald—The Last Laocoön, New Yorker*, 43 (June 3, 1967), 146–147.

vii.   Bruccoli, Matthew J. "In Able Defense of Scott Fitzgerald," Chicago *Daily News*, May 13, 1967, "Panorama" Section, p. 9.

viii.   ———. "The Last Laocoön," *Fitzgerald Newsletter*, No. 37 (Spring 1967), 5.

ix.   Bryer, Jackson R. "New Study of Fitzgerald," Baltimore *Sunday Sun*, July 9, 1967, Sec. D, p. 5.

x.   Callaghan, Morley. "The Lyric Touch," *NY Times Book Review*, July 9, 1967, pp. 16, 18.

xi.   Carroll, John. "A Thesis Rides Hard on Familiar Terrain," Toronto *Globe and Mail*, July 29, 1967, Magazine, p. 14.

xii.   Corbett, Edward P. J. Review of *F. Scott Fitzgerald— The Last Laocoön, America*, 117 (July 29, 1967), 117–118.

xiii.   Hicks, Granville. "Literary Horizons—Students of American Culture," 50 (June 10, 1967), 27–28.

xiv.   Kiessel, William C. Review of *F. Scott Fitzgerald—The Last Laocoön, Library Journal*, 92 (July 1967), 2559.

xv.   Lehan, Richard. Review of *F. Scott Fitzgerald—The Last Laocoön, American Literature*, 40 (March 1968), 101–102.

xvi.   Perley, Maie E. "Volume Seeks to Repair Fitzgerald's Defamed Image," Louisville *Times*, May 15, 1967, p. A9.

xvii.   Ryan, Frank L. Review of *F. Scott Fitzgerald—The Last Laocoön, Best Sellers*, 27 (June 15, 1967), 115–116.

xviii.   Skipp, Francis E. Review of *F. Scott Fitzgerald—The Last Laocoön, South Atlantic Quarterly*, 67 (Summer 1968), 565–566.

xix.   Stevenson, John W. "A Dream Issued in Time, Which Creates, Destroys," Roanoke *Times*, June 25, 1967, p. B–12.

xx.   White, William.   "Fitzgerald and Others," *American Book Collector*, 18 (April 1968), 4.

I322.   Smith, Scottie Fitzgerald.   "Foreword."   In *Bits of Paradise—21 Uncollected Stories By F. Scott and Zelda Fitzgerald.* London: Bodley Head, 1973; NY: Charles Scribner's, 1974. Pp. 1–7. F's daughter recalls "bits and pieces of the child's paradise" which her parents created for her, and advises reading these stories "as reports from another, more romantic world." This volume also includes (pp. 8–13) "Preface" by Matthew J. Bruccoli which explains what materials were included, their original publishing history, F's short story writing philosophy and practice, and comments on several individual stories.

I323.   ———.   "Foreword."   In *Zelda.*   Montgomery, Ala.: [Montgomery Museum of Fine Arts, 1974]. Unpaged. Brief introduction to catalogue of museum retrospective discusses her parents' relationship, with emphasis on Zelda's talents as a writer, dancer, and painter. This volume also includes "Introduction" by Edward Pattilo which gives a brief biographical sketch of Zelda and presents an overview of her career as an artist.

I324.   ———.   "Introduction."   In her, Matthew J. Bruccoli, and Joan P. Kerr, eds. *The Romantic Egoists.* NY: Charles Scribner's, 1974. Pp. ix-x. Gives rationale for this autobiography of her parents drawn from their scrapbooks and photograph albums which tries to convey an "interweaving of the inner ego and the outward expression," and comments on the sources of the material in the volume and on her father's concern with money. Volume also includes (pp. 240–244) "Restoration: Fitzgerald's Posthumous Vindication" by Matthew J. Bruccoli which gives an historical overview of the F revival from 1941 to 1974, discussing the critical, scholarly, and popular aspects of it and speculating on possible reasons for it.

———. See Bruccoli (I42).

———. See Bruccoli (I55).

———. See Bruccoli and Clark, eds. (I60)

I325.   Smith, William Jay.   "F. Scott Fitzgerald: A Poet's View."   In his *The Streaks of the Tulip—Selected Criticism.*   NY: Delacorte Press, 1972. Pp. 268–283. Reprinting of Smith's 1966 *Hollins College Bulletin* essay (H273).

I326.   Smoller, Sanford J.   *Adrift Among Geniuses—Robert McAlmon—Writer and Publisher of the Twenties.*   University Park: Pennsylvania State University Press, 1975. Pp. 1, 19, 102–103, 111-

112, 155–156, 188, 210, 211, 222–227, 230, 265, 322, 329.
Recounts incidents in the F-McAlmon relationship and tries to account for the acrimony which existed between them.

I327.   Sokoloff, Alice Hunt. *Hadley—The First Mrs. Hemingway.* NY: Dodd, Mead, 1973. Pp. 78, 79, 87.
Brief memories of F and Zelda in Paris and on the Riviera.

I328.   Solomon, Barbara H. "Introduction." In her ed. *Ain't We Got Fun?—Essays, Lyrics, and Stories of the Twenties.* NY: New American Library, 1980. Pp. 1–36 [15, 19, 21–23, 33–34].
Brief discussions of GG and "Bernice Bobs Her Hair."

Soskin, William. See Bryer, ed. (I73)

I329.   Spatz, Jonas. "Fitzgerald, Hollywood, and the Myth of Success." In Warren French, ed. *The Thirties: Fiction, Poetry, Drama.* Deland, Fla.: Everett/Edwards, 1967. Pp. 31–37.
Focuses on "The Diamond as Big as the Ritz," GG, and LT in exploring F's changing attitudes towards Hollywood and the success myth, suggesting that in the latter two works F became more sympathetic towards the myth of success, romanticizing his vision of the American dream in GG and of Hollywood as its embodiment in LT.
Reprinted: Spatz (I330).

I330.   ———. *Hollywood in Fiction—Some Versions of the American Myth.* The Hague: Mouton, 1969. Pp. 16–17, 29, 37, 53–67, 78, 87–88, 89–91, 95, 96–99, 102, 107–108, 113, 115–116.
Includes (pp. 53–67) slightly revised reprinting of Spatz's essay in *The Thirties* (I329), as well as considerable scattered discussion of LT, particularly as a vision of Hollywood as an American success story, and some discussion of GG, TITN, and "C-U."

I331.   Spencer, Benjamin T. "Fitzgerald and the American Ambivalence." In his *Patterns of Nationality: Twentieth-Century Literary Visions of America.* NY: Burt Franklin, 1981. Pp. 145–159; see also pp. 130, 207, 220, 224.
Reprinting of Spencer's *South Atlantic Quarterly* article (H324).

I332.   Spindler, Elizabeth Carroll. *John Peale Bishop—A Biography.* Morgantown: West Virginia University Library, 1980. Pp. 12–14, 18–22, 24–25, 34–43, 62–63, 114–115, 125–126, 134–135, 148–149, 156–157, 183–186, 192–195, 199–202, 205–207, 233–234, and *passim.*
Scattered mentions of the F-Bishop friendship and professional relationship which includes quotes of F's opinions of Bishop's writings.

I333. Stafford, William T. "Benjy Compson, Jake Barnes, and Nick Carraway—Replication in Three 'Innocent' American Narrators of the 1920s." In his *Books Speaking to Books—A Contextual Approach to American Fiction.* Chapel Hill: University of North Carolina Press, 1981. Pp. 25–50 [29–30, 43–50]; see also pp. 7, 14, 29–30, 58–59, 63, 65, 122–123, 157, 158.

Nick is seen as a "replica" of "a central aesthetic concern of some American novelists of the 1920s."

I334. Stanley, Linda C. THE FOREIGN CRITICAL REPUTATION OF F. SCOTT FITZGERALD—AN ANALYSIS AND ANNOTATED BIBLIOGRAPHY. Westport, Conn.: Greenwood Press, 1980. 276 pp.

Devotes individual chapters to France, Great Britain, Germany, Italy, and Japan, and one which includes Australia, Canada, Denmark, India, The Low Countries, Norway, Portugal, Russia, South Africa, Spain, and Sweden. Each chapter contains an analysis of the various critical reponses to F, a chronological list of translations and editions of F, and an annotated listing of books, parts of books, periodical and newspaper articles, and reviews about F.

REVIEWS:

i. Anonymous. Review of *The Foreign Critical Reputation of F. Scott Fitzgerald, Choice,* 18 (November 1980), 378.

ii. ———. Review of *The Foreign Critical Reputation of F. Scott Fitzgerald, Journal of Modern Literature,* 9 (December 1982), 447.

iii. Fried, Lewis. Review of *The Foreign Critical Reputation of F. Scott Fitzgerald, American Reference Books Annual,* 12 (1981), 577.

Nelson, Raymond S. Review of *The Foreign Critical Reputation of F. Scott Fitzgerald, Modern Fiction Studies,* 27 (Summer 1981), 364. See H1282.

Startsev, A. See Proffer, ed. (I289)

I335. Stavola, Thomas J. SCOTT FITZGERALD: CRISIS IN AN AMERICAN IDENTITY. NY: Barnes & Noble; London: Vision Press, 1979. 176 pp.

Uses Erik Erikson's psychoanalytic theories to examine "the American identity crisis of Scott Fitzgerald and those of the major male characters in his four completed novels," exploring the developmental stages outlined by Erikson in F and the four protagonists. Also contrasts the characters, all of whom are failures whose failings are rooted in their individual weaknesses and in "a more fundamental weakness in the American belief in unlimited possibility," with F himself, whose "personal failures taught him to make successful fictional images of basic psychological drives with which all of us contend."

REVIEWS:

    i.   Anonymous. Review of *Scott Fitzgerald: Crisis in an American Identity, Choice,* 16 (September 1979), 838.

    ii.   ————. Review of *Scott Fitzgerald: Crisis in an American Identity, Queen's Quarterly,* 86 (Winter 1979/80), 739.

    iii.   Beaver, Harold. "3. The American Scene," *Times Literary Supplement* (London), December 21, 1979, pp. 167–168 [168].

    iv.   Butler, Robert J. Review of *Scott Fitzgerald: Crisis in an American Identity, Best Sellers,* 40 (May 1980), 74.

    v.   B[utscher], E[dward]. Review of *Scott Fitzgerald: Crisis in an American Identity, The Booklist,* 76 (September 15, 1979), 86.

    vi.   Donaldson, Scott. Review of *Scott Fitzgerald: Crisis in an American Identity, Modern Fiction Studies,* 26 (Summer 1980), 333–334.

    vii.   Hawley, John C. Review of *Scott Fitzgerald: Crisis in an American Identity, America,* 141 (October 6, 1979), 179–180.

    viii.   Horder, John. Review of *Scott Fitzgerald: Crisis in an American Identity, Times Educational Supplement* (London), August 22, 1980, p. 19.

    ix.   Spindler, Michael. Review of *Scott Fitzgerald: Crisis in an American Identity, Journal of American Studies,* 14 (December 1980), 491.

    x.   Tucker, Deborah B. Review of *Scott Fitzgerald: Crisis in an American Identity, Kliatt Young Adult Paperback Book Guide,* 15 (January 1981), 16.

I336.   Stegner, Wallace. *The Writer in America.* Tokyo: Hakuseido, 1952; Folcroft, Pa.: Folcroft Library Editions, 1976. Pp. 38–39, 115–116.

Calls F one of American writers of the 1920s who celebrated "a purely personal nihilism" and sees F's and Zelda's "sad and draggled end" as having had "a great symbolic effectiveness."

Stein, Gertrude. See White, ed. (I369)

I337.   Stein, Rita. *A Literary Tour Guide to the United States: SOUTH and SOUTHWEST.* NY: William Morrow, 1979. Pp. 16, 41.

Mentions F's and Zelda's associations with Montgomery, Alabama, and F's visit to Marjorie Kinnan Rawlings in Florida.

I338.   ———.   *A Literary Tour Guide to the United States: WEST and MIDWEST.* NY: William Morrow, 1979. Pp. 35, 110, 112–113.
Discusses F's associations with St. Paul and briefly mentions his Hollywood experiences.

I339.   Stenerson, Douglas C.   *H. L. Mencken—Iconoclast From Baltimore.* Chicago: University of Chicago Press, 1971. Pp. 5, 191, 209, 210, 218, 221.
Passing reference to the F-Mencken relationship and F's association with *The Smart Set.*

I340.   Stern, Milton R.   THE GOLDEN MOMENT—THE NOVELS OF F. SCOTT FITZGERALD. Urbana: University of Illinois Press, 1970. 463 pp.
Sees at "the center of Fitzgerald's imagination" the "uses of history, the American identity, the moral reconstruction of the American past," and studies this theme in TSOP, B&D, GG, and TITN, using F's life "to illuminate his fiction" and finding in that fiction "the 'identity crisis' of our American time."

REVIEWS:

i.   Anonymous. "The American Dream Deferred," *Times Literary Supplement* (London), August 6, 1971, p. 941.

ii.   ———. Review of *The Golden Moment—The Novels of F. Scott Fitzgerald, Choice,* 8 (July 1971), 678.

        *Adams, Robert M. "Attis Adonis Osiris Fitzgerald & Co.," 17–18 (January 27, 1972), 26–29 [26–27]. See G91.

iii.   Buitenhuis, Peter. "Acadamicable Study of Auto-biografiction," *NY Times Book Review,* December 20, 1970, p. 4.

iv.   *Gross, Barry. Review of *The Golden Moment—The Novels of F. Scott Fitzgerald, Journal of Modern Literature,* 1 (Supplement 1971), 792–795.

v.   [Johnston, Albert]. Review of *The Golden Moment—The Novels of F. Scott Fitzgerald, Publishers' Weekly,* 198 (October 19, 1970), 48.

vi.   Jordan, Enoch P. Review of *The Golden Moment—The Novels of F. Scott Fitzgerald, Southern Humanities Review,* 11 (Winter 1977), 69–70.

vii.   Long, Robert Emmet. Review of *The Golden Moment—The Novels of F. Scott Fitzgerald, Saturday Review,* 54 (July 24, 1971), 40.

viii.   M[alkin], M[ary] A[nn O'Brian]. Review of *The Golden Moment—The Novels of F. Scott Fitzgerald*, *AB Bookman's Weekly*, 47 (February 15, 1971), 442.

ix.   Perosa, Sergio. Review of *The Golden Moment—The Novels of F. Scott Fitzgerald*, *Annali di Ca'Foscari*, 10 (Nos. 1–2, 1971), 314–316. In Italian.

x.   Piper, Henry Dan. Review of *The Golden Moment—The Novels of F. Scott Fitzgerald*, *American Literature*, 43 (November 1971), 469–470.

xi.   Rueckert, William. Review of *The Golden Moment—The Novels of F. Scott Fitzgerald*, *Criticism*, 13 (Summer 1971), 326–328.

xii.   Willingham, John R. Review of *The Golden Moment—The Novels of F. Scott Fitzgerald*, *Library Journal*, 96 (April 1, 1971), 1270–1271.

I341.   Stevenson, Elizabeth. *Babbitts and Bohemians—The American 1920s*. NY: Macmillan, 1967. Pp. 7, 122, 141, 168, 170, 237.
Brief passing references to F and to his works written in the 1920s.

I342.   Stewart, Donald Ogden. *By a Stroke of Luck!—An Autobiography*. NY: Paddington Press, 1975. Pp. 86–88, 94, 101, 102, 139, 243–244.
Memories of friendship with F in St. Paul in 1919, in NY, on the Riviera, and in Hollywood. Includes reprinting of Stewart's 1971 *Fitzgerald/Hemingway Annual* essay (H517).

I343.   Strode, Hudson. *The Eleventh House—Memoirs*. NY: Harcourt Brace Jovanovich, 1975. Pp. 74, 75, 89–93, 98, 162.
Recollections of F and Zelda during their courtship and early marriage, with emphasis on Zelda's behavior and F's hedonistic lifestyle. F had "an obliging and indulgent nature, unless he had had too much to drink. Then he could be rather horrible."

I344.   Styron, William. "An Elegy for F. Scott Fitzgerald." In his *This Quiet Dust and Other Writings*. NY: Random House, 1982. Pp. 77–84.
Reprinting of Styron's 1963 *New York Review of Books* review of *The Letters of F. Scott Fitzgerald* (A973).

I345.   Swanberg, W. A. *Dreiser*. NY: Charles Scribner's, 1965. Pp. 262, 263, 272.
Recounts (p. 272) F's appearance at a Dreiser party to present the host with a bottle of champagne.

I346.   Szladits, Lola L., comp. *1922—A Vintage Year—A Selection of Works From the Henry W. and Albert A. Berg Collection of English and American Literature.* NY: NY Public Library, 1972. Pp. 3, 5, 16, 29.
Exhibition catalogue includes mention and description of B&D and TJA.

Tate, Allen. See Young and Hindle, eds. (I390)

I347.   Thurber, Helen, and Edward Weeks, eds. *Selected Letters of James Thurber.* Boston: Little, Brown, 1981. Pp. 106, 122.
Brief references to LT and to Thurber's only meeting with F.

Thurber, James. See Thurber and Weeks, eds. (I347)

Tiessen, Paul. See Lowry and Lowry (I228).

I348.   Tomkins, Calvin. *Living Well Is the Best Revenge.* NY: Viking Press, 1971. Pp. 3–7, 35, 38, 42, 95, 100–116, 119–125, 127–128.
Slightly revised reprinting of Tomkins' 1962 *New Yorker* profile of Gerald and Sara Murphy (B516), here divided into chapters, with the addition of an "Album" of photographs with commentary and black and white reproductions of ten Gerald Murphy paintings with commentary.

I349.   Trachtenberg, Alan. "The Journey Back: Myth and History in *Tender Is the Night.*" In Roy Harvey Pearce, ed. *Experience in the Novel—Selected Papers From the English Institute.* NY: Columbia University Press, 1968. Pp. 133–162.
Contends that, if F's theme "is frequently disappointment in the failure of the American Dream to realize itself within history, then a conflict between history and myth as opposing ways of viewing the world lies at the heart of his vision." In GG, F had tried to grasp the world mythically; in TITN, his perspective is "unrelentingly historical."

I350.   Trilling, Lionel, Perry Miller, and Lyman Bryson. "*The Great Gatsby.*" In George D. Crothers, ed. *Invitation to Learning: English & American Novels.* NY: Basic Books, 1966. Pp. 319–328.
Text of CBS radio broadcast in which various aspects of GG are discussed: its conciseness and economy, the character of Daisy, the timelessness of its themes, and the reliability of Nick as a narrator.

I351.   Tsuboi, Kiyohiko. "Steinbeck's *Cup of Gold* and Fitzgerald's *The Great Gatsby.*" In Tetsumaro Hayashi, Yasuo Hashiguchi, and Richard F. Peterson, eds. *John Steinbeck: East and West.* Proceedings of the First International Steinbeck Congress Held at Kyushu Univ., Fukuoka City, Japan, in Aug. 1976 (Steinbeck Monograph Series, No. 8). Muncie, Ind.: Steinbeck Society of America, English Dept., Ball State University, 1978. Pp. 40–47.

Cites ten similarities between the two novels, most important of which is "the metamorphosis, or the transformation, of Elizabeth in *Cup of Gold* and Jay Gatsby."

I352.   Turnbull, Andrew. *Thomas Wolfe.* NY: Charles Scribner's, 1967. Pp. 133–135, 157–159, 190–194, 240–244, 217–277, and *passim.*

Account of Wolfe's contacts with F, mostly through Maxwell Perkins, but also through exchanges of letters, several of which are quoted.

I353.   Tuttleton, James W. "'Combat in the Erogenous Zone': Women in the American Novel Between the Two World Wars." In Marlene Springer, ed. *What Manner of Woman—Essays on English and American Life and Literature.* NY: New York University Press, 1977. Pp. 271–296 [278–282].

Surveys F's, Hemingway's, and Faulkner's responses to the "New Woman's declaration of war against traditional values," finding that at times "they were clearly hostile to what they felt as a threat she posed to an older ideal of women to which they clung." In F's "histories of the young men entrapped by their own fantasies," his "anxiety over the emasculating power of the New Woman of the Jazz Age" is revealed; but F's "saving grace...was his sensitivity to the social transformations liberating young American women (and men), the accuracy with which he recorded their moral experience, and the aesthetic power with which he organized and expressed his ambivalent feelings." Includes discussions of TSOP, B&D, GG, and TITN.

I354.   ———. "F. Scott Fitzgerald: The Romantic Tragedian as Moral Fabulist." In his *The Novel of Manners in America.* Chapel Hill: University of North Carolina Press, 1972. Pp. 162–183.

Deals with F as novelist of manners, noting that to "praise Fitzgerald as the Social Historian of the Jazz Age is...to pay homage to his powers of observation and intelligence in imaginatively recreating the socially significant detail in the form of art, to praise his gift for appropriating the moral fact and transforming it into the felt experience of his times." Includes long discussion of GG and briefer consideration of TSOP.

———. See Bryer, ed. (I74)

I355.   Vidal, Gore. "F. Scott Fitzgerald's Case." In his *The Second American Revolution—And Other Essays (1976–78)*. NY: Random House, 1982. Pp. 3–23.

Reprinting of Vidal's 1980 *NY Review of Books* review-essay (G414).

I356.   Voss, Arthur. *The American Short Story—A Critical Survey*. Norman: University of Oklahoma Press, 1973. Pp. 208–214.

Discusses "Winter Dreams," "The Rich Boy," and "Babylon Revisited," with emphasis on plot summaries and descriptive comments. Concludes that while F did "serious and important work in the short story,...his commercial fiction bulks very large, and there are only a few superb stories."

I357.   Walcutt, Charles C. *Man's Changing Mask: Modes and Methods of Characterization in Fiction*. Minneapolis: University of Minnesota Press, 1966. Pp. 239, 242, 280, 286–290.

Suggests (pp. 286–290) that the "ideal of democratic aristocracy" gives GG "its force" and that this idea inspires the successful characterizations of the novel because "they are expressed through significant actions."

I358.   Walker, Meredith. "Foreword." In Zelda Fitzgerald. *Scandalabra—A Farce Fantasy in a Prologue and Three Acts*. Bloomfield Hills, Mich., and Columbia, S.C.: Bruccoli Clark, 1980. Unpaged.

Discusses the composition, production, and biographical background of Zelda's play and compares the two surviving versions with the description of the play in the production program.

I359.   [Warren, Robert Penn]. "Scott Fitzgerald (1896–1940)." In his, Cleanth Brooks, and R. W. B. Lewis, eds. *American Literature: The Makers and the Making. Volume II*. NY: St. Martin's Press, 1973. Pp. 2282–2318.

Biographical/critical essay which discusses TSOP, B&D, GG, TITN, and, more briefly, LT, and stresses F's "capacity...to immerse himself in the life of his age" and his growing "ambivalence toward wealth, privilege and self-indulgence."

I360.   Watson, James G. "Faulkner's Short Stories and the Making of Yoknapatawpha County." In Doreen Fowler and Ann J. Abadie, eds. *Fifty Years of Yoknapatawpha—Faulkner and Yoknapatawpha—1979*. Jackson: University Press of Mississippi, 1980. Pp. 202–225 [206, 207, 208, 209–212].

Discusses influence of F's "Absolution" on Faulkner's "Nympholepsy" and *Flags in the Dust*.

I361.   Watts, Stephen. *The Ritz of Paris*. NY: W. W. Norton, 1964. Pp. 148–149.
Brief anecdote about a drunken F in the Ritz bar.

I362.   Way, Brian. F. SCOTT FITZGERALD AND THE ART OF SOCIAL FICTION. London: Edward Arnold; NY: St. Martin's Press, 1980. 171 pp.
Sees F as essentially a social novelist and explores the intellectual and cultural connections of his childhood and young adulthood; his affinities with Henry James, Henry Adams, and Edith Wharton; the trial and error process of his early writings through "The Diamond as Big as the Ritz"; and GG, TITN, "C-U," and LT, with a chapter devoted also to F's short stories.

REVIEWS:

i.   Anonymous. Review of *F. Scott Fitzgerald and the Art of Social Fiction*, *Choice*, 18 (March 1981), 956.

ii.   ———. Review of *F. Scott Fitzgerald and the Art of Social Fiction*, *Journal of Modern Literature*, 9 (December 1982), 447.

iii.   Glassco, David. Review of *F. Scott Fitzgerald and the Art of Social Fiction*, *British Book News*, August 1980, p. 496.

iv.   Gray, Richard. "Observed Manners," *Times Higher Education Supplement* (London), June 6, 1980, p. 17.

v.   Spangler, George M. Review of *F. Scott Fitzgerald and the Art of Social Fiction*, *American Literature*, 53 (November 1981), 521–522.

vi.   Wickes, George. Review of *F. Scott Fitzgerald and the Art of Social Fiction*, *Modern Fiction Studies*, 28 (Summer 1982), 292.

I363.   Wegelin, Christof. "The Image of Europe in Twentieth-Century American Fiction." In François Jost, ed. *Proceedings of the IVth Congress of the International Comparative Literature Association. Volume I*. The Hague: Mouton, 1966. Pp. 86–93 [88, 91].
Brief mention of TITN.

I364.   Weinhardt, Carl J. "The Rise of the Mormon Kid." In *The Most of John Held, Jr*. Brattleboro, Vt.: Stephen Greene Press, 1972. Pp. 12–14, 16–19 [12, 13].
Brief mention of F, with some comparison made between Held and F.

I365.   Wells, Walter. "The Hero and the Hack." In his *Tycoons and Locusts: A Regional Look at Hollywood Fiction of the 1930s*. Carbondale: Southern Illinois University Press, 1973. Pp. 103–121.
Traces through LT and the Pat Hobby stories elements found in oth-

er Hollywood fiction: "the loss or confusion of identity; the end of love
and of innocence; the corruption of normal sexuality; human decay; the
death of art, of values, and of dreams; the breakdown of language; an
all-pervading sense of the waste of human energies."

I366. West, James L. W., III. THE MAKING OF F. SCOTT
FITZGERALD'S "THIS SIDE OF PARADISE." [Columbia, S.C.]:
J. Faust, 1977. 122 pp.; THE MAKING OF "THIS SIDE OF
PARADISE." Philadelphia: University of Pennsylvania Press, 1983.
140 pp.

Studies "the gestation, composition, publication, reception, and textual history" of TSOP, with the intention of increasing "the reader's understanding of F. Scott Fitzgerald's first novel—of how he wrote it and
of what he wanted to say." Appendices include: "Physical Characteristics of the Manuscript" (pp. 112–113); "Manuscript-First Edition
Conversion Table" (pp. 114–118); and "Variants Between the First
English and American Editions" (pp. 118–120). New edition is "a
complete revision" of the earlier volume, but most changes are stylistic.
Adds to Appendices "Physical Characteristics of the *Romantic Egotist*
Fragments" (pp. 123–124).

I367. ————. "THIS SIDE OF PARADISE," THE
GRAMMARIAN, AND THE "AUTHOR'S FINAL INTENTIONS."
Blacksburg, Va.: James L. W. West III, 1972. [6 pp.]

Abstract of talk given at meeting of South Central Modern Language
Association in October 1972, and facsimiles of three pages from manuscript of TSOP. Most of this material is incorporated into West's longer
study (I366).

————. See Bryer, ed. (I74)

I368. Westbrook, Wayne W. "Debt in the Genteel Garden." In
his *Wall Street in the American Novel.* NY: New York University
Press, 1980. Pp. 124–151 [125, 145–148]; see also pp. 155, 169, 204.

Includes (pp. 145–148) analysis of F's portrait of the newly rich
class in B&D.

White, A. A. See Bryer, ed. (I73)

I369. White, Ray Lewis, ed. *Sherwood Anderson/Gertrude
Stein—Correspondence and Personal Essays.* Chapel Hill: University
of North Carolina Press, 1972. Pp. 74, 113.

Reprints Stein's comment on F from *The Autobiography of Alice B.
Toklas* (C149) and Anderson's comment about F's death in a January
26, 1941, letter to Stein.

I370. White, Sidney Howard. *Sidney Howard.* Twayne's United States Authors Series, No. 288. Boston: Twayne, 1977. Pp. 60, 65, 129, 134, 159n.
Brief references to parallels between GG and Howard's play "Lucky Sam McCarver" and to F and Howard in Hollywood.

I371. White, William. "Hemingway and Fitzgerald." In James Woodress, ed. *American Literary Scholarship—An Annual—1967.* Durham, N.C.: Duke University Press, 1969. Pp. 96–112.
Critical survey of the year's work in F studies.

I372. ———. "Hemingway and Fitzgerald." In J. Albert Robbins, ed. *American Literary Scholarship—An Annual—1968.* Durham, N.C.: Duke University Press, 1970. Pp. 107–117.
Critical survey of the year's work in F studies.

I373. ———. "Hemingway and Fitzgerald." In J. Albert Robbins, ed. *American Literary Scholarship—An Annual—1969.* Durham, N.C.: Duke University Press, 1971. Pp. 122–136.
Critical survey of the year's work in F studies.

I374. ———. "Hemingway and Fitzgerald." In J. Albert Robbins, ed. *American Literary Scholarship—An Annual—1970.* Durham, N.C.: Duke University Press, 1972. Pp. 132–148.
Critical survey of the year's work in F studies.

I375. Whitley, John S. F. SCOTT FITZGERALD: "THE GREAT GATSBY." Studies in English Literature, No. 60. London: Edward Arnold, 1976. 64 pp.
Attempts to "widen the range of references" and to suggest that GG is "a great world novel and that it can exert a tremendous effect on readers whose awareness of American history and culture is minimal." Includes chapters on Gatsby and Nick, as well as discussions of parallels with Keats' poetry, *Heart of Darkness, Moby-Dick,* and Poe's poetry.

I376. Wickes, George. *Americans in Paris.* Garden City, NY: Doubleday, 1969. Pp. 94, 147, 154, 166, 168, 171–172.
Scattered references to F in Paris, with emphasis on his relationships with Cummings, Harold Stearns, and Hemingway.

———. See Astro and Benson, eds. (I9)

I377. Williams, W. H. A. *H. L. Mencken.* Twayne's United States Authors Series, No. 297. Boston: Twayne, 1977. Pp. 45, 46, 85, 89, 90–91, 119, 140, 150.
Brief references to Mencken's influence on and championing of F.

I378.   Wilson, Edmund.   "Princeton—1912–1916" and "The Army—1917–1919." In his *A Prelude—Landscapes, Characters and Conversations From the Earlier Years of My Life*. NY: Farrar, Straus and Giroux, 1967. Pp. 71–148 [106] and 171–278 [180]; see also pp. 47, 68, 93, 148.

Reprinting of Wilson's 1967 *New Yorker* essays (H333, H334), along with other passing references to F.

I379.   ————.   *The Thirties—From Notebooks and Diaries of the Period*. Ed. by Leon Edel. NY: Farrar, Straus and Giroux, 1980. Pp. 301–303, 322–324, 353, 408, 473–474, 711–712, 714.

Brief mentions of F, along with accounts of encounters with F in NY City, at La Paix, and in Connecticut.

I380.   ————.   *The Twenties—From Notebooks and Diaries of the Period*. Ed. by Leon Edel. NY: Farrar, Straus and Giroux, 1975. Pp. 3–6, 16, 18, 29, 46, 48, 51–53, 55, 59–60, 67, 79, 82, 94–96, 138, 185–186, 214, 222, 278, 298, 340, 345, 355–356, 414, 450, 513.

Passing references to friendships with F and Zelda.

————.   See Karlinsky, ed. (I199)

————.   See Wilson, ed. (I381)

I381.   Wilson, Elena, ed.   *Edmund Wilson—Letters on Literature and Politics—1912–1972*. NY: Farrar, Straus and Giroux, 1977. Pp. 5, 24, 29–31, 34–35, 41, 44–47, 53, 56, 57, 61–63, 68, 73, 78–79, 82, 84–89, 94, 96–98, 105–106, 110, 118–119, 121–122, 129, 134, 140, 142, 152, 173, 201–202, 228–229, 231–234, 251–254, 307, 312–315, 327–331, 335, 337–351, 369–370, 388, 413, 433, 475–481, 487, 494, 562–563, 596, 643, 664–665, 699, 710.

Includes letters to F and comments about F in letters to others, with critical commentary on TSOP, B&D, "The Vegetable," GG, TITN, and LT, and considerable information on Wilson's editing of C-U and LT, as well as his opinions of Mizener's biography (C110) and Schulberg's novel (C139).

I382.   Wilson, Robert N.   "F. Scott Fitzgerald—Personality and Culture." In his *The Writer as Social Seer*. Chapel Hill: University of North Carolina Press, 1979. Pp. 17–41; see also pp. 42, 51, 60, 97, 109, 148.

First portion of the chapter (pp. 17–28) is a slightly revised reprinting of Wilson's 1957 *Antioch Review* essay (B359); second portion suggests that F's behavior and attitudes were consonant with major American values: beliefs in the future, in individualism, in human perfectibility, in man's ability to master nature, and in doing and becoming. Because of his identification with these attitudes and because of his concern with social class, F is a "cultural exemplar."

I383. Winnick, R. H. *Letters of Archibald MacLeish—1907–1982*. Boston: Houghton Mifflin, 1983. Pp. 179, 181, 236, 273–274, 425.

Two MacLeish to F letters (pp. 236, 273–274) and brief mention of F in letters to Dos Passos, Hemingway, and Robert Linscott.

Wolfe, Peter. See Bryer, ed. (I74)

I384. Wolff, Geoffrey. *Black Sun—The Brief Transit and Violent Eclipse of Harry Crosby*. NY: Random House, 1976. Pp. 88, 116.

Brief passing mention of F.

I385. Woodress, James. *Booth Tarkington*. Philadelphia: J. B. Lippincott, 1955. Pp. 116, 244, 265, 290.

Passing references to F and Zelda, including brief account of visit by F and Hemingway to Tarkington in Paris.

I386. ———. "F. Scott Fitzgerald (1896–1940)." In his *American Fiction, 1900–1950—A Guide to Information Sources*. Detroit: Gale Research, 1974. Pp. 103–108.

Brief and selective survey of research and criticism on F.

I387. Yardley, Jonathan. *Ring—A Biography of Ring Lardner*. NY: Random House, 1977. Pp. 5–6, 110, 127, 146, 182, 201, 217–218, 240, 254, 256–269, 272–274, 277, 279–281, 284, 285, 288–290, 292, 297, 302, 309, 313, 314, 319, 322, 326, 339, 354, 371, 377–378, 388, 390, 393.

Includes account of the F-Lardner friendship, recounting incidents from that relationship as well as commenting on their influence on one another's work.

I388. Yates, Norris W. *Robert Benchley*. Twayne's United States Authors Series, No. 38. NY: Twayne, 1968. Pp. 61–62, 64.

Mention of Nick Carraway and Dick Diver as manifestations of "the uncommon common man."

I389. Young, Philip, and Charles W. Mann. "Fitzgerald's *Sun Also Rises*: Notes and Comment." In Bertram D. Sarason, ed. *Hemingway and "The Sun" Set*. Washington, D.C.: NCR Microcard Editions, 1972. Pp. 247–255; see also pp. 6, 18, 68, 71.

Reprinting of Young and Mann's essay from 1970 *Fitzgerald/Hemingway Annual* (H448), as well as passing references to F and GG.

I390.   Young, Thomas Daniel, and John J. Hindle, eds. *The Republic of Letters in America—The Correspondence of John Peale Bishop & Allen Tate*. Lexington: University Press of Kentucky, 1981. Pp. 2, 15, 16, 17, 19–20, 134, 136, 174.

Passing references to F and Zelda, mostly about the latter's mental condition and F's antics.

I391.   Zelnick, Stephen. "The Incest Theme in *The Great Gatsby*: An Exploration of the False Poetry of Petty Bourgeois Consciousness." In Norman Rudich, ed. *Weapons of Criticism—Marxism in America and the Literary Tradition*. Palo Alto, Calif.: Ramparts Press, 1976. Pp. 327–340.

Sees GG as "a specific and historically definite portrayal of the American nineteen-twenties as it was perceived by a humane and talented writer, whose theme, although he was finally unable to grasp it firmly, is the tortuous contradictions of his own petty bourgeois class," and suggests that in the novel "the family romance, and particularly the aspect of the usurpation of the father, becomes the central expression of the petty bourgeoisie adventurer's dream of class usurpation...the bourgeoisie become parents whose wealth and power allow them an untrammeled and irresponsible will; all others are children doomed to live in Cinderella fantasies."

I392.   Zlotnick, Joan. "The Roaring Twenties." In her *Portrait of an American City: The Novelists' New York*. Port Washington, NY: Kennikat Press, 1982. Pp. 110–131 [111–116].

Explores F's "vivid—if sometimes one-sided—fictional recreation of New York during the Jazz Age" in "May Day," "The Rich Boy," TSOP, B&D, and GG.

J

Graduate Research on
F. Scott Fitzgerald

This listing of graduate research is based on *Dissertation Abstracts* and *Dissertation Abstracts International* for the Ph.D. dissertations and on reports from librarians at approximately one hundred American and Canadian universities for the Masters Essays. The list of dissertations updates the similar compilation in Section E of *The Critical Reputation of F. Scott Fitzgerald*; the list of Masters Essays both updates and supplements the earlier listing in that more universities were surveyed and, as a consequence, a number of pre-1967 essays are here included. Nonetheless, the Masters Essays list should be regarded as representative; and the dissertation list, while more complete, may well not include works done in English at some foreign universities which do not currently list in *Dissertation Abstracts International*.

DOCTORAL DISSERTATIONS

J1.   Allen, Joan Marie. "Residual Catholicism in Selected Works of F. Scott Fitzgerald," Ph.D., University of Massachusetts, 1973 [Abstract in *Dissertation Abstracts International*, 34 (July 1973), 302A].
See I4.

J2.   Allen, Louis David. "Prose Fiction as Symbolic Form," Ph.D., University of Nebraska, Lincoln, 1975 [Abstract in *Dissertation Abstracts International*, 36 (June 1976), 8029A–8030A].
Includes discussion of GG.

J3.   Anderson, William Richard, Jr. "The Fitzgerald Revival, 1940–1974: A Study in Literary Reputation," Ph.D., University of South Carolina, 1974 [Abstract in *Dissertation Abstracts International*, 36 (August 1975), 883A–884A].

J4.   Atkinson, Jennifer Elizabeth. "Author and Agent: Appendices to *As Ever, Scott Fitz—*," Ph.D., University of South Carolina, 1971 [Abstract in *Dissertation Abstracts International*, 32 (November 1971), 2671A–2672A].
See I42.

J5.   Bednick, David B. "The Changing Role of Anxiety in the Novel," Ph.D., New York University, 1975 [Abstract in *Dissertation Abstracts International*, 36 (December 1975), 3682A].
Includes discussion of TITN.

J6.   Bizzell, Patricia Lynn. "I. 'With an Opulent American Touch': The Development of F. Scott Fitzgerald's Romantic Ideal. II. Willful Simplicity: The Charm of John Bunyan's Poetry. III. The English Romantics on War: Revolution or Conquest," Ph.D., Rutgers University, 1975 [Abstract in *Dissertation Abstracts International*, 36 (November 1975), 2788A].

J7.   Bloom, Thomas Kenneth. "The Style of F. Scott Fitzgerald," Ph.D., Ohio University, 1972 [Abstract in *Dissertation Abstracts International*, 33 (August 1972), 746A].

J8.   Box, Patricia Ann Slater. "The Image of the Artist in the Works of F. Scott Fitzgerald," Ph.D., Texas Tech University, 1978 [Abstract in *Dissertation Abstracts International*, 39 (March 1979), 5509A].

J9.   Bridges, Lloyd. "Flight in the American Novel," Ph.D., University of Utah, 1971 [Abstract in *Dissertation Abstracts International*, 32 (December 1971), 3243A].
Includes discussion of GG.

J10.   Bronson, Dan E. "Vision and Revision: A Genetic Study of Scott Fitzgerald's Short Fiction With Some Excursions Into His Novels," Ph.D., Princeton University, 1972 [Abstract in *Dissertation Abstracts International*, 33 (November 1972), 2362A].

J11.   Buntain, Lucy Madden. "*The Great Gatsby*: A Romantic Masquerade," Ph.D., University of Nebraska, Lincoln, 1975 [Abstract in *Dissertation Abstracts International*, 36 (March 1976), 6096A].

J12. Busby, Mark Bayless. "Innocence, Suffering, and Release: The Merging Adam-Christ Figure in Contemporary American Fiction," Ph.D., University of Colorado, 1977 [Abstract in *Dissertation Abstracts International*, 38 (January 1978), 4164A]. Includes discussion of GG.

J13. Callahan, John Francis. "When That Greater Dream Had Gone: History and Self in *The Great Gatsby* and *Tender Is the Night*," Ph.D., University of Illinois at Urbana-Champaign, 1970 [Abstract in *Dissertation Abstracts International*, 31 (November 1970), 2376A]. See I79.

J14. Carlson, Constance Hedin. "Heroines in Certain American Novels," Ph.D., Brown University, 1971 [Abstract in *Dissertation Abstracts International*, 32 (March 1972), 5175A]. Principally F, Wharton, and Updike.

J15. Chipman, Bruce Lewis. "America's Dream-Dump: A Study of the American Hollywood Novel," Ph.D., Tufts University, 1981 [Abstract in *Dissertation Abstracts International*, 42 (October 1981), 1632A]. Includes section on LT.

J16. Collins, Angus Paul. "Three Apocalyptic Novels: *Our Mutual Friend*, *The Princess Casamassima*, *Tender Is the Night*," Ph.D., Indiana University, 1976 [Abstract in *Dissertation Abstracts International*, 37 (February 1977), 5109A].

J17. Cooper, Douglas Marshall. "Form and Function: The Writing Style of Zelda Sayre Fitzgerald," Ph.D., University of Delaware, 1979 [Abstract in *Dissertation Abstracts International*, 40 (October 1979), 2060A].

J18. Cree, Charles George. "The Pastoral and the Theme of the Validity of Authorship in American Fiction," Ph.D., Indiana University, 1980 [Abstract in *Dissertation Abstracts International*, 41 (March 1981), 4032A]. Includes discussion of TITN.

J19. Crosland, Andrew Tate. "A Concordance to *The Great Gatsby*," Ph.D., University of South Carolina, 1976 [Abstract in *Dissertation Abstracts International*, 37 (April 1977), 6483A–6484A]. See I97.

J20. Dardis, Thomas Anthony. "Some Time in the Sun: The Hollywood Years of Fitzgerald, Faulkner, Nathanael West, Aldous Huxley, and James Agee," Ph.D., Columbia University, 1980

[Abstract in *Dissertation Abstracts International*, 41 (April 1981), 4392A–4393A].
See I100.

J21.   Davidson, Colleen Tighe. "Beyond the Sentimental Heroine: The Feminist Character in American Novels, 1899–1937," Ph.D., University of Minnesota, 1975 [Abstract in *Dissertation Abstracts International*, 37 (July 1976), 306A].
Includes discussion of SMTW.

J22.   Dean, Sharon Welch. "Lost Ladies: The Isolated Heroine in the Fiction of Hawthorne, James, Fitzgerald, Hemingway, and Faulkner," Ph.D., University of New Hampshire, 1973 [Abstract in *Dissertation Abstracts International*, 34 (November 1973), 2616A].

J23.   Dixon, Wheeler Winston. "The Cinematic Vision of F. Scott Fitzgerald," Ph.D., Rutgers University the State University of New Jersey (New Brunswick), 1982 [Abstract in *Dissertation Abstracts International*, 43 (October 1982), 1150A–1151A].

J24.   Doyle, Phyllis Louise. "The Search For Selfhood in the Fiction of F. Scott Fitzgerald," Ph.D., University of Rhode Island, 1980 [Abstract in *Dissertation Abstracts International*, 41 (February 1981), 3578A–3579A].

J25.   Durrell, John Blaine. "The Other Side of Paradise," Ph.D., University of South Carolina, 1971 [Abstract in *Dissertation Abstracts International*, 32 (April 1972), 5784A–5785A].
Deals with F's attempts at "formal tragedy."

J26.   Elmore, Albert Earl. "An Interpretation of *The Great Gatsby,*" Ph.D., Vanderbilt University, 1968 [Abstract in *Dissertation Abstracts*, 29 (February 1969), 2706A].

J27.   Evans, Thomas Jeffrey. "Realism in the Novels of F. Scott Fitzgerald," Ph.D., University of California, Davis, 1974 [Abstract in *Dissertation Abstracts International*, 36 (July 1975), 310A].

J28.   Farley, Pamella. "Form and Function: The Image of Woman in Selected Works of Hemingway and Fitzgerald," Ph.D., Pennsylvania State University, 1973 [Abstract in *Dissertation Abstracts International*, 35 (December 1974), 3735A].

J29.   Feldman, Leonard Mark. "A Matter of Money: Money and the World of the American Novel, 1893–1940," Ph.D., University of California, Los Angeles, 1981 [Abstract in *Dissertation Abstracts International*, 42 (February 1982), 3599A–3600A].
Includes section on GG.

J30.　Funk, Ruth Christy.　"Order and Chaos: A Study of Cultural Dialectic in Adams, James, Cather, Glasgow, Warren, and Fitzgerald," Ph.D., Syracuse University, 1979 [Abstract in *Dissertation Abstracts International*, 40 (November 1979), 2679A]. Includes discussion of GG.

J31.　Fussell, Mary Burton.　"Last Testaments: Writers in Extremis," Ph.D., University of California, San Diego, 1976 [Abstract in *Dissertation Abstracts International*, 37 (March 1977), 5814A–5815A]. Includes discussion of TITN.

J32.　Gottlieb, Carole Patricia.　"The Armored Self: A Study of Compassion and Control in *The Great Gatsby* and *The Sun Also Rises*," Ph.D., University of Washington, 1970 [Abstract in *Dissertation Abstracts International*, 32 (July 1971), 429A–430A].

J33.　Gross, Barry Edward.　"The Novels of F. Scott Fitzgerald: 'The Dominant Idea,'" Ph.D., Ohio State University, 1966 [Abstract in *Dissertation Abstracts*, 27 (March 1967), 3048A].

J34.　Guthmann, Herbert Jordan.　"The Characterization of the Psychiatrist in American Fiction, 1859–1965," Ph.D., University of Southern California, 1969 [Abstract in *Dissertation Abstracts International*, 30 (April 1970), 4451A]. Includes discussion of TITN.

J35.　Haines, James Barr.　"Being and Becoming: The Dynamic of Image and Theme in the Novels of F. Scott Fitzgerald," Ph.D., University of Pittsburgh, 1975 [Abstract in *Dissertation Abstracts International*, 36 (January 1976), 4490A].

J36.　Hanley, Richard Eugene.　"Place to Place: A Study of the Movement Between the City and Country in Selected Twentieth-Century American Fiction," Ph.D., State University of NY at Binghamton, 1981 [Abstract in *Dissertation Abstracts International*, 42 (November 1981), 2130A–2131A]. Includes section on F.

J37.　Hartley, Dean Wilson.　"The Provincial Hero: Studies in the American Consciousness (1799–1970)," Ph.D., Indiana University, 1974 [Abstract in *Dissertation Abstracts International*, 35 (April 1975), 6714A–6715A]. Includes discussion of GG.

J38.   Hazel, Erik Richard. "The Hollywood Image: An Examination of the Literary Perspective," Ph.D., Case Western Reserve University, 1974 [Abstract in *Dissertation Abstracts International*, 35 (November 1974), 2991A].
Discussion of F and LT.

J39.   Hewitt, Rosalie. "Aristocracy and the Modern American Novel of Manners: Edith Wharton, F. Scott Fitzgerald, Ellen Glasgow and James Gould Cozzens," Ph.D., Purdue University, 1970 [Abstract in *Dissertation Abstracts International*, 31 (February 1971), 4163A–4164A].

J40.   Higgins, John A. "F. Scott Fitzgerald as a Writer of the Short Story: A Critical Study of His Basic Motifs and Techniques," Ph.D., St. John's University, 1968 [Abstract in *Dissertation Abstracts International*, 30 (September 1969), 1169A–1170A].
See I178.

J41.   Higgs, Robert Jackson. "The Unheroic Hero: A Study of the Athlete in Twentieth-Century American Literature," Ph.D., University of Tennessee, 1967 [Abstract in *Dissertation Abstracts*, 28 (April 1968), 4177A].
See I179.

J42.   Hindin, Beverly Narod. "Death and the Imaginative Vision of Modern and Post-Modern American Fiction," Ph.D., University of Pennsylvania, 1981 [Abstract in *Dissertation Abstracts International*, 42 (December 1981), 2676A].
Includes discussion of GG.

J43.   Hipkiss, Robert Arthur. "The Values of Expatriation for the Major American Novelists: 1914–1941," Ph.D., University of California, Los Angeles, 1966 [Abstract in *Dissertation Abstracts*, 27 (June 1967), 4254A].

J44.   Hirshfield, Robert. "The Success Ethic in America and Its Effect Upon Four American Novelists," Ph.D., University of Nebraska, Lincoln, 1974 [Abstract in *Dissertation Abstracts International*, 35 (November 1974), 2991A–2992A].
London, Dreiser, Herrick, and F.

J45.   Horodowich, Peggy Maki. "The Prose of F. Scott Fitzgerald," Ph.D., University of Delaware, 1978 [Abstract in *Dissertation Abstracts International*, 39 (September 1978), 1568A].

J46.   Huonder, E[ugen]. "The Func[t]ional Significance of Setting in the Novels of Francis Scott Fitzgerald," Ph.D., Universität Basel, 1974 [Abstract in *Dissertation Abstracts International*, 38 (Autumn 1977), 22C].
See I191.

J47.   Jeffery, Benjamin Miles.   "The *Saturday Evening Post* Short Story in the Nineteen-Twenties," Ph.D., University of Texas, 1966 [Abstract in *Dissertation Abstracts*, 27 (March 1967), 3050A].

J48.   Kenyon, Nina Naomi.   "Self-Hatred as a Basis For Criticism of American Society," Ph.D., St. Louis University, 1968 [Abstract in *Dissertation Abstracts*, 29 (February 1969), 2713A]. London, S. Lewis, and F.

J49.   Klug, Jack B.   "Satire in the Early Works of F. Scott Fitzgerald," Ph.D., Texas A&M University, 1976 [Abstract in *Dissertation Abstracts International*, 37 (June 1977), 7752A].

J50.   Kuhnle, John Harold.   "Conscious Artistry in the Major Novels of F. Scott Fitzgerald," Ph.D., Vanderbilt University, 1971 [Abstract in *Dissertation Abstracts International*, 32 (May 1972), 6431A].

J51.   Kumar, Sukrita Paul.   "Man-Woman Relationship in the Fiction of Theodore Dreiser, F. Scott Fitzgerald and Ernest Hemingway," Ph.D., Marathwada University, 1975 [Abstract in *Ideas—Indian Doctoral Engagements in American Studies*, No. 6 (June 1976), 31–32].

J52.   Latham, John Aaron.   "The Motion Pictures of F. Scott Fitzgerald," Ph.D., Princeton University, 1970 [Abstract in *Dissertation Abstracts International*, 31 (June 1971), 6617A–6618A]. See I218

J53.   Lawson, Jessie Edminster.   "The Other Side of the Window: An Essay on Structural Iconography in English and American Fiction," Ph.D., University of Missouri-Columbia, 1978 [Abstract in *Dissertation Abstracts International*, 40 (July 1979), 232A–233A].
Includes chapter on use of windows, literal and figurative, in works by Hawthorne, James, and F.

J54.   Lee, Lynn Allen.   "The Significant Popular Novel as American Literature, 1920–1930; 1950–1960," Ph.D., University of Minnesota, 1968 [Abstract in *Dissertation Abstracts International*, 30 (July 1969), 329A].
Includes discussion of GG.

J55.   Lhamon, William Taylor, Jr.   "The Horatio Alger Pattern in the Twentieth Century American Novel: Focus on Fitzgerald," Ph.D., Indiana University, 1972 [Abstract in *Dissertation Abstracts International*, 33 (May 1973), 6363A–6364A].

J56.   Long, Robert Emmet.   "The Hero and Society in the Earlier Novels of F. Scott Fitzgerald: A Study in Literary Milieu," Ph.D., Columbia University, 1968 [Abstract in *Dissertation Abstracts*, 29 (February 1969), 2715A–2716A].

J57.   Maimon, Elaine Plaskow.   "The Biographical Myth of F. Scott Fitzgerald (1940–1970)," Ph.D., University of Pennsylvania, 1970 [Abstract in *Dissertation Abstracts International*, 32 (July 1971), 442A–443A].

J58.   Mangum, Anthony Bryant.   "The Short Stories of F. Scott Fitzgerald: A Study in Literary Economics," Ph.D., University of South Carolina, 1974 [Abstract in *Dissertation Abstracts International*, 37 (October 1976), 2184A].

J59.   Margolies, Alan.   "The Impact of Theatre and Film on F. Scott Fitzgerald," Ph.D., New York University, 1969 [Abstract in *Dissertation Abstracts International*, 30 (February 1970), 3467A].

J60.   Margolin, Michael Paul.   "Three Studies in Contemporary American Fiction: Romantic, Mimetic, and Didactic Forms," Ph.D., University of Iowa, 1976 [Abstract in *Dissertation Abstracts International*, 37 (November 1976), 2873A].
Includes discussion of GG.

J61.   Mark, Winifred Agnes Nora.   "The Critical Reception of the Major Works of F. Scott Fitzgerald, 1920–1977," Ph.D., Catholic University of America, 1978 [Abstract in *Dissertation Abstracts International*, 39 (September 1978), 1574A].

J62.   Messenger, Christian Karl.   "Sport in American Literature (1830–1930)," Ph.D., Northwestern University, 1974 [Abstract in *Dissertation Abstracts International*, 35 (April 1975), 6724A].
Includes discussion of GG. See I255.

J63.   Michael, Subhashini.   "The Tragic Sense of Fitzgerald," Ph.D., Kanpur University, 1978 [Abstract in *Ideas—Indian Doctoral Engagements in American Studies*, No. 8 (August 1981), 19–20].

J64.   Millani, Sister Mary Elvira, M.Z.S.H.   "Irony and Symbolism: An Examination of the Longer Fiction of F. Scott Fitzgerald," Ph.D., St. Louis University, 1968 [Abstract in *Dissertation Abstracts*, 29 (February 1969), 2718A].

J65.   Miller, Linda Patterson.   "'That Rare Race of People': Gerald and Sara Murphy and the Expatriates," Ph.D., University of Delaware, 1979 [Abstract in *Dissertation Abstracts International*, 40 (August 1979), 856A].

J66.   Morse, Jonathan Irving. "Forms of Disillusion in Fitzgerald and Dos Passos," Ph.D., Indiana University, 1975 [Abstract in *Dissertation Abstracts International*, 36 (November 1975), 2826A].

J67.   Moyer, Kermit Wonders, II. "The Historical Perspective of F. Scott Fitzgerald," Ph.D., Northwestern University, 1972 [Abstract in *Dissertation Abstracts International*, 33 (April 1973), 5738A–5739A].

J68.   Murthy, Sikha, Satyanarayana. "Frank Norris and Scott Fitzgerald: Some Parallels In Their Thought and Art," Ph.D., University of Utah, 1976 [Abstract in *Dissertation Abstracts International*, 37 (December 1976), 3628A].

J69.   Nagel, Raymond Preston. "Romantic Reality in the Edwardian-Georgian Novel," Ph.D., University of New Mexico, 1973 [Abstract in *Dissertation Abstracts International*, 34 (November 1973), 2644A–2645A].
Includes discussion of GG.

J70.   Norris, Carolyn Brimley. "The Image of the Physician in Modern American Literature," Ph.D., University of Maryland, 1969 [Abstract in *Dissertation Abstracts International*, 31 (August 1970), 765A].
Includes discussion of TITN.

J71.   Oravets, Andrew Joseph, Jr. "Out of Kings: A Inquiry Into the Americanness of the Classic American Novel," Ph.D., Ohio State University, 1976 [Abstract in *Dissertation Abstracts International*, 37 (August 1976), 972A–973A].
Includes discussion of GG.

J72.   Petrie, Dennis Wayne. " 'Ultimately Fiction': A Study of Design in Modern American Literary Biography," Ph.D., Purdue University, 1979 [Abstract in *Dissertation Abstracts International*, 40 (March 1980), 5058A].
Includes section on Andrew Turnbull's *Scott Fitzgerald* (C167). See I285.

J73.   Podeschi, John Battista. "The Writer in Hollywood," Ph.D., University of Illinois at Urbana-Champaign, 1971 [Abstract in *Dissertation Abstracts International*, 32 (February 1972), 4629A].

J74.   Podis, Leonard Alan. "*The Great Gatsby*: A Stylistic Analysis," Ph.D., Case Western Reserve University, 1975 [Abstract in *Dissertation Abstracts International*, 36 (January 1976), 4496A].

J75.   Pomeroy, Charles William. "Soviet Russian Criticism 1960–1969 of Seven Twentieth Century American Novelists," Ph.D., University of Southern California, 1971 [Abstract in *Dissertation Abstracts International*, 32 (July 1971), 449A].

J76.   Potts, Stephen Wayne. "F. Scott Fitzgerald: His Career in Magazines," Ph.D., University of California, Berkeley, 1980 [Abstract in *Dissertation Abstracts International*, 41 (January 1981), 3110A].

J77.   Prigozy, Ruth Markoe. "The Stories and Essays of F. Scott Fitzgerald," Ph.D., City University of NY, 1969 [Abstract in *Dissertation Abstracts International*, 30 (December 1969), 2544A–2545A].

J78.   Probert, Kenneth Gordon. "Romance By Intent: A Study of Generic Procedure in *The Blithedale Romance, Moby-Dick, The American*, and *The Great Gatsby*," Ph.D., York University (Canada), 1979 [Abstract in *Dissertation Abstracts International*, 40 (March 1980), 5040A].

J79.   Reiter, Joan Govan. "F. Scott Fitzgerald: Hollywood as Literary Material," Ph.D., Northwestern University, 1972 [Abstract in *Dissertation Abstracts International*, 33 (April 1973), 5744A–5745A].

J80.   Rosenzweig, Paul Jonathan. "The Wilderness in American Fiction: A Psychoanalytic Study of a Central American Myth," Ph.D., University of Michigan, 1972 [Abstract in *Dissertation Abstracts International*, 33 (March 1973), 5140A].
Includes discussion of GG.

J81.   Ruppel, James Robert. "Narcissus Observed: The Pastoral Elegaic in Woolf, Faulkner, Fitzgerald, and Graeme Gibson," Ph.D., University of Toronto, 1977 [Abstract in *Dissertation Abstracts International*, 39 (January 1979), 4249A].
Includes chapter on GG.

J82.   St. Andrews, Bonnie Anne. "Forbidden Fruit: The Relationship Between Woman and Knowledge," Ph.D., Syracuse University, 1980 [Abstract in *Dissertation Abstracts International*, 41 (December 1980), 2620A].
Brief discussion of GG and TITN.

J83.   Schaeffer, Lynne Gail. "F. Scott Fitzgerald and the South," Ph.D., University of Detroit, 1977 [Abstract in *Dissertation Abstracts International*, 39 (March 1979), 5515A–5516A].

J84.   Scholz, Carol Krusen. "They Share the Suffering: The Psychoanalyst in American Fiction Between 1920 and 1940," Ph.D., University of Pennsylvania, 1977 [Abstract in *Dissertation Abstracts International*, 38 (April 1978), 6134A]. Includes discussion of TITN.

J85.   Schoonover, David Eugene. "The Long Way Home: American Literary Expatriates in Paris, 1919–1929," Ph.D., Princeton University, 1975 [Abstract in *Dissertation Abstracts International*, 37 (September 1976), 1556A].

J86.   Seidman, Barbara Ann. "The Filmgoing Imagination: Filmmaking and Filmgoing as the Subjects of Modern American Literature," Ph.D., University of Illinois at Urbana-Champaign, 1982 [Abstract in *Dissertation Abstracts International*, 42 (May 1982), 4827A–4828A].

J87.   Seiters, Dan Loren. "Image Patterns in the Novels of F. Scott Fitzgerald," Ph.D., Southern Illinois University, 1976 [Abstract in *Dissertation Abstracts International*, 37 (December 1976), 3629A–3630A].

J88.   Service, Eleanor Harnett. "Sense of Place in F. Scott Fitzgerald," Ph.D., Case Western Reserve University, 1976 [Abstracts in *Dissertation Abstracts International*, 37 (June 1977), 7754A–7755A and 43 (September 1982), 804A].

J89.   Seshachari, Neila C. "Myth in the Novels of F. Scott Fitzgerald," Ph.D., University of Utah, 1975 [Abstract in *Dissertation Abstracts International*, 36 (October 1975), 2203A–2204A].

J90.   Silver, Elizabeth Jane. "America Revisited: History and Setting in the Works of F. Scott Fitzgerald," Ph.D., University of California, Los Angeles, 1981 [Abstract in *Dissertation Abstracts International*, 42 (November 1981), 2133A].

J91.   Sivaramakrishna, M. "Fitzgerald Hero: The Anatomy of 'Crack-Up' Being a Study of the Theme of Deterioration," Ph.D., Osmania University, 1969 [Abstract in *Ideas—Indian Doctoral Engagements in American Studies*, No.3 (October 1972), 25–26].

J92.   Skenazy, Paul N. "Inarticulate Characters in Modern American Fiction: A Study of Fitzgerald, Hemingway, and Faulkner," Ph.D., Stanford University, 1974 [Abstract in *Dissertation Abstracts International*, 34 (June 1974), 7783A].

J93.   Stanley, Linda Claire. "The Foreign Critical Reputation of F. Scott Fitzgerald: An Analysis and Annotated Bibliography," Ph.D., New York University, 1976 [Abstract in *Dissertation Abstracts International*, 38 (August 1977), 777A].
See I334.

J94.   Stavola, Thomas John. "Crisis in an American Identity: An Application of Erik Erikson's Psychoanalytic Theories to the Life and Fiction of F. Scott Fitzgerald," Ph.D., Fordham University, 1977 [Abstract in *Dissertation Abstracts International*, 38 (October 1977), 2130A].
See I335.

J95.   Steinberg, Michael Jay. "Dream and Disillusion: The Major Theme in F. Scott Fitzgerald's Fiction," Ph.D., Michigan State University, 1974 [Abstract in *Dissertation Abstracts International*, 35 (March 1975), 6162A–6163A].

J96.   Steinbrink, Jeffrey Carl. "Attitudes Toward History and Uses of the Past in Cooper, Hawthorne, Mark Twain, and Fitzgerald," Ph.D., University of North Carolina, 1974 [Abstract in *Dissertation Abstracts International*, 36 (July 1975), 288A–289A].

J97.   Summers, Marcia Perry. "The Use of Subordinate Characters as Dramatized Narrators in Twentieth-Century Novels," Ph.D., University of Illinois, 1969 [Abstract in *Dissertation Abstracts International*, 30 (January 1970), 3024A–3025A].
Includes discussion of GG.

J98.   Talbott, Barbara Merlo. "The Material Ideal: Women as Symbols of Success in Selected American Fiction," Ph.D., University of Wisconsin-Milwaukee, 1978 [Abstract in *Dissertation Abstracts International*, 39 (March 1979), 5518A].
Includes chapter comparing GG with *An American Tragedy*.

J99.   Thornton, Patricia Elizabeth. "The Prison of Gender: Sexual Roles in Major American Novels of the 1920's," Ph.D., University of New Brunswick, 1976 [Abstract in *Dissertation Abstracts International*, 37 (May 1977), 7133A–7134A].
Faulkner, Hemingway, Dos Passos, and F.

J100.   Timson, Beth Snavely. "'In My Father's House': The Structure of Inheritance in Modern British and American Fiction," Ph.D., Vanderbilt University, 1978 [Abstract in *Dissertation Abstracts International*, 39 (November 1978), 2934A].
Includes discussion of GG.

J101. Walton, Dean Franklin. "A Chance For Preciseness: A Study and Collation of F. Scott Fitzgerald's Revisions to Selected Stories For His Four Collections," Ph.D., University of Delaware, 1982 [Abstract in *Dissertations Abstracts International*, 43 (November 1982), 1549A].

J102. Weingart, Seymour Leonard. "The Form and Meaning of the Impressionist Novel," Ph.D., University of California, Davis, 1964 [Abstract in *Dissertation Abstracts*, 26 (September 1965), 1656]. Includes chapter on F's indebtedness to Conrad.

J103. West, James Lemuel Wills, III. "Materials For an Established Text of F. Scott Fitzgerald's *This Side of Paradise*," Ph.D., University of South Carolina, 1971 [Abstract in *Dissertation Abstracts International*, 32 (April 1972), 5754A–5755A]. See I366.

J104. Wexelblatt, Robert Bernard. "Disintegration in Works of F. Scott Fitzgerald and Nathanael West," Ph.D., Brandeis University, 1973 [Abstract in *Dissertation Abstracts International*, 34 (January 1974), 4296A].

J105. Williams, Jere Lee. "The Cast of Glamour: A Study of Selected Short Stories of F. Scott Fitzgerald," Ph.D., Rice University, 1970 [Abstract in *Dissertation Abstracts International*, 31 (December 1970), 2945A].

J106. Winter, Keith John. "Paired Opposites as a Method of Composition in Fitzgerald's Novels," Ph.D., Washington State University, 1972 [Abstract in *Dissertation Abstracts International*, 33 (December 1972), 2909A].

J107. Woll, Harvey Stephen. "The Double World of F. Scott Fitzgerald's Short Stories," Ph.D., Duke University, 1976 [Abstract in *Dissertation Abstracts International*, 37 (December 1976), 3619A].

J108. Woodward, Jeffrey Harris. "F. Scott Fitzgerald the Artist as Public Figure, 1920–1940," Ph.D., University of Pennsylvania, 1972 [Abstract in *Dissertation Abstracts International*, 33 (June 1973), 6937A–6938A].

MASTERS ESSAYS

J109. Adkins, Carl Alan. "Toward a Dramatic Structure—The Evolution of F. Scott Fitzgerald's Artistry in His Short-Story Characterizations," M.A., University of Idaho, 1964.

J110.   Ahern, Eckor M. "A Comparison of the Syntax of Fitzgerald and Galsworthy," M.A., San Diego State University, 1968.

J111.   Anderson, William Hilton. "Characterization in the Novels of F. Scott Fitzgerald," M.A., University of South Carolina, 1962.

J112.   Angermeier, Brother Carol, C.S.C. "Themes and Patterns of Development in a Representative Group of F. Scott Fitzgerald's Short Stories," M.A., University of Notre Dame, 1952.

J113.   Antonin, Claudine. "The Legacy of Romantic Love in *The Great Gatsby* and *The Sun Also Rises*," M.A., University of North Carolina at Greensboro, 1970.

J114.   Arbo, Evelyn Andrews. "A Study of the Treatment of Wealth in the Fiction of F. Scott Fitzgerald and Edith Wharton," M.A., University of Maine, 1955.

J115.   Arndt, Murray. "A Structural Analysis of F. Scott Fitzgerald's *Babylon Revisited*," M.A., Catholic University of America, 1961.

J116.   Backstrom, Paul Meyer. "Jay Gatsby, Thomas Sutpen, and Humbert Humbert: Failed Idealists," M.A., University of Virginia, 1981.

J117.   Bacot, Lucia Blair. "Keats and the Novels of F. Scott Fitzgerald," M.A., University of South Carolina, 1976.

J118.   Baker, Christine. "F. Scott Fitzgerald: Portraits in Golden Girls and Fallen Heroes," M.A., Adelphi University, 1976 [Abstract in *Masters Abstracts*, 15 (June 1977), 103].

J119.   Baker, Lera Helen. "The Flapper Figure in American Fiction, 1919–1933," M.A., University of Louisville, 1974 [Abstract in *Masters Abstracts*, 13 (March 1975), 26].
Includes discussions of B&D, GG, and TITN.

J120.   Barton, George Lloyd, IV. "Narrative Artistry in *The Great Gatsby*," M.A., University of Virginia, 1971.

J121.   Bennett, Ellen E. "Three Uncollected Works of F. Scott Fitzgerald," M.A., California State University (Fresno), 1965.

J122.   Benson, Barbara P. "A Marriage and an Age: An Approach to the Novels of F. Scott Fitzgerald," M.A., North Carolina State University, 1977.

J123.   Bergmann, Lynn Suzanne.   "'Daddy's Girl': Rosemary Hoyt in Fitzgerald's *Tender Is the Night*," M.A., Pennsylvania State University, 1974.

J124.   Boyer, Ruther Edgerton.   "F. Scott Fitzgerald: The Development of Craft in *This Side of Paradise* and *The Beautiful and Damned*," M.A., North Carolina State University, 1971.

J125.   Bray, Phyllis M.   "F. Scott Fitzgerald's 'The Garden of Allah': An Unheralded Haven," M.A., Temple University, 1969.

J126.   Bremmer, John Frederick.   "The Function of the Women Characters in the Novels of F. Scott Fitzgerald," M.A., Oklahoma State University, 1967.

J127.   Brooke, Cheryl.   "Three Studies in English. William Shakespeare's *Henry IV*: A Study of Conscience; Prisoners of Society in *Bleak House*; Monroe Stahr: Scott Fitzgerald's Ideal Hero," M.A., Pennsylvania State University, 1967.

J128.   Brown, Paul Allen.   "A Study of the Women in the Novels of F. Scott Fitzgerald," M.A., Arizona State University, 1966.

J129.   Buchanan, William Fuller.   "Objectification of Women in the Major Fiction of F. Scott Fitzgerald," M.A., Vanderbilt University, 1979 [Abstract in Vanderbilt University. *Abstracts of Theses for Master's Degrees; and Titles of Doctoral Dissertations 1978–79*, p. 57].

J130.   Busch, Joan Mary.   "F. Scott Fitzgerald as Dreamer," M.A., University of Wyoming, 1968.

J131.   Carter, Susan Blythe.   "A Study of the Characterization of Dick Diver," M.A., University of North Carolina at Chapel Hill, 1967.

J132.   Collazo, Rosa Xnex.   "From Fact to Fiction: Characters in the Novels of F. Scott Fitzgerald," M.A., University of Akron, 1964.

J133.   Cook, Jerome Edward.   "Attitudes Toward Wealth in the Works of F. Scott Fitzgerald," M.A., University of Texas, 1965.

J134.   Cruoglio, Leonard Gerard.   "The Recognition of *The Great Gatsby*—Selected Criticism Since 1925," M.A., Villanova University, 1967.

J135.   Culmer, Angela Manette.   "Fitzgerald and the Phantasmagoric: Gatsby's Creator in Hollywood," M.A., Atlanta University, 1975.

J136.   Dambrauskas, Cynthia C. K.   "F. Scott Fitzgerald's Creation of a Character: A Study of the Artistic Transformation of Biographical Experience Into Fiction," M.A., Ball State University, 1970.

J137.   Derrington, Will.   *The Pat Hobby Stories* and the Maturity of F. Scott Fitzgerald," M.A., Middle Tennessee State University, 1978.

J138.   Dotterer, Donald William.   "'The Privileged and Precocious': A Study of F. Scott Fitzgerald's Basil and Josephine Stories," M.A., Drew University, 1977.

J139.   Duggan, Margaret Manning.   "F. Scott Fitzgerald's Portrait of the Artist as Nick Carraway," M.A., University of South Carolina, 1975.

J140.   Elkins, Marilyn Blake Roberson.   "F. Scott Fitzgerald's Use of the Bitch-Goddess Success," M.A., Vanderbilt University, 1970 [Abstract in Vanderbilt University. *Abstracts of Theses for Master's Degrees and Titles of Doctoral Dissertations 1969–70*, p. 38].

J141.   Fadden, Jean Therese.   "A Comparative Study of F. Scott Fitzgerald's *This Side of Paradise* With Compton Mackenzie's *Youth's Encounter* and *Sinister Street*," M.A., Villanova University, 1952.

J142.   Ferrante, Mary Elizabeth.   "F. Scott Fitzgerald's Portrayal of Women," M.A., Hofstra University, 1976.

J143.   Findley, Susan Tankersley.   "The Relationship of Maxwell Perkins, F. Scott Fitzgerald, and Ernest Hemingway," M.A., Clemson University, 1971.

J144.   Fluckiger, James.   "A Comparison of Wharton's *The Age of Innocence* and Fitzgerald's *The Great Gatsby*," M.A., Columbia University, 1978.

J145.   Fortner, Holloway.   "Psychological Study of Artificialities in the Life of Scott Fitzgerald and the Characters in His Novels," M.A., University of Wyoming, 1965.

J146.   Freeman, Maria R.   " 'All the Lost Youth in the World': Youth Worship in F. Scott Fitzgerald's *Tender is the Night*," M.A., College of William and Mary, 1979.

J147.   Gates, Michael F.   "F. Scott Fitzgerald's Basil Duke Lee Stories: An Archetypal Perspective," M.A., Brigham Young University, 1974.

J148. Goolsby, Rebecca J. "The Conflict of Eastern and Western Values in Three Novels By F. Scott Fitzgerald," M.A., Middle Tennessee State University, 1978.

J149. Gross, Barry Edward. "Gatsby and His Brethren: The Struggle and the Prize," M.A., Cornell University, 1962.

J150. Gross, Marilyn Frances. "The Acquisitive Rich: A Comparative Study of *The Theory of the Leisure Class* and *The Great Gatsby,*" M.A., East Tennessee State University, 1972.

J151. Gross, Robert Dillon. "F. Scott Fitzgerald's Short Story Narrators," M.A., University of North Carolina at Chapel Hill, 1973.

J152. Haberstroh, Charles. "The Phoenix That Never Was: A Study of the Failure of Love in the Completed Novels of F. Scott Fitzgerald," M.A., Villanova University, 1965.

J153. Haggard, Kay Burns. "The Impact of John Keats on F. Scott Fitzgerald," M.A., University of Tulsa, 1974.

J154. Hauenstein, Joyce. "F. Scott Fitzgerald's Heroines: A Study of the 'New' Woman and Her Destructive Influence," M.A., Bowling Green State University, 1966 [Abstract in Bowling Green State University. *Abstracts of Theses and Dissertations*, 11 (1965–1966), 192].

J155. Heldebrand, Carol Jamison. "A Study of the Heroines in the Novels of F. Scott Fitzgerald," M.A., Baylor University, 1968.

J156. Hertzog, Susan Kathryn. "The American Dream of Success in the 1925 Novels, *An American Tragedy*, *The Great Gatsby*, and *Arrowsmith*, in the Lives of Theodore Dreiser, F. Scott Fitzgerald, and Sinclair Lewis," M.A., University of Delaware, 1973.

J157. Hill, Fera Kornegay. "Francis Scott Fitzgerald, Chronicler of an Era," M.A., Atlanta University, 1963.

J158. Holland, James Elery. "The Idea of Honor in the Novels of Scott Fitzgerald," M.A., University of Texas, 1966.

J159. Houston, Clara Ruth Null. "Heroines in the Novels of F. Scott Fitzgerald," M.A., Louisiana State University, 1968.

J160. Ison, David Leslie. "Chiaroscuro and Color Symbolism in the Novels and Selected Short Stories of F. Scott Fitzgerald," M.A., Oklahoma State University, 1966.

J161.   Jacobs, Elizabeth Kahr. "The Business Man in the American Novel Since 1920," M.A., University of Cincinnati, 1958. Includes discussions of GG and LT.

J162.   Jensen, Vernon Hortin. "The Romantic Eden: A Study of Felt Alienation in the Short Fiction of Scott Fitzgerald; Who Is Sylvia? A Story; An Unfinished Fresco," M.A., Brigham Young University, 1967.

J163.   Johnson, Marcia A. "In Another Spectrum: F. Scott Fitzgerald and Impressionism," M.A., Murray State University, 1981.

J164.   Joslin, Richard Freeman. "The Heroine in the Fiction of F. Scott Fitzgerald," M.A., University of Connecticut, 1977.

J165.   Kirchhausen, James. "A Study of Humor in the Works of F. Scott Fitzgerald," M.A., Hofstra University, 1976.

J166.   Klug, Jack B. "F. Scott Fitzgerald's 'Top Girl': A Study of His Women Characters in Three Major Novels," M.A., Texas A&M University, 1965.

J167.   Kumar, P. Shiv. "The Valley of Ashes: Theme of Failure in the Novels of F. Scott Fitzgerald," M.A., Osmania University, 1967 [Abstract in *Ideas—Indian Doctoral Engagements in American Studies*, No. 2 (May 1972), 29–30].

J168.   Lackey, June Ellen. "Historical Reality and Illusion in F. Scott Fitzgerald's Fiction," M.A., Texas Technological College, 1966.

J169.   La May, Lauren Virginia. "In White Midnight: The Puritan Conscience of F. Scott Fitzgerald," M.A., Brown University, 1978.

J170.   Landrum, Roger L. "Imagery in F. Scott Fitzgerald's *The Great Gatsby*," M.A., Bowling Green State University, 1960 [Abstract in Bowling Green State University. *Abstracts of Theses and Dissertations*, 8 (1959–1960), 87].

J171.   Lascola, Linda M. "The Aesthetic Balance in the Romantic Point of View of the Male Protagonists in the Novels of F. Scott Fitzgerald," M.A., West Virginia University, 1970.

J172.   La Vista, Daniel J. "The Hollow Woman in F. Scott Fitzgerald's Early Fiction," M.A., University of Dayton, 1967.

J173.   Lawler, Daniel. "Symbolic Function of the Automobiles in *The Great Gatsby*," M.A., Columbia University, 1980.

J174.   Liles, Minette Roberson. "The Treatment of Time in *Tender Is the Night*," M.A., East Carolina University, 1977.

J175.   Lindsay, Julia Irene. "The Indictment of America in 1925: A Comparative Study of *The Great Gatsby* and *An American Tragedy*," M.A., University of North Carolina at Greensboro, 1969.

J176.   Lord, Mary Jean. "The First-Rate Intelligence in F. Scott Fitzgerald," M.A., Washington State University, 1963.

J177.   Love, Alan Carson. "Late Victorian Social Expression in the Novels of F. Scott Fitzgerald," M.A., Texas A&M University, 1966.

J178.   Luchtel, Patricia Moss. "F. Scott Fitzgerald's *Tender Is the Night*: A Discussion of the Development of the Novel and Its Alleged Credibility Gap," M.A., University of Louisville, 1969 [Abstract in *Masters Abstracts*, 8 (June 1970), 77].

J179.   Lynch, Cornelius D. "The Destructive Dreams of F. Scott Fitzgerald," M.A. (Liberal Studies), Wesleyan University, 1963.

J180.   MacCurdy, Carol Ann. "The Ironic Treatment of the Romantic Hero in the Novels of F. Scott Fitzgerald," M.A., University of South Carolina, 1975.

J181.   McFrederick, Carol Ann. "A Study of the Initiation Theme in the Works of F. Scott Fitzgerald," M.A., Florida Atlantic University, 1974 [Abstract in *Masters Abstracts*, 13 (March 1975), 27].

J182.   McKenna, Thomas A. "Shadow Imperfections: A Study of the Women in Three Novels of F. Scott Fitzgerald," M.A., Villanova University, 1969.

J183.   McMillan, Virginia. "Fitzgerald: The Faded Blue Room—A Study of the Critical Reception of *Tender Is the Night*," M.A., University of South Carolina, 1965.

J184.   Matthes, Carol Marie. "The Tragedy of F. Scott Fitzgerald," M.A., University of Georgia, 1969.

J185.   Miazga, Ronald C. "Views of Upper Class Americans By Fitzgerald, Santayana and Marquand," M.A., Illinois State University, 1967.

J186.   Mielke, Friederich. "F. Scott Fitzgerald's *The Great Gatsby* in German: A Comparative Analysis of Two Versions," M.A. (Comparative Literature), Indiana University, 1976.

J187.   Millet, Edwin Louis. "The Characterization of Fitzgerald's *The Last Tycoon*," M.A., University of Florida, 1968 [Abstract in *University of Florida Abstracts of Theses and Dissertations*, March 1968, p. 46].

J188.   Mizell, Elizabeth. "The Self and the Location of the Ideal in Fitzgerald's *The Beautiful and Damned*," M.A., University of Florida, 1972 [Abstract in *University of Florida Abstracts of Theses and Dissertations*, December 1972, p. 55].

J189.   Moore, Joan Scott. "F. Scott Fitzgerald—Ironist," M.A., University of Houston, 1962.

J190.   Mowery, Judith Kay. "Zelda Fitzgerald's Fiction: The Quest for Self," M.A., University of Akron, 1972.

J191.   Moyle, Thomas Michael. "F. Scott Fitzgerald After *Tender Is the Night*: A Study of the Late Stories," M.A., Clemson University, 1979.

J192.   Mullen, June Rhyne. "F. Scott Fitzgerald's Flashback Technique—A Study of Six Short Stories," M.A., University of North Carolina at Chapel Hill, 1969.

J193.   Norton, Sarah B. "The Jazz Age as Reflected in the Writing of F. Scott Fitzgerald," M.A., Baylor University, 1966.

J194.   O'Hanlon, Patricia. "The Social and Moral Significance of *This Side of Paradise*," M.A., Catholic University of America, 1958.

J195.   Olson, Larry Dean. "The Identity Crisis of Adolescence and *The Great Gatsby*," M.A., University of Northern Iowa, 1970.

J196.   Orcutt, Jo Ellen Lindh. "The Authority of Imagination: An Interpretative Study of Dick Diver in F. Scott Fitzgerald's *Tender Is the Night*," M.A., University of New Hampshire, 1973.

J197.   Ormsby, Rosemary. "A Comparison of F. Scott and Zelda Fitzgerald's Flower Imagery; The Function of Parties as Vehicles of Self Definition in Two Novels By Virginia Woolf; Reading for Author's Purpose: An Approach For Improving Reading in the Junior College," M.A., University of Vermont, 1976.

J198.   Pair, Joyce Morrow. "The Jazz Age Is Over: A Study of Dr. Richard Diver in *Tender Is the Night*," M.A., Georgia State University, 1975.

J199.   Parr, Mary Bryan. "Seductive Virgins and Callous Coquettes: Women in the Novels of Scott Fitzgerald," M.A., University of South Carolina, 1974.

J200.   Pfeiffer, John Franklin. "Fitzgerald and Glamor: An Interrelation of His Fact and Fiction," M.A., Duke University, 1965.

J201.   Polk, Donna J. "The Moral Dilemma of F. Scott Fitzgerald," M.A., University of South Carolina, 1971.

J202.   Price, Debora Marion. "Point of View and Vision in the Works of F. Scott Fitzgerald," M.A., Brown University, 1965.

J203.   Providente, Madeline Garbers. "F. Scott Fitzgerald: A Study of Personality and Personage," M.A., Hofstra University, 1977.

J204.   Puzio, Elaine M. "F. Scott Fitzgerald—The Fated Prophet of the Lost Generation," M.A., Fairleigh Dickinson University, 1969.

J205.   Rayner, Ricki Allyn. "A Study of the Jazz Age as Depicted in the Writings of F. Scott Fitzgerald," M.A., University of Mississippi, 1974.

J206.   Richards, George Michael. "The Thematic Evolution of *The Great Gatsby,*" M.A., West Virginia University, 1974.

J207.   Richards, Gloria Ellen. "A Psychoanalytical Study of the Narrator of F. Scott Fitzgerald's *The Great Gatsby,*" M.A., Ohio State University, 1978.

J208.   Riggs, Jerry Ann. "Insanity in the Novels of F. Scott Fitzgerald," M.A., University of Mississippi, 1967.

J209.   Robinson, Joan. "Elements of the Absurd in F. Scott Fitzgerald's *The Great Gatsby,*" M.A., Catholic University of America, 1970.

J210.   Robinson, Peter Guy. "Ritual Response in the Protagonists of F. Scott Fitzgerald's Major Novels," M.A., Vanderbilt University, 1970 [Abstract in Vanderbilt University. *Abstracts of Theses for Master's Degrees and Titles of Doctoral Dissertations 1970–71,* p. 49].

J211.   Rocheleau, Marcel. "Dreams, Dust, Despair: F. Scott Fitzgerald's Vision of America," M.A., University of Vermont, 1979.

J212.   Rogan, Elizabeth Gayle. "Innocence and Experience as Theme in the Novels of F. Scott Fitzgerald," M.A., University of Mississippi, 1974.

J213.   Rose, Elizabeth Dameron. "The Development of the Dominant Female in Selected Stories of F. Scott Fitzgerald, " M.A., North Texas State University, 1977 [Abstract in *Masters Abstracts*, 16 (March 1978), 43].

J214.   Ross, Dale Howard. "'The American Dream': Theme in the Major Novels of F. Scott Fitzgerald," M.A., University of Akron, 1961.

J215.   Ross, Patricia Anne. "The American Quest in *The Great Gatsby*," M.A., West Virginia University, 1975.

J216.   Rowe, Elizabeth Fitzmaurice. "The Heroine in the Novels of F. Scott Fitzgerald—Mirror and Shadow," M.A., Georgia State College, 1968.

J217.   Rumble, Allen Walker. "Gatsby and the Self-Made Man: *The Great Gatsby* As a Variant Statement of the Self-Made Man Ideal in America," M.A., University of Iowa, 1965.

J218.   Russell, Mary Patricia. "Zelda's Influence on Scott Fitzgerald's Major Heroines," M.A., Hofstra University, 1973.

J219.   Ruttonsha, Lakshmi. "F. Scott Fitzgerald's Novels: The Theme of Failure," M.A., Osmania University, 1970.

J220.   San Fratello, Father Sennen, O.F.M. "The Conscious Artistry of F. Scott Fitzgerald in *The Great Gatsby*," M.A., St. Bonaventure University, 1964.

J221.   Schoer, Marilyn Jean Herlitz. "Essays on American Culture and Literature," M.A., University of Utah, 1973.

J222.   Schroeder, Richard. "Personalities and Personages: A Study of the Protagonists in F. Scott Fitzgerald's Novels," M.A., University of New Mexico, 1965.

J223.   Seekins, Georgann Elizabeth. "F. Scott Fitzgerald: An Appraisal of His Reputation," M.A., University of Wyoming, 1955.

J224.   Shand, George Brian. "The Nature of Dreams—Theme and Imagery in Three Stories By F. Scott Fitzgerald," M.A., Cornell University, 1965.

J225.   Shull, Martha Smith. "An Investigation of the Autobiographical Elements in the Novels of F. Scott Fitzgerald," M.A., University of Dayton, 1965.

J226.   Simmons, Jean. "Eyes, Music, & Color: Imagery as Evidence of F. Scott Fitzgerald's Stylistic Development," M.A., Brigham Young University, 1975.

J227.   Skeels, Ralph Allan. "F. Scott Fitzgerald—The Futility of Success," M.A., University of Idaho, 1950.

J228.   Skwire, David. "*My Ántonia* and *The Great Gatsby*—A Single Voice," M.A., Cornell University, 1956.

J229.   Skyrms, Martha Ristine. "The Literary Heroes of Fitzgerald and Hemingway; Updike and Bellow," M.A., Iowa State University, 1979.

J230.   Smith, Mary Malone. "The Personal and Literary Relationship of Fitzgerald and Tennyson," M.A., University of Georgia, 1967.

J231.   Smock, Susan Wanlass. "A Thematic Study of the Relationship Between Hero and Heroine in Fitzgerald's Short Stories," M.A., University of North Carolina at Chapel Hill, 1975.

J232.   Soland, Carol Vivian. "Fitzgerald's Women Characters," M.A., Tufts University, 1965.

J233.   Solomon, Samuel Herschel. "Fitzgerald's Jay Gatsby and the American Dream," M.A., University of South Carolina, 1969.

J234.   Spiese, Richard Dale. "The Pattern of Despair in the Novels of F. Scott Fitzgerald," M.A., Pennsylvania State University, 1956.

J235.   Stadelman, Katherine Knopf. "Setting as Symbol in F. Scott Fitzgerald's *Tender Is the Night*," M.A., University of Florida, 1969 [Abstract in *University of Florida Abstracts of Theses and Dissertations*, January 1969, p. 51].

J236.   Stanton, Judith McNutt. "F. Scott Fitzgerald: The Function of the Money Motif," M.A., University of Maine, 1967.

J237.   Stern, Felice Abram. "Anatomy of a Failure: Structure, Theme and Point of View in F. Scott Fitzgerald's *The Beautiful and Damned*," M.A., Old Dominion University, 1968.

J238.   Stevens, Susan J. "The Misogyny of F. Scott Fitzgerald," M.A.L.S. (Liberal Studies), Drew University, 1978.

J239.   Storm, Donna O. "The Feminine Mystique in F. Scott Fitzgerald's Jazz Age," M.A. (American Studies), University of Wyoming, 1966.

J240.   Thomas, Carol Jeanet. "Outcast of Eden: Religious Motif in the Novels of F. Scott Fitzgerald," M.A., Eastern Kentucky University, 1972.

J241.   Unthank, Luisa Teresa Brown. "F. Scott Fitzgerald's Concept of the Rich," M.A., East Carolina University, 1965.

J242.   Vinson, Donna Harrington. "F. Scott Fitzgerald and the Romantic Quest," M.A., University of Mississippi, 1971.

J243.   Warren, Clifton Lanier. "F. Scott Fitzgerald: His Materials and Methods," M.A., University of Richmond, 1954.

J244.   West, Suzanne Jones. "Nicole and the Gardens in *Tender Is the Night*," M.A., College of William and Mary, 1975.

J245.   Weston, Elizabeth A. "Depiction of the American Abroad in F. Scott Fitzgerald's Fiction," M.A., University of Vermont, 1975.

J246.   White, Mary Ann. "A Study of the Three Published Versions of F. Scott Fitzgerald's *Tender Is the Night*," M.A., Auburn University, 1972.

J247.   Williams, Star Ann. "A Study of Nick Carraway's Contribution to *The Great Gatsby*," M.A., University of Mississippi, 1973.

J248.   Williams, Thomas W., Jr. "The Last Extremity: F. Scott Fitzgerald in Hollywood," M.A., University of Mississippi, 1967.

J249.   Woodard, Helena. "The Cruise and the Crack-up: F. Scott Fitzgerald and North Carolina," M.A., East Carolina University, 1979.

K

Reviews of
Save Me the Waltz
by Zelda Fitzgerald

Because of the interest in Zelda Fitzgerald generated by Nancy Milford's 1970 biography, *Zelda*, and because it is more clear now than ever before that F. Scott Fitzgerald's writing and that of his wife were inextricably interdependent (as were their lives), this listing of reviews of *Save Me the Waltz* is included. The reviews of the novel's 1932 first edition were gathered from clippings in the Princeton University scrapbooks and from a search of newspapers and magazines; the result can be no more than a representative sampling of responses. No reviews were located for the 1953 Grey Walls Press first English edition; reviews of the 1967 American and 1968 English editions were gathered from publishers' files. Reviews which are extensive re-evaluations of the Fitzgeralds' careers and are thus Review-Articles are marked with an asterisk. There is no corresponding section in *The Critical Reputation of F. Scott Fitzgerald*.

SAVE ME THE WALTZ
(1932)

K1.   Anonymous. "Alabama Steps Fast in Europe," Sacramento *Union*, January 8, 1933, p. 11.
"Mrs. Fitzgerald...has written this novel in charming style, although her plot is not extremely new."

K2.   ———. "The Bookworm," San Francisco *Call-Bulletin*, October 8, 1932, p. 9.
This is "a snappy book."

K3.   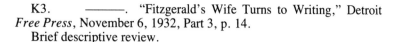. "Fitzgerald's Wife Turns to Writing," Detroit
Free Press, November 6, 1932, Part 3, p. 14.
Brief descriptive review.

K4.   ———. "Looking at Life," Rochester (NY) *Democrat
and Chronicle*, February 26, 1933, p. 3D.
"Mrs. Fitzgerald has drawn her characters with keen understanding,
and rare discernment."

K5.   ———. "Mrs. Fitzgerald's First Novel Places Her on
Scott's Level," Baltimore *Post*, October 15, 1932, p. 4.
Descriptive review. Mrs. F is "truly" a "writer."

K6.   ———. "New Books of the Week," Boston *Evening
Transcript*, October 8, 1932, Book Section, p. 3.
Descriptive brief review.

K7.   ———. "Of the Jazz Age," *NY Times Book Review*,
October 16, 1932, p. 7.
"Mrs. Fitzgerald's book is a curious muddle of good psychology and
atrocious style." It is burdened "with a weight of unwieldy metaphor;
and in searching for the startling phrase," she "has often descended to
the ludicrous."

K8.   ———. Review of *Save Me the Waltz*, *Forum and
Century*, 88 (December 1932), xi.
"Gifted with a talent for crisp dialogue and with a pleasant sense of
the humorous, Mrs. Fitzgerald has for some reason seen fit to subordinate this element in her first novel to an extremely involved prose
style which fails to do anything but clog both the action of the plot and
the reader's understanding of the characters."

K9.   ———. Review of *Save Me the Waltz*, *NY Herald
Tribune Books*, October 30, 1932, pp. 10–11.
Although "at times the story comes dangerously near losing all emotional credibility," it can nonetheless "be read with considerable pleasure. The writing has a masculinity that is unusual; it is always vibrant
and always sensitive."

K10.   ———. "'Save Me the Waltz,'" Detroit *News*,
November 6, 1932, Arts Section, p. 16.
"It is a light, loose-jointed romance that pleases with its portrait of
Alabama Beggs, but rather tires with its pictures of commonplace
affairs."

K11.   Becker, Charlotte. "A Stormy Passage From Youth's
Urge to Days of Reason," Buffalo *Evening News*, October 8, 1932,
Magazine, p. 3.
"It is odd to see wisdom handled with the methods one has so often

seen applied to the Follies....More than delightful is it to encounter anyone who can treat contemporary life with such a gift, and the talented wife of F. Scott Fitzgerald has obviously a sensitive talent of this sort."

K12.   Brande, Dorothea. "Seven Novels of the Month," *The Bookman* (NY), 75 (November 1932), 731–735 [735].
"There is a warm, intelligent, undisciplined mind behind *Save Me the Waltz.* Mrs. Fitzgerald should have had what help she needed [from 'the elementary services of a literate proofreader'] to save her book from the danger of becoming a laughing-stock."

K13.   Brickell, Herschel. "The Literary Landscape," *North American Review*, 234 (December 1932), 567–576 [573].
Brief review. "It is a period Mrs. Fitzgerald seems to know very well, and she has some gifts as a writer of fiction."

K14.   Currie, George. "Passed in Review," Brooklyn *Eagle*, October 12, 1932, p. 27.
"The book seeks to dramatize a state of mind, rather than to build up to a climax any exciting human experience. But the author has a remarkable gift of speech figures, not all of which she is at pains to keep from mixing."

K15.   Daniel, Frank. "'Save Me the Waltz,'" Atlanta *Journal*, October 30, 1932, Magazine, p. 18.
"'Save Me the Waltz' is written in lively fashion, sprightly with conversations and adventures among the gay young post-war cynics of America and Europe."

K16.   Dutton, Edna S. "'Save Me the Waltz' Is First Novel," Marion (Ohio) *Star*, September 10, 1932, p. 9.
"This is a book of strong colors and distinct characters, an account of a young woman's stormy passage from the safe harbor of childhood to that of maturity and a fixed point of view."

K17.   G., L. "With a Halo of Sad Absurdity," Memphis *Commercial Appeal*, December 18, 1932, Sec. 1, p. 20.
"Gazing on the struggles of these flies in amber is as melancholy a business as attending the benefit of a once cherished actress now fallen on evil days."

K18.   Green, Elizabeth Lay. "The Lantern," *The State* (Columbia, S.C.), October 16, 1932, p. 23.
Mrs. Fitzgerald "has written a modern, an almost excessively modern, novel, in some places glassy hard and sophisticated, in others tender and guardedly emotional. In vocabulary and style it is coruscating,

brilliant, and at moments over-rich." This review also appeared in Louisville *Courier-Journal*, October 30, 1932, Sec. 3, p. 7; Norfolk *Virginian-Pilot*, October 16, 1932, Part 1, p. 6.

K19.   H., P. Review of *Save Me the Waltz*, Providence *Sunday Journal*, October 23, 1932, "Features" Section, p. 8.

"One need not fear boredom from this book but neither need one expect satisfaction."

K20.   H., W. E. "Save Me the Waltz—A Girl as She Emerges From Adolescence," Boston *Evening Transcript*, November 30, 1932, Part Four, p. 2.

"The detachment that builds two parallel lines of thought: that of the character, unconscious of being examined, and that of the author who cooly appraises, either sympathetically or with eyes creased in mirth or horror—this is strangely missing in Mrs. Fitzgerald's first novel. Without it her story becomes merely a creditable piece of narrative, vividly arraying certain highly flavored scenes."

K21.   Hansen, Harry. "The First Reader," San Francisco *News*, October 19, 1932, Sec. 1, p. 6.

"If anyone knows what the gay, brilliant life of young Americans was like in those first years after the war she should know and be able to tell it" and, in this novel, she "has done this." This review also appeared in NY *World-Telegram*, October 10, 1932, p. 23; Norfolk *Virginian-Pilot*, October 21, 1932, p. 4; Minneapolis *Tribune*, October 16, 1932, p. 5; Greensboro (N.C.) *Daily News*, October 13, 1932, p. 6; Pittsburgh *Press*, October 23, 1932, Society Section, p. 10.

K22.   Hasbrook, Irene. "Prose That Is Near Poetry," Richmond (Va.) *Times-Dispatch*, October 23, 1932, Sec. 3, p. 4.

Author "writes prose that is near poetry. Beautifully and expressively, she tosses us moving passages for our delectation...." It is a "bright and lovely book."

K23.   Hellman, Geoffrey. "Beautiful and Damned," *Saturday Review of Literature*, 9 (October 22, 1932), 190.

Although the book "evokes, quite effectively at times," the post-war era, its "most noticeable feature...is the steady stream of strained metaphor with which Mrs. Fitzgerald manages to make what should be a light novel a study in the intricacies of the English language."

K24.   Horan, Kenneth. "Dance Mad—Story About Artists," Chicago *Journal of Commerce*, October 22, 1932, p. 2.

Mrs. Fitzgerald "tells a story about some artistic people which is interesting because they are interesting, but before she is done with it they are talking in such metaphors, and with such affectations of manner and diction that their peculiarities mar their attractive qualities."

K25.   Jackson, Joseph Henry. "A Book a Day," San Francisco *Chronicle*, October 24, 1932, p. 9.

"If you are willing to accept the author's gaucheries for the sake of the really charming story she tells, you will find 'Save Me the Waltz' a pleasant hour's light reading."

K26.   K., W. S. "Zelda Sayre Fitzgerald Writes Story With Setting in Montgomery," Montgomery *Advertiser*, October 16, 1932, p. 7.

"Mrs. Fitzgerald's style is delightfully akin to her heroine, bubbling, emotional, unhampered by convention and with a devilish sense of humor."

K27.   McCarroll, Marion Clyde. "That 'Younger Generation,'" NY *Evening Post*, October 29, 1932, p. 7.

Descriptive review.

K28.   McD., M. I. "Two Zelda Fitzgeralds Seen Present in 'Save Me the Waltz,'" Milwaukee *Journal*, November 5, 1932, p. 6.

"An abrupt transition, not only in mood but in the mechanics of style, so separates the early portion of the book from its later incident that it seems scarcely possible the same author could have produced both."

K29.   M'Fee, William. "During the Jazz Age," NY *Sun*, October 8, 1932, p. 12.

"In this book, with all its crudity of conception, its ruthless purloinings of technical tricks and its pathetic striving after philosophic profundity, there is the promise of a new and vigorous personality in fiction."

K30.   Minot, John Clair. "Realm of Books," Boston *Herald*, October 31, 1932, p. 10.

"Mrs. Fitzgerald leaps into labyrinths of flowery language at times, but succeeds well in getting certain sections of our post-war youth into her pages."

K31.   Morrison, Jane. "Modern Story By Fitzgerald Seems Unreal," Charlotte *News*, November 27, 1932, Sec. B, p. 6.

"The action is slow, the events drawn out over a surprising quantity of paper. Now and then one comes upon a delightfully colorful and impressionistic bit of description or a very clever line. In short the novel is a wordy and voluminous portrayal of twentieth century life as it is imagined, rather than it really is."

K32.   R., C. F.   Review of *Save Me the Waltz*, Philadelphia *Public Ledger*, October 15, 1932, p. 15.
Novel is "constructive in thought, clever in execution, individual, fascinating and brisk."

K33.   Seldes, Gilbert.   "True to Type—Books For Week Leading to Election," NY *Evening Journal*, October 29, 1932, p. 5.
"The whole book is…a pendant to the stories of the lost generations of the 1920's, told with profound feeling and profound unhappiness."

K34.   V., B.   "Reviewing the Latest Contributions in the Book World," Evanston (Ill.) *News-Index*, October 11, 1932, p. 6.
Descriptive review.

K35.   West, Duffy R.   "Those Writing Fitzgeralds," Cincinnati *Star*, January 3, 1933, p. 18.
"This novel conveys the impression that the writer can turn her hand to a number of things and she has tried a fling at novel writing mainly because she had a lot to say and that was the only way of saying it."

K36.   Willson, Robert H.   "Cognomen Revived," Chicago *Herald and Examiner*, October 22, 1932, p. 9.
"It may be that the author is so busy plucking strange phrases out of the air, arranging fantastic sentences full of awkward adjectives, that she has no time to put flesh and blood into the puppets who cavort through her pages."

1967 American Edition

K37.   Anonymous.   Review of *Save Me the Waltz*, *Contemporary Review*, 212 (February 1968), 112.
Brief descriptive review.

K38.   ———.   Review of *Save Me the Waltz*, *Publishers' Weekly*, 191 (March 13, 1967), 62.
"As a novel, it is interesting in itself, with its picture of the life of a 1920's glamor girl; as a companion volume to studies of Fitzgerald, or read in conjunction with his novels, it's invaluable."

K39.   ———.   Review of *Save Me the Waltz*, Worcester *Sunday Telegram*, July 9, 1967, p. 10E.
Brief descriptive review.

K40.   Billings, Claude.   "Book Review—'Save Me the Waltz,'" Terre Haute *Star*, July 8, 1967, p. 4.
Novel "comes near to capturing the spirit of the 20s."

K41. Brockman, Zoe. "'Save Me the Waltz' Has Become a Collector's Item," Gastonia (N.C.) *Gazette*, May 12, 1968, p. P4.
Descriptive favorable review.

K42. Callaway, Leslie. *"Save Me the Waltz*—Zelda Fitzgerald's Novel Can Hardly Interest Anyone," Baton Rouge *Sunday Advocate*, August 20, 1967, p. 2-E.
"Zelda Fitzgerald's novel can hardly be of interest to anyone except the most devoted student of F. Scott Fitzgerald....Probably never before has any writer worked so hard to use words in a peculiar way and to concoct figures of speech that are effective only insofar as they startle."

K43. Cavell, Marcia. "Susan and Zelda: Reviewed Posthumously," *Westside News*, October 26, 1967.
The first half of the novel is "a study in bad writing and bad faith"; the second half is "a quite interesting account of the several years in which Zelda Fitzgerald did in fact devote herself single-mindedly to becoming a great ballet dancer." This review, seen as a clipping in the Publicity Department files of the Southern Illinois University Press, could not be verified.

K44. Collins, L. M. "Solo Novel Is Fitzgeraldana Curio," Nashville *Tennessean*, July 2, 1967, p. 8-C.
This is "a novel of unusual merit and interest."

K45. Comans, Grace. "The Golden Girl," Hartford *Courant*, July 2, 1967, Magazine, p. 14.
"If one can overcome one's resistance to her literary style in the first third of the book, one discovers a picture of an era and the tragic story of a tormented, driven woman. But the style is not easy to ignore."

K46. Cowan, Harry. "About Books," *Pensador* (Angelo State College, San Angelo, Tex.), 2 (May 1968), 15.
"The work derives its vitality from the current of life that runs throughout this thinly disguised autobiography."

K47. Cromie, Alice. "Paperbacks," Chicago *Tribune*, June 26, 1968, p. 16.
"Whether your interest is literary detection or merely nostalgia, Zelda's story is far more than a curiosity and a beguilement."

K48. Daughtrey, Anita. "Waltz With Zelda: A Haunting Refrain," Fresno *Bee*, August 13, 1967, p. 18-F.
While "unevenly written, it catches a quality of tragic enchantment, bringing to life not only the South prior to World War I and the merry-

go-round life of the Riviera during the Jazz Age, but also the backstage battling necessary for a career as a ballerina."

K49.   F., C. A.   "Fitzgerald Reissued," New Orleans *Times-Picayune*, August 27, 1967, Sec. 3, p. 6.
Descriptive favorable review.

K50.   Felts, Dave.   "Someday, Maybe Even a Musical About JFK," *Southern Illinoisan* (Southern Illinois University, Carbondale), June 12, 1967, p. 4.
Novel "is not good literature for its faults are apparent to the casual reader for pleasure. But it has a certain charm of its own, particularly to those who have read books by and about the F. Scott Fitzgeralds."

K51.   Fizpatrick, Tom.   "In Review—Zelda's Only Novel," *The Foghorn* (University of San Francisco), May 5, 1967, p. 6.
Novel "has real appeal only to a special kind of Fitzgerald admirer, one who combines nostalgia with a sincere regard for Scott's work."

K52.   Hatfield, Don.   "Wilson, Dos Passos, Millay...and the Fitzgeralds—Time Remembered: The 20's," Huntington (W.Va.) *Herald-Advertiser*, July 23, 1967, "Amusements" Section, p. 9.
This "is a powerfully written book which can be read for its own sake, not simply because it was written by the wife of F. Scott Fitzgerald. It is moving, the vocabulary is surprisingly good, and it is gripping in spite of its unevenness."

K53.   Hogan, William.   "Between the Lines—A Dusting-Off of the Zelda Fitzgerald Novel," San Francisco *Sunday Examiner & Chronicle*, June 18, 1967, "This World" Section, p. 40.
Novel is "a literary bauble which should be of some interest to scholars and Fitzgerald collectors."

K54.   H[onig, Nat].   "Portrait of Woman of 1920s," Long Beach (Calif.) *Independent Press Telegram*, August 27, 1967, "Southland" Section, p. 15.
Novel is "somewhat of a curiosity,...but, though hardly to be mentioned in the same breath with the best of Fitzgerald's work, there are many glints of talent."

K55.   James, Elizabeth.   "Wife's Tale Focuses Fitzgerald Viewpoint," Buffalo *Courier-Express*, August 6, 1967, p. 16A.
"In her attempt to exercise the frustrations of her own life, the author airs some characteristics which may have directly influenced the emotional climate and motivational background of her husband's works."

K56.   Martin, Rana.   "Zelda Has Curio Value," Houston *Chronicle*, July 16, 1967, "Zest" Section, p. 15.
"Beyond the curio value," the novel "has little merit."

K57.   *Mizener, Arthur. "The Good Gone Times," *NY Times
Book Review*, August 13, 1967, pp. 1, 32–33.

The "essential subject" of the novel is the "conflict between the un-
compromising romantic and the irrepressible realist within her that
finally destroyed Zelda Fitzgerald. To the description of that conflict
she sacrificed boldly—perhaps even unconsciously—the conventional
uses of the novel."

K58.   Newquist, Roy. Review of *Save Me the Waltz*, Chicago
Heights *Star*, June 11, 1967, p. 1A–10.
Brief review. "It is entertaining enough to stand on its own."

K59.   O'Neill, John. "Zelda's Novel—When Nobody Knew
Whose Party It Was," Atlanta *Journal and Constitution*, July 2, 1967,
p. 7-D.

"The major value of the book lies in the sense of its time that it expresses and in its depiction of her relationship with her husband, and
his failure to live up to the father image she projected onto him."

K60.   Sayre, Nora. "What Zelda Wrote," *Book Week* (NY
World Journal Tribune, Washington [D.C.] *Post*, Chicago *Sun-Times*),
May 28, 1967, pp. 9–10.

"If biography is sometimes intolerably like fiction, this novel is an
attempt to improve and reprove the past: a spell cast against the ogres of
repetition. The effort seems as sane as the sanity was temporary."

K61.   Schlueter, Paul. "Notable Fiction From SIU Press,"
Daily Egyptian (Southern Illinois University, Carbondale), October 7,
1967, p. 4.

"No doubt this novel will have most appeal on sheerly extrinsic
matters, such as the light it sheds, implicitly, on the Fitzgeralds' own
marriage and years as expatriates. But it also has intrinsic value as a
lively, sensitive book,...."

K62.   T[horpe], D[ay]. "Zelda Fitzgerald's Novel," Washington (D.C.) *Sunday Star*, July 2, 1967, p. E–2.

"It is hectic, caustic, original, and provocative. The reader never has
an urge to put the book aside—and that is more than can be said for
nine out of ten novels I find myself reading these days."

K63.   Wharton, Will. "Scott Fitzgerald's Zelda As a Novelist,"
St. Louis *Globe-Democrat*, July 1–2, 1967, p. 5F.

"Even as an oddity the work has a fugitive charm, even in the pathetic efforts of the girl who never grew up, to scintillate...."

K64.   Yardley, Jonathan. "About Books," Greensboro (N.C.) *Daily News*, June 25, 1967, p. D3.

"The difference between husband and wife is evident: He not merely saw, he perceived. She was but a mirror of the times. Yet what a sad and beautiful mirror she was; and how lucky we are that her one effort to put down her reflections has now been preserved."

1967 English Edition

K65.   Anonymous. "Back Numbers," *Times Literary Supplement* (London), October 5, 1967, p. 934.

Novel's narrative is "slipshod," its style "tends to be highly charged, incandescent with verbal fireworks," and Zelda's "eyes and ears were rapacious."

1968 English Edition

K66.   Anonymous. Review of *Save Me the Waltz*, *Times Literary Supplement* (London), January 23, 1969, p. 77.

Brief descriptive review.

K67.   *Ackland, Rodney. "Great Scott! Great Zelda!" *The Spectator*, 222 (February 28, 1969), 273–274.

"For all its occasionally turgid patches, Zelda's style is like electricity: it sparks off, flashes, whizzes along, packed with meaning, concentrated to bursting point." Novel is "a profoundly original creation, a coruscating literary firework, unique in both senses of the word."

K68.   Berridge, Elizabeth. "Poor Dizzy Zelda," *Books and Bookmen*, 14 (March 1969), 23–24.

"The best part of the novel—apart from the perceptive handling of the neglected child—where sheer drive and exuberance triumphs over the hysterical verbiage, is the description of Alabama...working—too late—to become a ballet dancer."

K69.   Burns, Jim. "Setting—The United States," London *Tribune*, March 7, 1969, p. 11.

"No one could claim that it's a major work, but it has enough to recommend it to a discerning reader."

K70.   Churchill, R. C. Review of *Save Me the Waltz*, Birmingham (England) *Post*, January 18, 1969, "Midland" Magazine, p. II.

"One admires the honesty of the presentation, if inevitably there must be two opinions about whether the tragedy of their married life was caused primarily by their being helpless victims of the Lost Generation or by some weakness in their own characters."

K71.   Coleman, John.   "A Page Out of His Book," *The Observer* (London), January 12, 1969, p. 29.

"How good much of the quick, nervous prose" is, "earning the rewards of the risks it takes." Overall, "Zelda proves as much a mistress of the fast, disillusioned line as Scott was master of it."

K72.   Connolly, Cyril.   "One Side of Paradise," London *Sunday Times*, January 19, 1969, p. 59.

Novel reveals that its author "was capable of patient craftsmanship and some tragic intuitions even while her mind was going."

K73.   Jacobson, Dan.   "Pre-Emptive Strike," *The Listener*, 81 (January 23, 1969), 118.

Although Zelda's "deficiencies as a novelist are spectacular," SMTW is "nevertheless the record of a life, or of scenes from a life, by a woman who is not afraid to acknowledge what she felt and wanted and how different these often were from what she managed to achieve."

K74.   Lister, Richard.   "What Jealousy Did to Zelda Fitzgerald," London *Evening Standard*, January 14, 1969, p. 13.

"There are many incidental pleasures" in SMTW, but it is "mostly as an interesting literary footnote that it is likely to be read in the future."

K75.   Moynihan, John.   "Not So Tender," London *Sunday Telegraph*, January 12, 1969, p. 11.

Novel is "outrageously autobiographical" and the writing "is always extraordinarily alert, the story described at a pace that would leave many boring contemporary authors on their hands and knees."

K76.   Stanford, Derek.   "The Dishonest Heart," *The Scotsman* (Edinburgh), January 25, 1969, "Week-end Scotsman" Section, p. 3.

Novel is "an interesting literary curiosity and a disguised autobiographical document on the domestic life. The reader, whose palate can endure the prinked pretentious prose of Zelda's opening pages, will find sensuous colour and a natural transcription of affected dialogue in later passages."

K77.   Tomalin, Claire.   "Chews Gum—Shows Knees," *New Statesman*, n. s. 77 (January 17, 1969), 89.

"What strikes one forcibly about *Save Me the Waltz* is that most of the best passages are not concerned with the life she lived with her husband."

K78.   Whateley, Rosaleen.   "Novel Notebook," Liverpool *Daily Post*, February 19, 1969, p. 10.

"This is more a biographical curiosity than a work of art and is an interesting addition to any study of the life of the Fitzgeralds."

K79.   Williamson, Bruce.   "Clamour of the Footlights," *Irish Times* (Dublin), January 18, 1969, p. 10.

"The trouble with the book—apart from the over-writing—is that it confuses extraordinarily....It is a novel—or, rather, an autobiographical fragment—of great poignancy."

Appendix

Checklist of the First Appearances of Publications Containing Items by Fitzgerald

This checklist updates and supplements the listing in *The Critical Reputation of F. Scott Fitzgerald.* It is based almost entirely on Matthew J. Bruccoli's *F. Scott Fitzgerald—A Descriptive Bibliography* (I40) and his *Supplement* (I56). It includes only the first appearances of Fitzgerald's publications. Within the "Books" section only those items *by* Fitzgerald within collections are listed. Thus, in *F. Scott in His Own Time: A Miscellany,* the various reprinted interviews, reviews, and essays are not included. They are listed in Section I of this volume.

I. BOOKS

1971   *F. Scott Fitzgerald in His Own Time: A Miscellany.* Edited by Matthew J. Bruccoli and Jackson R. Bryer. Kent, Ohio: Kent State University Press, 1971. *Contents*: "Football"; *Fie! Fie! Fi-Fi!*—Opening Chorus, Gentlemen Bandits We, A Slave to Modern Improvements, In Her Eyes, What the Manicure Lady Knows, Good Night and Good Bye, 'Round and 'Round, Chatter Trio, Finale Act I, Rose of the Night, Men, In the Dark, Love or Eugenics, Reminiscence, Fie! Fie! Fi-Fi!, The Monte Carlo Moon, Finale Act II; A Cheer for Princeton; *The Evil Eye*—Act I Opening Chorus, I've Got My Eyes on You, On Dreams Alone, The Evil Eye, What I'll Forget, Over the Waves to Me, On Her Eukalali, Jump Off the Wall, Finale Act I, Act II Opening Chorus, Harris from Paris, Twilight, "The Never, Never Land," My

Idea of Love, Other Eyes, The Girl of the Golden West, With Me; *Safety First!*—(A) Prologue, (B) Garden of Arden, Act I Opening Chorus, Send Him to Tom, One-Lump Percy, Where Did Bridget Kelly Get Her Persian Temperament?, It Is Art, Safety First, Charlotte Corday, Underneath the April Rain, Dance, Lady, Dance, (A) Safety First, (B) Hello Temptation, When That Beautiful Chord Came True, Rag-Time Melodrama, Scene II, Take Those Hawaiian Songs Away, The Vampires Won't Vampire for Me, The Hummin' Blues, Down in Front, Finale; To My Unused Greek Book; Rain Before Dawn; Princeton—The Last Day; On a Play Twice Seen; The Cameo Frame; City Dusk; My First Love; Marching Streets; The Pope at Confession; A Dirge; Sleep of a University; To Anne; untitled poem; Lamp in a Window; Obit on Parnassus; There was once a second group student...; May Small Talk; How They Head the Chapters; The Conquest of America; Yais; Little Minnie McCloskey; One from Penn's Neck; A Litany of Slang; "Triangle Scenery by Bakst"; Futuristic Impressions of the Editorial Boards; "A glass of beer kills him"; Oui, le backfield est from Paris; "When you find a man doing a little more"; Things That Never Change! Number 3333; The Old Frontiersman; Boy Kills Self Rather Than Pet; Precaution Primarily; Things That Never Change. No. 3982; McCaulay Mission—Water Street; Popular Parodies—No. I; The Diary Of A Sophomore; Undulations Of An Undergraduate; Yale's swimming team will take its maiden plunge to-night; Kenilworth Socialism; True Democracy; A Few Well-Known Club Types And Their Futures; The Prince of Pests; "These rifles *** will probably not be used..."; "It is assumed that the absence of submarines..."; "Ethel had her shot of brandy..."; The Staying Up All Night; Intercollegiate Petting Cues; Our American Poets; Cedric the Stoker; Our Next Issue; The Usual Thing; Jemina; review of *Penrod and Sam*; review of *David Blaize*; review of *The Celt and the World*; review of *Verses in Peace and War*; review of *God, The Invisible King*; review of *Prejudices, Second Series*; review of *Three Soldiers*; Three Cities; review of *Brass*; review of *Crome Yellow*; review of *Gentle Julia*; review of *Margey Wins the Game*; review of *The Oppidan*; review of *The Love Legend*; review of *Many Marriages*; review of *Being Respectable*; review of *Through the Wheat*; How to Waste Material; F. Scott Fitzgerald Is Bored by Efforts at Realism in "Lit";

blurb for *Babel*; blurb for *Lily-Iron*; introduction to *The Great Gatsby*; blurb for *Cast Down the Laurel*; foreword to *Colonial and Historic Homes of Maryland*; blurb for *What Makes Sammy Run?*; blurb for *The Day of the Locust*; self-interview; The Author's Apology; The Credo of F. Scott Fitzgerald; What I Was Advised To Do—And Didn't; How I Would Sell My Book If I Were a Bookseller; Confessions; In Literary New York; Censorship or Not; Fitzgerald Sets Things Right About His College; Unfortunate "Tradition"; False and Extremely Unwise Tradition; Confused Romanticism; An Open Letter to Fritz Crisler; comments on stories; statement on Huck Finn; Anonymous '17; letter to Harvey H. Smith; "Why Blame It on the Poor Kiss if the Girl Veteran of Many Petting Parties Is Prone to Affairs After Marriage?"; Does a Moment of Revolt Come Sometime to Every Married Man?; What Kind of Husbands Do "Jimmies" Make?; "Wait Till You Have Children of Your Own!"; What Became of Our Flappers and Sheiks?; Girls Believe in Girls; What I Think and Feel at 25; A Short Autobiography; This is a Magazine; Reminiscences of Donald Stewart; *The St. Paul Daily Dirge*; The Most Disgraceful Thing I Ever Did; Salesmanship in the Champs-Elysées; The True Story of Appomattox; A Book of One's Own; testimonial for Constant Tras.

Dear Scott/Dear Max—The Fitzgerald-Perkins Correspondence. Edited by John Kuehl and Jackson R. Bryer. NY: Charles Scribner's Sons, 1971.

1972 *As Ever, Scott Fitz—: Letters Between F. Scott Fitzgerald and His Literary Agent Harold Ober 1919–1940.* Edited by Matthew J. Bruccoli. With the Assistance of Jennifer McCabe Atkinson. Philadelphia: J. B. Lippincott, 1972.

1973 *The Basil and Josephine Stories.* Edited by Jackson R. Bryer and John Kuehl. NY: Charles Scribner's Sons, 1973. *Contents*: That Kind of Party; The Scandal Detectives; A Night at the Fair; The Freshest Boy; He Thinks He's Wonderful; The Captured Shadow; The Perfect Life; Forging Ahead; Basil and Cleopatra; First Blood; A Nice Quiet Place; A Woman with a Past; A Snobbish Story; Emotional Bankruptcy.

F. Scott Fitzgerald's Ledger—A Facsimile. Washington, D.C.: NCR/Microcard Editions, 1973.

"The Great Gatsby"—A Facsimile of the Manuscript. Edited

by Matthew J. Bruccoli. Washington, D.C.: Microcard Editions, 1973.

Bits of Paradise—21 Uncollected Stories By F. Scott and Zelda Fitzgerald. Selected by Scottie Fitzgerald Smith and Matthew J. Bruccoli. London: Bodley Head, 1973. Contents: The Popular Girl; Love in the Night; Our Own Movie Queen; A Penny Spent; The Dance; Jacob's Ladder; The Swimmers; The Hotel Child; A New Leaf; What a Handsome Pair!; Last Kiss; Dearly Beloved.

1976   *The Cruise of the Rolling Junk.* Bloomfield Hills, Mich., and Columbia, S.C.: Bruccoli Clark, 1976.

1974   *The Romantic Egoists.* Edited by Matthew J. Bruccoli, Scottie Fitzgerald Smith, and Joan P. Kerr. NY: Charles Scribner's Sons, 1974.

1978   *F. Scott Fitzgerald's Screenplay for "Three Comrades" by Erich Maria Remarque.* Edited by Matthew J. Bruccoli. Carbondale: Southern Illinois University Press, 1978.

The Notebooks of F. Scott Fitzgerald. Edited by Matthew J. Bruccoli. NY: Harcourt Brace Jovanovich/Bruccoli Clark, 1978.

F. Scott Fitzgerald's St. Paul Plays 1911–1914. Edited by Alan Margolies. Princeton, N.J.: Princeton University Library, 1978. Contents: The Girl From Lazy J; The Captured Shadow; Coward; Assorted Spirits.

1979   *The Price Was High—The Last Uncollected Stories of F. Scott Fitzgerald.* Edited by Matthew J. Bruccoli. NY: Harcourt Brace Jovanovich/Bruccoli Clark, 1979. Contents: The Smilers; Myra Meets His Family; Two For a Cent; Dice, Brassknuckles & Guitar; Diamond Dick and the First Law of Woman; The Third Casket; The Pusher-in-the-Face; One of My Oldest Friends; The Unspeakable Egg; John Jackson's Arcady; Not in the Guidebook; Presumption; The Adolescent Marriage; Your Way and Mine; The Love Boat; The Bowl; At Your Age; Indecision; Flight and Pursuit; On Your Own; Between Three and Four; A Change of Class; Six of One—; A Freeze-Out; Diagnosis; The Rubber Check; On Schedule; More than Just a House; I Got Shoes; The Family Bus; In the Darkest Hour; No Flowers; New Types; Her Last Case; Lo, the Poor Peacock!; The Intimate Strangers; Zone of Accident; Fate in Her Hands; Image on the Heart; Too Cute for Words; Inside the House; Three Acts of Music;

"Trouble"; An Author's Mother; The End of Hate; In the Holidays; The Guest in Room Nineteen; Discard [Director's Special]; On an Ocean Wave; The Woman from Twenty-One.

1980 *Correspondence of F. Scott Fitzgerald.* Edited by Matthew J. Bruccoli and Margaret M. Duggan. With the assistance of Susan Walker. NY: Random House, 1980.

1981 *Poems—1911–1940.* Edited by Matthew J. Bruccoli. Bloomfield Hills, Mich., and Columbia, S.C.: Bruccoli Clark, 1981. *Contents*: Football; *Fie! Fie! Fi-Fi* (1914)—Act I Opening Chorus, Gentlemen Bandits We, A Slave to Modern Improvements, In Her Eyes, What the Manicure Lady Knows, Good Night and Good Bye, 'Round and 'Round, Chatter Trio, Finale Act I, Rose of the Night, Men, In the Dark, Love or Eugenics, Reminiscence, Fie! Fie! Fi-Fi!, The Monte Carlo Moon, Finale Act II; May Small Talk; A Cheer For Princeton; *The Evil Eye* (1915)—Act I Opening Chorus, I've Got My Eyes On You, On Dreams Alone, The Evil Eye, What I'll Forget, Over The Waves To Me, On Her Eukalali, Jump Off The Wall, Finale Act I, Act II Opening Chorus, Harris From Paris, Twilight, The Never, Never Land, My Idea of Love, Other Eyes, The Girl Of The Golden West, With Me; To My Unused Greek Book; One from Penn's Neck; *Safety First!* (1916)—(A) Prologue, (B) Garden of Eden, Act I Opening Chorus, Send Him to Tom, One-Lump Percy, Where Did Bridget Kelly Get Her Persian Temperament?, It Is Art, Safety First, Charlotte Corday, Underneath the April Rain, Finale Act I—Dance, Lady, Dance, Act II—(A) Safety First, (B) Hello Temptation, When That Beautiful Chord Came True, Rag-Time Melodrama, Scene II, Take Those Hawaiian Songs Away, The Vampires Won't Vampire For Me, The Hummin' Blues, Down in Front, Finale; Rain Before Dawn; From "Precaution Primarily"; Popular Parodies—No. 1; Undulations of an Undergraduate; Princeton—The Last Day; On a Play Twice Seen; The Cameo Frame; Our American Poets; City Dusk; The Pope at Confession; My First Love; Marching Streets: First Printed Text; Marching Streets: Revised *Notebooks* Text; We keep you clean in Muscatine; A Dirge; Verse included in *This Side of Paradise*—Untitled: "Marylyn and Sall*ee*...," Untitled: "So the gray car crept...," In a Lecture-Room, Untitled: "Victorians, Victorians, who never learned to weep...," Untitled: "Songs in

the time of order...," Untitled: "We leave to-night...,"
Boston Bards and Hearst Reviewers, Untitled: "The February streets...," Untitled: "When Vanity kissed Vanity...," A
Poem That Eleanor Sent Amory Several Years Later, A
Poem Amory Sent to Eleanor and Which He Called
"Summer Storm," Untitled: "A fathom deep in sleep I
lie..."; Untitled: "Carrots and peas..."; Untitled: "Oh
down—..."; Sleep of a University; To Anne; Untitled: "For
the lads of the village triumph..."; Untitled: "Then wear the
gold hat, if that will move her;..."; Untitled: "We sing not
soft, we sing not loud..."; Untitled: "Oh—oh—oh—oh...";
Lamp in a Window; Obit on Parnassus; Poems from
Fitzgerald's *Notebooks*—Answer to a Poem, Apology to
Ogden Nash, Untitled: "The barber's too slick...," Beg You
to Listen, Clay Feet, Untitled: "Colors has she in her
soul...," Untitled: "Come in! Come in!...," Counter Song to
the "Undertaker," Untitled: "Don't you worry I
surrender...," The Earth Calls, Untitled: "Everytime I blow
my nose I think of you...," Untitled: "First a hug and tease
and a something on my knees...," For a Long Illness,
Untitled: "For Song—Idea—," Untitled: "For the time that
our man spent in pressing your suit...," Untitled: "A god intoxicated fly...," Half-and-Half Girl, Untitled: "Hooray...,"
Hortense—To a Cast-Off Lover, Untitled: "I don't need a bit
assistance...," Untitled: "If Hoover came out for the
N.R.A....," Untitled: "If you have a little Jew...," Untitled:
"I hate their guts...," Untitled: "In a dear little vine-covered
cottage...," Untitled: "Keep the watch!...," Untitled: "Life's
too short to...," Untitled: "Listen to the hoop la...,"
Untitled: "Little by little...," Untitled: "Mr. Berlin wrote a
song about forgetting to remember...," Untitled: "Mother
taught me to—love things...," Untitled: "Now is the time for
all good men to come to the aid of the party...," Oh, Sister,
Can You Spare Your Heart, Untitled: "Oh where are the
boys of the boom-boom-boom...," One Southern Girl, Our
April Letter, Pilgrimage, Untitled: "Pretty Boy Floyd...,"
Prizefighter's Wife, Refrain for a Poem. How to Get to So
and So., Sad Catastrophe, Untitled: "Scott Fitzgerald so they
say...," Untitled: "She lay supine among her Pekinese...,"
Song, Song—, A Song Number Idea:, Untitled: "'Sticking
along.' The voice so faint sometimes I could scarcely hear
it...," Thousand-and-First Ship, To Carter, a Friendly
Finger, Untitled: "Touchdown song based on...," Untitled:
"Truth and—consequences...," Untitled: "You'll be reckless

if you...," Untitled: "You'll never know...," Untitled: "You've driven me crazy..."; Martin's Thoughts; Untitled: "My mind is all a-tumble..."; On My Ragtime Family Tree; Untitled: "My Very Very Dear Marie..."; For Dolly; A Letter to Helen; Untitled: "Ruth..."; Untitled: "There was a young lady named Ruth...", When We Meet Again; Ellerslie; Untitled: "Ah May, Shall I splatter my thoughts in the air..."; 1st Epistle of St. Scott to the Smithsonian; To the Ring Lardners; [Dog! Dog! Dog!]; Untitled: "Of wonders is Silas M. Hanson the champ..."; Untitled: "There was a young man of Quebec..."; Untitled: "All the girls and mans..."; Untitled: "Orange pajamas and heaven's guitars..."; Untitled: "'Oh papa—...'"; Untitled: "DONT EXPECT ME..."; "Momishness"; Untitled: "East of the sun, west of the moon..."; For 2nd Stanza Baoth Poem; Because; Untitled: "Oh Misseldine's, dear Misseldine's..."; Spring Song; Lines on Reading Through an Autograph Album; Untitled: "Valentine was a Saint;..."; Untitled: "SING HOTCH-CHA SING HEY-HI NINNY..."; Some Interrupted Lines to Sheilah; Untitled: "This book tells that Anita Loos..."; For Mary's Eighth Birthday; Les Absents Ont Toujours Tory; To a Beloved Infidel; The Big Academy Dinner; Lest We Forget; Untitled: "From Scott Fitzgerald..."; Untitled: "Frances Kroll..."; On Watching the Candidates in the Newsreels; Untitled: "Now your heart is come so near..."; [Vowels]; Tribute; Choke down another Hic and Hail the king; Colds in the Head; Dopey Sal + Penthouse Jerry; The girls I met at the Chicago Fire; Untitled: "Mr. McDonald was keen to lay eyes on his daughter..."; Untitled: "Strombergs assorted pickels gather near..."; Untitled: "There was no firelight..."; To My Grandfather; Omitted Poems.

II. PERIODICALS

1910 S. P. A. Men in College Athletics (essay). *St. Paul Academy Now and Then*, December.

1911 "Football" (verse). *Newman School News*, Christmas(?).

1912 Untitled news feature about school election. *Newman School News*, ?.

1913 Untitled news feature about school dance. *Newman School News*, ?.

1914   Untitled: "There was once a second group student..." (essay). *Princeton Tiger*, December.

1915   May Small Talk (verse). *Princeton Tiger*, June.

How They Head the Chapters (essay). *Princeton Tiger*, September.

The Conquest of America (as some writers would have it) (essay). *Princeton Tiger*, Thanksgiving.

Three Days at Yale (essay). *Princeton Tiger*, December.

1916   Yais (verse). *Princeton Tiger*, June.

Little Minnie McCloskey A Story for Girls (essay). *Princeton Tiger*, December 1.

One from Penn's Neck (verse). *Princeton Tiger*, December 18.

A Litany of Slang (essay). *Princeton Tiger*, December 18.

"Triangle Scenery by Bakst" (essay). *Princeton Tiger*, December 18.

Futuristic Impressions of the Editorial Boards (essay). *Princeton Tiger*, December 18.

"A glass of beer kills him" (joke). *Princeton Tiger*, December 18.

Untitled: "Oui, le backfield est from Paris..." (verse). *Princeton Tiger*, December 18.

Untitled: "'When you find a man doing a little more...'" (joke). *Princeton Tiger*, December 18.

Things That Never Change! Number 3333 (essay). *Princeton Tiger*, December 18.

The Old Frontiersman A Story of the Frontier (essay). *Princeton Tiger*, December 18.

1917   Untitled book review of *Penrod and Sam* by Booth Tarkington. *Nassau Literary Magazine*, January.

Untitled: "Boy Kills Self Rather Than Pet..." (joke). *Princeton Tiger*, February 3.

Things That Never Change. No. 3982 (joke). *Princeton Tiger*, February 3.

Precaution Primarily (burlesque musical comedy). *Princeton Tiger*, February 3.

Untitled book review of *David Blaize* by E. F. Benson. *Nassau Literary Magazine*, February.

A Few Well-Known Club Types And Their Futures (cartoon). *Princeton Tiger*, March 17.

Untitled: "McCaulay Mission—Water Street..." (joke). *Princeton Tiger*, March 17.

Popular Parodies—No. 1 (verse). *Princeton Tiger*, March 17.

The Diary of a Sophomore (essay). *Princeton Tiger*, March 17.

True Democracy (cartoon). *Princeton Tiger*, March 17.

Undulations of an Undergraduate (verse). *Princeton Tiger*, March 17.

Kenilworth Socialism (cartoon). *Princeton Tiger*, March 17.

The Prince of Pests A Story of the War (essay). *Princeton Tiger*, April 28.

Untitled: "'These rifles *** will probably not be used...'" (joke). *Princeton Tiger*, April 28.

Untitled: "'It is assumed that the absence of submarines...'" (joke). *Princeton Tiger*, April 28.

Untitled: "Ethel had her shot of brandy..." (verse). *Princeton Tiger*, April 28.

Untitled: "Yale's swimming team will take its maiden plunge to-night" (joke). *Princeton Tiger*, April 28.

Untitled book review of *The Celt and the World* by Shane Leslie. *Nassau Literary Magazine*, May.

Untitled book review of *Verses in Peace and War* by Shane Leslie. *Nassau Literary Magazine*, June.

Untitled book review of *God, The Invisible King* by H. G. Wells. *Nassau Literary Magazine*, June.

The Dream and the Awakening (cartoon). *Princeton Tiger*, June 15.

The Staying Up All Night (essay). *Princeton Tiger*, November 10.

Intercollegiate Petting-Cues (joke). *Princeton Tiger*, November 10.

Our American Poets (verse). *Princeton Tiger*, November 10.

Cedric the Stoker (The True Story of the Battle of the Baltic) (essay). *Princeton Tiger*, November 10.

1919   My First Love (verse). *Nassau Literary Magazine*, February.

Marching Streets (verse). *Nassau Literary Magazine*, February.

The Pope at Confession (verse). *Nassau Literary Magazine*, February.

A Dirge (Apologies to Wordsworth) (verse). *Judge*, December 20.

1920   The Claims of the *Lit*. (letter). *Princeton Alumni Weekly*, March 10.

Contemporary Writers and Their Work, A Series of Autobiographical Letters—F. Scott Fitzgerald (letter). *The Editor*, Second July Number.

Who's Who—and Why (essay). *Saturday Evening Post*, September 18.

Sleep of a University (verse). *Nassau Literary Magazine*, November.

1921   Public letter to Thomas Boyd.   St. Paul *Daily News*, February 20.

The Baltimore Anti-Christ (review of *Prejudices, Second Series* by H. L. Mencken). *The Bookman*, March.

Three Soldiers (review of *Three Soldiers* by John Dos Passos). St. Paul *Daily News*, September 25.

Three Cities (essay). *Brentano's Book Chat*, September-October.

Poor Old Marriage (review of *Brass* by Charles Norris). *The Bookman*, November.

Reminiscences of Donald Stewart by F. Scott Fitzgerald (in the Manner of............) (parody). St. Paul *Daily News*, December 11.

1922   Aldous Huxley's "Crome Yellow" (review of *Crome Yellow* by Aldous Huxley). St. Paul *Daily News*, February 26.

What I Was Advised To Do—And Didn't (essay). Philadelphia *Public Ledger*, April 22.

"Margey Wins the Game" (review of *Margey Wins the Game* by John V. A. Weaver). NY *Tribune*, May 7.

Tarkington's "Gentle Julia" (review of *Gentle Juliu* by Booth Tarkington). St. Paul *Daily News*, May 7.

Homage to the Victorians (review of *The Oppidan* by Shane Leslie). NY *Tribune*, May 14.

A Rugged Novel (review of *The Love Legend* by Woodward Boyd). NY *Evening Post*, October 28.

1923 How I Would Sell My Book If I Were a Bookseller (essay). *Bookseller and Stationer*, January 15.

Minnesota's Capital in the Role of Main Street (review of *Being Respectable* by Grace Flandrau). *Literary Digest International Book Review*, March.

Sherwood Anderson on the Marriage Question (review of *Many Marriages* by Sherwood Anderson). NY *Herald*, March 4.

10 Best Books I Have Read (essay). Jersey City *Evening Journal* (syndicated elsewhere as well), April 24.

Confessions (letter). Chicago *Daily Tribune*, May 19.

Under Fire (review of *Through the Wheat* by Thomas Boyd). NY *Evening Post*, May 26.

Letter to A. Philip Randolph (Great Neck, Long Island, 25 May 1923). *The Messenger*, June.

Censorship or Not (essay). *Literary Digest*, June 23.

The Most Disgraceful Thing I Ever Did: 2. The Invasion of the Sanctuary (essay). *Vanity Fair*, October.

In Literary New York (letter). St. Paul *Daily News*, December 23.

1924 What Kind of Husbands Do "Jimmies" Make? (essay). Baltimore *American* (syndicated elsewhere as well), March 30.

Who's Who in this Issue (letter). *Woman's Home Companion*, July.

1926 Letter to Class Secretary. *Princeton Alumni Weekly*, April 14.

1928 F. Scott Fitzgerald Is Bored by Efforts At Realism In "Lit" (review of March issue of *Nassau Literary Magazine*). *Daily Princetonian*, March 16.

1929   Fitzgerald Sets Things Right About His College (letter). Washington (D.C.) *Herald*, June 28.

1930   False and Extremely Unwise Tradition (letter). *Daily Princetonian*, February 27.

Letter to H. N. Swanson. *College Humor*, April.

1932   Confused Romanticism (letter). *Princeton Alumni Weekly*, April 22.

1934   An Open Letter to Fritz Crisler. *Princeton Athletic News*, June 16.

Anonymous '17 (statement). *Nassau Literary Magazine*, June.

My Ten Favorite Plays (essay). NY *Sun*, September 10.

1938   Letter to Harvey H. Smith. *Princeton Alumni Weekly*, January 28.

1939   Letter to Harvey H. Smith (MGM, 3 January 1939). *Princeton Alumni Weekly*, February 3.

1952   The Boy Who Killed His Mother (verse). *Neurotica*, Winter.

1954   The High Cost of Macaroni (essay). *Interim*, Nos. 1 and 2.

1961   Martin's Thoughts (verse). *Fitzgerald Newsletter*, Spring.

1968   My Generation (essay). *Esquire*, October.

1969   Dearly Beloved. *Fitzgerald/Hemingway Annual*.

Untitled: "Valentine was a Saint..." (verse). *Fitzgerald/Hemingway Annual*.

1970   Letter to Ernest Hemingway (1925). *Fitzgerald/Hemingway Annual*.

Six Letters to the Menckens. *Fitzgerald/Hemingway Annual*.

1971   Lo, the Poor Peacock! *Esquire*, September.

Preface to *This Side of Paradise*. *Fitzgerald/Hemingway Annual*.

Oh, Sister, Can You Spare Your Heart (verse). *Fitzgerald/Hemingway Annual*.

1973   Infidelity (screenplay). *Esquire*, December.

1977   The Defeat of Art (unlocated review of *The Boy Grew Older* by Heywood Broun). *Fitzgerald/Hemingway Annual*.

Checklist of the First Appearances of Publications Containing Items by Zelda Fitzgerald

This checklist provides a listing of the first appearances of Zelda Fitzgerald's publications. It is based on the information in Matthew J. Bruccoli's *F. Scott Fitzgerald—A Descriptive Bibliography* (I40) and his *Supplement* (I56). In several instances, publications which were, in *The Critical Reputation of F. Scott Fitzgerald*, listed among F. Scott Fitzgerald's writings are here listed as actually written by Zelda Fitzgerald, based on information in Fitzgerald's *Ledger*, despite the fact that they were usually published under their joint by-line. Within the "Books" section only those items *by* Zelda Fitzgerald within a collection are listed. Thus, in *Bits of Paradise*, the stories by F. Scott Fitzgerald are listed under his publications above; the one exception is "Our Own Movie Queen," which apparently was genuinely written in collaboration and is thus listed here and in the listing of F. Scott Fitzgerald's writings above.

I. BOOKS

1932 *Save Me the Waltz*. NY: Charles Scribner's Sons, 1932.

1973 *Bits of Paradise—21 Uncollected Stories By F. Scott and Zelda Fitzgerald*. Selected by Scottie Fitzgerald Smith and Matthew J. Bruccoli. London: Bodley Head, 1973. *Contents*: Our Own Movie Queen; The Original Follies Girl; The Southern Girl; The Girl the Prince Liked; The Girl with Talent; A Millionaire's Girl; Poor Working Girl; Miss Ella; The Continental Angle; A Couple of Nuts.

1974 *The Romantic Egoists*. Edited by Matthew J. Bruccoli, Scottie Fitzgerald Smith, and Joan P. Kerr. NY: Charles Scribner's Sons, 1974.

1980 *Scandalabra* (play). Bloomfield Hills, Mich., and Columbia, S.C.: Bruccoli Clark, 1980.

Correspondence of F. Scott Fitzgerald. Edited by Matthew J. Bruccoli and Margaret M. Duggan. With the assistance of Susan Walker. NY: Random House, 1980.

II. PERIODICALS

1922   Friend Husband's Latest (review of *The Beautiful and Damned* by F. Scott Fitzgerald). NY *Tribune*, April 2.

Eulogy on the Flapper (essay). *Metropolitan Magazine*, June.

1924   Does a Moment of Revolt Come Sometime to Every Married Man? (essay). *McCall's*, March.

1925   Our Own Movie Queen. Chicago *Sunday Tribune*, June 7.

What Became of the Flappers? (essay). *McCall's*, October.

1928   The Changing Beauty of Park Avenue (essay). *Harper's Bazaar*, January.

Looking Back Eight Years (essay). *College Humor*, June.

Who Can Fall in Love After Thirty? (essay). *College Humor*, October.

1929   Paint and Powder (essay). *Smart Set*, May.

The Original Follies Girl. *College Humor*, July.

Southern Girl. *College Humor*, October.

1930   The Girl the Prince Liked. *College Humor*, February.

The Girl with Talent. *College Humor*, April.

A Millionaire's Girl. *Saturday Evening Post*, May 17.

1931   Poor Working Girl. *College Humor*, January.

Miss Ella. *Scribner's Magazine*, December.

1932   The Continental Angle. *New Yorker*, June 4.

A Couple of Nuts. *Scribner's Magazine*, August.

1934   "Show Mr. and Mrs. F. to Number—" (essay). *Esquire*, May and June.

Auction—Model 1934 (essay). *Esquire*, July.

1974   Zelda Fitzgerald's Tribute to F. Scott Fitzgerald (essay). *Fitzgerald/Hemingway Annual.*

1975   A Letter from Zelda Fitzgerald. *Fitzgerald/Hemingway Annual.*

Introduction to
the Index

The aim of this index has been to be as comprehensive and as inclusive as possible. As in *The Critical Reputation of F. Scott Fitzgerald*, all the names of authors, titles of books, and titles of journals, magazines, and newspapers from the individual bibliographical citations have been entered directly into the index. Once again, varying titles of newspapers and other periodicals have been cited as they appeared at a particular time and have not been cross-referenced; for example, both titles for the same scholarly journal, *Bulletin of the Rocky Mountain Modern Language Association* and *Rocky Mountain Review of Language and Literature*, appear at their respective places in the index.

There has been a concerted effort to be comprehensive in compiling the subject entries. However, the subject entries have been drawn from the annotations and titles of the individual bibliographical citations and, therefore, reflect the limitations of the annotations themselves. The subject entries, which are fully integrated into the index with those for author and title, include persons, titles of books and periodicals, places, titles of works by F. Scott Fitzgerald, names of Fitzgerald characters, and literary terms (e.g., point of view, stylistic analysis, etc.). The titles of books have been entered under the author's name unless the book is an entry in Section I, "Books and Book Sections About F. Scott Fitzgerald." Because this bibliography is ostensibly a compilation of works about F. Scott Fitzgerald, all entries for Zelda Sayre Fitzgerald, including her literary works, appear under her name in the index.

Unlike the index to the first volume of the bibliography, there are some entries for F. Scott Fitzgerald. It may be argued that all of the entries in the index are technically about Fitzgerald, and, therefore, such entries are superfluous. In the interest of clarity and of the user, a few entries have been made under Fitzgerald's name. Some of the entries seemed necessitated as, for example, when the annotations did not specify titles of specific short stories in a discussion of Fitzgerald's short fiction. Therefore, there is an entry for "Short stories" under

Fitzgerald. These entries are only for general discussions where no specific short stories are mentioned individually. These stories are indexed directly by title. The typographical format of the entries varies slightly to indicate at a glance certain types of entries. Authors and subjects are listed in upper and lower case roman type and titles of books and periodicals appear in upper and lower case italic type with the following exceptions. Books wholly about Fitzgerald which appear in Section I in Roman capitals appear in Roman capitals in the index as well. Book-length works by Fitzgerald appear in the index in italic bold face capitals while shorter works (short stories and essays) appear in bold face upper and lower case.

Ruth M. Alvarez
University of Maryland

Index

The Novel of Manners in America, I354
Novelist's America: Fiction as History,
1910–1940, I25
Novyi Mir, I289II
Now!, G523
Now & Then, H851
Now Playing at Canterbury, I30
Nugent, Elliott, H136, I278
Nye, Robert, G202, G271, I54lviii,
I78xxxiv, I218xlii

Oakes, Philip, H893
Ober, Harold, H451, H1160, I27, I42.
See also *AS EVER SCOTT FITZ—*
Oberbeck, S. K., G350
Oboler, Arch, H845, H933
O'Brien, John H., G171
The Observer (London), G197, G273,
G518, H723a, H829a, H1045a, I55vii,
I159vi, I160xiv, I218xxxi, I258xix,
K71
O'Connor, Bijou, H893
O'Connor, John J., H793, H1069
O'Donnell, John, H16
O'Donoghue, Michael, H575
"The Offshore Pirate," H11, H12, H695,
H1028, I74VI, I96
"The Offshore Pirate" (film), H12
O'Flaherty, Terrence, H795, H796, H995
Oglebay, Kate, H116
Ogunsanwo, Olatubosun, H1284
O'Hanlon, Patricia, J194
O'Hara, John, H204, H266, H363, H797,
H866, I52, I57II, I58, I123, I147,
I235, I279; *Appointment in Samarra*,
I235
O'Hara, John Myers, H1131
O'Hara, I123
*The O'Hara Concern—A Biography of
John O'Hara*, I52
*Okayama Daigaku Hōkei Tanki
Daigakubu Kiyō: Bungaku Renshū*,
H236
Oklahoma City *Sunday Oklahoman*,
G303, G434, I49vii, I258cii
Oklahoma Journal (Oklahoma City),
G225
Oldsey, Bernard, I49xii
O'Leary, Theodore M., G84, G172,
G570, I160xxxvi, I258lxxiv
Oleksy, Walter, H798
Olevnik, Peter P., I97viii
Oliver, Ruth Hale, H661
Olsen, Carol, G500

Olson, Larry Dean, J195
Omaha *Sunday World-Herald*, G108,
G510, I258xliv
Omaha *World-Herald*, H523
Omarr, Sydney, H662
On the Sound, H734, H746, H789, H815,
H835
"On Your Own," H1158, H1193
"One Trip Abroad," H933, H1136
O'Neill, Eugene, H866, I147
O'Neill, John, K59
O'Neill, William L., I280
Orangeburg (S.C.) *Times-Democrat*,
I252xxxviii
Oravets, Andrew Joseph, Jr., J71
Orcutt, Jo Ellen Lindh, J196
Oregon Journal (Portland), G528
"The Original Follies Girl," H100
Orlando *Sentinel-Star*, I54xlv
Ormsby, Rosemary, J197
Ornstein, Robert, I118VI, I223IV
O'Rourke, Matthew R., G392
Orwell, George: *1984*, I138
Osborn, E. W., G53, H74, I73LXVII,
I73CXLII
Osborne, Charles, I35
Osborne, Lorraine, I252lii
Oshawa (Canada) *Times*, I54xvi
Osmania Journal of English Studies, H516
*Otemon Gakuin Daigaku Bungakubu
Kiyō*, H954
Ottawa *Citizen*, G185
Ottawa *Revue*, G459
"Our Own Movie Queen," I74X
Our Sunday Visitor (Ottawa, Canada),
I252xliv
Ousby, Ian, I281
The Outing Magazine, H1167
Overstreet, Richard, H283
Overton, Grant, I73CCIX
Owen, Isabel, H1289
Owens, Robert J., Jr., I268
Ower, John, H894
Owett, Trudy, H799
*The Oxford Book of American Literary
Anecdotes*, I167
Oxford (England) *Mail*, I258xli
Oxnard (Calif.) *Press-Courier*,
I252xxxviii

P., F., G85
Pace, Eric, H1070
Page, Geraldine, H1244
Pages: The World of Books, Writers, and